The Lorette Wilmot Library
Nazareth College of Rochester

WITHDRAWN

WILLIAM GRANT STILL

William Grant Still, circa 1933. Photograph by George Manuel. Courtesy of the William Grant Still and Verna Arvey Papers, University of Arkansas Libraries, Fayetteville.

WILLIAM GRANT STILL

A Bio-Bibliography

Judith Anne Still,
Michael J. Dabrishus,
and Carolyn L. Quin

Bio-Bibliographies in Music, Number 61
Donald L. Hixon, Series Adviser

GREENWOOD PRESS
Westport, Connecticut • London

Library of Congress Cataloging-in-Publication Data

Still, Judith Anne.
  William Grant Still : a bio-bibliography / Judith Anne Still,
Michael J. Dabrishus, and Carolyn L. Quin.
    p. cm.—(Bio-bibliographies in music, ISSN 0742–6968 ; no.
61)
  Includes bibliographical references, discography, and index.
  ISBN 0–313–25255–6 (alk. paper)
  1. Still, William Grant, 1895– —Bibliography. I. Dabrishus,
Michael J. II. Quin, Carolyn L. III. Title. IV. Series.
ML134.S8S75 1996
016.78′092—dc20   96–21946

British Library Cataloguing in Publication Data is available.

Copyright © 1996 by Judith Anne Still, Michael J. Dabrishus,
and Carolyn L. Quin

All rights reserved. No portion of this book may be
reproduced, by any process or technique, without the
express written consent of the publisher.

Library of Congress Catalog Card Number: 96–21946
ISBN: 0–313–25255–6
ISSN: 0742–6968

First published in 1996

Greenwood Press, 88 Post Road West, Westport, CT 06881
An imprint of Greenwood Publishing Group, Inc.

Printed in the United States of America

The paper used in this book complies with the
Permanent Paper Standard issued by the National
Information Standards Organization (Z39.48–1984).

10 9 8 7 6 5 4 3 2 1

Every reasonable effort has been made to trace the owners of copyright materials in this book, but in some instances this has proven impossible. The authors and publisher will be glad to receive information leading to more complete acknowledgments in subsequent printings of the book and in the meantime extend their apologies for any omissions.

In memory of the Composer

CONTENTS

Preface	*ix*
Acknowledgments	*xi*
A Personal Reminiscence of William Grant Still by Judith Anne Still	1
Biographical Sketch of William Grant Still by Carolyn L. Quin	15
Works and Performances	45
Writings by William Grant Still and Verna Arvey	213
General Bibliography	231
Discography	287
Appendix A: Alphabetical List of Works	295
Appendix B: Preliminary List of Arrangements and Orchestrations	303
Index	307

PREFACE

It is fitting that this volume appears in 1996, right after the centennial year of the birth of William Grant Still. Orchestras and individual musicians across the country have taken part in the celebration by performing Still's compositions. Organizations and institutions have encouraged research into aspects of the composer's professional career and life through conferences and special programs. Hopefully, this volume will stimulate additional research and writings on Still, as well as encourage performances of his music by those unfamiliar with one of America's most significant composers.

This book consists of six major sections:

1) A personal reminiscence of the composer from the viewpoint of his daughter, Judith Anne Still, accompanied by passages from his theme books, diaries, and sketch books.

2) A biographical sketch of his professional life and career.

3) Entries on works (arranged alphabetically by title), performances, and reviews.

4) A bibliography of the writings of William Grant Still and Verna Arvey. This section is sub-divided into three groups: writings by Still; writings by Still and Arvey as joint authors, and writings by Arvey that pertain to Still.

5) A general bibliography that includes 453 entries divided into two sections. The first section pertains to information contained in general reference works, and the second includes information found in monographs, journals, newspapers, magazine articles, newsletters, theses, and dissertations. Each citation is preceded by the mnemonic **B** followed by a sequential number.

6) A *selected* discography of commercially-produced recordings, whether or not currently available. Entries are preceded by the mnemonic **D** and numbered sequentially. Each entry includes the record label, date of release, performers, album title, and series title. Space limitations preclude the inclusion of annotated references to reviews.

In "Works and Performances," each composition is identified by the mnemonic **W** for "Work" followed by a sequential number (**W1**, **W2**, etc.). Each work is provided with descriptive information that includes publisher, medium, place and date of composition, commission, dedication, contents, instrumentation, duration, and location of holographs or facsimiles. The following terms are used to describe the musical scores: *holograph,* an autograph signed by the composer; *autograph,* an unsigned manuscript in the composer's handwriting; *manuscript,* a handwritten score not identified as that of the composer; and *facsimile,* a copy of any original, including photostat and photocopy processes. An added feature is information and inscriptions, placed within quotations, from the composer or Verna Arvey drawn from sketches, scores, or other records that comprise the William Grant Still and Verna Arvey Papers, located in the Special Collections Division of the University of Arkansas Libraries, Fayetteville. It is the authors' belief that such information materially strengthens a work's description when it exists.

Many of Still's works were assigned to publishers but never actually published or distributed. William Grant Still Music has recovered the copyrights on many of the compositions. Whenever a piece is available from William Grant Still Music, the authors have indicated that in the publication information. The address of William Grant Still Music is 4 South San Francisco Street, Suite No. 422, Flagstaff, Arizona 86001-5737.

First performances and selected performances are listed after the descriptive information for each work. These are listed in chronological order and are identified by the "Works" number followed by a sequential lower-case letter (W1a, W1b, etc.). We focused on performances that occurred during Still's lifetime, except for works which premiered after the composer's death, or for special occasions honoring the composer. Even so, space limitations prevented a more inclusive listing.

Bibliographical references to works and performances, usually in the form of reviews, follow the selected performances. These are identified by WB with the Works number, followed by a decimal point and a sequential number (WB1.1, WB1.2, etc.). These entries are arranged chronologically by date of publication. References to other citations are identified by "See" or "See also."

The first appendix is an alphabetical list of works, including all movements within each work which have distinct titles. This list includes entry numbers for those works with separate entries and cross references for the movements within a work or for variant titles. The second appendix is a preliminary alphabetical list of currently identified titles of arrangements and orchestrations by Still, including those done for musical theater, radio, television, and film.

ACKNOWLEDGMENTS

This is a publication that required a great deal of research over a long period of time. It was completed only through the assistance of many individuals and libraries. First of all, we want to extend our sincere gratitude to the staff of the University of Arkansas Libraries, Fayetteville, where the William Grant Still and Verna Arvey Papers are located. John A. Harrison, director of libraries, encouraged this project from the beginning. This volume, in a sense, serves as an example of his support and of his own deep appreciation for the value of manuscript collections.

The Still and Arvey Papers, housed in the Special Collections Division of the University of Arkansas Libraries, are certainly in good company. Staff members E. Betty Austin, Andrea E. Cantrell, Věra Ekechukwu, Ellen C. Shipley, Ethel C. Simpson, Todd Lewis, Cassandra McCraw, and Christopher Wright provided professional assistance of the highest caliber. We would like to draw attention to two staff members who deserve special recognition: Ramona Willis, who created and maintained databases, and checked and revised entries; and Nan Lawler, who set the pages, prepared the final camera-ready copy, and provided thoughtful editorial suggestions that proved to be invaluable. We cannot thank each of them enough.

Personnel from other departments also merit our praise. E. Beth Juhl, Elizabeth McKee, and L. Stephen Perry, all from the Reference Department, helped to locate resources in the main collection or to assist with database searches. Staff members from the Interlibrary Loan Department frequently were called upon to secure books, theses, dissertations, and microfilm of newspapers and journals held by other libraries, providing timely and friendly assistance. To Regina French, Allison Levene, Laura Norsworthy, Susanna Price, Kim Smith, and Michelle Tabler, thank you very, very much! Deborah Cochran, formerly head of the ILL Department, provided early assistance with the project, and we thank you, too. Jenny K. Quintin, from the Automation Department, provided helpful computer expertise.

Alicia S. Merritt, Acquisitions Editor at Greenwood Press, provided support and assistance at crucial times. Donald L. Hixon, Bio-Bibliographies in Music Series Advisor and former Fine Arts Librarian at the University Library of the University of California at Irvine, provided helpful encouragement and insight throughout the project.

The National Endowment for the Humanities recognized the significance of the William Grant Still and Verna Arvey Papers when, in 1991, it awarded a grant to the University of Arkansas Libraries to arrange, describe, and preserve the collection, amounting to nearly ninety linear feet of materials. The completion of that work by

Norma Ortiz-Karp, project archivist, enabled research on this volume to proceed systematically. Judy Culberson, Melissa Gatlin, Michelle King, Jennifer Kolmes, and Cathy Reineka, all of the Technical Services Division, and Jaya Kilambi, of the Audio Visual Department of the library, also provided a valuable service during the grant project.

Also, we would like to acknowledge the assistance and services of a number of additional individuals and institutions: Sylvia Kennick Brown, College Archivist and Special Collections Librarian, The Paul Whiteman Collection, Williams College Archives and Special Collections; Joyce Clinkscales, Music Librarian, Emory University; the NEH Summer Seminar Program and the Center for Black Music Research, in particular Samuel Floyd; D. Antoinette Handy; Sharon Herfurth, formerly assistant head of the Fine Arts Department, Dallas Public Library; Barbara Garvey Jackson and Kern Jackson, emeritus professors of the University of Arkansas, Fayetteville; Robert Y. McMahon, Trenton State College; Gayle Murchison, Department of Music, University of Arkansas, Fayetteville; Edward C. Oetting, Head of Archives and Manuscripts, Hayden Library, Arizona State University; Bruce Raeburn, Curator, William Ransom Hogan Jazz Archive, Tulane University; Louise Sherby, Assistant Director for Public Services, University of Missouri-Kansas City Libraries; Wayne Shirley, Music Specialist, Library of Congress; Andrea Watson, W. S. Hoole Special Collections Library, University of Alabama, Tuscaloosa; Linda Whitesitt; the Wisconsin State Historical Society; and the Mills Library at the University of Wisconsin, Madison; the Andrew W. Mellon Foundation and the United Negro College Fund, Inc.; the Music Library at the University of Tennessee, Knoxville.

Finally, we would like to thank members of our families, including the Headlee children; Carroll, Rose, and Betty Quin; Anna and Mara Dabrishus; and especially Nancy E. Dabrishus, who provided encouragement, support, patience, and strength throughout. Without them this volume would not exist.

WILLIAM GRANT STILL

A PERSONAL REMINISCENCE OF WILLIAM GRANT STILL

Judith Anne Still

"The Coercive Smile of a Winking Saint"

The following passages are from the theme book, diaries, and sketchbooks of William Grant Still.

Theme book, 1924: Humbly have I sought the aid of my Father in composing. . . . This is the result. May it glorify Him in the highest.

Ode to the American Negro.

Despised—Rejected. He struggles. His struggles are futile, for he relies on his own strength that is naught but weakness. He falls back into the pit of misery, and sinks to deeper depths. A ray of hope penetrates the stygian gloom. From Celestial heights it comes bearing a message of comfort from the throne of God: a reminder that Divine aid is ever given one who will accept. The Negro hears. . . . (Having risen) he triumphantly voices the truth . . . (as a man thinks, so is he.)

July 10, 1930 (Thurs): Cloudy today. Yet one feels no depression because of it. God seems so near. Grace [Grace Bundy was Still's first wife.] in ill humor. Unpleasant scene at home. Thanks to God, I did not lose my temper.

July 11, 1930 (Fri): Thank God for another day. Still scoring *Sahdji*. Nine pages today. Tired now. Picture show to rest my brain. . . . I often feel discouraged over the way things are mis-managed in my home. Feel that way today and wish that I might be able to go away. But, would that be what God would have me do?

July 12, 1930 (Sat): Beautiful day. Semi-finals of tennis tournament. Slept well last night. Dreamed that I was walking through mud that clung to my feet but soon came to clear water. Feel that God is telling me not to lose courage.

September 4, 1930 (Thurs): God bestowed honor on me today. Received catalog of the works of the leading American composers. In spite of my color, my works and name were included.

October 9, 1930 (Thurs): My orchestration of *Deep River* acclaimed unusually good by so very many. Thanks to God to whom the credit is due.

October 10, 1930 (Fri): Purchased radio today, in spite of very large obligations ahead. I do not know how, but I am assured that my Father will open the way for me.

October 24, 1930 (Fri): God sent me success today. *Africa* was a sensation.

October 27, 1930 (Mon): Today I discovered that Grace has again drawn my money from the bank without telling me of it. . . . I wrote a check for $39.00 . . . and discovered . . . that I had not enough to cover the amount of the check. But I believe that God will clear away my trouble.

February 24, 1938 (Thurs): Concert [in San Francisco where Still conducted]. Audience enthusiastic. Had to repeat *Lenox Ave.* Just as we did in Los Angeles and Oakland. Met other people, autographed programs and shook hands after the concert. Was almost given a ticket for driving 44 miles per hour.

March 27, 1938 (Sun): At times it seems that I am almost able to understand the purpose of my present incarnation.

April 4, 1938 (Mon): Dreamed of being the hungry guest of honor at a banquet where all ate except me.

April 18, 1938 (Mon): My spirit worked on music most of the night conveying with force ideas to my brain.

May 4, 1938 (Wed): Worked on material for Act II [*Troubled Island*]. Cleaned more in the alley. . . . Watered lawn. Worked out May chart for V [Verna Arvey]. . . . Old German lady across alley said to me, "Niggers don't think."

June 7, 1938 (Tues): Shep messed up back porch. I rec'd. telepathically his appeal to be let out when sleeping.

January 1, 1939 (Sun): Prayed as New Year entered. V. called. Plans for Stenio's aria [from *Troubled Island*] progressed beautifully, thanks to God's aid administered by my Friends [spirit forces].

February 8, 1939 (Wed): Up early. Ate. Drove to Tijuana. Terrific wind. V & I married. Got a ticket for speeding at National City. Ate lunch in San Diego. Got back to L.A. around 6:00. Marketed. Called Klemperer. . . . Read proofs of *Rising Tide*. Worked on revision of orchestra score of *Troubled Island*.

August 31, 1942 (Mon): Judith born at 1 p.m. [high noon] exactly. . . . Worked on score of *Victory Tide* [same as *Rising Tide*] for Sweeten. Letter from Kramer.

January 28, 1945 (Sun): Went out for some things but was unable to get them. War (or probably the desire of some people for wealth) causes us to do without many things.

February 14, 1945 (Wed): Thank God for the solution of a problem that arose in 3rd movement of symphony [*Symphony No. 5, "Western Hemisphere"*]. Composed. In fact I was composing all night in my sleep. Sawed part of puzzle. Jas., Flo, Mrs. Philips and Mrs. Jordan came.

April 24, 1945 (Tues): Painted walls. Sowed onions. Scored page 86. Worked on circus [for the children].

January 23, 1946 (Wed): *Southern Interlude* [later revised as *Highway 1, U.S.A.*] failed in Metropolitan Opera contest. Again prejudice has struck us. Truly, there is but little freedom for colored Americans.

January 11, 1947 (Sat): Listened to broadcast of Roger's opera. Terrible music. One may easily believe that the Met[ropolitan] Opera Co. chose it for the purpose of discrediting operas written by native Americans. Worked on bookcase. No important mail.

January 3, 1949 (Mon): Several letters. None important. Truly it seems that we are confronted by a stone wall. Men ignore my efforts and contributions on all sides. But, I believe that God will bring it to a happy conclusion. Went through Act III. Worked on wooden dolls. The children returned to school.

March 10, 1949 (Thurs): God is good. I pray that His blessed hand will guide *Troubled Island* through to success and a position where it can accomplish good.

March 31, 1949 (Thurs): Tr. Is. Premiere. Thank God for the results. He blessed it. Received an ovation. Thank God.

May 5, 1949 (Thurs): Rec'd clipping from *Boston Post* [April 17, 1949]. A splendid review of the opera refuting the false statements of the New York critics.

April 2, 1952 (Wed): A period has come when most everything seems useless.

October 30, 1952 (Thurs): Verna became ill in the evening. . . . Judith prepared a nice party for us. Worked on *Bayou Legend*. Judith's party for Duncan and me touched me deeply. I pray that our children may be blessed with happiness and with unhampered opportunity to do good for others. I pray that Verna may be rewarded for her sacrifices.

December 19, 1952 (Fri): I long for the time when my music will receive the consideration it merits. Those who are in power in the field of music certainly deal unfairly with me.

January 1, 1953 (Thurs): There are in these United States too many who think it only right for me to be denied the right to live. They connive to stop performances of my work, to pooh pooh my efforts, to keep us from expressing ourselves through the press, to cause others to hold us in contempt, and to force me out of music. These are the people who turned my opera's success into failure. . . . God forgive them! Worked on Symphony today [*The Third Symphony*]. With God's aid I will continue as best I can even though our unethical opponents seek to destroy all that would offer us reason to hope. I'm glad that I do not hate them for what they do.

Sketchbook for Minette Fontaine, *1958:* Give me, O Father, the friendship of my fellow men.

August 19, 1959. William Grant Still ceased to write in his diary. He pasted a clipping of the music of Diron's Swan Song, from *Minette Fontaine*, into his diary as the last "entry."

William Grant Still wrote in his diaries, or his journals, or his sketchbooks every day for almost twenty years. He had, in fact, one of the most minutely-chronicled careers of any composer in history, for what he failed to set down himself, his wife, Verna Arvey, noted or compiled for him in articles, scrapbooks, scratchpads and letters. Moreover, in response to Still's public life and activities, critics, historians and musicologists also published references to him, characterizing his work and listing his accomplishments. Between 1950 and 1980, Still's music was more discussed or alluded to than it was heard in concert: at the end of his life he was the most well-known unknown composer in the United States.

    The diaries of William Grant Still seem to reveal accurately who he was: a man of obdurate purpose, insoluble faith and permanent domestic energy and responsibility. These things he was, without question. And yet, when all the private papers have been absorbed, much remains to be said, asked and answered. What kind of personality did he have? Was he always so serious? What did those outside of his family think of him? How did he dress, compose, spend his free time? What was his actual and ultimate contribution to music, beyond all the conjectural verbiage?

    Indeed so many questions grip the cliff-edge after the commentary has slipped into the abyss, that one wonders how Peter Shaffer could have arrived at the core of Mozart's character through a side-long glance at slurs of the composer's detractors, and a soppy preoccupation with a young man's bawdy trifles. The seeming credibility that *Amadeus* wrests from the truth should warn even the staunchest biographical scholar against the dangers of assumption. A man whose labors alter human consciousness is always more than anything he says of himself, or anything that people say of him.

    Certainly Still was more than the sum of the words that surrounded him. Even his physical presence carried implied meaning. He had large, infusive eyes, and a head-on attitude toward the world that swung gently heavenward at the corners—a look that almost effortlessly captured those he looked upon, held them, then let them go, in the same way that the smiling mother gives her babies to adulthood. Even in later years, when watersheds of opposition eroded the last of his hopes for major publications and recordings, his love of his fellows and his sense of humor survived, winking in the dark background of his thoughts, then hiding shyly like a firefly overtaken by daybreak.

As a young man, he was said to be "as handsome as a movie star," arrestingly clean and slim, invariably finely-pressed, polished and polite. He was 5 feet 8¾ inches tall, weighed 135 pounds, and, when he walked near, there was about him a decorous hint of men's talcum and stately-sweet shaving lotion. When he had money he spent it on operatic scores, tailored suits, and presents for his friends. He was high-spirited yet devout, interested yet preoccupied, charming yet positive.

When he was in love, he was an irredeemable romantic. Clarissa Cumbo, one of his lady loves in college, never forgot the evenings wherein he stood beneath her dormitory window, playing radiant serenades for her on his violin. At parties he danced with the most intriguing girls, whirling them around in fantastic arcs of laughter and motion until the music sighed away. Then, beaming with pleasure, he paused to accept a serving of homemade ice cream, which he took into the kitchen and put into the oven for a moment so that the outside would soften a little. (His teeth, somewhat subject to decay, were also sensitive to excessive cold).

Eubie Blake, Still's employer in the *Shuffle Along* orchestra in the twenties, said that Still "was quite the natty man about town in those early years," in addition to being "one of the kindliest, gentlest men he ever met."[1]

Still's sense of fun was evident in the early copies of his sheet music. Occasionally he drew round monkey faces with big ears in his orchestral parts, and, at the edge of the last page of his *Black Man Dances* is his stick-figure monkey running away, with the words, "He's through." Often he inserted messages to the players at the end of his parts, in order to establish a personal relationship with the members of the orchestra. The messages said, "See you again sometime," or, "Glad to have met you."

In the twenties his songs had a humorous bent, as suggested by titles such as *The Tumblebug's Lament*, *Sister Heavy Hips*, *Brother Lowdown* and *The Cross-Eyed Monkey*. Verna Arvey's personal notes on her husband indicate that the composer's arrangements for Willard Robison and the *Deep River Hour* in New York were a "storehouse of humor." She goes on to say that "Robison asked for an arrangement of *Way Down Yonder in de Confiel'*. Still couldn't find a copy of the music, so he wrote one of his own, and titled it, *A Cornfield. Which One?* While he was scoring *Oh, Miss Hannah*, he put these words in lieu of numbers at the top of each page: Hannah (Smith), Hannah (Brown), Hannah (Jones), etc."

Later on, this ebullient joviality surfaced again in his *Quit Dat Fool'nish* for piano, dedicated to his dog Shep. On the toy buildings that he built for his son's train set, he put business names such as, the "Yipp and Arff" pet store, the "Hydro and Chloric Acid Co.," and the "Out to Lunch" diner. Also, when he wrote story lines for his operas to be used by his wife to create the libretti, he inserted chuckling asides for her, such as, "The two men fight. Bow, Bam, Biff, Bop. How do you like that ending, Momsey?"

The composer's ingenuously soaring spirits were greatly loved by his friends and colleagues. Only a few Hollywood movie-makers didn't care for his wit, especially when he inserted a jazz trumpet playing *The Music Goes 'Round and 'Round* into Dimitri Tiompkin's score for the funeral march in *Lost Horizons*. (Of course, the film moguls didn't care for him when he was serious either; they habitually rejected his music because it was not "typically Negroid," that is, it was "too dignified.")

Truly, the composer's humor and optimism might be thought to be unusual, considering the prejudices that existed in the nation while he was growing up. Like other colored people of his day, he was called names, pushed off the sidewalk, prevented from eating, travelling and sleeping in the best circumstances, and forced to enter hotels and houses at service entrances. Yet, his self-confidence and sense of personal worth remained intact, probably as much owing to his talent as to the inculcations of his mother and stepfather when he was a child.

He was born in Woodville, Mississippi, a town whose racial feelings had erupted in the shameless killing of Negroes called "the Woodville Massacre." Rumors in the Still family suggested that certain white folk in Woodville were jealous of Still's father, William Grant Still, Sr., who was said to be too good-looking, too smart, too clever, and too well-to-do "for a Nigger." The light-skinned descendant of a Scotch-Irish overseer and a slave woman, the elder Still taught mathematics, owned half-interest in a colored grocery store, and, with his gleaming cornet, led the Negro band in Woodville on festive occasions.

The elder Still's sudden death in 1895, when his son was three months old, was a mystery that remains unsolved. Townspeople said that an angry ex-girlfriend had poisoned him, while later observers have determined that he must have died of malaria. However, members of the family, now dead themselves, once whispered that white people paid the ex-girlfriend to murder the young man. Racial hatred had found a focus when a friend of Still's was shot to death for complaining that colored teachers received less pay than white: it seemed obvious that the math teacher was in sympathy with the trouble-maker, and that he ought to be dealt with in a similar fashion. Soon afterward Still died of poison.

Perhaps aware of the murder, Carrie Still, the composer's mother, looked at the body of her husband and ran screaming out of the house into the night. Later she collected herself, and, hoping to save her son from the horror of Woodville, she took him to live in Little Rock, Arkansas, where prejudice was less dangerous.

Carrie's decision to move to Little Rock was carefully considered. The daughter of a Spanish plantation owner and a Choctaw-Negro servant (once a slave), Still's mother was adored by her white father, who had considerable holdings and land in Florida. The latter offered her a house and an orange grove if she would bring her son and live near him after the elder Still died. But the Jim Crow laws in Florida were as distasteful to Carrie as the racial climate in Woodville, and, because her son was darker-skinned than she and could not be mistaken for white, it was important to her to live where repression was minimal.

In Little Rock, mother and son lived on West 14th Street, between Chester and Ringo, on the north side of the roadway. Still's grandmother, Anne Fambro, lived with them, and took care of the cooking and the housework while Carrie taught English in the colored schools and involved herself in community service.

Carrie Still was strict, thorough and dynamic. She played the piano for her own choral group, went into the backwoods to teach the poor people to read and write, and produced Shakespearean plays using student actors. With the money earned from her productions, she established the first library that colored people could use in Little Rock. In her free time she painted china and did needlework, creating things of such refinement that they won prizes at the county fair. In addition, she attended to her son's literary, musical and spiritual education.

While Anne Fambro was teaching little William her beloved Negro spirituals, it was Carrie who took him to Negro church services where he was exposed to intrinsically American music with its natural rhythmic content. This is not to say that the boy appreciated the experience: when they went to a service of the "Holy Rollers," where worship was rambunctious and physical, she had to spank him for laughing out loud at the obese Sisters who were rolling and shouting in the sanctuary aisles. He hardly realized that he had begun his education in the growth of American folk music.

It might be mentioned here that the spanking given Still for laughing in church was not the only incidence of corporal punishment in his childhood. He was a mischievous lad who would try anything if it piqued his curiosity, and most everything did. He played with matches, slid down the hall bannister into the decor below, dug a private cave in the backyard so large that the woodshed almost fell in, threw crayons at kindly Professor Gillam when his back was turned in class, stole sherbet from the kitchen pantry when the adults were eating dinner, and played hookey from school to gad about the blacksmith shop and the train station.

All of his pranks were cause for an application of his mother's whipping strap, regardless of how he pleaded for absolution. If he crawled under the bed to escape, the leather whip curled under after him, catching him around the ankles. When the beating was over, Still vowed that he would never cross his mother again, but, of course, he always did and he was always punished for it.

The worst period came when his mother was his English teacher at M. W. Gibbs High School. The days of throwing crayons and snickering in class ended, as any uncalled-for noise from his direction caused the ruler to be brought down on his knuckles. Outside of class his study habits were monitored, and he was given extra instruction in grammar, spelling, and literature. On Saturdays he was taken to Lotus Club meetings, which were gatherings reminiscent of the parlor concerts of the French aristocracy. At these conclaves, the leading Negro musicians, actors and writers of the time appeared to perform in recitals of classical music and literature. It was at these recitals that Still was able to hear Clarence Cameron White on the violin, and Richard B. Harrison performing Shakespeare.

Still was not always happy over being forced to live a life of culture and manners, but, without his being aware, the noble influences of the church and the Lotus Club were drawing him into his natural artistic element. He began to gravitate toward music, and to try to make music on his own. Soon, he was fashioning toy violins out of cigar boxes, sticks and cat gut, and trying to play them.

By this time his second father had joined forces with his mother in forging his character. At the turn of the century his mother married Charles B. Shepperson, a railway postal clerk who loved stage shows and opera. It was Mr. Shepperson who bought his stepson a real violin to play, who led Carrie to give him violin lessons, and who took him to musicals in town where he could gain exposure to the best expressions of popular music and comic opera.

In December of 1911, Mr. Shepperson brought home a Victor talking machine, the product of Emile Berliner's 1887 invention of the gramophone. With the machine came Red Seal recordings of grand opera, from Puccini to Wagner; and with the grand opera came Still's head-over-heels decision to become a serious composer.

His mother opposed his decision, naturally, because in 1911 there was no possibility for a Negro to make a living as a composer. She insisted that he pursue a Bachelor of Science degree at Wilberforce University, hoping that he would become a doctor. He tried to please her for awhile, but when he learned that Wilberforce had a band, and the band needed a clarinetist, he quickly taught himself to play the clarinet and joined the group. From there he began to learn to play other instruments in the band, and formed his own string quartet. After that, most of his money went toward acquiring music texts and sheet music, and to writing his own short compositions.

Somewhere in between the band concerts and string recitals, however, there were moments devoted to courting the ladies and to college escapades: he had not ceased to be the precocious source of all forms of devilment. He, along with the boys who considered him their leader, were adroit at stealing pies from windowsills or putting dead creatures in the beds of other students. Once they undressed a foppish lad and left him tied up in front of the girls' dormitory.

Their last caper at Wilberforce was the most disastrous. A girl named Grace Bundy suggested that a group of them go walking in the woods where it was forbidden for male and female students to be seen together, and they decided that there was no harm to the proposal. Still volunteered to be Miss Bundy's escort on the expedition. Unfortunately the faculty caught them before they reached the woods, and they were threatened with expulsion. Still left Wilberforce without graduating, married Grace Bundy out of shame, and, against his mother's wishes, embarked on an attempt to earn a living in music.

He secured odd jobs in bands and orchestras to support his new wife, and the child born a year after the marriage, but starvation was a definite prospect until he met W. C. Handy. Handy had just opened a music publishing house in Memphis, Tennessee, and he had a band which toured the cities from Memphis to New Orleans. It was Handy who gave Still his first real job, in his publishing house as an arranger, and on the road as a performer.

Still profited from the opportunity to learn orchestration, but he disliked the road trips to ignoble Southern nightclubs and cafes. In the tiny sawmill towns in Tennessee, where the men had to slap at the mosquitos while they played, he saw deep-seated racial prejudice for the first time. To his enormous dismay, Negroes were beaten bloody on the street without provocation; to his horror, colored men were lynched without arrest or trial. He felt suddenly compelled to work against this injustice in some way, though he was not at that time sure how he might do so.

His first attempt to correct injustice was his enlistment in the Navy in 1918. Many colored people felt that, if they fought for their country in World War I, they might be afforded greater respect by the nation. The fact that their efforts were unrewarded was a source of disappointment for Still, but, when he left the War behind him, he was more determined than ever to be an orchestral composer.

His mother softened somewhat, seeing how resolute he was, and she gave him a legacy that had been left for him from the late William Grant Still Sr.'s grocery business. With this money, he studied at Oberlin Conservatory for a year and a half, acquiring his first formal training in theory and composition.

When the money ran out, he had no recourse but to leave Oberlin and to go back to work for Handy, who had moved his music business to New York City. When Handy had no work for him he was hired to play in Eubie Blake's orchestra, and, while he was with Blake in Boston, he was given a scholarship to study with George Chadwick at the New England Conservatory. Then, back in New York from Boston, he conducted and composed in the Pace-Handy Black Swan Phonograph Company, and he was given musical training without charge by the avant-garde composer, Edgard Varèse. When the Black Swan folded, he played his violin in speakeasies in the dingy part of town.

Thus the years from 1919 to the early thirties passed for him, carrying him through Prohibition into the Depression, alternating periods of work and study with periods of no work and unspeakable poverty. He almost froze in a blizzard when someone at a nightclub stole his overcoat, and he did not eat for over a week when a speakeasy comedian smashed his violin and he could not work. Once he had to buy a banjo in a pawn shop and pretend he knew how to play it, since the only job available anywhere was for a banjo player.

It was during one of these very dark periods in New York that he finally arrived at his philosophy of life and of music. He was lying on a cold and sagging mattress in his Harlem apartment, praying silently, wondering how he was to go on under such adverse circumstances. His life was not yet half done, and yet he was weary, despondent; he had grown up in a world that was full of frolics and laughter, but had stumbled off that world somehow, into a vast sea of joylessness. Perhaps he should give up his music, and seek elsewhere for fulfillment.

The instant that the doubt formed itself in his mind, a shocking thing happened: in the doorway of the room an explosive white light appeared, and a Being which seemed to be part of the light was there before him. The Being, without speaking, somehow had dialogue with him, telling him secrets of human life, and insisting that he make some firm decision about his career.

When the light dissipated, he had the feeling that everything was made clear to him. He was given a choice, and if he chose to continue in music, he was given the promise that he would always be able to feed his family and that he would, ultimately, achieve respect and acclaim. Moreover, he had made a promise to the Being, swearing that, if he were allowed to make a living through composing, he would use his music to bring peoples together in spirit; he would pour the essence and the worth of all the races and cultures into his work, revealing human creative and emotional kinships and encouraging brotherhood.

When the commitment was made, and the anchor raised, Still's existence, while not easy, was inspired with aspiration and vivification. Edgard Varèse and Howard Hanson helped him to get some of his earliest works performed by the International Composers' Guild Orchestra, and the American Composers' Orchestra; in the popular field, he was given work arranging for Don Voorhees, Sophie Tucker, Paul Whiteman and Artie Shaw. He scored *Earl Carroll's Vanities,* and on radio, the *Deep River Hour* for stations CBS and WOR. He became the first colored man to conduct a radio orchestra in the United States, and through his composing and conducting, he was credited with bringing a unique sound to early radio.

The praise for Still's work in the twenties and thirties is copious. Gunther Schuller, in the liner notes for Paul Whiteman's *Happy Feet* album (Golden Crest Records, CRSQ 31043), said that Still was one of the three "greatest arrangers that ever worked in the field" of popular music, and that he was responsible for "one of the half-a-dozen most original sounds ever to have been created." Frank Chase, who played in the *Deep River* orchestra in New York, said that Still's arrangements of spirituals were so beautiful and so innovative that it was the only time in his life during which he "felt close to God." In addition, according to Chase, Still was loved and respected by the members of the orchestra for his talent, his gentility, his gentleness and his humor. Artie Shaw echoed the sentiments of Chase, and added that, "Bill had a rare thing: a sense of musicality or savvy. He invariably did the right thing musically."[2]

It was Still's sense of musicality, and his familiarity with both popular and classical strengths and techniques, that helped him to create the first truly American idiom in orchestral music. Though Gershwin is usually cited for the American popular-classical fusion, Negro musicians like Eubie Blake and Still often testified that Gershwin and other white songwriters "borrowed things" from the poor colored songwriters in Harlem, and that even *I Got Rhythm* was Still's own improvisation when he was playing for the stage show, *Shuffle Along.*[3]

Howard Hanson, who premiered Still's first major work, *The Afro-American Symphony,* affirmed the pioneering character of the symphony when he declared, "William Grant Still came on the American scene at the time when the new music of America was being born . . . [and he] brought to music a new voice, a voice filled with lovely melodies, gorgeous harmonies, insidious rhythms and dazzling colors." Moreover, continued Hanson, "Still brought a new ingredient to music, an ingredient which was a purely American idiom couched in the "grandeur of simplicity"—a simplicity which was the "measure of genius."[4]

Certainly Hanson must have recognized the American quality of Still's music when he played *The Afro-American Symphony* overseas. Foreign audiences reacted strongly to the work, and, in Berlin in 1933, the concert-goers demanded the third movement be repeated twice, something that has never happened again in that city. Critic Alfred Einstein, having been present at the concert, commented upon the "rhythmic, sonorous vitality and humor" of Still's music, and observed that Europeans thought the composer's work to be "the most American in character." It was this comment, and many others, that led John Briggs to state that "Still may well become the American Tchaikovsky."[5]

After the success of *The Afro-American Symphony,* the young composer knew that he would be able to stay with his music, so he began a concerted effort to complete his first opera. Yet, even though he was doing things he that had never been done by a Negro before, he was not as ecstatic as he might have been in earlier years. His fun-loving nature slightly confined by a dreamy sober-mindedness, he was no longer a frequent guest at parties and dances; his only diversions were an occasional game of tennis or an afternoon at the moving picture show. The years of struggling in the Depression were wearing on his temperament, and he and Grace were not getting along.

Grace wanted to travel in Europe, to enjoy aristocratic luxuries, and to be admired by many. Grace's mother, who lived with them, not only wanted to be admired, but she also wished to be obeyed. Still never made enough money to suit either wife or mother, nor did he seem inclined to go into a line of work that would be more lucrative. The fact that his compositions were drawing worldwide attention was of scant importance; it only made Grace angry that her own poems and other writings were not similarly triumphant.

By the early thirties Still and Grace had four children, and these offspring were the only element that kept the marriage intact. Still was an indulgent father, known in the neighborhood for his playfulness and good nature where children were concerned. When his own or the neighbor's youngsters were home from school, he was frequently in the yard with them, joining them in games of catch or helping them to ride their bicycles. As long as he could be with the little ones, he would stay with his wife.

Because he was steeped in fatherhood and in his music, the composer was oblivious to the basic seriousness of the domestic friction in his home. His friend and librettist, Carlton Moss, recalled in later years that everyone in Harlem except Still knew that the marriage was dissolving. Moss told the story of an evening meal at the YMCA with Still, wherein Moss chatted about personal things that were going on in town and Still tapped his foot absently. In the midst of a rendition by Moss of a particularly interesting bit of gossip, the composer looked up placidly and said, "Carlton, give me a name [for the opera] with music in it." Moss realized instantly that his companion hadn't heard a word that he had said, nor did he care what was going on in town or in his own home. He was thinking about his opera.[6]

When Grace took the children and ran away to Canada in 1932, Still's only regret was the loss of his progeny. He could not avoid the feeling of relief, as if an unbearable weight had been lifted from him, and he determined that there was no longer any reason for him to continue living in New York. He remembered that he had been captivated by California when he went there with Paul Whiteman in 1929, and it seemed to him that now was a good time to move west.

In May of 1934 he arrived in Los Angeles to stay for the rest of his life, having driven across the country in his Ford automobile. He brought little with him except his clothes, his Bible, his 1929 diary, his most important pieces of music, and his dog, Shep. With the support of a Guggenheim Fellowship, he began work on his opera, *Blue Steel,* and he hired Verna Arvey, a Jewish concert pianist and journalist, as his press secretary.

It was Verna Arvey who, owing to her friendship with Mrs. Irish of the Los Angeles Philharmonic Society, helped him to garner an invitation to conduct at the Hollywood Bowl in 1936, thereby making him the first Negro to lead a major symphony orchestra in the United States.

In 1939 Still succeeded in divorcing Grace, who had returned from Canada sometime back and had made a futile attempt to regain her husband's confidence. The composer had no intention of going back to New York, or of giving up the productive and reciprocal relationship that he was developing with Miss Arvey.

By 1939 Still and Arvey had made the decision to marry, but they had to go to Mexico to do so because interracial marriages were illegal in California at the time. They drove across the border in Still's '36 Ford, obtained a license, went through the ceremony, then started home. Still was in a hurry to get back home to work on a revision of his opera, and, in his haste, he was given a traffic ticket in National City. The police required that he post bail right on the spot, and, discovering that he did not have the necessary $20, he was detained in jail until his new wife could find a friend who would bring them the money.

Fortunately the difficulties of the wedding day did not portend a shaky future: Still and Arvey were to remain comfortably together for 39 years, producing two children, making countless friends, and collaborating on hundreds of articles and compositions. Their years together were highly-structured, artistically fecund, and endearingly lacking in disagreement.

Every morning Still dressed in a light blue or white cotton shirt over a sleeveless undershirt, dark pleated slacks, black belt and polished black shoes. A terry cloth robe remained on unless he went out or received guests. For breakfast he prepared toast with an abundance of butter, perhaps melon or fruit, and instant coffee for him and his wife, milk for the children. Verna Arvey made the beds, set the table, and let the dog out.

After the morning meal, he retired to his small workroom, where he sat for awhile praying and meditating, inviting the spiritual forces to bless him with inspiration. Then, at the piano, he tried themes that had been given to him spiritually, working them out in detail at the keyboard. Sometimes he did not have to seek his themes in the morning, as they had already come when he slept. Sometimes, during the night, he got up to jot his ideas down, or he invited inspiration during the day by going back to bed after breakfast (with a notebook and several sharpened #1 pencils in his hand).

After twelve noon he did the mechanical work of making piano scores or abstracting orchestral parts. In the thirties he used a music typewriter for this work, but later he went back to copying by hand when he found that it was less tedious and less time-consuming. When the master sheets were finished, he had them copied at the blue print shop downtown, and bound them himself in covers made of colored construction paper, cardboard and horse glue. On occasion he included title pages that were made with designs and pictures fashioned at the typewriter. If the score was for a stage production, he also made a miniature set to go with it out of cardboard, paint and wood.

At 3:30 p.m. his wife served the second meal of the day, a substantial repast with a starchy entree and vegetables from the garden. One day the main dish might be spaghetti, one day enchiladas, one day blintzes, one day potato pancakes. When the food was consumed, she cleaned the dishes and the kitchen, and he recorded in ink the music he had sketched earlier in the day, or went outdoors to mow the lawn, to play with the dog and/or the children, or to work in the garden.

His garden was a source of satisfaction to him and to his wife, for it brought extra food into the household. On the other hand, it could at times be an annoyance when the composer planted too much of something. Growing as if by some hidden power, the vegetables were always two or three times as large as ordinary produce, so that they amply supplied the Still's table as well as the stores of all of the neighbors and friends. If a crop were over-planted, the result was exasperating, as Verna Arvey's notes on the garden relate:

> The zucchini that came from the Still garden were as large as small watermelons. . . . As I say, the Stills were proud of that zucchini at first. It was big and it was plentiful. They ate zucchini for days on end. All their friends ate zucchini. They cooked it with sausages, with butter, with tomatoes, with cheese, and with various sauces. Their ingenuity was finally exhausted, so were their palates. When the time for the next planting arrived, the Stills and their friends held a hasty conference. This year the Stills aren't planting zucchini.

If there was nothing to do in the garden on a particular afternoon, Still built furniture for the house or toys for the children. In his garage he produced tea wagons, lazy susans, bookcases, tables, swings, teeter totters, doll furniture, circus trains, locomotives, and jigsaw puzzles. He especially delighted in making train sets, for they reminded him of his jaunts to the train station in long-ago Little Rock.

At dusk he went indoors, ate a dish of ice cream that had been slightly softened in the oven, and looked over his wife's shoulder while she sat at the piano to play measures that he had composed earlier in the day. If he was content with those measures, he developed them immediately into a conductor's score.

When the orchestrating was finished, he put the children on his lap and read them the OZ Books or *Treasure Island*, after which he tucked them into bed around eight o'clock. That done, he lay on his bed to read his historical novels or philosophical books, or he worked on numerology charts. From eleven to midnight he did crossword puzzles, said his prayers and went to sleep.

Sundays were days of relaxation whereon many friends came to call. (Friends came during the week, also, but on Sundays the numbers were greater). On occasion people were invited to Sunday dinner, or they invited the Stills to dinner, but the composer and his wife never went to any gatherings where they could not take their children. The youngsters grew up without ever knowing that their father had once known how to dance.

On special weekends the composer took his family on drives to museums, parks and train stations, or to downtown Los Angeles to the picture shows. In the late fifties, when city traffic made driving an ordeal for him, he bought a television set and stayed home to watch Dodger baseball, the prize fights, *Perry Mason, Ozzie and Harriet,* and various sorts of travelogues.

In general, Still was an affectionate father and husband, though he was not given to embracing or kissing. When the offspring were babies he held them on his lap to sing *Bye Baby Bunting* to them, or *Frog Went a Courtin'*. These songs were always followed by a session of "this little piggy" on their toes. When they got older he read passages from his philosophy books to them, or rubbed their backs, foreheads and the bridges of their noses when they did not feel well.

When he was not writing music or reading he was childlike in his pleasures, sometimes reciting nonsense rhymes when he was in a good mood, or reading license plates aloud when he was driving, rolling the sounds of the letters around on his tongue. If someone told an especially good joke he laughed until the tears came to his eyes. Sometimes he teased his wife because she had become too fat, even though he was essentially undisturbed about her appearance. Once when he walked into the kitchen in the late evening and found her downing an enormous serving of peach cobbler, he chirped, "Hello, there, appetite, how's Verna?" She almost choked with laughter, but he felt guilty about his teasing and went out the next day to buy a peace-offering of eight pounds of See's chocolate.

And so the days passed, with the garden, and the toys and the crossword puzzles, and, as they passed, the composer wrote a few measures of music every morning and every evening for almost sixty years. Between the thirties and the early fifties many important orchestras played the music, bringing notoriety and material essentials to Still and his family. Among these orchestras were the New York Philharmonic, the Boston Symphony, the Philadelphia Orchestra, the Chicago Symphony, the Cleveland Orchestra, the Los Angeles Philharmonic, the Oklahoma Symphony, the Detroit Symphony, the Liverpool Philharmonic, the B.B.C. Orchestra, the National Symphony in Panama, the Pittsburgh Symphony, the A.B.C. Symphony in Australia, the London Symphony, the Pasdeloup Orchestra, the Cincinnati Symphony, the Helsinki Municipal Orchestra, the Charleston Symphony, and the Institut National Belge de Radiodiffusion (INR) Symphony.

Moreover, everywhere that the music was played the effect was pervasive, involving ovations and praises for its color and rhythm. When the Los Angeles Philharmonic, with

Verna Arvey at the piano and Otto Klemperer on the podium, presented Still's *Kaintuck'* in concert, the *Los Angeles Times* said,

> *Kaintuck'* has the syncopated rhythms one would expect from a natural rhythmist who cut his musical teeth on Whiteman's band music. But its beauty lies in the lazy, flowing melodies and the fine instrumentation. . . . The audience liked it at once. Klemperer, Still and Miss Arvey were returned to the stage several times.[7]

Indeed, it was not only the music that made an impression, but it was also the attractive nature of the composer. The morning before Still conducted the San Diego Symphony Orchestra in his *Kaintuck'* and *Lenox Avenue,* the *San Diego Sun* declared that,

> spontaneous applause, such as the orchestra gave William Grant Still yesterday morning at the close of his rehearsal . . . indicated that the orchestra acknowledged Still's great gifts as a composer, and that both his conducting and his pleasant personality were approved.[8]

Although this public approbation was what he strived to gain, and what he silently appreciated, Still never knew quite how to deal with it when it bore him aloft. If asked to speak before crowds he shrank shyly and stammered a bit, usually deferring to someone else. If he had a chance to prepare, he always read his remarks from a notebook typed and organized by his wife; if not, he thought of some way to escape the situation. The anecdote told by Madeleine Goss in *Modern Music-Makers* is absolutely to the purpose:

> Once at a meeting when he was called on to contribute a few words following a succession of lengthy speeches, he rose—said quietly, 'I wonder if everyone is as hungry as I am?'—and sat down amid loud applause.[9]

Of course, he did not always have to worry about the discomforts of standing in the spotlight, for his fame was merely temporary. The peak of his success came in 1949 when the efforts of Eleanor Roosevelt and Mayor Fiorello La Guardia of New York led, obliquely, to the staging of his opera, *Troubled Island,* on the City Center stage. Still thought that this production, the first such for a Negro composer in the United States, would bring wide acceptance of his music, operatic performances in all of the major houses, and recordings with the top recording companies. Instead, however, the premiere of *Troubled Island* led to an effort among the New York critics to discredit his work; his opera was panned in spite of audience ovations, and future performances of his compositions were discouraged.

Still came home from his opera premiere a shattered man, aware that his flight toward the highest dream of the serious composer—that of operatic performance—was stifled. Even worse, from 1949 on he seemed to be blackballed by the musical community: he was given fewer and fewer performances, fewer commissions and no commercially-promoted recordings whatsoever. He was reduced to writing chamber works, or solos, because major orchestras ceased to play his compositions with regularity.

Still's humor and optimism, long-pressed by the demands of survival, became veiled by an immortal wistfulness. He felt tired and cheated, and turned more and more toward his spiritual beliefs to find self-justification. His disappointment in the prejudices of his fellow adults led him, in the fifties and sixties, to seek out the company of children: if those who were grown were unable to accept him for what he was rather than for his color, he would rely on young minds for better awareness. He and his wife went into the public schools to speak, to play music, and to talk about human understanding; at Christmas he played Santa Claus and handed out little candy-filled stockings at 36th Street School. In 1954 he wrote *The Little Song That Wanted to be a Symphony*, a work that was predicated on the notion that brotherhood could be taught to the younger generation. In an interview with Bob Martin on KPFK radio, Los Angeles, he told why the piece was written:

> We'd noticed how children, under natural circumstances, seem to get along so well, and to have not some of the . . . mistaken ideas that some of the elders have, [in other words], ideas that are taught them. So, the first thought that came was how to get the idea of

brotherhood . . . over in a musical way to young folks, and to have a little story [along with it], some sort of 'catch' story that would be palatable. So, the idea of *The Little Song That Wanted to Be a Symphony* came.[10]

During this period he also wrote spiritual arrangements for school textbooks, and a song with the theme of brotherhood called *Minorities*. Finances were dwindling, however, and only a brief period of writing background music for television shows such as *Gunsmoke*, *Three Stooges*, *Have Gun Will Travel* and *Perry Mason* helped to keep food on the table. This studio work required long hours of labor, and, because he was his own copyist, he frequently stayed up all night extracting parts. As the light in his workroom was poor, his eyes suffered.

In the later years, he had trouble with his eyes, his teeth and his stomach, but few outsiders could tell that he was uncomfortable. Everyone commented upon his youthful appearance, and, on February 12, 1968, when he conducted the Seattle Youth Symphony, the *Seattle Post-Intelligencer* observed that Still was "the image of courtesy and courtliness," and although "73 years of age, barely looks to be 50." John B. Parker said, "Still's smooth skin, twinkling eyes and the general vibrant impression he gives belie his years."[11]

From 1963 to 1969 he became the willing Grandfather to the four children born to his daughter, Judith. Because his daughter was going to college, he and his wife were often called upon to babysit, a task which returned a lifting smile to his aspect, and a brightness that winked and fluttered behind a serene exterior. If he opened the door to find the children arriving unexpectedly, he exclaimed with elation,

"Verna, come quick! The babies are here. Now, you just come right on in, darlings."

Then followed hours of reading stories, singing songs, piggies on the toes and several choruses of *24 Robbers at My Door*. If the babies were unruly, he shook his head helplessly and went on to some new game—he had forgotten the virtues of Carrie Still's whipping strap.

His health failed in 1970, right after his much-beloved son-in-law, geologist Larry Headlee, was killed in a mini-submarine accident. Four months after the funeral he had a heart attack and a stroke, and his mind was batted like a shuttlecock between vacancy and desperate confusion. In 1975 he was placed in a sanitarium near his home in Los Angeles, and he died there in December of 1978.

Many of his friends, in referring to him after his death, spoke of his humility, his manners, his august way of speaking, his considerate yet distinguished air. Mrs. John Wright, a long-term friend of the family, said that he was the closest thing to a saint that she had known in her life. All agreed that he was a singular man of the spirit about whom God would say, "Well done, thou good and faithful servant."

Thus the course was run from bon vivant, serenading sweethearts in the evening air, to saint. It was a passage teeming with exuberance, self-conscious spirituality, struggle, triumph and disappointment, with comment, praise and criticism.

Now the job of making the final, detached assessment begins. Now that the composer's papers have been transferred to the University of Arkansas for study, much more will be written and compiled, much will be presumed and assumed. As with all human endeavor, and despite every effort to the contrary, study may fail to see accurately into the past, as it did in Shaffer's *Amadeus*.

And yet, where facts and presences have been overtaken by critical observance, where memorabilia do not say all that needs to be said, it is hoped that the music itself will retrace a long progress, digging channels through which all can stream toward the open sea of human vision. If Peter Shaffer had really listened to Mozart's music—had truly heard the composer's melodic heart beating—he could not have written *Amadeus*. Only the creative product has a pure voice. Only the product can take William Grant Still from his place as "Dean of Negro Composers," to his larger place as a "Dean of American Composers," the progenitor of works that are the "most American in character."

Not only do Still's works stretch the scope of American serious music to admit minority idioms, but, as Hanson pointed out, they also bridge the enormous chasms in American culture between radio and film music, folk music and symphonic music. Moreover, his works have made these grand leaps without having forced the composer to abandon his role as a helpmate of mankind, or, in the words of Hanson, "as a gentle man," full of "simplicity, friendship, love and beauty."[12]

The music, when all is finished, is the voice which whispers and winks, smiles and coerces, hiding behind the diaries, journals and critical publications, answering the unanswered questions, unearthing the composer's intent, and revealing the arresting personality that peeked shyly around that intention.

Notes

1. Letter from Bob Martin, KPFK (Los Angeles) radio host, to Judith Anne Still, May 25, 1986, in possession of the author.

2. Artie Shaw, conversation with the author, September 10, 1986.

3. Verna Arvey, "Afro-American Music Memo," *Music Journal* 27 (November 1969), 36, 68, 69.

4. Howard Hanson speech at the University of Southern California, May 24, 1975.

5. Albert Einstein, unidentified newspaper clipping, Berlin, Germany, March 6, 1933. John Briggs, "Rodzinski and the Philharmonic Perform Two New Compositions," *New York Post*, January 6, 1944.

6. Carlton Moss, telephone conversation with the author, July, 1983.

7. Isabel Morse Jones, "New Music Work Lauded," *Los Angeles Times*, February 18, 1939.

8. Constance Herreshoff, "Still to Lead Symphony in Bowl Tonight," *San Diego Sun*, August 9, 1938.

9. Madeleine Goss, *Modern Music-Makers* (New York: E.P. Dutton, 1952), 217.

10. Interview of William Grant Still by Bob Martin, KPFK (Los Angeles) radio, May, 1964.

11. Rolf Stomberg, "Something to Harp About," *Seattle Post-Intelligencer*, February 12, 1968. John B. Parker, "Composer Praises Individuality He Developed At OC," Elyria, Ohio, *Chronicle-Telegram,* November 10, 1970.

12. Howard Hanson speech, May 24, 1975.

BIOGRAPHICAL SKETCH OF WILLIAM GRANT STILL

Carolyn L. Quin

The life and career of William Grant Still (1895-1978) spanned an important period in the development of an American style of composed music which gradually became distinct from European models. Often judged by those European models and criticized for taking an alternative path, Still, the composer, followed his convictions with courage. Throughout his career, he sought to create an American style in his music. He studied the folk music of indigenous people of the Americas, African Americans, Africans in the Caribbean, and southerners as source material for his melodies and rhythms. He found expression in his music for his own heritage. He studied and arranged jazz and used those rich harmonies in his style. He felt strongly that any composer who called himself an American must study jazz whether he used it in his composition or not. Still experimented with his orchestrations in musical revues of the 1920s and radio broadcasts in the early 1930s. He used the instruments and the special effects he found in commercial music in his operas, ballets, and symphonies, composed, for the most part, after 1934.

Working as he did outside of a secure academic position, concentrating on composing, conducting only occasionally, Still showed a rare focus and a distinct, self-imposed discipline. Everyday, throughout most of his life, he studied, sketched, copied, scored, arranged, composed, or revised music. He loved his work. Once he knew what he wanted to do with an idea, he would select a title for the composition and work on that piece until he finished it. Often he drew on the resources of his own sketchbooks, theme books, and other notes as he brought an idea to fruition.

Born in Woodville, Mississippi, on May 11, 1895, William Grant Still was the son of William Grant Still, Sr. (1871-1895), and Carrie Lena Fambro Still (1872-1927), both college graduates and teachers. His father, a native of Woodville, had completed his education in 1892 at Alcorn Agricultural and Mechanical College in nearby Lorman, Mississippi, where he had distinguished himself in music and mathematics. For the 1892-1893 academic year, he took a position as instructor of bookkeeping, instrumental music, and vocal music at Alabama Agricultural and Industrial College in Normal, Alabama. There he met Carrie Fambro, an 1886 graduate of Atlanta University, who was also teaching at the Alabama college headed by President William Harper Councill. On June 26, 1894, they were married and they decided to live in Woodville, Mississippi. There Mr. Still had family, property, and contacts. He shared ownership in a grocery store with his friend, Harry Anderson, and he had the respect of both black and white leaders of the community.

A friend of the Stills recollected in later years that the young couple brought their infant son to a six-day Teachers Institute in the summer of 1895. That fall, on September 26, 1895, the elder Still died. The exact circumstances of his death remain a mystery. Very soon after, Carrie Fambro Still left Woodville for Little Rock, Arkansas, where her mother and sister lived. With the life insurance funds she had, she purchased a home for herself and her son and invited her mother to live with them. She established herself in Little Rock as a strict and highly respected English teacher in the public schools where she taught until her death in 1927.

Anne Fambro, who had been a slave in a plantation home in Milner, Georgia, became the primary caretaker for her grandson. When she took the five-year old child to Atlanta to visit his relatives for the first time, a cousin of his mother gave this account of the relationship: "His mother was a teacher and their sole support. So he was left mainly to his grandmother who was devoted to him and he to her. She was his protector."[1]

In a 1969 interview with Dr. Eileen Southern, Still said of his mother, Carrie Fambro Still, "she had many talents. She painted, played piano, embroidered, even wrote a piece of fiction . . . called *Orange and Lemon* . . . I must have been about five or six—when she put on *A Midsummer's* [sic] *Night's Dream* to raise money to start a school library. The next year, either 1901 or 1902, it was the *Merchant of Venice*."[2] Carrie Still was active in the neighborhood where they lived in Little Rock and during the course of her life achieved considerable wealth through her investments in real estate. She also started the first library open to African Americans in Little Rock at the Capitol Hill School. She spent her summers traveling to rural areas to teach less fortunate children, usually with her son in tow.

In 1904, Carrie Still married Charles Benjamin Shepperson, a railway postal clerk who loved music and the theatre. He often took his stepson to traveling productions when they came through Little Rock, and he encouraged him in his musical interests. It was Shepperson who helped Billy convince his mother to allow him to study violin in 1908 with William Price, an American violinist who lived briefly in Little Rock.[3]

Still graduated as valedictorian of his class at M. W. Gibbs High School in 1911, having just turned sixteen. Although he had long expressed an interest in music, his mother was adamant in her opposition to music as a career. He enrolled in Wilberforce College, a distinguished school established and operated by the African Methodist Episcopal Church, in the fall of 1911. Mabel Mute recollected that "many funny incidents were related by the girls from Little Rock who were his classmates. . . . One girl told of his going to class with a music book on harmony instead of taking his history book. . . . She reminded him that he had this music book and he was perfectly dazed and said, 'Oh, yes.' He was always dreaming about his music and really lived in another world."[4]

Still later recalled,

> The big turning point in my life came during the summer of 1912. When I went home [from Wilberforce College] for spring vacation that year, I found that my step-father . . . had purchased a victrola. . . . That summer [at the age of seventeen] I lay on the floor day after day, all summer long, listening to records of operas. I even remember the make—Red Seal records . . . [the operas were] *Il Trovatore, Rigoletto, Elixir of Love,* and others. I should say that my deep love of opera dates from that time. I knew then that I had to learn how to compose operatic music. (Southern, 168)

While he was a student at Wilberforce, he joined the important social fraternity, Kappa Alpha Psi. His interest in music became so strong that he once spent his entire allowance ($8.50) on an oboe he ordered through a mail order catalogue. The college did not have a music department at the time, so, according to Still, the students

> handled their own music. . . . after I got settled I took over the band . . . I made arrangements for the band. I would borrow instruments from the band's supply and teach

myself the basics until I learned what kinds of things each instrument could do . . . I also made arrangements for the student string quartet that I organized. (Southern, 169)

Still was inspired during his college years by the Afro-British composer, Samuel Coleridge-Taylor (1875-1912), who served as a role model for the first generation of African American composers. Coleridge-Taylor, whose most famous work was *Hiawatha's Wedding Feast,* made three successful visits to the United States in 1904, 1906, and 1910. He was an admirer of Antonin Dvořák and became acquainted with the African American singer and composer Harry T. Burleigh during his visits. "Coleridge-Taylor saw it as his mission in life to help establish the dignity of the black man. He was greatly influenced by the black American poet Paul Laurence Dunbar (some of whose poems he set), by the Fisk Jubilee Singers of Nashville, by W. E. B. DuBois, Frederick Douglass, Booker T. Washington and others, whose works he studied zealously."[5] As Still recalled, "although I did not get to know him personally . . . I tried to imitate him in every way possible, even tried to make my rather straight hair stand up on my head bushily like he wore his." (Southern, 167-168)

By 1914, his ambitions were growing. A relative recalled,

This summer of his nineteenth year, he entered a national contest of composers. . . . He would slip up at night in his pajamas and sit at the dining room table far into the morning hours absorbed in his writing. . . . The critics of the contest wrote him that his music was not understood by them, but it was of merit. . . . After all his mother's trying to discourage him with being a musician or composer, he would remark, when she left the room . . . "It is settled, Mabel, I am to be a composer." He was very respectful to his mother and he never crossed her, but he was quietly determined.[6]

In the spring of 1915 he left Wilberforce without graduating and began to play in dance bands and orchestras in Columbus and Dayton. In Columbus he played in a small combo that consisted of piano, clarinet, violin, flute, and cello. They played at the Athletic Club and "got involved with some white vaudeville shows. Then we went to Cleveland for the summer, where we played at Luna Park . . . I played the cello. As for music, they wanted dinner music at the Athletic Club. We would play things like *Chocolate Soldier* [Oscar Strauss]. . . . We played 'straight' [no improvisation]." (Southern, 168)

On October 4, 1915, he married Grace Bundy. Since he had not completed his degree, Still's allowance ended, and he had to support himself and his new wife with his professional playing. The marriage seemed ill-fated from the beginning, and Grace moved back to Danville, Kentucky, with her parents in May, 1916. Their first child, William Bundy Still, was born in November. Still recalled later, that, even though he rented and furnished a house in Columbus, he was not able to persuade Grace to come to live with him until July of 1921.[7]

In the summer of 1916, he got an opportunity to go to Memphis, Tennessee, to arrange for William Christopher Handy's band. While it is possible that Still's stepfather, Mr. Shepperson, knew Handy and helped him make the contact, the young Still would have been no stranger to the man who would be called "The Father of the Blues." Handy had succeeded William Grant Still, Sr., as the band director at the Alabama Agricultural and Industrial College. Mr. Still had directed the band with such distinction that in 1900, when W. C. Handy had taken his place on the faculty, President W. H. Councill remarked, "My, my, what a delightful program. Mr. Handy is the best band teacher we've had since the days of Mr. Still."[8] Handy left the college after two years.

Still's position with Handy required that he travel with the band on the road, riding in train cars and eating and sleeping in private homes, since blacks were not allowed to stay or eat in white-owned hotels or restaurants. Although from this experience Still came to understand why his mother had been so adamant about not wanting her son to choose music as a profession, it was even more important that he had the opportunity to learn and understand the blues. Pace and Handy Music Company, Memphis, Tennessee, published some of his first arrangements, *Florida Blues* by William King Phillips and *Old Miss* (a ragtime piece) by W. C. Handy, in 1916. As he reflected in later years on the importance of his work with Handy,

> It brought me closer to Negro music, because . . . I didn't come in contact much with Negro music until I had become of age and had entered professional work. I had to go out and learn it. . . . Now, in the blues, I saw this: a unique musical creation of Negroes. . . . [the blues] were looked down upon . . . they were considered to be connected with the dives. . . . I felt that there was something more in them than that. . . . I wanted to dignify it through using it in major symphonic composition.[9]

When he turned twenty-two in May of 1917, he received an inheritance from his father's interest in the grocery store in Woodville, Mississippi. Still decided to use it to study music at Oberlin. He studied composition and theory at Oberlin with Friedrich Lehmann and George Whitfield Andrews.[10] He also studied violin there with Maurice Kessler, to whom he later dedicated his fourth symphony. He had a concert of his own works on a student recital which included a song setting of a poem by Paul Laurence Dunbar, *Good Night*. When asked later in life why he chose Oberlin, Still said, "The reason was this: that quite a number of colored Americans had gone to Oberlin. . . . [I went] because it was . . . recognized as a good school." (Brown, 21) Still continued to visit his wife whenever his schedule permitted at her parents' home in Kentucky.

World War I interrupted his study. He enlisted in the Navy as a mess attendant in 1918. Still gave an account of his nine months of service:

> I was so bad at being a mess attendant—and someone found out I could play violin—that they put me to work playing with a white pianist in the Officers Mess . . . [we played] popular tunes of the day: "You Made Me Love You," "Roses of Picardy," "After You've Gone," things like that. . . . Even when we were attacked by torpedos . . . we had to keep the music going. (Southern, 168-169)

After his discharge from the Navy, Still went to work in a shipyard at Port Newark, New Jersey, where he remained until he received a telegram in January, 1919, stating that his wife was dead. He quit his job and went to Danville, only to find that the message was a prank. By then they had a second child, Gail Lynton Still, who had been born in 1918. (Papers, 52:9)

Still decided to go back to Oberlin for additional study, but he left the school in 1919 to go to New York. W. C. Handy's business was expanding in New York, and he asked him to work for the Pace and Handy Music Publishing Company as a full-time staff arranger and to perform with Handy's touring band. Still recalled later,

> It was a very wonderful thing for me [to get a job with Handy] because I wanted to be in New York. I realized that it was necessary at the time, that I just had to be there. . . . I saw no way whatsoever [to get ahead unless I could find work in New York] . . . so this opportunity to work with Handy was one that I regarded as remarkable. . . . As far as Handy was concerned, it was all orchestrating, and, of course, he had an orchestra too [which traveled]. We weren't in New York all the time. We traveled to a large extent in the South. . . . And we would go out for periods—we'd go out for a month or so, and then come back to New York—making several trips during the course of the year. And then I would work there in the office when I was in New York. (Brown, 4)

Still remembered that Handy's orchestra had "six pieces. Handy played the cornet, of course. Then there was a piano, trombone, and clarinet. Also strings—I played violin or cello, whichever was needed . . . we played for dances and gave concerts on college campuses." (Southern, 169-170) Once back in the office, Still was busy, preparing at least seven tunes for publication in 1919, including *Frisco Jazz Band Blues* (Freddie Rich) and *I Never Had the Blues* (Straight P. Williams).[11]

Because he did not have the funds when he arrived in New York to join the Clef Club, Still free-lanced on the oboe, violin, and cello and "got involved with the Negro groups there." (Southern, 169) Musical groups, led and populated by black musicians, sprang up all over New York to fulfill the needs of the dance crazed white population. Eileen Southern noted, "A tiny item appeared in *Variety* magazine in 1915: 'Since the turkey-trot craze, the colored musicians in New York have been busy dispensing syncopated music for the 400' (i.e., the cream of white society)."[12]

In 1919 as staff arranger at the Pace and Handy Music Publishing Company, Still did an arrangement of the *St. Louis Blues,* which was recorded by James Reese Europe's "Hellfighters" of the 369th Infantry Regiment Band. This is the first known recording of an arrangement by Still. Europe credited the band with innovations: "With the brass instruments we put in mutes and make a whirling motion with the tongue, at the same time blowing full pressure. With wind instruments we pinch the mouthpiece and blow hard." W. C. Handy always credited Still with being the first person to arrange the *St. Louis Blues* (composed in 1914) for orchestra, although that first version was probably done in 1916.[13]

The Pace and Handy partnership dissolved in January, 1921, even though Still's arrangement of *Whistling Blues* (Joe Diamond, Jack Barnett, and Saxi Holtsworth) carried a 1921 publication date. On Sunday evening, October 30, 1921, Still's art song *Good Night* was performed by soprano Revella E. Hughes at St. Mark's Hall on 138th Street, marking the first New York performance of an original work by Still.[14]

In May of 1921, he began to play oboe in the pit orchestra for *Shuffle Along*. "Deacon Johnson's group," as Still called it, was the orchestra led by Hall Johnson (who also played viola) of this successful show. Eubie Blake and Noble Sissle wrote the music and lyrics for *Shuffle Along* and Flournoy Miller and Aubrey Lyles wrote the libretto or "book." According to Still, "there were several associated with that show who later would become well known in their respective fields. In addition to Blake and Sissle themselves, there were Paul Robeson, Caterina Jarboro, Florence Mills, and Josephine Baker." (Southern, 170)

After a brief road tour to raise funds for a New York production, *Shuffle Along* had its premieres on May 22 and 23, 1921, at the 63rd Street Theatre.

> Eubie Blake explained: "It was really off-Broadway, but we caused it to be Broadway.... It was the price of the ticket that mattered. Our tickets cost the same as any Broadway show. That made it Broadway!" *Shuffle Along,* which had charged $1.00 . . . upped its admission to $2.00 for half the orchestra seats. The rest of the orchestra seats was [sic] priced at $1.50.[15]

Variety assumed that the show would attract a black audience, but the reviewer found the clientele almost ninety percent white. The show ran for 504 performances, and

> James Weldon Johnson credited *Shuffle Along* with breaking the rigid barriers of segregation in New York City's legitimate theatres that restricted blacks to the balcony. *Variety*'s critic noted on opening night that "colored patrons were noticed as far front as the fifth row," as though he were surprised by such a sight . . . *Variety* calmed its readers by noting that "the two races are rarely intermingled."[16]

Theatrical producer John Cort, who had backed the show initially

> eventually persuaded a Boston producer to open his theatre for the show in July, 1922. . . . Initially set for a two-week run, *Shuffle Along* attracted audiences in surprising numbers. . . . the run stretched into three months. . . . after threat of a lawsuit, *Shuffle Along* had to vacate the theatre.[17]

In Boston with the show from July until early October of 1922, Still decided to see if he could study composition at The New England Conservatory of Music. Still recalled,

> Now Boston is where my life took an unusual turn. . . . the secretary recommended Mr. Chadwick. He looked at something I had written and offered to teach me free of charge. I learned a great deal from that man. It was he more than anyone else who inspired me to write American music. (Southern, 170)

George Whitefield Chadwick was at that time the Director of the New England Conservatory of Music. Still studied with him for about three months.

In the orchestra for *Shuffle Along* he was paid $60 a week to play oboe. His wife, Grace, had come to New York in July of 1921 to live with him, and at her request, he rented rooms in the Bronx near Pelham Bay Park, despite the inconvenience it caused him in getting to work. A third child, a daughter, June Allen Still, had been born in 1920. As Still remembered, "I took her [Grace] to Boston where she made my life miserable by nagging and constantly finding fault with me. She decided I must quit the show and get a job in New York." (Papers, 52:9)

When *Shuffle Along* went on to Chicago, Still returned to New York to work as an arranger for Harry Pace at the Pace Phonograph Company at $30 per week. The Pace Phonograph Company, which pressed records on the Black Swan label, is "credited with being the first recording company owned by blacks."[18] Still was promoted to Musical Director when Fletcher Henderson, who was Recording Manager, "went down town to play at a dance hall [the exclusive Club Alabam on forty-fourth street]." (Southern, 170) In the meantime, Grace had rented an apartment on St. Nicholas Avenue for $75 a month. "There my life was made miserable again by lack of good management. Every cent we had went as soon as it came to us. Her parents came, and lived on me for the entire winter." (Papers, 52:9)

Fletcher Henderson had worked as a house pianist for the Pace and Handy Music Publishing Company in 1920 while Still was an arranger there. Henderson had subsequently gone on tour with his Black Swan Dance Masters with blues singer Ethel Waters. (*See:* B128) When Still put some of his popular songs on the Black Swan label, Fletcher Henderson was the pianist who recorded *I Want To* in a piano solo version and who played piano for Isabelle Washington in the vocal version of the same piece. Ethel Waters and Her Jazz Masters recorded three of Still's songs, *Brown Baby, Memphis Man,* and *Lost Out Blues.*

Using the pseudonym Willie M. Grant, Still authored at least three additional recorded songs, *How I Got Dem Twilight Blues, Love Me in Your Own Time,* and *Go Get It.* These 1923 works are the first known recordings of original compositions by Still. The other artists on his recordings on the Black Swan label were Inez Wallace, C. Carroll Clark, Helen Woodruff, and Josie Miles. On the same label were two spiritual arrangements attributed to William Grant Still, *Swing Low, Sweet Chariot* and *Steal Away,* and a Still/Henderson cut, *Pretty Ways.*[19] Still had two more arrangements published that year.

In the meantime, Still's family situation worsened in 1923 when, as Still remembers, Grace decided to buy a home, using money she had borrowed from his mother and money he had saved. Then, she filled the house at 225 West 127th Street with "roomers, some of whom were objectionable . . . the police had to be called." (Papers, 52:9)

Carrying on professionally despite the conflicts at home, Still conducted, arranged, and composed for the Pace Phonograph Company in his position as Musical Director. The business soon began to have its own troubles. As Eileen Southern concluded, "Although Pace engaged some of the best artists of his time, the competition from the white recording companies proved to be overwhelming. In 1923 his business began to falter; he declared bankruptcy in December of that year, and in March 1924 he sold the Black Swan label to Paramount Records."[20]

While working in the offices at the Pace Phonograph Company in 1923, Still got an opportunity that would set the course of his first successes as a composer. He intercepted a letter sent to Pace by the French composer, Edgard Varèse, who, by then, lived in New York. Varèse inquired if there might be some Negro musician working there who would like to study composition with him on a scholarship. Still recalled, "I said, 'Now wait. Hold it. Give that to me. I want that.' And so I managed to get that scholarship." (Brown, 5)

Still began his study with the French modernist that year. His association with Varèse provided many of the important professional contacts of Still's early career and made opportunities for performances of his first works possible. His time with Varèse until 1925 represented the longest period of formal study of composition he would ever have with a single teacher. Varèse promoted and supported him in every way. Still often said, "When I was groping blindly in my efforts to compose, it was Varese [*sic*] who pointed out to me the way to individual expression and gave me the opportunity to hear my music performed."[21]

As a student of Varèse, Still composed a number of works for which he would later be recognized with performances and publications. The works dating from these important years in his development as a composer were *From the Black Belt, From the Land of Dreams, From the Journal of a Wanderer, Levee Land,* and *Death Song* (with a text by Paul Laurence Dunbar). During this time, he first sketched the important suite, *Africa,* and began to keep a theme book and a sketch book with ideas for later use.

While he was studying with Varèse and after the dissolution of the Pace Phonograph Company, Still and his family went through a period of time when he was not working regularly. When Still's mother came to visit in the summer of 1924, Grace left and went to visit her family in Danville. "She disliked my mother, [even] after having accepted my mother's financial favors. . . . My mother was left to look after the children." When Grace returned, she brought her parents to live with them permanently. In September, 1924, their fourth child, Caroline Elaine, was born. By April or May of 1925, they lost their house on 137th Street and the money that had gone into it. When Grace selected a $90 a month apartment at 83 St. Nicholas Place, Still lost the job he had at the time. In frustration he reflected, "She never realized that my work was uncertain and that we should conserve for the time we needed the money." (Papers, 52:9)

During these years, Still orchestrated for a number of Broadway and off-Broadway shows and musical revues. Among his orchestrating and arranging credits are *Runnin' Wild* (1923), a Miller and Lyles show with music by James P. Johnson; *Dixie to Broadway* (1924), written by whites but starring black singer, Florence Mills of *Shuffle Along* fame; *Creole Follies,* a Leonard L. Harper production with music by Johnson and lyrics by Henry Creamer; *Struttin' Time,* music by C. Lucketh Roberts, lyrics by Eddie Hunter and Alex Rogers, and book by Alex Rogers; several editions of *Earl Carroll's Vanities,* one edition of J. P. McEvoy's *Americana;* and *Rain or Shine* (1928), music by Milton Ager and Owen Murphy, book by James Gleason and Maurice Marks. A reviewer of *Runnin' Wild* said, "whoever arranged the music of James Johnson and Cecil Mack is something of a genius, we think."[22] Still's reputation as a fine orchestrator grew.

Still played oboe in the short-lived Harlem Orchestra conducted by E. Gilbert Anderson, along with Fletcher Henderson (piano), Marion Cumbo (violin), Rudolph Dunbar (clarinet), and others.[23] That experience made such a lasting impression that Still would later dream of establishing an all-Negro orchestra.

Finally on February 8, 1925, the premiere of a work billed as Still's "first" work, *From the Land of Dreams,* took place on an International Composers' Guild concert, a culmination of his two seasons of study with Varèse. The performance was at Aeolian Hall, and it was the fourth season of the ICG. The reviews appeared in major newpapers in New York. Louise Varèse said, "after the concert, Still wrote his teacher: 'That was one of the greatest moments of my life. . . . Through it all I never lost sight of the one who befriended me.'"[24]

After the opening, Still hosted a celebration event which Mrs. Varèse described from her special perspective:

> Still gave a dinner at his house [on West 127th Street] in Harlem (wonderful fried chicken) in honor of Varèse and afterward a very large and formal reception with all the women in elaborate evening gowns. It was a very dignified and even solemn occasion. Varèse and I stood together and were introduced individually in an exactly repeated formula to each one of the fifty or more guests. Still, as well as many of his dark guests, had ceremonious and even courtly manners that would have graced any embassy or king's court—the genetic memory of ancestral pride and ritualistic formality.[25]

Almost a year later on January 24, 1926, the International Composers' Guild premiered another Still work, *Levee Land,* conducted by Eugene Goossens, the second concert of its fifth season. According to the report in the *Musical Courier,* the concert included a "galaxy of stars:" Florence Mills, for whom *Levee Land* was written, Elsa Respighi (wife of the composer), Alfredo Casella (the pianist), Guiseppe Respighi, Germaine Tailleferre, Carlos Salzedo, and Eugene Goossens. Incidentally, the only other American composer on the program that night besides Still was Carl Ruggles. The reviewer said, "This year he [Still] . . . gave the public four foolish jazz jokes—sung by Florence Mills in true and proper Broadway manner—and greatly enjoyed by the public. These works are so good, healthy, sane—such good musical fooling—that they place this Negro composer on a high plane in the super-jazz field just now in vogue." Louise Varèse remembered, "The previous spring, Still had brought her [Mills] to the house and had taken us to hear her sing at the Palace, a vaudeville theater."[26]

Still was invited to enter the Orchestral Composition Contest of The Chicago North Shore Festival Association. He submitted *From the Journal of a Wanderer.* While he waited on word from the Festival, he began to sketch his first grandiose ideas for *Sahdji* in March of 1926. He sent the ballet to the Chicago Allied Arts, Inc., who rejected it, but commissioned him to write another based on a legend of Martinique. On May 3, Ruth Page, the dancer who suggested the story, wrote, "I am so happy you are going to write the music for my Martinique ballet—I have heard so much about you, and I think you are a great person to do it."[27]

On April 3, 1926, the North Shore Festival informed Still that his piece was one of five finalists in their contest.[28] While Still ultimately did not win the prize, his piece was performed in public at the Festival by the Chicago Symphony Orchestra with Frederick Stock conducting in May of 1926, marking the first performance of a work by Still by a major orchestra outside of New York City.

In the summer of 1926, Still free-lanced again as a performer, playing oboe in a pit orchestra for Leroy Smith in Atlantic City, New Jersey. A cable from Don Voorhees, for whom Still did a lot of arranging, ended that job. It said, "PUT IN YOUR NOTICE IMMEDIATELY SO THAT YOU WILL BE BACK HERE NO LATER THAN THE TWENTY SIXTH SOONER IF POSSIBLE LET ME KNOW IF OK."[29] Still's career as a performer is to date largely undocumented, except for the *Shuffle Along* position and the stints with Handy's band, but he played frequently when he needed money and was not able to find jobs arranging or orchestrating. Providing a rare glimpse into that aspect of his career, he said, "I used to play with that orchestra after they left the Cotton Club. We played downtown at Ciro's, one of Jack Legs Diamond's places . . . there was no difference [in the music] whatsoever. They played the same type of music down there as at the Cotton Club." (Brown, 13)

In September, Still sent the score of his ballet, *La Guiablesse,* to Ruth Page who had written the scenario. A letter to Still dated October 5, 1926, acknowledged that the "piano and orchestra score of La Guiablesse reached Chicago. . . . Enclosed please find our check constituting the balance unpaid."[30] Still had completed his first commissioned original work, but there would not be a production of *La Guiablesse* until 1933. The Chicago Allied Arts, Inc., however, announced *La Guiablesse* as part of a group of ballets that were to be produced by Adolph Bolm in December, 1926, but Still's work was not performed. The only work advertised that made it to production was a commissioned ballet by Ralph Vaughn Williams based on the *Christmas Carol* of Charles Dickens. Other works also announced in the series, but not performed, included *Symphony for Small Orchestra* by Darius Milhaud, Igor Stravinsky's *L'Histoire du Soldat*, a Venetian ballet by Ottorino Respighi, one by Moussorgsky, and a new ballet by John Alden Carpenter.

Darker America was the third work of Still to be performed on an International Composers' Guild concert. It premiered in Aeolian Hall in New York on November 28, 1926, with Eugene Goossens conducting. The *Musical Courier* reported that "The actual high spot was a new work by that greatly gifted negro [sic] composer, William G. Still." Olin Downes supported the work by declaring, "The best music last night was that of 'Darker America.'" *Musical America* praised the work by pointing out the "earnestness of the writing, the driving energy of the rhythmic movement and the ingenious scoring. . . . The music has a powerful emotional urge and convincing sincerity."[31]

In November of 1927 *Darker America* premiered in Rochester, New York, and won a professional jury's approval in a program of American music presented at The Eastman School of Music, under the direction of Dr. Howard Hanson. The audience was given the opportunity to vote on the new music heard. They selected another work for their second choice, but were overuled by the distinguished jury which included Olin Downes, critic of the *New York Times*; Eugene Goossens, conductor of the Rochester Philharmonic Orchestra; and Stewart B. Sabin, music critic of the *Rochester Democrat and Chronicle*. A note from Claire R. Reis, sent to Still in care of Edgard Varèse, informed him that *Darker America* was sent abroad by the United States Section of the International Society for Contemporary Music.[32] The result was that Still's works began to be introduced in Europe.

From the Black Belt, for chamber orchestra, premiered in New York on March 20, 1927, performed by Georges Barrère's Little Symphony. It had been completed in 1924. Reviewers did not fail to point out that Still was a student of Varèse, for whom they had little regard because of his encouragement of experimentation and his free use of dissonance, but they praised Still's music, despite his teacher, for clever scoring, and called his *Blues* an "artistic example." The Barrère Little Symphony kept *From the Black Belt* in their repertoire for several years after that. In 1930, Still himself conducted this work in a concert at the Park Avenue Theatre.[33]

On April 16, 1927, in a concert at the New School for Social Research, Jessie Zachary performed three art songs by Still in a group called "Dialect Songs." The songs were *Winter's Approach, The Breath of a Rose,* and *Mandy Lou*. A month later, Still received a letter from G. C. Sonneck who at that time worked at the publisher, G. Schirmer, Inc., informing him that *Winter's Approach* and *The Breath of a Rose* had been accepted for publication. A set of three pieces for orchestra, *Log Cabin Ballads,* and the song, *Mandy Lou*, were rejected by the same publisher that year. He also arranged and recorded with Don Voorhees, *Fantasy on St. Louis Blues,* on a Columbia disc.[34]

Personal tragedy struck for Still when his stepfather died in a drowning accident. Soon after, in February, 1927, his mother's health began to fail, just as she was finally beginning to see that her son would achieve success as a composer and to approve of his chosen profession. In February, "when the doctors informed me that my mother suffered a fatal illness, I wrote her a letter in which I spoke of my love for her, my pride in her accomplishments and my admiration for her moral integrity." (Papers, 52:9) His mother died on May 18, 1927.

Early the next year, Still received notice that he had been chosen for the Second Award of the William E. Harmon Awards for Distinguished Achievement among Negroes in Music and that the prize of $100 and a bronze metal would be presented to him on Lincoln's birthday, February 12, 1928. A letter of congratulations from the Grace Congregational Church of Harlem, where Still attended, noted that this award was especially important because it was "in the difficult field of musical composition." The letter indicated that they had missed Still in church recently, and they supposed that he was out of town.[35]

Still became a charter member of the Pan American Association of Composers, founded in 1928 by Edgard Varèse, Henry Cowell, and Carlos Chavez. As a concert sponsor, the Association emphasized repeated performances of works, rather than premieres like the ICG. Among his associates in this organization, in addition to the founders, were Ruth Crawford, Howard Hanson, Roy Harris, Charles Ives, Heitor Villa-Lobos, Colin McPhee, Wallingford Riegger, Carl Ruggles, and Adolph Weiss.

His reputation as an arranger became firmly established, and his scrapbooks included notices of radio broadcasts of his orchestrations over WNAC Boston, WEEI Boston, and WOR New York. Don Voorhees and his concert orchestra were the stars of a program on WOR, and the works by Still that were listed in a program announcement were *Dance of Love* and *Juba,* both now lost. A 1939 biography of Still suggested that "*Dance of Love* (played over the radio many times) was put into the *Sorcerer Ballet* . . . and the *Dance of the Carnal Flowers* [another lost work] was inserted, with few changes, into the ballet *La Guiablesse.*"[36]

When he began to make $100 a week arranging for Voorhees, Still decided to buy a place in Westchester for his family to live, but his wife decided that they should get a place in Jamaica, Long Island. They moved to 108-15 172nd Street, Jamaica, Long Island, probably in April 1928 and remained there until 1932. The couple published a popular song together, *No Matter What You Do,* with Grace providing the lyrics. In the meantime, Still entered a symphonic work in the Victor Symphonic Contest, but his entry was not successful.

Still met Paul Whiteman "through Jack Robbins, a music publisher, who gave Whiteman one of Still's arrangements without identifying the arranger. Paul liked the piece immediately."[37] Still did two arrangements for him in February. In March of 1929 the number of arrangements increased and included several medleys. By April, Still supplied the busy band with an arrangement of *My Girl,* and six more medleys, including *Irving Berlin, Inc.,* and *Ancient History Medley.*

Then Still was hired for one year to do arrangements for Paul Whiteman and His Orchestra for the "Old Gold Hour," sponsored by Old Gold Cigarettes on radio in California. Still, who became full-time just as the group was leaving for the West Coast, traveled with Whiteman and his bandsmen to Hollywood in May. They all returned to New York in September, because of an important engagement Whiteman's band had to fulfill in New York, and, in October, the entourage went back to California, remaining there until April of 1930. Still's employment with Whiteman ended in May of 1930. (Papers, 52:9)

The opportunity to travel to the West Coast with The Paul Whiteman Orchestra turned out to be a pivotal point in Still's life. He immediately liked the area and knew that he wanted to live there permanently some day. Although Whiteman and his band were filming the movie, *The King of Jazz,* Still's responsibilities lay with the weekly, one-hour radio broadcast only. He said, "I had to finish only three pieces a week; the rest of the time was free. Since I am a pretty fast worker, that gave me a great deal of time to myself. . . . I would average about thirty pages of score a day. Once I did ninety pages in a day." (Southern, 170) Among the fine musicians in Whiteman's orchestra at that time were Frankie Trumbauer, Charles Teagarden, Charles Strickfaden, and, for a brief time, Bix Beiderbecke. Ferde Grofé was Whiteman's longstanding arranger.

It was indeed a productive period for Still. Among the other arrangements Still did was another orchestration of *St. Louis Blues* (Handy). The version for Whiteman, dated September 6, 1929, contains a part for the legendary trumpeter, Bix Beiderbecke.[38] He composed at least two original works for Whiteman, *Three Portraits* and *Jungle Episode: The Origin of Jazz*. The first biography of Still was completed in February 1930 by a Los Angeles native and African American musician, Harold Bruce Forsythe. It was dedicated to Edgard Varèse. That document pointed to *Darker America* as his most significant work to date.[39]

During that year in California, Still completed about 118 of his 127 arrangements that have been preserved in The Paul Whiteman Collection. Three years later, Paul Whiteman would commission him to compose five original works for his orchestra, including *A Deserted Plantation* (dated 1933), *Land of Superstition* from *Africa* (a reorchestration dated 1933), *Ebon Chronicle* (performed in 1936), *Down Yonder* (undated) and *Blues from Lenox Avenue* (about 1937). Another piece written for Whiteman, *Beyond Tomorrow,* was later renamed *A Song at Dusk* and arranged for full orchestra by the composer. The original version of *Beyond Tomorrow* was, according to Verna Arvey, "dedicated to Still's four children."[40]

Still started again to compose his ballet *Sadhji* on the lot at Universal Studios during the filming of *The King of Jazz*. (Brown, 10) He finished the important suite, *Africa,* in early 1930. This new suite, *Africa,* was first performed on April 6, 1930, by the Barrère Little Symphony under the direction of Georges Barrère in a reduced orchestra version and then on October 24, 1930, for full orchestra by the Rochester Philharmonic under the direction of Howard Hanson. Hanson had also repeated *Darker America* in a retrospective concert in honor of the Fifth Anniversary of the founding of the American Composers' Concerts. Barrère indicated in his announcement of the April concert that Still had written *Africa* for him two years before, but the Barrère Little Symphony ceased its concerts in March of 1928 (for financial reasons) and did not resume them until April, 1930. *Africa* was the first serious work by Still to get consistently enthusiastic reviews.

After his return to New York, Still wrote the first entry on July 7, 1930, in what is known today as his earliest diary. He recorded that he had just finished scoring *Sadhji,* thereby establishing a pattern in his diaries that he would maintain during subsequent years. That is, rather than dating manuscripts consistently or using opus numbers, he simply recorded in his diary what he had done that day. For instance, on Wednesday and Thursday, August 20 and 21, Still noted that he started "mapping out spirituals for Birchard. ["]Holy Spirit, Don't You Leave Me" the first . . . "Every Time I Feel The Spirit" today.[41]

Later that same year, his diary provided documentation of the completion of the *Afro-American Symphony* and noted the first performance of *Africa* in Rochester, which he attended. The inside cover of the diary listed the arrangements that Still completed and the amount he was paid for each. He also mentioned in his 1930 diary that his name and a list of his works were included in a catalogue of American composers that was just published, "in spite of my color."[42] The book, *American Composers of Today and Their Works,* compiled by Claire Reis with the assistance of the Juilliard Foundation, was published by the United States Section of the International Society for Contemporary Music. It included fifty-five composers and Still was the only African American.

The important premiere of the ballet *Sahdji* came on May 22, 1931, when the Rochester Philharmonic Orchestra, again under the direction of Howard Hanson, presented it with Thelma Biracree as the principal dancer and choreographer, an orchestra of sixty-five, about 100 in the chorus, and a corps de ballet of about thirty. Still's collaborators for the work were the playwright, Bruce Nugent (who used the pseudonym, Richard Bruce) and the great articulator of the Harlem Renaissance, Alain Locke. Still later explained the nature of the collaboration by saying, "I had received the scenario back in the early twenties. So much time passed [because] I still had a lot of preparation to go through before I was ready." (Brown, 10) The report by Olin Downes on the Rochester performance of *Sahdji* said, "Mr. Still is a composer of marked talent . . . this is real music, music of a composer of exotic talent and temperament, who has a keen sense of beauty, sensuousness which is controlled by taste, and incipient aptitude for the theatre."[43] (*See:* WB132.1)

On July 7, 1931, Still had his European premiere with a performance of *Darker America* in Bad Homburg, Germany, at the first European festival of American Music. Dr. Oscar Holger conducted the Frankfurter Rundfunk Symphonie Orchestra. The festival was under the direction of Irving Schwerké, music critic of the Paris edition of the *Chicago Tribune,* who became a mentor of Still as they exchanged letters about music. The other American composers who were represented were Charles Griffes, Edward MacDowell, Howard Hanson, and Carl McKinley.

With sketches dating back to 1928 and the idea germinating since his first days with W. C. Handy, the actual process of composing his first symphony, the *Afro-American,* took place between October 30 and December 6, 1930. When the first performances came on October 28 and 29, 1931, Still's fame was assured for the rest of his life. The *Afro-American Symphony* became Still's signature piece, cited often for its symphonic use of the banjo and for its inspiration from the Blues. It would be performed all over the world and remain his most well-known composition. The score would also be subjected to the never-ending revisions that became so characteristic of this self-critical artist.

Program notes for the *Afro-American Symphony* were included in a letter by the composer to Irving Schwerké on October 5, 1931. Missing are the poems by Paul Laurence Dunbar (now closely associated with the work) that Still added, probably at the time of publication (1937). Instead, the composer wrote simply,

> The Afro-American Symphony is not a tone picture of the "New Negro" [a reference to Alain Locke's publication of 1925]. It portrays that class of American Negroes who still cling to the old standards and traditions; those sons of the soil who differ, but little, if at all, from their forbears [sic] of ante-bellum days.
>
> These are an humble people. Their wants are few and are generally childlike. Theirs are lives of utter simplicity. Therefore no complex or elaborate scheme of harmonization would prove befitting in a musical picture of them. 'Tis only the simpler harmonies, such as those employed, that can accurately portray them.
>
> From the hearts of these people sprang Blues, plaintive songs reminiscent of African tribal chants. I do not hesitate to assert that Blues are more purely Negroid in character than very many Spirituals. And I have employed as the basic theme of the symphony a melody in the Blues style. This theme appears in each movement.[44]

With problems at home continuing, Still rented a small office where he began in earnest to fulfill his goals as a serious composer. Buoyed by the self-consciousness of having had his biography written while he was in California and increasingly aware of the importance of his ideas, Still resolved to get on with his business. Despite his ample salary when he worked with Paul Whiteman and a generous household budget, Grace had forged a check while he was away and left many unpaid bills that he had to settle upon his return. She "forged another check for $500 and then went to the bank before I had a chance to go on that particular morning so that she might again destroy the cancelled check." (Papers, 52:9) Then, about the time of the premiere of the *Afro-American Symphony,* she began the practice of staying away from home. . . . I had then gotten another job [with Willard Robison]. To secure peace in the house and to try to make her happy, I agreed to give her $60 a week and to pay her something extra for the food I ate. This condition lasted for awhile. Then she announced she was going to Montreal to work for a magazine (this, I learned later, was a lie) and that she would take her mother and children with her. (Papers, 52:9)

In September, 1932, when his family left for Montreal, Still moved from the home on Long Island, to 408 Manhattan Avenue, New York. His scrapbooks from 1932-1934 include drawings by Gail and Elaine and a Christmas card from Elaine. He continued to send money for the children until the youngest became twenty-one (about 1943), but he never saw Grace again, even though he was able to see the children occasionally. He eventually lost contact with them.

On December 17, 1931, Still had signed a contract with Willard Robison to provide arrangements for Willard Robison's Deep River Orchestra program on WOR Radio Monday, Tuesday, and Wednesday afternoons of each week. A clipping from the black press illuminated the importance of this position in the context of the times:

> William G. Still, the youthful colored composer and arranger, is not generally known as the director and arranger of the WOR radio presentation of the Willard Robinson [sic] Orchestra. Many of us have listened to the rich, colorful playing of this unusual orchestra and failed to know that a colored musician arranged the orchestration and personally was directing this splendid organization of all-white musicians. The name Willard Robinson [sic] was always announced but no mention was made of the talented colored director, Mr. Still.[45]

The same article pointed to a situation that would haunt Still for the better part of his life; his growing popularity among whites, while those of his own race knew little of his activities. The writer said,

> Among prominent white musicians, Mr. Still is highly regarded, as he has made arrangements for Paul Whiteman and for Don Voorhees and other leading white orchestras. . . . His arrangements. . . . have been used at the Lewisohn Stadium. . . . Mr. Still, it is said, started arranging years ago in Memphis with the redoubtable "Father of the Blues," W. C. Handy.[46]

Another newspaper clipping began, "The achievements of William Grant Still seem to be more generally known by the white race than by his own."[47]

There was a great deal of truth in that statement, as Still's compositions were presented in "white" venues such as Aeolian Hall, Kilbourn Hall at The Eastman School of Music, and in The Auditorium at the Chicago Civic Opera. This disparity worried the composer, and he remarked later in life that "during all that period [of the International Composers' Guild concerts at Aeolian Hall], I saw one Negro at the concerts, and that was Hall Johnson." (Brown, 12)

On March 3, 1932, the *Afro-American Symphony* was repeated in Kilbourn Hall in Rochester as part of the seventh season of the American Composers' Concerts. The review in the *Rochester Democrat and Chronicle* from March 4 said,

> Last came Mr. Still's symphony, repeated from an earlier concert that the composer might hear it . . . he was given a fine tribute of applause by the audience at its close. This is unquestionably the most directly appealing of Mr. Still's orchestral works. He has done what has, in a way, been done before but he has done it with great skill. . . . he has written a symphonic piece that will be heard with pleasure by audiences at large.[48]

All the while, Still continued to earn his living in radio. He said that working for Willard Robison and the Deep River broadcast in New York,

> was the most remarkable opportunity that I'd ever had, because, while I had been working with orchestras that permitted me the opportunity to experiment, I hadn't been working with orchestras that were large enough to have complement like the symphony orchestras. We

didn't have the bassoons and the English horns, and so on. . . . we didn't play only at WOR. . . . There were times when we would broadcast at CBS, and we'd use that symphony orchestra, and then we would broadcast at NBC. . . . we just used all of the musicians that were connected with the studio and had a very worthwhile orchestra. Splendid musicians! And I had a chance to experiment. During all the years prior to that, I had made many notes. They were my theories about orchestration, effects that I had dreamed up, and I was just waiting for an opportunity to see whether they were practical or not. Now, here came the Deep River idea, and I had a chance to do them, because I had absolute freedom there. In choosing material of a serious nature [to] be played on the program, we played all sorts of things—Debussy and things of that sort—and then we would take a piece like "Frankie and Johnnie" and make a symphonic poem out of it. I would do [arrangements like] that. (Brown, 8-9)

In a press release contained in his scrapbook from 1932, with the heading "WOR Shorts," the station promoted the accomplishments of its arranger:

It is William Grant Still, a young negro [sic] with a flair for unusual harmony, who makes the arrangements for Willard Robison's Deep River program on WOR. Glancing through Still's scrapbook you will find notes and telegrams from Schwerké, Covarrubias and Countee Cullen congratulating him on some composition, asking for the loan of a special manuscript. In print Still's name rarely appears except in small letters at the foot of a program.[49]

Minutes of a meeting of the committee for "The (Ninth) Annual Music Week Effort in Harlem" showed that Still, Eva Jessye, W. C. Handy, Edward Margetson, Hall Johnson, H. Lawrence Freeman, and Consuella Pappy among others were expected to participate. The minutes indicated that the entire program would be sponsored by the New York branch of the National Association of Negro Musicians. Interestingly, Still is identified as director of the Deep River Hour on the radio, not as a composer of orchestral works or ballets. Eva Jessye's talk was to be on "The Qualifications Needed for Radio Work," and Edward Margetson was assigned the topic, "Classical Works."[50]

In January of 1933 Howard Hanson conducted a very successful concert of American music with the Berlin Philharmonic Orchestra. The program included works by Hanson, Charles Griffes, Leo Sowerby, and Still's *Scherzo* from the *Afro-American Symphony*. The enthusiasm was so great that "the audience demanded a repetition of Still's scherzo."[51] On January 25, The Paul Whiteman Orchestra performed *Land of Superstition* from *Africa* on a concert at Carnegie Hall with great success.

Still mentioned scoring *Africa* for Whiteman in his diary of 1930, but Whiteman apparently did not hire Still to do the arrangement until 1933. Still also worked with Whiteman at the Ziegfield Follies and was among the celebrities who placed his autograph in the large gold oval on Whiteman's dressing room door.[52] A new vocal group, the "Rhythm Boys," had a young singer, Bing Crosby, who "was considered unimportant!" (Brown, 26) When Crosby did a recording in New York with Whiteman, Still did the orchestration. The tune was probably *My Kinda Love* (Alter).

By now, however, Still's works were being played with some frequency in Europe by the Concerts Pasdeloup. A concert featuring *Africa* was in the Théâtre des Champs-Élysées on February 4, 1933. Irving Schwerké reviewed the performance very favorably in the *Chicago Daily Tribune,* European edition, Paris, February 5, 1933. In his letter to "My dear composer," Schwerké said,

In Paris AFRICA had an overwhelming public success—I have heard thousands of concerts here, but seldom a first performance that so completely gripped a Parisian audience. . . . Some of the criticisms are not good, but that need not trouble you in the least: you do not write for critics, but for the human heart, and the way your audience responded was proof of your success.[53]

Still's response to Schwerké reflected joy over the enthusiasm for *Africa*. As the long-distance friendship grew between the two men, Still decided to dedicate the *Afro-*

American Symphony to Schwerké. In a number of letters, the composer and the critic discussed the dedication until Schwerké began to refer to the work as "my" symphony, a designation he never forsook. In a letter of March 17, 1937, Still explained, "I have always thought of it as being dedicated to you, and have agreed with the publisher that whenever a new edition is made, your name will appear on it as it should have done in the first place."[54] Those anticipated editions would never be forthcoming, so the special dedication was almost forgotten.

The first performances of the ballet commissioned in 1926, *La Guiablesse,* took place in May and June, 1933. Still, who revised the score in 1932, was present for the first performance at The Eastman School of Music with Thelma Biracree as the choreographer. He did not have the opportunity, however, to attend the performance that summer in Chicago produced by Ruth Page, who danced the title role, supported by a cast of African American dancers, on June 16. In the cast in Chicago was Katherine Dunham, an African American dancer, who would perform the leading role in the production the next year. Certainly encouraged by the performances of *La Guiablesse,* Still completed a little known work for pantomimists and dancers, *The Sorcerer: Fantastic Scene,* in late summer of 1933. It was based on a scenario by Harold Bruce Forsythe, his California biographer. Although completed and copied, the work seems never to have been performed.

On December 15, 1933, *A Deserted Plantation* was given its first performance at the Metropolitan Opera House in the "Sixth Experiment in American Music" presented by Paul Whiteman and His Orchestra augmented to seventy-five players. Framing the program were two works by George Gershwin, *An American in Paris* (1928) and the famous *Rhapsody in Blue* (1924), a piece commissioned by Paul Whiteman and orchestrated by Ferde Grofé. Thus, *A Deserted Plantation* became the first work by Still to be performed in the Metropolitan Opera House. Paul Whiteman's biographer said, "*A Deserted Plantation* reaffirmed the Mississippi-born composer's skill in longer works and revealed the influence of Grofé's musical-picture approach." Freddie Rich's orchestra played *A Deserted Plantation* on radio station WABC, because "we found it the most interesting of the novelties." In the third movement, the composer used an adaptation of the spiritual, *I Want Jesus to Walk with Me.* Doing that represented a distinct departure from his usual philosophy of writing original themes based on spirituals, rather than quoting the spirituals themselves.[55]

Still became a charter member of The Composers' Protective Society, organized in May, 1933, to promote American music. Among his associates in this group were Howard Hanson, Morton Gould, Bernard Rogers, Henry Cowell, Irving Kolodin, Robert Russell Bennett, Marc Blitzstein, Vivian Fine, George Gershwin, Percy Grainger, Wallingford Riegger, Carlos Salzedo, and Elie Siegmeister.

Spurred on by his successes in the United States and abroad in both commercial music and serious music, Still completed work on a large-scale orchestral composition called *A Negro Epic,* on January 15, 1934. It was dedicated to Verna Arvey, a Jewish pianist and admirer who lived in Los Angeles and with whom he was corresponding at the time. This piece, with its title changed to *Ebon Chronicle,* was orchestrated for Paul Whiteman in 1936 for a performance in Fort Worth, Texas.

Still received notice that he had been awarded a Guggenheim Fellowship in musical composition for one year, beginning on May 14, 1934. Many doors now began to open for him. Henry Cowell wrote on April 16, "I am so delighted to hear of your Guggenheim Award. It could be given to no one who deserves it more!" On April 28, the Carl Diton Branch of the National Association of Negro Musicians, Inc., gave a musicale and reception in honor of Still.[56] Wherever he would go in the succeeding years, the prestigious name of the Guggenheim Foundation would follow him. Once he received the fellowship, he no longer sought jobs as a performer, instead preferring to compose and arrange music. Except for some short-term contracts to compose background music for movie studios and television, he devoted the rest of his life to his own compositions. He was thirty-nine years old before he had the opportunity to fulfill his lifelong goals and dreams.

Having requested permission to do his work in California, rather than to study abroad, Still arrived in Los Angeles on May 22, 1934, coincidentally, exactly thirteen years to the day after the successful New York opening of *Shuffle Along*. Some of his admirers met him upon his arrival and that group included the pianist Verna Arvey.

His initial project was to complete his first opera, *Blue Steel*, which he had already begun in New York. The opera was based on a story by Carlton Moss, then a young Harlem playwright and radio actor. The African American composer and pianist, Harold Bruce Forsythe (Still's first biographer), was designated to write the libretto. A 1934 article from the *Los Angeles Times* said,

> the new opera, like others of Still's works, is based on his people's themes and rhythms but has a decidedly modern-European influence. . . . He is an extremely modest, rather shy person in regard to his composing, but from hearing the first act of *Blue Steel* it is apparent he has a high regard for melody. . . . The story of *Blue Steel* begins with the African jungle.[57]

Arvey described *Blue Steel* as

> by far his most powerful completed work to date [1939]. . . . Still has used every element possible to bring about a powerful and compelling climax, from the moment the arresting '*Blue Steel*' motif introduces the opera, to the final chords. . . . when Blue Steel tells of the bright lights and glories of the cities, the music assumes a jazz form, harmonically and rhythmically speaking . . . when Blue Steel becomes terrified and looks toward his own God for aid, the music assumes the outward characteristics of a Negro spiritual.[58]

In the fall of 1934, Still traveled to Chicago for the second presentation of his ballet, *La Guiablesse,* at the Chicago Civic Opera House on November 30. His arrival was noted in the black and white presses, and he was interviewed by both. *La Guiablesse* was being presented in Chicago by the Chicago Grand Opera Company in a special all-ballet program. Ruth Page, who had danced the lead in the Chicago premiere in 1933, was now the *première danseuse* and director of the Chicago Opera Ballet.

According to the black press, "Katherine Dunham, dancer of fame and an accomplished teacher, dances the title role in tonight's (Friday) performance supported by a group of dancers of our own race."[59] A review from the white press vividly describes the exoticism of the experience for members of the white audience:

> It was an astonishing performance, both last year and last night. The ease and grace that this Negro group put into their evolutions, the eloquence of their swaying bronze bodies, made a perfect performance of this tale of the Martinique siren.[60]

Once back in California, Still started a new work for piano and orchestra, *Kaintuck',* which he finished in February, 1935, "a tone poem . . . depicting my emotions as I passed through a certain section of Kentucky on a misty summer day."[61] (*See:* WB74.6) It was about this time that the composer began to inscribe on each of his manuscripts a phrase which would become his trademark: "With humble thanks to God, the source of inspiration." He had used similar expressions on earlier works, but this version is the one on which he finally settled. This dedication of sorts to God appeared on the score of *Kaintuck'* and on most major works afterward.

The work was premiered by Verna Arvey on Sunday, May 5, 1935, in a Lecture-Recital sponsored by the Twelfth Street Branch of the YMCA at the Musart Theatre in Los Angeles. The program also included *The Bamboula* by Still's early idol, Samuel Coleridge-Taylor, and *Jubal* by Bruce Forsythe. Verna Arvey played piano arrangements of Still's suite, *Africa,* and two excerpts from his ballet, *La Guiablesse.* Leola Longress

On his birthday, May 11, 1935, Still founded a Library of Music at the Gray Conservatory of Music in Los Angeles, just as his mother had done in Little Rock, Arkansas, about thirty years before. He donated musical scores, violin music, and books on theoretical subjects. (*See:* B162) On May 15, the Guggenheim Foundation renewed his fellowship in musical composition for another six months.

Still composed *Quit Dat Fool'nish,* a whimsical piano solo, allegedly dedicated to Bruce Forsythe, even though the printed inscription is to his dog, Shep. It was first performed by Forsythe in its original piano solo version on July 11, at Second Baptist Church in Los Angeles.[62] Other works followed quickly, as the experienced composer and orchestrator devoted most of his energies to implementing ideas and theories from years of dreaming and planning. The Guggenheim Fellowship allowed him the freedom to compose without having to work in commercial music to support himself. Still cherished those years and conscientiously worked hard composing new works.

Still had Guggenheim Fellowships in 1934, 1935, and 1938. After 1934 Still reported the new works, publications, and performances of his music to the Guggenheim Foundation regularly, so that their biannnual reports became an excellent source for information on his serious music. (*See:* B252) The wealth of detail in those reports and in the yearly summaries given in the *Pan Pipes of Sigma Alpha Iota* beginning in 1950 give detailed information on new compositions, performances, commissions, awards, and other activities of the composer. (*See:* B273)

To support himself and his family between Guggenheim stipends, Still did some freelance work in the movie studios. He and the former unknown member of the "Rhythm Boys," Bing Crosby, worked together on the movie starring Crosby, *Pennies from Heaven* (1936). In a letter dated June 6, 1936, Still wrote to his daughter Gail, who had returned to New York with her mother and siblings in the interim:

> When I was receiving the Fellowship stipend [about $200 a month] I gave you over three fourths of it, and sent you money for clothes in addition. I was able to send the clothing through getting a little extra work. . . . I have recently gotten a job in one of those studios. The salary is not large, but it enables me to meet expenses. I do not enjoy the work. I find it quite taxing, and am bothered with my nerves because of it.[63]

The works for piano were also written during this time.[64] Other works from these years, besides the opera *Blue Steel,* were *Dismal Swamp* (sketch completed June 21, 1935), a poem for orchestra with piano solos; *The Black Man Dances,* for solo piano and orchestra; *Central Avenue* (1935); and *Lenox Avenue* (1937). Still also revised his ballet *Sahdji,* and he revised the *Afro-American Symphony* for publication (1935, 1937).

In 1936, Still joined the American Society of Composers, Authors, and Publishers (ASCAP), a prestigious society for which he had to be nominated and recommended. Designed to promote and protect the legal interests of those who did creative work, ASCAP monitored broadcasts and publications and collected royalties. Realizing that his life now needed to be documented more carefully, the composer made an agreement with Verna Arvey that she would compile the facts of his early life and career for a biography. On her behalf, Still wrote to some of his friends and family members asking them to send any information they had on him to Arvey.

Because his focus had always been on his music, and little else, he sought help with the tasks associated with promoting his career and getting performances of his works. For a small stipend he hired Arvey to help him with the correspondence and paperwork that he needed to follow through on to advance his career. A trained journalist, she began to write letters to newspapers informing them of his activities.

Once he moved to California, Still felt it was time to broaden his music. (*See:* B201) He said,

Once he moved to California, Still felt it was time to broaden his music. (*See:* B201) He said,

> while I still intended to devote myself to giving expression . . . to the use of the Negroid idiom, I did not want to confine myself to that particular idiom because I think [that] here in America we have so many idioms. . . . I would like to write music that expresses America rather than confine myself to writing just Negro music. [Even so], the Negro, being part of America [is important, and I am] not leaving him out. (Brown, 18-19)

Still's music was being heard in two worlds and highly regarded in both. In 1935 the New York Philharmonic gave Still's *Afro-American Symphony* its New York premiere. On July 29, "Whiteman set a record when 9,100 Philadelphians heard one of his longest programs—26 selections, plus an encore."[65] The program included Still's *Land of Superstition* from *Africa*. Whiteman also commissioned another original work from Still, *The Black Man Dances*, inspired by four short verses attributed to Bruce Forsythe.

Still started composing his *Symphony in G Minor*, "Song of a New Race," in 1936 and completed it in 1937. He sent the program notes to music critic Irving Schwerké and described the piece as,

> related to my Afro-American Symphony (composed in 1930) being, in fact, a sort of extension or evolution of the latter. This relationship is implied musically through the affinity of the principal theme of the first movement of the Symphony in G Minor to the principal theme of the fourth, or last, movement of the Afro-American. . . . I prefer to think of it as an abstract piece of music but, for the benefit of those who like interpretations of their music, I have written the following notes: The Afro-American Symphony represented the Negro of the days not far removed from the Civil War. The Symphony in G Minor represents the American colored man of today, in so many instances a totally new individual produced through the infusion of white, Indian and Negro bloods.[66]

A review from December 11, 1937, after the premiere of the work by The Philadelphia Orchestra with conductor Leopold Stokowski, said, "Symphony in G Minor, entitled 'Song of a New Race' by the Negro composer, William Grant Still, was of absorbing interest . . . ranging from the exuberance of jazz to brooding wistfulness."[67]

On July 23, 1936, Still was the guest conductor for the Los Angeles Philharmonic concert at the Hollywood Bowl. He conducted excerpts from two of his works, *Land of Romance* from *Africa* and the *Scherzo* of the *Afro-American Symphony*. Still also received his first honorary degree, a Master of Music degree, from his undergraduate school, Wilberforce University in 1936. He joined a new organization, The California Society of Composers, whose purpose was to bring "better conditions for American composers of the larger forms of composition."[68] On October 30, *Dismal Swamp* was premiered by the Rochester Civic Orchestra, and on November 3, Paul Whiteman debuted *Ebon Chronicle* with the Fort Worth Symphony on a program that also included the works of Grofé and Gershwin. Still continued to find venues in both worlds while also becoming involved in the world of film.

Still explained how he got the opportunity to work in the movie studios:

> My friend, Howard Jackson, was doing a lot of composing at that time for Columbia Studios. . . . they chose him to be the head of the Music Department [at the studio]. So Howard was enabled, thereby, to get me in the studio as a composer. (Brown, 24) (*See:* B274)

Still eventually left because there was so little for him to do and because Jackson was replaced by someone else. "Incidentally, before I left Columbia, the picture 'Lost Horizon' came up (in 1937), and I orchestrated some of that, [specifically], the funeral procession of the dead lama." (Brown, 25)

On Sunday, May 23, 1937, Still's *Lenox Avenue* had its premiere on WABC radio with Howard Barlow conducting the orchestra. Submitted in response to a commission for a work for radio broadcast, *Lenox Avenue* was a piece for orchestra with announcer (narrator) and choir. The original ideas were conceived and written into a piano vocal score in 1935 titled

Central Avenue, after the street in Los Angeles that compared with the Harlem street of the final version. Still reworked it, adapted it to the special sound effects possible on radio, and changed the title to *Lenox Avenue* to complete the commission. Explaining the origin of the work, Arvey wrote,

> The themes had been gathering for many years, and Still had even made a tentative effort to shape them into a composition. When the commission from CBS . . . arrived, Still realized that the perfect form for this musical material was at hand, in a symphonic work to be built directly for radio audience. . . . on the Deep River programs long before, the announcer had spoken over musical interludes.[69]

He was paid $500 for his score and commended for his timeliness in submitting it. The executives at The Columbia Broadcasting System sent each composer who had been commissioned to write a work some scores especially prepared for broadcast that illustrated the special effects one could get on radio. Excerpts of two letters from Deems Taylor gave an indication of the respect Still had already earned in the field while he was in New York. Taylor wrote, "Incidentally, none of us here think that the broadcast [workshop] could tell you anything that you didn't already know. . . . I must congratulate you on the completeness and clarity of the technical setup. You certainly know your radio."[70]

Davidson Taylor from the Program Department wrote to Still, reflecting on the broadcast of *Lenox Avenue,* "I also wish I could have persuaded Mr. Barlow to use a Negro chorus. I feel they would have sung with more gusto and better rhythm. . . . Again, our gratitude for your excellent work. . . . I wish the rest of the composers were as prompt and businesslike."[71] *Lenox Avenue* was broadcast again in October. The next year it was converted into a ballet with the addition of a scenario and complete stage directions by Verna Arvey. It was presented by the Dance Theatre Group of Los Angeles with Norma Gould, choreographer, and the Hall Johnson Choir singing the spiritual in the mission scene.

From May 24-26, 1937, The California Society of Composers presented a "Composers' Festival" at the Friday Morning Club. Sixteen members of the Society had their works performed in the festival including Charles Wakefield Cadman, Mary Carr Moore, and William Grant Still. Verna Arvey performed three piano pieces by Still, *Dark Horseman, Summerland,* and *Radiant Pinnacle,* the set known as *Three Visions,* which had been composed in 1935 and published by J. Fischer in 1936.

He also completed the first six of the spiritual arrangements for *Twelve Negro Spirituals.* These were published by Handy Brothers Music, Inc., in an elaborate volume featuring a photograph and biography (by Arvey) of Still, illustrations by Albert Barbelle, and literary treatments by Ruby Berkley Goodwin. Still treasured the old spirituals of his people, first taught to him by his beloved grandmother, and, in his career, he would set no less than forty-five individual titles of spiritual melodies, many of them in more than one setting, an indication of the personal devotion he had for these precious reminders of the past. In many other works that were not settings of existing spirtuals, Still would often say that he had written an original melody based on the spirituals, like them, but not quoted from them, showing his synthesis of their musical traits.

His old friend from New York, Clarence Williams, did not forget his excellent arranging skills either. As president of The Clarence Williams Music Publishing Company, he wrote to Still in 1937 to ask him to write two new arrangements. When Williams had received the arrangements, he wrote, "The arrangement [of *Passionette*] is wonderful. I tried it out the other night with 'Fats' Waller and his band and he liked it so much that he had his arranger copy it and had extra parts made."[72]

The opera, *Troubled Island,* had its beginnings in 1937. In a letter to Irving Schwerké dated May 5, 1937, Still said, "Last week, Langston Hughes (the poet) arrived in Los Angeles to collaborate with me on a new opera. We are both enthused over the subject, and by the musical possibilities inherent in the libretto that has been sketched." A newspaper clipping in Still's scrapbook pointed to the origin of the idea in a play, "Drums of Haiti," by Hughes. Hughes went to Detroit to see his play produced before going to California to work with Still upon its operatic version.[73]

As a composer, Still had an intellectual interest in providing for his audience music based on materials that were as authentic as possible. He struggled often with library collections of the day seeking as much information as he could on music that existed mostly in the oral tradition, music of the folk. When frustrated by what he found in print, he would consult friends who had recordings or acquaintances who had traveled to countries about whose music he wished to learn. In contemplation of the opera on Haiti, he began his research in the usual fashion, asking friends to help him locate some sound resources. Henry Cowell replied, "As far as Haitian records, I had two in New York (they are very scarce), and think that I copied them for my California collection. . . . Strang will give them to you if he has them. . . . Did you know that Lomax (the younger one) has just returned [from] Haiti with a very complete collection of native records?"[74]

Composition of the music for *Troubled Island* would continue for at least the next two years with parts still being extracted as late as 1941. Spending such a long time on one work was not something to which Still was especially accustomed. He once remarked that he had been amazed at how long it took him to write it. This opera represented the fulfilment of a dream that began that summer of 1914 when he sat up at night in Little Rock to prepare a naive work for a contest. Even before its completion, Still began to seek a venue for its performance. As early as 1939, he wrote to CBS, which had broadcast *Lenox Avenue,* to see if they would be interested in the opera for broadcast. He would spend the next decade making contacts, getting his hopes up, planning, and seeing his plans shattered before he would finally see it produced.

In 1937, after some serious soul searching and immense frustration over the situation with his wife and the children, Still started compiling the information needed to proceed with getting a divorce. He had not seen Grace since their separation in September, 1932, and he had found a new life in California free from the worries he had had in New York. In early 1938, he made the official application for the divorce. It would take a year for the decree to be finalized. In the meantime, he continued to compose in a fury, and he began to keep a diary on a regular basis.

On June 3, 1938, the Guggenheim Foundation renewed Still's fellowship for another six months, that is, until December 3. Ulysses Kay, an aspiring African American composer to whom Still would become a mentor and friend, performed *Three Visions* for piano solo at a concert in Tucson, Arizona, on May 11, 1938. William Duncan Allen, to whom the composer later dedicated one of his piano pieces, played the same pieces in New York City on November 9. Later in 1938, he was notified that he would receive a commission from the 1939-1940 New York World's Fair Committee to write theme music for "The City of Tomorrow." The selection committee, advised by Kay Swift who had been a close friend of George Gershwin, chose a composer after they listened to radio air checks of works by Americans. They determined that the winner of the commission should be either the composer of *A Deserted Plantation* or *Lenox Avenue.* As it turned out, Still was the composer of both pieces.

Still traveled to New York in November of that year to meet with the committee and to see the drawings for the large perisphere where his work would be performed. The resulting work, published in various arrangements with the titles *Rising Tide, Victory Tide,* and *Song of a City* was broadcast over loud speakers during the entire run of the New York Fair. The *New Yorker* magazine calculated that it had 31,857 performances. (*See:* WB141.3) It was recorded by an orchestra conducted by André Kostelanetz and first performed for broadcasting over the Mutual Radio Network by the same conductor on April 13, 1939.[75]

On February 6, 1939, the divorce from Grace was final, permitting Still to marry his Jewish friend and supporter, Verna Arvey, with whom he had developed a strong friendship. (*See:* SA3) Two days later they drove to Mexico and were married. The relationship with Arvey would turn out to be not unlike the close camraderie Edgard Varèse had with his wife and collaborator, Louise. As a pianist, she performed and played his works with great enthusiasm, and, as a journalist, she wrote articles about him which she submitted to major magazines and newspapers for publication. She even syndicated many of her articles to black newspapers across the country through Calvin's News Service, giving Still copious coverage on almost every event of his life after 1939. She eventually became his librettist for most works that needed words, including all but two of his operas, supplying the words usually only after he had finished the musical score. She became his closest confidant and a full partner in his work. He was forty-three years old when they married, and she was twenty-nine. They would work and live together, both focused on his music, for the next thirty-nine years.

On the day of their marriage, Henry Cowell responded to a package he had received from Arvey, saying, "It was awfully good of you to send me a copy of your new book on Still. . . . The book . . . give[s] a very fine and truthful picture of Still as a person of charm, refinement, dignity, and genuine modesty, all of which are wonderfully true, and accounts for some of the high esteem in which his friends hold him."[76] Still scored the music for the World's Fair on his wedding night, and on February 17 and 18, 1939, just nine days later, Arvey was the piano soloist in *Kaintuck'* with the Los Angeles Philharmonic Orchestra, Otto Klemperer, conducting. The composer then wrote another important set of piano works in seven short movements, *Seven Traceries,* dedicating each movement to a close friend. In April of 1939, he received a Julius Rosenwald Foundation Fellowship in musical composition for one year which was renewed for a second year in 1940.

The year 1940 brought two important collaborations. The major one was for a cantata to a text by Katherine Garrison Chapin, *And They Lynched Him on a Tree.* It was written for orchestra, black chorus, white chorus, narrator, and contralto solist. It was first performed at Lewisohn Stadium in New York on June 25 by the New York Philharmonic-Symphony Orchestra, Artur Rodzinski conducting, the Wen Talbot Negro Choir, and fifty members of the Schola Cantorum. Louise Burge was the soloist and Abner Dorsey the narrator.[77]

For the second collaboration, Still worked with the African American anthropologist Zora Neale Hurston on a group of folk song settings which he later published as *Caribbean Melodies.* As he completed these comparatively smaller projects, he continued to score and prepare parts for his large-scale opera, *Troubled Island.* Early in 1941, possibly inspired by his contact with Hurston who had been to Haiti collecting folk materials, he even sketched a fourth act for the opera. In January or early February, Langston Hughes wrote to his friend Arna Bontemps, "I have withdrawn from the board of the revue. . . . Did I tell you Still resigned, too, to devote his time to a WPA version of our opera to be done in April, which he will conduct." The next month Hughes reported that rehearsals had begun in Los Angeles with a mixed cast, chorus of one hundred and an orchestra of seventy, but on March 22, he wrote, "Did I tell you the Still opera is off? WPA appropriations cut out half the cast when they were reduced. So it goes with theatre!"[78]

A second Chapin collaboration on *Plain-Chant for America* followed in 1941, along with the composition and performance of *Old California* and the completion of his third opera, *A Bayou Legend. Plain-Chant for America* was performed by the New York Philharmonic-Symphony Orchestra, John Barbirolli, conducting, at Carnegie Hall. This important work would be repeated early the next year by the Pittsburgh Symphony Orchestra under the baton of Fritz Reiner.[79] That year Howard University gave him the first of the eight honorary doctorates that he would receive in his lifetime.

In 1940, Still and Arvey had the first of their two children, Duncan Allan Still. On August 31, 1942, their daughter, Judith Anne Still was born. Still and his children with Arvey were extremely close. Because of their own sensitivity to their interracial marriage and the effect it might have on other people's perceptions of their children, Still and Arvey were quite protective of Duncan and Judith. They took them to performances and included them when visitors came to their home. The composer made toys for them and crafted train sets, furniture, and other items from wood. His woodworking became a hobby that brought him a deep sense of satisfaction, and the greatest beneficiaries of his gifts of love were his two children. After the death of her parents, Judith Anne Still (Headlee) would take over William Grant Still Music and begin to travel around the country promoting her father's music. It is largely through her efforts that Still's music is enjoying the popularity it is today. She has made long forgotten scores available to the public and has generously sponsored recordings so that all may hear and enjoy this music. The world of American music owes her a great debt.

In 1943, Still did some work at Fox Studio on the film *Stormy Weather*, which featured Lena Horne, Ethel Waters, Bill "Bojangles" Robinson, and Katherine Dunham, before he started working with Dimitri Tiompkin. Still remembered the experience:

> I was in on that because—as I was told when I was approached to be musical advisor—the plans were for a portion of the picture to have to do with some of the achievements of colored Americans in music. When I got there, I found out that was not so. It was all popular music, so there was very little for me to do. . . . Finally I resigned. . . . Then, after that, I did a great deal of orchestrating for Dimitri Tiompkin. . . . I was working so constantly and so hard that I had trouble with my eyes. (Brown, 26) (*See:* B271, B276, B278)

It was an important year for some of Still's more serious and respected works. Inspired by a report that the first soldier to die in the second World War was African American, he composed *In Memoriam: The Colored Soldiers who Died for Democracy*. (*See:* WB69.2) This piece received its premiere in Carnegie Hall on January 5, 1944, performed by the New York Philharmonic-Symphony Orchestra, and was broadcast on the CBS network four days later. An important collaboration with violinist Louis Kaufman led to the composition of a difficult piece, the *Suite for Violin and Piano*, inspired by three paintings of African American artists, which had been published in 1940 in *The Negro in Art* by Alain Locke. Louis Kaufmann and his wife, Annette, a pianist, played this piece for many years on their concert tours. Still would later write an arrangement for solo violin with orchestra and an arrangement of two of the movements for flute, chamber orchestra, and piano.

The *Festive Overture* of 1944 won the Cincinnati Symphony Orchestra's Golden Jubilee Season Composition Competition and was premiered on January 19, 1945, in Music Hall with Eugene Goossens conducting. Still's dedication on the holograph says, "To my dear friend, Rudolph Dunbar." The version distributed by Carl Fischer is dedicated to the memory of Eugene Goossens. In November Rudolph Dunbar conducted a performance of the work in Paris with the Orchestre National, the second in a long succession of performances with other conductors that included the Denver Symphony, the Hollywood Bowl Symphony, the New York Philharmonic, the Los Angeles Philharmonic, and symphony orchestras in Nashville, Charleston (WV), Seattle, San Jose, Richmond, and Detroit, among many others. Rudolph Dunbar, who had played clarinet in the Harlem Orchestra with Still about 1924, championed Still's works in Europe and in the United States from about 1942 until 1946.

Still received a commission from the Fynette H. Kulas American Composer's Fund to write a piece for the Cleveland Orchestra. *Poem for Orchestra* (1944) had its premiere in Severance Hall on December 7, 1944, with Rudolph Ringwall conducting. It was subsequently performed in New York in Carnegie Hall by the New York Philharmonic in 1946 with Artur Rodzinski conducting, in Dallas by the Dallas Symphony in 1948 with Antal Dorati, and in Chicago by the Chicago Symphony Orchestra under Rafael Kubelik in 1950.

In December of 1943, Still finished his third important solo piano group, *Bells,* containing *Phantom Chapel* and *Fairy Knoll.* The latter is dedicated to the young concert pianist, Philippa Schuyler, who passed away prematurely while on a concert tour in 1967. Schuyler's parents were also an interracial couple who felt a special closeness to the Stills because of their shared beliefs in the brotherhood of all people and in promoting the advancement of African Americans. *Bells* was published by Delkas in 1944. The *Scherzo* of the *Afro-American Symphony* was recorded by Leopold Stokowski and the All-American Orchestra on a Columbia recording in 1944.

Still's important song cycle, *Songs of Separation,* came in 1945, even though it was not published until 1949. (*See:* B310) Selecting significant African American poets for his texts, the composer sought to bring expression to his people through the art song. In a letter from Arna Bontemps to Langston Hughes, the former said, "Start dusting off a chair for me at ASCAP. My first song just came through, a poem called 'Idolatry,' set by Still. A very impressive job for the more profound music lovers."[80] Jerome Hines would include this outstanding song cycle in his 1951-52 concert tour.

During the next three years, Still wrote several notable works, including *From the Delta* for band (1945), *Pastorela* for violin and piano (1946), *Danzas de Panama* for string quartet based on folk songs collected by Elisabeth Waldo (1948), *From a Lost Continent* for chorus and piano or orchestra (1948), and *Miniatures for Flute, Oboe, and Piano* (before 1948). In 1947 he received an honorary doctorate in music from Oberlin College.

In November of 1948, Still wrote about the long-awaited premiere of *Troubled Island* in New York, saying, "I have been spending so much time and energy on the opera that I haven't written anything new." The composer revealed his innermost thoughts on the importance of the opera in a statement to Leopold Stokowski: "This opera is the dream of my life, and no one but you thought it worth hearing." He dedicated the opera to Stokowski, his friend and supporter. Langston Hughes, the librettist, who was on hand in New York a month before the production, wrote, "The City Center is humming with preparations for *Troubled Island.* (Premiere March 31). . . . the music . . . sounds very lovely indeed. It has a lot of melody and so should prove to be a popular opera with the public."[81]

After the New York City Center performances of his opera, *Troubled Island,* Still was awarded a citation by the National Association for American Composers and Conductors for his outstanding service to American music. The critics, however, were not as enthusiastic. John Briggs wrote, it "was received with cheers, whistles and noisy applause" (*See:* WB164.22), but Robert Sabin said, "Mr. Still's score is largely unsuited to the nature of the subject." (*See:* WB164.27) Other critics were even harsher. (*See:* B171) Once again encouraging words came from Leopold Stokowski, "I suppose we have to be patient. Apparently, it was not too well understood by some of the writers. This is not the first time I have heard that certain critics write their articles before they listen to the music. What could be more intellectually dishonest?"[82]

The Department of State recorded *Troubled Island* for distribution abroad and presented recordings of its dress rehearsal on a Voice of America broadcast. In a letter to Stokowski, Still explained that it was having great success on radio in Paris until it was suddenly removed from the air and returned. The reason was that it was *mauvais* (bad).[83] Subsequent letters to Stokowski from Still revealed that after some intervention on the part of influential politicians, a new tape was recorded, citing technical difficulties as the reason for the return, and sent to Europe for additional broadcasts.

When Stokowski wrote a year later to say, "I'm afraid there has been some intrigue going on against your TROUBLED ISLAND,"[84] he had summed up an unexplainable situation succinctly. More importantly, Still was able to recover from the disappointments of the severe criticisms and to learn from the musical experience of seeing and hearing his opera produced. In 1952, he wrote to Stokowski,

> I'm very glad that I did not become discouraged over the many things that happened after "Troubled Island" was presented in 1949—since then I have finished two new operas. One [*Costaso*] has a colorful Western setting and is an expression of Faith. The other [*Mota*] is set in Africa, with native choruses, and so on. . . . I think I learned a great deal from seeing "Troubled Island" staged, and hope that it (this new knowledge) will be evident whenever the new operas are done.[85]

Still's works continued to receive international exposure. In 1950, *Pan Pipes of Sigma Alpha Iota* reported that the INR in Brussels played *Troubled Island, Poem for Orchestra*, the *Scherzo* from the *Afro-American Symphony, Sahdji, Old California, From the Black Belt*, and excerpts from *Lenox Avenue* on broadcasts.[86] The next year his *Symphony No. 4, "Autochthonous,"* which had been written in 1947, was played for the first time by the Oklahoma Symphony over the Mutual Radio Network. In 1951, the first two of many songs that Still would be commissioned to write for music education textbooks were published.

In 1953 the Freedoms Foundation presented an honor medal and cash award to Still for his symphonic work, *To You, America!* In February, he received the George Washington Carver Achievement Award of Phi Beta Sigma Fraternity in Los Angeles.[87]

When Still received an honorary Doctor of Humanities in Music from Bates College in Lewistown, Maine, in 1954 he said,

> I felt very, very highly complimented to have received the degree from Bates [in the Humanities, because] I've always wanted to do everything [that] I could to build up better race relations. From the very beginning, in the time when I was in the Navy in World War One, I made up my mind that, when I got out. . . . I would devote myself to establishing friendships, [and to] building good will. So, to have received a degree in the Humanities . . . seemed. . . . to be sort of a recognition of those efforts. (Brown, 18)

Within a few days of receiving this degree, Dr. Still delivered the keynote address at the American Symphony Orchestra League Convention in Springfield, Ohio. His topic was, "Toward a Broader American Culture."[88] (*See:* B184, B324, S52) As Still grew older, he wrote and published articles on his philosophies and opinions about music, race, American culture, and his opposition to communism. He continued to stress his lifelong commitment to the equality of all people. His ideas on Americanizing the American concert hall were ahead of their time, misunderstood and resisted by the opera companies and symphony halls who presented primarily repertoire by European composers. Along with such diverse musical leaders as W. C. Handy, Henry Cowell, Paul Whiteman, Leopold Stokowski, Howard Hanson, and John Alden Carpenter, Still believed that the United States should promote its own culture and that music written by Americans represented that culture in positive ways. From Whiteman's "Experiments in American Music," to Hanson's "Festivals of American Music," Still and his colleagues in various composers' alliances fought to have their music recognized and played in their own country. Through music, Still believed, the various races could come together, understand each other, and put aside their differences, if only for a moment. It was to this end that Still would devote his later years as he visited schools, gave speeches, accepted awards, and contemplated his life.

A work that represented in many ways the synthesis of his ideas was *The Little Song that Wanted to be a Symphony*, written in 1954 for narrator, voices, and orchestra and first performed in Mississippi in 1955 by the Jackson Symphony Orchestra (now called the Mississippi Symphony). He used a theme and variations form to take the theme around the world as it tried to become a symphony. In the program notes for the 1968 performance in Rochester, New York, Still provided the following remarks: "[Since 1938], the idea of building a composition around a little melody that would bring friendship to American children of many different racial groups had been in the back of my mind . . . [the theme] gives up its idea of becoming a symphony in order to make the children of America happy and to bring them together in harmony and brotherhood."[89]

In 1956 Still wrote *Four Indigenous Portraits* for flute and string quartet which he dedicated to Bessie Lawson Blackman, an African American nurse who befriended the Stills and devoted her life to helping others. The work had four movements, each based on an original theme by the composer. He chose the spiritual of the North American Negro, folk themes of the Brazilian Negro, folk themes of Brazilian and Peruvian Indians, and music of North American Indians as his inspiration. As he grew older and began to evaluate the merits of his works, he discarded those he felt were not good enough. This work was among many that he judged to be not up to the standard he had set. In his later years, as he rejected the influence of the "ultra-modern," most of the works he composed during the years with Varèse also fell into the "discarded" category.

Still composed only one original work for harp solo and orchestra, *Ennanga* (1958), although he used the harp extensively in his orchestral compositions throughout his life. It was dedicated to Lois Adele Craft who premiered the work with Verna Arvey on piano, and who subsequently performed it with string quartet and piano, with string orchestra, and with full orchestra. The program notes indicated that *Ennanga* was an African word for harp with themes based on the composer's impressions of African folk music.

By the late 1950s the number of performances began to diminish and the composer became discouraged. In 1959, Still made his last entry in a diary, officially signaling his retirement from documenting his life, if not also expressing a sense of frustration over the lack of interest in his music. He would have other commissions during the next two decades and his works would be performed, but the numbers would be smaller, the venues less prestigious, and the works shorter, mostly songs and choral pieces. In 1960, he had many large works which were collecting dust on the shelves, unpublished and unperformed.

Still came to the attention of the American Accordionists' Association in 1960 and received a commission to write a piece for that instrument. The result was a difficult piece, *Aria,* which was performed in a Carnegie Hall recital as part of the National Accordionists' Association Convention that year. This piece was a landmark of sorts, because it was one of the early pieces written especially for the instrument, rather than arranged from an existing piece. Because of its popularity and the familiarity of Still's name to accordionists, the Association commissioned him to write an easier piece, *Lilt,* suitable for students. He would also receive a commission from the American Guild of Organists for their national convention in the 1960s. Many works for chambers groups came in that decade, including the *Folk Suites, Nos. 1, 2, 3, and 4,* and the *Folk Suite for Band.*

Still recalled a significant award from that time: "In 1961, the National Federation of Music Clubs and the Aeolian Music Foundation offered a prize for a composition dedicated to the United Nations, and I wrote 'The Peaceful Land' which won that [prize]." (Brown, 17) *The Peaceful Land,* for orchestra, was premiered on October 22, 1961, by the University of Miami Symphony Orchestra with Fabien Sevitsky conducting.

In 1962 Still completed another opera, *Highway 1, U.S.A,* which was premiered by the University of Miami Opera at Coral Gables High School with Fabien Sevitsky conducting. The precursor of *Highway 1, U.S.A.,* was *A Southern Interlude,* completed twenty years before in June of 1942, with a libretto by Verna Arvey. The reviews of the 1963 performance were enthusiastic. Mark Polo wrote in the *Miami Hurricane,* "On the surface, the work sounds like a Bernstein Broadway musical, but it is much deeper and more complex." (*See:* WB62.3) Another reviewer wrote, "It is lively, free in spirit, and with a touch of nobility about it." (*See:* WB62.1) When the opera was performed in Jackson, Mississippi, in 1972, in the landmark production by Opera/South conducted by Margaret Harris, Frank Hains noted, "It's rich in tunes, from a rousing, hand-clapping, revivalistic chorus to lyrical solos and duets, some with a vaguely Porgy-and-Bessish quality." (*See:* WB62.8)

Recognition for his achievements in music continued to come during the 1970s in the form of honorary doctorates. The University of Arkansas degree in 1971 was followed by Pepperdine University and the New England Conservatory of Music in 1973 and the Peabody Conservatory of Music in 1974. In 1974 Still was cited as "a distinguished Mississippian" by the governor of Mississippi and his opera, *A Bayou Legend,* composed in 1941, had its debut by Opera/South, the same company that had performed *Highway 1, U.S.A.* two years before. This opera "about black folkways in the bayou country of Mississippi in the nineteenth century was produced on nationwide public television in June 1981, and thereby made history as the first opera written by a black composer to be telecast on a national network."[90]

In 1974 Still was one of the first composers represented on the Columbia Records/AAMOA (Afro-American Music Opportunities Association) Black Composers Series releases. Volume two of that set included a recording of his *Afro-American Symphony* conducted by Paul Freeman. In 1975 Still received an honorary doctorate at the University of Southern California at Los Angeles in what was to be his last public appearance. He died on December 3, 1978.

Still's efforts to gain recognition parallel the story of the struggle for the credibility of American music. He and his professional associates in the Hanson and Varèse circles represented the first generation of American composers to fight the battle for nationalism in the United States. During his lifetime, he created music as a composer and performer, and he skillfully arranged the music of others in unique and distinguishable ways. He wrote possibly as many as four hundred arrangements and scores used in musical theatre, jazz, popular music, and television from 1916 until the 1950s, and he earned recognition for his pioneering work in radio.

Still's music did not fit into easily defined categories, even though he preferred to use melody as the basis for his compositions. His harmonies ranged from modal constructions and diatonic triads to nebulous tonalities, but he always kept his listener in mind. Above all, he wanted to please his audience. Experimenting as he did in some early works, he found a style that worked for him derived from the music of his race. As he matured, he became comfortable with employing whatever style he felt suited the message he wanted to convey, and he possessed the skill in composition to select appropriate techniques. He was a masterful orchestrator. He believed that inspiration came from God, and his humble spirit never failed to acknowledge that his talent came from a higher source.

Still earned the title "Dean of Afro-American Composers" for his courage to be the first of his race to break away from traditional roles. If he had a good idea, he could be the witty experimentalist who was not afraid to break the rules. He was also the serious composer of five symphonies based on carefully sketched and planned themes and transitions, striving to make a statement in an art form that transcends written language. Largely self-taught as an arranger and performer, he avoided the rigid, traditional college curriculum that a degree in music would have given him. Instead, he pioneered his own way, working in commercial music for the experience he would gain, studying jazz for the richness it added to his sound, and seeking out qualities in all music that could be formulated into a uniquely American sound.

He credited George Chadwick with inspiring him, more than anyone, to write American music. He thanked Edgard Varèse, the "ultra-modernist," with allowing him to experiment with his own ideas and showing him that breaking the rules could lead to exciting new possibilities. Yet it was his college idol, the Afro-British composer, Samuel Coleridge-Taylor, whose philosophies he followed throughout his life. More than anything, he wanted to uplift his people and elevate the music of his people by using their music in symphonic works. From his first exposure to the blues in 1916 with W. C. Handy's band until the first performances of his *Afro-American Symphony* in 1931, Still kept his resolution deep in his heart. In addition to that goal, he wanted to contribute even greater works to the operatic repertoire, and it is in this area that his works have been the most neglected. Any hope of evaluating his achievements in that field rests with the future.

Once Still felt that he had elevated the music of his people, he broadened his focus to include the brotherhood of all people, as he set about writing his own definition of an American style of composed music. Drawing on folk songs of all regions, and recognizing the unique and important contributions of African Americans to music in the United States, William Grant Still synthesized the melodies, harmonies, and rhythms of a melting pot culture into a style recognizable as his own.

Notes

1. Mabel Mute (White), "Notes on Life of William Grant Still," typescript, 1936, William Grant Still and Verna Arvey Papers, Special Collections Division, University of Arkansas Libraries, Fayetteville (hereafter cited as WGS/VAS Papers), Box 75. Mabel Mute, later White, was a cousin of Still's mother.

2. Eileen Southern, "Conversation with William Grant Still," *The Black Perspective in Music* 3 (May 1975): 166; interviews from June 20-22, 1969. Hereafter this conversation will be indicated within the text as (Southern, page).

3. Verna Arvey, *In One Lifetime* (Fayetteville, Arkansas: University of Arkansas Press, 1984), 30, 231.

4. Mute, "Notes," WGS/VAS Papers, Box 75.

5. Stephen Banfield, "Samuel Coleridge-Taylor," *The New Grove Dictionary of Music and Musicians,* 6th ed., edited by Stanley Sadie (New York: MacMillan, 1984), 4:528.

6. Mute, "Notes," WGS/VAS Papers, Box 75.

7. William Grant Still, "Divorce Document and Information, and Marriage Document," 1937, WGS/VAS Papers, Box 52, folder 9. Hereafter this box and folder will be indicated within the text as (Papers, 52:9).

8. W. C. Handy, *Father of the Blues: An Autobiography,* edited by Arna Bontemps (1941; reprint, New York: Da Capo Press, n.d.), 60.

9. William Grant Still, interviews by R. Donald Brown, November 13, 1967, and December 4, 1967, transcript, "Negro Serious Music," edited by Judith Anne Still, California Black Oral History Project (Fullerton: California State University), 7-8, 29. Hereafter this interview will be indicated within the text as (Brown, page).

10. Arvey, *In One Lifetime,* 49; Eileen Southern, *Biographical Dictionary of Afro-American and African Musicians* (Westport, Connecticut: Greenwood Press, 1982), 359.

11. The author is indebted to Mark Tucker for sharing with her information which he obtained from Vince Giordano on Still's arrangements.

12. Eileen Southern, *The Music of Black Americans,* 2nd ed. (1971; New York: W. W. Norton, 1983), 344; quote from Samuel B. Charters and Leonard Kunstadt, *Jazz: A History of the New York Scene* (New York, 1962), 32.

13. Southern, *Music of Black Americans,* 351-352; quote from James Reese Europe, "A Negro Explains Jazz," *Readings in Black American Music* (New York, 1983), 226. The recording of Still's 1919 arrangement of *St. Louis Blues* is currently available on *William Grant Still: A Centennial Tribute (1895-1995),* a Two-Hour Radio Documentary, produced by Lance Boling and Cambria Records, 1995.

14. Southern, *Music of Black Americans,* 366; WGS/VAS Papers, scrapbook, vol. 1, p. 1 (hereafter cited as 1:1).

15. *Variety,* May 27, 1921; quoted in Allen Woll, *Black Musical Theatre from Coontown to Dreamgirls* (Baton Rouge and London: Louisiana State University Press, 1989), 62.

16. *Variety,* May 27, November 25, December 9, 1921; in Woll, *Black Musical Theatre,* 72.

17. Woll, *Black Musical Theatre,* 73.

18. Southern, *Music of Black Americans,* 366.

19. Patricia Turner, *Dictionary of Afro-American Performers* (New York: Garland Press), 362-363.

20. Southern, *Music of Black Americans,* 367.

21. Verna Arvey, *Studies of Contemporary American Composers: William Grant Still* (New York: J. Fischer & Bro., 1939), 13.

22. Newspaper clipping, "Runnin' Wild," n.d., WGS/VAS Papers, scrapbook, 1:1.

23. Personnel list from a program of the Harlem Orchestra, n.d., WGS/VAS Papers, scrapbook, 1:1.

24. Louise Varèse, *Varèse: A Looking Glass Diary,* vol. 1 (New York: W. W. Norton, 1972), 226-227.

25. Louise Varèse, *Varèse,* 227.

26. *Musical Courier,* "International Composers' Guild," [1926], WGS/VAS Papers, scrapbook, 1:5.; *ibid;* Louise Varèse, *Varèse,* 243.

27. Carl D. Kinsey to William Grant Still, September 8, 1925, WGS/VAS, scrapbook, 1:6; Ruth Page to Still, May 3, [1926], WGS/VAS Papers, Box 36.

28. Charles W. Spofford to Still, April 3, 1926, WGS/VAS Papers, scrapbook, 1:8.

29. Southern, *Biographical Dictionary,* 359; Don Voorhees, telegram to Still, [1926], WGS/VAS Papers, scrapbook, 1:10.

30. Thomas H. Fisher to Still, October 5, 1926, WGS/VAS Papers, scrapbook, 1:12.

31. *Musical Courier,* "International Composers' Guild," [1926], WGS/VAS Papers, scrapbook, 1:13.; Olin Downes, "Music," *The New York Times,* November 29, 1926, WGS/VAS Papers, scrapbook, 1:13 (*See:* WB26.1); *Musical America,* WGS/VAS Papers, scrapbook, 1:13.

32. Olin Downes, "Fair Play for Young America," *The New York Times,* [1927], WGS/VAS Papers, scrapbook, 1:12; Claire Reis to Still, [1926], WGS/VAS Papers, scrapbook, 1:11.

33. Harold Bruce Forsythe, *William Grant Still: A Study in Contradictions,* typescript (February, 1930), 14, WGS/VAS Papers, Box 75; "Barrere's Little Symphony Plays," *The New York Times,* March 21, 1927, WGS/VAS Papers, scrapbook, 1:16; Forsythe, *Still,* 21.

34. Arvey, *Still,* 13.

35. George E. Haynes to Still, [n.d.], WGS/VAS Papers, scrapbook, 1:18; A. G. Garner to Still, January 12, 1928, WGS/VAS Papers, scrapbook, 1:18.

36. Arvey, *Still,* 15.

37. Thomas A. DeLong, *Pops: Paul Whiteman, King of Jazz* (Piscataway, NJ: New Century Publishers, Inc., 1983), 102.

38. Still wrote on the score at rehearsal number 8, "1st time only Bix Hot solo—2nd time—later Trum [Trumbauer] Hot solo second time—Andy and Bix inversion to the end." The Paul Whiteman Collection, Williams College Special Collections and Archives, Williamstown, Massachusetts, No. 2138-9.

39. Forsythe, *Still,* 6.

40. Arvey, *Still,* 34. *Beyond Tomorrow* and Still's orchestration of *After You've Gone* both were once in The Paul Whiteman Collection, Williams College Archives and Special Collections. They were officially listed as missing in 1989.

41. Still, *Diary 1930,* August 20 and 21, 1930, WGS/VAS Papers, Box 54.

42. Still, *Diary* 1930, September 4, 1930, WGS/VAS Papers, Box 54.

43. Olin Downes, "Ballet Presented at Rochester Fete," *The New York Times*, [May 23, 1931], WGS/VAS Papers, scrapbook, 1:34.

44. Still to Irving Schwerké, October 5, 1931, WGS/VAS Papers, Box 40.

45. Unidentified newspaper clipping, [New York, 1932], WGS/VAS Papers, scrapbook,1:47.

46. Ibid.

47. Cora Gary Illidge, "Music News," *New York Amsterdam News*, 1931, WGS/VAS Papers, scrapbook, 1:32.

48. Stewart B. Sabin, "Concerts: American Composers' Concert," *Rochester Democrat and Chronicle*, March 4, 1932, WGS/VAS Papers, scrapbook, 1:53.

49. Press release, "WOR Shorts," 1932, WGS/VAS Papers, scrapbook, 1:49.

50. Henry C. Parker, Jr., secretary, "Minutes of the (Ninth) Annual Music Week Effort in Harlem," [1932], WGS/VAS Papers, scrapbook, 1:52.

51. "Berlin Hails Hanson Offering Our Music," *The New York Times*, January 8, 1933, WGS/VAS Papers, scrapbook, 2:3.

52. This wooden door with the large gold oval and a wooden star is part of the memorabilia in The Paul Whiteman Collection, Williams College Archives and Special Collections, Williamstown, Massachusetts.

53. Irving Schwerké to Still, February 10, 1933, WGS/VAS Papers, Box 40.

54. Still to Schwerké, March 17, 1937, WGS/VAS Papers, Box 40; facsimile of the original in the Library of Congress.

55. DeLong, *Pops*, 177; "High Spots on the Air," unidentified newspaper clipping, February 13, 1934, WGS/VAS Papers, scrapbook, 3:5; Arvey, *Still*, 33.

56. Henry Cowell to Still, April 16, 1934, WGS/VAS Papers, Box 10; J. H. P. Eckles, president, National Association of Negro Musicians, postcard, n.d., WGS/VAS Papers, scrapbook, 3:2.

57. "Afro-American Composer Here To Write New Opera," *Los Angeles Times*, [1934], WGS/VAS Papers, scrapbook, 4:8.

58. Arvey, *Still*, 39.

59. "Composer Here for Showing of *La Guiablesse*," unidentified newspaper clipping, [1934], WGS/VAS Papers, scrapbook, 4:17.

60. Edward Moore, "Critic Praises Innovation of Ballet Night," [1934], WGS/VAS Papers, scrapbook, 4:19.

61. Still to Schwerké, April 10, 1938, WGS/VAS Papers, Box 40.

62. Concert Program, July 11, [1935], WGS/VAS Papers, scrapbook, 4:8.

63. Still to Gail Still, June 6, 1936, WGS/VAS Papers, Box 44.

64. For a study of the piano works, see Carolyn L. Quin, "Fusion of Cultures in the Piano Works of William Grant Still," *William Grant Still and the Fusion of Cultures in American Music*, 2nd ed., edited by Judith Anne Still, Celeste Anne Headlee, and Lisa M. Headlee-Huffman (1972; Flagstaff, Arizona: Master Player Library, 1995), 174-187.

65. DeLong, *Pops*, 177.

66. Still to Schwerké, December 20, 1937, WGS/VAS Papers, Box 40; also quoted in Arvey, *Still*, 30.

67. Linton Martin, "Stokowski Mute in Exit from Phila. Orchestra," *Philadelphia Inquirer*, December 11, 1937.

68. "Composer's Festival on May 24-26," unidentified newspaper clipping, May 8, 1937, WGS/VAS Papers, scrapbook, 3:18.

69. Arvey, *Still*, 41.

70. Deems Taylor to Still, November 18, 1936, and February 3, 1937, WGS/VAS Papers, Box 10.

71. Davidson Taylor to Still, May 24, 1937, WGS/VAS Papers, Box 10.

72. Clarence Williams to Still, March 16, 1937, WGS/VAS Papers, Box 9.

73. Still to Schwerké, May 5, 1937, WGS/VAS Papers, Box 40; "Hughes-Roxborough Drama Will Be Scored for Opera By W. Grant Still," unidentified Detroit newspaper, 1937, WGS/VAS Papers, scrapbook, 3:17.

74. Cowell to Still, June 4, 1937, WGS/VAS Papers, Box 10.

75. John Simon Guggenheim Memorial Foundation, *Report of the Secretary and Treasurer,* 1939 and 1949 (New York), 172.

76. Cowell to Verna Arvey, February 8, 1939, WGS/VAS Papers, Box 10.

77. Guggenheim Foundation, *Report* 1939 and 1940, 172.

78. Langston Hughes to Arna Bontemps, January or February 1941, *Arna Bontemps-Langston Hughes Letters, 1925-1967,* edited by Charles H. Nichols (New York: Dodd Mead & Co., 1980), 73; Hughes to Bontemps, *Letters,* 75; Hughes to Bontemps, *Letters,* 78. (*See:* B325)

79. Guggenheim Foundation, *Report* 1941 and 1942, 209.

80. Bontemps to Hughes, November 19, 1945, *Letters,* 200.

81. Still to Leopold Stokowski, November 27, 1948, WGS/VAS Papers, Box 45; Still to Stokowski, November 27, 1948, WGS/VAS papers, Box 45; Hughes to Bontemps, February 26, 1949, *Letters,* 251-252.

82. Stokowski to Still, August 22, 1949, WGS/VAS Papers, Box 45.

83. Still to Stokowski, August 27, 1949, WGS/VAS Papers, Box 45.

84. Stokowski to Still, September 18, 1950, WGS/VAS Papers, Box 45.

85. Still to Stokowski, July 24, 1952, WGS/VAS Papers, Box 45.

86. Marguerite Kelly Kyle, "AmerAllegro," *Pan Pipes of Sigma Alpha Iota* 43 (December 1950): 131.

87. Kyle, *Pan Pipes* (January 1954): 62.

88. Kyle, *Pan Pipes* (January 1955): 69.

89. Ruth Watanabe, "Program Notes," Thirty-Eighth Annual Festival of American Music, Rochester, May 2, 1968. (*See:* WB91.6)

90. Southern, *Music of Black Americans,* 425.

WORKS AND PERFORMANCES

W1 *Africa,* variants of title: *Darker Africa* and *Darkest Africa* (available from William Grant Still Music).
Suite for orchestra in three movements; also in piano solo arrangement.
Completed in Hollywood, CA, February 1930; based on sketches dating from as early as 1924 and additional sketches in 1928; revised five times until 1935; reduced orchestra version, April, 1930; full orchestra version, November, 1930; *Land of Superstition* arranged for The Paul Whiteman Orchestra, 1933; piano solo version and final revision of full score, 1935.
Dedicated to Georges Barrère "as an expression of gratitude for his kindness and encouragement."
Contents: I. Lento-Moderato: Land of Peace, II. Lento: Land of Romance, III. Moderato con moto: Land of Superstition.
On the condensed autograph score, the composer wrote this program: "An American Negro has formed a concept of the land of his ancestors, based largely on its folklore, and influenced by his contact with American civilization. He beholds in his mind's eye not the Africa of reality, but an Africa mirrored in fancy, and radiantly ideal.
   1. He views it first as a land of peace; peace that is partly pastoral in nature, and partly spiritual.
   2. It is to him also a land of fanciful and mysterious romance; romance tinged with ineffable sorrow.
   3. Contact with American civilization has not enabled him to completely overcome his inherent superstitious nature. It is *that heritage* [composer's emphasis] of his forbears [*sic*] binding him irrevocably to the past, and making it possible for him to form the most accurate concept of Africa."
Instrumentation: 3 flutes (3rd doubles on piccolo), 2 oboes, English horn, 3 clarinets (3rd doubles on bass clarinet), 2 bassoons; 4 horns, 3 trumpets and 3 trombones (Harmon and fiber mutes), tuba; timpani, snare drum, 3 tom-toms, wood block, gourd, triangle, vibraphone, wire brush, bells (originally chime), cymbals; harp, piano, celesta, strings.
Duration: 30 minutes.
Autograph sketches, bound condensed autograph score with orchestration notes and revisions, fair copies of parts (for viola, cello, bass, and harp) for *Land of Romance,* and the autograph score for the piano solo arrangement are in

the William Grant Still and Verna Arvey Papers at the University of Arkansas Libraries, Fayetteville.

Holograph score of *Land of Superstition* and a set of 60 parts dated 1933 are in The Paul Whiteman Collection, Williams College Archives and Special Collections, Williamstown, Massachusetts. (Parts designated for individual players like Charles Strickfaden, Fud Livingston, and Frankie Trumbauer.)

Holograph full score of the first version is in the Library of Congress, gift of Irving Schwerké.

Autograph fair copy of the full score, final revision of 1935, is in The William Grant Still Estate.

Still and Arvey Papers indicate this piece was later "discarded by the composer."

W1a **First Performance:** 1930 (April 6): New York, NY; Guild Theater; Barrère Little Symphony Orchestra, Georges Barrère, conductor. (Reduced orchestra version)

W1b 1930 (October 24): Rochester, NY; Kilbourn Hall; Rochester Philharmonic Orchestra, Howard Hanson, conductor. (Full orchestra version)

Selected Performances

W1c 1933 (January 25): New York, NY; Carnegie Hall; The Paul Whiteman Orchestra, Paul Whiteman, conductor. (III)

W1d 1933 (February 4): Paris, France; Pasdeloup Symphony Orchestra, Richard Lert, conductor.

W1e 1933 (March 1): New York, NY; Town Hall; Sinfonietta of New York, Quinto Maganini, conductor.

W1f 1933 (mid Summer): Lewisohn Stadium; The Paul Whiteman Orchestra with the Philharmonic-Symphony Orchestra, Paul Whiteman, conductor.

W1g 1935 (April 2): Rochester, NY; Eastman Theater; Eastman School Symphony and Chorus, Howard Hanson, conductor.

W1h 1935 (May 5): Los Angeles, CA; Musart Theater; Verna Arvey, piano. (*See:* WB76.6)

W1i 1935 (July 29, 30): Philadelphia, PA; Fairmont Park; Philadelphia Symphony Orchestra and the Paul Whiteman Orchestra, Paul Whiteman, conductor.

W1j 1935 (December 8): San Francisco, CA; Sorosis Club; Verna Arvey, piano.

W1k 1936 (July 23): Los Angeles, CA; Hollywood Bowl; Los Angeles Philharmonic Orchestra, William Grant Still, guest conductor.

W1l 1938 (January 19): Los Angeles, CA; Belasco Theatre; Los Angeles Federal Symphony Orchestra, William Grant Still, guest conductor, Verna Arvey, piano. (*See also:* WB80.8, WB80.9)

W1m 1938 (May 2): San Diego, CA; Savoy Theatre; San Diego Symphony Orchestra, Julius Leib, conductor.

Bibliography

WB1.1 Sabin, Stewart B. "American Composers' Concert." *Rochester Democrat and Chronicle*, October 25, 1930.

Review of the October 24, 1930, performance of the Rochester Philharmonic Orchestra. "Mr. Still's *Africa* was heard by the writer with genuine pleasure . . . the first movement has much—almost too much—material; but there is charming music in it; the second movement lingers a bit, but it is characteristic and it is lyric; the finale hints at something that one believes comes individually in conception to the composer."

WB1.2 Shulsky, Samuel. "Moderns Strike New Note in Kilbourn Concert." Rochester *Times-Union*, October 25, 1930.

"To my mind the highlight of the evening came in the superb playing of William Grant Still's third movement entitled *Land of Superstition*, of his suite *Africa*. Daring rhythm backed up by a friendly welded theme and strength in motive are combined in this movement. Mr. Still, one of the foremost of American negro [sic] composers, does not shy at melody or musical figure and his suite proves it. The ovation which followed his number well illustrated how pleasing modern music, handled intelligently, can be. In *Land of Romance*, the second movement, his clever use of the piano is praiseworthy. The first movement, *Land of Peace* seems a bit too long, extending beyond its climax."

WB1.3 Schwerké, Irving. "American Negro's Tone-Poem 'Africa' Scores Success in Concert Here." Paris *Tribune*, February 5, 1933, p. 3. (Also appears in *The Left Bank Revisited: Selections from the Paris* Tribune *1917-1934*, Hugh Ford, ed., [University Park: Pennsylvania State University, 1972]: 227-28.)

Review of the February 4, 1933, performance of the Pasdeloup Symphony Orchestra. "The work [*Africa*] made a deep impression and was enthusiastically received by the large audience, and Richard Lert, who conducted, gave a reading of the difficult and penetrating composition that was perfect in detail and made felt the essence of Still's music, so sincere, so curiously and beautifully orchestrated, so unaffectedly, even primitively lyrical. If I had a regret, it was that Still was not present in person to approve his interpreters and to receive the plaudits of the crowd."

WB1.4 H., H. "Music." *New York Times*, March 2, 1933.

Review of the March 1, 1933, performance of the Sinfonietta of New York. Still's *Land of Romance*, from his *Africa* suite, appears on the program. "It was an Africa faintly suggesting the 'blues' which a sensitive, intelligent Negro might take back to that continent with him; lush in color, effective in writing; rhythmically interesting without being powerfully original. It was warmly applauded and the composer had to rise and bow thrice."

WB1.5 Reichard, Carolyn. "The Concert." *Rochester Times-Union*, April 3, 1935.

"From the compositions of the Negro musician, William Grant Still, were selected two sections of his *Africa* suite. Wistful and lyric, their intended mood and impression were at all times clear. Mr. Still writes to enhance by musical development the negro [sic] themes which form his bases. Although primitive in suggestion, this suite is never crude, and does not strain for its effects. The performance of the orchestra at times had a tendency to be disjointed."

WB1.6 Shulsky, Samuel. "Eastman Orchestra and Chorus Open Fifth Annual Festival of American Music." *Rochester Journal*, April 3, 1935.

"The Still [*Africa*] suite, of which the last two movements were played last evening, is a good example of the admirable work this composer has done in incorporating Africa [sic]-American themes into American music. It is a fine example of orchestral color in modern composition."

WB1.7 Jones, Isabel Morse. "Noted Composer's Music Heard at Lecture-Recital." *Los Angeles Times,* May 8, 1935.

Review of a performance at the Musart Theater on May 5, 1935. "Miss Arvey played the parts of *Africa,* a symphonic poem, and of the new Still opera, *Blue Steel*, as well as *Kaintuck'* and an introductory group by Coleridge-Taylor, Villa-Lobos, and Bruce Forsythe. Her knowledge of the composers of the dark races enabled her to make interesting comparisons and to point out certain characteristics in Still's work which enhanced her performance at the piano."

WB1.8 Taylor, Deems. "Program Notes." Robin Hood Dell Concerts Review. (Philadelphia Symphony Orchestra), July 29-30, 1935, p. 24.

Land of Superstition, the third movement from *Africa*, appears on the program. "*Africa* . . . is an American Negro's concept of the cradle of his race, formed on the folklore which has come down through the generations. . . . the concept is wholly fanciful. . . . This is most definitely marked in the third movement where all of the stories, myths and lore, have been concentrated . . . as a *Land of Superstition*. . . . Mr. Still has employed a unique rhythmic treatment to portray this concept in music."

WB1.9 Laciar, Samuel L. "Music: Paul Whiteman Scores Huge Success at Dell." Philadelphia *Evening Public Ledger*, July 30, 1935.

Review of the July 29, 1935, performance of the Philadelphia Symphony Orchestra and the Paul Whiteman Orchestra, conducted by Paul Whiteman, at Fairmont Park. "The third movement from William Grant Still's symphony *Darkest Africa* [sic], entitled *Land of Superstition* . . . proved to be one of those works which are on the borderline between classic and jazz and are convincing from neither angle."

WB1.10 "Whiteman Draws Overflow at Dell." *Philadelphia Inquirer*, July 30, 1935.

Review of the July 29, 1935, performance of the Philadelphia Symphony Orchestra and the Paul Whiteman Orchestra. "[*Land of Superstition*], the third movement of Still's *Darkest Africa* [sic] . . . sounded more Indian than Negroid."

WB1.11 Fisher, Marjory. "William G. Still Tells of Own Music." *San Francisco News*, December 9, 1935.

Short article based upon a program presented by the New Music Society of California, on December 8. The program included *Africa*, three dances from the ballet *La Guiablesse*, two dances from *Central Avenue [Lenox Avenue]*, and *Kaintuck'*. Verna Arvey performed as pianist. "Mr. Still is one of the more gifted among young American composers, as those who have heard his works in orchestral form can well testify."

WB1.12 Frankenstein, Alfred. "Wolski, Morini Give First of Recital Series; Third of Dance Council Programs Staged at Playhouse." *San Francisco Chronicle*, December 9, 1935.

Review of two programs, one of which was a Still concert at the Sorosis Club on December 8, 1935. "In the evening the composer, William Grant Still, was presented in a concert of his own works by the New Music Society of California. Verna Arvey played Still's symphonic suite, *Africa*, in a piano reduction, and Nathan Emanuel sang several of his songs in the first half of the program. If this portion of the proceedings is any criterion, it would indicate that Still lands very well in straight forward compositions with a jazz or folk flavor, like the setting of a Dunbar poem Mr. Emanuel sang."

WB1.13 Gowdy, Alma. "Afro-American Music Stirs Bowl Crowd." *Los Angeles Evening Herald and Express*, July 24, 1936.

The program included *Land of Romance* from *Africa* and the *Scherzo* from the *Afro-American Symphony*. "From a point of unity and taste in building an evening of music, the concert rightfully began with these two sincere and individualistic tributes to the African heritage of the American Negro. Mr. Still's music came from the fertile soil of the jungle and it borrowed only the laws of logic in form from the ways of the white man."

WB1.14 Jones, Isabel Morse. "Variety Found Keynote of Interesting Bowl Concert." *Los Angeles Times*, July 24, 1936.

"William Grant Still, the first of his race to conduct a major orchestra in the United States, presented his *Land of Romance* [from *Africa*] and the *Scherzo* from the *Afro-American Symphony*. . . . Still's two numbers are significant. They mark the advance of a people. The *Scherzo* with its jazz rhythms reminds one of the beginning of the race, and the mystical *Land of Romance* is expressive of its poetry. Dignity, sincerity and a certain pride characterize Still's writing."

WB1.15 Norton, Mildred. "Divine Ouster." Los Angeles *Evening News*, July 24, 1936.

Review of the July 23, 1936, performance of the Los Angeles Philharmonic Orchestra, with William Grant Still as guest conductor of *Land of Romance*, from *Africa*, and the *Scherzo* from the *Afro-American Symphony*, at the Hollywood Bowl. "In both of these he proved himself sensitive to the trends of modern orchestration, and invested the numbers with poetry and harmonic color. His *Land of Romance* especially, depicting the American Negro's concept of the birthplace of his people, painted a picture that might have illustrated one of the darker and more somber passages of Poe. Haunted with mystery and shadowed by a sense of brooding, it epitomized the pathos inherent in the history of his race."

WB1.16 Saunders, Richard D. "Sevitsky and Still Conduct Varied Musical Fare at Hollywood Bowl." *Hollywood Citizen-News*, July 24, 1936.

"Still . . . led the orchestra in two of his own works. Both were invariably melodic, with a racially characteristic wistful sentimentality. The instrumentation was adequate, but suggestive of an augmented dance band, a resemblance accentuated by the typical modulations at phrase endings. *The Land of Romance* [from *Africa*] was reflective, contrasting with the vivid and choreographic *Scherzo* from Still's *Afro-American Symphony*."

WB1.17 Spivak, Rose. "Negro Spirituals Well Received At Hollywood Bowl." *West Adams Tribune*, July 27, 1936.

Review of the July 23, 1936, performance of the Los Angeles Philharmonic Orchestra, with William Grant Still as guest conductor of *Land of Romance* from *Africa* and the *Scherzo* from *Afro-American Symphony*, at the Hollywood Bowl. "He employed all the modern devises [sic], syncopation, Polyrhythms [,] discords, and turned out a perfect description of an American Negro's conception of the land of his ancestors."

WB1.18 "Concerts at the Hollywood Bowl." *Pacific Coast Musician*, August 1, 1936.

Review of the July 23, 1936, performance of the Los Angeles Philharmonic Orchestra, with William Grant Still as guest conductor of *Land of Romance* from *Africa* and the *Scherzo* from the *Afro-American Symphony*. "Mr. Still . . . proved to be very much on the quiet, unobtrusive order. His *Land of Romance* is serene, tranquil, poetical and grateful to the ear. In marked contrast in style is his *Scherzo*. Melodious, effectively harmonized and strongly rhythmic, and with well-spiced syncopations, playing on an interestingly colored orchestration, this number proved to be utterly charm-

WB1.19 LaMar, Lawrence F. "Wm. Grant Still Conducts Symphony at Los Angeles." *California Eagle*, August 1, 1936.
   Lengthy review of the July 23, 1936, performance of the Los Angeles Philharmonic Orchestra, with William Grant Still as guest conductor, at the Hollywood Bowl. "After each of the two compositions, Still was showered with wave upon wave of sustained applause. . . . About 250 of the 12,000 people assembled in the Hollywood Bowl that seats 20,000 were of the Race. This number, although small in comparison to the whole, represents an increase over past regular season bowl attendance of Negroes. . . . The concert was in every way a success."

WB1.20 Lawrence, Florence. "William Still Wins Ovation In Symphony." Los Angeles *Examiner*, January 20, 1938.
   Review of the Los Angeles Federal Music Project Symphony Orchestra performance at the Belasco Theater, January 19, 1938. "Still's works have been heard here before, but last night his *Land of Superstition*, the third movement from his *Africa* suite, was well played and conducted by the composer with fine contrasts both of tempo and dynamics. Verna Arvey appeared as guest pianist both in this number and in the *Lenox Avenue* which followed and proved as fine a piece of descriptive writing as Los Angeles concert goers have heard."

W2 *Afro-American Symphony* (1930), also known as *Symphony No. 1* (copyright by Carl Fischer & Co., conductor's score, 1935, and orchestra parts, 1937; copyright renewed and transferred in 1962 to Novello and published by Novello & Co., Ltd., Novello Orchestral Series, 1970. Full orchestral score and orchestral parts available for rental from Novello. Study score prepared by Still, revised 1969, available from Novello).

Composed in New York: diary entries identify October 30, 1930, as the beginning of the first movement and December 6, 1930, as the date of completion of scoring for the third movement.

Dedicated to Irving Schwerké.

Contents: I. Moderato assai, II. Adagio, III. Animato; scherzo, IV. Lento, con risoluzione; the movements have programmatic titles also: I. Longing, II. Sorrow, III. Humor, IV. Aspiration.

The composer later added excerpts from the poems of Paul Lawrence Dunbar.

Additional inscriptions from the Novello Study Score by Still: "With humble thanks to God, the source of inspiration. He who develops his God-given gifts with a view to aiding humanity, manifests truth."

Instrumentation: 3 flutes (3rd doubles on piccolo), 2 oboes, English horn, 3 clarinets, bass clarinet, 2 bassoons; 4 horns, 3 trumpets, 3 trombones (Harmon mutes), tuba; timpani, vibraphone, triangle, bells, wire brush, wood block, snare drum, cymbals, gong; harp, celesta, strings, tenor banjo.

Duration: 28 minutes.

Holograph melodic score with conductor's cues and published (Novello, revised 1969) study score are in the William Grant Still and Verna Arvey Papers at the University of Arkansas Libraries, Fayetteville. (*See:* W133)

Several manuscript versions exist. One was given to Paul-Elliott Cobbs, author of a D.M.A. thesis (University of Washington, 1990) on the work.

Holograph full score of first version is in the Library of Congress, gift of Irving Schwerké.

Holograph full score of third version is in the Library of Congress, gift of J. Fischer & Bro., 1935.

Holograph excerpt from the fourth movement (one page) signed and dated May 5, 1963, is in the Northwestern University Library, Evanston, Illinois.

Manuscript version with notes dated 1936 and later corrections by the composer and a title page saying "J. Fischer & Bro. No. 0318" on the front and the poems of Paul Lawrence Dunbar (copyright 1935) on the verso is in The William Grant Still Estate. Cover has written on it, "hold this score."

W2a **First Performance:** 1931 (October 29): Rochester, NY; Kilbourn Hall, Rochester Philharmonic Orchestra, Howard Hanson, conductor.

Selected Performances

W2b 1932 (March 3): Rochester, NY; Kilbourn Hall, Rochester Philharmonic Orchestra, Howard Hanson, conductor.

W2c 1933 (January 6): Berlin, Germany; Berlin Philharmonic Orchestra, Howard Hanson, conductor.

W2d 1935 (October 30): Rochester, NY; Eastman Theater; Rochester Philharmonic Orchestra, Howard Hanson, conductor.

W2e 1935 (November 20): New York, NY; Carnegie Hall; New York Philharmonic-Symphony Orchestra, Hans Lange, conductor.

W2f 1936 (April 27, 28): Los Angeles, CA; Pan-Pacific Auditorium; Philadelphia Symphony Orchestra, Leopold Stokowski, conductor.

W2g 1936 (May 2, 3): San Francisco, CA; Exposition Auditorium; Philadelphia Symphony Orchestra, Leopold Stokowski, conductor.

W2h 1937 (January 21, 22, 26): Chicago, IL; Orchestra Hall; Chicago Symphony Orchestra, Hans Lange, conductor.

W2i 1937 (May 12): Los Angeles, NY; Los Angeles Federal Music Project Orchestra, Manuel Compinsky, conductor.

W2j 1937 (December 2): San Bernardino, CA; Fox Court Theater; Federal Symphony Orchestra, Vernon Robinson, conductor.

W2k 1938 (February 3-4): Kansas City, MO; Music Hall, Municipal Auditorium; Kansas City Philharmonic Orchestra, Karl Krueger, conductor.

W2l 1939 (October 2): New York, NY; Carnegie Hall; Negro Symphony Orchestra, William Grant Still, guest conductor.

W2m 1940 (July 23); Los Angeles, CA; Hollywood Bowl; Los Angeles Philharmonic Orchestra, David Broekman, conductor.

W2n 1942 (April 26): London, England; Royal Albert Hall; London Philharmonic Orchestra, Rudolph Dunbar, conductor.

W2o 1942 (November 28): London, England; Royal Albert Hall; London Symphony Orchestra, Rudolph Dunbar, conductor.

W2p 1942 (December 20): Liverpool, England; Philharmonic Hall; Liverpool Philharmonic Orchestra, Rudolph Dunbar, conductor.

W2q 1943 (March 12): Sheffield, England; City Hall; National Philharmonic Orchestra, Rudolph Dunbar, conductor.

W2r 1943 (March 18): Nottingham, England; Theatre Royal; National Philharmonic

Orchestra, Rudolph Dunbar, conductor.

W2s 1943 (March 24): Manchester, England; Palace Theatre; National Philharmonic Orchestra, Rudolph Dunbar, conductor.

W2t 1943 (April 2): Bristol, England; Stoll Hippodrome; National Philharmonic Orchestra, Rudolph Dunbar, conductor.

W2u 1944 (March 12): Liverpool, England; Philharmonic Hall; Liverpool Philharmonic Orchestra, Rudolph Dunbar, conductor.

W2v 1944 (November 19): Paris, France; Salle Gaveau; Pasdeloup Symphony Orchestra, Rudolph Dunbar, conductor.

W2w 1945 (June 12): Paris, France; Théâtre des Champs-Élysées; Orchestre de la Société des Concerts Du Conservatoire, Rudolph Dunbar, conductor.

W2x 1945 (September 2-3): Berlin, Germany; Titania-Palast; Berlin Philharmonic Symphony, Rudolph Dunbar, conductor.

W2y 1945 (November 19): Paris, France; Théâtre des Champs-Élysées; National Orchestra, Rudolph Dunbar, conductor.

W2z 1946 (August 22): Los Angeles, CA; Hollywood Bowl; Hollywood Bowl Symphony, Rudolph Dunbar, guest conductor.

W2aa 1946 (November 15): Helsinki, Finland; Konsorvatorium; Helsinki Municipal Orchestra, Martti Similä, conductor.

W2bb 1952 (March 23): Brussels, Belgium; Institut National Belge de Radiodiffusion (INR) Symphony Orchestra, Franz Andre, conductor.

W2cc 1955 (March 4): Baton Rouge, LA; Southern University; University Auditorium; New Orleans Philharmonic-Symphony Orchestra, William Grant Still, guest conductor.

W2dd 1963 (November 24): Detroit, MI; Ford Auditorium; Detroit Symphony Orchestra, William Grant Still, guest conductor.

W2ee 1965 (November 26): San José, Costa Rica; Teatro Nacional; Orquesta Sinfónica Nacional de Costa Rica, Hugo Mariani, conductor.

W2ff 1968 (April 16): New Orleans, LA; Tulane University; McAlister Auditorium; New Orleans Philharmonic-Symphony Orchestra, William Grant Still, guest conductor. (*See:* WB36.17, WB117.18)

W2gg 1970 (March 1): Indianapolis, IN: World War Memorial Auditorium; Philharmonic Orchestra of Indianapolis, Wolfgang Vacano, conductor.

W2hh 1971 (October 26); Rochester, NY; Auditorium Theatre; Rochester Philharmonic Orchestra, Samuel Jones, conductor.

W2ii 1974 (November 17): Pasadena, CA; Civic Auditorium; Los Angeles Philharmonic Orchestra, Sidney Harth, conductor.

W2jj 1976 (February 15): New York, NY; Carnegie Hall; Symphony of the New World, Everett Lee, conductor.

W2kk 1986 (October 11): Jackson, TN; Jackson Civic Center; Jackson Symphony Orchestra, Jordan Tang, conductor.

Bibliography

WB2.1 Croughton, Amy H. "The Concert." *Rochester Journal*, October 30, 1931.
Review of the October 29, 1931, performance of the Rochester Philharmonic Orchestra. "Mr. Still's *Afro-American Symphony* is built up from a 'Blues' theme which he develops into a composition of poignant beauty through which

one feels intense and compelling emotion held within bounds by a fine intelligence. There is not a cheap or banal passage in the composition."

WB2.2   Kessler, David. "New Symphonic Work Acclaimed at First Playing in American Composers' Concert." *Rochester Evening Journal and Post Express*, October 30, 1931.

Review of the October 29, 1931, performance of the Rochester Philharmonic Orchestra. "Mr. Still's [*Afro-American Symphony*] was especially intriguing. . . . Throughout the symphony has life and sparkle when needed and a deep, haunting beauty that aids in conveying a picture of the mercurial temperament of the Negro. The symphony sometimes shuffles its feet, at other times dances. It laughs unrestrainedly, it mourns dolefully and sways often in the barbaric rhythm of its subject. And always it sings."

WB2.3   Sabin, Stewart. "American Composer's Concert." *Rochester Democrat and Chronicle*, October 30, 1931.

Review of the October 29, 1931, performance of the Rochester Philharmonic Orchestra. In the *Afro-American Symphony* "his motive is suggestion of the spirit in the older American Negro life and music, [and] Mr. Still logically uses a characteristic idiom; his material is tuneful; his pathos is characteristic of what the spirituals have made familiar; his humor is jazz-like without jazz vulgarities. . . . Mr. Still has done his work well in this new composition, but to some extent he has replaced that arresting vigor one has admired by deft sophistication."

WB2.4   Croughton, Amy H. "The Concert." *Rochester Times-Union*, March 4, 1932.

Review of the March 3, 1932, performance of the Rochester Philharmonic Orchestra. "It [*Afro-American Symphony*] is honest, sincere music in which the underlying quality of the 'blues' idiom, with its pathos, its humanness and its humor, is developed without resort to theatrical invention."

WB2.5   Kessler, David. "Kilbourn Hall Filled with Enthusiasts." *Rochester Evening Journal and Post Express*, March 4, 1932.

Review of the March 3, 1932, performance of the Rochester Philharmonic Orchestra. "Using a simple little 'blues' theme, the composer wrought a miracle in rhythm and mood. It is music with color, and with life. Mr. Still has not been particularly inventive in themes or harmony. But he evinced real ability in adapting them to an idea of his own."

WB2.6   Reichard, Carolyn. "The Concert" *Rochester Times-Union*, October 31, 1935.

Review of the October 30, 1935, performance of the Rochester Philharmonic Orchestra. "The simplicity of [the *Afro-American Symphony*] only adds to its great appeal and the temperament of the composer reveals the simplicity of his racial feelings for mood and emotion . . . the whole work indicates the composer's excellent ability to trace the course of feeling through musical phrases. Certain musical arrangements have the quality of eliciting an almost universal response, and Mr. Still has the faculty of chosing [*sic*] the most simple of them without falling into harmonic cliches."

WB2.7   Sabin, Stewart. "American Music Series Starts Successfully." *Rochester Democrat and Chronicle*, October 31, 1935, p. 20.

Review of the October 30, 1935, performance of the Rochester Philharmonic Orchestra. "The [*Afro-American Symphony*] was given a fine performance. Doctor Hanson spoke of his regard for this music, and then he conducted that regard into the playing of the symphony. It is quite simple; it is a voicing by so many solo instruments of characteristically racial melodies; it is, if you will, almost naive, but it is wholly musical statement made in all sincerity. The performance was a tribute to the composer."

WB2.8 Downes, Olin. "Two Premiers Offered By Lange." *New York Times*, November 21, 1935.

Review of the November 20, 1935, performance of the New York Philharmonic-Symphony. "Mr. Still has written better music [than the *Afro-American Symphony*]. We have heard other compositions of his, better worked out, with more substance and with no less color and mood. There is little true development in this symphony. . . . The music is best when it lapses whole-heartedly into a jazz tune. . . . The composition wavers, in a word, between the symphonic intention and the style of purely popular music."

WB2.9 Gilman, Lawrence. "Music." *New York Herald Tribune*, November 21, 1935.

Review of the November 20, 1935, performance of the New York Philharmonic-Symphony. "This work is remarkably scored. Mr. Still's [*Afro-American Symphony*] laments and rejoices, longs and aspires, with a prismatic beauty and exquisiteness of hue. . . . The work was brilliantly conveyed by the orchestra under Mr. Lange."

WB2.10 Henderson, W.J. "Lange Conducts Philharmonic." *New York Sun*, November 21, 1935.

Review of the November 20, 1935, performance of the New York Philharmonic-Symphony. The *Afro-American Symphony* "is a straightforward work, making no pretense of profundity, but saying what it has to say in forthright and melodious idioms. . . . But again one is tempted to ask whether the colored race must musically dominate the United States. If there is no other idiom native to the soil, it might be well to give over trying to be national in black face. . . . The symphony was excellently performed and the audience would surely have liked to see the composer and bestow its blessings upon him."

WB2.11 Sanborn, Pitts. "Lange Gives 2 Novelties at Carnegie." *New York World Telegram*, November 21, 1935.

Review of the November 20, 1935, performance of the New York Philharmonic-Symphony. The *Afro-American Symphony* "is melodious, frank in the expression of mood, cumulative in effect. Thus, the finale 'Be proud, my Race, in mind and soul,' unlike many symphonic finales, is, from its stately introduction on, no anti-climax, but the true culmination, the crowning glory of the design."

WB2.12 "Philharmonic Orchestra." *Musical Courier* 111 (November 30, 1935): 16.

Comments on the November 20, 1935, performance of the New York Philharmonic-Symphony. "Still keeps his [*Afro-American Symphony*] in the spirit of his intention, and that makes for simple and direct statement, with melodic content at all times prominent and treated with welcome transparency of harmonization and orchestration. . . . The entire work displays an expert hand and rare taste in a refined method of workmanship which avoids any suggestion of the banal."

WB2.13 Simon, Robert A. "Musical Events: Three Native Composers, Many Orchestras, and a Few Virtuosi." *New Yorker* 11 (November 30, 1935): 55.

Includes a review of the November 20, 1935, performance of the New York Philharmonic-Symphony. "The [*Afro-American Symphony*] is melodious, and for clarity of construction and instrumentation, it's one of the best American works to appear on symphonic programs for several years. The first two movements are charming and sometimes touching; the third, however, isn't much more than a clever fox trot, and the fourth doesn't come through as majestically as it might. Nevertheless, the symphony was well worth the excellent performance with which Mr. Lange graced it, and it deserved a rather less condescending reception from some of the customers."

WB2.14 "Lange Gives Bach Works and American Novelties." *Musical America* 55 (December 10, 1935): 12.

Review of the November 20, 1935, performance of the New York Philharmonic-Symphony. The *Afro-American Symphony* "is a first-class production. In its four movements there is a wealth of melodic material, always handled with taste and a genuine mastery of the orchestral apparatus. . . . Judged by it Mr. Still is one of the ablest symphonists this country has produced."

WB2.15 Bigelow, Stanley. "Stokowski Plays Modern Music." *Los Angeles Herald Examiner*, April 28, 1936.

Review of the April 27, 1936, performance of the Philadelphia Symphony Orchestra in Los Angeles. "A portion of Still's *Afro-American Symphony*, indicated a more serious musical conception; the passage chosen by Stokowski was a long andante [IV. Lento, con risoluzione] movement, scored principally for the strings. It revealed a most original and thoughtful creative ability, and genuine beauty in thematic material and orchestration."

WB2.16 Jones, Isabel Morse. "Stokowski Plays Again." *Los Angeles Times*, April 29, 1936.

Review of the April 28, 1936, performance of the Philadelphia Symphony Orchestra in Los Angeles. "William Grant Still, who is now in Los Angeles on a Guggenheim Fellowship, has written an arresting composition on Negro melodies, using American jazz rhythms. His 'blues' in the fourth movement of the *Afro-American Symphony* played by Stokowski are soft, insinuating blues which came from the South and not from Gershwin's Broadway. Still knows his craft but he has not hesitated to write straight Negro music and let it stand without ornamentation."

WB2.17 Mines, Harry. "Stokowski Concert Great." *Los Angeles Morning News*, April 29, 1936.

Review of the April 28, 1936, performance of the Philadelphia Symphony Orchestra in Los Angeles. "A Negro composer from Mississippi, William Grant Still, is represented in a portion [fourth movement] of the *Afro-American Symphony*, a pretentious and meritorious musical piece which whets further interest in Still. It is typically American, of definite value and while not overpowering, it should find its way into the class of the worthwhile."

WB2.18 Saunders, Richard D. "Native Music Gains Favor of Audience." *Hollywood Citizen-News*, April 29, 1936. (Essentially the same review appears in the May 9, 1939, issue of *Musical Courier* under the title "Philadelphia Orchestra's Concerts Are Outstanding Events in Los Angeles.")

Review of the April 28, 1936, performance of the Philadelphia Symphony Orchestra. "The excerpt [fourth movement] from Still's *Afro-American Symphony* was definitely Negroid in its emotional concept, with spontaneous melodic flow infused with a characteristically wistful tenderness. The climax was dynamic and effective, but the modulation preceding it was banal, with some quite unnecessary and [s]illy contrasting jazz treatment which somewhat let the work down in that place."

WB2.19 Davidson, Marie Hicks. "Great Audiences Again Join in Acclaim for

Stokowski Music." *San Francisco Call-Bulletin*, May 4, 1936.

Review of the May 3, 1936, performance of the Philadelphia Symphony Orchestra. Still's music "was represented with a fragment from the *Afro-American Symphony*. He has fused aboriginal and civilized American themes and achieved a delightful concoction in the melting pot, the indefinable haunting quality of the Negro spiritual flavoring the rich substance of modern orchestration."

WB2.20 Stinson, Eugene. "Music Views." *Chicago Daily News*, January 22, 1937.

Preview of the January 21, 22, and 26, 1937, performances of the Chicago Symphony Orchestra. Still's *Afro American Symphony* appears on the program. "Mr. Still writes as a Negro and in behalf of the Negro, and all lovers of music who are touched with the wonderful qualities of his race will rejoice to find in this work a simple straight-forward, unpretentious but extremely beautiful account of how the composer, from a decidedly superior viewpoint, beholds the world that is open to the Negro in the United States."

WB2.21 Borowski, Felix. "Program Notes." (Chicago Symphony Orchestra), January 26, 1937.

Program notes for the performance of the *Afro-American Symphony*, with Hans Lange as conductor. Still provides the following on his symphony: "The *Afro-American Symphony* is based on an original theme in the 'Blues' idiom. . . . It is possible that some may regard the employment of this theme as an undignified and insincere step on my part. But I harbor no delusions as to the triviality of 'Blues', the secular folk-songs of the American Negro, despite their lowly origin and the homely sentiment of their texts, for the pathos of their melodic content belies the banality associated with them due to their origin and to their texts."

WB2.22 Jones, Isabel Morse. "Moderns United in Federal Concert." *Los Angeles Times*, May 13, 1937.

Review of the May 12, 1937, performance of the Los Angeles Federal Music Project Orchestra. "The effect of this symphony is more impressive each time it is heard. The 'blues' are raised to an emotional dignity in this work that commands respect."

WB2.23 "Orchestra in Third Concert." *San Bernardino Sun*, December 3, 1937.

"In the *Afro-American Symphony* . . . there is a 'skillful and sympathetic blending of melodies to give the hearer an understanding of the emotional structure of the colored people—a deep racial sadness together with a delightful child-like sense of happiness,' according to Mr. [Vernon] Robinson [conductor]."

WB2.24 P., M. K. "A Concert Stirs Talk." *Kansas City Times*, February 4, 1938.

"The *Afro-American Symphony* . . . may not be a jazz symphony, but it certainly gives a vivid description of the music known as jazz. . . . Still has recorded with keen insight in his symphony almost everything that belongs to the Negro temperament. There are some very beautiful passages in the work, compensation enough for passages that are a bit harsh and uncivilized. Wilbert Peske played the tenor banjo with admirable effect."

WB2.25 Taubman, Howard. "Negro Music Given At ASCAP Recital." *New York Times*, October 3, 1939.

Review of October 2, 1939, performance. Still's *Afro-American Symphony* "had not the freshness and daring in its genre of the blues and stomps that came later in the programs."

WB2.26 Jones, Isabel Morse. "Outstanding Bowl Event Lures 23,000." *Los Angeles Times*, July 24, 1940.
Review of the July 23, 1940, program at the Hollywood Bowl. "It [*Afro-American Symphony*] is a work symphony and appropriate to this concert for the 'everybodies' as the 'Ballad' has it. There is melody easy to sing, blues harmonies that reach the heart and a clever *Scherzo* with a sense of humor."

WB2.27 "Negro Conductor at Albert Hall." *Daily Telegraph*, April 27, 1942.
Review of the April 26, 1942, performance of the London Philharmonic Orchestra, which included the *Afro-American Symphony*. "Its substance seemed elusive; but the scoring was exactly what one expected from a musician familiar with every device of modern popular orchestration."

WB2.28 "Sunday Orchestral Concert." *London Times*, April 28, 1942.
Review of the April 26, 1942, performance of the London Philharmonic Orchestra. "The question has often been asked when is a symphony not a symphony. One historic answer was 'When it contains a cor anglais.' Still's *Afro-American Symphony* begins with a cor anglais solo, and aggravates the offence by including two 'Blues' movements, of which one takes the place of an opening allegro. . . . The finale is the only movement of the four which tries to present an issue of symphonic dimensions in the extended dialogue form of a symphony."

WB2.29 "Music." *News Review*, April 30, 1942, p.23.
Review of the April 26, 1942, performance of the London Philharmonic Orchestra, which included the *Afro-American Symphony*. "With snatches of *Rhapsody in Blue*, *Song of the Bayou*, and *I've Got Rhythm* wrapped around *Old Black Joe*, it irritates rather than haunts, lacks significance, colour and life, chiefly because it is too erratic, never pauses long enough to develop anything more than a general theme."

WB2.30 Newman, John. "Dunbar's Albert Hall Triumph." *Melody Maker*, May 2, 1942.
Review of the April 26, 1942, performance of the London Philharmonic Orchestra. "This music, expressing the emotions of black colonies the world over, cannot offend the ears of those who hate either lowbrow jazz, as they would term it, or highbrow, unintelligible discord. I think it merits frequent repetition. It grows on one, as did the *Rhapsody in Blue*, and will appeal to a wider circle."

WB2.31 "A Coloured Conductor Has An Albert Hall Triumph." *Picture Post* (London), May 9, 1942, p. 20.
"The [*Afro-American Symphony*] . . . is an interesting work, sometimes genuinely exciting and for the most part nostalgic in its effects. Its main interest lies in its experimental nature."

WB2.32 H., A. K. "Rudolph Dunbar." *Liverpool Daily Post*, December 21, 1942.
"The coloured symphony [*Afro-American Symphony*] is a very lively composition, obviously influenced in style by Negro music, but while the ideas are comparatively slight, the orchestral material is both ingenious and pleasantly scored."

WB2.33 "Ovation for Rudolph Dunbar." *Liverpool Echo*, December 21, 1942.
Review of the December 20, 1942, performance of the Liverpool Philharmonic Orchestra. "It [*Afro-American Symphony*] is rich in musical feeling and orchestral colour. Mr. Dunbar seemed to have a real affinity with this symphony, and secured a performance of great liveliness and beauty."

WB2.34 Linstead, Dr. George F. "Gifted Negro Made Jaded Music Fresh." *Sheffield Telegraph*, March 13, 1943.

Review of the March 12, 1943, performance of the National Philharmonic Orchestra at Sheffield, England. "This symphony [*Afro-American*] was broadcast some months ago, and last night's performance only confirmed one's previous opinion as to its diffuse character. . . . It was reasonably well played by the orchestra."

WB2.35 H., G.A. "The Palace." *Manchester Guardian*, March 25, 1943.

Review of the March 24, 1943, performance of the National Philharmonic Orchestra at Manchester, England. "Still's African Symphony [*sic*] contains some rather clever treatment of dance rhythms."

WB2.36 A., M. "Symphony Concert at Hippodrome." *Western Daily Press*, April 3, 1943.

Review of the April 2, 1943, performance of the National Philharmonic Orchestra at Bristol, England. "The most interesting work was a contribution to symphonic literature based mainly on the spiritual effect of Christianity on the Negro mentality, founded on native melodies mostly heard in the past at revival meetings. The composer uses muted brass a great deal, giving at times a purely jazz effect. The title is *Afro-American Symphony*."

WB2.37 Dixon, Randy. "Symphony Thrills Audience; Still's Music Is Featured." *Pittsburgh Courier*, April 17, 1943.

The correspondent indicates the significance of the performance of Still's *Afro-American Symphony* by the National Philharmonic Orchestra, at Bristol, England, to the three hundred African American soldiers who were part of the audience.

WB2.38 "American Music." *Liverpool Echo*, March 13, 1944.

Review of March 12, 1944, performance of the Liverpool Philharmonic Orchestra. "No one could pretend that the music of the *Plain-Chant for America*, by William Grant Still, comes anywhere near its terrific text. . . . The *Afro-American Symphony* of Still (which isn't really a symphony) is, if one admits Blues rhythms and melodies into the rubric, pleasant and accomplished music though quiet and uneventful."

WB2.39 Pendleton, Edmund J. "*Music in Paris*." *New York Herald Tribune* (European Edition), June 16, 1945.

Review of the June 12, 1945, performance of the Orchestre de la Société des Concerts du Conservatoire. "Still's *Afro-American Symphony* particularly interested the audience by its characteristic local color and rhythms which reflect good jazz and the nostalgia of Negro spirit not without warm musical expression; it presents, however, no particularly novel aspect."

WB2.40 Dunbar, Rudolph. "William G. Still Tops to Paris." Los Angeles *Sentinel*, July 19, 1945.

Dunbar's article is based upon performances of Still's *Afro-American Symphony* and *In Memoriam: The Colored Soldiers Who Died for Democracy*, conducted by Dunbar in France.

WB2.41 "Negro Wins Plaudits Conducting in Berlin." *New York Times*, September 3, 1945.

Review of the September 2, 1945, performance of the Berlin Philharmonic Symphony. "The audience of 3,500 German civilians, with a sprinkling of Allied service men, applauded Mr. Dunbar's conducting of works by Tchaikovsky and von Weber, but saved its loudest cheers for something Berliners had never heard before—William Grant Still's *Afro-American Symphony*."

WB2.42 "Dunbar Conducts Berlin Philharmonic Orchestra." *Pittsburgh Courier*, September 8, 1945.

Review of the September 2, 1945, performance. "Loudest applause for the young conductor came after the orchestra played the syncopated strains of composer William Grant Still's *Afro-American Symphony*. This was something Berliners had never heard before."

WB2.43 "Music." *Time* 46 (September 10, 1945): 64.

Review of the September 2, 1945, performance of the Berlin Philharmonic Symphony. "They broke into cheers, and called him back five times, when he [Rudolph Dunbar] gave them Berlin's first hearing of fellow-Negro William Grant Still's boisterous, bluesick *Afro-American Symphony*."

WB2.44 "Paris to Hear American Music." *Paris Post* (Week End), October 13-15, 1945.

Preview of the first of four concerts that will be performed by the National Orchestra. "He [Dunbar] claims Still is the outstanding contemporary American composer: 'He has an exceptional gift for national expression,' he said. 'The minute you hear his work you think American.'"

WB2.45 Swing, Sally. "Negro's Symphonic Music to be Heard." *Paris Post* (Week End), November 17-19, 1945.

Preview of the November 19, 1945, performance of the National Orchestra. "'It isn't because Still is Negro that I am playing his works,' Dunbar said. 'It is simply that I consider Still one of America's important composers.' Dunbar, who is the first foreign conductor to perform in Paris since the liberation, was asked by many Paris musicians to give an all-Negro concert. He believes that Still is the most representative of contemporary Negro composers."

WB2.46 "Rudolph Dunbar to Conduct Negro Culture Program at Hollywood Bowl." Los Angeles *Sentinel*, August 22, 1946, p. 18.

Article focuses on Dunbar and his work. However, Still is mentioned in conjunction with performances of his *Afro-American Symphony*, which Dunbar will conduct at the Hollywood Bowl.

WB2.47 Bronson, Carl. "Dunbar Impressive." Los Angeles *Herald-Express*, August 23, 1946.

"[Dunbar's] feeling in the William Grant Still *Afro-American Symphony* placed that work among the forefront of moderns and impressed the audience deeply."

WB2.48 Jones, Isabel Morse. "Dunbar Wins Approval in Bowl Debut." *Los Angeles Times*, August 23, 1946.

"The one work possible to judge Dunbar by was William Grant Still's *Afro-American Symphony*. It made a deep impression. . . . Dunbar's tempi were careful and his beat effective. The orchestra responded admirably with only one rehearsal. Dunbar conducts with skill and definite loyalty to the score."

WB2.49 Norton, Mildred. "Music Review." Los Angeles *Daily News*, August 23, 1946.

Review of the August 22, 1946, performance of the Hollywood Bowl Symphony. "William Grant Still's *Afro-American Symphony* was the orchestral highlight of the evening. I have not heard everything Still has written but this work is certainly among his best."

WB2.50 Fentress, J. Cullen. "Dunbar to Introduce Serious Negro Music to Europeans." *Pittsburgh Courier*, August 24, 1946.

Article on Dunbar, based upon an interview at the Still residence after Dunbar conducted the Hollywood Bowl Symphony on August 22. On the Bowl program, Still is quoted: "'I think Dunbar's interpretation of the *Afro-American Symphony* perfectly splendid.'"

WB2.51 "British Gov't. Films Hollywood Bowl Debut of Rudolph Dunbar." *Los Angeles Tribune*, August 31, 1946.

Article on the fanfare associated with the August 22, 1946, performance of the Hollywood Bowl Symphony, when Dunbar conducted the *Afro-American Symphony*.

WB2.52 Fentress, J. Cullen. "Noted Conductor Directs Still's Opus at Jubilee." *Pittsburgh Courier*, August 31, 1946.

"Best indication of Dunbar's greatness as a conductor was his handling of Still's *Afro-American Symphony* . . . the symphony carried bowl enthusiasts back to the 'yesterday' of the American Negro and they literally [were] thrilled as the orchestra responded to Dunbar's interpretations."

WB2.53 "Music: Debut in the Bowl." *Time* 48 (September 2, 1946): 41-42.

Article on Rudolph Dunbar, who served as guest conductor of the August 22, 1946, performance of the Hollywood Bowl Symphony. "Last fall . . . he conducted the Berlin Philharmonic in Berlin. . . . Some in the audience, accustomed to Brahms and Wagner, found the cacophony of William Grant Still's *Afro-American Symphony* a little hard to take. So did some in the audience at [the] Hollywood Bowl last week."

WB2.54 Beaufort, Robert. "Ears Across the Sea." *Musical Digest* (May 1947):5-7+.

Article relative to the cultural music programs operated by the Office of International Information and Cultural Affairs (OIC), a branch of the State Department. On November 15, 1946, the Helsinki Municipal Orchestra, with the assistance of the OIC, performed the *Afro-American Symphony* which one reviewer stated, in part, "is a work which arouses interest, particularly because its music, rhythm and manner of instrumentation contain something which flows direct from the life-of-today in America."

WB2.55 "N.O. Symphony Gets Hand From Southern U. Audience." Baton Rouge *Morning Advocate*, March 5, 1955.

Review of the March 4 performance of the New Orleans Philharmonic-Symphony Orchestra. "Still . . . conducted his own *Afro-American Symphony*. . . . It is a lush work, the kind of thing Kostelanetz would be happy with, and it received effective treatment last night. There are shades of *Deep River* of various blues, of Porgy and Bess—none of them tangible, but strongly suggested. It may be some common denominator blues music has generally, that suggested such other compositions. Strings, oboe and harp were particularly well used in this composition. Hilsberg returned after intermission to conduct a second Still work, *Suite of Three Dances*, representing two small boys dancing mischievously around a forbidden cake (*Boy's Dance*), a sensuous love dance, quite lovely (*Dance Before the Hut*), and *Tribal Dance*, featuring a kind of restrained frenzy, if that's not too much of a contradiction. The work is pleasing, descriptive, possibly overstated, but nonetheless a worthwhile effort, and it was well received."

WB2.56 Wolter, Beverly. "Composer Conducts N.O. Symphony In Performance of

Own Work Here; Urges U.S. to Cultivate Heritage." Baton Rouge *State Times*, March 5, 1955.

Review of the March 4 performance of the New Orleans Philharmonic-Symphony Orchestra "The audience . . . came to life with the poignant blues melodies and jaunty, vigorous jazz rhythms of Still's [*Afro-American Symphony*]. A comparison with Gershwin's earlier *Rhapsody in Blue* was inevitable and on the whole, could be favorably made, save in the adagio movement which seemed cluttered and lacking in coherence. A rollicking third movement, reminiscent of laughter and dancing in the night, preceded the broad and dignified phrases of the final movement. . . . Colorful harmonics, and bright buoyant rhythmic effects distinguished the [*Suite of Three Dances*]. More original in conception than the symphony, the three showed to advantage Still's sensitive grasp of native emotions and his deepfelt urge to give expression to his people and his generation through music in their idiom."

WB2.57 "William G. Still scores as guest conductor in Louisiana." New Jersey *Afro-American*, March 19, 1955.

Review of the March 4 performance of the New Orleans Philharmonic-Symphony Orchestra. The program included the *Afro-American Symphony* and the *Suite of Three Dances*. "The sheer elegance with which Still directed this ensemble of young gifted white artists qualifies him among America's best conductors."

WB2.58 George, Collins. "Concert Honors Lincoln." *Detroit Free Press*, November 25, 1963, sec. C, p. 10.

Review of the November 24, 1963, performance of the Detroit Symphony Orchestra. "It is a pleasant work, not a great one, but somehow evocative of the era, the late 20's, the era of Gershwin and Whiteman, in which it was born. One wishes that the orchestra had rehearsed it more. Still dedicated the slow movement of the work to the memory of President Kennedy."

WB2.59 Patrick, Corbin. "Philharmonic Plays Premieres." *Indianapolis Star*, March 2, 1970, p. 26.

Review of the March 1, 1970, performance of the Philharmonic Orchestra of Indianapolis. "William Grant Still . . . was called on stage to acknowledge a standing ovation, the audience response to his *Afro-American Symphony*. It's an interesting piece of music, as presented by Wolfgang Vacano, who conducted the Philharmonic. . . . His slow movement, which recalls other folk material, is followed by a tremendously vital 'animato' and finale in which a broad melody with character fulfills the quotation from a Dunbar poem on which the movement is based, according to the program notes: 'Be proud, my Race, in mind and soul. Thy name is writ on Glory's scroll in characters of fire.'"

WB2.60 Sherman, Robert. "Carnegie Concert Salutes Black History Week." *New York Times*, February 16, 1976.

Review of the February 15, 1976, program at Carnegie Hall which included Still's *Afro-American Symphony*, performed by the Symphony of the New World. "Mr. Still's 1930 symphony is very much a period piece, rather corny in its evocation of minstrel, blues and spiritual expression. It's great fun to hear, though, its naive enthusiasm cemented by the composer's craftsmanship and bolstered by the vigorous performance Mr. [Everett] Lee conducted."

W3 *All That I Am* (available from William Grant Still Music).
Hymn for SATB chorus with piano or organ.

Composed in Los Angeles, 1965.
Text by Verna Arvey.
Duration: 2 minutes.
Manuscript is in the William Grant Still and Verna Arvey Papers at the University of Arkansas Libraries, Fayetteville.

W4 ***Alnados de España, Los*** (available from William Grant Still Music).
Suite for orchestra.
Composed in Los Angeles, 1962.
Inspired by Spanish-Colonial life in the Western Hemisphere.
Contents: I. Prólogo y Narración, II. El Valle Escondido, III. Serenata, IV. Danza.
Instrumentation: 3 flutes (3rd doubles on piccolo), 2 oboes, English horn, 3 clarinets, 2 bassoons; 4 horns, 3 trumpets, 3 trombones, tuba; timpani, percussion, claves, castanets, triangle, bells, glockenspiel, xylophone, cymbals; harp, celesta, strings.
Duration: 16 minutes.
Autograph location unknown.

W5 ***American Scene, The*** (available from William Grant Still Music).
Five suites for orchestra; excerpts arranged for band, wind ensemble, or chamber ensemble.
Composed in Los Angeles, 1957.
The five suites are dedicated to different individuals: Marjorie Lange (1), Miriam Matthews (2), Joseph Portanova (3), the Pasadena Inter-racial Women's Club (4), Helen Thompson (5).
The composer's program notes describe the suites as "presenting musical pictures of America and Americans past and present."
Contents:
  Suite 1: The East: I. On the Village Green, II. Berkshire Night, III. Manhattan Skyline (New York, the Gracious City).
  Suite 2: The South: I. Florida Night, II. Levee Land ("Where the Blues were Born, Birthplace of Blues & Spirituals"), III. A New Orleans Street (also titled "Mardi Gras").
  Suite 3: The Old West: I. Song of the Plainsmen, II. Sioux Love Song ("Based on a Sioux Melody"), III. Tribal Dance.
  Suite 4: The Far West: I. The Plaza ("Los Angeles, Latin American charm and grace"), II. Sundown Land ("A mystic region, far beyond the Golden West"), III. Navaho Country ("Based on a Navajo Melody").
  Suite 5: A Mountain, A Memorial, and A Song: I. Grand Teton ("A Symbol of American Strength"), II. Tomb of the Unknown Soldier ("Let us never forget 'Our Boys'"), III. Song of the Rivermen (originally called "Father Mississippi").
Instrumentation: 3 flutes (3rd doubles on piccolo), 2 oboes, English horn, 3 clarinets (including clarinets in A), 2 bassoons (2nd doubles on contrabassoon); 4 horns, 3 trumpets, 3 trombones, tuba; timpani, percussion, maracas, claves, castanets, rattle, glockenspiel, bells, chimes, triangle, tambourine, xylophone, drums, tom-tom, cymbals, gong; harp, celesta, strings.
Duration: 50 minutes.
Holograph with revisions of the five suites is in the William Grant Still and Verna Arvey Papers at the University of Arkansas Libraries, Fayetteville. Folder also includes first sketches of melodies and other melodies derived

from folk songs along with the composer's notes on titles and the order for the movements of each suite.

W5a **First Performance:** 1959 (January 20): Tucson, AZ; University Auditorium; Tucson Symphony Orchestra, Frederic Balazs, conductor. (Only *Tribal Dance* performed.) (*See:* WB103.4)

Selected Performances

W5b 1959 (March 31): Standard School Broadcasts, Standard School Broadcast Symphony Orchestra, Carmen Dragon, conductor. (Suite 5. I. *Grand Teton*.)

W5c 1962 (February 18): Beverly Hills, CA; Beverly Hills H.S. Auditorium; Beverly Hills Symphony Orchestra, Herbert Weiskopf, conductor.

W5d 1964 (December 13): Inglewood, CA; George Green Auditorium; Inglewood Philharmonic, Philip Kahgan, conductor.

W5e 1968 (April 16): New Orleans, LA; Tulane University; McAlister Auditorium; New Orleans Philharmonic-Symphony Orchestra, William Grant Still, conductor. (Suite 2: The South. II. *Levee Land*, III. *A New Orleans Street*.) (*See:* WB36.17, WB117.18)

Bibliography

WB5.1 Saunders, Richard D. "Pony-Tail Pianist Stars As Soloist." *Hollywood Citizen-News*, February 19, 1962.

Review of the February 18, 1962, performance of the Beverly Hills Symphony Orchestra, Herbert Weiskopf, conductor. "Of musical importance was the premiere of a new portion of William Grant Still's noble *The American Scene*, for which the composer was given a personal ovation." Three scenes were presented, however, they were not identified.

W6 *And They Lynched Him on a Tree* (J. Fischer & Brothers, 1941, no. J.F.&B. .46, and J.F.&B. 0409-46, piano vocal score; available from William Grant Still Music).

For 2 SATB choruses, contralto soloist, narrator, and orchestra; also in piano vocal score.

Composed in Los Angeles, 1940.

Text by Katherine Garrison Chapin, wife of Francis Biddle who was the United States Attorney General in 1940.

Dedicated to Henry Allen Moe.

Subject: Tolerance and the brotherhood of man.

Still specifies in the piano vocal score, "White Chorus, Negro Chorus," and says, "The narrator should be a man with a low pitched, resonant voice. His lines are to be spoken." (The narrator's lines are written in rhythmic notation on the staff.)

Oh, Sorrow has been recorded separately. (*See:* D34)

Instrumentation for orchestra: 2 flutes (2nd doubles on piccolo), 2 oboes (2nd doubles on English horn), 2 clarinets, 2 bassoons; 3 horns, 3 trumpets, 3 trombones, tuba; timpani, percussion; harp, strings; 2 SATB choruses, narrator, contralto soloist; optional off-stage sounds of starting motors and occasional auto horns.

Duration: 19 minutes.

Program for the music: "It is night. In a clearing by the roadside among the turpentine pines, lit by the headlights from parked cars, a Negro has just been lynched. The white crowd who hung him, and those who watched, are breaking up now, going home. They sing together, get into their cars and drive away. Darkness falls on the roads and woods. Then slowly the Negroes come out from hiding to find the body of their friend. Among them is the mother of the man who was hung. In darkness they grope for the tree; when they find it the mother sings her dirge. The Negro chorus joins her and they retell the story of the man's life and rehearse the tragedy. She is humble and broken but as long as they sing together, the white voice joining the Negroes', the song becomes strong for its impartial protest against mob lawlessness and pleads for a new tolerance to wipe this shadow of injustice off the land."

Two copies of the 1941 published piano vocal score are in the William Grant Still and Verna Arvey Papers at the University of Arkansas Libraries, Fayetteville. Holograph is in The William Grant Still Estate.

W6a **First Performance:** 1940 (June 25): New York, NY; Lewisohn Stadium; New York Philharmonic-Symphony Orchestra, Artur Rodzinski, conductor; Wen Talbot Negro Choir and fifty members of the Schola Cantorum; Louise Burge, contralto; Abner Dorsey, narrator.

Selected Performances

W6b 1941 (June 23): New York, NY; Lewisohn Stadium; New York Philharmonic-Symphony Orchestra, Hugh Ross, conductor; Chorus of 100 Voices of Schola Cantorum and Eva Jessye Choir; Louise Burge, contralto; Ruth Kenworthy, soprano; Abner Dorsey and George Headley, narrators.

W6c 1942 (April 14): New York, NY; Radio City; NBC Symphony Orchestra, Leopold Stokowski, conductor; Collegiate Choir, Robert Shaw, director; Eva Jessye Choir, Eva Jessye, director; Louise Burge, contralto; Lawrence Whisonant, narrator.

W6d 1957 (February 23): New York, NY; Town Hall; Westchester Interracial Fellowship Chorus, David Katz, conductor, Carol Brice, contralto, Jonathan Brice, piano, David Allen, narrator.

W6e 1967 (March 25): Beverly Hills, CA; Beverly Hills High School Auditorium; Los Angeles Jubilee Singers, Albert J. McNeil, director.

W6f 1974 (April 28): Los Angeles, CA; Ingalls Auditorium; Los Angeles Jubilee Singers, Albert J. McNeil, director; East Los Angeles College Concert Choir, William P. Pearson, director; Virginia White, contralto, and Elmer Bush, narrator.

Bibliography

WB6.1 Ussher, Bruno David. "Sounding Board." Los Angeles *Daily News*, June 5, 1940.
In announcing that *And They Lynched Him on a Tree* will receive its premiere in New York, the author laments the fact that the composition could not have been performed in Los Angeles first.

WB6.2 "Whites, Negroes to Perform Lynch Ballad." Kansas City *Call*, June 7, 1940.
Preview of the performance of *And They Lynched Him on a Tree* by the New York Philharmonic-Symphony Orchestra.

WB6.3 Chapin, Katherine Garrison. "And They Lynched Him on a Tree." *Nation* 150 (June 8, 1940): 707-08.
The complete text of the author's poem.

WB6.4 Bohm, Jerome D. "American Novelties." *New York Herald Tribune*, June 23, 1940, sec. 6, p. 6.

Lengthy article previewing the premiere of *And They Lynched Him on a Tree*. "From a brief examination of the piano-vocal score and attendance at partial choral rehearsals thereof under Hugh Ross's discerning and energetic direction, Mr. Still's music impresses one as being deeply moving and tellingly dramatic. . . . His harmonies are often poignant and the closing lines, ending on an unresolved ninth chord, provide a fitting climax."

WB6.5 Sanborn, Pitts. "Program Notes." *Stadium Concerts Review* 23 (June 24, 25, 26, 1940): 7+.

Program notes for the premiere of *And They Lynched Him on a Tree*, performed by the New York Philharmonic-Symphony Orchestra, at Lewisohn Stadium. Mr. Sanborn provides a good account of the development of the poem to music, identifying Alain Locke as the person who brought the poem to the attention of Still, who was at the time a Rosenwald Fellow.

WB6.6 King, William G. "Music." *New York Sun*, June 25, 1940.

Brief article announcing that inclement weather forced the postponement of the concert program at Lewisohn Stadium and that it was rescheduled for June 25. *And They Lynched Him on a Tree* appears on the program.

WB6.7 Bohm, Jerome D. "'Democracy' Is Concert Theme at the Stadium." *New York Herald Tribune*, June 26, 1940.

"Mr. Still's ballad-poem [*And They Lynched Him on a Tree*] contains some stirring pages, more especially those dealing with the sentiments of the Negroes concerned in its unfolding. . . . Mr. Still's instrumentation seemed at times too weak for an outdoor concert."

WB6.8 Taubman, Howard. "American Music Heard in Stadium." *New York Times*, June 26, 1940.

A lengthy and favorable review of the premiere performance of *And They Lynched on a Tree*. "Mr. Still has written with utter simplicity and with deep feeling. . . . The music achieves its greatest eloquence in the pages devoted to the Negro men and women and especially to the solo sung by the boy's mother. . . . the Still-Chapin work had a moving performance."

WB6.9 Thompson, Oscar. "American Works Performed." *New York Sun*, June 26, 1940.

Review of the June 25, 1940, performance of the New York Philharmonic-Symphony Orchestra. "*And They Lynched Him on a Tree* opens with a stabbing intensity that is permitted to sag thereafter. Though much of it is commonplace and some of it thin, there are some warmly lyrical passages."

WB6.10 Roosevelt, Eleanor. "My Day." *Los Angeles News*, June 27, 1940.

In describing some of her thoughts and activities while in New York, Mrs. Roosevelt states that "rain spoiled my chance last evening [June 24] to hear Mrs. Frances Biddle's poem sung at the Lewisohn Stadium."

WB6.11 Crawford, Lenore. "Advance Is Steady." *Windsor* (Ontario) *Daily Star*, June 29, 1940.

In her remarks associated with the premiere of *And They Lynched Him on a Tree*, the author states that "no composer is more American in feeling and interpretation of life in America than this colored composer whose works have hit instruments with jazz notes, expressed the speed, enthusiasm and quick laughter of the American people, and added telling pathos."

WB6.12 DuBois, W.E.B. "As the Crow Flies." *New York Amsterdam News*, July 6, 1940.
"The greatest event of the month [June] was the premiere of William Grant Still's ballad poem: *And They Lynched Him to* [sic] *a Tree.*"

WB6.13 Simon, Robert A. "Musical Events." *New Yorker* 16 (July 6, 1940): 43.
"*And They Lynched Him on a Tree* . . . is the most ambitious effort yet heard from its skillful composer. The first passage, concerning the callous reactions of a mob, sounded somewhat uncertain, possibly because the adjustment of the music to the words was awkward. After that, the work developed logically and dramatically, with singularly persuasive solo moments, well sung by Louise Burge, a young Negro contralto."

WB6.14 "Music." *Time* 36 (July 8, 1940): 46.
Includes a review of the premiere of *And They Lynched on a Tree*. "[T]he music was by shy, devout Negro William Grant Still, who inscribed the score: 'Humble thanks to God, the source of inspiration.' Composer Still's inspiration often ran to obvious ear-catching effects, but it kept pace with Mrs. Biddle's ballad."

WB6.15 Locke, Alain. "Ballad for Democracy." *Opportunity: Journal of Negro Life* 18 (August 1940): 228-29.
Locke reviews the development and initial presentation of *And They Lynched Him on a Tree*, which serves as a very good general description of the work, concluding, "For the discriminating in poetic and musical taste, this is, for our decade thus far, *the* ballad of democracy."

WB6.16 "Mrs. Roosevelt Gets Still's New Cantata." *Pittsburgh Courier*, May 31, 1941.
Brief announcement that Mrs. Eleanor Roosevelt received an autographed score of *And They Lynched Him on a Tree*.

WB6.17 Perkins, Francis D. "Robeson Draws Enthusiasts to Lewisohn Bowl." *New York Herald Tribune*, June 25, 1941.
Review of the June 23, 1941, performances at Lewisohn Stadium. "*And They Lynched Him to* [sic] *a Tree* proved to be well worth a rehearing. . . . There is some looseness of form, but the musical ideas and their treatment are appropriate and generally effective." Paul Robeson was also part of the program, although he was not involved with any of Still's works.

WB6.18 Briggs, John. "Stokowski Ends Series at NBC." *New York Post*, April 15, 1942.
"Last night the music [of *And They Lynched Him on a Tree*] seemed even more impressive than at first hearing. Few present writers can spin a melody like Mr. Still, and he is adept also at heightening the dramatic content of a verbal text. It is to be hoped that he will produce an opera one of these days."

WB6.19 Lawrence, Robert. "Two Choirs Join In Stokowski's N.B.C. Concert." *New York Herald Tribune*, April 16, 1942.
"[T]he score [of *And They Lynched Him on a Tree*], though sensitively created and well blocked out for orchestra, lacks a feeling of unity . . . the poem remained statuesque and the music lacking in dramatic life."

WB6.20 Allen, Donald Vail. "Jubilee Singers Perform." *Los Angeles Times*, March 27, 1967.
Review of the March 25, 1967, performance of the Los Angeles Jubilee Singers, Albert McNeil, conductor, for the Festival of Negro Music presented in the Beverly Hills High School Auditorium. "These singers are responsive,

accurate and wonderfully disciplined. Nothing stands out particularly, the effect being one of carefully coordinated ensemble. William Grant Still's *O, Sorrow!* (an excerpt from the composer's *And They Lynched Him On A Tree*) and *Psalm for the Living* are pleasant pieces. Mr. Still, who was in the audience, is not the most daring of contemporary composers."

W7 **Archaic Ritual** (available from William Grant Still Music).
Suite for orchestra in three movements.
Composed in Los Angeles; manuscript dated February, 1946.
Contents: I. Chant, II. Incantation: Dance Before the Altar, III. Possession.
Instrumentation: 3 flutes (3rd doubles on piccolo), 2 oboes, English horn, 3 clarinets, 2 bassoons (2nd doubles on contrabassoon); 4 horns, 3 trumpets, 3 trombones, tuba; timpani, bells, resonator bells in G & D, chimes, drums, 3 tom-toms (holograph says "Indian tom-toms preferably"), cymbals, gong; harp, celesta, strings.
Duration: 20 minutes.
A holograph sketch of the piano conductor score with orchestration notes and revisions is in the William Grant Still and Verna Arvey Papers at the University of Arkansas Libraries, Fayetteville.

W7a **First Performance:** 1949 (August 25): Los Angeles, CA; Hollywood Bowl Symphony Orchestra, Izler Solomon, conductor.

Selected Performances

W7b 1955 (April 21): Santa Monica, CA; Barnum Hall; Santa Monica Symphony Orchestra, Arthur Lange, conductor.

W7c 1962 (July 30): Santa Fe, Argentina; Teatro Ocean; Orquesta Sinfónica Provincial de Santa Fe, Washington Castro, director.

Bibliography

WB7.1 Kendall, Raymond. "Soprano Davis Heard At Bowl." *Los Angeles Mirror*, August 26, 1949.
Review of the August 25, 1949, premiere of *Archaic Ritual* by the Hollywood Bowl Symphony Orchestra. "While possessed of some of the unique instrumentation for which this well-known resident composer is remembered, the score is not one of his best. It is repetitious, episodic; reminds one of a fair to middlin' score for a nondescript 'B' movie."

WB7.2 Norton, Mildred. "Music Review." Los Angeles *Daily News*, August 26, 1949.
Review of the August 25, 1949, premiere of *Archaic Ritual* by the Hollywood Bowl Symphony Orchestra. "Like all of Still's music, it is imaginative, vividly colored and adroitly handled. The orchestra performed it beautifully and the audience was enthusiastic."

WB7.3 Scott, Phyllis. "NANM Convention Ends on Note of Triumph." *California Eagle*, September 1, 1949.
The National Association of Negro Musicians met in Los Angeles in 1949, at which time Still's *Archaic Ritual* was performed at the Hollywood Bowl. It "was a pleasant blending of harmonious movements. It was listenable and enjoyably pleasant on a hot summer evening."

W8 **Aria** (Sam Fox Publishing Co., Inc., New York, 1960; available from William Grant Still Music).
Accordion solo.

Composed in Los Angeles, 1960.
Commissioned by the American Accordionists' Association.
Duration: 5 minutes.
Holographs and a copy of the published version are in the William Grant Still and Verna Arvey Papers at the University of Arkansas Libraries, Fayetteville.

W8a **First Performance:** 1960 (May 15): New York, NY; Town Hall; Myron Floren, accordion.

Selected Performances

W8b 1961 (April 17): New York, NY; Carnegie Recital Hall; Carmen Carozza, accordion.

W8c 1962 (May 4): Miami, FL; University of Miami, Beaumont Lecture Hall; Mogens Ellegaard, accordion.

W8d 1964 (February 21): New York, NY; Donnell Library Auditorium; Janice Simon, accordion.

W8e 1977 (November 3): Baltimore, MD; Morgan State University, Murphy Auditorium; Robert Young McMahon, accordion.

Bibliography

WB8.1 P[erkins], F[rancis] D. "Sano Accordion Symphony Plays At Town Hall." *New York Herald Tribune*, May 16, 1960, p. 12.

Review of the May 15, 1960, world premiere of Still's *Aria*. "The Sano Accordion Symphony, conducted by Eugene Ettore, gave the first half of yesterday afternoon's concert at Town Hall and then left the stage to a skillful solo accordionist, Myron Floren, who began his share of the program with Robert Russell Bennett's *Four Nocturnes* and an aria by William Grant Still. . . . Possessing melodic appeal and variety of mood, they also revealed their composers' understanding of the accordion's requirements and resources and received an admirable performance."

WB8.2 Bennett, Elsie M. "William Grant Still Joins Ranks of AAA-Commissioned Composers." *American Accordionists Association Monthly Bulletin* 3 (June 1960): 5-6.

Article pertaining to Still's composition for the accordion. "*Aria for Accordion* is written for unaccompanied accordion, in Rondo form. It is built around two major themes which recur throughout the composition's nine parts. It is comprised of lots of development, contrast and transition; it includes a *codetta* at the half-way point, and an interesting coda at the end. . . . 'My [Still's] association with Mr. [Myron] Floren made me realize what the instrument can accomplish in the way of virtuosity and in sustained and flowing melodies. One can no longer speak simply of 'the sound' of an accordion, because of the variety of its tonal effects. After hearing some of the striking and appealing things that can be done on it, I would say that it not only has many resources, but it could very well be used with marked effectiveness in the orchestra.'"

WB8.3 Perkins, Francis D. "Conductor-Composer Unit in Season's Final Concert." *New York Herald Tribune*, April 18, 1961, p. 19.

"The compositions, skillfully played by Carmen Carrozza—William Grant Still's *Aria*, Virgil Thomson's *Lamentations* and Paul Creston's *Prelude and Dance*, all commissioned by the American Accordionists' Association—were engaging and instrumentally grateful."

WB8.4   Bergh, Frances Hovey. "Program Notes." University of Miami Third Annual Festival of American Music, May 2-5, 1962.

Program notes for the May 4, 1962, performance of Still's *Aria for Accordion*, performed by Mogens Ellegaard. "Mr. Still has this to say about the accordion: 'In the old days I thought of the accordion as an instrument to be used only be entertainers, for light moments. Now I realize that this instrument has a tremendous potential, worthy of every composer's thoughtful consideration.'"

WB8.5   Reno, Doris. "Artist Turns Accordion Into a Concert Triumph." *Miami Herald*, May 5, 1962, Section B, p. 4.

Review of the May 4, 1962, program of the University of Miami's Third Annual Festival of American Music, which included the performance of Still's *Aria for Accordion* by Mogens Ellegaard, a Danish artist. "Young Mr. Ellegaard had learned four important American works for accordion especially for this concert, and it would be hard to imagine better performances. . . . The bagpipe-drone of the instrument is still heard, but the technical virtuosity of the performer keeps everything at concert level. He can play as softly as on a piano, and varies tone and timbre with marvelous deftness."

WB8.6   Bennett, Elsie M. "William Grant Still and Accordion Music." *Black Perspective in Music* 3 (May 1975): 193-95.

As chair of the Composers' Commissioning Committee for the American Accordionists' Association, the author was in a position to promote the development of compositions for the accordion. Her article describes how *Aria* and *Lilt* (also by William Grant Still) were proposed and supported.

W9   ***Bayou Legend, A*** (available from William Grant Still Music).
Opera in 3 acts.
Libretto by Verna Arvey, inspired by an authentic legend of the Biloxi (Mississippi) region, concerning a man who fell in love with a spirit.
Composed in Los Angeles, 1941.
For: Cast: Principle roles: tenor, mezzo-soprano, soprano, baritone, bass; Secondary roles: 3 tenors, baritone, bass; chorus.
Instrumentation: 3 flutes (3rd doubles on piccolo), 2 oboes, English horn, 3 clarinets, 2 bassoons; 3 horns, 3 trumpets, 2 trombones, tuba; timpani, percussion, drums, cymbals; celesta, harp, strings.
Duration: 75-90 minutes.
A manuscript fair copy prepared by the composer of a piano vocal score and one of a full orchestra score are in The William Grant Still Estate.

W9a   **First Performance:** 1974 (November 15, 17): Jackson, MS; Municipal Auditorium; Opera/South; Opera/South Chorus; Opera/South Ballet; Leonard de Paur, conductor; Donald Dorr, designer-director; Raymond I. Johnson, choral coordinator; Bobbie Mason, choreographer; Francois Clemmons as the Minstrel; Naymond Thomas as Father Lestant; Francois Clemmons as First Blade; Earl Taylor as Second Blade; Eddie Goins as Third Blade; John Miles as Bazile; Barbara Conrad as Clothilde; Robert Mosley as Leonce; Juanita Waller as Aurore.

Selected Performances

W9b   1976 (February 13, 14): Los Angeles, CA; East Los Angeles College; Ingalls Auditorium; East Los Angeles College Orchestra, Calvin Simmons, conductor; East Los Angeles College Chorus; East Los Angeles College Dancers; Gary

Fisher, director; Roger Cantrell, music director; Russell Fox, chorus master; Alicia Jones, choreographer; Eileen Moss as Clothilde; Fredrick Winthrop as Bazile; Delcina Stevenson as Aurore; James Vincent Pickens as Leonce; James Sterrett-Bryant as The Minstrel; Marvin Samuels as Father Lestant; Rod Rodriguez as First Blade; Wardell Howard as Second Blade; William Bales as Third Blade.

W9c 1976 (April 10): Jackson, MS; Municipal Auditorium; Opera/South, Leonard de Paur, conductor, Donald Dorr, designer-director, Raymond I. Johnson, choral coordinator, Bobbie Mason, choreographer; Curtis Rayam as the Minstrel; Naymond Thomas as Father Lestant; Curtis Rayam as First Blade; Oliver Sueing as Second Blade; Eddie Goins as Third Blade; William Brown as Bazile; Barbara Conrad as Clothilde; Robert Mosley as Leonce; Juanita Waller as Aurore; Chorus: Jackson State University and Utica Junior College.

W9d 1981 (June 15): Public Broadcasting System: Videotaped on location near Vicksburg, Mississippi, October, 1979; Produced by the Mississippi Center for Educational Television and Opera/South; Opera/South Orchestra, Leonard de Paur, musical director and conductor; Ed Van Cleef, executive producer, Mississippi ETV; Curtis W. Davis, producer; John Thomson, director; Dolores Ardoyno, Opera/South general manager; Donald Dorr, Opera/South artistic director; students from Jackson State University and Utica Junior College, chorus; Bobby G. Cooper and Raymond I. Johnson, chorus directors; Students from Utica Junior College, dancers; Bobbie Mason, choreographer. Cast: Carmen Balthrop as Aurore; Peter Lightfoot as Leonce; Raeschelle Potter as Clothilde; Gary Burgess as Bazile; Ben Holt as Third Blade; Irwin Reese as Second Blade; Cullen Maiden as Father Lestant; Francois Clemmons as the Minstrel/First Blade.

W9e 1994 (April 28): San Diego, CA; San Diego State University, Don Powell Theatre; San Diego State University Orchestra, Donald Barra, conductor; David Tucker, III, director; Stefani Wells Pastorini, choreographer; Susan Ali as Clothilde; Jody L. Ashworth as Father Lestant; Martin Chambers as Bazile; Kerry Hogan as The Minstrel; Tom Roy as Leonce; Shouna Shoemake as Aurore; San Diego State University Ensemble; Chris Allen, musical director.

Bibliography

WB9.1 Gagnard, Frank. "New Jackson Opera a Southern *Sylphide*." New Orleans *Times-Picayune*, November 10, 1974.

Lengthy preview of Still's *A Bayou Legend*, including a description of each of the three acts. The opera was produced by Opera/South and premiered November 15, 1974, at Jackson, Mississippi.

WB9.2 Hains, Frank. "Just Three Words." *Jackson Daily News*, November 14, 1974, sec. F, p. 12.

Lengthy article on Leonard de Paur based upon an interview with de Paur prior to the world premiere of *A Bayou Legend* at Jackson, Mississippi. "What made him decide to conduct *Bayou Legend*? 'As I've told Dolores Ardoyno (general manager of Opera/South) since, all she would have had to say—she could have saved a lot of conversation—was three words: William. Grant. Still. . . . he was one of the heroes of my youth. . . . I lived near Mr. Still, and I used to walk out of my way down his block, just hoping to see him come out so that I could be able to say, 'hello, Mr. Still. . . . ' Some of the things that man could put on paper—as an arranger and of course as a composer—were just fabulous."

WB9.3 ———. "Arms Measured." *Jackson Daily News*, November 15, 1974, sec. D, p. 6.

Lengthy article based upon an interview with William Grant Still and Verna Arvey Still two days before the world premiere of *A Bayou Legend*. "Dr. Still has a 'very clear memory' of the writing of *Bayou Legend*. 'Sometimes you know, I try to avoid thinking of things I've written, to keep from repeating, but not in that instance. I had the type of story that orchestrates well—lots of variety and drama—there was nothing to do but just orchestrate it.' Mrs. Still recalled that 'we developed the story just as a playwright would; letting the characters develop it for us after they were established. I suppose it's an economical way of saying it, that he wrote the music and I wrote the libretto, but actually, while I had nothing to do with the music, HE had a lot to do with the libretto. He was—the creative thing.'"

WB9.4 Bunge, Jean. "Opera/South's *Bayou Legend*: Magic." Jackson *Clarion-Ledger*, November 16, 1974.

"There was something magical about the world premier of William Grant Still's *Bayou Legend* by Opera/South Friday night . . . the audience enthusiastically received his work and approved the company's presentation. [Donald] Dorr's production qualities were nearly flawless. . . . The chorus always has been one of Opera/South's strongest points, and the current production is no exception. . . . The good orchestra sound probably was a combination of Dr. Still's score and conductor [Leonard] de Paur, who kept the volume exactly right, which is unusual in that auditorium."

WB9.5 Hains, Frank. "Still's Bayou Legend Is Given Enthusiastic Welcome In City" *Jackson Daily News*, November 16, 1974.

Review of the November 15, 1974, world premiere of *A Bayou Legend*. "In what was perhaps the single most notable event in Jackson musical history, Opera/South Friday night presented the world premiere of *Bayou Legend*, a major work by William Grant Still. . . . The opera is a richly theatrical piece, filled with gloriously romantic writing for the four principals and the lush and vividly colored orchestrations for which Dr. Still is noted. . . . Visiting conductor Leonard de Paur gave the score the warm and lyrical reading it demands, presiding over an excellent pit orchestra."

WB9.6 Gagnard, Frank. "*Bayou Legend* Heard." New Orleans *Times-Picayune*, November 18, 1974, sec. 3, p. 8.

Review of the world premiere performance of *A Bayou Legend*. "Still's music is a mixture . . . though adhering conservatively to the 'number'—opera scheme of set pieces—arias, ensembles, sung recitative, ballet. . . . What regionalism there is—the chorale, the ballet music—has a musical sophistication that refuses to be pinpointed on the map. One gets the impression that composer Still was writing more for the world market than for recognition by a local audience."

WB9.7 Hains, Frank. "Legend Marvelous." *Jackson Daily News*, November 18, 1974, sec. D, p. 5.

Review of the November 17, performance of *A Bayou Legend*. "I thought *Bayou Legend* was marvelous in Friday night's world premiere. A second hearing at Sunday's student matinee not only confirmed it but made me even more aware of the work's genuine greatness . . . it is far and away the most richly melodic contemporary opera I have heard. Dr. Still is a masterful melodist as well as an endlessly inventive and fascinating orchestrater [sic]. The depth and variety and coloration of the orchestral sounds is phenomenal."

WB9.8 LaRose, Joseph. "Opera-South premiere." New Orleans *Clarion Herald*, November 21, 1974.

Review of the world premiere of *A Bayou Legend* produced by Opera/South at Jackson, Mississippi, November 15, 1974. "Still's music has no resemblance to the dissonance or bizarre harmonies of modern music. It is warmly melodious and lushly orchestrated, but never overwhelms the singers and allows the chorus almost a cappella freedom. It is in the tradition of 19th century French and Italian opera . . . Leonard de Paur conducted the orchestra and directed the singing with understanding and appreciation for Still's music."

WB9.9 Eggler, Bruce. "*Verismo* Comes to the Bayou." New Orleans *States-Item*, November 23, 1974.

Review of the world premiere performance of *A Bayou Legend* produced by Opera/South at Jackson, Mississippi. "Written in a mostly conservative idiom, though with occasional hints of jazz influence, it is often well-crafted and tuneful, . . . but it only intermittently strikes sparks of real musical vividness or dramatic urgency. . . . Conductor Leonard de Paur paced the proceedings with a sure hand and drew some of the best work from his orchestra and chorus heard yet in any Opera-South production."

WB9.10 DeMers, John. "Still's Lyrical *Bayou Legend* Sparkles in World Premiere." Baton Rouge *Advocate*, November 24, 1974, sec. F, p. 6.

Review of the world premiere performance of *A Bayou Legend* by Opera/South at Jackson, Mississippi. "The score of *A Bayou Legend* is such a miracle that even a cursory listing of highlights would take too long. From the first lyric offering of a balladeer to the soaring religious chorale to the vocal fireworks of the love duet, there is a scintillating magic in the music that transcends national idiom. . . . Leonard de Paur of New York's Lincoln Center conducted the orchestra with spirit and understanding, taking special care to accent the jazz and blues innovations that spangle the score."

WB9.11 "Opera In Mississippi." *Time* 104 (November 25, 1974): 84.

Review of the November 15, 1974, world premiere performance of *A Bayou Legend* by Opera/South. "*Legend* is not a great work. It does not introduce any innovations in musical or dramatic style. . . . It has the directness (though not the genius) of Verdi, the misty orchestral hues of Delius and a soulful melodic style that both Puccini and Sigmund Romberg might have liked. . . . *A Bayou Legend* reveals him [Still] as a kind of American Grieg—a miniaturist gifted with melody, an unerring sense of color and a fondness for the folklore."

WB9.12 Saggus, James. "Black Opera Rises in South." *Los Angeles Times*, November 29, 1974, sec. 4, p. 20.

Article on Opera/South with comments on *A Bayou Legend*. "With composer William Grant Still beaming his benediction, the premiere production of his *Bayou Legend* by the Opera/South company became a happy union of two romantic endeavors. . . . 'I liked it very much,' Still told newsmen afterward. 'I thought they did it with a wonderful spirit. They were singing it as though they loved it.'"

WB9.13 Hains, Frank. "Opera/South: *Bayou Legend*." *High Fidelity/Musical America* (March 1975): MA 25-26.

Review of the world premiere performance of *A Bayou Legend* produced by Opera/South at Jackson, Mississippi, November 15, 1974. "Written in 1941, *Legend* is virtually undatable; it draws on a musical reservoir in which each listener can find a reflection of his choice; comparisons have been drawn to composers from Strauss (R.) to Grieg, Verdi to Weill. Actually, Still's music has a quality distinctly his own, marked by an extraordinarily rich orchestral palette whose complexities are superbly controlled in juxtaposition to a direct and lyrical melodic line. . . . Conductor Leonard de Paur's vast choral experience may have had something to do with his effective control of orchestra as partner rather than accompanist; Donald Dorr's richly colored, impressionist set matched the music's moods perfectly."

WB9.14 Pirtle, Caleb, III. "Opera As You Like It." *Southern Living* 10 (November 1975): 92-94+.

Article focuses on Opera/South. Included are remarks William Grant Still and Verna Arvey made at the world premiere of *A Bayou Legend* which Opera/South produced. "Some refer to [Still] as the 'dean of American black composers.' He smiles and says, 'All I know is that the minute I learned how to read music, I wanted to write it.' Verna Arvey points out, 'He writes the music; I write the libretto. He has the creative mind and develops the characters. They tell me the story . . . I can't write poetry. But when I set words to his music, they suddenly become poetry.'"

WB9.15 Cariaga, Daniel. "Still's *Bayou Legend* at ELAC." *Los Angeles Times*, February 16, 1976.

Review of the February 13, west coast premiere of *A Bayou Legend*, at East Los Angeles College. "The short, 75-minute piece requires no extramusical justifications. Joyously and disarmingly melodious, dramatically effective and beautifully crafted, it is an attractive and poignant work inexplicably neglected for 33 years after its composition. . . . The performance Friday, apparently thoroughly rehearsed, did justice to the work. In the pit, Calvin Simmons, assistant conductor of the Los Angeles Philharmonic, led the ad hoc orchestra of 45 skilled members authoritatively, observed sensitively the many facets of the work and seldom swamped the singers."

WB9.16 Leydon, Joe. "Conductor Returns to Jackson For *Bayou Legend*." Jackson *Clarion-Ledger*, April 2, 1976, p. 10.

Article based on an interview of Leonard de Paur, conductor for Still's *A Bayou Legend*, which was produced by Opera/South on April 10. "[Leonard] de Paur feels that the major strength of the opera is 'its orchestration. I am constantly learning from his orchestration. I always have been. He has an absolute genius for the orchestral craft.'"

WB9.17 ———. "Still's *Bayou Legend* Given Wonderful Revival." Jackson *Clarion-Ledger*, April 12, 1976, p. 17.

Review of the April 10, 1976, performance of *A Bayou Legend*. "The diverse melodies of Still's music are a joy to the ear. *Bayou Legend* combines many different influences—19th century Italian opera, Negro spirituals, English drinking songs and even square dancing—to produce a constantly surprising, many-faceted composition. . . . The libretto by Verna Arvey tells its story with disarming simplicity, colored with welcome flashes of humor and dark mysticism. . . . Conductor Leonard de Paur's respect for Still's creating was demonstrated by his masterful direction of the orchestra, carefully weaving the music among the vocal efforts of the cast."

WB9.18 Tipton, Nancy. "Second *Bayou Legend* Was Miraculous." *Jackson Daily News*, April 12, 1976, sec. B, p. 4.

Review of the April 10, 1976, performance of *A Bayou Legend*. "Dr. Still's music is full and rich—a masterful combination of bayou sounds and classical methods—and Verna Arvey's libretto tells a legend that smacks with the mysticism-religiosity of early 19th-century Mississippi."

WB9.19 DeMers, John. "William Grant Still: Requiem For A Heavyweight." *Jackson Daily News*, December 6, 1978.

Lengthy review of Still's life after his death on December 3, 1978. The article covers *A Bayou Legend* considerably.

WB9.20 Verongos, Helen. "Opera/South officials resign over broadcast." Jackson *Clarion-Ledger*, August 28, 1980.

Article on the resignations of the general manager and the artistic director of Opera/South, resulting from a disagreement over the PBS network broadcast of *A Bayou Legend*, filmed by Mississippi Educational Television. The Opera/South management team believed that: "allowing a teletape with 29 musical errors to broadcast on national television will ruin the opera company's reputation."

WB9.21 Mayer, Martin. "TV Opera Hits a High Note." *American Film* 6 (January-February 1981): 53-55.

Preview of the Public Broadcasting System telecast on June 15, 1981, of *A Bayou Legend*, produced by the Mississippi Center for Educational Television and Opera/South. "Like [Ildebrando] Pizzetti, [Still] has more melodic imagination than has been fashionable in the last generation, and huge skill at writing for chorus. The vocal writing is graceful, with few wide skips or notes at the extremes of the range, and the orchestration is supportive throughout, though rarely striking. Not many American operas are so professional in craft and so available to the sort of singers to be found in small opera houses. And being mostly duets, the opera works well as television."

WB9.22 Speer, David. "Van Cleef took 'Bayou Legend' on location as a physical drama." *Natchez Democrat*, April 13, 1981.

Lengthy article on the production of *A Bayou Legend*, based upon an interview with Ed Van Cleef, executive producer of Mississippi Educational Television.

WB9.23 Chamberlain, Carl. "*Legend* Makes TV Debut." *Los Angeles Sentinel*, June 11, 1981, sec. A, p. 2+.

Preview of the PBS telecast on June 15 of *A Bayou Legend*, produced by the Mississippi Center for Educational Television and Opera/South. The article is based in part on an interview with Verna Arvey Still. "For the most part Mrs. Still is happy with the television production and said, 'I feel very good about the work.' However, Mrs. Still did have uncomplimentary words for the producer who reportedly tampered with one of the opening sequences of the opera. 'He thought we didn't know how to be Negroes,' she said."

WB9.24 Perlmutter, Donna. "Celebrating the black artists." *Los Angeles Herald-Examiner*, June 14, 1981, sec. E, p. 1+.

Preview of the PBS debut of *A Bayou Legend*. "If one chooses to categorize [Still] at all it must be as a reactionary—whose love for Negro spirituals and simple harmonic structures did not result in lapel-grabbing music. *Legend*, which has much to recommend it in this production, bears signs of considerable craft. Still wrote gracefully for the voice and his orchestral parts have enough color, detail and drama to retain interest."

WB9.25 Cariaga, Daniel. "*A Bayou Legend* Airs On KCET At 9." *Los Angeles Times*, June 15, 1981.

Preview of the PBS telecast of *A Bayou Legend*. "It is an affectionate treatment of Still's charming score, though the small-screen sound does not do justice to the composer's full orchestration or his choral pieces. Both seem tiny . . . Leonard de Paur's musical direction proves correct rather than inspired, the chorus of college students more than a little raucous. Mixing of the studio-recorded orchestra and the location-recorded singers results in some weird and incompatible harmonies in the church scene, as well as elsewhere."

WB9.26 Shepard, Richard F. "TV: Still's Opera of the Southland, *A Bayou Legend*." *New York Times*, June 15, 1981, p. 24.

Preview of the PBS debut of *A Bayou Legend*. "This is a simple but effective tale told in a standard musical form. But Still's music often soars with the spirit of his legend, particularly in the love-song duets. He injects small-town humor in the persons of the Three Blades, a trio of happy-go-lucky neer-do-wells who mean trouble but are lighthearted relief from the heavy romance. The village folk serve as a sort of Greek chorus representing the social forces of the community. A dance festivity at the start of Act III gives us the only musical intimation of geography in the work. The cast of black performers is an exceptionally handsome and talented one, and under the musical direction of Leonard de Paur, the singers bring heart and soul to their performances."

WB9.27 Verongos, Helen. "The legend lives: Opera shares tale of state's bayous." Jackson *Clarion-Ledger*, June 15, 1981.

Preview of the PBS debut of *A Bayou Legend*. "The television debut of the romantic tragedy in three acts represents a number of firsts. It's Opera/South's first television production of one of Still's works. It's the first television opera with an all-black cast, and it represents a pioneering technical approach in bringing opera to the television screen. . . . Opera/South's television debut has won four awards: a Chris Bronze Plaque from the Columbus International Film Festival; a Bronze Award from the International Film and Television Festival of New York; A Bronze Award from the Houston International Film Festival, and a Certificate of Merit from the Chicago International Film Festival."

WB9.28 "A Bayou Legend." *Opera News* 45 (July 1981): 27.

This is a very good preview of the PBS telecast of *A Bayou Legend*, describing each act in detail, with background on its creation.

W10 ***Bells*** (Piano version: Delkas Music Publishing Company, Los Angeles, 1944; available from William Grant Still Music; Orchestral version: Delkas Music Publishing Company, Los Angeles, CA, 1944; MCA Music).

Piano solo; also arranged as a suite for orchestra, and for smaller orchestra.
Composed in Los Angeles; manuscript dated December, 1943.
Dedicated to Dolores Calvin (I) and Philippa Schuyler (II).
Contents: I. Phantom Chapel, II. Fairy Knoll.
Instrumentation (Delkas, 1944 edition): 3 flutes (3rd doubles on piccolo), 3 oboes, (3rd doubles on English horn), 3 clarinets (3rd doubles on bass

clarinet), 2 bassoons (2nd doubles on contrabassoon); 4 horns, 3 trumpets, 3 trombones, tuba; timpani, cymbals, vibraphone, marimba, chime, bells; harp, piano, celesta, strings.

Instrumentation for smaller orchestra: 3 flutes (3rd doubles on piccolo), 2 oboes, English horn, 4 clarinets, 3 bassoons (3rd doubles on contrabassoon); 4 horns, 3 trumpets, 3 trombones, tuba; timpani, bells, vibraphone, chimes, cymbals; harp, piano, celesta, strings.

Duration: 7 minutes.

Autograph of the piano score for *Fairy Knoll* (II), sketches of the orchestration, and the published miniature orchestral score are in the William Grant Still and Verna Arvey Papers at the University of Arkansas Libraries, Fayetteville.

Autograph of *Phantom Chapel* location unknown.

W10a **First Performance:** 1946 (November 29, 30): St. Louis; Kiel Auditorium; St. Louis Symphony Orchestra, Vladimir Golschmann, conductor. (Suite for orchestra.)

Bibliography

WB10.1 Burke, Harry R. "Symphony Presents Great Music by Negro Composer." *St. Louis Globe Democrat*, November 30, 1946.

Review of the November 29, 1946, performance of the St. Louis Symphony Orchestra, which included the premiere of *Bells*. "But of all the experiments in modernization he has heard in a quarter of a century . . . this chronicler enjoyed none like this. So simple, so sincere, so colorful. So dramatic in its texture of tone."

WB10.2 Sherman, Thomas B. "Fine Performance by Violinist Stern." *St. Louis Post-Dispatch*, November 30, 1946.

Review of the November 29, 1946, performance of the St. Louis Symphony Orchestra. "The bells were euphonic and impressionistic but had little interest aside from being a display of delicate orchestral coloring."

WB10.3 C., O. "St. Louis Premieres." *Musical Courier* 134 (December 15, 1946): 21.

"William Grant Still's charming, suggestive work, *Bells*, was given its initial hearing in St. Louis, proving the composer a master craftsman in achieving unusual effects."

W11 *Beyond Tomorrow,* also known as *A Song at Dusk* (available from William Grant Still Music as *A Song at Dusk*).

Poem for orchestra.

Composed in Los Angeles, 1936.

Commissioned by Paul Whiteman.

Dedicated to the composer's children from his marriage to Grace Bundy from 1915-1939: William (Billy), Gail, June, and Elaine; *A Song at Dusk* dedicated "To My Mother."

Instrumentation for *A Song at Dusk*: 3 flutes (3rd doubles on piccolo), 2 oboes, English horn, 3 clarinets, 2 bassoons; 4 horns, 3 trumpets, 3 trombones, tuba; timpani, percussion, bells, chime, cymbals, drums; harp, celesta, strings.

Duration: 9 minutes.

The autograph score of *Beyond Tomorrow* was at one time in The Paul Whiteman Collection, Williams College Archives and Special Collections, Williamstown, Massachusetts. It was listed as missing on February 23, 1989.

Autograph condensed conductor's score and full score are in The William

Grant Still Estate. Full score has *A Song at Dusk* at the top and *Beyond Tomorrow* at the bottom.

The family papers indicate that "this composition has been scrapped."

W12 ***Black Bottom*** (available from William Grant Still Music).
For chamber orchestra.
Composed in New York "about" 1922 (composer's inscription).
Composer's notes provide the following program: "A swamp where, between the hours of 4 a.m. and 6 a.m., Death and the fiends of darkness revel. Death, disguised as a siren, dances and sings a song which is repeated by the fiends. All join in the revelry which is interrupted at its heighth by a distant clock striking the hour of six."
Instrumentation: 3 flutes (3rd doubles on piccolo), 1 oboe, 3 clarinets, 2 bassoons; 2 horns, 3 trumpets, 2 trombones, tuba; timpani, percussion, gourd, slap stick, bells, drums, cymbals; piano (partial score), strings.
Autograph is in The William Grant Still Estate.

W13 ***Black Man Dances, The*** (available from William Grant Still Music; conductor's score only).
Suite for orchestra with solo piano; also known as *Four Negro Dances* for piano and orchestra in four brief movements.
Composed in Los Angeles, 1935.
Commissioned by Paul Whiteman.
Verses, attributed to [Harold] Bruce Forsythe, are attached to the four movements. Inscription by the composer at the end: "(He can't dance anymore)."
Inscription by the composer on the holograph: "Acknowledging with gratitude the helpful suggestions of Miss Verna Arvey concerning the preparation of the piano part."
Contents: I. Allegro-Moderato assai, II. Piu Lento, III. Moderato assai, IV. Lento-Allegro moderato.
Instrumentation (version for orchestra): flute, oboe, clarinet; 3 saxophones; horn, 2 trumpets, trombone, tuba; bells, drums; piano, guitar, strings.
Instrumentation (The Paul Whiteman Collection score): flute, English horn, B-flat and E-flat clarinets, bass clarinet, 2 alto saxophones, C and B-flat tenor saxophones; horn, 3 trumpets, 3 trombones; timpani, bells, tom-tom, vibraphone, wire brush, snare drum, cymbal; guitar, strings, solo piano.
Duration: 10 minutes.
Holograph of the piano and orchestra version, with sketches for a fifth piece and orchestration notes, is in the William Grant Still and Verna Arvey Papers at the University of Arkansas Libraries, Fayetteville.
Holograph conductor's score and parts are in The Paul Whiteman Collection, Williams College Archives and Special Collections, Williamstown, Massachusetts.
Notes in the composer's files indicate that this composition was later "scrapped."

W14 ***Blue Steel*** (available from William Grant Still Music).
Opera in 3 acts; 3 stage sets.
Composed in Los Angeles, 1934-1935.
"Dedicated to the Founders of the Guggenheim Fellowships."
Libretto by [Harold] Bruce Forsythe, based on a story by Carlton Moss.
Inscription by the composer says, "With humble thanks to God, the Source of Inspiration."
For: Cast: baritone, soprano, contralto, tenor, chorus.

Partial contents: Entrance of Priests, Dance of the Priestesses.
Instrumentation: 3 flutes, 2 oboes, English horn, 4 clarinets, 3 bassoons; 4 horns, 3 trumpets and 3 trombones (with Ray Robinson, Harmon, and straight mutes), tuba; timpani, percussion, 3 tom-toms; celesta, harp, strings.
Duration: 120 minutes.
Holograph piano vocal score and typescript libretto are in the Library of Congress, deposited for copyright January 28, 1935.
Autograph fair copy of a piano vocal score and of a full orchestral score are in The William Grant Still Estate. This autograph includes a synopsis and stage setting designs.
The Still and Arvey Papers indicate that this work was "discarded by the composer" and that the composer incorporated the musical material into other works.

Selected Performances

W14a 1935 (April 3): Rochester, NY: Kilbourn Hall; Eastman School Little Symphony, Karl Van Hoesen, conductor. (*Entrance of Priests* and *Dance of the Priestesses* only).

W14b 1935 (May 5): Los Angeles, CA; Musart Theater; Verna Arvey, piano. (*See:* WB1.7, WB76.6)

Bibliography

WB14.1 Reichard, Carolyn. "The Concert." *Rochester Times-Union*, April 4, 1935.
Review of the April 3, 1935, performance of the Eastman School Little Symphony. "An excerpt [*Entrance of Priests* and *Dance of the Priestesses*] from William Grant Still's new and unfinished opera, *Blue Steel*, opened the program. It shows good use of color, a better welding of thematic material and easier transitions than compositions of this writer played Tuesday night."

WB14.2 Sabin, Stewart B. "Little Symphony Has Capacity Audience." *Rochester Democrat and Chronicle*, April 4, 1935.
Review of the April 3, 1935, performance of the Eastman School Little Symphony. *Entrance of Priests* and *Dance of the Priestesses,* excerpts from the opera *Blue Steel*, received its premiere performance. "One would look to knowledge of Still's opera, *Blue Steel*, to explain why he wrote the piquante, bizarrely scored music last night; probably the music fits the scheme of the work as a whole."

WB14.3 Shulsky, Samuel. "Ensemble Plays in Kilbourn." *Rochester Journal*, April 4, 1935.
Review of the April 3, 1935, performance of the Eastman School Little Symphony. The program included *Entrance of Priests* and *Dance of the Priestesses,* an excerpt from the opera *Blue Steel*, receiving its premiere performance. "A bit of the Still work . . . was heard from a vantage point near the orchestra entrance and indicated that this latest of his works possesses his remarkable flair for rhythm."

W15 ***Blues, The,*** from ***Lenox Avenue*** (J. Fischer & Brothers, New York, 1938, no. 0379, piano vocal score; the ***Blues*** section published for small orchestra in 1939, no. 0391 and 0391a; available from William Grant Still Music).
For violin and piano (violin part edited by Louis Kaufman); also for chamber orchestra, solo piano, and solo violin with chamber orchestra.

Blues is the music for the House-Rent Party scene (IX) from **Lenox Avenue**. (*See:* W80)

Instrumentation (for chamber orchestra version): flute, oboe, 2 clarinets, bassoon; 2 alto saxophones, tenor saxophone, baritone saxophone; 2 horns, 2 trumpets, trombone cues (only if saxophone is not available); drums; piano (piano conductor score).

Instrumentation for a version for solo violin and chamber orchestra: solo violin with flute, oboe, 3 clarinets, 2 bassoons (2nd doubles on contrabassoon); 4 saxophones; 2 (more or less) horns, 2 (more or less) trumpets, 1 trombone; drums, strings.

Duration: 3 minutes, 50 seconds.

Manuscript copy in Verna Arvey's hand of the violin and piano score and a set of parts for the chamber orchestra version are in the William Grant Still and Verna Arvey Papers at the University of Arkansas Libraries, Fayetteville.

W15a **First Performance:** 1944 (February 4): New York, NY; Carnegie Hall; National Orchestral Association, Leon Barzin, conductor; Louis Kaufman, violin. (Solo violin and chamber orchestra version.)

Selected Performances

W15b 1937 (November 21): Los Angeles, CA; Pacific Institute of Music and Fine Art; Verna Arvey, piano.

W15c 1938 (May 18): Los Angeles, CA; Ruskin Club; Verna Arvey, piano.

W15d 1942 (March 25): New York, NY; Town Hall; Louis Kaufman, violin; Vladimir Padwa, piano.

W15e 1944 (April 30): Standard Symphony Orchestra, Meredith Willson, conductor. Radio broadcast over NBC.

W15f 1949 (January 6): New York, NY; Lobero Theatre; Louis Kaufman, violin; Annette Kaufman, piano.

W15g 1959 (March 30): Milan, Italy; Accademia Csaky; Nelly Csaky, violin; Efram Casagrande, piano.

Bibliography

WB15.1 Simon, Robert A. "Musical Events." *New Yorker* 20 (February 26, 1944): 74-75.

"Mr. Kaufman and the orchestra added the *Blues* movement from William Grant Still's *Lenox Avenue Suite*, to the great approval of the audience."

W16 ***Breath of a Rose, The*** (G. Schirmer, 1928, publication no. 33804 [low voice]; published with **Winter's Approach** as "2 poems set to music for voice and piano by William Grant Still"; included in Schirmer's *A New Anthology of American Song,* 1942, publication no. 39639; also in G. Schirmer, *Romantic American Art Songs*, currently Hal Leonard; available from William Grant Still Music).

For vocal solo and piano.

Composed in New York, probably in 1927.

Poem by Langston Hughes.

Performed in 1927 in a set called "Dialect Songs" with **Winter's Approach** and **Mandy Lou**. (*See:* W171, W96)

Holograph is in the Research Division, New York Public Library for the Performing Arts at Lincoln Center.

Selected Performances

W16a 1927 (April 16): New York, NY; New School of Social Research Auditorium; Jessie Zachary, soprano. Concert arranged by Paul Rosenfeld.

W16b 1935 (May 5): Los Angeles, CA; Musart Theater; Leola Longress, soprano; John A. Gray, piano.

W16c 1935 (December 8): San Francisco, CA; Sorosis Club; Nathan Emanuel, tenor; Verna Arvey, piano. (*See:* WB1.11, WB1.12)

W16d 1947 (October 7): Fort Worth, TX; Will Rogers Memorial Auditorium; Muriel Rahn, soprano.

W16e 1953 (July 1): Stockton, CA; Civic Auditorium; Ruth Daniel, soprano; Margaret Thomas, piano.

W16f 1956 (April): San Francisco, CA; First A.M.E. Zion Church; Ruth Daniel, soprano; Irving Pearson, piano.

W16g 1966 (August 19): Detroit, MI; Wayne State University, Community Arts Auditorium; Adele Addison, soprano; John Carter, piano.

W16h 1966 (October 15): Los Angeles, CA; Wilshire-Ebell Theatre; Cathryn Flewellyn Ballinger, soprano; Geyen Sherrill, piano.

W16i 1968 (February 12): Detroit, MI; Detroit Public Library; Gloria Hill, soprano; Geraldyne Duncan, piano.

W16j 1969 (December 28): Washington DC; National Gallery of Art, East Garden Court; Reginald Farrar, heldentenor; Wendell Pritchett, piano.

W16k 1976 (June 6): New York, NY; Lincoln Center; Alice Tully Hall; Diane Wilson, soprano; Marjorie De Lewis, piano.

W16l 1982 (October 17): New York, NY; Symphony Space; The Triad Chorale, Noel Da Costa, director; Alpha Brawner-Floyd, soprano.

Bibliography

WB16.1 B., T. E. "Music" *New York Amsterdam News*, April 27, 1927, p. 24.
"Compositions of William G. Still were among those of the five modern composers presented by the New School of Social Research, 465 West Twenty-third Street, at a recital there last Saturday week. Mr. Still's compositions—three dialect selections—were beautifully interpreted by Jessie A. Zachary, soprano." The compositions performed were *Breath of a Rose*, *Winter's Approach* and *Mandy Lou*.

WB16.2 Whitlock, E. Clyde. "Negro Soprano Sings Here To Appreciative Audience." *Fort Worth Star-Telegram*, October 8, 1947.
Review of October 7, 1947, performance by Muriel Rahn. "*Breath of a Rose* . . . was one of the most appealing items of the program."

W17 ***Brown Baby*** (Edward B. Marks, New York, 1923; available from William Grant Still Music).
Popular song.
Published under the pseudonym Willie M. Grant.
Composed in New York, about 1923.
Lyrics by Paul Henry.
Performed by Ethel Waters and Her Jazz Masters on a recording by The Black Swan Phonograph Company in the 1920s. (*See:* B113)
Autograph location unknown.

W18 ***Can'tcha Line 'Em,*** variant title, ***Can't You Line 'Em*** (available from William Grant Still Music).
For orchestra.
Composed in Los Angeles; manuscript dated January, 1940.
Commissioned by the Columbia Broadcasting System, 1940 (radio).
Instrumentation: 1 flute, 1 oboe, 2 clarinets, 1 bassoon; 2 horns, 2 trumpets, 1 trombone; percussion; strings.
Duration: 5 minutes.
The holograph has the following inscriptions by the composer: "(With humble thanks to God, The Source of Inspiration) Based on a Negro folk melody from the collection of John A. and Alan Lomax."
Sketches with orchestration notes are in the William Grant Still and Verna Arvey Papers at the University of Arkansas Libraries, Fayetteville.

W18a **First Performance:** 1940 (February 17): CBS Radio Network on the program *American School of the Air.*

Selected Performance

W18b 1941 (september 25): Standard Symphony Orchestra, Paul Lemay, conductor. Radio broadcast over KHJ Mutual Network.

W19 ***Caribbean Melodies*** (Oliver Ditson Company, Philadelphia, 1947, no. 78751-62; available from William Grant Still Music).
Folk song settings for SATB chorus, male chorus, soloists, percussion, piano, and dancers.
Composed in Los Angeles, in collaboration with Zora Neale Hurston between September 1941 and February 1942.
Based on melodies, rhythms, dances, and unpublished folk materials collected by Hurston in the Bahamas during the 1930s.
Dances described by Verna Arvey in the preface.
Contents:
  Hand A' Bowl (mixed chorus), Jamaica, British West Indies.
  Baintown (tenor solo, chorus, piano), New Providence, Bahamas.
  Two Banana (Jumping Dance), New Providence.
  Woman Sweeter Than Man (tenor solo, piano), Cat Island.
  Peas and Rice (Jumping Dance), Cat Island.
  Bellamina (contralto solo, piano), New Providence.
  Mama, I Saw a Sailboat (Ring Play), New Providence.
  Ah, La Sa Wu! (chorus, tenor, drum, piano), Fox Hill.
  Evalina (baritone solo, piano), Eleuthera Island.
  Doo Ma (chorus, dancers, drum, piano), Abaco Island.
  Héla Grand-Père (chorus, drum, piano), Haiti.
  Going to My Old Home (chorus, dancers, and piano), New Providence.
  Mister Brown (dancers, a cappella chorus), New Providence.
  Ten Poun' Ten (tenor solo, dancers, grater, piano), Jamaica.
  Do an' Nannie (soprano solo, piano), New Providence.
  Eh, Bi Nango (soprano solo, piano), Abaco Island.
  Carry Him Along (soprano solo, tenor, chorus, dancers, drums, piano), Nassau, Bahamas (*See:* W20).
Autograph dated September 1941 with additional notes on the folk materials is in the William Grant Still and Verna Arvey Papers at the University of Arkansas Libraries, Fayetteville. (*See also:* W67, W130)

W20 *Carry Him Along* (Oliver Ditson Company, Philadelphia, 1945, no. 15218-78584-6; available from William Grant Still Music).
Folk song setting for SATB chorus, soprano and tenor soloist, and piano.
Composed in Los Angeles, in collaboration with Zora Neale Hurston between September 1941 and February 1942 (also published in 1947 with *Caribbean Melodies,* W19).
Based on a folk tale, melody, and rhythm collected by Hurston in Nassau, the Bahamas, during the 1930s (folk tale printed on published octavo edition).
Autograph fair copy in pencil is in the William Grant Still and Verna Arvey Papers at the University of Arkansas, Fayetteville.

W21 *Choreographic Prelude* (available from William Grant Still Music).
For orchestra; also a version for organ, piano, and strings.
Composed in Los Angeles, 1970.
Instrumentation: 2 flutes (2nd doubles on piccolo), 2 oboes, 2 clarinets, 2 bassoons; 3 horns, 2 trumpets, 2 trombones, tuba; timpani, tambourine, conga drum, cymbals; harp, strings.
Sketches with revisions are in the William Grant Still and Verna Arvey Papers at the University of Arkansas Libraries, Fayetteville.

W21a **First Performance:** 1970 (January 25): Los Angeles, CA; Los Angeles County Museum of Natural History Concert, William Grant Still, guest conductor.

W22 *Christmas in the Western World (Las Pascuas)* (Southern Music Publishing Co., Inc., New York, 1967 no. 1075-32; Peer Music Co., New York; Theodore Presser).
Cantata based on folk song material for mixed chorus with piano, string quartet, orchestra, or string quartet and piano; can be performed by string quartet and piano, string orchestra and piano; or mixed vocal quartet, string quartet, and piano, according to the cover of the published score.
Narration and texts by Verna Arvey.
Contents: I. A Maiden was Adoring God, The Lord (Argentina), II. Ven, Niño Divino (Nicaragua), III. Aguinaldo (Venezuela), IV. Jesous Ahatonhia (Canadian Indian), V. Tell Me, Shepherdess (French Canadian), VI. De Virgin Mary Had a Baby Boy (Trinidad), VII. Los Reyes Magos (Puerto Rico), VIII. La Piñata (Mexico), IX. Glad Christmas Bells (Brazil), X. Sing! Shout! Tell the Story! (American Negro).
Duration: 20 minutes.
A copy of the printed score with the composer's five-page manuscript of errata is in the William Grant Still and Verna Arvey Papers at the University of Arkansas Libraries, Fayetteville.
Holograph is in The William Grant Still Estate.

W23 *Citadel* (available from William Grant Still Music).
For voice and piano; also for voice, string orchestra, and piano.
Poem by Virginia Brasier begins, "Love can lace leaves together and make them proof against the world."
Duration: 2 minutes.
Autograph sketches and a fair copy are in the William Grant Still and Verna Arvey Papers at the University of Arkansas Libraries, Fayetteville.

W24 *Costaso* (available from William Grant Still Music).
Opera in 3 acts with ballet, 4 stage sets.
Composed in Los Angeles, 1949-1950.

Libretto by Verna Arvey.

Dedicated "To my friend Don Voorhees, in appreciation of his service to American music."

Setting: Spanish-Colonial America; The days of the Spanish Dons in the American Southwest, inspired by a legend of that region; A Pueblo near the desert.

For: Cast: Principle roles: 2 tenors, soprano, baritone, mezzo-soprano; Secondary roles: baritone, 3 basses, 2 tenors; chorus.

The arias, *Love Bids Me Stay at Home* and *Ballad* have been performed separately. *Golden Days,* an aria for Carmela (soprano), is in separate arrangements for soprano with string quartet and harp or piano, or for soprano with string orchestra and harp.

A duet from Act II, *Ave Maria,* sung by Ramon Costaso and his friend Manuel Parron, has been performed separately.

Two instrumental dances, *Waltz* and *Corrido,* have been performed separately. Two other instrumental interludes have been performed separately, *Introduction to Desert Scene* and *Promenade. Dance from Costaso* exists as a piano solo.

Instrumentation: 2 flutes (2nd doubles on piccolo), 2 oboes, English horn, 2 clarinets, 2 bassoons; 3 horns, 3 trumpets, 3 trombones, tuba; timpani, percussion, snare drum, cymbals, bells, castanets, claves, gong, wire brush; celesta, harp, strings.

Duration: 85 minutes, 42 seconds.

Holograph with performance notes, sketches of the libretto, and orchestration notes throughout, bound together by the composer, is in the William Grant Still and Verna Arvey Papers at the University of Arkansas Libraries, Fayetteville.

Autograph full score and piano vocal score are in The William Grant Still Estate.

W25 ***Danzas de Panama*** (Southern Music Publishing Company, Inc., New York, 1953, no. 197-31; available from William Grant Still Music).

For string quintet, or string orchestra; also arranged for string quartet.

Composed in Los Angeles, 1948.

Based on Panamanian folk themes collected by Elisabeth Waldo.

Contents: I. Tamborito, II. Mejorana y Socavon, III. Punto, IV. Cumbia y Congo.

Instrumentation: violin I, violin II, viola, cello, bass.

The composer's notes in the sketches: "Whenever the indication, 'tap,' occurs, instruments are to be tapped on."

Duration: 15 minutes.

Autograph sketches and a copy of the published score for string orchestra or string quintet are in the William Grant Still and Verna Arvey Papers at the University of Arkansas Libraries, Fayetteville.

W25a **First Performance:** 1948 (May 21): Los Angeles, CA; Los Angeles County Museum of Natural History, Harrison Gallery; Waldo Latin American String Quartet.

Selected Performances

W25b 1948 (December 12): Los Angeles, CA; Assistance League Playhouse; Waldo Latin American String Quartet.

W25c 1956 (May 13): Washington, DC; National Gallery of Art, East Garden; National Gallery Orchestra, Richard Bales, conductor.

W25d 1957 (March 17): Benevento, Italy; Nelly Csaky String Quartet (Under the auspices of the Centro de Cultura, this group performed *Danzas de Panama* in sixteen cities in Italy between March 17 and April 10 in 1957.)

W25e   1964 (April 27): Los Angeles, CA; Lindy Opera House; Spinoza Paeff Quartet: Spinoza Paeff, viola; Harris Goldman, violin; William Van Den Burg, cello; Bernard Gerrard, violin.

W25f   1966 (February 18): Houston, TX; Texas Southern University, University Auditorium; Texas Southern University String Quartet, William Grant Still, guest conductor.

W25g   1968 (February 12): Seattle, WA; Seattle Center Opera House; Seattle Youth Symphony Orchestra, Vilem Sokol, conductor. (*See:* WB154.1)

W25h   1968 (March 22): Argentina; Teatro Rosario; Orquesta Sinfónica Provincial de Rosario, Luis Milici, conductor.

W25i   1970 (January 29): Dallas, TX; Bishop College; Dallas Symphony Orchestra, Paul Freeman, conductor. (*See also:* WB133.3)

W25j   1970 (November 9): Oberlin, OH; Oberlin College, Warner Concert Hall; Ronald Copes, violin; John Schoening, violin; Noah Chaves, viola; Norman Fischer, cello. (*See:* WB155.2, WB155.3)

W25k   1971 (March 21): Richmond, VA; The Mosque; Richmond Symphony, Paul Freeman, guest conductor.

W25l   1972 (December 9): Washington DC; Pan American Health Organization; National Gallery Strings, Richard Bales, conductor.

W25m   1973 (March 23): Rosario, Argentina; Teatro Rosario; Orquesta Sinfónica Provincial de Rosario, Jorge Rotter, conductor.

W25n   1977 (September 2): New York, NY; Avery Fisher Hall; New York Philharmonic Chamber Orchestra, Leon Thompson, conductor.

W25o   1979 (October 18): Los Angeles, CA; Arnold Schoenberg Institute; University of Southern California String Quartet: Steven Mohler, violin; Kevin Lancaster, violin; Philip Tietze, viola; Michael Matthews, cello. (*See:* WB112.4)

W25p   1980 (March 9): Los Angeles, CA; St. John's Episcopal Church; Harmonians String Quartet: Lesa Terry, violin; Dale Almond, violin; Robin Moore, viola; Clavis Ballard, cello.

W25q   1984 (February 15): Fayetteville, AR; University of Arkansas, Fine Arts Center Concert Hall; University Chamber Orchestra, Carlton R. Woods, conductor.

Bibliography

WB25.1   Waldo, Elisabeth. "Program Notes." *Latin American Concert* (Waldo Latin American String Quartet), May 21, 1948.

           Program notes for the premiere performance of *Danzas De Panama* in the Harrison Gallery of the Los Angeles County Museum of Natural History, May 21, 1948. "This suite embodies authentic folk material gathered by Elisabeth Waldo during two tours to Central America, in the course of which Miss Waldo studied folk culture. The first and last of these dances are Negro in origin, probably brought by the first slaves imported into Panama. The Mejorana and Punto are both of Spanish derivation with Indian influence. There is a distinct unity and a touch of Caribbean color in these four dances."

WB25.2   Quinn, Alfred Price. "Music." Los Angeles *B'nai B'rith Messenger*, May 28, 1948.

Brief review of the Waldo Latin American String Quartet performance of *Danzas De Panama* in the Harrison Gallery of the Los Angeles County Museum of Natural History, May 21, 1948. "This proved to be an effective work which should have no difficulty finding a place on quartet programs. Although short on finesse and at times somewhat course, nevertheless the Latin American Quartet played the work with vigor, verve and vehemence."

WB25.3 Faber, Charles. "Quartet Plays Music of Latin America." *Los Angeles Mirror*, December 13, 1948.

Brief review of the December 12, 1948, Waldo Latin American String Quartet performance at the Assistance League Playhouse. "While the selected works may not have the full-bodied consistency of the traditional European chamber music to which the North American ear is accustomed, they manage, sometimes with brilliant effect, to say what they have to in a style which is both adequate to their content and provocative to the listener. The suite, *Danzas de Panama*, is folk art formalized. The dances were collected by Miss Waldo and brilliantly arranged by William Grant Still, who sacrificed none of the coruscating rhythms in transcription."

WB25.4 Ardoin, John. "Black Composers Played by DSO." *Dallas Morning News*, January 31, 1970.

Review of the January 29, 1970, performance of the Dallas Symphony Orchestra, Paul Freeman, conductor. The program included Still's *Scherzo*, from his *Afro-American Symphony*, and *Cumbia y Congo*, from *Danzas De Panama*. "Perhaps the reason Still's music can even now fall on our ears with a faded enchantment is that his roots stem from an age of greater directness in the arts, a time of less pressure, a moment which seems almost simple next to the emotional tanglements of now. . . . A very large audience seemed to appreciate the efforts of Freeman and the orchestra, and cheered enthusiastically."

WB25.5 Scarborough, Charles. "Music." *Richmond News Leader*, March 22, 1971.

Review of the March 21, 1971, performance of the Richmond Symphony. "William Grant Still has explored African music in all its aspects as it developed after slaves were brought to various parts of the New World. In this music rhythm was always a primary element, the syncopated, contagious rhythm that became the basis of what first was called in this country 'ragtime' and later 'jazz.' The first example of Still's music played yesterday was a folk dance, *Cumbia y Congo*, from a dance suite, *Danzas de Panama*. More extended in form and more sophisticated musically was the *Scherzo* movement from Still's *Afro-American Symphony*, one of his best known works. Hardly anyone could have missed the theme that sounds like Gershwin's *I've Got Rhythm*. It appears that Gershwin borrowed this theme, whether consciously or subconsciously, from Still."

WB25.6 Southern, Eileen. "Program Notes." *Stagebill* 4 (August 1977): 16-17.

Program notes for the Lincoln Center performance of *Danzas de Panama* by the New York Philharmonic Chamber Orchestra, Leon Thompson, conductor, September 2, 1977. "[*Tamborito*] is of African origin, probably brought over by the first slaves imported into Panama. It is typically performed with percussive instruments and the voice or with percussions and strings. . . . *Mejorana y Socavon* [is] of Spanish-Indian derivation, [and] is usually accompanied by the rabel, or three-stringed violin, and mejoraneras, or guitars, playing countermelodies. *Punto*. Also of Spanish-Indian origin

this dance includes a paseo, or promenade, and a zapates, or shoe-tapping section. The composer suggests the latter through his use of pizzicato.
Cumbia y Congo. An African dance, this is the most sensuous of the four. When it is danced in the streets, the men dance with wild abandon and the women hold lighted candles in their hands. When danced inside, the dance is more decorous. The composer uses his 'taps,' along with reiterated-note motives, to great effect."

WB25.7 Davis, Peter G. "Stimulating Celebration of Music." *New York Times*, September 4, 1977, p. 4.
Review of the September 2, 1977, performance of the New York Philharmonic. The program was the fifth and last of a "Celebration of Black Composers Week." "The concert opened pleasantly enough with two lightweight items, Samuel Coleridge-Taylor's *Danse Nègre* (1897) and William Grant Still's *Danzas de Panama* (1948). Both made effective use of their indigenous dance rhythms and the congenial pop-concert flavor contrasted nicely with the more serious fare on the program."

W26 ***Darker America*** (Carl Fischer, Inc., 1924; C.C. Birchard & Company, Boston, 1928, N555 no. 21, for The University of Rochester, The Eastman School of Music; available for rental from Theodore Presser).
For chamber orchestra, a tone poem; also scored for full orchestra.
Composed in New York, 1924-1925.
Winner of a publication prize in 1928 at the Eastman School of Music.
Instrumentation: 2 flutes, 1 or 2 oboes, English horn, 2 clarinets, 2 bassoons; 1 horn, 1 trumpet, 1 trombone; cymbal, bass drum; piano, strings.
Duration: 17 minutes.
Composer's program notes: "is representative of the American Negro. His serious side is presented and is intended to suggest the triumph of a people over their sorrows through fervent prayer. At the beginning the theme of the American Negro is announced by the strings in unison . . . English horn announces the sorrow theme . . . theme of hope . . . to muted Brass. . . . Then the prayer is heard (given to oboe); the prayer of numbed rather than anguished souls."
Autograph location unknown.

W26a **First Performance:** 1926 (November 28): New York, NY; Aeolian Hall; International Composers' Guild Concert, Eugene Goossens, conductor.

Selected Performances

W26b 1927 (November 21): Rochester, NY; Kilbourn Hall; Rochester Philharmonic Orchestra, Howard Hanson, conductor.

W26c 1930 (May 1): Rochester, NY; Kilbourn Hall; Rochester Philharmonic Orchestra, Howard Hanson, conductor.

W26d 1941 (April 16): New York, NY; NYA Orchestra, Ben Steinberg, conductor. Broadcast on WNYC radio.

W26e 1946 (March 19): Oberlin, OH; Finney Memorial Chapel; Oberlin Conservatory Orchestra, Maurice Kessler, conductor.

W26f 1971 (November 13): White Plains, NY; Highlands School; Westchester Symphony Orchestra, Siegfried Landau, conductor.

W26g 1975 (October 7, 8, 9): Oakland, CA; Paramount Theatre; Oakland Symphony Orchestra, Harold Farberman, conductor.

Bibliography

WB26.1 Downes, Olin. "Music." *New York Times*, November 29, 1926, p. 16.

Review of the November 28, 1926, performance of the International Composers' Guild Concert at Aeolian Hall. "The best music last night was that of *Darker America* . . . an improvement in clearness and consecutiveness of statement over *Levee Land*, played at a Guild concert last season, and the polyharmonic treatment of the theme in the opening and the concluding measure is more than ingenious. It communicates an atmosphere. What is lacking is actual development and organic growth of the ideas. This music, however, has direction and feeling in it, qualities usually lacking in contemporaneous music."

WB26.2 Sabin, Stewart B. "Composers Present As Works Given." *Rochester Democrat and Chronicle*, May 2, 1930.

Review of the May 1, 1930, performance of the Rochester Philharmonic Orchestra. "Still's *Darker America* arrests attention because of its strong individuality; one believes that it could only have been written by an American Negro; its racial derivation is plain to hear, and there is pathos and deep feeling revealed in it. But it seems to the writer the least technically expert composition played last night; there is in it variation from passages that bespeak imaginative inspiration and poignant feeling to others that sound contrived with little of either."

WB26.3 "Orchestra Program to Feature Two Works of Local Interest." *Oberlin Times*, March 14, 1946.

Preview of the March 19, 1946, program of the Oberlin Conservatory Orchestra, which includes *Darker America*.

W27 ***Deserted Plantation, A*** (Robbins Music Corporation, New York, 1936, piano solo version; available from William Grant Still Music).
Suite for orchestra in five movements; for piano solo in three movements.
Composed in New York, 1933.
Commissioned by Paul Whiteman. (*See:* W29)
Based on a poem with the same title by Paul Laurence Dunbar.
Composer's notes describe this piece as "a musical picture of the meditations of Uncle Josh, an old colored man who is the sole occupant of the dying plantation, and who delights in dreaming of its past glory."
Contents of the orchestra version, which includes solo piano interludes between all movements except I and II: I. Prologue, II. Yistiddy—an' Today, III. Spiritual, IV. Young Missy, V. Dance; piano solo version has movements III, IV, and V. Movement III, *Spiritual,* is an adaptation of "I Want Jesus to Walk with Me."
Instrumentation in The Paul Whiteman Collection for one version: 2 flutes, 3 oboes, 4 clarinets; 5 saxophones; 1 horn, 3 trumpets, 3 trombones, tuba; timpani, percussion, drums; harp, piano, celesta; strings. (The conductor's score no longer exists.) Version dated December 1933: 1 flute, 4 clarinets; 3 trumpets, 3 trombones; drums; 2 pianos, 2 violins, 1 string bass. Additional notes say, "use tuba and guitar parts from the other arrangement."
Duration: 15 minutes.
Autographs of two versions for orchestra are in The Paul Whiteman Collection, Williams College Archives and Special Collections, Williamstown, Massachusetts.

W27a **First Performance:** 1933 (December 15): New York, NY; Metropolitan Opera House, The Paul Whiteman Orchestra, Paul Whiteman, conductor.

Selected Performances

W27b 1934 (March 6): Cincinnati, OH; Music Hall; Cincinnati Musicians' Association Symphony and The Paul Whiteman Orchestra, Paul Whiteman, conductor.

W27c 1937 (March 16): Tucson, AZ; University of Arizona, College of Fine Arts; Ulysses Kay, piano. (Only *Young Missy.*)

W28 ***Dismal Swamp*** (The New Music Society of California, *New Music Orchestra Series,* No. 21, San Francisco, January, 1937; available from William Grant Still Music).
Poem for orchestra with piano solos.
Composed in Los Angeles, 1935; manuscript says, "Sketch completed June 21." Dedicated to Quinto Maganini.
Instrumentation: 3 flutes (3rd doubles on piccolo), 2 oboes, 4 clarinets,
   3 bassoons (3rd doubles on contrabassoon); 4 horns, 3 trumpets, 3 trombones, tuba; timpani, percussion, vibraphone, triangle, drums, cymbals; piano, strings.
Duration: 11 - 15 minutes.
Holograph piano score with orchestration notes is in the William Grant Still and Verna Arvey Papers at the University of Arkansas Libraries, Fayetteville.

W28a **First Performance:** 1936 (October 30): Rochester, NY; Kilbourn Hall; Rochester Civic Orchestra, Howard Hanson, conductor.

Selected Performances

W28b 1937 (January 14): Rochester, NY; Eastman Theater; Rochester Philharmonic Orchestra, Howard Hanson, conductor, Irene Gedney, piano.

W28c 1938 (February 3 and 8): Mexico; Sinfónica de Yucatan, Samuel Marti, conductor.

W28d 1939 (October 12): Rio de Janeiro, Brazil; Instituto Brasil-Estados Unidos, O. Lorenz Fernandez, conductor.

Bibliography

WB28.1 Kessler, David. "Howard Hanson Leads Philharmonic."*Rochester Journal and Post Express*, January 15, 1937.
   "For three-quarters of its length, [*Dismal Swamp*] was an atmospheric, ingenious development of a constantly repeated phrase, sometimes five notes and at others six notes long. Then it lapsed into a commonplace finale that did not help the earlier impression. But this composer contrived the best score on the program, even if his piece was barren of ideas."

WB28.2 Sabin, Stewart B. "Strong Contrast in Music by Americans." *Rochester Democrat and Chronicle*, January 15, 1937.
   "The widely-known Negro composer in his music [*Dismal Swamp*] last night is busy, as of old, in devotion to a mood. His orchestration, or that played last night, is interesting and extensive. His color scheme is dark, little brightened by contrast and thus somewhat monotonous."

W29 ***Down Yonder.***
Suite for orchestra.
Commissioned by Paul Whiteman.

Dedicated "To my friend, Paul Whiteman."

Contents: I. Dance, II. Honey Chile, III. From a Deserted Plantation. (*See:* W27)

Instrumentation: flute, oboe, 4 clarinets, C melody saxophone, B-flat soprano saxophone, alto saxophone, tenor saxophone, bassoon; 3 trumpets,
3 trombones (one has a "hot" solo); triangle, vibraphone, timpani, damped cymbal and bass drum, slapstick, bells; piano, celesta, violins (1st and 2nd desk), string bass, banjo.

Parts for specific players who double on several instruments include the names Strickfaden, Daly, Hazlett, and Friedman. Margulis plays first trumpet.

Autograph parts for all three movements are in The Paul Whiteman Collection, Williams College Archives and Special Collections, Williamstown, Massachusetts. The Collection includes a melodic cue score with melodies only for the conductor.

W30 ***Ebon Chronicle,*** also known as *A Negro Epic* (conductor's score available from William Grant Still Music).

Poem for orchestra.

Composed in New York; manuscript dated January 14 and 15, 1934.

Performed by The Paul Whiteman Orchestra and other orchestras with Paul Whiteman conducting.

Dedicated "To V.A." [Verna Arvey].

Composer's inscription says, "Humbly asking the aid of God."

Inscription, written in Verna Arvey's hand, in the autograph: *"Ebon Chronicle* is a tone picture of the Negro Race."

Instrumentation: 3 flutes (3rd doubles on piccolo), 2 oboes, English horn, 3 clarinets, bass clarinet, 3 bassoons (3rd doubles on contrabassoon); 4 horns, 3 trumpets and 3 trombones (Shastock, Harmon, and Kazoo mutes), tuba; timpani, percussion, vibraphone, temple blocks, wire brush, wind machine, glockenspiel, snare drum, 2 tom-toms, cymbals; harp, 2 pianos, celesta, strings, banjo.

Duration: 9 minutes.

Players' names given on some parts include Bonnacio, Strickfaden, Trumbauer, and Cordero.

Autograph conductor's score and sketches of *A Negro Epic* are in the William Grant Still and Verna Arvey Papers at the University of Arkansas Libraries, Fayetteville.

Autograph score and 58 parts of *Ebon Chronicle* with stamp on facsimile negatives for string parts that say "Harold M. Solstad, S1225, or Rube Thomas, T688, Local 802, copyright 1936," are in The Paul Whiteman Collection, Williams College Archives and Special Collections, Williamstown, Massachusetts.

W30a **First Performance:** 1936 (November 3): Fort Worth, TX; First Baptist Auditorium; Fort Worth Symphony Orchestra and The Paul Whiteman Orchestra, Paul Whiteman, conductor.

Selected Performance

W30b 1936 (November 27, 28): Philadelphia, PA; Academy of Music; Philadelphia Orchestra and The Paul Whiteman Orchestra, Paul Whiteman, conductor.

Bibliography

WB30.1 "Jazz on the Verge." *Time* 28 (December 7, 1936): 62-63.

90   William Grant Still: A Bio-Bibliography

Examination of the work of Paul Whiteman, which includes a review of a performance of Whiteman's band with the Philadelphia Symphony Orchestra. Still's *Ebon Chronicle* is described as "dull, pretentious."

W31 ***Elegy*** (Avant Music, West Coast chapters of the American Guild of Organists, 1963, no. 7 in a series; available from William Grant Still Music).
For organ.
Composed in Los Angeles, 1963.
Duration: 3 minutes.
Autograph is in the William Grant Still and Verna Arvey Papers at the University of Arkansas Libraries, Fayetteville. It has "Trio" and "II" at the top in ink. The word "organ" is in pencil in another hand.

Selected Performances

W31a   1964 (January 19): New Orleans, LA; Dillard University, Lawless Memorial Chapel; Ralph Simpson, organ.

W31b   1970 (July 5, 12, 19, 26): Los Angeles, CA; First Baptist Church; Irene Robertson, organ.

W31c   1984 (February 18): Fayetteville, AR; University of Arkansas, Fine Arts Center Concert Hall; Campbell Johnson, organ.

W32 ***Ennanga*** (Southern Music Company, San Antonio, Texas; available on rental).
Suite for harp and orchestra in three movements (without pause); arranged for harp and piano; also harp, piano, and string quartet; harp and string orchestra.
Composed in Los Angeles, 1958.
Dedicated to Lois Adele Craft.
Program notes written by the composer indicate that "Ennanga" is an "African word" for harp. He writes, "the themes in the Suite are original with the composer, but are based on his impressions of African folk music."
Instrumentation: 2 flutes (2nd doubles on piccolo), 2 oboes (2nd doubles on English horn), 2 clarinets, 2 bassoons; 3 horns, 2 trumpets (trumpet in C and one trumpet in B-flat), 2 trombones, tuba; timpani, percussion, cymbals, 3 (Chinese) tom-toms (or Rada drums), drums, wood block, maracas, (claves), xylophone, triangle, bells; celesta, strings.
Duration: between 15 and 19 minutes.
Autographs of the original version for harp and orchestra written in open score with revisions and a piano reduction are in the William Grant Still and Verna Arvey Papers at the University of Arkansas Libraries, Fayetteville. The Still and Arvey Papers also include the complete original sketches of the themes with indications of the form.
Holograph of full score is in The William Grant Still Estate. Typed note indicates that *Ennanga* means a Ganda harp that resembles the ancient Egyptian harp. (The Ganda are a Bantu-speaking people of Uganda.)

W32a   **First Performance:** 1958 (October 12): Los Angeles, CA; Westside Jewish Community Center; Lois Adele Craft, harp; Verna Arvey, piano.

Selected Performances

W32b   1965 (May 16): Los Angeles, CA; Los Angeles Music Center; Lois Adele Craft, harp; Mrs. William Grant Still (Verna Arvey), piano.

W32c   1965 (August 15): Los Angeles, CA; Scottish Rite Masonic Temple; Coppin

String Quartet: John Coppin and David Margetts, violin; Ross Beckstead, viola; Margaret Coppin, cello; Verna Arvey, piano; Lois Adele Craft, harp.

W32d   1966 (October 28): Los Angeles, CA; University of California at Los Angeles, Royce Hall; Lois Adele Craft, harp; Verna Arvey Still, piano. *(See also:* WB125.1)

W32e   1967 (January 29): Los Angeles, CA; West Hollywood Park Auditorium; American Harp Society of Los Angeles; William Grant Still, guest conductor; Lois Adele Craft, harp; Aeolian String Quartet: David Margetts, violin; Diana Ezmirlian, violin; Ross Beckstead, violin; Margaret Coppin, cello; Mrs. William Grant Still, piano.

W32f   1971 (January 10): Las Vegas, NV; University of Nevada, Las Vegas, Social Science Lecture Hall; University String Symphony, William Gromko, conductor, Lois Adele Craft, harp.

W32g   1979 (December 2): Las Vegas, NV; Charleston Heights Arts Center; Las Vegas Studio Orchestra, Bob Barclay, conductor, Lois Adele Craft, harp.

Bibliography

WB32.1   Arlen, Walter. "Series Spotlighting Negroes Falls Short." *Los Angeles Times*, October 30, 1966, sec. C, p. 6.

Review of a performance held at UCLA which included *Ennanga* and *A Psalm for the Living*. "Only William Grant Still, the dean of them all, maintained the equilibrium of his position, namely that of a lyricist. Both his *Psalm for the Living* (conducted by Albert McNeil), and *Ennanga*, a suite for harp, string orchestra and piano . . . displayed all the ingratiating elements of his muse."

WB32.2   Foreman, T.E. "Music leaders fail to attend concert." *Riverside Press*, November 2, 1966, sec. D, p. 2.

Review of a performance held at UCLA which included *Ennanga* and *A Psalm for the Living*. "Most conventional and consequently least interesting of the works was William Grant Still's *A Psalm for the Living*. . . . However, when the 71-year-old Still conducted his *Ennanga* suite for harp, string orchestra and piano, he revealed a work with as much freshness, charm and originality as any of those of the younger composers."

WB32.3   Jenkins, Walter D. "University Strings Play Local Program." *Las Vegas Sun*, January 17, 1971, p. 12.

Review of the January 10 performance of the University of Nevada, Las Vegas, University String Orchestra, which included Still's *Ennanga*. "One of America's outstanding Negro composers, William Grant Still, created *Ennanga* in three movements for harp and string orchestra especially for harpist Lois Craft. The music, which is based on African folk songs, was both moving and exciting in its minor keys. An aura of syncopation punctuated with the undertone of African rhythms were well-controlled and well-balanced by Conductor [William] Gromko and his strings. Miss Craft again displayed her technically difficult solos with ease and moving feelings."

WB32.4   Still, Judith Anne. "The Genesis of *Ennanga*." *American Harp Journal* 9 (Winter 1984): 15-17.

This article traces the history and development of the composition.

W33   ***Ev'ry Time I Feel the Spirit,*** see also *Four Octavo Songs*, W44 (Galaxy, New York, 1948, no. 17242; E.C. Schirmer; available from William Grant Still Music).

Spiritual arrangement for solo voice and piano; also for SATB chorus and piano in the keys of E-flat major or F major.

Arranged in New York, 1930.

Duration: 2 minutes.

Manuscript copy of the solo voice and piano arrangement in the key of F major is in the William Grant Still and Verna Arvey Papers of the University of Arkansas Libraries, Fayetteville.

Selected Performances

W33a 1953 (May 22): San Jose, CA; Scottish Rite Temple; Robert Lancaster, bass; Richard Corbett, piano. (solo voice and piano version)

W33b 1959 (July 5): Malibu, CA; Pepperdine College Auditorium; Leonardo Watts, baritone. (*See:* WB136.2, WB136.3)

W34 *Fanfare for American War Heroes* (available from William Grant Still Music).

For orchestra.

Composed in Los Angeles, 1943.

Instrumentation: 3 flutes (3rd doubles on piccolo), 2 oboes, English horn, 3 clarinets, 2 bassoons; 4 horns, 3 trumpets, 3 trombones, tuba; timpani, cymbal; harp, strings.

Duration: 1 minute.

Sketch with orchestration notes and a one-page piano reduction are in the William Grant Still and Verna Arvey Papers at the University of Arkansas Libraries, Fayetteville. Date on facsimile of piano reduction is Mar[ch] 30, 1943.

Holograph piano score is in the Library of Congress, deposited for copyright March 30, 1943.

W35 *Fanfare for the 99th Fighter Squadron,* also known as *Chamber Music for Brass and Percussion* (available from William Grant Still Music).

For brass and percussion.

Instrumentation: 4 horns, 3 trumpets, 3 trombones, tuba; timpani, cymbal, snare drum.

Duration: 1 minute.

Fair copy of this 17-measure work is in the William Grant Still and Verna Arvey Papers at the University of Arkansas Libraries, Fayetteville.

W35a **First Performance:** 1945 (July 22): Los Angeles, CA; Hollywood Bowl; Los Angeles Philharmonic Orchestra, Leopold Stokowski, conductor.

W36 *Festive Overture* (Carl Fischer, Inc., New York).

For orchestra.

Composed in Los Angeles, 1944.

Winner, Cincinnati Symphony Orchestra's Golden Jubilee Season Composition Competition.

Dedication on the holograph says, "To my friend, Rudolph Dunbar."

Dedicated to the memory of Eugene Goossens in the published version.

Instrumentation: 3 flutes (3rd doubles on piccolo), 2 oboes, English horn, 2 clarinets (bass clarinet), 2 bassoons; 4 horns, 3 trumpets (Harmon mutes), 3 trombones, tuba; timpani, snare drum, military drum, marimba, chime, bells, xylophone, resonator bells; harp, celesta, strings.

Duration: 10 minutes.
Autograph with orchestration notes and revisions is in the William Grant Still and Verna Arvey Papers at the University of Arkansas Libraries, Fayetteville.

W36a **First Performance:** 1945 (January 19, 20): Cincinnati, OH; Music Hall; Cincinnati Symphony Orchestra, Eugene Goossens, conductor.

Selected Performances

W36b 1945 (November 19): Paris, France; Théâtre des Champs-Élysées; Orchestre National, Rudolph Dunbar, conductor.

W36c 1945 (December 18): Denver, CO; Denver Municipal Auditorium; Denver Symphony Orchestra, Saul Caston, conductor.

W36d 1946 (August 8): Los Angeles, CA; Hollywood Bowl; Hollywood Bowl Symphony Orchestra, Izler Solomon, guest conductor.

W36e 1947 (April 3): New York, NY; Carnegie Hall; New York Philharmonic-Symphony Orchestra, Leopold Stokowski, conductor.

W36f 1964 (October 24, 25): Indianapolis, IN; Clowes Hall; Indianapolis Symphony Orchestra, Izler Solomon, conductor.

W36g 1966 (March 29): Tucson, AZ; University Auditorium; Tucson Symphony Orchestra, William Grant Still, guest conductor.

W36h 1966 (May 1): Nashville, TN; Fisk University, Fisk Memorial Chapel; Nashville Symphony Orchestra, William L. Dawson, guest conductor.

W36i 1967 (April 1): Los Angeles, CA; Music Center; Los Angeles Philharmonic Orchestra, James K. Guthrie, conductor.

W36j 1968 (February 12): Seattle, WA; Seattle Center Opera House; Seattle Youth Symphony, William Grant Still, guest conductor. (*See:* WB154.1)

W36k 1968 (April 16): New Orleans, LA; Tulane University, McAlister Auditorium; New Orleans Philharmonic-Symphony Orchestra, Werner Torkanowsky, conductor. (*See also:* WB117.18)

W36l 1972 (February 24): Petersburg, VA; Virginia Hall; Richmond Symphony, Leon Thompson, conductor.

W36m 1972 (May 21): Los Angeles, CA; Music Center; Los Angeles Philharmonic Orchestra, Zubin Mehta, conductor.

W36n 1973 (February 18): Los Angeles, CA; Scottish Rite Cathedral; Southeast Symphony Orchestra, Louis Palange, conductor.

W36o 1973 (February 25): Detroit, MI; Wayne County Community Arts Auditorium; Detroit Metropolitan Orchestra, Charles Sumner, conductor. (*See:* WB155.6)

W36p 1974 (February 24): New York, NY; Avery Fisher Hall; Symphony of the New World, Kermit Moore, conductor.

W36q 1975 (March 24): New York, NY: Avery Fisher Hall; New York Philharmonic-Symphony Orchestra, Leon Barzin, conductor.

W36r 1976 (February 22): Charleston, WV; Municipal Auditorium; Charleston Symphony Orchestra, Leon Thompson, guest conductor.

W36s 1981 (May 22): New Orleans, LA; New Orleans Theatre of the Performing Arts; New Orleans Philharmonic-Symphony Orchestra, Andrew Massey, conductor.

Bibliography

WB36.1 *A Half Century of Golden Music*. Cincinnati: Cincinnati Symphony Orchestra, 1944.

Booklet published in commemoration of the Golden Jubilee Year of the Cincinnati Symphony Orchestra. Background to Still's composition *Festive Overture* is included. "The prize-winning composition . . . which was written and scored in the space of a few weeks, has a definite American flavor. It bespeaks the pride of the composer in his native land, the warmth of the American people, the grandeur of scenic America."

WB36.2 Walker, George G. "The Negro Community." *Arkansas Democrat*, December 31, 1944.

Announcement with highlights of his career that Still has received a $1000 war bond as first prize (for *Festive Overture*) in a competition sponsored by the Cincinnati Symphony Orchestra.

WB36.3 Bell, Eleanor. "Prize Winning Overture Given World Premiere." *Cincinnati Post*, January 20, 1945.

Review of the January 19, 1945, performance of the Cincinnati Symphony Orchestra. "[*Festive Overture*] is colorful writing, sometimes brilliant and grand. There is nothing to offend the reactionaries, which may mean that it is not aggressive enough to be important."

WB36.4 Hess, Howard W. "Symphony Program Displays Varied Instrumentation Styles." *Cincinnati Times-Star*, January 20, 1945.

Review of the January 19, 1945, performance of the Cincinnati Symphony Orchestra. "The prize-winning Still overture caught the composer in a studious rather than inspired mood. The work is good; its instrumentation is solid, with a short, spirited, first section; an all too short slow movement (considering that the theme of that section was the best) and an over-extended last part."

WB36.5 Leighton, Mary. "Symphony Concert." *Cincinnati Enquirer*, January 20, 1945.

Review of the January 19, 1945, performance of the Cincinnati Symphony Orchestra. "I find [*Festive Overture*] pleasant enough and a deserving account of Mr. Still's acclaimed talent, but not a distinguished one. . . . Its nature is not jubilant, however—in fact I found it somewhat nostalgic in cast. It would make effective background music for a visual medium, perhaps a movie or some kind of show. It is not too stirring melodically, but it does move the listener by harmonic richness, mood coloring and admirably pointed scoring that heightens it appeal."

WB36.6 Jones, Isabel Morse. "Conductor, Soloist Win Bowl Favor." *Los Angeles Times*, August 9, 1946.

Review of the August 8, 1946, performance of the Hollywood Bowl Symphony. "It [*Festive Overture*] is gay and lighthearted for the most part, but there is a moment of lament before he continues with a joyous mood. The work is one of Still's best and shows solid advance in orchestration."

WB36.7 Norton, Mildred. "Music Reviews." Los Angeles *Daily News*, August 9, 1946.

Review of the August 8, 1946, performance of the Hollywood Bowl Symphony. "William Grant Still's *Festive Overture* is an engaging work, with a strong lyric strain despite its active rhythmic interest."

WB36.8   Downes, Olin. "Stokowski Offers Music for Easter." *New York Times*, April 4, 1947.

Review of the April 3, 1947, performance of the New York Philharmonic-Symphony Orchestra. "William Grant Still's *Festival* [sic] *Overture* was heard for the first time in this city, and was welcomed. . . . The score is well orchestrated and ingeniously developed. It sounds well and it betokens increasing mastery on the part of the composer."

WB36.9   Bohm, Jerome D. "Philharmonic." *New York Herald Tribune*, April 5, 1947.

"It [*Festive Overture*] is a well-made, effectively orchestrated product, its melodic substance being of a kind which should make its addition to the music performed at 'pops' concerts assured. It was warmly received by last night's audience."

WB36.10   Simon, Robert A. "Musical Events." *New Yorker* 23 (April 12, 1947): 94-97.

"The occasion was not entirely without its novelty, for it included the local première of William Grant Still's *Festive Overture*, which won first prize two years ago in a Cincinnati Symphony Orchestra competition for short overtures by American composers. Mr. Still's winner proved to be tuneful, handsomely orchestrated, and brisk."

WB36.11   Butler, Henry. "Symphony 'A Joy' in 2d Pair." *Indianapolis Times*, October 25, 1964, p. 32.

"This cheerful, mildly syncopated work [*Festive Overture*] . . . holds up well. It's nicely scored, cheerful and bouncy."

WB36.12   Patrick, Corbin. "Symphony and Soloist Dazzling in Concerto." *Indianapolis Star*, October 25, 1964.

"[*Festive Overture*] . . . is a stream of charming melody in which the composer makes discreet use of a wide range of percussion instruments."

WB36.13   Pavillard, Dan. "Mezzo-Soprano Thebom Thrills Capacity Audience." *Tucson Daily Citizen*, March 30, 1966, p. 26.

Review of the March 29, 1966, performance of the Tucson Symphony Orchestra. "Dr. William Grant Still of Los Angeles was given the baton by conductor Frederic Balazs to conduct his own composition *A Festive Overture*. The selection, programmed to honor Still for his 70th birthday, is unmistakably modern and distinctively American in both its rhythms and orchestration. Still is considered a major contemporary composer and has received numerous accolades from critics and musicians alike. The work is permeated with a light-hearted, half-martial air that opens as bright as sunshine and ends in radiance. The brass supplies support for a flowing melody line carried in the string section."

WB36.14   Saltzberg, Geraldine. "Soloist's Voice Highlights Tucson Symphony Concert." *Arizona Daily Star*, March 30, 1966.

Review of the March 29, 1966, performance of the Tucson Symphony Orchestra. "*A Festive Overture* by William Grant Still, which the composer conducted himself, was scheduled to honor his 70th anniversary year. It received hearty audience acclaim as well as the approval of the orchestra, especially winds and brasses, the work is nevertheless lyrical and melodious."

WB36.15   Nicholas, Louis. "Fisk Music Fitting Centennial End." *Nashville Tennessean*, May 2, 1966, p. 15.

Review of the May 1, 1966, performance of the Nashville Symphony Orchestra, which included *A Festive Overture*. "Still's thickly scored overture was thematically attractive, and had lively and contemplative moods nicely contrasted."

WB36.16 Zepernick, Werner. "Fisk Festival Closes With Negro Symphonic Works." *Nashville Banner*, May 3, 1966, p. 3.

Review of the May 1, 1966, performance of the Nashville Symphony Orchestra. "The concert began with *A Festive Overture* by William Grant Still. This prize-winning work, never heard here before, was first performed in 1945. It is a pleasant-sounding, though somewhat meandering composition of considerable melodic interest. It makes intensive use of percussion instruments."

WB36.17 Dufour, Charles L. "All-Still Performance Offers Happy Evening." *New Orleans States-Item*, April 17, 1968.

Review of the April 16, 1968, performance of the New Orleans Philharmonic-Symphony Orchestra, which included five Still compositions: *Festive Overture*, *Afro-American Symphony*, *Old California*, *Levee Land* and *A New Orleans Street* (both excerpts from the suite *From The South*), and *Plain-Chant for America*. "It is pleasant, easy, graceful music, completely traditional in approach. But inside the framework of the conventional, composer Still has exercised originality. Albeit non-taxing to the listeners, Mr. Still's rhythms and readily discernable melodic lines do not obscure in any way the solid substance of his music nor diminish his considerable stature among living American composers."

WB36.18 Hauri, Erin. "New Conductor Leads San Jose Symphony." *Palo Alto Times*, May 15, 1970.

Review of the May 14, 1970, performance of the San Jose Symphony. "William Grant Still's *Festive Overture* was far better suited to Guthrie's fanfare approach. He was able to realize all the humor of the work, while maintaining amazing control of the rhythmic and metrical irregularities. What with the klip klop of the xylophone and violins a-swaying, the orchestra successfully depicted the colorful Americana imagery of yesterday."

WB36.19 Morgan, Marta. "Variety Abounds At S. J. Symphony Concert." *San Jose News*, May 15, 1970, p. 45.

Review of the May 14, 1970, performance of the San Jose Symphony. "Dr. Still's *Festive Overture* is an intelligently constructed score, rich in melodic content and harmonic invention. His musical idiom is perhaps a little old-fashioned in this age of harsh cacophonies and raucous sounds, but it is refreshingly straightforward and to the point. The composer, who was present, was given a standing ovation by audience and orchestra alike."

WB36.20 Bernheimer, Martin. "Zubin Mehta Leads 'Tribute'." *Los Angeles Times*, May 23, 1972, sec. 4, p. 11.

Review of the May 21 performance of the Los Angeles Philharmonic Orchestra, Zubin Mehta, conductor. "Mehta conducted a spirited performance of William Grant Still's sensitively crafted *Festive Overture* (1945). . . . The concert left the incidental impression that no black composer today is concerning himself with the 'serious' avant garde. I refuse to believe it."

WB36.21 Monson, Karen. "Philharmonic in 'Tribute to Black Music.'" *Los Angeles Herald-Examiner*, May 23, 1972.

Review of the May 21 performance of the Los Angeles Philharmonic Orchestra, Zubin Mehta, conductor. "William Grant Still, the first black man to conduct an American symphony orchestra . . . was in the audience to acknowledge the applause for his bright, well-crafted *Festive Overture*. . . . This "Tribute" was billed as the 'first annual' . . . and one hopes that subsequent 'annuals' will be met with as much enthusiasm."

WB36.22 Kimball, Robert. "Symphony of New World Plays Black Composers." *New York Post*, February 25, 1974.

Review of the February 24, 1974, performance of the Symphony of the New World, Kermit Moore, conductor. "Two of the mere dozen black composers who have been recorded at all are William Grant Still and Howard Swanson. Still was represented yesterday by his *Festive Overture*, a jubilant, exciting work which had won a special contest sponsored by the Cincinnati Symphony in 1945."

WB36.23 Bowers, Violet George. "Program Notes." May 22, 1981. New Orleans Philharmonic-Symphony Orchestra.

Program notes for the May 22, 1981, performance of the New Orleans Symphony Orchestra. The program included Still's *Festive Overture*. "Mr. Still's music will always enrich lives because he was always striving to compose music that everyone would understand, enjoy, and appreciate. The prime motivating factor in his life was his love of God, his people, and humanity. Mr. Still has made extraordinary contributions to the literature of symphonic music, opera, ballet, chamber songs and solo works. Today William Grant Still's music is played around the world."

W37 *Five Animal Sketches* (Silver Burdett, New York, 1952, in *Music for Early Childhood,* pp. 49-53, New Music Horizons Series; available from William Grant Still Music).

For piano solo.

Composed in Los Angeles, 1951.

Contents of the published group: I. Camel, II. Bear, III. Horse, IV. Lamb, V. Elephant.

Contents of the autograph: I. Swan (Graceful Swan), II. Camel (also titled Bear, then Clumsy Bear), III. Chipmunk (Busy Chipmunk), IV. Bear (also titled Camel, then Swaying Camel), V. Horse (Galloping Horse),
VI. Lamb (Gamboling Lamb), VII. Mischievous Monkey, VIII. Elephant (Pacing Pachyderm).

Autograph fair copy with revisions for the eight short character pieces listed above and sketches are in the William Grant Still and Verna Arvey Papers at the University of Arkansas Libraries, Fayetteville.

W38 *Folk Suite for Band* (Bourne Company, Inc., 1967; available from William Grant Still Music).

Spiritual arrangements for band.

Contents: I. Get on Board, Little Children, II. Deep River, III. The Old Ark's a Moverin, IV. Sinner, Please Don't Let This Harvest Pass.

Autograph location unknown.

W38a **First Performance:** 1963 (August 18): Los Angeles, CA; MacArthur Park; Los Angeles Bureau of Music Symphonic Band, Dale Eymann, conductor.

Selected Performance

W38b 1974 (July 4): New York, NY; Damrosch Park; Goldman Band, Richard Franko Goldman, conductor. (I, II)

W39 ***Folk Suite No. 1*** (available from William Grant Still Music).
Folk song arrangements for flute, string quartet, and piano; *Bambalelé* has been arranged by the composer for violin or viola and piano.
Composed in Los Angeles, 1962.
Contents: I. Bambalelé e Espingarda Pá Pá Pá, II. Sometimes I Feel Like A Motherless Child, III. Two Hebraic Songs: Artsah Alinu and Ayzeh Peleh.
Program notes by the composer provide information about these selections:
    I. "[*Bambalelé* is] an Embolada from the State of Pernambuco in the North of Brazil: that is to say, a popular folk song with marked Negro influence. . . . its syncopated rhythms give it an insouciant and lilting character. The second melody . . . may be compared to the *Samba* of the South of Brazil, because of its lively rhythms."
    II. "Among the most haunting of all North American Negro Spirituals is this memorable tune, born of loneliness, frustration, hopelessness."
    III. "These Hebraic Songs, to both of which was danced the Hora, are of a different character due to their different racial origin."
Autograph with revisions is in the William Grant Still and Verna Arvey Papers at the University of Arkansas Libraries, Fayetteville.

W40 ***Folk Suite No. 2*** (available from William Grant Still Music).
Folk song arrangements for flute, clarinet, cello, and harp (or piano).
Composed in Los Angeles, 1962.
Dedicated to Dr. and Mrs. Fabien Sevitzky.
Contents: I. El Zapatero (The Shoemaker), II. Mol'e, III. Chink, Pink, Honey, IV. Mom'selle Zizi, V. Peruvian Melody.
Program notes by the composer provide the following information:
    I. "From the days of the Spanish occupation of the State of California comes this spirited little song. It tells the story of a shoemaker."
    II. "This plaintive song [from Peru] . . . has to do with a tree called 'the false pepper tree.'" (*See:* W88, W101)
    III. "(The Bean Picker's Song) Louisiana, U.S.A., The women who pick beans in the fields have devised these nonsense syllables."
    IV. "This memorable Creole melody [from Louisiana] strongly influenced by the music of the Frenchmen who settled in Louisiana."
    V. "In contrast to the previous Peruvian song (II. Mol'e), this one is a lively tune customarily played on flutes."
Autograph sketches of all five pieces and a fair copy made by Verna Arvey of the full score with piano and instrumental parts (except harp) for sections I, II, IV, V are in the William Grant Still and Verna Arvey Papers at the University of Arkansas Libraries, Fayetteville. Autograph location for III unknown.

Selected Performance

W40a 1984 (February 18): Fayetteville, AR; University of Arkansas, Fine Arts Center Concert Hall; Leonard Garrison, flute; Robert Umiker, clarinet; Samuel Magill, cello; Arthur Tollefson, piano.

W41 ***Folk Suite No. 3*** (available from William Grant Still Music).
Folk song arrangements for flute, oboe (originally clarinet), bassoon, and piano.
Composed in Los Angeles, 1962.
Contents: I. An Inca Dance (Peru), II. An Inca Song (Yaravi: Peru), III. Bow and Arrow Dance (Santa Domingo Pueblo, New Mexico).
Program notes by the composer provide the following information:

I. "Rhythms similar to this appear in the music of the North American Indians, also in certain African music."
II. "In contrast is this simple melody, in the style of a Yaravi. No more nostalgic songs have been derived than the Yaravis of Peru's ancient people." (*See:* W101)
III. "Following the Winter Solstice ceremony, the Shiwana (men masked and dressed like supernatural beings) dance all day for the people, to bring rain to their crops."

Autograph sketches are in the William Grant Still and Verna Arvey Papers at the University of Arkansas Libraries, Fayetteville.

W42 *Folk Suite No. 4* (available from William Grant Still Music).
Folk song arrangements for flute, clarinet, cello, and piano.
Composed in Los Angeles, 1962.
Contents: I. El Monigote (Venezuela), II. Anda Buscando de Rosa en Rosa (Mexico), III. Tayêras (Brazil).
Duration: 6 minutes, 41 seconds.
Program notes on the fair copy (by Arvey from Still's notes):
I. "'El Monigote,' though speaking of a grotesque puppet, is in the form of a waltz."
II. "This haunting melody . . . is still sung in Mexico. 'I am,' say the words, 'the worthless butterfly that goes flying through the region, seeking from rose to rose the soft breath of a passion.[']"
III. "Brazil's Negro folk singers have given us 'Tayêras,' a religious song corresponding to the Negro Spirituals of North America, but more vivacious. The Tayêras are three women, each one of whom sings a couplet and is answered by the trio singing the refrain."

Autograph sketches by the composer and a fair copy of the score and parts made by Verna Arvey are in the William Grant Still and Verna Arvey Papers at the University of Arkansas Libraries, Fayetteville.

Selected Performance

W42a 1984 (February 18): Fayetteville, AR; University of Arkansas, Fine Arts Center Concert Hall; Leonard Garrison, flute; Robert Umiker, clarinet; Samuel Magill, cello; Arthur Tollefson, piano.

W43 *Four Indigenous Portraits* (available from William Grant Still Music).
For flute and string quartet; also for flute and string orchestra.
Composed in Los Angeles, 1956.
Dedication on a fair copy says, . . . to "our dear friend, Bessie Lawson Blackman, who has devoted her life to helping others."
Contents: I. Slowly: North American Negro, II. Gracefully: South American Negro, III. Slowly: South American Indian, IV. Vigorously: North American Indian.
The manuscript contains the following information on the derivation of the themes used by the composer:
I. "An original theme in the style of a Spiritual."
II. "Based on folk themes of the Brazilian Negro, collected by Elsie Houston."
III. "Based on folk themes of Brazilian and Peruvian Indians."
IV. "An original theme in the style of Indian folk music."
Duration: approximately 10 to 13 minutes.

Fair copies of string parts in the William Grant Still and Verna Arvey Papers at the University of Arkansas Libraries, Fayetteville, indicate that this piece was prepared, in addition to the quartet version, for flute and string orchestra. The Still and Arvey Papers also include a manuscript fair copy of the score for the string quartet and flute version signed by the composer and facsimiles of the parts for flute, violin I, violin II, viola, and cello.
Family papers indicate that this work was "discarded by the composer."
Aboriginal Dance from *Four Indigenous Portraits* is in The William Grant Still Estate.

W44 ***Four Octavo Songs*** (Gemini Press, Inc., 1977, numbers GP-405, GP-406, GP-407, GP-408, Gemini Choral Series; sole selling agents, Alexander Broude, Inc., New York; Gemini, Music Division of the Pilgrim Press, New York, 1981; available from William Grant Still Music).
For SATB chorus and piano; *The Blind Man* also arranged for SSA and SATB chorus with tenor solo and piano.
Text by Judith Anne (Still) Headlee for *Toward Distant Shores*.
Contents: I. Ev'ry Time I Feel the Spirit (*See:* W33), II. The Blind Man, III. Toward Distant Shores, IV. Where Shall I Be? (*See also:* W84)
Original copy of the published octavo edition of *Toward Distant Shores* is in the William Grant Still and Verna Arvey Papers at the University of Arkansas Libraries, Fayetteville.
Autograph locations unknown.

W45 ***From a Lost Continent*** (available from William Grant Still Music).
Suite for chorus and piano; also for chorus and orchestra.
Composed in Los Angeles, 1948.
Text consists of syllables only (see composer's notes below).
Dedicated to the "Gordons of Berkeley."
Contents of autograph version: I. Song of Worship, II. Song for Dancers, III. Song of Yearning, IV. Song of Magic, V. [no title].
Instrumentation for orchestra: Soprano and tenor soloists and SATB chorus with 2 flutes, 1 oboe, 2 clarinets, 2 bassoons; (no brass); timpani, bells, chime, triangle, maracas, snare drum, tom-tom, cymbals; harp, strings.
Duration: 15 minutes.
The composer's notes provide the following insights into the intent of this piece: "My interest in the legend of Mo, the continent said to have been engulfed in the Pacific Ocean eons past, caused me to attempt this imaginative concept of the music of that age. To impart archaic feeling and avoid incongruity, special syllables are used instead of a text in English."
Example of text: "I-To-A Me di-Ra Su-le Ta-Mo." Composer's inscription: "they enable the music to present its message more clearly."
Autograph fair copy of the piano vocal score, sketches, and sketches of the version for orchestra are in the William Grant Still and Verna Arvey Papers at the University of Arkansas Libraries, Fayetteville.

W45a **First Performance:** 1953 (May 22): San Jose, CA; Scottish Rite Temple; The Choral Guild of San Jose: Yvonne Long, soprano; Theodore Simmons, tenor; Barbara Simmons, piano; James Pelkey and Bernard Woods, percussion; LeRoy V. Brant, conductor.

Selected Performances

W45b 1954 (May 23): Saratoga, CA; Villa Montalvo; The Choral Guild of San

Jose: Theodore Simmons, tenor; Melita Franusich, soprano; Jean Pasmore, contralto; Barbara Simmons, piano; James Pelkey and William Pedigo, percussion; LeRoy V. Brant, conductor.

W45c 1955 (March 27): Brussels, Institut National Belge de Radiodiffusion (INR) (Flemish Divison).

W45d 1965 (May 7): Los Angeles, CA; Second Baptist Church; Second Baptist Church Choir, John Shaw, director.

W45e 1972 (April 6): Far Rockaway, NY; Bethel A.M.E. Church; North Carolina A. & T. State University Choir, Dr. Howard T. Pearsall, conductor.

W45f 1976 (June 6): New York, NY; Lincoln Center, Alice Tully Hall; Triad Chorale and Chuck Davis Dance Company, Noel Da Costa, director; Linda Hardwick, soprano; Walter Hight, tenor. (*See:* WB144.8)

W45g 1978 (July 22): Washington, DC; Frederick Douglass National Historic Site at Cedar Hill; Afro-American Chorale, J. Weldon Norris, director.

Bibliography

WB45.1 "Keys of City Presented to Composer." *San Jose Mercury-News*, May 24, 1953.

Article describing activities associated with the premiere performance of *From A Lost Continent*, on which occasion Still was presented the keys to the city of San Jose. "[Still] described Barbara Simmons' interpretation of the intricate piano scores as highly sympathetic. 'It seemed to me to be a complete expression of my feelings and thoughts in the composing of the work,' Dr. Still added."

W46 ***From the Black Belt*** (Carl Fischer, Inc., New York, 1946, no. C117).
Suite for chamber orchestra; also for full orchestra.
Composed in New York, 1924.
Contents: I. Li'l' Scamp, II. Honeysuckle, III. Dance, IV. Mah Bones is Creakin', V. Blue, VI. Brown Girl, VII. Clap Yo' Han's.
First performance program lists movements as I. Dance, II. Blue, III. Dance, IV. Serenade, V. Sorrow Song, VI. Des Keep on Shovin' (variant of title in review: "Jes Keep on Shovin'").
Instrumentation for chamber orchestra (does not include movement VI): 2 flutes, 1 oboe, 3 clarinets, bassoon; 3 horns, 3 trumpets (Harmon and fiber mutes); timpani, vibraphone, percussion; harp, strings.
Duration: approximately 20 minutes.
Holograph lead sheet is in the Library of Congress, deposited for copyright November 3, 1941.
Autograph location of full score unknown.

W46a **First Performance:** 1927 (March 20): New York, NY; Henry Miller Theatre; Barrère Little Symphony Orchestra, Georges Barrère, conductor.

Selected Performances

W46b 1932 (December 4): New York, NY; Civic Repertory Theatre; Barrère Little Symphony Orchestra, Georges Barrère, conductor.

W46c 1933 (May 3): Rochester, NY; Kilbourn Hall; Eastman School Little Symphony, Karl D. Van Hoesen, conductor.

W46d 1935 (February 17): New York, NY; American Museum of Natural History; Greenwich Sinfonietta, Gerald McGarrahan, conductor.

W46e 1935 (June 11): Denver, CO; Elitch Gardens Theatre; Pro Musica Concert, Small Orchestra of Denver musicians, Nicholas Slonimsky, guest conductor.

W46f 1936 (December 13): Los Angeles, CA; Pacific Institute Concert Hall; Pacific Institute Symphony Orchestra, Constantin Bakaleinikoff, conductor.

W46g 1938 (August 27): Bogotá, Columbia; Teatro de Colón; Orquesta Sinfónica Nacional, Nicholas Slonimsky, guest conductor.

W46h 1943 (July 25): Los Angeles, CA; Hollywood Bowl; Los Angeles Philharmonic Orchestra, Vladimir Bakaleinikoff, conductor, Richard Tetley-Kardos, piano.

W46i 1947 (May 3, 4, 5): Charleston, WV; Charleston Symphony Orchestra, Antonio Modarelli, conductor.

W46j 1952 (December 7): Charleston, WV; West Virginia State College, College Auditorium; Charleston Symphony Orchestra, Leon Thompson, guest conductor.

W46k 1973 (February 18): Los Angeles, CA; Scottish Rite Cathedral; Southeast Symphony Orchestra, Louis Palange, conductor.

Bibliography

WB46.1 Perkins, F.D. "Little Symphony Program Varied In Second Recital." *New York Herald Tribune*, March 21, 1927.
"Mr. Barrère warned his hearers that Mr. Still was a pupil of Edgard Varèse, but his music, after starting with a suggestion of jazz, seemed unlikely to shock conservative ears. Mr. Still's opening 'dance' closed abruptly at about the sixth measure. The ensuing music proved tuneful and showed skill in the use of instrumental sonorities while not seeming, itself, of the highest importance. This last section, 'Jes' keep on shovin' was another fragment, closing a likable piece."

WB46.2 Sabin, Stewart B. "Music." *Rochester Democrat and Chronicle*, May 4, 1933.
Review of the May 3, 1933, performance of the Eastman School Little Symphony. "This [*From the Black Belt*] is fragmentary music, appealing by humor and sentimentality, as well as by ingratiating instrumentation. People at large will like to hear it as did the audience of last night. Mr. Still heard it, too, and was boisterously applauded at its close."

WB46.3 Saunders, Richard D. "New Works Offered for Recital Fans." *Hollywood Citizen-News* December 14, 1936.
Review of the December 13, 1936, performance of the Pacific Institute Symphony Orchestra. "Another new work, *From The Black Belt*, by William Grant Still, was a series of seven short pieces, charmingly capturing the Southern Negro spirit. To secure this the harmony was necessarily banal, but the composer achieved color through well handled instrumentation. He made the most of the sentimental items, *Honeysuckle, Blue* and *Brown Girl*, but the livelier episodes, *Li'l' Scamp, Dance* and *Mah Bones is Creakin'* were really overshort, and could have been developed to more advantage. The finale, *Clap yo' Han's*, was purely jazz."

WB46.4 Jones, Isabel Morse. "Bakaleinikoff Leads Bowl." *Los Angeles Times*, July 26, 1943.
Review of the July 25 performance of the Los Angeles Philharmonic Orchestra. "The melodies [of *From the Black Belt*] are characteristic but the instrumentation and the choral coloring belong to Still. This style of his, which is so subtle a refinement that it is difficult to define, might be termed American impressionistic."

WB46.5 Thompson, Leon. "Black Belt Suite." (Program Notes for the December 7, 1952, performance of *From The Black Belt* by the Charleston Symphony Orchestra at the West Virginia State College Auditorium).

"*From the Black Belt* is a suite of seven short orchestral pieces, written frankly to amuse and to please those who listen to them. Because the first episode is loud and vigorous, one might suppose that this fellow, who delights in playing childish pranks, is a big scamp. But the aptness of the title is not determined by the volume of sound, for it is the brevity of the piece and unexpected ending which tells us that he is a *Li'l' Scamp*. In the second piece, the composer has tried to give a musical impression of the saccharine odor of the *Honeysuckle*. The third title, *Dance*, is self-explanatory. In the fourth episode, an old man afflicted with rheumatism, complains loudly that *Mah Bones Is Creakin'*. A plaintive melody suggestive of the Blues songs of the southern Negro appears in the fifth section, *Blue*, while the sixth, *Brown Girl*, is a tone picture of [a] lovely mulatto girl. Last comes *Clap Yo' Han's*, in which the participants in a dancing game for children clap their hands rhythmically."

W47 *From the Delta* (Leeds, New York, 1947; available from William Grant Still Music).

For band; *Work Song From the Delta* (I) scored for strings and percussion (available from William Grant Still Music).

Composed in Los Angeles, 1945.

Contents: I. Moderately: Work Song, II. Spiritual, III. Dance.

Instrumentation: flutes, piccolo, 2 oboes, 3 clarinets (including clarinet in E-flat and bass clarinet), 2 bassoons, contrabassoon and string bass; 4 saxophones; 4 horns, 2 trumpets and/or 3 cornets, 3 trombones, euphonium, tuba; timpani, cymbals, snare drum, bass drum, wire brush.

Duration: 8 minutes.

Holograph sketch dated January 1945 with instrumentation notes is in the William Grant Still and Verna Arvey Papers at the University of Arkansas Libraries, Fayetteville.

W47a **First Performance:** 1947 (June 13): New York, NY; Central Park Mall; Goldman Band, Richard Franko Goldman, conductor.

Selected Performances

W47b 1949 (January 16): Oberlin, OH; Oberlin Conservatory of Music, Finney Memorial Chapel; Conservatory Symphony Band, Arthur L. Williams, director.

W47c 1952 (March 30): Oberlin, OH; Oberlin Conservatory of Music, Warner Concert Hall; Conservatory Symphony Band, Arthur L. Williams, director.

W47d 1956 (July 22): New York, NY; Central Park; Goldman Band, Richard Franko Goldman, conductor.

W47e 1965 (July 1, 2): Brooklyn, NY; Prospect Park; Goldman Band, Richard Franko Goldman, conductor.

W47f 1967 (July 20): New York, NY; Central Park; Goldman Band, Richard Franko Goldman, conductor.

W47g 1971 (February 13): Orangeburg, SC; South Carolina State College, Smith-Hammond-Middleton Memorial Center; South Carolina All-State College Band, William Grant Still, guest conductor.

W47h 1976 (March 20): Cambridge, MA; Harvard University, Sanders Theatre; Harvard University Concert Band, Thomas G. Everett, conductor.

W47i 1992 (November 5): Fayetteville, AR; Walton Arts Center; University of Arkansas Band, Chalon Ragsdale, conductor.

Bibliography

WB47.1 Kastendieck, Miles. "Goldman Band Opens at Mall." *New York Journal American*, June 14, 1947.
"Still's *From the Delta* had its premiere. . . . The three parts . . . lived up to their designations: *Work Song*, *Spiritual*, and *Dance*. Of these, the *Dance* was a disappointment, but the others had persuasive qualities."

WB47.2 Perkins, Francis D. "Goldman Band." *New York Herald Tribune*, June 14, 1947.
"Mr. Still's *From the Delta* is in three parts, *Work Song*, *Spiritual*, and *Dance*. . . . With considerable appeal and effectiveness, the work, in the treatments of its tunes, does not always escape conventionality; the scoring, often skilled, is sometimes weighty."

WB47.3 Hague, Robert A. "Dr. Goldman Presents Band Concert No. 1697." *PM* (New York), June 16, 1947.
"Containing much skillful and expressive writing for woodwinds and brasses, it [*From the Delta*] is an engaging and appealing work, and should prove a popular addition to band repertoire."

WB47.4 Simon, Robert A. "Musical Events." *New Yorker* 23 (June 28, 1947): 60.
Includes a review of the June 13 performance of the Goldman Band.
"William Grant Still's attractive *From the Delta* . . . was ably directed by Richard Franko Goldman, Dr. Goldman's son and the associate conductor of the band."

W48 ***From the Furnace of the Sun,*** additional title: *The Negro in America, A Revue of the Race* (available from William Grant Still Music).
Opera fragment; Scene I: The Black Land.
Inscription on the manuscript says, "Music about 1936."
Text and scenario by Sherwood Trask, New York.
Subject: Abstract concept of Africa.
Instrumentation indicated in the conductor's score: woodwinds, including clarinets; horns, other brass; timpani, woodblock, gourd, tom-tom, cymbals; strings.
Holograph of conductor's score of Scene I, *The Black Land,* with stage directions and vocal parts and facsimile of the complete libretto of 15 scenes by Sherwood Trask are in the William Grant Still and Verna Arvey Papers at the University of Arkansas Libraries, Fayetteville.
An incomplete fair copy of the vocal score with accompaniment by two pianos and orchestration notes in the composer's hand is in The William Grant Still Estate.

W49 ***From the Heart of a Believer*** (conductor's score available from William Grant Still Music).
Poem for orchestra.
Composed in New York, 1927.
Instrumentation: 3 flutes (3rd doubles on piccolo), 2 oboes, English horn, 3 clarinets, 3 bassoons (3rd doubles on contrabassoon); 4 horns, 3 trum-

pets, 3 trombones (small bore trombones preferable), tuba; timpani, drums, cymbals, gong, glockenspiel; celesta, strings.
Duration: 10 minutes.
Autograph conductor's score is in The William Grant Still Estate.

W50 *From the Hearts of Women* (available from William Grant Still Music).
Song cycle for solo voice and piano; soprano with string orchestra and harp; and soprano with string quartet, flute, oboe, and piano.
Composed in Los Angeles, 1959.
Poems by Verna Arvey.
Contents: I. Little Mother (A child talks to her doll), II. Midtide (A woman reaches middle age), III. Coquette or Creole Belle (a young girl enjoys life), IV. Bereft (a mother loses her son).
Duration: 9 minutes.
Autograph fair copies and sketches for the piano vocal version, an autograph for harp and string orchestra, and a facsimile of a final version of the piano vocal score are in the William Grant Still and Verna Arvey Papers at the University of Arkansas Libraries, Fayetteville.

W50a **First Performance:** 1962 (February 19): Los Angeles, CA; Los Angeles State College, Music Hall; William Grant Still Ensemble: William Grant Still, conductor; Pearl Whitelow, soprano; Verna Arvey, piano; Leon Trebacz and Iris Trebacz, violins; Walter Rower, cello; Charles Hubbard, flute; and Arthur Gault, oboe.

Selected Performance

W50b 1964 (August 9): Los Angeles, CA; Second A.M.E. Zion Church; Pearl Whitelow, soprano; Barbara Geyen Sherrill, piano. (version for solo voice and piano)

W51 *From the Journal of a Wanderer* (conductor's score available from William Grant Still Music).
Suite for orchestra in five movements.
Composed in New York, 1924.
Dedicated to Edgard Varèse.
Entry in The North Shore [Illinois] Festival Association's Orchestra Composition Contest, 1926; original title: "With God There is No Failure."
Contents: I. Phantom's Trail, II. Magic Bells, III. Valley of Echoes, IV. Mystic Moon, V. Devil's Hollow.
Instrumentation: 3 flutes (3rd doubles on piccolo), 3 oboes (3rd doubles on English horn), 4 clarinets, 3 bassoons (2nd plays solo on contrabassoon); 4 horns, 3 trumpets, 3 trombones, tuba; timpani, percussion, bells, chimes, triangle, tam-tam, tom-tom, wood block, snare drum, gourd, cymbals; harp, celesta, strings.
Duration: 20 minutes .
Autograph location unknown.

W51a **First Performance:** 1926 (May): Chicago, IL; North Shore Festival, Chicago Symphony Orchestra, Frederick Stock, conductor.

W52 *From the Land of Dreams.*
For three voices and chamber orchestra, in 3 movements.
Composed in New York, 1924.
Dedicated to Edgard Varèse.

The composer's notes printed in a 1925 International Composers' Guild, Inc., program say, "In the first two movements I have sought to depict, or rather to suggest, the flimsiness of dreams which fade before they have taken definite form. The varying moods of these movements may be construed as suggestions of the ever changing scenes which dreams unfold to the dreamer's vision. Some may contend that the last movement is too vigorous to be a part of the composition, but there are vivid dreams with clearly defined outlines. From these we often awake abruptly dwelling, as it were, on the borders of both the realm of fancy and of reality. The three movements are *Lento, Allegretto, Allegro Moderato.* The work is scored for flute, oboe, clarinet, bassoon, horn, viola, cello, double bass, bells, triangle, and three voices (high soprano, soprano, mezzo-soprano) used instrumentally."
Duration: 8 minutes.
Autograph lost (before 1938).

W52a **First Performance:** 1925 (February 8): New York, NY; Aeolian Hall; International Composers' Guild, Vladimir Shavitch, conductor.

Bibliography

WB52.1 Downes, Olin. "Music." *New York Times*, February 9, 1925, p. 15.
"One hoped for better things from Grant Still and his *From the Land of Dreams*, for he knows the rollicking and often original and entertaining music performed at negro revues. But Mr. Varese [*sic*] . . . has driven all that out of him. Is Mr. Still unaware that the cheapest melody in the revues he has orchestrated has more reality and inspiration in it than the curious noises he has manufactured? . . . This is music unprofitable to compose or listen to."

W53 *Gateway to the Temple* (sketches, no date).
Choral episode, inspired by the life of Mirza Ali Muhammad, the Bab.
Text by Verna Arvey.
Arvey's notes suggest that an extended work was planned for tenor and bass soloists, several female voices, and SATB chorus. Arvey's scenario is complete in three pages, ending with "When the lights of brotherhood surround us—God's shining favors are bestowed. etc. etc. etc."
Melodic sketches and preliminary notes on musical form by the composer and a typed scenario (complete) by Verna Arvey are in the William Grant Still and Verna Arvey Papers at the University of Arkansas Libraries, Fayetteville.

W54 *Get on Board* (available from William Grant Still Music).
Spiritual arrangement for chamber ensemble. (*See:* W38, W147)
Instrumentation: flute (piccolo), oboe, clarinet, bassoon, piano, and string quartet.
Manuscript is in the William Grant Still and Verna Arvey Papers at the University of Arkansas Libraries, Fayetteville.
Autograph is in The William Grant Still Estate.

W55 *Glory to the Newborn King* (available from William Grant Still Music).
Spiritual arrangement for SATB chorus, string orchestra, and piano.
Autograph full score is in The William Grant Still Estate.

W56 *Go Get It.*
Popular song.
Recorded under the pseudonym Willy M. Grant.

Composed in New York, about 1923.
Performed by Inez Wallace with orchestra on a recording by The Black Swan Phonograph Company in the 1920s. (*See:* B113)
Autograph location unknown.

W57 ***God's Goin' To Set This World on Fire*** (Holt, Rinehart and Winston, New York, 1968, in *Exploring Music*).
Spiritual arrangement, SAT with piano for a music education textbook.
Facsimile of the performance notes is in the William Grant Still and Verna Arvey Papers at the University of Arkansas Libraries, Fayetteville.
Holograph is in The William Grant Still Estate.

W58 ***Good Night.***
Voice and piano.
Composed at Oberlin College, 1917, while Still was a student there.
"Dedicated to Mr. Bell" [William Service Bell].
Poem by Paul Laurence Dunbar.
Autograph location unknown.

Selected Performances
W58a 1921 (October 21): Newark, NJ; Newark YWCA, Sayre Hall; William Service Bell, baritone; Tourgee DeBose, piano.

W58b 1921 (October 30): New York, NY; St. Mark's Hall; Revella E. Hughes, soprano; James Walker, piano.

W59 ***Grief*** (Oliver Ditson Company, Bryn Mawr, PA, 1955, C 131-41053; for high voice, C 131-41053-2; available from William Grant Still Music).
For voice and piano; also for voice and orchestra.
Composed in Los Angeles, 1953.
Poem by LeRoy V. Brant; text begins "Weeping angel with pinions trailing."
Instrumentation for orchestra: 2 flutes, 2 oboes, 2 clarinets, 2 bassoons; 3 horns, 2 trombones, tuba; celesta, harp, strings.
Published version for high voice is in the William Grant Still and Verna Arvey Papers at the University of Arkansas Libraries, Fayetteville. Inscription on published version: "With humble thanks to God, the source of inspiration."
Autograph copy at one time in the library of LeRoy V. Brant.

W59a **First Performance:** 1954 (May 23): Saratoga, CA; Villa Montalvo; Theodore Simmons, tenor; Barbara Simmons, piano.

Selected Performances
W59b 1963 (April 28): San Jose, CA; Scottish Rite Temple; Ralph Laris, tenor; Arpha MacIntyre, piano.

W59c 1964 (May 24): Los Angeles, CA; First A.M.E. Church; Earl Green, tenor; Jonathan Collins, piano.

W60 ***Hallelujah 'Tis Done.***
Spiritual arrangement for solo voice and piano.
Inscription by Arvey says, "Negro spiritual arr. by WGS."
Fair copy in Verna Arvey's hand is in the William Grant Still and Verna Arvey Papers at the University of Arkansas Libraries, Fayetteville.

W61 ***Here's One*** (John Church Company, Philadelphia, 1941, nos. 30823 and 322-40037; published in *The Etude,* January 1942; SATB chorus and piano version, Theodore Presser Co., Bryn Mawr, PA, n.d.).
Spiritual arrangement for SATB chorus and piano; voice and piano (published in *The Etude*); flute, piano, violins I and II, viola, cello, and bass; voice, string quartet, and paino.
Facsimile of *The Etude* publication for solo voice and piano in E minor and a facsimile of a manuscript transposed to A minor ("for Dr. McPhierson") are in the William Grant Still and Verna Arvey Papers at the University of Arkansas Libraries, Fayctteville.
Holograph of instrumental arrangement is in The William Grant Still Estate.

Selected Performances

W61a 1942 (January 18): New York, NY; Carnegie Chamber Music Hall; Wilson Woodbeck, baritone; pianist not identified.

W61b 1945 (December 16): Los Angeles, CA; Wilshire Ebell Theatre; Louis Kaufman, violin; Annette Kaufman, piano. (Arrangement by Louis Kaufman.)

W61c 1946 (March 15): New York, NY; Town Hall; Louis Kaufman, violin; Paul Meyer, piano. (Arrangement by Louis Kaufman.)

W61d 1953 (May 22): San Jose, CA; Scottish Rite Temple; Robert Lancaster, bass; Richard Corbett, piano.

W61e 1960 (October 29): San Francisco, CA; The Century Club; Norma J. Levister, mezzo-soprano; William Duncan Allen, piano.

W61f 1963 (June 6): New York, NY; St. Martin's Little Theatre; Helen Phillips, soprano; Frederick Bell, piano.

W61g 1969 (October 14): Los Angeles, CA; University of Southern California, Hancock Auditorium; Anthony David Thomas, bass; Leon G. Simmons, piano.

Bibliography

WB61.1 Harford, Margaret. "Louis Kaufman Introduces New Khachaturian Violin Concerto." *Hollywood Citizen-News*, December 17, 1945.
Review of the December 16, 1945, performance of Louis and Annette Kaufman. "Kaufman is consistently interesting. . . . Bringing the beloved Negro Spirituals into the violin repertoire is a very pleasing idea, we think, after hearing . . . Kaufman's own arrangement of Still's *Here's One.*"

WB61.2 L., R. "Kaufman Pleases in Violin Program." *New York Times*, March 16, 1946.
Review of a performance by Louis Kaufman on March 15. "All of these numbers and Mr. Kaufman's own arrangement of William Grant Still's Negro spiritual, *Here's One*, were well accounted for by the player."

WB61.3 Perkins, Francis D. "Louis Kaufman: Violinist Gives Recital at Town Hall." *New York Herald Tribune*, March 16, 1946.
"Mr. Kaufman's own arrangement of William Grant Still's *Here's One* completed a group which provided a pleasing variation from the standard assortment of last-group recital favorites."

W62 ***Highway 1, U.S.A.,*** see also ***A Southern Interlude,*** W146 (available from William Grant Still Music).
Opera in 2 acts, one stage set.

Revised in Los Angeles, 1962; holograph of *A Southern Interlude* dated June, 1942.

Libretto by Verna Arvey.

"Dedicated to Judy [the composer's daughter], Larry [Headlee, her husband], Daniel and Lisa [their son and daughter]."

Setting: an incident in the life of an American family; set in a filling station (gasoline station) near the highway.

For: Cast: Principle roles: baritone, soprano, tenor; Secondary roles: mezzo-soprano, bass; chorus.

The arias, *A Dream Wasted, What Does He Know of Dreams?,* and *You're Wonderful, Mary,* have been performed separately.

Instrumentation: 2 flutes (2nd doubles on piccolo), 2 oboes (2nd doubles on English horn), 2 clarinets (2nd doubles on bass clarinet), 2 bassoons; 4 horns, 2 trumpets, 2 trombones; timpani (2), percussion; harp, strings.

Autograph conductor's score, orchestral parts, and piano vocal score are in The William Grant Still Estate.

W62a **First Performance:** 1963 (May 11): Coral Gables, FL; Coral Gables H.S. Auditorium; University of Miami Opera; Cheryl Claiborne as Mary; Patrick Mathews as Bob; Ben Laney as Nate; Frances Maddaford Whitney as Aunt Lou; Nicholas Shipskie as The Sheriff; Donald Smith as The Doctor; University of Miami Orchestra, Fabien Sevitsky, producer and director; Gordon Bennett, stage director; Clayton Charles and Robert Stoetzer, scenery; Lina Maddaford, coach and ensemble director.

Selected Performances

W62b 1967 (April 30, May 3): Charleston, WV; West Virginia State College, John W. Davis Fine Arts Theatre; Charleston Symphony Orchestra, Leon Thompson, producer and conductor; Carol Bohnert as Mary; James Knorr as Bob; Betty Hamilton as Aunt Lou; Otis Laury as Nate; Reginald Billups as The Sheriff; Harold Bradford as the The Doctor.

W62c 1968 (March 15, 16): Azusa, CA; Citrus College; Citrus College Auditorium; Citrus College Community Opera Association; Phyllis Michell as Mary; John C. Lasher as Bob; Mary Ann Brazzel as Aunt Lou; Thomas Schultz as Nate; Ed Keith as The Sheriff; Harriet Guse; conductor; John Kniest, stage and production director.

W62d 1972 (November 17, 19): Jackson, MS; Municipal Auditorium; Wilma Shakesnider as Mary; Clyde Walker as Bob; Gladys Scott as Aunt Lou; William Brown as Nate; ballet principals: Linda Cleveland, Joseph Gordon, and Hollis Pippins; Jackson State College Chorale, Margaret Harris, conductor; Donald Dorr, designer and director; Sister M. Elise, S.B.S., general director; Willy Patton, sets.

W62e 1974 (April 4, 6): Richmond, VA; Virginia Union University, Wall Auditorium; The Opera Workshop; The University Players; Gail Parker as Mary; Cornell Gaulmon as Bob; Charmaine Sims as Aunt Lou; James Bryant as Nate; Edward Smith as The Sheriff; August Bullock as The Doctor; Elgin Lowe, musical director; William W. Kramer, stage director; Russell Wilson, piano; Denise Bennett, costume design.

W62f 1975 (March 21): Norfolk, VA; Norfolk State College, Chrysler Hall; Renee Williams as Mary; Otis Alexander as Bob; Corliss Fulton as Aunt Lou; Ferman Convington as Nate; Maurice Joyner as The Sheriff; Clarence Sykes as The Doctor; The Norfolk State College Orchestra, Glenn Hull, conductor; Gloria Amos, musical director; Catherine Clarke, stage manager.

W62g 1977 (December 3): New York, NY; Beacon Theatre; National Opera/Ebony; Leavata Johnson as Mary; Arthur Thompson as Bob; William Brown as Nate; Elvira Greene as Aunt Lou; Margaret Harris, conductor; Richard Isaekes, scenic designer; Bennet Avery, costumes and lighting; stage by Franco Gentilesca.

W62h 1979 (November 18-19): Washington, DC; Gateway Theater; Annette Pierson Poulard as Mary; Samuel Bonds as Bob; Teresa Gilmore as Aunt Lou; John LeSane as Nate; Jonathan Hughes as The Sheriff; Starling Hatchett as The Doctor; Southwest Philharmonic, Dingwall Fleary, conductor-director; Harry Poe, co-director dramatic supervision; Thomasena Davis Allen, producer.

Bibliography

WB62.1 Reno, Doris. "Premier Enthralls Audience." *Miami Herald*, May 12, 1963, p. 22A.
Review of the first performance of *Highway 1, U.S.A.* "The music is highly original, yet fits the ordinary material for which it was intended. It is lively, free in spirit, and with a touch of nobility about it. The arias, ensembles, and choral sections were expertly handled. Mr. Still . . . got a standing ovation at the conclusion of the work."

WB62.2 "New Opera Given Miami Premiere." *New York Times*, May 13, 1963.
Brief report on the premiere of *Highway 1, U.S.A.*

WB62.3 Polo, Mark O. "Opera Premiere Scores Sweet Success." *Miami Hurricane*, May 17, 1963, p. 15.
Review of the premiere of *Highway 1, U.S.A.* "On the surface, the work sounds like a Bernstein Broadway musical, but it is much deeper and more complex. Interesting interplay of melodies depict moods of the personalities characterized in this work."

WB62.4 Armstrong, George. "Locally Produced Opera Impressive." *Charleston Daily Mail*, May 1, 1967, p. 17.
Review of the April 30 performance of *Highway 1, U.S.A.*, at West Virginia State College. "*Highway No. 1, U.S.A.* offers some splendid musical moments and is well worth attending. The opera is unmistakably modern, but its dissonances are mild and largely confined to the brief orchestral interludes. It is very singable, and well suited to the voices of the soloists and cast."

WB62.5 Ennis, Bayard F. "*Highway* Credit To W. Va. State College." *Charleston Gazette*, May 7, 1967.
Review of the April 30 and May 3 performances of *Highway 1, U.S.A.*, at West Virginia State College. "In *Highway One, U.S.A.*, Still has in the main abandoned his use of Negro themes to convey his message. In any event, only the second choral number in the final scene conveys the impression of being in the nature of a spiritual or having an origin indigenous to the Negro race. What Still has composed, though notably melodic and outwardly appealing, actually is much deeper in its depiction of the moods and personalities of the characters involved in the opera."

WB62.6 "Citrus College Opera Group Sets Two Performances." *Azusa Herald*, March 14, 1968.

Preview of the West Coast premiere of *Highway 1, U.S.A.* by the Citrus College Community Opera Association, March 15-16, 1968.

WB62.7 Mangum, David. "Opera South's Twin Bill Neatly Written, Executed." Jackson *Clarion-Ledger*, November 18, 1972.
Review of *The Juggler of Our Lady* by Ulysses Kay and *Highway 1, U.S.A.* by Still, operas produced by Opera/South of Jackson, Mississippi. "Opera librettos are rarely narrative marvels and therefore rarely as good as that of *Highway 1*. Conceived in realism and executed with tight simplicity, the story of Bob, Mary, and Bob's no good brother, Nate, is strongly reminiscent of Jesse Hill Ford's short fiction and would have been enough to carry the performance on its own strength. . . . *Highway 1* is soulful, though definitely not the hot buttered variety. It is decently and elegantly expressive of the loves and hates of a good, hardworking American gas station owner, and the rendition of this opera is no small achievement."

WB62.8 Hains, Frank. "On Stage." *Jackson Daily News*, November 20, 1972.
Lengthy review of *The Juggler of Our Lady* by Ulysses Kay and *Highway 1, U.S.A.* by Still. "*Highway 1, U.S.A.* is in its way quite as sentimental as *Juggler*, but far more melodramatic. The music is lush and probably over-cinematic for either the classical or the contemporary taste in 'serious' music, but it has tremendous popular appeal. It's rich in tunes, from a rousing, hand-clapping, revivalistic chorus to lyrical solos and duets, some with a vaguely Porgy-and-Bessish quality. . . . The chorus came into its own in the Still work, with the aforementioned hand-clapper, which was repeated as an encore. . . . The orchestra sounded as well as a pit orchestra has ever sounded in Jackson and maybe at times better."

WB62.9 Hemeter, Mark. "Opera South Opens With 2 Black Works." *New Orleans States-Item*, November 20, 1972.
Review of *The Juggler of Our Lady* by Ulysses Kay and *Highway 1, U.S.A.* by Still. "Mississippi-born Still's slice of 'verismo' Americana about a down-and-out couple who run a filling station charmed more easily than the ambitious Kay work and on the whole, got the better performances. To a tautly melodramatic libretto by Verna Arvey, Still has added music of appealing tunefulness—call it that, and nothing more."

WB62.10 LaRose, Joseph. "Takes bold artistic step." *New Orleans Clarion Herald*, November 30, 1972.
Review of *The Juggler of Our Lady* by Ulysses Kay and *Highway 1, U.S.A.* by Still. "William Grant Still's *Highway 1, U.S.A.* is a worthy dramatic piece about a struggling black couple, who have sacrificed themselves to see the husband's brother through college to honor their mother's dying request. The chorus 'Mary and Bob,' sung by neighbors, extolling the couple's friendliness and goodness, has a sort of gospel-spiritual quality about it. . . . Still's music is appealing, dramatic and melodious. Dorr's staging was highly effective and interesting though the skeletal single room set made a rather bare stage centerpiece."

WB62.11 "Divas in Dixie." *Newsweek* 80 (December 4, 1972): p. 67-68.
Review of *The Juggler of Our Lady* by Ulysses Kay and *Highway 1, U.S.A.* by Still. "Donald Dorr designed and staged both *The Juggler* and Still's *Highway 1, U.S.A.*, which is a far piece from thirteenth-century France. Still the 77-year-old doyan [sic] of American black composers, is much more conventional in his musical approach than Kay, using arias,

duets and ensembles. . . . Demonstrating one of Opera/South's strengths—it's knack of attracting first-rate singers—the cast of *Highway 1* was led by Wilma Shakesnider, Clyde Walker and William Brown (a Jackson State alumnus), all seasoned veterans of opera and concert."

WB62.12 Durrett, C. William. "Jackson." *Opera News* 37 (January 13, 1973): 23.

Review of the November 17, 1972, Opera/South production of *Highway 1, U.S.A.* "[Donald] Dorr's set for *Highway 1* consisted only of an open room with exposed beams, reflecting appropriately the caged feeling that the main characters frequently express. . . . Still's rather lushly romantic score reveals a strong sense of musical characterization. In the major roles, Wilma Shakesnider (Mary) and Clyde Walker (Bob) gave admirable performances, both vocally secure and convincing dramatically. The success of the evening owed much to Margaret Harris, who conducted . . . with an effective blend of spirit and control, and to the Jackson State College Chorale."

WB62.13 Hains, Frank. "Opera/South: All-Black And Hopeful." *High Fidelity/Musical America* (May 1973): 23+.

Article centers on Opera/South and a review of two of its productions—William Grant Still's *Highway 1, U.S.A.* and Ulysses Kay's *The Juggler of Our Lady*. "Still's *Highway 1, U.S.A.* is equally sentimental [as *Juggler*] but far more melodramatic. The music is lush and probably overcinematic for either the classical or the contemporary taste in 'serious' music, but it has tremendous popular appeal. It's rich in tunes, from a rousing, hand-clapping, revivalistic chorus to a vaguely *Porgy-and-Bess*ish quality in some of the solos and duets . . . but in the main is an unusually successful attempt to combine operatic form and popular harmonies."

WB62.14 Griffin, Alison. "Opera Echoes Black History." Richmond *Times-Dispatch*, April 4, 1974, sec. D, p. 7.

Preview of the April 4, 1974, production of *Highway 1, U.S.A.* at Virginia Union University. "In this piece, [Elgin Lowe, musical director] said, 'the music doesn't sound like jazz, nor like classical music—it sounds like American music that is reflective of the historical growth of black people.'"

WB62.15 Morton, Tim. "College's Songs Stimulate." Norfolk *Virginian-Pilot*, March 22, 1975, p. B9.

Review of the March 21, 1975, performance of *Highway 1, U.S.A.* produced by Norfolk State College. "There are problems with the libretto. Some of the lines, unintentionally, came out sounding funny; and there is a plot twist at the end that strains credulity, though not much more than most any Italian opera. The music is fine: persuasive, fitted neatly to the voice, melodic and with blue notes that sharply define character and give variety, and seamlessly connected to the story."

WB62.16 Davis, Peter G. "Opera Ebony In Debut Work." *New York Times*, December 5, 1977.

Review of the New York premiere of *Highway 1, U.S.A.*, performed by National Opera/Ebony at the Beacon Theatre, December 3. "Opera Ebony gave the work a superior production. Arthur Thompson (Bob), Leavata Johnson (Mary) and William Brown (Nate) possess fine, healthy voices and then effectively took every advantage of the music's expressive possibilities. The detailed setting by Richard Isaekes, Franco Gentilesca's economical staging and Margaret Harris's conducting proved to be sympathetically in tune with the material. The opera was prefaced by a performance of Mr. Still's *Afro-American Symphony*, composed in 1930."

WB62.17 Abdul, Raoul. "Reading The Score: Opera Ebony Comes Home." *New York Amsterdam News*, December 17, 1977, sec. D, p. 6.

Review of the New York premiere of *Highway 1, U.S.A*. "Despite the mediocre text by Verna Arvey, the composer has created a work for the musical theatre which gives a great deal of pleasure. It is musically conservative, filled with lovely melodies, and orchestrated with his characteristic technical skill. . . . The performance of the *Afro-American Symphony*, which opened the evening, was a little rough in spots, but nevertheless spirited. But, the large audience which filled the theatre came out to hear the opera. And, they were rewarded with a production which exceeded all expectations."

W63 ***Hiking Song*** (Silver Burdett, possibly published in *The New Music Horizons Series*).
Solo voice and piano for a music education textbook.
Autograph location unknown.

W64 ***How I've Got Dem Twilight Blues.***
Popular song.
Recorded under the pseudonym Willy M. Grant.
Composed in New York, about 1923.
Performed by Josie Miles with orchestra on a recording by The Black Swan Phonograph Company in the 1920s. (*See:* B113)
Autograph location unknown.

W65 ***I Feel Like My Time Ain't Long*** (Theodore Presser Co., Bryn Mawr, PA, 1956, no. 312-40304).
Spiritual arrangement for mixed chorus and piano.
Facsimile of a manuscript for SSATB chorus and piano is in the William Grant Still and Verna Arvey Papers at the University of Arkansas Libraries, Fayetteville.
Holograph is in The William Grant Still Estate.

Selected Performance

W65a 1984 (February 15): Fayetteville, AR; University of Arkansas, Fine Arts Center Concert Hall; University of Arkansas Schola Cantorum

W66 ***I Want To.***
Popular song.
Recorded under the pseudonym Willy M. Grant.
Composed in New York, about 1923.
Performed by Isabelle Washington with Fletcher Henderson, piano, and as a piano solo (by Henderson) on recordings by The Black Swan Phonograph Company in the 1920s. (*See:* B113)
Autograph location unknown.

W67 ***Igama Lo Kusina.***
For SATB chorus, tenor soloist, piano, and drums with hand clapping and foot stomping.
Folk song setting of a melody probably collected by Zora Neale Hurston in the Bahamas.
Composed in Los Angeles, probably 1941. (*See:* W19)

Holograph in a style similar to the settings in *Caribbean Melodies* is in the William Grant Still and Verna Arvey Papers at the University of Arkansas Libraries, Fayetteville.

W68 ***I'm Pickin' My Last Row of Cotton*** (published as *Bayou Home*, Robbins Music Corporation, 1944, H-2786-4; available from William Grant Still Music).
For (male) chorus, pantomime, orchestra; available for solo voice and piano.
Composed in Los Angeles, 1941.
Original lyrics by Paul Webster. Solo character is "Old John; this ballad tells the story of a man who earned a meager living picking cotton and who now has to face the harsh realities of finding a job, because he has been replaced by a cotton picking machine." The score calls for the projection of an illustration of a cotton picker at a specific place in the performance.
Text for *Bayou Home* by Verna Arvey.
Instrumentation lost.
Duration: 3 minutes.
Holograph for baritone solo, mixed chorus, and piano in the key of F minor with text for *Bayou Home* written over original text is in the William Grant Still and Verna Arvey Papers, University of Arkansas Libraries, Fayetteville. There is also a fair copy of *Bayou Home* in the key of D minor/Dorian in the Still and Arvey Papers.
Holographs of lead sheet dated January 25, 1941, with title, *Cotton Pickers' Song,* are in The William Grant Still Estate and the Library of Congress.

W69 ***In Memoriam: The Colored Soldiers Who Died for Democracy***
(Delkas Music Publishing Company, Los Angeles, 1943; later Leeds, New York; MCA Music Publishing, New York).
For orchestra.
Composed in Los Angeles; manuscript dated August 1943.
Poem by Verna Arvey.
Commissioned by the League of Composers.
Instrumentation: 3 flutes (3rd doubles on piccolo), 3 oboes (3rd doubles on English horn), 3 clarinets (3rd doubles on bass clarinet), 2 bassoons; 4 horns, 3 trumpets, 3 trombones, tuba; timpani, cymbals, drums, chimes; harp, strings.
Duration: 6 minutes.
Published score and autograph with orchestration notes and revisions are in the William Grant Still and Verna Arvey Papers at the University of Arkansas Libraries, Fayetteville.

W69a **First Performance:** 1944 (January 5, 7): New York, NY; Carnegie Hall; New York Philharmonic-Symphony Orchestra, Artur Rodzinski, conductor.

Selected Performances

W69b 1944 (February 6): Rochester, NY; Rochester Civic Orchestra, Guy Fraser Harrison, conductor.

W69c 1944 (August 3): Los Angeles, CA; Hollywood Bowl; Los Angeles Philharmonic Orchestra, George Szell, conductor.

W69d 1945 (January 19, 20): Boston, MA; Symphony Hall; Boston Symphony Orchestra, George Szell, guest conductor.

W69e 1945 (June 12): Paris, France, France; Théâtre des Champs-Élysées;

Orchestre de la Société des Concerts Du Conservatoire, Rudolph Dunbar, conductor.

W69f 1945 (November 3): New York, NY; Carnegie Hall; New York Philharmonic-Symphony Orchestra, George Szell, guest conductor.

W69g 1946 (June 20): New York, NY; Lewisohn Stadium; New York Philharmonic-Symphony Orchestra, George Szell, conductor.

W69h 1946 (November 7, 9): Cleveland, OH; Severence Hall; Cleveland Orchestra, George Szell, conductor.

W69i 1946 (December 3): Oberlin, OH; Finney Chapel; Cleveland Orchestra, George Szell, conductor.

W69j 1948 (November 11, 12): Los Angeles, CA; Philharmonic Auditorium; Los Angeles Philharmonic Orchestra, Alfred Wallenstein, conductor.

W69k 1959 (November 11): New York, NY; Carnegie Hall; The Orchestra of America, Richard Korn, conductor.

W69l 1965 (January 7, 9): Cleveland, OH; Severance Hall; Cleveland Orchestra, George Szell, conductor.

W69m 1965 (April 20): Moscow, USSR; Cleveland Orchestra, George Szell, conductor.

W69n 1965 (May 21): Los Angeles, CA; Second Baptist Church; Southeast Symphony Orchestra, Leon Thompson, conductor.

W69o 1965 (May 29): Hamburg, West Germany; Musikhalle; Cleveland Orchestra, George Szell, conductor.

W69p 1965 (June 22): London; Royal Festival Hall; Cleveland Orchestra, George Szell, conductor.

Bibliography

WB69.1 Downes, Olin. "Composers On War." *New York Times*, October 10, 1943.
Long article on the League of Composers commissioning sixteen compositions on patriotic themes associated with the war. Still, who is among the composers selected, provides background on how *In Memoriam: The Colored Soldiers Who Died for Democracy* came to his mind.

WB69.2 Bagar, Robert and Louis Biancolli. "Notes on the Program." (The Philharmonic-Symphony Society of New York): January 5 and 7, 1944, p. 2.
Still writes of this work: "When it was suggested to me that I compose something patriotic there immediately flashed through my mind the press release which announced that the first American soldier to be killed in World War II was a Negro soldier. Then my thoughts turned to the colored soldiers all over the world, fighting under our flag and under the flags of the countries allied with us."

WB69.3 Bennett, Grena. "Philharmonic Goes Modern at Carnegie." New York *Journal-American*, January 6, 1944.
Review of January 5, 1944, performance of the New York Philharmonic-Symphony Orchestra, which included *In Memoriam*. "Still utilized refrains stemming from Negro spirituals of doleful, reverent and jubilant character, deftly wrought into appealing harmonization and orchestrated with craftmanship."

WB69.4 Bohm, Jerome D. "New Concerto Is Offered by Philharmonic." *New York Herald Tribune*, January 6, 1944.

"Still's [*In Memoriam*] might be described as a Negro spiritual styled and orchestrated à la Tchaikovsky."

WB69.5 Briggs, John. "Rodzinski and the Philharmonic Perform Two New Compositions." *New York Post*, January 6, 1944.

"Mr. Still's [*In Memoriam*] was a stirring work, put together with great skill. . . . I have long been a believer in Mr. Still's talent and last night didn't change my mind. Mr. Still may well become the American Tchaikovsky."

WB69.6 Downes, Olin. "Rodzinski Offers W.G. Still's Music." *New York Times*, January 6, 1944.

Review of the January 5, 1944, performance of the New York Philharmonic-Symphony Orchestra, which included *In Memoriam*. "He preludes with a few notes of a semi barbaric chant, first hinted at and later used extensively, sometimes alone, sometimes in combination with a second lyrical melody of the 'spiritual' type, and this with simplicity and feeling, without affectation or attitudizing in the music. The emotional and sincere character of this simple elegiac piece was also of some relation to the *New World Symphony*."

WB69.7 Simon, Robert A. "Musical Events." *New Yorker* 19 (January 15, 1944): 63-64.

"Mr. Still's composition [*In Memoriam*], one of the most successful of the works on war themes commissioned by the League of Composers, was an effective presentation of mood expressed by a grave and charming melody that was like a spiritual."

WB69.8 Norton, Mildred. "Music Review." Los Angeles *Daily News*, August 4, 1944.

Review of the August 3, 1944, performance of the Los Angeles Philharmonic Orchestra. "It [*In Memoriam*] is a short but effective requiem in which fanfare by full orchestra is counterposed against the elegiac melodic line of the strings. Still did not intend it to be an ambitious work, but as sometimes happens with understatement, its force is in inverse ratio to its simplicity."

WB69.9 Elie, Jr., Rudolph. "Music." *Boston Herald*, January 20, 1945, p. 10.

Review of the January 19, 1945, performance of the Boston Symphony Orchestra. "Still's tribute [*In Memoriam*] is a beautiful and touching composition, one of utmost sincerity and certainly well worth hearing."

WB69.10 Stutsman, Grace May. "Szell Conducts Boston Series." *Musical America* 65 (February 1945): 208.

In her review of the January 19-20 performances of the Boston Symphony Orchestra, the author writes that *In Memoriam* "is a sincere and genuine tribute to those Negroes who have paid the supreme sacrifice. Mr. Szell and the orchestra gave the work a beautiful performance."

WB69.11 Dunbar, Rudolph. "William G. Still Tops to Paris." *Los Angeles Sentinel*, July 19, 1945.

Dunbar's article is based upon performances of Still's *Afro-American Symphony* and *In Memoriam*, conducted by Dunbar in Paris, France.

WB69.12 K., I. "Still Work Played By Philharmonic." *New York Sun*, November 5, 1945.

Review of the November 3, 1945, performance of the New York Philharmonic-Symphony Orchestra. "The composer has written a thoughtful, impassioned piece . . . but, considering the extent to which segregation has been deplored in this Army, it would have been more attractive of Still had he dedicated his moving piece [*In Memoriam*] to the men of all colors and creeds who faced the common bullet with common mortality."

WB69.13 L., H. W. "Summer Events Set a Rapid Tempo." *Musical Courier* 134 (July 1946): 5.

Brief review of the June 20, 1946, performance of the New York Philharmonic-Symphony Orchestra. "William Grant Still's *In Memoriam* was again the moving experience it had proved at first hearing in Carnegie Hall."

WB69.14 Elwell, Herbert. "Conductor Szell Hailed for 'Inspired' Work with Baton." *Cleveland Plain Dealer,* November 8, 1946.

"Still's *In Memoriam* . . . proved a piece of sincere and beautiful writing, as well as a touching tribute. It also suggested that this leading Negro composer of America is progressing in the right direction, toward freedom of melodic utterance and simplicity of harmonic idiom."

WB69.15 Loesser, Arthur. "Erica Morini Puts Interest into Well-Worn Concerto." *Cleveland Press*, November 8, 1946.

"A high-minded aspiration is discernable in this work [*In Memoriam*]; and it evidently was written by someone with a good understanding of large orchestral sonorities."

WB69.16 Hall, James H. "Critic Busy; Writes of Jones, Szell & Co., the Stuyvesants." *Oberlin News-Tribune*, December 12, 1946, p. 6.

"Oberlin may be proud of the small part she had in training William Grant Still whose symphonic sketch, written to commemorate *The Colored Soldiers Who Died for Democracy*, was more than a lament. Its lonely melody in English Horn with its modal and rhythmic reminiscences of Spirituals, led to a prophetic close in which the full orchestra mounted to a huge fortissimo whose last chord was dramatically climaxed by a crash of the cymbals left vibrating."

WB69.17 Callin, Owen. "Wallenstein Superb as L.A. Symphony Season Opens." *Los Angeles Evening Herald and Express*, November 12, 1948, p. 4B.

Review of the November 11, 1948, performance of the Los Angeles Philharmonic Orchestra. "In observing the holiday, Wallenstein opened the season with William Grant Still's tone poem, *In Memoriam*. . . . After its completion Wallenstein brought the composer out on the stage for a warm ovation from the pleased audience. The Still music is a poem of mournful and contemplative sadness. It is an elemental bit of melody with a rather haunting central theme in keeping with its purpose and the orchestra did homage to the intent. The result was satisfactory, if the applause was any criterion."

WB69.18 Goldberg, Albert. "Philharmonic Season Opened." *Los Angeles Times*, November 12, 1948.

Review of the November 11, 1948, performance of the Los Angeles Philharmonic Orchestra. "Mr. Still's *In Memoriam*, which opened the concert in observance of Armistic[e] Day, bears the subtitle *'The Colored Soldiers Who Died for Democracy.'* But it is not at all a doleful elegy. It is warm and melodious, and its themes constantly suggest a rarefied sort of Negro spiritual in a manner that is both touching and fitting. The writing is broad, effective, and unpretentious, and the composer was given a warm reception when he was finally persuaded to appear before the footlights."

WB69.19 Norton, Mildred. "Music Review." Los Angeles *Daily News*, November 12, 1948.

Review of the November 11, 1948, Los Angeles Philharmonic Orchestra performance. "Still's *In Memoriam* . . . is, as its name implies, an elegy and tribute to the Negro servicemen of World War II, a purpose it fulfills with quiet eloquence and appropriate musical honesty. Opening with a muted fanfare, it presents a gentle threnody of songful, folklike character, which Still has handled resourcefully but without pretentiousness. I think it can stand as one of the finest things he has done so far."

WB69.20 Sargeant, Winthrop. "Musical Events." *New Yorker* 35 (November 21, 1959): 208-09.

Review of the November 11, 1959, performance of the Orchestra of America, Richard Korn, conductor, at Carnegie Hall. "I was particularly impressed with William Grant Still's *In Memoriam,* . . . which is an essay in pure lyricism—a very difficult thing for a contemporary composer to achieve, since it lays upon him the obligation of having something to say and deprives him of the technical devices with which most composers nowadays tend to obscure their personalities from their listeners. On the whole, I thought Mr. Still's work the finest on the program. He said what he had to say unaffectedly, and what he had to say was dignified and moving."

WB69.21 Roy, Klaus G. "Notes On The Program." The Cleveland Orchestra, January 7 and 9, 1965, p. 541+.

Program notes for *In Memoriam*. "The work, a single movement in generally moderate tempo, is hymnic in tone; the basic tonality is B flat minor. Its substance features an alternation between the fanfare motive first heard from the muted trumpets and the song—like a Negro spiritual—intoned by the English horn. The more agitated music of the strings derives itself from aspects of both song and fanfare. The music ends with a growing proclamation of the full orchestra."

WB69.22 Hruby, Frank. "Violinist Gives All to Viotti." *Cleveland Press*. January 8, 1965.

Review of the January 7, 1965, performance of the Cleveland Orchestra, George Szell, conductor. The program included *In Memoriam*. "It was good to renew acquaintance with a work of William Grant Still. *In Memoriam* is a typically American work in the sense that it is utterly sincere, warm and rich in texture, and obviously constructed to achieve its dedicatory purpose in as direct and easily understandable terms as possible."

WB69.23 Leacacos, John P. "Izvestia Praises Orchestra." *Cleveland Plain Dealer*, April 21, 1965.

Review of the Cleveland Orchestra's tour of the Soviet Union, and of its April 20, 1965, performance in Moscow. "Russians specially noted that last night's concert opened with a work by an American Negro composer, William Grant Still [*In Memoriam*]. It was on the program as a symbolic reminder that America is progressing in its civil rights struggle in a democratic way."

WB69.24 "Triumph Abroad." *Time* 85 (May 28, 1965): p. 69.

Review of the opening performances of the Cleveland Orchestra's five-week tour of the Soviet Union and Western Europe. *In Memoriam* was part of the program. "The only sour note of the tour was sounded privately by the musicians, who rightfully questioned [George] Szell's generally lightweight selection of American works, including two insipidities by composers William Grant Still and Herbert Elwell, a native of Cleveland."

WB69.25 Weyland, John. "Hamburg Shouts Bravo for Szell." *Cleveland Plain Dealer*, May 30, 1965.

Review of the May 29, 1965, performance of the Cleveland Orchestra in Hamburg, West Germany, which included *In Memoriam*. "The piece by Still, an American Negro, brought two curtain calls."

WB69.26 "Orchestra Wins Praise Again in London." *Cleveland Plain Dealer*, June 23, 1965.

Review of the June 22, 1965, performance of the Cleveland Orchestra at the Royal Festival Hall. "The second half of the concert began with William Grant Still's *In Memoriam*. . . . The American Negro composer's requiem was received well. Szell was called back once for the applause."

W70 *Incantation and Dance* (Carl Fischer, New York, 1945, sheet music edition no. W 1867 or 29843-8-2).
For oboe and piano.
Composed in Los Angeles; holograph dated 1941.
Dedicated to Mr. and Mrs. Loyd (Betty) Rathbun.
Holograph for oboe and piano dated November 1941 is in the William Grant Still and Verna Arvey Papers at the University of Arkansas Libraries, Fayetteville. Inscription by the composer on the holograph says, "score for solo oboe, flute, clarinet, harp, strings, tom-tom."

W70a **First Performance:** 1942 (February 5): Elmira, NY; Elmira College Chapel; Robert McBride, oboe; Gregory Tucker, piano.

Selected Performances

W70b 1942 (February 12): Boston, MA; Simmons College, Assembly Hall; Robert McBride, oboe; Gregroy Tucker, piano.

W70c 1942 (February 15): Los Angeles, CA; University of Southern California, Hancock Auditorium; Loyd Rathbun, oboe; Dorothy Bishop, piano.

W70d 1970 (April 1): New York, NY; New York Public Library, Countee Cullen Regional Branch; Harry Smyles, oboe; Alan Booth, piano.

W70e 1970 (May 3): Grambling, LA; Grambling College, T.H. Harris Auditorium; Larry Pierson, oboe; Walton Phillips, piano.

W70f 1976 (April 23): Fayetteville, AR; University of Arkansas, Arkansas Union; Roger Widder, oboe; Beatriz Pilapil, piano.

W70g 1979 (February 4): Los Angeles, CA; Los Angeles County Museum of Natural History, Jean Delacour Auditorium; James McCullough, oboe; Charles Gould, piano.

W71 *Is There Anybody Here (Who Loves My Jesus)?* (Theodore Presser Co., Bryn Mawr, PA, 1956, no. 312-40305-3 for SATB chorus with piano).
Spiritual arrangement for a cappella chorus; also for SATB chorus with piano.
Facsimile of the published version for SATB chorus with piano is in the William Grant Still and Verna Arvey Papers at the University of Arkansas Libraries, Fayetteville.
Autograph location unknown.

Selected Performance

W71a 1984 (February 15): Fayetteville, AR; University of Arkansas, Fine Arts Center Concert Hall; University of Arkansas Schola Cantorum.

W72 ***Jungle Drums*** (available from William Grant Still Music).
Composed by William Grant Still and Phil Boutelse, date unknown.
For orchestra and chorus.
Piano conductor sketch is in The William Grant Still Estate.

W73 ***Jungle Episode: The Origin of Jazz.***
For orchestra.
Composed in Hollywood, CA, 1929 or 1930, possibly for the weekly radio show, *The Old Gold Hour.*
Commissioned by Paul Whiteman.
Contents: Gloom, Mystery, Beauty.
Instrumentation: solo violin (Paul Whiteman) with flute, oboe, English horn, clarinet, saxophone, bassoon; 2 horns, 3 trumpets, 3 trombones, tuba; tom-tom, triangle, timpani, bells, bass drum, wire brush, snare drum, gong, cymbal; piano, celesta, banjo, strings.
Autograph parts are in The Paul Whiteman Collection, Williams College Archives and Special Collections, Williamstown, Massachusetts.

W74 ***Kaintuck'*** (available from William Grant Still Music).
Poem for piano and orchestra; also scored by the composer for two pianos.
Composed in Los Angeles, February, 1935.
Commissioned by the League of Composers.
Dedicated to Verna Arvey.
Inscription by the composer says, "With humble thanks to God, the source of inspiration."
Contents: Languidly, Faster, Tempo I, Much faster, Moderately, At a convenient speed [cadenza], Languidly. Arvey's note on the holograph says, "The Cadenza, from (A) to No. 18, is optional, and may be omitted."
Instrumentation: 3 flutes (3rd doubles on piccolo), 2 oboes, English horn, 3 clarinets, bass clarinet, 2 bassoons; 4 horns, 3 trumpets (cup and Harmon mutes), 3 trombones (soft hat mutes), tuba; timpani, percussion; strings
Duration: 13 minutes.
Holograph with orchestration notes and a facsimile of the two-piano version (with orchestra cues) are in the William Grant Still and Verna Arvey Papers at the University of Arkansas Libraries, Fayetteville.
Manuscript master for blueprint reproduction with pencilled corrections for the piano and orchestra version is in the James Weldon Johnson Memorial Collection of Negro Arts and Letters at Yale University.

W74a **First Performance:** 1935 (May 5): Los Angeles, CA; Musart Theater; Verna Arvey, piano; Dale Arvey (Verna Arvey's brother), second piano. (*See:* WB1.7, WB76.6)

Selected Performances

W74b 1935 (October 28): Los Angeles, CA; Biltmore Hotel; Pro Musica All American Program, two piano version; Verna Arvey, principal piano; Miss Robert V. Edwards, second piano.

W74c 1935 (December 8): San Francisco, CA; Sorosis Club; Verna Arvey, piano; Dale Arvey (Verna Arvey's brother), second piano. (*See:* WB1.11)

W74d 1936 (January 16): Rochester, NY; Eastman Theater; Rochester Philharmonic Orchestra, Howard Hanson, conductor, Henry Watts, piano.

W74e 1936 (March 27): Cincinnati, OH; Emery Auditorium; Cincinnati Symphony Orchestra, Eugene Goossens, conductor, John Quincy Bass, piano.

W74f 1937 (April 18): Los Angeles, CA; Pacific Institute of Music and Fine Art; Pacific Symphony Orchestra, William Grant Still, guest conductor, Verna Arvey, piano.

W74g 1938 (February 22): Oakland, CA; Oakland Auditorium Theatre; Bay Region Federal Symphony, William Grant Still, guest conductor, Verna Arvey, piano. (*See:* WB80.10)

W74h 1938 (February 24): San Francisco, CA; Scottish Rite Auditorium; Bay Region Federal Symphony, William Grant Still, guest conductor, Verna Arvey, piano.

W74i 1938 (August 9): San Diego, CA; Ford Bowl; San Diego Symphony Orchestra, William Grant Still, guest conductor, Verna Arvey, piano. (*See also:* WB80.14, WB80.15)

W74j 1939 (February 17, 18): Los Angeles, CA; Philharmonic Auditorium; Los Angeles Philharmonic Orchestra, Otto Klemperer, conductor, Verna Arvey, piano.

W74k 1939 (April 23): Salt Lake City, UT; Utah State Art Center; Verna Arvey, principal piano; Rudolph E. Hainke, second piano. (*See:* WB164.4)

W74l 1942 (December 5, 6, 10): Indianapolis, IN; Murat Theater; Indianapolis Symphony Orchestra, Fabien Sevitsky, conductor.

W74m 1984 (February 18): Fayetteville, AR; University of Arkansas, Fine Arts Center Concert Hall; John Keene, piano; Arthur Tollefson, piano.

Bibliography

WB74.1 Saunders, Richard D. "New Works Offered by Pro-Musica." *Hollywood Citizen-News*, October 29, 1935.

Review of the program at the Biltmore Hotel, October 28, 1935. "William Grant Still's *Kaintuck'* was given with lovely tone and splendid pianism by Verna Arvey at the solo piano, while Miss Robert V. Edwards played the orchestral accompaniment on a second piano. It was a work of attractive caliber, imbued with a languorous atmosphere properly typical of the old South, while some passages were appropriately equine in suggestiveness. On two pianos the work was naturally a monochrome, with the colors of the original orchestral concept lacking."

WB74.2 Jones, Isabel Morse. "Pro Musica Concert Event." *Los Angeles Times*, October 30, 1935.

Review of the program at the Biltmore Hotel, October 28, 1935. "*Kaintuck'* . . . was written for piano and orchestra for the League of Composers. Judging by the two-piano arrangement played . . . by Verna Arvey as soloist and Miss Robert V. Edwards at the second piano, the work is a credit to the league and to the Guggenheim Fellowship committee, whose award made its composing possible. Still has used Negro themes, naturally, but has not been content to lease them in the rough. It is smoothly written, ingratiating music which will be liked in America."

WB74.3 Kessler, David. "Musical 'Mississippi' Impressive Work." *Rochester Journal*, January 17, 1936.

Review of the January 16, 1936, performance of the Rochester Philharmonic Orchestra. "I am afraid the promising young Negro composer is going in for 'knick-knacks' in [*Kaintuck'*]. It seemed like retrogression instead of an advance from his fine *Afro-American Symphony*. It has basically primitive motif characteristic of this composer's works. One hears also the inevitable and catchy syncopation and rhythm. The development and unimaginative orchestration . . . are strongly suggestive of Harlem in a Prix de Rome setting."

WB74.4   Sabin, Stewart B. "Honors Are Paid To American Musician." *Rochester Democrat and Chronicle*, January 17, 1936.
Review of the January 16, 1936, performance of the Rochester Philharmonic Orchestra with Henry Watts on piano. "Still, in his *Kaintuck'*, is quite within his typical manner. His material is not startling but it has the dainty dissonance, the lightly accentuated syncopation that he knows how to use with skill. And he knows how to choose an occasional instrumentation that is both arresting of attention and often of charm. The piano adds much to the distinctiveness of this piece and Harry [Henry] Watts played it admirably."

WB74.5   R., G. "Rochester American Composers' Event Honors Stillman-Kelly." *Musical Courier* 112 (February 8, 1936): 8.
Comments on the January 16, 1936, performance of the Rochester Philharmonic Orchestra. "Harry [Henry] Watts of the Eastman School of Music faculty was soloist in Still's new work [*Kaintuck'*]. This music is charming and so characteristically in the personal idiom of its composer that it is inconceivable to imagine any other composer writing it. Facile, delicate orchestration, novel coloristic effects, and a lazy yet none the less insidious rhythmical pattern, are the salient features of this young Negro composer's music."

WB74.6   Yeiser, Frederick. "Blue Grass." *Cincinnati Enquirer*, March 22, 1936.
Preview of the March 27, 1936, program of the Cincinnati Symphony Orchestra. This article describes how Still conceived of *Kaintuck'*, quoting from a letter he wrote, in part, as follows: "'Several years ago, when going from Cincinnati to Lexington on what was then the Queen and Crescent Railroad, I was so greatly impressed by the beauty of the country that I decided to attempt at some future time to describe in musical terms my reaction. And it is my feeling of peacefulness, and the more active emotions inspired by the more rugged sections that I seek to present in the piece.'"

WB74.7   Rhodes, John P. "Music Lovers Elgar Charms." *Cincinnati Post*, March 28, 1936.
Review of the March 27, 1936, performance of the Cincinnati Symphony Orchestra. "[*Kaintuck'*] is typical of a certain type of Americanism rampant in our music to date. It has . . . slightly more dignity, grace and originality than the work of most of our contemporary would-be symphonists."

WB74.8   Smith, Nina Pugh. "Beethoven's 'Pastoral' Delicately Played." *Cincinnati Times Star*, March 28, 1936.
Review of the March 27, 1936, performance of the Cincinnati Symphony Orchestra. "*Kaintuck'* in its way seems sufficiently well written for orchestra. . . . It is lively, without presenting a firm line. It suggests the L & N or the Q & C going past Latonia—if they do go. There sounds the grating of rusty wheels, the clang of some signal iron, the unrest of things in general. Very melodious, all of it. Mr. John Quincy Bass, who played the pianoforte lines of *Kaintuck'*, was actually soloist of the afternoon."

WB74.9 Yeiser, Frederick. "Symphony Concert." *Cincinnati Enquirer*, March 28, 1936.

Review of the March 27, 1936, performance of the Cincinnati Symphony Orchestra with John Quincy Bass as piano soloist. "*Kaintuck'* discloses the principal substances apparent in other of Still's compositions, namely a sincerity of mood and feeling, a considerable melodic gift, and a marked competence in acquiring clear, almost transparent, orchestral color."

WB74.10 Jones, Isabel Morse. "Work of Resident Composers Featured in Two Concerts." *Los Angeles Times*, April 20, 1937.

"*Kaintuck'* for piano and orchestra, played by Verna Arvey and the Pacific Orchestra, made an impression. It is a wholly sincere work in which the piano accentuates or underlines the musical delineations in the orchestration. The writing for the orchestra is richer than for the piano. Miss Arvey has the sympathetic understanding of this composer's work which makes her the ideal pianist to convey its message to the outside."

WB74.11 Fisher, Marjory M. "American Music Featured By Bay Region FMP Groups." *San Francisco News*, February 25, 1938.

Review of the February 24, 1938, performance of *Kaintuck'* with Verna Arvey at the piano and *Lenox Avenue* at the Scottish Rite Auditorium by the Bay Region Federal Symphony, guest conducted by William Grant Still. "Neither [*Kaintuck'* or *Lenox Avenue*] work seemed to represent the composer at his best. He has written many far better works. *Kaintuck'* established the mood intended—that of a laz[y] sunny summer day—although it had moments far more energetic than any we have ever associated with lackadaisical moods. . . . If *Lenox Avenue* had been given without verbal interruptions, more than one person would have found it more enjoyable and, musically, more effective."

WB74.12 Fried, Alexander. "Guest Batonists and Pianist Share Concert Honors." *San Francisco Examiner*, February 25, 1938.

"With all due ease and security [Still] conducted his own *Kaintuck'* and *Lenox Avenue*. The latter work was the more valuable of the two. *Kaintuck'* . . . succumbs to its composer's technical and imaginative limitations by becoming monotonous. [Still] can make an orchestra sing blues with a swarming persuasive nostalgia. He can jazz up a dance pace delightfully. The problem that he ambitiously faces—and that still faces him—is to develop these elementary though valuable talents into symphonic form."

WB74.13 M., F. "Symphony Offers Cross-Section of America." *San Diego Union*, August 10, 1938.

"*Kaintuck'* is a work of haunting loveliness, and *Lenox Avenue* is spine-tingling stuff. These rhythms are the rhythms of our time, and these astringent harmonies are a musical speech to which we respond. . . . [T]he composer was brilliantly aided by Miss Arvey. She is manifestly in sympathy with the spirit of these works and has the technical skill to reveal it."

WB74.14 Jones, Isabel Morse. "New Music Work Lauded." *Los Angeles Times*, February 18, 1939.

Review of the February 17, 1939, performance of the Los Angeles Philharmonic Orchestra. "[*Kaintuck's*] beauty lies in the lazy, flowing melodies and the fine instrumentation. Modern tone colors are used with fine taste and a sure knowledge. The mood is hauntingly sad. The audience liked it at once. Klemperer, Still and Miss Arvey were returned to the stage several times."

WB74.15 Mittauer, Frank. "Quality in Variety." Los Angeles *Evening News*, February 18, 1939.

Review of the February 17, 1939, performance of the Los Angeles Philharmonic Orchestra. "[*Kaintuck'*] is original without being bizarre, novel without straining after novelty. The piano part around which the whole opus revolves was well played by Verna Arvey, who showed at the keyboard a fire and assurance unforeshadowed in her meek demeanor as she came on stage. *Kaintuck'* makes ingenious use of what sound vaguely like traditional southern melodies. Its tonal structure, however, is definitely modern, making frequent use of unorthodox combinations."

WB74.16 Saunders, Richard D. "Orchestra Fare Varied." *Hollywood Citizen-News*, February 18, 1939.

Review of the February 17, 1939, performance of the Los Angeles Philharmonic Orchestra. "*Kaintuck'* proved a work which ingeniously blended melodic appeal and impressionistic style. Although the piano took a leading part in the thematic exposition, it was not a concerto. A languorous theme, introduced by the solo instrument, was the principal motive, contrasted with material of lively character. . . . Verna Arvey gave the solo part with lovely tone and musicianly skill, making no attempt at virtuoso display but balancing effectively with the orchestra, while Klemperer handled the work with sympathy and understanding. Still, undoubtedly the leading Negro composer of the generation, appeared in person and was recalled for several bows by an enthusiastic audience."

WB74.17 Ussher, Bruno David. "Music." Los Angeles *Daily News* February 18, 1939.

Review of the February 17, 1939, performance of the Los Angeles Philharmonic Orchestra. "Verna Arvey shared honors as a sensitively phrasing soloist in the piano part which forms an integral feature of [*Kaintuck'*]. Still's work is a languorous reverie characteristic of racial tendencies yet couched in a musical idiom derived from the French impressionists, from advocates of harmonic freedom and not unreminiscent of Gershwin. There is no doubt, however, that Still speaks of himself and for himself."

W75 *Keep Me F'om Sinkin' Down* (Handy Brothers Music Company, New York, 1938; European representatives: Francis, Day, and Hunter, London, England).

Spiritual arrangement for mixed chorus (SAATTBB) and piano. (*See:* W165) Text is in dialect: "Oh Lawd! Oh, mah Lawd!"

Facsimile of the published version is in the William Grant Still and Verna Arvey Papers at the University of Arkansas Libraries, Fayetteville.

A different musical setting by William Grant Still of this spiritual was published in the same year by Handy Brothers for SATB chorus without dialect: "Oh, Lord, Oh, my Lord! Keep me from sinking down." (*See:* W78)

Autograph locations unknown.

W76 *La Guiablesse* (available from William Grant Still Music).

Ballet, 4 solo dancers, corps de ballet, one stage set; also arranged by the composer as an orchestral suite.

Composed in New York; original holograph date is partial: Mar[ch, possibly 1926 or 1927; revised 1932]; later holograph labeled "revised" is dated September 30, 1944.

Commissioned by Chicago Allied Arts, Inc., in 1926, at the suggestions of Adolph Bolm and Ruth Page.
Dedicated to Adrian Michaelis.
Scenario by Ruth Page based on a book by Lafcadio Hearn on a legend of the West Indian Island of Martinique.
Inscription by the composer says, "(Asking the aid and guidance of God. May this effort be pleasing in His Sight)."
Contents of orchestral suite: I. Dance of the Children, II. Dance of Yzore and Adou, III. Entrance of Les Porteuses [the Basket Woman].
Three Dances from La Guiablesse: Orchestral parts indicate the following sections: *First Dance of the Children, Second Dance of the Children,* and *Entrance of Les Porteuses.*
Instrumentation: 3 flutes (3rd doubles on piccolo), 2 oboes, English horn, 3 clarinets, 2 bassoons; 4 horns, 3 trumpets, 3 trombones, tuba; timpani, percussion, drums, tom-toms, cymbals, gong, triangle, xylophone, tambourine, wire brush; harp, strings.
Duration: 30 minutes.
The holdings, in the William Grant Still and Verna Arvey Papers at the University of Arkansas Libraries, Fayetteville, are varied and extensive:
  There is a holograph of the orchestration with revisions, an autograph of the *First Dance of the Children* for piano and 2 violins, an autograph of the *Second Dance of the Children* for two pianos with orchestration notes, sketches, and full orchestration with handwritten notes in addition to Still's (possibly by his collaborators).
  The Still and Arvey Papers also include a manuscript fair copy in full score of the orchestral suite. There is a reproduction of the composer's completed manuscript piano score ("as of the late Twenties, or early Thirties [typewritten note]") with stage directions throughout and the holograph revision, dated September 30, 1944, with orchestration notes.
"Complete manuscript of full score" listed in *Selected Items from the George Gershwin Memorial Collection of Music and Musical Literature* (Nashville: Fisk University Library, 1974).
Two facsimiles of an unsigned manuscript with dance notations are in The University of Rochester, The Eastman School of Music, Sibley Music Library, from the Thelma Biracree Schnepel Collection.
First Dance of the Children, arranged for 2 violins and piano by the composer, in autograph manuscript full score; *Entrance of les Porteuses* scored for string orchestra by the composer and *Dance of the Porteuses* for piano solo are in The William Grant Still Estate.
Holograph of full score for orchestra is in The William Grant Still Estate.

W76a **First Performance:** 1933 (May 5): Rochester, NY; Eastman Theater; Rochester Civic Orchestra, Howard Hanson, conductor; Thelma Biracree as La Guiablesse and choreographer; Evelyn Sabin as Yzore; Nathan Emanuel as Adou; Alice Couch, costumes; Clarence J. Hall, scenery.

Selected Performances

W76b 1933 (June 16): Chicago, IL: The Auditorium; Chicago Symphony Orchestra, Isaac Van Grove, conductor; Ruth Page Ballet Company, Ruth Page, choreographer and principle dancer, with Katherine Dunham and Jack Smith; Nicholas Remisoff, lighting; Harry Beatty, stage.

W76c 1934 (October 28): Los Angeles, CA; Wilshire Methodist Episcopal Church, Verna Arvey, piano.

W76d 1934 (November 4): Los Angeles, CA; Norma Gould Studios; Verna Arvey, piano.

W76e 1934 (November 30, December 7 and 14): Chicago, IL: Chicago Grand Opera Company; Katherine Dunham, principal dancer.

W76f 1935 (May 5): Los Angeles, CA; Musart Theater; Verna Arvey, piano. (*Dance of the Porteuses.*)

W76g 1935 (December 8): San Francisco, CA; Sorosis Club; Verna Arvey, piano. (*See:* WB1.11)

W76h 1937 (April 18): Los Angeles, CA; Pacific Institute of Music and Fine Art; Verna Arvey, piano.

W76i 1937 (April 30): Rochester, NY; Eastman Theatre; Rochester Civic Orchestra, Howard Hanson, conductor; Thelma Biracree as La Guiablesse and choreographer; Evelyn Sabin as Yzore and guest soloist; Harold Kolb as Adou and guest soloist; Alice Couch: costumes; Clarence J. Hall: scenery.

W76j 1940 (September 24): San Francisco, CA; Federal Plaza; San Francisco Symphony, William Grant Still, guest conductor.

W76k 1945 (November 19): Paris, France; Théâtre des Champs-Elysées; Orchestre National, Rudolph Dunbar, conductor.

Bibliography

WB76.1 "Rochester Hails Ballet By Still." *New York Times*, May 6, 1933.
Review of the May 5, 1933, performance of the Rochester Civic Orchestra. The program included the premiere performance of Still's *La Guiablesse*. "The score has rarity, lyric charm and dramatic suggestion. . . . The final scene made a marked impression on the audience. This ballet was written originally in 1926, but was not produced. Last year [1932] Mr. Still completely revised the score, retaining only a small part of the original music. . . . Dr. Hanson, with his orchestra, conducted an impressive musical performance."

WB76.2 Sabin, Stewart B. "Music." *Rochester Democrat and Chronicle*, May 6, 1933.
Review of the May 5, 1933, performance of the Rochester Civic Orchestra. "Mr. Still's music is charming, picturesque and dramatically suggestive, never padded, never divorced from the action yet with individual appeal of its own. In Miss [Thelma] Biracree, Miss [Evelyn] Sabin and Mr. [Nathan] Emanuel, the cast had performers of stage experience and professional knowledge."

WB76.3 Stinson, Eugene. "Music Views." *Chicago Daily News*, June 19, 1933.
Review of the June 16, 1933, performance of the Chicago Symphony Orchestra. "The primitive note it sounded was beautifully echoed in Miss [Ruth] Page's choreography, which gave numerous pictures at once modernistic and racial. . . . Katherine Dunham and Jack Smith as the native lovers gave a performance at once poetic and sensual. . . . The novelty was received with unbounded enthusiasm."

WB76.4 Saunders, Richard Drake. "Modern Piano Recital Given." *Hollywood Citizen-News*, November 5, 1934.

"Some very interesting modern piano music characterized the program given last night by Verna Arvey at the Norma Gould Studio auditorium under the auspices of the Dance Theater Group. It was announced as a program of idealized dance music, and this theme was admirably carried out. . . . Two short dances of Still from *La Guiablesse* were set in a rather stately rhythmic pattern."

WB76.5 Jones, Isabel Morse. "Words and Music." *Los Angeles Times*, November 11, 1934.

"Verna Arvey played for the Dance Theater Group Sunday [November 4] evening, a program of idealized dance music of particular interest . . . two dances from a *La Guiablesse* by Still, the Negro composer now resident here . . . attracted well-merited attention."

WB76.6 ———. "Noted Composer's Music Heard at Lecture-Recital." *Los Angeles Times*, May 8, 1935.

Review of a lecture-recital given by Verna Arvey at the Musart Theater, May 5, 1935. "Miss Arvey played piano arrangements of [Still's] orchestra works and had the assistance of a talented mezzo-soprano, Leola Longress. An excerpt from Still's *La Guiablesse* was skillfully interpreted by the dancer Teru. Miss Arvey played the parts of *Africa*, a symphonic poem, and of the new Still opera, *Blue Steel* as well as *Kaintuck'* and an introductory group by Coleridge-Taylor, Villa-Lobos and Bruce Forsythe. The music of [Still] is strongly centered in rhythm and the simple melodic ideas which are used to express emotions in the South. Their treatment is anything but naive, however. The ideas are clothed with rich harmonies, many of them delving into modern resources, but few could be called ultra or atonal."

WB76.7 Saunders, Richard D. "Varied Music Proffered at Concert Hall." *Hollywood Citizen-News*, April 19, 1937.

"The second portion of the program was devoted to works by William Grant Still, under the composer's direction. He handled the orchestra adroitly and secured well balanced effects. From his ballet, *La Guiablesse*, a *Dance of the Children* was short and lively, and the spiritedly prancing *Entrance of the Basket-Woman* [*Les Porteuses*] had to be repeated. From the ballet, *Sahdji*, the *Invitation Dance* cleverly contrived the effect of beckoning, followed by an ebullient *Dance before the Chieftain*. Verna Arvey showed an appealing tone and virtuoso pianistic ability in the solo part of *Kaintuck'*, a tone-poem for the piano and orchestra which appealingly blended the languor and activity of the South. For encore there was a humorously delicate *Footsteps Foolish* [*Quit Dat Fool'nish*], executed with gay charm. In conclusion were excerpts from Still's opera, *Blue Steel*. *Ritual and Dance of the Priestesses* was orchestrally well scored and effective."

WB76.8 Fisher, Marjory. "ASCAP Gives Rare Programs." *San Francisco News*, September 25, 1940, p. 11-12.

Review of a program sponsored by ASCAP of the San Francisco Symphony Orchestra on September 24, 1940, William Grant Still, guest conductor for *La Guiablesse* and two movements from *Symphony No. 2 in G Minor, "Song of a New Race."* "Mr. Still proved a composer who can qualify as one of the most graceful conductors ever seen on a podium."

WB76.9 "Gene Buck Goes to Town." *Time* 36 (October 7, 1940): 66-67.

Review of September 24, 1940, performance of the San Francisco Symphony. The concert was held in the open-air Federal Plaza, with 25,000 people in attendance. "The amplification was tinny, airplanes zoomed, firecrackers popped, a military band zing-boomed past but everyone thought the concert was swell."

W77 ***Lament*** (Silver Burdett Company, New York, 1951, in *New Music Horizons*, p. 99).
For chorus in a music education textbook.
Composed in Los Angeles, 1950.
Text by Verna Arvey.
Autograph of a sketch for SAA chorus and piano in the composer's hand with text in Arvey's hand is in the William Grant Still and Verna Arvey Papers at the University of Arkansas Libraries, Fayetteville.

W78 ***Lawd, I Want(s) to be a Christian*** (Handy Brothers Music Co., Inc., 1938, octavo version for SATB chorus with piano).
Spiritual arrangement for mixed chorus and piano.
Original published edition in the series *Negro Spirituals for Mixed Voices arranged by William Grant Still* is in the William Grant Still and Verna Arvey Papers at the University of Arkansas Libraries, Fayetteville. The edition lists two other arrangements in the series: *Keep Me From Sinking Down* (a different setting from the SAATTBB, *Keep Me F'om Sinkin' Down*) and *Gwinter Sing All Along De Way*. (*See:* W165) A portion of the SATB arrangement of the former appears on the back of the octavo. The text is not written in dialect. (*See:* W75)
Autograph location unknown.

W79 ***Legend*** (conductor's score available from William Grant Still Music).
For orchestra.
Composed in Los Angeles; manuscript dated "Nov 27, 1959."
Instrumentation: 3 flutes (2nd doubles on piccolo), 2 oboes, English horn, 3 clarinets (3rd doubles on bass clarinet), 2 bassoons; 4 horns, 3 trumpets, 3 trombones, tuba; timpani, triangle, tambourine, marimba, cymbals, tom-toms; harp, celesta, strings.
Autograph conductor's score with orchestration notes and revisions is in the William Grant Still and Verna Arvey Papers at the University of Arkansas Libraries, Fayetteville.

W80 ***Lenox Avenue*** (J. Fischer & Brothers, New York, 1938, no. 0379, piano vocal score; the *Blues* section published for small orchestra in 1939, no. 0391 and 0391a; available from William Grant Still Music).
Choreographic Street Scene (ballet) for orchestra, chorus, and piano solo; originally for radio broadcast with orchestra, announcer (narrator), chorus, and piano solo.
Composed in New York and Los Angeles, 1935, revised in 1937; excerpts from a similar work, *Central Avenue*, were performed in 1935.
Commissioned by the Columbia Broadcasting System for radio broadcast, 1937.
Scenario by Verna Arvey.
Setting: A street in Harlem, New York.
Version for ballet with orchestra, chorus, piano solo, corps de ballet and 2 solo dancers (no narrator) includes an elaborate scenario by Verna Arvey and complete stage directions coordinated with the musical selections by Verna Arvey (1938).
Contents (complete work, with annotations from the composer's papers): A

series of episodes outlined as follows: "I. Lenox Avenue: Racial (in the musical idiom of the contemporary Afro-American) also known as 'The Crap Game,' II. The Flirtation: Capricious, III. The Fight: Exciting and Intense, IV. The 'Law': Humorous, V. Dancing Gamins, also known as 'Dance of the Boys': Light and Graceful, VI. Dancing Drunkard, also known as 'Dance of the Man from Down South': Grotesquely humorous, VII. The Philosopher, also known as 'Thought Forms': Racial (Suggests reflection, followed by mental or spiritual turmoil which, in turn, is followed by reflection on a higher plane), VIII. The Mission: Negroid (In the style of the more animated rhythmic Spirituals, 'I'm Gonna Tell What Ma Lawd Has Done fo' Me'), IX. The House Rent Party: *Blues* (*See:* W15), X. The Orator: Blantant and repetitious, XI. Finale: This Episode begins with a choral chant in the vein of a Spiritual. . . . In conclusion the orchestra sounds in unison the Lenox Avenue motive."

Instrumentation (full orchestra): 2 flutes (2nd doubles on piccolo), 2 oboes (second doubles on English horn), 4 clarinets, 2 bassoons; 2 alto saxophones (2nd doubles on baritone saxophone), tenor saxophone (doubles on bass clarinet); 3 horns, 3 trumpets, 2 trombones; timpani, percussion; piano (doubles on celesta); strings (10 violins, 2 violas, 2 cellos, 2 basses); mixed chorus.

Duration: 23 minutes.

The materials in the William Grant Still and Verna Arvey Papers at the University of Arkansas Libraries, Fayetteville, include complete ballet production descriptions, drawings of the stage design, directions for the stage manager, and complete narration with musical cues.

Holograph for *Central Avenue* dated May 30, 1935, Los Angeles, in two versions, complete with scenario (author not identified) placed throughout the manuscript, is in the William Grant Still and Verna Arvey Papers at the University of Arkansas Libraries, Fayetteville. Characters include Rev. Wantmore, a man and woman in love, the woman's husband, a police officer, two boys who compete in a dance, and the two mothers of the boys who also dance. The scenes take place on the street, in the Hills of Zion Mission, and in the Club Hotsy Afriola.

Holograph of full score with copyright 1938 J. Fischer and Brother is in The William Grant Still Estate.

W80a **First Performance** of *Lenox Avenue*: 1937 (May 23): New York, NY; CBS Symphony Orchestra, Howard Barlow, conductor; *Central Avenue*: 1935 (December 8): San Franciso, CA; Sorosis Club; Verna Arvey, piano. (*Blues* and *Soft Shoe Dance* performed.) (*See:* WB1.11)

Selected Performances

W80b 1937 (October 17): New York, NY; CBS Symphony Orchestra, Howard Barlow, conductor. (Radio broadcast.)

W80c 1938 (January 19): Los Angeles, CA; Belasco Theatre; Los Angeles Federal Symphony Orchestra, William Grant Still, guest conductor; Verna Arvey, piano; Clarence Muse, narrator; Colored Chorus. (*See also:* WB1.20)

W80d 1938 (February 22): Oakland, CA; Oakland Auditorium Theatre; Bay Region Federal Symphony, William Grant Still, guest conductor; Verna Arvey, piano; Phillip Stearns, narrator; Colored Chorus of Oakland.

W80e 1938 (February 24): San Francisco, CA; Scottish Rite Auditorium; Bay

130   William Grant Still: A Bio-Bibliography

Region Federal Symphony, William Grant Still, guest conductor; Verna Arvey, piano; Phillip Stearns, narrator; Colored Chorus of Oakland. (*See:* WB74.11, WB74.12)

W80f 1938 (May 1, 2): Los Angeles, CA; Dance Theater on LaBrea; Dance Theater Group; Verna Arvey: scenario and piano; Norma Gould: director and choreography; Hall Johnson Choir; Charles Teske as the Man from Down South; Ted Meredith as the First Crap Shooter and Philosopher; Wood Spears as the Second Crap Shooter; David Tihmar as The Lover; Anastine Rowell as The Girl; Archie Royall as The Husband; Tom Ladd as the Policeman; Dorothee Jarcac as First Boy; Helen Lucas as Second Boy; Edward Lewis as The Loafer and Slave Driver; Joseph Stevenson as the Savage; Margaret Simcock, Eleanor Gleason, and Dorothy Cornell as Slaves; Marjorie Dougan as Mammy; Richard Irvin, stage; Charles Teske, costumes.

W80g 1938 (August 9): San Diego, CA; Ford Bowl; San Diego Symphony Orchestra, William Grant Still, guest conductor; Verna Arvey, piano; Jewell Smith, narrator; Los Angeles Federal Colored Chorus, Carlyle Scott, director.

W80h 1942 (March 15): Los Angeles, CA; Norma Gould Studios; Verna Arvey, piano. (*Muted Laughter* and *Blues*.)

Bibliography

WB80.1 "Mr. Still Offers 'Lenox Avenue' as Music Adapted for Broadcasting." *New York Times*, February 14, 1937.

   Long article on *Lenox Avenue*, with emphasis on its development as a radio broadcast for CBS.

WB80.2 Rowe, Billy. "Billy Still Submits First Serious Work." *Pittsburgh Courier*, February 20, 1937.

   Still's *Lenox Avenue* was the first score submitted to CBS radio from a group of composers invited to write music specifically for radio. This article provides background on the initiative.

WB80.3 Gross, Ben. "Listening In." *New York Daily News*, May 24, 1937.

   "The first of six compositions especially written for the CBS radio network was presented by Howard Barlow's symphony orchestra. . . . *Lenox Avenue* [is] a glittering panorama of life in Harlem. Score one for Columbia!"

WB80.4 Rowe, Billy. "Lenox Avenue Presented In Song Over NBC [sic]." *Pittsburgh Courier*, May 29, 1937, p. 21.

   "Over a nation-wide hook-up last Sunday [May 23], the first product of the Columbia Composers' Commission formed by the Columbia Broadcasting System to enable six American composers to explore the musical possibilities of the microphone and to write expressly for that instrument, was given its premiere. [*Lenox Avenue*] came over the [air] at 3 p.m. via WABC on the Everybody's Music program by an orchestra and a chorus directed by Howard Barlow. Commenting on the works of the great Negro composer, Deems Taylor, composer-critic and music consultant for Columbia, said the work is 'an interesting experiment by a composer whose long association with radio has given him an exceptional command of the medium.'"

WB80.5 Jones, Isabel Morse. "Native Composers Aided By Radio." *Los Angeles Times*, October 31, 1937.

   Review of the Federal Music Project and its efforts to broadcast the compositions of American composers. The first group of composers included

Aaron Copland, Roy Harris, Howard Hanson, Louis Gruenberg, William Grant Still and Walter Piston. The second group consisted of Quincy Porter, Robert Russell Bennett, Leo Sowerby, Jerome Moross, R. Nathaniel Dett and Vittorio Giannini. Still wrote *Lenox Avenue* expressly for the program. "Life moves fast on the *Lenox Avenue* of William Grant Still. There is more real Negro character in it than in all of *Porgy and Bess*. Episodes are clearly set forth in the music and emphasized by a well-written continuity by Verna Arvey. Rhythm patterns in the *Rent Party Blues* [*Blues*] are fascinating in their variation. The mood of the old philosopher's melody will be remembered. A marching chorus strongly indicates that contemporary Negroes are picking up their feet, not just shufflin' along."

WB80.6 Hughes, Albert D. "Radio Proves Valuable Agent for Promotion of Good Music." *Christian Science Monitor*, November 9, 1937.

Lengthy article on the Columbia Composers Commission of 1937, an adjunct of the Columbia Broadcasting System. Still's *Lenox Avenue* was among the works commissioned under the auspices of this program.

WB80.7 Bronson, Carl. "Woman['s] Lyric Chorus Given Big Ovation." Los Angeles *Herald-Express*, January 20, 1938.

"Still's personal directing of his own *Land of Superstition* . . . was the highlight and his . . . *Lennox* [sic] *Avenue* was so well liked that a repetition was demanded of the last movement, the Negro chorus, especially, contributing some beautifully harmonious singing. Still conducted with interpretive impressiveness, held the respect of his instrumentalists and revealed his works effectively."

WB80.8 Jones, Isabel Morse. "Women Give Concert At Auditorium." *Los Angeles Times*, January 20, 1938.

Two reviews of musical programs, one of which included Still compositions. "Los Angeles Federal Music Project presented its symphony orchestra at the Belasco Theater last night in a dominantly American program. William Grant Still directed his own works, *Land of Superstition*, the third movement from his suite for orchestra, *Africa*, and a *Symphonic Symposium* called *Lenox Avenue*. The last number on the program proved the most popular with the audience. Part of it had to be repeated, an unusual occurrence for a symphony concert. Mr. Still is advancing as a conductor as well as a composer. *Lenox Avenue* is an involved piece [for] orchestration but its valuable melodies always cut through and reach the listener. Clarence Muse made a fine interlocutor. The Negro chorus joined Verna Arvey, pianist, and the full orchestra in picturing a street in Harlem that is almost human in its personal characteristics."

WB80.9 VanGundy, Palmer. "Native Music Fare Offered." *Hollywood Citizen-News* January 20, 1938.

"The second half of the concert was conducted by William Grant Still, who led the orchestra and the Federal Music Project Colored Chorus in two masterful productions of his own pen: *Land of Superstition* from his suite *Africa* and his symphonic symposium, *Lenox Avenue*. In the latter number excellent piano accompaniments were provided by Verna Arvey, Clarence Muse acted as narrator, reading lines written by Miss Arvey, which are descriptive of various scenes and episodes of the central street of New York's Harlem, Lenox Avenue. Compositionally these works of Still's are exceptionally praise worthy."

WB80.10 Mason, Jack. "*Lennox* [sic] *Ave.* Cheered at Concert Here." *Oakland Tribune,* February 23, 1938.
"The music [of *Lenox Avenue*] is graphic enough to make the commentaries read from time to time unnecessary, if not irritating. Why not let music of this kind alone, without sandwiching in explanatory readings. . . . If the composer wants to call attention to his story, let him write a few remarks on the program. . . . The composer led the orchestra for the number, and for another of his compositions, *Kaintuck'*—a tone poem of lazy and ruminating description, technically sound, however, as is all of Still's writing."

WB80.11 Swisher, Viola Hegyi. "Life of Harlem Limned for Dance Lovers." *Hollywood Citizen-News*, May 2, 1938.
"Still's colorful music, at once graphic and insinuating, together with the realistic philosophy of Miss Arvey's book, has provided Miss Gould with good balletic material."

WB80.12 Jones, Isabel Morse. "Youthful Artists Perform At Belasco." *Los Angeles Times*, May 3, 1938.
Review of the premiere performance of *Lenox Avenue* in ballet form. "The piano version is utterly inadequate to portray the worth of this score. . . . Josef Stevenson, the only Negro in the cast, walked through in a shadow scene depicting a savage with handsome dignity and also aided Miss Gould in direction."

WB80.13 Pierre, Dorathi Bock. "Dance Events." *American Dancer* (July 1938).
Review of the premiere performance of *Lenox Avenue* in ballet form. "The music is rather short, and as a consequence the scenario should have been very simple and strong in a single theme, but trying to present everything significant of the street and of Negro character, made the ballet very episodic. . . . Broken into separate parts, the ballet is very good, but its fault lies in the fact that it is too short and that its central theme is not stressed with sufficient strength to hold all of the episodes together."

WB80.14 Herreshoff, Constance. "Still To Lead Symphony In Bowl Tonight." *San Diego Sun*, August 9, 1938.
Preview of the August 9, 1938, performance of the San Diego Symphony Orchestra. "Spontaneous applause, such as the orchestra gave William Grant Still yesterday morning at the close of his rehearsal, is a lucky sign. It means that a good concert is brewing for tonight. The applause also indicated that the orchestra acknowledged Still's great gifts as a composer, and that both his conducting and his pleasant personality were approved."

WB80.15 ———. "Moon And Symphony At Best As Leib And Still Conduct." *San Diego Sun*, August 10, 1938.
"Miss Arvey, to whom *Kaintuck'* is dedicated, had an important role in that work also. Her pianistic comments were always to the point. . . . Orchestra and audience, alike, found *Lenox Avenue* a thrilling experience. Ovations were in order for the composer, a particularly modest man who does not like to bow."

W81 ***Levee Land*** (facsimiles of "restored photostats" of the autograph available from William Grant Still Music).
Suite for chamber orchestra and soprano solo.

Composed in New York, 1925, while he was a student of Edgard Varèse.
Text by William Grant Still.
Written for Miss Florence Mills.
Contents (with the composer's notes) "Humorous Suite": I. Levee Song ("plaintive in character, a Blues type"), II. Hey-Hey ("humorous, without words"), III. Croon (also without words), IV. The Backslider ("is not a musical satire on religion").
Instrumentation: Soprano solo with 3 clarinets, bassoon, alto saxophone; drums; tenor banjo, piano, 2 violins.
Duration: 10 minutes.
Composer's notes say, "This is one of the very first efforts toward a symphonic treatment of jazz motifs." (*See:* W5, Suite 2)
Autograph location unknown.

W81a **First Performance:** 1926 (January 24): New York, NY; Aeolian Hall; International Composers' Guild, Eugene Goossens, conductor; Florence Mills, soloist. (*See also:* WB26.1)

Bibliography

WB81.1 Downes, Olin. "Music." *New York Times*, January 25, 1926, p. 25.
"Miss Mills sang four songs of William Still, two of them to verses, one of them a croon, the other a song in which the singer ejaculates 'Hey, Hey,' between very queer noises made by the orchestra. . . . The verses come collectively under the heading of *Levee Land*. The first is a 'Blue' ditty, with words, as the bard would say, of homely grief and longing, and the last song is one concerning the individual who lost religion through the lure of jazz. The first is the best. The last is effective when it has Miss Mills do it. Both of them seem artificial, neither real jazz nor real modernism, with forced wit and sentimental affectation. But the audience was enjoying the comedienne. The last song was repeated."

WB81.2 B., R. C. "Novelties at Modernist Concert Range from Atonality to Sophisticated Jazz." *Musical America* 43 (January 30, 1926): 4, 23.
"William Grant Still has attempted in *Levee Land* to combine jazz with sophisticated harmony, and the result of the union is not happy. His music does not have definite enough melodic character for the folk-music it purports to be, while its harmonic acidity is too deliberate. Trying to be both realistic and fantastic, it fails of becoming either. The 'Levee Song,' a plaintive 'Blues,' is the most worthy of the group. The second is a wordless croon and in the third the singer exclaims 'Hey! Hey!' at intervals with varying expression. 'The Backslider' owed its marked success . . . to the inimitable ways of Florence Mills. . . . In fact, the entire suite would have fallen flat without her piquant inflections, her peculiar reedy quality of voice and her contagious humor."

WB81.3 Osgood, Henry O. *So This Is Jazz.* Boston: Little, Brown, and Co., 1926: 46.
The author recalls the performance of *Levee Land*. "The music, cleverly utilizing what might be called the earmarks of jazz, was most ingenious—sane and healthy, yet of decided originality. Particularly interesting were the variety and ingenuity of the rhythmic devices. Miss Mills, learning the difficult voice parts by heart, since she does not read music, sang the songs with just the right freedom of expression and with mischievous nuances. Mr. Still succeeded in accomplishing what he set out to do. Further efforts of his along this same line will be awaited with interest."

W82 *Lilt* (Pietro Deiro Publishers; available from William Grant Still Music).
For accordion solo ("teaching piece").
Composed in Los Angeles, 1960.
Commissioned by the American Accordionists' Association.
Duration: 4 minutes.
Autograph with fingerings and additional notes from the composer and further notes in another hand and a facsimile of the manuscript without these additional notes are in the William Grant Still and Verna Arvey Papers at the University of Arkansas Libraries, Fayetteville.

Selected Performances

W82a 1977 (November 3): Baltimore, MD; Morgan State University, Murphy Auditorium; Robert Young McMahon, accordion.

W82b 1993 (February 6): Trenton, NJ; Trenton State College, Bray Recital Hall; Robert Young McHahon, accordion.

Bibliography

WB82.1 "William Grant Still Writes Second Work for Accordion." *Accordion Horizons* 4 (Fall 1968): 11.
Lilt was the second work for accordion by Still. In a letter dated June 23, 1968, to Mrs. Elsie Bennett, chair of the Composers Commissioning Committee of the American Accordionists' Association, Still says, "*Lilt* is a jaunty, good-humored little tune with an easy, infectious rhythm. The middle section, also melodic, offers a sparkling contrast to the basic theme." (*See also:* WB8.6)

W83 *Little David, Play on Your Harp* (available from William Grant Still Music).
Spiritual arrangement for SSATB chorus with piano.
Facsimile of a fair copy of the autograph of this arrangement of the spiritual for SSATB chorus with piano is in the William Grant Still and Verna Arvey Papers at the University of Arkansas Libraries, Fayetteville. (*See:* W147)
Autograph is in The William Grant Still Estate.

W84 *Little Folk Suite from the Western Hemisphere for Brass Quintet* (Peer Music Company, formerly Southern Music Publishing Company, Inc., New York; available from William Grant Still Music).
Folk song arrangements for brass quintet.
Contents: I. Where Shall I Be (When the Great Trumpet Sounds)? (Spiritual) II. En Roulant Ma Boule (French Canadian).
Instrumentation: 2 trumpets, trombone, horn, tuba.
Duration: 2 minutes, 30 seconds.
Autograph sketches and a fair copy of the score and parts are in the William Grant Still and Verna Arvey Papers at the University of Arkansas Libraries, Fayetteville.
Holograph is in The William Grant Still Estate.

W85 *Little Folk Suite from the Western Hemisphere No. 1* (Peer Music Company, formerly Southern Music Publishing Company, Inc., New York; available from William Grant Still Music).
Folk song arrangements for string quartet.
Contents: I. Salangadou (Louisiana), II. El Capotin (California).

Duration: 3 minutes, 45 seconds.
Autograph sketches are in the William Grant Still and Verna Arvey Papers at the University of Arkansas Libraries, Fayetteville.
Manuscript is in The William Grant Still Estate.

W86 *Little Folk Suite from the Western Hemisphere No. 2* (Peer Music Company, formerly Southern Music Publishing Company, Inc., New York; available from William Grant Still Music).
Folk song arrangements for string quartet.
Contents: I. El Nido (Argentina), II. Sweet Betsy from Pike (United States).
Duration: 4 minutes.
Autograph sketches, which include a third movement, *Whoopee Ti Yi Yo* are in the William Grant Still and Verna Arvey Papers at the University of Arkansas Libraries, Fayetteville.
Manuscript is in The William Grant Still Estate.

W87 *Little Folk Suite from the Western Hemisphere No. 3* (Peer Music Company, formerly Southern Music Publishing Company, Inc., New York; available from William Grant Still Music).
Folk song arrangements for string quartet.
Contents: I. Aurore Pradere (Louisiana) and Tant Sirop est Doux (Martinique), II. Wade in the Water (Spiritual).
Duration: 3 minutes.
Autograph sketches are in the William Grant Still and Verna Arvey Papers at the University of Arkansas Libraries, Fayetteville.
Manuscript is in The William Grant Still Estate.

W88 *Little Folk Suite from the Western Hemisphere No. 4* (Peer Music Company, formerly Southern Music Publishing Company, Inc., New York; available from William Grant Still Music).
Folk song arrangements for string quartet.
Contents: I. Los Indios (Brazil) and Yaravi (Peru), II. The Crawdad Song (Louisiana).
Duration: 3 minutes, 30 seconds.
Autograph is in The William Grant Still Estate.

W89 *Little Folk Suite from the Western Hemisphere No. 5* (Peer Music Company, formerly Southern Music Publishing Company, Inc., New York; available from William Grant Still Music).
Folk song arrangements for string quartet.
Contents: I. Tutu Maramba (Brazil), II. La Varsoviana (Spanish Colonial, United States).
Duration: 4 minutes.
Autograph is in The William Grant Still Estate.

W90 *Little Red Schoolhouse* (Peer Music Company, formerly Southern Music Publishing Company, Inc., 1967; *Little Red Schoolhouse* and *Pages From a Mother's Diary* available from William Grant Still Music).
Suite for orchestra.
Completed in Los Angeles, 1956; based on *Pages From a Mother's Diary*, composed in 1953.
Contents: I. Little Conqueror, II. Egyptian Princess, III. Captain Kidd, Jr., IV. Colleen Bawn, V. Petey.

Instrumentation for orchestra: 2 flutes (2nd doubles on piccolo), 2 oboes (2nd doubles on English horn), 2 clarinets (2nd doubles on bass clarinet), 2 bassoons; 3 horns, 3 trumpets, 2 trombones, tuba; timpani, bells, triangle, cymbals, wood block, drums; harp, celesta, strings.
Duration: 15 minutes.

Autograph sketches of portions of a work, including *Petey* and *Little Mother* with revisions, are in the William Grant Still and Verna Arvey Papers at the University of Arkansas Libraries, Fayetteville. The composer's notes indicate that *Little Red Schoolhouse* contains material from another work called *Pages From a Mother's Diary*.

Sketches in the Still and Arvey Papers with notes on orchestration of *Pages From a Mother's Diary* dated June 1953, "second draft," indicate the following contents: I. Little Conqueror, II. Egyptian Princess "(to Catherine Mary Lawrence)," III. [no title], IV. Little Song From Nowhere "(to Catheryn Lynne Smithwick)," V. Bundle of Energy. The Still and Arvey Papers include a sketch for a *Rhythmic Song for Orchestra* (unfinished).

W90a **First Performance:** 1954 (January 8): Santa Clara, CA; Montgomery Theater; Santa Clara County Symphonette, Edward Azhderian, conductor. (*Pages From a Mother's Diary*)

W90b **First Performance:** 1957 (March 30): Redlands, CA; University of Redlands Memorial Chapel; The University-Community Symphony Orchestra, Edward C. Tritt, conductor. (*Little Red Schoolhouse*)

Selected Performances

W90c 1957 (October 30): Sacramento, CA; San Juan High School; Sacramento Philharmonic Orchestra, Fritz Berens, conductor. (*Little Red Schoolhouse*)

W90d 1958 (March 18): Sacramento, CA; Sacramento High School; Sacramento Philharmonic Orchestra, Fritz Berens, conductor. (*Little Red Schoolhouse*)

W90e 1966 (March 27): Tucson, AZ; Tucson High School Auditorium; Tucson High School Symphonic Band, William Grant Still, guest conductor. (*Little Red Schoolhouse,* arrangement for band by Charles Bucky Steele)

W90f 1984 (February 15): Fayetteville, AR; Hilton Hotel, Sequoyah Ballroom; University of Arkansas Symphonic Winds, Eldon Janzen, conductor. (*Little Red Schoolhouse,* arrangement for band by Charles Bucky Steele)

Bibliography

WB90.1 Morgan, Marta. "Still's New Suite Warmly Applauded." *San Jose Mercury*, January 9, 1954.

Review of the January 8, 1954, performance of the Santa Clara County Symphonette, Edward Azhderian, conductor. The program included the world premiere of *Pages from a Mother's Diary*. "Suite itself is divided into five sections and, on first hearing, it seemed marked by imaginative, energetic and impish qualities usually associated with the innocence, imagery and high spirits of childhood. The short movements are well contrasted and imbued with genuine sensitivity, charm and creative inventiveness. Dr. Still . . . was enthusiastically applauded by the audience, as were conductor Azhderian and members of the Symphonette for their performance of the suite."

WB90.2 Glackin, William C. "Philharmonic's Preview Shows Strong Makeup." *Sacramento Bee*, October 31, 1957, p. A-14.

Review of the final pre-season concert. "This [*Little Red Schoolhouse*] is interesting and completely charming music."

WB90.3 De Pinto, Geraldine. "Program Notes." Metropolitan Symphony Orchestra, September 17, 1961.

Program notes for the September 17, 1961, performance of the Metropolitan Symphony Orchestra. "William Grant Still . . . has never lost the ability nor the inclination to think in terms of music for and about young people. *Little Red Schoolhouse* is just such a composition, an orchestral suite written for adults *about* children. Each of its sections describes a different student who attended the little red schoolhouse, an important part of early American life. *Little Conqueror* is descriptive of the boy who wanted to become a great general, and who always played soldier. The little girl who liked to pretend that she was the daughter of a Pharaoh is pictured in *Egyptian Princess*. Her parents came from Ireland and she was Irish too! *Colleen Brown* gives a musical portrait of the prettiest girl in school, while *Petey* was just Petey, a good-natured, popular, lively red-headed boy with a captivating grin." (III. *Captain Kidd, Jr.,* is not mentioned.)

W91 ***Little Song that Wanted to Be a Symphony, The*** (Carl Fischer, Inc., New York, and The Eastman School of Music in the American Composers' Edition, Rochester, NY, 1954; copyrighted by William Grant Still in 1954; copyright assigned 1973, copyright 1974 The Eastman School of Music).

For orchestra, narrator, women's vocal trio.

Composer's notes indicate that sketches began as early as 1938; completed in this form in Los Angeles, 1953.

Narration [and text] by Verna Arvey.

Contents: Theme and variations divided into sections I. Introduction, II. Episode, III. Interlude One, IV. Indian, V. Interlude Two, VI. Bayou, VII. Interlude Three, VIII. Oriental, IX. Interlude Four, X. Latin American, XI. Interlude Five, XII. Afro-American, XIII. Interlude Six, XIV. Italian American, XV. Interlude Seven, XVI. Romance, XVII. Interlude Eight, XVIII. Mountain Folk, XIX. Interlude Nine, XX. Finale.

Instrumentation: 2 flutes (2nd doubles on piccolo), 2 oboes (2nd doubles on English horn), 2 clarinets, 2 bassoons; 3 horns, 3 trumpets (straight and cup mutes), 2 trombones (straight and cup mutes and soft hats), tuba; timpani, bells, glockenspiel, xylophone, slap stick, maracas, castanets, triangle, tambourine, wood block, cymbals, drums; harp, celesta, strings.

Additional information provided by the composer on instrumentation: "The following parts, which do not appear in the score, are included to substitute for the female trio: solo 1st violin, solo 2nd violin, solo viola and solo cello. The following extra parts, which do not appear in the score, are included: flute 3, English horn, bass clarinet, horn 4, and trombone 3."

Duration: 19 minutes.

Autograph score with notes on orchestration in the order of the sections of the published version, including narration, are in the William Grant Still and Verna Arvey Papers at the University of Arkansas Libraries, Fayetteville.

W91a First Performance: 1955 (February 15): Jackson, MS; Bailey Auditorium; Jackson Symphony Orchestra, Theodore Russell, conductor; Dee Tankersley Faulkner, narrator.

Selected Performances

W91b 1957 (November 6): Redlands, CA; University of Redlands Memorial Chapel; The University-Community Symphony Orchestra, Edward C. Tritt, conductor; Marc Jack Smith, narrator; Women's Vocal Trio: Judy Pearce, Ann Thomason, Sandra Snebly.

W91c 1958 (December 14): Detroit, MI; Ford Auditorium; Detroit Symphony Orchestra, Valter Poole, conductor; Anita Goldman, narrator; Women's Vocal Trio sung by: Edith Babb, Evelyn Grimes, Mary Jean Hess, Susan Simmons, and Janet Thompson.

W91d 1963 (February 2): Philadelphia, PA; Academy of Music; Philadelphia Orchestra, William Smith, conductor; Isaiah Roossin, narrator; Women's Vocal Trio: Patricia Kelby, Alma Johnson, and Onyett Love.

W91e 1968 (May 2): Rochester, NY; Kilbourn Hall; Eastman-Rochester Symphony Orchestra, Howard Hanson, conductor; Ann Yervanian, mezzo-soprano and narrator; Women's Vocal Trio: Ann Yervanian, Barbara Morris, and Candace Wilson.

W91f 1971 (November 1): El Paso, TX; Liberty Hall; El Paso Symphony Orchestra, William Kirschke, conductor; William Grant Still, narrator.

Bibliography

WB91.1 Feldman, Goldie. "Program Notes." (Jackson Symphony Orchestra), February 15, 1955. p. 23+.

"Tonight marks the premiere performance of the *Little Song*, by the distinguished American composer, William Grant Still. Dr. Still has generously offered the Jackson Symphony Orchestra the opportunity to present it for the first time. Written in the theme and variations form, *Little Song* depicts the transformations of a theme as it visits young people in various parts of the United States, entering into the fluteplaying of an Indian boy in the Southwest, the dance of a Chinese girl in California, the lullaby of a Creole mother in Louisiana. The music is written in short sections, without extended development of the ideas, but with skill and care."

WB91.2 Herrington, Tommy. "Gibson, Faulkner 'Star' At Concert." *Clarion-Ledger*, February 16, 1955.

"Mrs. Faulkner completely charmed the audience with her narration on the *Little Song*,—a symphonic work built around a little theme, a little melody, that mixes and mingles on earth among all kinds of people and in all kinds of places. The Jackson Symphony seemed to play Still's piece with an unusual amount of pride."

WB91.3 Perlee, Charles D. "Orchestra Concert at UR Is Up to High Standards." *San Bernardino Daily Sun*, November 8, 1957.

Review of November 6, 1957, performance at the University of Redlands. "It [*The Little Song That Wanted To Be A Symphony*] . . . is most charming, but with strong appeal to adults, as well as children, because of the subtleties of melody, texture and rhythm. . . . [I]t is a cleverly achieved theme and variations."

WB91.4 Gill, Frank P. "Boy, 14, A Hit in Concert." *Detroit Times*, December 15, 1958, p. 16.

"[*The Little Song That Wanted To Be A Symphony*] has a simple charm and many delightful little themes, handled expertly by Still to create a very pleasant few minutes of music. . . . Yet, although it is obviously aimed at the young, it is the kind of work that adults would enjoy just as completely, because it has a serious underlying motif."

WB91.5 Singer, Samuel L. "Orchestra Delights Children." *Philadelphia Inquirer*, February 3, 1963.

"This [*The Little Song That Wanted To Be A Symphony*] is a thoroughly engaging musical story. . . . Isaiah Roossin was the personable and clear-voiced narrator, and got the kids to clap, in time, at one point in the story. . . . Still's work ended in full-throated symphonic splendor."

WB91.6 Watanabe, Ruth. "Program Notes." Thirty-Eighth Annual Festival of American Music. (Eastman-Rochester Symphony Orchestra), May 2, 1968.

Program notes for *The Little Song That Wanted To Be a Symphony*, which includes the following remarks by Still: "For at least fifteen years [since 1938], the idea of building a composition around . . . a little melody that would bring friendship to American children of many differing racial groups had been in the back of my mind. It appeared in various forms in notebooks and in plans for future creations. When [I] finally began the actual work, it took the form of a theme and variations, the latter rather unorthodox because they simulated the musical idioms of the distinct racial groups, rather than the conventional type of variation which we have come to expect. The *Little Song* is only four notes long. It gives up its early dream of becoming a symphony in order to make the children of America happy and to bring them together in harmony and brotherhood. The composition is scored for narrator, three female voices and orchestra, and is held together by a narration written by Verna Arvey."

WB91.7 Kimball, George H. "Highlights of Festival: 2 Memorable Works." *Times-Union*, May 3, 1968, sec. C, p. 9.

Review of the May 2, 1968, performance of the Eastman-Rochester Symphony Orchestra. "Still's *The Little Song That Wanted to Be a Symphony* is a four-note theme with variations, the orchestra and a trio of treble singers musically illustrating a narration in which the personalized 'song' gives up the symphony idea—after meeting a big, beautiful melody —in favor of 'bringing friendship to American children of many differing racial groups,' to quote the composer. It's a kind of magic, born of a free spirit, that Still conjures here, and the orchestra and singers—Barbara Morris, Candace Wilson and Ann Yervanian, the latter also as a very persuasive narrator—gave it all a magical touch."

WB91.8 Southgate, Harvey. "Festival Displays Native Talent." *Rochester Democrat and Chronicle*, May 3, 1968.

Review of the May 2, 1968, performance of the Eastman-Rochester Symphony Orchestra. "[*The Little Song That Wanted To Be a Symphony*] is about a little four-note song that wants to be a symphony, and Mr. Still has made it just that in enlarging, developing and particularizing it through concert halls, a lovely rustic setting and finally bringing it back to simple charm. It calls for a narrator, a role well filled last night by mezzo-soprano Ann Yervanian, and with two soprano parts, sung last night by Barbara Morris and Candace Wilson. Here is musical imagination at work in a genuinely creative form."

WB91.9 Funkhouser, Barbara. "Challenging Program Met By EP Symphony Orchestra." *El Paso Times*, November 2, 1971, sec. A, p. 1+.

Review of the November 1, 1971, performance of the El Paso Symphony Orchestra. "[*The Little Song That Wanted To Be A Symphony* begins] with four notes and [builds] into almost complete symphonic structure. It includes several musical styles including that of almost popular. . . . Dr. Still proved an able narrator. The concert was opened with the orchestra playing Dr. Still's *Festive Overture*, its broad, swinging sounds proving a showcase especially for muted trumpets. It is a happy piece with woodwinds, violins and harps sharing in the honors."

WB91.10 Quarm, Joan. "Symphony Orchestra Presents Special Arts Festival Offering." *El Paso Herald-Post*, November 2, 1971, sec. A, p. 4.

Review of the November 1, 1971, performance of the El Paso Symphony Orchestra. "Still's *Little Song* began as a four-note melody, with ambitions to become a symphony, but, on hearing that it would then be confined to concert halls, decided instead to join all the children of the nation. Composed years ago—'I never remember dates or Opus [numbers],' explained Still—the work involves different races of children and the kind of music they play. The *Little Song* entered into all of them, and helped them live in harmony."

W92 ***Log Cabin Ballads.***
Suite for chamber orchestra.
Composed in New York, 1927.
Contents: I. Long To'ds Night, II. Beneaf de Villers, III. Miss Malindy.
Instrumentation: woodwinds; percussion; 3 violins, viola, cello, bass.
Autograph location unknown.
The composer's notes indicate that this piece was later "discarded."

W92a **First Performance:** 1928 (March 18): New York, NY; Booth Theatre; Barrère Little Symphony Orchestra, Georges Barrère, conductor.

W93 ***Lost Out Blues.***
Popular song.
Recorded under the pseudonyn Willy M. Grant.
Composed in New York, about 1923.
Performed by Ethel Waters and Her Jazz Masters on a recording by The Black Swan Phonograph Company in the 1920s. (*See:* B113)
Autograph location unknown.

W94 ***Love Me in Your Old Time Way.***
Popular song.
Recorded under the pseudonyn Willy M. Grant.
Composed in New York, about 1923.
Performed by Josie Miles with orchestra on a recording by The Black Swan Phonograph Company in the 1920s. (*See:* B113)
Autograph location unknown.

W95 ***Lyric Quartette; Musical Portraits of Three Friends: Impressions,***
variant of title: *Lyric String Quartette* (Composer's original title: *Musical Portraits of Three Friends: Impressions;* available from William Grant Still Music).
For string quartet.
Composed in Los Angeles, 1960, registered in the copyright office September, 1970.
"Dedicated to my friend Joachim Chassman."
Contents: I. Moderately: On a Plantation, II. Moderately slow: In the moun-

tains of Peru (inspired by an Inca melody), III. Moderately fast: In a pioneer settlement.
Original titles: I. The Sentimental One, II. The Quiet One (based on an Inca melody), III. The Jovial One.
Instrumentation: violin I, violin II, viola, cello.
Duration: 9 minutes.
The composer's notes on the holograph identify the movements with the following subtitles: I. The Sympathetic One, II. The Quiet One, III. The Jovial One. Movements I and III are reversed in one version. An inscription by the composer on the sketch says, "I am now at home—Have come home where I may enjoy the happiness that comes only from the companionship of friends."
Holograph score titled *Three Friends,* a fair copy of the score and parts, and sketches are in the William Grant Still and Verna Arvey Papers at the University of Arkansas Libraries, Fayetteville.
The composer's notes indicate that this piece was later "discarded."

W96 *Mandy Lou.*
For voice and piano.
Composed in New York, possibly 1927.
Performed in 1927 in a set called "Dialect Songs" with *The Breath of a Rose* (*See:* W16) and *Winter's Approach.* (*See:* W171)
Rejected for publication by G. Schirmer, Inc., when *The Breath of a Rose* and *Winter's Approach* were accepted. Letter of May 16, 1927, from G. C. Sonneck, Director of Publication, says, "We consider the song, 'Mandy Lou,' not quite so desirable as the other two . . . it is not suitable because, while entirely different, commercially it would conflict with another song of a similar title." (G. Schirmer published *Mandy Lou* by Will Marion Cook in 1904.)
Autograph location unknown.

Selected Performance

W96a 1927 (April 16): New York, NY; New School of Social Research Auditorium; Jessie Zachary, soprano; pianist not identified. (*See:* WB16.1)

W97 *Marionette* (Delkas Music Publishing Company, Los Angeles, 1946, *U.S.A., 1946* collection; available from MCA Music Publishing, New York).
For piano solo.
Composed in Los Angeles, 1946.
Dedicated to Adelaide and Kenneth Winstead.
Duration: 1 minute.
Facsimile of the published edition is in the William Grant Still and Verna Arvey Papers at the University of Arkansas Libraries, Fayetteville.
Autograph location unknown.

Selected Performance

W97a 1971 (March 23): New Orleans, LA; Dillard University; Lawless Memorial Chapel; Jonnie Smith, piano.

W98 *Memphis Man* (Edward B. Marks Music Company, New York, 1928; available from William Grant Still Music).
For solo voice and piano.
Recorded and published under the pseudonym Willy M. Grant.
Composed in New York, about 1923.

142 *William Grant Still: A Bio-Bibliography*

Lyrics by Paul Henry.
Performed by Ethel Waters and Her Jazz Masters on a recording by The Black Swan Phonograph Company in the 1920s. (*See:* B113)
Autograph location unknown.

W99 ***Minette Fontaine*** (available from William Grant Still Music).
Opera in 3 acts, 5 stage sets.
Composed in Los Angeles, 1958; corrections in December, 1960.
Libretto by Verna Arvey.
Dedicated to Joan Palevsky "in appreciation."
Setting: 19th-century, about 1845; leading character is a prima donna with the old New Orleans Opera Company, New Orleans, Louisiana.
For: Cast: Principle roles: coloratura soprano, tenor, soprano, contralto, bass; Secondary roles: 3 mezzo-sopranos, bass, baritone; chorus.
Radiant Night has been recorded separately. (*See:* D34)
Instrumentation: 3 flutes (2nd and 3rd double on piccolo), 2 oboes (2nd doubles on English horn), 3 clarinets, 2 bassoons (2nd doubles on contrabassoon); 3 horns, 2 trumpets (straight, Harmon, and cup mutes), 3 trombones (soft hats or derbies), tuba; timpani, percussion; harp, strings.
Duration: 120 minutes.
Autograph score with corrections and revisions, complete scenario, and sketches for the complete opera are in the William Grant Still and Verna Arvey Papers at the University of Arkansas Libraries, Fayetteville.
Manuscript fair copy of full score and piano vocal score are in The William Grant Still Estate.

W99a **First Performance:** 1984 (October 22, 24, 26): Baton Rouge, LA; Centroplex Theatre; Baton Rouge Opera Company; Charles Rosekrans, conductor; Donald Dorr, director; Dolores Ardoyno, general manager; Cast: Gail Dobish as Minette; Donald George as Diron; Suzanna Gusman as Marie Laveau; Nancy Ross Assaf as Clarice; Andrew Wentzel as Claude; Stephen Markuson as Lucien; Cynthia Parker as Felice; Terry Patrick Harris as Madame de Noyan.

Bibliography

WB99.1 Deermont, Helen. "'Minette Fontaine' Meets Audience's Expectations." Baton Rouge *State Times*, October 25, 1984, p. 3D.
"Still's understating and sympathy for the traditions and haunting moods of New Orleans comes through in almost every passage in the opera. The libretto, written by his wife, Verna Arvey, ties in with the score and rounds out the imagery with skillful detail."

WB99.2 Campbell, Cynthia V. "Baton Rouge Opera: Still 'Minette Fontaine.'" *Musical America* (February 1985): 19-20.
"Still, who is recognized as perhaps the major black composer of his generation, combined his love of Puccini and his interest in the avant-garde to create an opera that is recognizably a product of the 1930s and 40s, tinged throughout by a coloration of jazz and the blues."

W100 ***Miniature Overture*** (available from William Grant Still Music).
For orchestra.
Composed in Los Angeles, 1965.
Instrumentation: 3 flutes, 2 oboes, English horn, 3 clarinets, 2 bassoons;

4 horns, 3 trumpets, 3 trombones, tuba; timpani, triangle, glockenspiel, xylophone, drums, cymbals; harp, strings.
Duration: 2 minutes.
Holograph with orchestration notes, revisions, and sketches is in the William Grant Still and Verna Arvey Papers at the University of Arkansas Libraries, Fayetteville.

W100a **First Performance:** 1965 (October 17, 18): Miami, FL; Greater Miami Philharmonic Orchestra, Fabien Sevitsky, conductor.

W101 *Miniatures for Flute, Oboe, and Piano* (Oxford University Press, London, 1963).
Folk song arrangements for flute, oboe, and piano.
Composed in Los Angeles, about 1948.
Dedicated to Sir John and Lady Barbirolli.
Contents: I. I Ride an Old Paint (Cowboy Song—U.S.A.), II. Adolorido ("Corrido del Bazio—Mexico"), III. Jesus is a Rock in a Weary Land ("Negro Spiritual—U.S.A."), IV. Yaravi ("Indian Lament—Peru") (*See:* W41, W88), V. A Frog Went A' Courtin' ("U.S.A.").
Autograph sketches and scores are in the William Grant Still and Verna Arvey Papers at the University of Arkansas Libraries, Fayetteville.

W101a **First Performance:** 1948 (October 11): London, England; Chelsea Town Hall; Evelyn Barbirolli and the Zephyr Trio.

Selected Performances

W101b 1949 (July 3): London, England; Evelyn Barbirolli and the Zephyr Trio. Radio broadcast over the BBC.

W101c 1960 (April 28): Glasgow, Scotland; Glasgow University; Geraldine Purser, flute; Gabriel Hay, oboe; and Elspeth Low, piano.

W101d 1967 (February 13): Detroit, MI; Detroit Public Library, Main Auditorium; Detroit Musicians Association; Marilyn Jones, flute; John Perry, oboe; Arthur LaBrew, piano.

W101e 1975 (August 31): Los Angeles, CA; Los Angeles Museum of Natural History; Sheridan Stokes, flute; John Ellis, oboe; Annette Kaufmann, piano.

W101f 1992 (November 5): Fayetteville, AR; Walton Arts Center; Alan Zoloth, flute; Theresa Delaplain, oboe; Robert Mueller, piano.

Bibliography

WB101.1 M., L. "Light and Agreeable." *Glasgow Bulletin*, April 29, 1960.
Review of the April 2, 1960, chamber music concert at Glasgow University. The program included Still's *Miniatures*. "As time goes on and the 12-tone composers become more numerous, the gulf between serious music and good light music seems likely to increase, with light music staying on the side of tonality. The sort of thing we shall always find agreeable is the arrangement of five American folk songs for flute, oboe and piano by the Negro composer [William] Grant Still, which Geraldine Purser, Gabriel Hay and Elspeth Low included in their programme at yesterday's lunch-hour concert in Glasgow University. Originally written for Lady Barbirolli [see dedication], they fall piquantly on the ear."

W102 *Minorities: Minorities and Majorities* (ABC Choral Art Series, Gemini Press; available from William Grant Still Music, copyright 1973).

For SATB chorus and piano.
Composed in Los Angeles, 1971.
Text by Verna Arvey.
Duration: 2 minutes.
Facsimile of a manuscript fair copy is in the William Grant Still and Verna Arvey Papers at the University of Arkansas Libraries, Fayetteville.

W103 *Miss Sally's Party* (available from William Grant Still Music).
Ballet, scored for orchestra, one stage set, corps de ballet, 7 solo dancers.
Composed in Los Angeles, 1940.
Dedicated to Thelma Biracree.
Synopsis printed on holograph begins, "Miss Sally gave a party with a cakewalk as its theme, but, though her guests were skillful dancers, to win that cake was Sally's dream. . . . moral: never make a little boy mad—especially if he owns a pet frog."
Scenario by Verna Arvey; Setting: Old South, climaxed by a *Cake Walk*.
Inscription on the sketch and on the fair copy in the composer's hand: "The composer acknowledges gratefully the kindness of The Julius Rosenwald Foundation whose assistance made possible the writing of this ballet. For details concerning the dancing of the Cake Walk the scenarist [Verna Arvey] is indebted to W. C. Handy."
Contents include: Boy's Dance, Cake Walk.
Instrumentation: 2 flutes (2nd doubles on piccolo), 1 oboe, 2 clarinets, 2 bassoons; tenor saxophone; 3 horns, 1 trumpet, 1 trombone; percussion; piano, strings.
Duration: 30 minutes.
Facsimile of the autograph signed by the composer with dance notations is in The University of Rochester, The Eastman School of Music, Sibley Music Library, from The Thelma Biracree Schnepel Collection.
Sketches of full orchestration of portions of the ballet, including the *Cake Walk,* are in the William Grant Still and Verna Arvey Papers at the University of Arkansas Libraries, Fayetteville.
Holograph of full score and fair copy of the piano vocal score are in The William Grant Still Estate.

W103a **First Performance:** 1941 (May 2): Rochester, NY; Eastman Theatre; Rochester Civic Orchestra, Howard Hanson, conductor; Thelma Biracree, choreographer and Miss Sally.

Selected Performance

W103b 1959 (January 20): Tucson, AZ; University Auditorium; Tucson Symphony Orchestra, Frederic Balazs, conductor.

Bibliography

WB103.1 Warner, A.J. "Ballet Closes Festival." *Times Union*, May 3, 1941.
Guest review of the May 2, 1941, performance of the Rochester Civic Orchestra. "*Miss Sally's Party* was a disappointment. . . . Still's score was very placid and all too much like a Sunday School. I wanted some sandpaper in the score, and was completely surprised at the gentle quality."

WB103.2 Will, Mary Ertz. "Annual American Music Festival in Rochester." *Musical America* 61 (May 10, 1941): 7.
Review of the Eleventh Annual Festival of American Music. "Dr.

Hanson and the orchestra gave it [*Symphony No. 2 in G Minor*] a fine performance; it is graceful music to listen to. . . . Still's *Miss Sally's Party* was a first performance, gay lively music with suggestions of the old South, and Miss [Thelma] Biracree, who took the lead, worked out the choreography most appropriately."

WB103.3   Hanson, Howard. "Summing Up an American Festival." *New York Times*, May 11, 1941. (Similar article appears in the University of Rochester *Alumni Bulletin* of The Eastman School of Music 12 [May 1941]: 1-2.)

"This [*Miss Sally's Party*] music has many of the well-known elements of Still's other works. The orchestration is deft and the melodic material homespun and frequently charming."

WB103.4   Saltzberg, Geraldine. "Symphony Has Trouble With Sibelius Concerto." *Arizona Daily Star*, January 21, 1959.

Review of the January 20, 1959, performance of the Tucson Symphony Orchestra. The program included Still's *Dance Before the Hut (Sahdji)*, *Boy's Dance (Miss Sally's Party)*, and *Tribal Dance (The American Scene)*. "Still's compositions made an excellent curtain raiser, modern in idiom, fresh and appealing. A ripple of laughter went through the auditorium in response to *Boy's Dance*, a scene from a ballet, in which two mischievous boys dance around the cake prepared for the winner of the Cakewalk."

W104   *Mississippi,* other titles are *Arkansas, Mississippi March, March-Finale,* and *Men of the Army* (available from William Grant Still Music).
For vocal solo with piano; also for SATB chorus with piano.
Composed in Los Angeles, 1942, as *March-Finale*.
Texts by Verna Arvey (texts are different for each title).
Duration: 3 minutes.
Holograph lead sheet of *March-Finale* is in the Library of Congress, deposited for copyright on November 2, 1942.
Autograph sketches of melody with text, solo vocal version with piano (no text), and SATB chorus version with piano, and a facsimile of the manuscript fair copy for the vocal solo and piano version of *Mississippi* are in the William Grant Still and Verna Arvey Papers at the University of Arkansas Libraries, Fayetteville. The composer wrote the title, *Mississippi,* on the autograph of *March-Finale*. The fair copy has a different introduction.

W104a   **First Performance:** 1948 (July 26): U.S. Army broadcast on the *Sound Off* program over the ABC Radio Network.

W105   *Mota* (available from William Grant Still Music).
Opera in 3 acts, scored for orchestra, with ballet, 4 stage sets.
Composed in Los Angeles, 1951.
Libretto by Verna Arvey.
Setting: A village of Ancestral Africa.
For: Cast: Principle roles: tenor, soprano, bass, mezzo-soprano; Secondary roles: 2 tenors, 2 basses; chorus.
Instrumentation: 2 flutes (2nd doubles on piccolo), 2 oboes, 2 clarinets, 2 bassoons; 4 horns (non-transposing mute), 3 trumpets and 3 trombones (with straight and cup mutes), tuba; timpani, percussion; harp, strings.
Duration: 120 minutes.
Holograph sketches and conductor's score with corrections and stage direc-

tions are in the William Grant Still and Verna Arvey Papers at the University of Arkansas Libraries, Fayetteville.
Manuscript full score and fair copy of piano vocal score are in The William Grant Still Estate.

W106 *My Brother American* (American Book Company [Litton Educational Publishing], 1972, in *New Dimensions in Music;* available from William Grant Still Music).
For solo voice, piano, triangle, and wood block in a music education textbook.
Text by Verna Arvey.
Inscription says: "This music was written especially for this book by William Grant Still."
Duration: 2 minutes.
Sketch with revision to the piano part, typed text, and a facsimile of the manuscript fair copy are in the William Grant Still and Verna Arvey Papers at the University of Arkansas Libraries, Fayetteville.

W107 *Nigeria, We Hail Thee.*
For solo voice and piano; SATB chorus a cappella.
Text written in the composer's hand with the following inscription: "The Independence Celebrations Officer 34/36 Iroyi Road, Lagos, Nigeria. Natnl. [National] Anthem."
Autograph of a solo voice and piano arrangement with revisions, the complete text, and an SATB arrangement (a cappella) are in the William Grant Still and Verna Arvey Papers at the University of Arkansas Libraries, Fayetteville.

W108 *No Matter What You Do* (Handy Brothers, [n.d.]).
Popular song for voice and piano.
Lyrics by Grace Bundy.
Autograph location unknown.

W109 *[Ohio, Ohio: Your Beacon Burns Brightly].*
For solo voice and piano; title above derived from first line of text.
Untitled autograph with text written in Arvey's hand is in the William Grant Still and Verna Arvey Papers at the University of Arkansas Libraries, Fayetteville. The autograph bears an inscription by the composer, "In the tempo of a stately march."

W110 *Old California* (available from William Grant Still Music).
For orchestra; also arranged for symphonic band by the composer.
Composed in Los Angeles; holograph date August, 1941 (composed between August 23 and September 1).
Composed at the request of Werner Janssen to honor the 160th birthday of the City of Los Angeles.
Band arrangement has the inscription: "Dedicated to the memory of my friend, the late George Fischer."
Contents: three principal sections, a tone poem.
Instrumentation for orchestra: 3 flutes (3rd doubles on piccolo), 2 oboes, English horn, 3 clarinets, 3 bassoons; 4 horns, 3 trumpets, 3 trombones, tuba; timpani, claves, vibraphone, chime, resonator bell, maracas, castanets, tambourine, costume bells, gong, drums, tom-tom, cymbals; harp, strings.
Instrumentation for band includes all of the above (except strings) and the

following additional instruments: E-flat alto clarinet, bass clarinet, 2 alto saxophones, tenor saxophone, 4 cornets, baritone horn, E-flat tuba, and BB-flat tuba.
Duration: 10 minutes.
Holograph sketches for orchestra and band are in the William Grant Still and Verna Arvey Papers at the University of Arkansas Libraries, Fayetteville.
Holograph full score is in the Library of Congress, deposited for copyright on October 30, 1941.
Manuscript of conductor's score prepared on the music typewriter is in The William Grant Still Estate.

W110a **First Performance:** 1941 (September 4): Standard Symphony Orchestra, Werner Janssen, conductor. (A Mutual Radio Broadcast.)

Selected Performances

W110b 1941 (October 30); Los Angeles, CA; Wilshire Ebell Theater; Werner Janssen Symphony Orchestra, Werner Janssen, conductor.

W110c 1942 (July 28): Brooklyn, NY; Prospect Park; Goldman Band, Edwin Franko Goldman, conductor.

W110d 1943 (July 25): Pasadena, CA; Brookside Theatre; Werner Janssen Symphony Orchestra, Werner Janssen, conductor.

W110e 1944 (November 4): New York, NY; Carnegie Hall; New York Philharmonic-Symphony Orchestra, Pierre Monteux, guest conductor.

W110f 1945 (August 21): Los Angeles, CA; Hollywood Bowl; Hollywood Bowl Symphony Orchestra, Leopold Stokowski, conductor.

W110g 1945 (November 19): Paris, France; Théâtre des Champs-Élysées; Orchestre National, Rudolph Dunbar, conductor.

W110h 1950 (May 21): New York, NY; Town Hall; New York Chamber Orchestra, Dean Dixon, conductor.

W110i 1959 (September 4): Los Angeles, CA; Old Plaza; Los Angeles County Symphonic Band, Arthur Babich, conductor.

W110j 1965 (July 1, 2): Brooklyn, NY; Prospect Park; Goldman Band, Richard Franko Goldman, conductor.

W110k 1966 (December 11): Los Angeles, CA; J.L. Caston Fellowship Hall; Southeast Symphony Orchestra, Louis Palange, conductor.

W110l 1968 (April 16): New Orleans, LA; Tulane University, McAlister Auditorium; New Orleans Philharmonic-Symphony Orchestra, Werner Torkanowsky, conductor. (*See:* WB36.17, WB117.18)

W110m 1969 (May 15): Torrance, CA; Torrance High School Auditorium; The South Bay-Torrance Symphony Orchestra, William Grant Still, guest conductor.

W110n 1974 (February 24): Los Angeles, CA; Occidental College, Thorne Hall; Occidental College Band, Felix McKernan, conductor.

Bibliography

WB110.1 "William Grant Still's New Tone Poem." *Pacific Coast Musician*, September 20, 1941.

Provides insight to the development of *Old California*, which was broadcast on the Standard Symphony Hour on September 4, 1941, by the

Janssen Symphony Orchestra. According to Still, "[T]he piece was written very quickly as Mr. Janssen telephoned me on August 23rd and asked me to have it ready by September 3rd. I had only a short time to do the research and the subject (which he had outlined to me beforehand) was one which I had very little previous knowledge. However, I began to work on it and it was ready on September 1."

WB110.2 Jones, Isabel Morse. "Janssen Concert at Ebell Success." *Los Angeles Times*, October 31, 1941.

"[*Old California*] began with a basic, primitive bit of atmospheric writing and soon brightened into an Indian dance with a touch of whoopee. A brief religious theme gave the middle part character and then Mexico and the Spanish dancing were introduced. The American finale was blurred with strange combinations of tone which were not always effective last night."

WB110.3 Saunders, Richard D. "Janssen Wins Applause as Season Opens." *Hollywood Citizen-News*, October 31, 1941.

Review of the October 30, 1941, performance of the Werner Janssen Symphony Orchestra. "A prolonged ovation was accorded William Grant Still after a fine initial presentation of his tone-poem, *Old California*, depicting the history of the State. A work of strong melodic appeal, magnificently orchestrated, it is worth a permanent place in orchestral repertory."

WB110.4 ———. "Orchestra at Brookside Park Lauded." Los Angeles *Citizen-News*, July 26, 1943.

Review of the July 25, 1943, performance of the Janssen Symphony Orchestra. "Essaying a tonal picture of California's development, [*Old California*] holds thematic charm, enunciated with deft orchestration."

WB110.5 Straus, Noel. "Leon Fleisher, 16, Scores as Soloist." *New York Times*, November 5, 1944.

Review of the November 4, 1944, performance of the New York Philharmonic-Symphony Orchestra. "*Old California* . . . received its first New York presentation. It proved a commonplace work, elaborately scored, but hardly of the type deserving a hearing on a serious program."

WB110.6 Biancolli, Louis. "San Francisco Boy Pianist [Leon Fleisher] Impressive in Carnegie Hall Debut." *New York World Telegram*, November 6, 1944.

Review of the November 4, 1944, performance of the New York Philharmonic-Symphony Orchestra. "*Old California* is a frank piece of program music, mingling Indian and Spanish motifs in obvious development but rather shallow in content and probably best adapted as accompaniment to a movie panorama showing Los Angeles growth as a meeting place of racial cultures."

WB110.7 Jones, Isabel Morse. "Shostakovich 'Seventh' Bowl Symphonic Event." *Los Angeles Times*, August 22, 1945.

Review of the August 21, 1945, performance of the Hollywood Bowl Symphony. "When the scheduled *Plow That Broke the Plain* by Virgil Thomson failed to arrive yesterday morning. . . . *Old California* was hastily substituted. This work is short and direct."

WB110.8 Biancolli, Louis. "All-Negro Program at Town Hall." *New York World Telegram and Sun*, May 22, 1950.

Review of the May 21, 1950, New York Chamber Orchestra performance, at Town Hall, which included William Grant Still's *Old California.* "In putting together this diversified material Mr. [Dean] Dixon [conductor] was doing more than assembling a group of Negro composers who happened to turn out symphonic scores. These were all composers with something to say and capable of saying it in accepted symphonic form, modified to suit their own purposes."

WB110.9 Perlee, Charles D. "Concert Season Off To A Fine Start." San Bernardino *Evening Telegram*, October 30, 1967.

Review of the October 29, 1967, performance of the Riverside Symphony Orchestra at the Riverside Municipal Auditorium. "[*Old California*] recounts the Indian and Spanish influences on our lives and showed Still's abilities in translating for the modern orchestra the simple melodies of our forebears. I wish Dr. Still could have been there to hear it, especially the oh-so-lovely oboe solo of Karen Carmack."

W111 ***Pages from Negro History*** (Carl Fischer, Inc., *Music of Our Time*, New York, 1943, no. 03195).
Suite for school orchestra (can include narrator); also for solo voice and piano.
Composed in Los Angeles; holograph dated April 1941.
Inscription by the composer says, "For Duncan" (Duncan Allan Still, b. 1940, the son of Verna Arvey and William Grant Still).
Optional narration by Verna Arvey.
Contents: I. Moderately fast: Africa, II. Slower: Slavery, III. Moderately: Emancipation.
Inscription in II. *Slavery* on the holograph says, "In the style of a Negro chant" at the tempo marking "Mournfully."
Instrumentation: 2 flutes (2nd optional), 2 oboes (2nd optional), 2 clarinets, 2 bassoons (2nd optional); alto and tenor saxophone (optional); 4 horns (3rd and 4th optional), 2 trumpets, 3 trombones (1st and 2nd optional), tuba; percussion, harp or piano, strings.
Duration: 10 minutes.
Holograph with orchestration notes is in the William Grant Still and Verna Arvey Papers at the University of Arkansas Libraries, Fayetteville.

W111a **First Performance:** 1944 (March 17): Westminster, MD; Western Maryland College Little Symphony Orchestra, Philip Royer, conductor, Esther Smith, narrator.

Selected Performances

W111b 1944 (July 31): Rochester, NY; Kilbourn Hall; Eastman School Summer Orchestra, Karl D. Van Hoesen, conductor; Joseph Lupkiewicz, narrator.

W111c 1946 (March 31): Washington, DC; National Gallery of Art; National Gallery Sinfonietta, Richard Bales, conductor.

W111d 1969 (April 20): Södertälje, Sweden; Mattiwilda Dobbs, soloist; Ernst Arndal, piano.

W111e 1974 (March 3): Los Angeles, CA; Martin Luther King Auditorium; Watts Symphony Orchestra, Octave Bonomo, conductor; Barbara Scott, narrator.

W111f 1977 (March 7): Los Angeles, CA; University of Southern California, Bovard Auditorium; Watts Symphony Orchestra, Octave Bonomo, conductor; William Marshall, narrator.

Bibliography

WB111.1 Eversman, Alice. "Vladimir Horowitz Delights Audience With Performance." Washington *Evening Star*, April 1, 1946.

"The American Music Festival in the National Gallery of Art concluded last night with the hearing of several new works, performed by the National Gallery Sinfonietta under Richard Bales' direction. Noteworthy among these was William Grant Still's impressive *Pages From Negro History*."

W112 *Pastorela,* variant of title: *Pastorella* (M. Witmark & Sons, New York, 1947, no. 20603-19; available from William Grant Still Music).
For violin and piano; also for violin and orchestra.
Composed in Los Angeles, 1946.
Published inscription: "Dedicated to my friend Samuel Marti."
Foreword by the composer says, " . . . I have sought to present a tone picture of a Western Landscape."
Instrumentation: solo violin with 3 flutes (3rd doubles on piccolo), 2 oboes, English horn, 3 clarinets, 2 bassoons; 4 horns, 3 trumpets, 3 trombones, tuba; timpani, chimes, cymbals; harp, strings.
Duration: 11 minutes.
Holograph with orchestration notes for violin and orchestra, holograph of violin part with original editorial markings from Louis Kaufman, and a facsimile of the published edition for violin and piano are in the William Grant Still and Verna Arvey Papers at the University of Arkansas Libraries, Fayetteville. Holograph has notes from the composer: "(Please mark bowings and return)" and "Violin part edited by Louis Kaufman."

W112a **First Performance:** 1947 (March 14): New York, NY; Town Hall; Louis Kaufman, violin; Erich Itor Kahn, piano.

Selected Performances

W112b 1947 (July 9): Louis Kaufman, violin; Columbia Broadcasting System Orchestra, Bernard Herrman, conductor. Broadcast over the CBS Radio Network.

W112c 1970 (March 29): Los Angeles, CA: Los Angeles County Museum of Natural History; Louis Kaufman, violin; Annette Kaufman, piano.

W112d 1970 (October 29): Long Beach, CA; Long Beach Museum of Art; Louis Kaufman, violin; Annette Kaufman, piano.

W112e 1971 (September 12): Portland, OR; Portland Art Museum Auditorium; Louis Kaufman, violin; Annette Kaufman, piano.

W112f 1973 (August 5): Los Angeles, CA; Exposition Park, Jean Delacour Auditorium; Louis Kaufman, violin; Annette Kaufman, piano.

W112g 1975 (August 31): Los Angeles, CA; Los Angeles County Museum of Natural History; Louis Kaufman, violin; Annette Kaufman, piano.

W112h 1976 (May 2): Fayetteville, AR; University of Arkansas, Newman Center; Alan Pedigo, violin; Billigene Pedigo, piano.

W112i 1979 (October 18): Los Angeles, CA; Arnold Schoenberg Institute; Yukiko Kamei, violin; Doris Stevenson, piano.

W112j 1980 (January 14): Washington, DC; Kennedy Center; Vincent Esposito, violin; Pablo Zinger, piano.

W112k 1984 (February): Fayetteville, AR; University of Arkansas, Fine Arts Center Concert Hall; Margaret Magill, violin; John Keene, piano.

Bibliography

WB112.1 P[erkins], F[rancis] D. "Kaufman Recital." *New York Herald Tribune*, March 15, 1947.

Review of the March 14, 1947, recital by Louis Kaufman. "William Grant Still was represented by the first public performance of his *Pastorela*, written at Mr. Kaufman's suggestion. . . . The music itself did not give a sense of any particular color, but it had contrast of mood."

WB112.2 P., W. A. "Violin Recital by Kaufman." *New York Sun*, March 15, 1947.

Review of the March 14, 1947, recital by Kaufman. "William Grant Still's *Pastorela* received its world premiere. Somewhat too long for its own good, it is a quietly lyrical tone picture of vaguely Oriental flavor."

WB112.3 T., H. "Louis Kaufman, Violinist, Presents Music by Six Contemporaries in Lively Program." *New York Times*, March 16, 1947.

Review of the March 14, 1947, recital by Louis Kaufman. "William Grant Still's skillful and pleasant *Pastorela* . . . had its première."

WB112.4 Goldberg, Albert. "A USC Tribute to William Grant Still." *Los Angeles Times*, October 20, 1979, part 2, p. 9.

Review of the October 18, 1979, performance of the University of Southern California School of Music in a "Tribute Concert to William Grant Still" at the Arnold Schoenberg Institute. "The more ambitious side of his art was represented on this program by a *Pastorela* that belied its title in its length and sturdy development. . . . Smaller in scale, but equally imaginative were four pieces from a set of seven *Traceries*, played by Cynthia Summerville, pianist. *Songs of Separation*, settings of five poems by black poets, should attract more recitalists by reason of their strong dramatic impulse. . . . Still's cleverness in handling folk material in dance form was exemplified in five *Vignettes*. . . as well as in four *Danzas de Panama* played by the USC String Quartet, and three *Rhythmic Spirituals*, sung with fine precision and clarity of enunciation by the USC Chamber Singers, directed by Rodney Eichenberger."

W113 ***Path of Glory, The*** (available from William Grant Still Music).
For bass-baritone solo and narrator with orchestra.
Composed in Los Angeles, 1962.
Text by Verna Arvey on the "glory and fall of the Aztec Empire."
Contents: I. Prologue, II. Evocation, III. Interlude, IV. Call to Battle, V. Interlude, VI. Judgment, VII. Interlude, VIII. Elegy.
Instrumentation: bass-baritone solo with 3 flutes, 2 oboes, English horn, 3 clarinets, 2 bassoons; 4 horns, 3 trumpets, 3 trombones, tuba; timpani, percussion; harp, strings.
Duration: 15 minutes.
Holograph with revisions and sketches is in the William Grant Still and Verna Arvey Papers at the University of Arkansas Libraries, Fayetteville. "Song Cycle with orchestration" is written on the sketches by the composer.
Autograph is in The William Grant Still Estate.

W113a **First Performance:** 1990 (April 22); Grand Forks, ND; Holy Family Church; Grand Forks Symphony Orchestra, John Deal, conductor; Herbert V. R. P. Jones, soloist.

W114 *Patterns* (available from William Grant Still Music).
Suite for small orchestra; also for harp and string sextet.
Composed in Los Angeles, 1960.
Dedicated to Ernst Gebert and the Inglewood Symphony Orchestra.
Program notes by the composer say, "it is frankly experimental music, brief, but varied as to harmonies. The word 'Patterns' as an overall title refers to the rather persistent rhythmic designs in each section."
Contents: I. Magic Crystal, II. A Lone Teardrop, III. Rain Pearls, IV. Tranquil Cove, V. Moon-Gold.
Instrumentation for small orchestra: 2 flutes (2nd doubles on piccolo), 2 oboes, English horn, 2 clarinets, 2 bassoons; 2 trumpets; strings.
Duration: 15 minutes.
Sketches with orchestration notes for *Magic Crystal, A Lone Teardrop, Rain Pearls,* and *Moon-Gold* (originally called "Voices in the Night" and "The Shape of a Moonbeam") are in the William Grant Still and Verna Arvey Papers at the University of Arkansas Libraries, Fayetteville. The Still and Arvey Papers include an autograph of the arrangement of *Magic Crystal* for harp and string sextet (violin I, violin II, violin III, viola, cello, bass) with the indication "Csaky Ensemble" at the top left.
Autograph is in The William Grant Still Estate.

W114a **First Performance:** 1961 (April 22, 23): Torrance, CA; El Camino College Campus Center; Inglewood Symphony Orchestra, Ernst Gebert, conductor.

Selected Performances

W114b 1961 (April 29): Hollywood, CA; Bancroft Auditorium; Hollywood Symphony Orchestra, Ernst Gebert, conductor.

W114c 1964 (December 13): Los Angeles, CA; E.B. Crocker Gallery; Little Symphony, James Adair, conductor.

Bibliography

WB114.1 Summo, Beverly. "Inglewood Symphony's Last Concert Triumph." *Inglewood Daily News*, April 24, 1961.

Review of the April 23, 1961, performance of the Inglewood Symphony Orchestra. "Mr. Still's work [*Patterns*] is a tone poem 'written in a polytonal, post-romantic style,' very beautiful with unusual harmonies, and haunting melodies. Each of the five sections is distinctive and compelling."

WB114.2 Saunders, Richard D. "Last Hollywood Symphony Concert Well Presented." *Hollywood Citizen-News*, May 1, 1961.

Review of the April 29, 1961, performance of the Hollywood Symphony Orchestra. The program included Still's suite *Patterns*, which had its world premiere on April 22, 1961, by the Inglewood Symphony Orchestra. "World premiere of William Grant Still's suite, *Patterns*, revealed a work of imaginative character and pervasive beauty, both in concept and execution. Each of its five movements was a different flight of fancy. Where so many modern composers attempt to overpower the listener with tonal force, Still has been content to intrigue him with delicate, tasteful utterance and the result was delightful."

W115 *Peaceful Land, The* (American Music Education, New York, 1960; available for rental from Theodore Presser Co., Bryn Mawr, PA).
For orchestra.

Composed in Los Angeles, 1960.
Dedicated to the United Nations.
Winner of a contest sponsored by the National Federation of Music Clubs and Aeolian Music Foundation for an orchestral work dedicated to the United Nations, 1961.
Instrumentation for orchestra: 2 flutes, 2 oboes, 2 clarinets, 2 bassoons; 3 horns, 2 trumpets, 2 trombones, tuba; harp, strings.
Duration: 9 minutes.
Sketches, originally titled *The Quiet Land,* with orchestration notes and revisions are in the William Grant Still and Verna Arvey Papers at the University of Arkansas Libraries, Fayetteville.
Autograph location unknown.

W115a **First Performance:** 1961 (October 22): Miami, FL; Miami Beach Auditorium; University of Miami Symphony Orchestra, Fabien Sevitzky, conductor.

Selected Performance

W115b 1962 (September 12): Boise, ID; Methodist Cathedral of the Rockies; Boise Philharmonic Orchestra, Jacques Brourman, conductor.

Bibliography

WB115.1 Bergh, Frances Hovey. "Program Notes." University of Miami Symphony Orchestra, October 22, 1961, p. 28.

Program notes for the October 22, 1961, performance of the University of Miami Symphony Orchestra. The program included the world premiere of *The Peaceful Land,* which came to Still in the following manner: "One morning a few months ago I awoke after having had a most uplifting dream. In my dream I was in a beautiful land with some friends of mine . . . it was a land of peace, of freedom and of exalted beings. . . . I immediately started to write a composition descriptive of my dream. While I was writing it, my wife noted the title and said, 'That sounds like a composition that stands for the same ideals the United Nations has. Why don't you dedicate it to the UN?' This seemed like a good idea, so I agreed."

WB115.2 Reno, Doris. "Symphony Opens On High Note." *Miami Herald*, October 24, 1961.

Review of the October 22, 1961, performance of the University of Miami Symphony Orchestra. "The world premiere of William Grant Still's prize-winning United Nations work, *The Peaceful Land,* provided a less spectacular peak for listeners, mainly because it is so quiet, expressive, undramatic, genuine, and non-showy a work. Mr. Still, who was hearing his work for the first time, praised the performance, and afterwards in a little ceremony on-stage received the $1,500 prize check with a short, modest speech of thanks to everybody involved in the premiere."

WB115.3 S., S. K. "Philharmonic, Guest Soloist, Premiere Captivate Audience." *Morning Statesman*, September 13, 1962.

Review of the September 12, 1962, performance of the Boise Philharmonic Orchestra. "*The Peaceful Land,* a relatively short work, was given a poetic reading by Brourman. Written primarily for strings, it was rich in harmony."

W116 *Pillar, The* (available from William Grant Still Music).
Opera in 3 acts with ballet, 3 stage settings, orchestra, chorus.

154 William Grant Still: A Bio-Bibliography

Composed in Los Angeles, 1954 and 1955; research started in January, 1954, sketch started in July, 1955.
Libretto by Verna Arvey on "an American Indian theme."
Dedicated to Mrs. Leiland Atherton Irish "in appreciation of her service to American music and in gratitude for her friendship."
Scene: A valley in the Southwest where the Indians once roamed.
For: Cast: 3 tenors, 2 baritones, bass, soprano, mezzo-soprano, 2 contraltos, chorus.
Instrumentation: 2 piccolos, or 2 flutes with 2nd doubling on piccolo, 2 oboes, English horn, 3 clarinets, 2 bassoons, contrabassoon; 3 horns, 3 trumpets, 2 trombones, tuba; timpani, drums, tom-toms, cymbals, chimes, tambourine, triangle, temple blocks, maracas; celesta, harp, strings.
Duration: 120 minutes.
Holograph conductor's score with corrections, stage directions, scenario, and additional sketches are in the William Grant Still and Verna Arvey Papers at the University of Arkansas Libraries, Fayetteville.
Autograph fair copy of full score and piano vocal score are in The William Grant Still Estate.

W117 ***Plain-Chant for America*** (J. Fischer & Brothers, New York, 1941, no. 7800; piano vocal score published as no. 7800-14; available from William Grant Still Music).
For baritone solo and orchestra with organ; chorus with orchestra.
Composed in Los Angeles; holograph dated July 1, 1941.
Composed for the Centennial of the New York Philharmonic Orchestra.
"Dedicated to the President of the United States and Mrs. Franklin Delano Roosevelt."
Text by Katherine Garrison Chapin, the wife of Francis Biddle who was the United States Attorney General in 1941.
Instrumentation: Baritone solo (or SATB chorus) with 3 flutes (3rd doubles on piccolo), 2 oboes, English horn, 3 clarinets, 2 bassoons; 4 horns, 3 trumpets, 3 trombones, tuba; timpani, drums, cymbals; harp, strings; an organ part is in the autograph score in the Still and Arvey Papers.
Duration: 10 minutes.
Holograph dated July 1941 written in open score with orchestration notes is in the William Grant Still and Verna Arvey Papers at the University of Arkansas Libraries, Fayetteville. It includes an unpublished organ part. (The authors would like to thank Wayne Shirley of the Library of Congress for discovering the organ part.) The Still and Arvey Papers also include the published piano vocal score.
Autograph is in The William Grant Still Estate.

W117a **First Performance:** 1941 (October 23, 24): New York, NY; Carnegie Hall; New York Philharmonic-Symphony Orchestra, John Barbirolli, conductor; Wilbur Evans, solo baritone.

Selected Performances

W117b 1941 (November 29): New York, NY; Concert Hall; Juilliard School of Music Orchestra, Albert Stoessel, conductor.

W117c 1942 (January 2): Pittsburgh, PA; Syria Mosque; Pittsburgh Symphony, Fritz Reiner, conductor; Wilbur Evans, baritone.

W117d 1942 (November 19, 20): Los Angeles, CA; Philharmonic Auditorium; Los

Angeles Philharmonic Orchestra, John Barbirolli, conductor; Jerome Hines, baritone; Alfred LeRoy Urseth, organ.

W117e 1943 (March 26, 27, 30): Washington DC; Constitution Hall, Philadelphia Orchestra, Eugene Ormandy, conductor; James Pease, baritone.

W117f 1943 (August 25): London, England; Royal Albert Hall; National Symphony Orchestra, Rudolph Dunbar, conductor; Swales Atkinson, baritone.

W117g 1944 (March 12): Liverpool, England; Philharmonic Hall; Liverpool Philharmonic Orchestra, Rudolph Dunbar, conductor; Swales Atkinson, baritone.

W117h 1944 (November 23): London; Royal Albert Hall; London Symphony Orchestra, John Barbirolli, conductor; Swales Atkinson, baritone.

W117i 1967 (August 14): Los Angeles, CA; Statler-Hilton, Pacific Ballroom; Angel City Symphony Orchestra, Leroy E. Hurte, conductor; Albert McNeil Singers; Louis J. Johnson, baritone; Georgia Laster Branch Chorus.

W117j 1968 (April 16): New Orleans, LA; Tulane University; McAlister Auditorium; Dillard University Choir; New Orleans Philharmonic-Symphony Orchestra, Werner Torkanowsky, conductor. (Version for chorus with orchestra.) (*See also:* WB36.17)

W117k 1970 (May 3): Grambling, LA; Grambling College; T.H. Harris Auditorium; Grambling College Band and Orchestra, William Grant Still, guest conductor.

Bibliography

WB117.1 Ussher, Bruno David. "New William Grant Still Score for New York." Los Angeles *Daily News*, September 23, 1941.

Article surrounding the development of *Plain-Chant for America*. "Beginning stirringly, Still's composition reflects on the American way of life, on the danger of mechanization of life in this country, on Nazi denial of democracy, the work ending with an exultant promise that 'if freedom falls, we'll fight for more freedom.' Symphonically the music is linked together with a melody expressive of such avowal."

WB117.2 Bagar, Robert. "Philharmonic Draws a Full House." *New York World Telegram*, October 24, 1941.

Review of the October 23, 1941, performance of the New York Philharmonic-Symphony Orchestra. "There is melody in the number [*Plain-Chant for America*], good popular-type melody. And the composer has not inhibited himself in distributing it. The harmonic scheme is modern in a mildly dissonant way, and the music rises to dramatic power several times."

WB117.3 Briggs, John. "Barbirolli and Hofmann Heard with Philharmonic." *New York Post*, October 24, 1941.

Review of the October 23, 1941, performance of the New York Philharmonic-Symphony Orchestra. "Pleasant listening was afforded by the new William Grant Still piece [*Plain-Chant for America*], which, like most of its predecessors, is a neatly constructed score, well orchestrated and with thematic material of a melodious kind. . . . Mr. Wilbur Evans was sonorous and impressive in the solo part."

WB117.4 Downes, Olin. "New Work Given by Philharmonic." *New York Times*, October 24, 1941.

Review of the October 23, 1941, performance of the New York Philharmonic-Symphony Orchestra. "It [*Plain-Chant for America*] was competently sung by Mr. Evans, and energetically conducted by Mr. Barbirolli. . . . This performance was vehemently applauded."

WB117.5 Lewando, Ralph. "Symphony Gets 1942 Off To Musical Start." *Pittsburgh Press*, January 3, 1942.

Review of the January 2, 1942, performance of the Pittsburgh Symphony. "For the first time in this city, we listened to a thrilling offering of . . . *Plain-Chant for America* in which Mr. [Wilbur] Evans was the effective soloist. . . . The music is forthright. It appeals, it grips. The score is set to the text with fine craftsmanship and poetic understanding by a Negro composer who is one of America's foremost creative musicians."

WB117.6 Bronson, Carl. "Symphony in Opening Triumph." Los Angeles *Herald-Express*, November 20, 1942, p. B-20.

Review of the November 19, 1942, performance of the Los Angeles Philharmonic. "The composer was present and shared in the many recalls until he was positively embarrassed."

WB117.7 G., P. "Philharmonic Season Opens Under Direction of Barbirolli." Los Angeles *Examiner*, November 20, 1942.

"In a first performance on the Pacific Coast, [*Plain-Chant for America*] . . . proved to be a fine piece of craftsmanship, sincerely written, with well integrated themes and effective orchestration."

WB117.8 Jones, Isabel Morse. "Symphony Group Opens Season Here." *Los Angeles Times*, November 20, 1942.

Review of the November 19, 1942, performance of the Los Angeles Philharmonic. "The music [of *Plain-Chant for America*] is straightforward and mounts to a splendid climax. . . . Still says what he has to say with conviction and with no loss of inspiration. The work is rhythmical but its spiritual intent is nonetheless clear."

WB117.9 Saunders, Richard D. "Philharmonic Presents Native Work." *Hollywood Citizen-News*, November 20, 1942.

"Still's music in *Plain-Chant for America* . . . made a stirring opening. The harmonic structure was simple, yet artistically achieved effects without striving for effects. It was firm, strong and martial, rising to a great climax with the orchestra augmented by organ. . . . Unfortunately, Baritone Hines' enunciation was so poor that not a single word was comprehensible."

WB117.10 Middleton, Emanuel. "Middleton praises Still work played by Philharmonic here." *Los Angeles Tribune*, November 23, 1942.

Review of the November 20, 1942, performance of the Los Angeles Philharmonic. "*Plain-Chant for America* is the work of a technical master, who knows how to work within the laid-down laws and still not become academic. There is melody in the work; good, popular melody, the melodic style broad but not vulgar; the instrumentation sure handled and rather pleasantly dissonant."

WB117.11 C., H. D. "Los Angeles Philharmonic." *Christian Science Monitor*, December 5, 1942.

Of the November 19, 1942, performance of *Plain-Chant for America*, the reviewer has these remarks: "Mr. Still knows well the roots from which stem the ideals and aspirations of our national character. His work is moving, often profound, as he has succeeded in translating lofty thought into volumes of compelling sound."

WB117.12 Brown, Ray C. B. "Piatigorski Bright Star of Concert." *Washington Post*, March 31, 1943.
Review of the March 30, 1943, performance of the Philadelphia Orchestra. "The work [*Plain-Chant for America*] has a surging and vital movement appropriate to the text, some pleasing melodic contours and a warmly colored instrumentation."

WB117.13 Eversman, Alice. "Ormandy and Piatigorsky Share Concert Honors." Washington *Evening Star*, March 31, 1943.
Review of the March 30, 1943, performance of the Philadelphia Orchestra. "The spiritual quality of the music [*Plain-Chant for America*] is constantly uppermost but Mr. Still has left its expression almost wholly to the orchestra, the writing for the voice being meager."

WB117.14 Gunn, Glenn Dillard. "New Hindemith Concerto Thrills Capacity Crowd." *Washington Times Herald*, March 31, 1943.
Review of the March 30, 1943, performance of the Philadelphia Orchestra. "This [*Plain-Chant for America*] is a fine example of patriotic verse. . . . The composer . . . has surrounded the vocal line with expertly contrived sound effects."

WB117.15 "Newspaper Press Fund Concert." London *Times*, August 26, 1943.
"The 'plain chant' is a theme, recalling to English musicians a phrase in Coleridge-Taylor's *Hiawatha*, which recurs through the work and so unifies what otherwise tends to be discursive. It was not possible to make out exactly what the message of the aria was, but the music was certainly evocative of the American scene. It is an instance of geography, as much as nationalism, making itself felt in music."

WB117.16 Padmore, George. "Negro Conducts British National Symphony Again." *Chicago Defender*, September 18, 1943.
Plain-Chant for America was performed by the National Symphony Orchestra in London, England, on August 25, 1943, and resulted in these remarks: "Still's work was warmly received, though heavy orchestrations tended to eclipse the baritone voice of the soloist. . . . Still has definitely established his reputation in England, as one of the most stimulating composers doing first-rate work in America today."

WB117.17 "Colonial Comforts' Fund Concert." Liverpool *Evening Express*, March 13, 1944.
Very brief review of the March 12, 1944, performance of the Liverpool Philharmonic Orchestra. "William Grant Still's descriptive composition, *Plaint* [sic] *Chant for America* . . . was rich in tone, and another work by the same composer, the *Afro-American Symphony*, offered a wide scope for the orchestra."

WB117.18 Gagnard, Frank. "Still's Music Easy to Enjoy." *Times-Picayune*, April 17, 1968.
Review of the April 16, 1968, performance of the New Orleans Philharmonic-Symphony Orchestra. "Dr. Still led the performances of his *Afro-American Symphony* and the *Levee Land* and *New Orleans Street* sections of the suite *From the South*. The Philharmonic Symphony's Werner Torkanowsky conducted the opening *Festive Overture*, the musical history lesson *Old California*, and the concluding *Plain-Chant for America*, for chorus and orchestra, which understandably brought the audience to its feet."

W118 *Poem for Orchestra* (1944) (Delkas, Los Angeles, 1945; MCA Music; Theodore Presser, Bryn Mawr, PA).
For orchestra.
Composed in 1944, Los Angeles.
Commissioned by the Fynette H. Kulas American Composers' Fund for the Cleveland Symphony Orchestra.
Dedicated to Arthur Judson.
Based on a poem by Verna Arvey in which man is revealed as undergoing toil and tribulation, but overcoming evil and redeeming himself and the world in an understanding of God.
Instrumentation: 3 flutes (2nd and 3rd double on piccolo), 2 oboes, English horn, 2 clarinets, 2 bassoons (2nd doubles on contrabassoon); 4 horns, 3 trumpets, 3 trombones, tuba; timpani, percussion; harp, celesta, strings.
Duration: 15 minutes.
Holograph in open score with original title, "This Day Must Come," orchestration notes, and revisions is in the William Grant Still and Verna Arvey Papers at the University of Arkansas Libraries, Fayetteville.

W118a **First Performance:** 1944 (December 7, 9, 31): Cleveland, OH; Severance Hall; Cleveland Symphony Orchestra, Rudolph Ringwall, conductor.

Selected Performances

W118b 1946 (April 4): New York, NY; Carnegie Hall; New York Philharmonic-Symphony Orchestra, Artur Rodzinski, conductor.

W118c 1948 (February 8): Dallas, TX; Fair Park Auditorium; Dallas Symphony Orchestra, Antal Dorati, conductor.

W118d 1948 (February 9): Fort Worth, TX; Will Rogers Memorial Auditorium; Dallas Symphony Orchestra, Antal Dorati, conductor.

W118e 1948 (April 25): Pasadena, CA; Civic Auditorium, Pasadena Civic Orchestra, Richard Lert, conductor.

W118f 1950 (November 2): Chicago, IL; Orchestra Hall; Chicago Symphony Orchestra, Rafael Kubelik, conductor.

W118g 1965 (May 14): Los Angeles, CA; Bovard Auditorium; Southeast Symphony Orchestra, Leon Thompson, conductor.

W118h 1970 (November 6): Los Angeles, CA; University of Southern California; steps of Bovard Auditorium; University of Southern California Symphony Orchestra, Phillip Lehrman, conductor.

W118i 1979 (October 19): Los Angeles, CA; Bovard Auditorium; University of Southern California Symphony Orchestra, Daniel Lewis, conductor.

Bibliography

WB118.1 G., M. B. "Year-End Concert Delights Crowd." *Cleveland Plain-Dealer*, January 1, 1945.
Review of the December 31, 1944, performance of the Cleveland Orchestra. "Deeply moving and reminiscent of the Negro spiritual, the work [*Poem for Orchestra*] was well received by new and old hearers. . . . The sad, sorrowing beginning in dissonance of brass builds to a musical climax of hope and coming to spiritual consciousness expressed in a singing melody of strings."

WB118.2 Bacon, Elmore. "Still's 'Poem' Given Cleveland Premiere." *Musical America* 15 (January 10, 1945): 3.

Review of the December 7, 1944, performance of the Cleveland Orchestra. "[*Poem for Orchestra*] was indeed beautiful, with distinctive themes, clever orchestration, lovely lyrical passages and stirring, forthright vitality. . . . Still's inspiration is most evident in the closing passages of the finale."

WB118.3 Bagar, Robert. "Miss Anderson [Marian Anderson] Disappointing with Symphony." *New York Telegram*, April 5, 1946.

"Like all of Still's music, this piece is well orchestrated. . . . For all its good intentions, the *Poem for Orchestra* is not arresting music, nor does it seem to be articulate enough of its literary philosophy."

WB118.4 Downes, Olin. "Music of Negroes Concert Feature." *New York Times*, April 5, 1946.

"We went with special anticipation of Mr. Still's score [*Poem for Orchestra*], but were disappointed. It is fluently written and orchestrated. . . . But the composer's expression is diluted in a way that deprives it of racial essence, or any strongly individual note. . . . [H]e appears to have been smoothed out as a composer—conventionalized. It is to be hoped that in later scores Mr. Still will return to what hide-bound academicians might call the original error of his ways."

WB118.5 Perkins, Francis D. "The Philharmonic." *New York Herald Tribune*, April 6, 1946.

"Mr. Still's *Poem* [*for Orchestra*] . . . is sincere and expressive music, skillfully scored, and generally conservative in its style and harmonies. Apart from the close, the range of expressive color was less wide than that suggested by the composer's program note; the musical color also inclined toward the darker instrumental hues."

WB118.6 Hague, Robert. "Musical Diary." *PM*, April 7, 1946.

Review of the April 4, 1946, performance of the New York Philharmonic-Symphony Orchestra. "The purely orchestral part of the program had few redeeming moments. Its most interesting feature was the first performance [in New York] of William Grant Still's *Poem for Orchestra*, an ambitious, worthy, ably written and occasionally impressive work."

WB118.7 Simon, Robert A. "Musical Events." *New Yorker* 22 (April 13, 1946): 92-93.

"[T]he Philharmonic-Symphony gave the New York première of William Grant Still's *Poem for Orchestra*. . . . Mr. Still's familiar clarity and orchestral skill were agreeably evident, but the materials of the music weren't as noteworthy as the craftmanship."

WB118.8 "Concerts in New York." *Musical America* 56 (April 25, 1946): 10.

Notes on the April 4, 1946, performance of the New York Philharmonic-Symphony Orchestra. "Of the contemporary works, Gould's *Spirituals* made out rather better than the Still work [*Poem for Orchestra*] which proved to be surprisingly slick and conventional."

WB118.9 Miers, Virgil. "Dallas Symphony, Kapell Thrill Concert-Goers." *Dallas Times Herald*, February 9, 1948.

Review of the February 8, 1948, performance of the Dallas Symphony Orchestra. "*Poem for Orchestra* by William Grant Still and *Symphony in B Minor* by Borodin completed the first part of the program. Best received was the selection by Still, written as recent as 1944 by this great

160   William Grant Still: A Bio-Bibliography

American Negro composer. The symphony was in brilliant form for both presentations, and both received hearty approval of the audience."

WB118.10   Rosenfield, John. "Kapell Has At Another Rachmaninov Opus." *Dallas Morning News*, February 9, 1948.
Review of the February 8, 1948, performance of the Dallas Symphony Orchestra. "More emotional and less expressive than the overture [*Concert Overture*, by Daniel Sternberg] was William Grant Still's *Poem for Orchestra*, commissioned by Cleveland four years ago. The Negro composer has followed a Verna Arvey poem that views a desolate world, rallies to the hope of its redemption and ends in an ecstacy of atuned [*sic*] spirituality. While Mr. Still's handling of orchestral resources is firm, his musical language is obvious and banal."

WB118.11   Marsh, William J. "Kapell's Playing, Borodin Music Warmly Approved." *Fort Worth Star-Telegram*, February 10, 1948.
Review of the Fort Worth performance of the Dallas Symphony Orchestra. "Opening the program with one of the novelties, *Poem for Orchestra* by William Grant Still, we were introduced to the music of perhaps the most widely played Negro composer in this country. A work of serious intent, and the product of a thoroughly trained musician, this poem is more properly a rhapsody of force, with strong themes of a characteristic vein. It made an exciting start for the evening."

WB118.12   Perlee, Charles D. "Young Flutist and Still Work Mark Opening of Music Fete." *Pasadena Star-News*, April 26, 1948.
Review of a performance by the Pasadena Civic Orchestra, April 25, 1948. "Dr. Lert [conductor] presented the first Western performance of William Grant Still's *Poem* and there was a heart-warming and tremendous ovation for this great American composer. . . . The triumphant theme, coming after passages of misery and frustration, sent chills up and down the spine."

WB118.13   Sablosky, Irving. "Symphony Concert A Musical Showcase." *Chicago Daily News*, November 3, 1950.
Review of the November 2, 1950, performance by the Chicago Symphony Orchestra. "Kubelik paid Still's *Poem* the compliment of conducting it from memory. The work is written with skill, taste and perhaps a bit of rhetoric, but Still neatly avoids cliche in an idiom that sometimes bears close to movie style. The performance had vigor and direction."

WB118.14   Lebow, Roger. "Program Notes." University of Southern California Symphony, October 19, 1979, p. 2.
Program notes for the October 19, 1979, performance of the University of Southern California Symphony. The program included Still's *Poem for Orchestra*. "The work is in three sections. The chaotic, bitonal introductory passage superimposes the keys of A and B flat. This gives way at once to a cantabile D minor threnody, punctuated by rhythmic figures from the opening. In the quicker second section the unison strings give out a martial, marcato theme in B minor. Material from the first section is subsequently introduced, reaching a great climax in F major and leading into the final section, an A major pastorale. A brief coda recalls previous material. The final cadence, a major chord turning minor (a device used to dramatic ends by Schubert and Mahler), underscores the essentially somber mood of this piece."

WB118.15 Cariaga, Daniel. "USC Symphony Opens Season." *Los Angeles Times*, October 22, 1979.

> Review of the October 19 performance of the University of Southern California Symphony Orchestra. "Still's *Poem [for Orchestra]* is a heroic, lushly textured work which uses the entire resources of the orchestra tellingly, an American *Heldenleben*, if you will, but one compressed into less than 10 minutes. Its Hansonian idiom and extreme attractiveness, two qualities once again acceptable in our concert halls, make it worthy of a currency previously withheld."

W119 **Pompous March** (available from William Grant Still Music).
For piano and a solo instrument; possibly a student work.
Autograph is in The William Grant Still Estate.

W120 **Preludes I-V** (for piano; *II. Placidly* was published in the *New Scribner Music Library*, edited by Howard Hanson, volume IV, New York: Charles Scribner's Sons, 1972; available from William Grant Still Music).
For solo piano; also for string orchestra, flute, and piano.
Adapted for piano in Los Angeles, 1964; these are derived substantially from the *Preludes for String Orchestra and Piano. (See:* W121)
Dedicated to Consuelo Pappy.
Contents: I. Briskly, II. Placidly, III. Delicately, IV. Moderately, V. Liltingly.
Autograph sketches, a bound manuscript copy with title and dedication page and additional markings from the composer, and an unbound copy are in the William Grant Still and Verna Arvey Papers at the University of Arkansas Libraries, Fayetteville.

W121 **Preludes for String Orchestra and Piano** (available from William Grant Still Music).
For string orchestra and piano; also for flute and piano.
Composed in Los Angeles, 1962.
Dedicated to Consuelo Pappy.
Contents: I. Moderately fast, II. Moderately slow, III. Delicately, IV. Moderately, V. Energetically. *(See:* W120)
Extensive sketches and a holograph of a final version titled *Preludes* (with a fair copy of the piano part) for string orchestra and piano are in the William Grant Still and Verna Arvey Papers at the University of Arkansas Libraries, Fayetteville.

W121a **First Performance:** 1968 (May 26): Westchester, CA; Westchester High School Auditorium; Westchester String Symphony, George Berres, conductor.

W122 **Pretty Ways.**
Popular song by William Grant Still and Fletcher Henderson.
Composed in New York, about 1923.
Performed by the Black Swan Dance Orchestra on a recording by The Black Swan Phonograph Company in the 1920s. *(See:* B113)
Autograph location unknown.

W123 **Prince and the Mermaid, The** (available from William Grant Still Music).
Incidental music for a fairy tale for children, play by Carol Stone.
Originally composed for piano; adapted for small instrumental combination and for string quartet.

Composed in Los Angeles, 1965.
Contents: I. Song of the Sea, II. Waltz, III. Minuet, IV. Scherzo.
Instrumentation: flute, clarinet, trumpet; percussion: drums, cymbals, vibraphone, wood block, triangle, bells, gong, chimes; piano.
Duration: 20 minutes.
Sketches are in the William Grant Still and Verna Arvey Papers at the University of Arkansas Libraries, Fayetteville. They include fragments with the following titles: *Romance* for piano, *Song, The Jester* (melodic material "assigned to bassoon for droll effect"), *Song of the Sea,* or *Spell of the Sea,* also *The Mermaid, Fanfare, The Sorcerer,* and *Dance.* The Still and Arvey Papers include two facsimiles of the play by Carol Stone with the composer's handwritten notes throughout. His notes indicate that he planned a larger orchestra initially.
Autograph is in The William Grant Still Estate.

W123a **First Performance:** 1966 (March 4): Northridge, CA; San Fernando Valley State College; Campus Theatre; Roy Atherton, piano; Justus Matthews, flute and clarinet; Larry Glenn, percussion; Carol Stone, playwright; Mary Jane Evans, director; Hanley Jackson, musical director; Pamela Roberts, choreographer.

Bibliography

WB123.1 Denney, Jane. "Costumes, Jester, Music Glitter in Winning *Prince.*" *Valley State Daily Sundial*, March 8, 1966, p. 4.
Review of the March 4, 1966, world premiere performance of *The Prince and the Mermaid*, staged at San Fernando Valley State College. "*Prince* is actress Carol Stone's first play and hopefully not her last. Unlike so many kiddie shows, *Prince* is not a syrupy, singsong play which downgrades even the dullest child's intelligence. There is wit and wisdom in the little couplets and quatrains found throughout the dialogue. William Grant Still's music blends harmoniously into the entire fantasy."

W124 *Promised Land* (available from William Grant Still Music).
Sacred cantata.
Text by Frederick Martens.
Sketches from the composer's journal are in The William Grant Still Estate.

W125 *Psalm for the Living, A* (Bourne Company, Inc., New York, 1965, no. 3159-19).
For SATB chorus and piano; also for chorus and orchestra.
Composed in Los Angeles, 1954.
Text by Verna Arvey.
Dedicated to Dr. Bessie Arvey (mother of Verna Arvey).
Instrumentation for orchestra: SATB chorus with 2 flutes, 2 oboes, 2 clarinets, 2 bassoons; 4 horns, 2 trumpets, 2 trombones, tuba; percussion; harp, piano, strings.
Autograph sketches in open score for orchestra and the piano part are in the William Grant Still and Verna Arvey Papers at the University of Arkansas Libraries, Fayetteville. There is no chorus part included in the Still and Arvey Papers. There is an additional autograph score which says, "Special parts 'Psalm for the Living' University of California Concert," in the conductor's hand. The parts are for horns and piano.
Autograph of chorus parts location unknown.

W125a **First Performance:** 1966 (February 18): Houston, TX; Texas Southern University Orchestra and Choir; William Grant Still, guest conductor.

Selected Performances

W125b 1966 (October 28): Los Angeles, CA; University of California at Los Angeles, Royce Hall; McNeil Singers, Albert McNeil, conductor. *(See also:* WB32.1, WB32.2)

W125c 1967 (March 25): Beverly Hills, CA; Beverly Hills H.S. Auditorium; Los Angeles Jubilee Singers, Albert McNeil, conductor.

W125d 1972 (March 22): Fayetteville, AR; University of Arkansas, Fine Arts Center Concert Hall; Chamber Ensemble, Jack Groh, director.

W125e 1980 (February 17): Brooklyn, NY; Lafayette Avenue Presbyterian Church; Festival Ensemble Chorus, Frederick Bell, conductor; Sophie Williams, piano.

W125f 1984 (February 15): Fayetteville, AR: University of Arkansas, Fine Arts Center Concert Hall; University of Arkansas Schola Cantorum and Concert Choir, Jack Groh, director.

W125g 1986 (October 11): Jackson, TN; Jackson Civic Center; Jackson Symphony Orchestra, Jordan Tang, conductor; Lane College Concert Choir.

Bibliography

WB125.1 Nelson, Burt. "Negro Art Music: Variety of Moods." *Hollywood Citizen-News*, October 31, 1966, sec. B, p. 3.
   Review of a performance at UCLA. "Mr. Still—dean of American Negro composers—scored the biggest success of the evening with two works: *A Psalm for the Living*, for chorus and strings—a strongly romantic affirmation of faith, with long, flowing lines and soaring obbligatos . . . and *Ennanga* . . . a rhapsodic suite for harp and strings, with the composer on the podium and Lois Craft distinguishing herself as soloist."

WB125.2 Greene, Patterson. "Full House for Rubenstein; McNeil Choir Excels." *Los Angeles Herald-Examiner*, March 27, 1967.
   Review of the March 25, 1967, performance of the Los Angeles Jubilee Singers. "Fine voices in a smooth blending distinguished Albert McNeil's Jubilee Singers, who offered Negro spirituals in traditional and jazz idiom in the auditorium of the Beverly Hills High School on Saturday Night. William Grant Still was in the audience to hear the applause for his tragic *O, Sorrow* [from *And They Lynched Him on a Tree*] . . . and *Psalm for the Living*—two works in a highly cultured idiom that still carried the force of elemental emotion."

W126 ***Quit Dat Fool'nish*** (J. Fischer & Brothers, New York, 1938, no. 7460-3; piano solo, flute and piano, and violin and piano versions are available from William Grant Still Music; orchestra arrangement, saxophone and chamber orchestra version, and saxophone and piano version are available from Bourne Company, Inc., International Music Catalog, New York).
   For piano solo; also arranged for flute and piano; violin and piano; orchestra; saxophone and chamber orchestra; and saxophone and piano.
   Composed in Los Angeles, 1935.
   Dedicated "To Shep, my mischievous dog" in the published version. It was actually written for Harold Bruce Forsythe.
   Instrumentation in arrangement for orchestra: 2 flutes, 2 oboes, 2 clarinets,

2 bassoons; saxophone; 3 horns, 2 trumpets, 2 trombones (no tuba); timpani, harp, strings .
Duration: 2 minutes.
Autograph of the violin and piano version, sketches of the orchestration in open score, and a facsimile of the published edition for solo piano with a few orchestration notes in the composer's hand are in the William Grant Still and Verna Arvey Papers at the University of Arkansas Libraries, Fayetteville.
Autograph for original piano solo location unknown.

W126a **First Performance:** [1935] (July 11): Los Angeles, CA; The Booster Club, Second Baptist Church, Harold Bruce Forsythe, piano.

Selected Performances

W126b 1937 (March 16): Tucson, AZ; University of Arizona, College of Fine Arts; Ulysses Kay, piano.

W126c 1937 (April 18): Los Angeles, CA; Pacific Institute of Music and Fine Art; Verna Arvey, piano. (*See:* WB76.7).

W126d 1939 (April 23): Salt Lake City, UT; Utah State Art Center; Verna Arvey, piano.

W126e 1941 (February 16): Nashville, TN; Fisk University; William Allen, piano.

W126f 1941 (April 20): New York, NY; Carnegie Chamber Music Hall: Hugo Bornn, piano.

W126g 1942 (March 25): New York, NY; Town Hall; Louis Kaufman, violin; Vladimir Padwa, piano.

W126h 1961 (September 10): Los Angeles, CA; Los Angeles County Museum of Natural History, Hancock Auditorium; Gretel Shanley, flute; George Covell, piano. (First performance for flute.)

W127 ***Reverie*** (Avant Music, West Coast Chapter of the American Guild of Organists, *A.G.O. Prelude Book,* 1962; available from Western International Music, Inc., Greeley, Colorado).
For organ.
Composed in Los Angeles, 1961.
Duration: 3 minutes.
Holograph is in the Library of Congress, deposited for copyright September 25, 1961.
Autograph is in the William Grant Still and Verna Arvey Papers at the University of Arkansas Libraries, Fayetteville.

W127a **First Performance:** 1962 (March 12): Pasadena, CA; Pasadena Presbyterian Church; Robert Prichard, organ.

Selected Performances

W127b 1963 (April 28): San Jose, CA; Scottish Rite Temple; Reginald G. Greenbrook, organ.

W127c 1970 (July 5, 12, 19, 26): Los Angeles, CA; First Baptist Church; Irene Robertson, organ.

W127d 1984 (February 18): Fayetteville, AR; University of Arkansas, Fine Arts Center Concert Hall; Campbell Johnson, organ.

Works and Performances   165

W128   ***Rhapsody*** (available from William Grant Still Music).
        Song cycle for voice and orchestra; voice and piano; arranged by the composer for vocal solo or chorus and orchestra; coloratura soprano, string quartet, and piano; and chorus and piano.
        Composed in Los Angeles; holograph dated March 14, 1955.
        Text by Verna Arvey.
        Commissioned for Mattiwilda Dobbs by the Southwide Conference Educational Fund.
        Dedicated later to the memory of the composer's beloved son-in-law, Larry Allyn Headlee (died 1970).
        Program notes written by Arvey say it "is a cycle of songs encompassing the whole of a woman's life, from girlhood to marriage, motherhood and the awareness of her role in the world."
        Inscription by the composer says, "Great deal should be made of the portamento [at the end]."
        Contents: I. Pastorale, II. Romance, III. Lullaby, IV. Paean.
        Contents of piano vocal autograph score: I. Moderately slow: Pastorale (Duration: 4:13); II. Moderately slow: Romance (Duration: 4:09); III. Moderately slow: Lullaby (Duration: 3:21); IV. Moderately slow: Paean (Duration: 4:00).
        Instrumentation for orchestra: soprano solo and (or) SATB chorus with 2 flutes, 2 oboes, English horn, 2 clarinets, 2 bassoons; 3 horns, 3 trumpets, 2 trombones, tuba; timpani, small triangle, bell, cymbal; harp, celesta, strings.
        Duration: 15-16 minutes.
        Holograph dated March 14, 1955, of a four-section vocal solo with piano version and an autograph dated March 14, 1955, with the indication that it is the "orchestral version" called "Universal Woman" are in the William Grant Still and Verna Arvey Papers at the University of Arkansas Libraries, Fayetteville. The autograph orchestral version is an extended work that includes a vocal solo part and the sketch of a chorus part with sections marked "Moderately slow," "Gracefully," "II. Moderately slow—Faster: Romance," III. "Moderately slow—Slowly: Lullaby," "Rhapsody," and IV. "Moderately slow: Paean."

W129   ***Ring Play*** (J. Fischer & Brothers, Glen Rock, New Jersey, 1964, in *Twentieth Century Piano Music*, edited by Bernice Frost, Book II B, no. 9499-26; available from William Grant Still Music).
        For piano solo.
        Composed in Los Angeles, 1962.
        Autograph location unknown.

W130   ***Ritual.***
        Folk song setting, sketch fragment, unfinished.
        For baritone solo, piano, and percussion (gourd, maracas); also planned for baritone solo with strings, harp, celesta, and percussion.
        Sketched in Los Angeles, probably 1941.
        Probably originally part of the ***Caribbean Melodies*** plan (*See:* W19) from material collected in the Bahamas by Zora Neale Hurston.
        Autograph of incomplete sketch with orchestration notes for baritone solo with strings, percussion (including timpani, gourd, maracas, triangle, marimba), celesta, and harp is in the William Grant Still and Verna Arvey Papers at the University of Arkansas Libraries, Fayetteville.

W131 ***Romance for Saxophone*** (Bourne Company, Inc., International Music Catalog, New York, 1966; orchestral parts available from William Grant Still Music).
For saxophone and piano; also for saxophone and chamber orchestra.
Composed in Los Angeles, 1954.
Dedicated to Sigurd Rascher; written at the request of Sigurd Rascher.
Instrumentation: saxophone solo with 2 flutes, 2 oboes, 2 clarinets, 2 bassoons; 2 horns, 2 trombones; harp, strings.
Duration: 3 minutes.
Autograph of saxophone and piano original with orchestration notes, a sketch for orchestra, the initial melodic sketches, and a copy of the published edition are in the William Grant Still and Verna Arvey Papers at the University of Arkansas Libraries, Fayetteville.

Selected Performances

W131a 1973 (January 21): Frankfort, KY; Kentucky State University, Bradford Hall Little Theatre; Lee Patrick, alto saxophone; David A. Browning, piano.

W131b 1974 (July 29): Lexington, KY; University of Kentucky, Memorial Hall; Lee Patrick, alto saxophone; Jay Flippin, piano; Mary Combs, alto saxophone.

W131c 1975 (July 21): Louisville, KY; University of Louisville, Recital Hall; Lee Patrick, alto saxophone; Peggy DeArmand, piano.

W131d 1984 (February 18): Fayetteville, AR; University of Arkansas, Fine Arts Center Concert Hall; Robert Umiker, saxophone; Arthur Tollefson, piano.

W132 ***Sahdji*** (The University of Rochester, The Eastman School of Music, American Composers' Edition, Rochester, NY, 1961; Carl Fischer, Inc., New York).
Ballet for 3 solo dancers and corps de ballet, scored for orchestra, mixed chorus, bass solo. *Four Dances from Sahdji* arranged for harp, piano, and strings.
Composed in Hollywood, CA, and finished in New York, 1930; sketches were begun initially in 1926, again in April 1928; copyright 1941 by William Grant Still.
Dedicated to Howard Hanson.
Scenario from 1925 or 1926 by Richard Bruce (pseudonym for Bruce Nugent) with additions by Alain Locke; the original story is printed in *The New Negro: An Interpretation,* edited by Alain Locke, New York, 1925.
Setting: Ancestral Central Africa. A hunting feast of the Azanda tribe.
Contents: (partial titles): Introduction, Festive Dance, Dance of the Warriors, Invitation Dance, Dance Before the Chieftain, Dance Before the Hut, Death Chant, Death Dance of Sahdji.
Instrumentation: 2 flutes (2nd doubles on piccolo), 2 oboes, English horn, 4 clarinets, 2 bassoons; 4 horns, 2 trumpets, 2 trombones, 2 tubas; timpani, percussion; strings.
Duration: 30-45 minutes.
Initial sketches dated April 1928 of melodic and rhythmic materials, including the "Sahdji motif," are in the William Grant Still and Verna Arvey Papers at the University of Arkansas Libraries, Fayetteville.
Autograph version in pencil for SATB chorus with piano, an autograph fair copy in blue pencil and ink labelled "Part One" and "Part Two" with stage directions typed into the score, a diagram of the stage set, descrip-

tions of the costumes, lighting directions, information on properties, the argument, and a detailed summary of the action are in the William Grant Still and Verna Arvey Papers, University of Arkansas Libraries, Fayetteville. Other materials include an autograph with orchestration notes labelled "Final revision" by the composer which has, on the verso of two pages, notes by the composer on his philosophy of composition.

Autograph copy in ink with dance notations is in The University of Rochester, The Eastman School of Music, Sibley Music Library, from The Thelma Biracree Schnepel Collection.

Manuscript orchestral score, with comments by Alain Locke and Bruce Nugent who collaborated on the scenario, is in the James Weldon Johnson Memorial Collection of Negro Arts and Letters at Yale University.

Holograph of full orchestral score is in The William Grant Still Estate.

W132a **First Performance:** 1931 (May 22): Rochester, NY; Eastman Theatre; Rochester Civic Orchestra, Howard Hanson, conductor; Thelma Biracree as Sahdji; William Wing as Konumbju; Nathan Emanuel as Mrabo; Martin Vogt as the Medicine Man; Eugene Loewenthal as the Chanter; Alice Couch, costumes; and Clarence Hall, scenery.

Selected Performances

W132b 1934 (May 4): Rochester, NY; Eastman Theatre; Rochester Philharmonic Orchestra, Howard Hanson, conductor; Thelma Biracree as Sahdji; Richard Andrews as the Chief, Konumbju; Martin Vogt as the Medicine Man; Alice Couch, costumes; Clarence Hall, stage.

W132c 1950 (May 6): Rochester, NY; Eastman Theatre; Eastman-Rochester Symphony Orchestra, Howard Hanson, conductor; Thelma Biracree as Sahdji and choreographer; Emmett Steele as Konumbju; Earl Cage, assistant choreographer and Mrabo; Tomas Del Solar as the Medicine Man and costumes; Wilton Laurence as Chanter; Alice Couch, costumes; and Clarence J. Hall, scenery.

W132d 1965 (May 15): Los Angeles, CA; East Los Angeles Junior College Auditorium; Civic Arts Orchestra, Richard Robinson, conductor; Carol Kaufman as Sahdji; Laurence Henry as Konumbju; Glenn Stadifer as Mrabo; Floyd Chatman as the Medicine Man; Marvin Samuels, Chanter; Jeni LeGon, choreography and stage director; Judith Wood, costumes; John Ingle, scenery and production manager; West Los Angeles Chorus; Crenshaw-Leimert Chorus; and West Valley Chorus.

W132e 1973 (February 18): Los Angeles, CA; Scottish Rite Cathedral; Southeast Symphony Orchestra, Louis Palange, conductor; Wanda Evans as Sahdji; Westley Gayle as Konumbju; Ronald Bush as Mrabo; William Couser as the Witch Doctor; Rudy Williams as the Chanter; Lloyd Hardy, stage manager; Charles Carter and Bob Mitchell, costumes and props.

W132f 1973 (September 27): Baltimore, MD; Goucher College; Baltimore Symphony Orchestra, Paul Freeman, guest conductor; Morgan State College Choir. (*See:* D8)

Bibliography

WB132.1 Downes, Olin. "Ballet Presented At Rochester Fete." *New York Times*, May 23, 1931.

Lengthy review of the May 22, 1931, performance of the Rochester Civic

Orchestra. "[*Sahdji*] is real music, music of a composer of exotic talent and temperament, who has a keen sense of beauty, sensuousness which is controlled by taste, and incipient aptitude for the theatre. It is not Negro music diluted with conventions of the white, nor yet is it cast in the forms of negroid expression which has also become conventional. Mr. Still does not indulge in Harlem jazz, but backs to more primitive sources for brutal, persistent and barbaric rhythms."

WB132.2 Sabin, Stewart B. "Highly Interesting Works Close Music School Festival." *Rochester Democrat and Chronicle*, May 23, 1931.

Lengthy review of the May 22, 1931, performance of the Rochester Civic Orchestra. "[*Sahdji*] is a vividly impressive work. Mr. Still . . . uses a chorus both greatly to enrich the musical component of his piece and to add advantageously to the dramatic action; and the music given to the chorus is admirable. His rhythmic fertility of invention is remarkable; the actual dances, apart from the pantomimic dramatic action, are given highly original music."

WB132.3 "New Native Ballet and Opera Given in Rochester." *Musical America* 51 (June 1931): 13.

Review of the May 22, 1931, performance of the Rochester Civic Orchestra. "The music [of *Sahdji*] is vital and primitive, expressive of the tribal rhythms of the jungle. The score contains beauty. Mr. Still achieves a vivid atmosphere with very simple means."

WB132.4 "Festival Ballet Program Draws Usual Throng to Eastman." *Rochester Democrat and Chronicle*, May 8, 1950, p. 13.

Review of the May 6, 1950, performance by the Eastman School of Music's twentieth annual festival of American music, which included *Sahdji*. "Concluding number was a revival of William Grant Still's choral ballet *Sahdji*, given at the first Eastman Festival in 1931. . . . Miss [Thelma] Biracree, who choreographed the opus, also took the role of Sahdji, with technical resource in both pantomime and dance. There was real abandon in her provocative moments with Earl Kage as the subject of her infatuation, and drama in her dance of death. Kage who had choreographed the warriors' dance, did an especially fine piece of work here."

WB132.5 Doernberg, Jerry. "Musical Premiere Due at E.L.A." *Los Angeles Times*, May 13, 1965.

Preview of the West Coast premiere of Still's choral ballet *Sahdji*, scheduled for presentation May 15, 1965 at East Los Angeles Junior College. The article also reviews Still's fifty years as a composer. "The composer . . . is the last one to blow his own horn. . . . Still said, 'I don't know if there is any significance to my work. All of it may be valueless. It's for people and posterity to judge.'"

WB132.6 Segal, Lewis. "Black Opera-Ballet Presented at Temple." *Los Angeles Times*, February 20, 1973.

Review of the February 18, 1973, performance of *Sahdji* produced by the Southeast Symphony Orchestra on their 25th anniversary. "*Sahdji* is atmospheric and accessible, yet—unlike Stravinsky or Orff—Still cannot quite unify his borrowings, influences and references into a convincing personal style. . . . [C]onductor Louis Palange led his orchestral forces with brisk assurance, attention to detail and appreciation of the humor, if not all the lyricism, in Still's scores."

WB132.7 Galkin, Elliott. "Panorama of styles in composers' music." Baltimore *Sun*, September 28, 1973, sec. B, p. 6.

Review of the September 27, 1973, performance of the Baltimore Symphony Orchestra. "The composition which provoked the greatest audience response was *Sahdji* by the dean of black composers, William Grant Still. . . . *Sahdji* is a hyper-romantic evocation, its textures at times recalling César Franck. It is urgent music, its melodies luxurious, its harmonies lush and its rhythms insistent. It received an impassioned reading by the Morgan State College Choir and the orchestra."

W133 *Scherzo,* from *Afro-American Symphony,* **III.** movement (*See:* W2) (parts and score for "reduced instrumentation" J. Fischer & Brothers, New York, 1937, no. J. F. & B. 0366; published separately in a version for two pianos by Verna Arvey, J. Fischer & Brothers, New York, 1936; available from William Grant Still Music).

For orchestra; scored for full band by the composer.

Composed in New York, 1930.

Cover of the "reduced instrumentation" score indicates, "This Scherzo of the *Afro-American Symphony* has been rescored for a smaller combination of instruments than in its original form, and in this arrangement is playable in one of the following combinations: (A) flute, oboe, two clarinets, bassoon, two horns, two trumpets, trombone, percussion, piano, strings; (B) two alto saxophones, tenor saxophone, trombone, two trumpets, percussion, piano, one or more violins, bass, tenor banjo; and, (C) five woodwinds, three saxophones, two horns, two trumpets, trombone, percussion, piano, tenor banjo, strings."

Duration: 4 minutes.

Published instrumental parts (J. Fischer & Bro., 1937) are in the William Grant Still and Verna Arvey Papers at the University of Arkansas Libraries, Fayetteville. The Still and Arvey Papers also contain a published (J. Fischer & Bro., 1937) piano reduction and a facsimile of a manuscript of a two-piano arrangement by Arvey of *Scherzo*.

Autograph of full orchestral score location unknown.

Selected Performances

W133a 1933 (January 6): Berlin, Germany; Berlin Philharmonic Orchestra, Howard Hanson, conductor.

W133b 1936 (July 23): Los Angeles, CA; Hollywood Bowl; Los Angeles Philharmonic Orchestra, William Grant Still, guest conductor. (*See:* WB1.13-WB1.19)

W133c 1937 (July 30): Los Angeles, CA; Hollywood Bowl; Los Angeles Philharmonic Orchestra, Howard Hanson, guest conductor.

W133d 1942 (February 14): WOR Symphony Orchestra, Alfred Wallenstein, conductor. Radio Broadcast on the *MBS Treasury Hour.*

W133e 1942 (June 17): Cleveland, OH; Cleveland Orchestra, Rudolph Ringwall, conductor.

W133f 1943 (February 14): Rochester, NY; Eastman Theatre; Rochester Civic Orchestra, Paul White, conductor.

W133g 1943 (March 6): San Francisco, CA; San Francisco Symphony Orchestra, Rudolph Ganz, conductor.

W133h 1944 (June 26): Boston, MA; Symphony Hall; Boston Pops Orchestra, Arthur Fiedler, conductor.

W133i 1947 (June 13): Washington, DC; National Symphony Orchestra, Richard Bales, conductor.

W133j 1955 (February 12): Los Angeles, CA; Shrine Auditorium; Los Angeles Philharmonic Orchestra, John Barnett, conductor.

W133k 1959 (November 6): Buffalo, NY; Kleinhans Music Hall; Buffalo Philharmonic Orchestra, Joseph Wincenc, conductor.

W133l 1966 (November 27): Detroit, MI; Ford Auditorium; Detroit Symphony Orchestra, Valter Poole, conductor.

W133m 1970 (January 29): Dallas, TX; Bishop College; Dallas Symphony Orchestra, Paul Freeman, conductor. (*See:* WB25.4)

W133n 1970 (May 16): Oakland, CA; Oakland Auditorium Theatre; Oakland Youth Chamber Orchestra, William Grant Still, guest conductor. (*See:* WB144.6)

W133o 1971 (March 21): Richmond, VA; The Mosque; Richmond Symphony, Paul Freeman, guest conductor. (*See:* WB25.5)

W133p 1972 (February 20): St. Louis, MO; Powell Symphony Hall; St. Louis Symphony Orchestra, Leonard Slatkin, conductor.

Bibliography

WB133.1 "Berlin Hails Hanson Offering Our Music." *New York Times*, January 9, 1933, p. 22.

On January 6, 1933, Howard Hanson conducted the Berlin Philharmonic Orchestra in Berlin. The *Afro-American Symphony* was on the program. "The audience demanded a repetition of Still's *scherzo*."

WB133.2 Peyser, Herbert F. "American Music Gains Respect Under Hanson's Baton in Berlin." *Musical Courier* 106 (February 4, 1933): 5.

Short review of activities associated with the January 6, 1933, performance of the Berlin Philharmonic Orchestra, with Dr. Howard Hanson, guest conductor, in Berlin. "[T]he audience re-demanded the jaunty *scherzo* of Still's *Afro-American Symphony*."

WB133.3 Chism, Olin. "Negro Composers Heard." *Dallas Times Herald*, January 30, 1970.

Review of the January 29, 1970, performance of the Dallas Symphony Orchestra. "Overall, the program was impressive in the high quality of the music offered, music that not only reflected the level of professionalism of the composers represented, but in several cases talents that draw deep emotional involvement and excitement from the listener. . . . *Cumbia y Congo* [from *Danzas de Panama*] and the *Scherzo* movement from his *Afro-American Symphony* were both solidly tonal, melodically pleasing and catchy. They are immediately accessible audience-pleasers."

W134 ***Sentimental Song*** (available from William Grant Still Music).
For chamber orchestra.
Instrumentation: flute, oboe, 2 clarinets, bassoon; 2 horns, trumpet, 2 trombones; harp celesta; strings.
Autograph is in The William Grant Still Estate.

W135   ***Serenade*** (available from William Grant Still Music).
        For orchestra; also for solo violin, string orchestra and piano; also flute, clarinet, harp, and string quintet; chamber orchestra.
        Composed in Los Angeles, 1957.
        Commissioned by the Great Falls (Montana) High School Symphony Orchestra.
        Dedicated to Ruth and LeRoy V. Brant.
        Duration: 8 minutes.
        Autograph is in The William Grant Still Estate.

W135a   **First Performance:** 1958 (May 7): Great Falls, MT; Great Falls High School; Great Falls High School Symphony Orchestra, Paul Shull, conductor.

Selected Performances

W135b   1965 (June 13): Los Angeles, CA; Trinity Baptist Church; Angel City Symphony Orchestra, Leroy E. Hurte, conductor.

W135c   1966 (February 18): Houston, TX; Texas Southern University, Small Chamber Orchestra.

W135d   1967 (January 16): Los Angeles, CA; Westchester String Symphony Orchestra; George Berres, conductor; Joachim Chassman, violin; J. Arnold Varney, flute.

W135e   1974 (February 17): Los Angeles, CA; Dorsey High School; Southeast Symphony Orchestra, Louis Palange, conductor.

W136   ***Seven Traceries*** (J. Fischer & Brothers, New York, 1940, no. 7632; *Muted Laughter* published separately, no. 7635-3; available from William Grant Still Music).
        For piano solo; also for piano and strings; flute, piano, and string orchestra (arranged for the Csaky Ensemble).
        Composed in Los Angeles, 1939.
        Each movement dedicated to friends of the composer: Helen and Allan (I), Josephine Harreld (II), Jessie, Marge, Adrian and Charles (III), William Duncan Allen (IV), Kay Swift (V), Militza and James (VI), Florence and James (VII).
        Contents: I. Cloud Cradles, II. Mystic Pool, III. Muted Laughter, IV. Out of the Silence, V. Woven Silver, VI. Wailing Dawn, VII. A Bit of Wit.
        Autograph, sketches, facsimiles of a manuscript edition, and the 1940 published edition are in the William Grant Still and Verna Arvey Papers at the University of Arkansas Libraries, Fayetteville.

Selected Performances

W136a   1959 (June 7): Los Angeles, CA; Avalon Christian Church; Waldemar Hille, piano.

W136b   1959 (July 5): Los Angeles, CA; Pepperdine College; Waldemar Hille, piano.

W136c   1975 (April 27): Washington, DC; National Gallery of Art, East Garden Court; Frances Walker, piano.

W136d   1975 (September 14): New York, NY; Carnegie Hall; Frances Walker, piano.

W136e   1977 (August 29): New York, NY; Auditorium of the Lincoln Center Library and Museum of the Performing Arts; Leon Bates, piano.

W136f   1979 (October 18): Los Angeles, CA; Arnold Schoenberg Institute; Cynthia Summerville, piano. (*See:* WB112.4)

W136g   1992 (November 5): Fayetteville, AR; Walton Arts Center; Alan Chow, piano.

172 William Grant Still: A Bio-Bibliography

Bibliography

WB136.1 Everett, Chestyn. "Carl Gipson not a tenor or a baritone, says critic." *Los Angeles Tribune,* June 12, 1959.

Review of the June 7, 1959, program at the Avalon Christian Church, which included selections from Still's *Seven Traceries* and *Songs of Separation*. "The second group was *Five Traceries* [sic] by the distinguished Negro composer, William Grant Still (present in the audience), beautifully and delicately played, by the pianist Waldemar Hille, who was [Carl] Gipson's accompanist [sic]. . . . It is a pity that we do not hear more of the music of our own composers like Mr. William Grant Still, whose music Sunday, eloquently stated his claim to distinction."

WB136.2 Arlen, Walter. "Leonardo Watts Heard at Pepperdine College." *Los Angeles Times,* July 7, 1959, sec. 4, p. 8.

Review of the July 5, 1959, program at Pepperdine College, which included selections from Still's *Seven Traceries* and *Songs of Separation*. It also included *Ev'ry Time I Feel The Spirit*. "William Grant Still, in the audience, could acknowledge the success of two groups of his compositions which included *Six Traceries* [sic] for piano solo nicely performed by Mr. [Waldemar] Hille, and *Songs of Separation* by Mr. [Leonardo] Watts. All were sensitive vignettes of considerable evocative power, expertly written for both the piano and the voice. The finest in the sets was no doubt the song *If You Should Go*, a little poem surrounded by static music of particular persuasiveness." (*See:* W144g)

WB136.3 Everett, Chestyn. "Leonardo Watts' recital enjoyable, but uneven." *Los Angeles Tribune,* July 10, 1959.

Review of the July 5, 1959, program at Pepperdine College, which included selections from Still's *Seven Traceries*, *Songs of Separation*, and *Ev'ry Time I Feel The Spirit*. "Prior to his playing William Grant Still's *Five Traceries* [sic], Mr. [Waldemar] Hille announced: 'These are very delicate little pieces, different from the usual ones you might hear on the piano, and in order to hear them you must be very quiet.' No sooner than the pianist began to play, one child, then a second, began to cry. . . . The evening was never quite the same. Mr. Watts returned to sing Mr. Still's *Five Songs of Separation*. . . . His voice had begun to falter in pitch; he was not infrequently flat . . . the results of these efforts were mainly without merit." (*See:* W144g)

WB136.4 Henahan, Donal. "Music: Tasteful Survey of Black Spirit." *New York Times,* September 15, 1975.

Review of the September 14, 1975, recital given by Frances Walker at Carnegie Recital Hall. "The bulk of the program offered music that had stylistic roots in the same international soil from which composers everywhere have been sprouting in the last couple of centuries. Thus, one heard Scriabin's influence in a wistful *Poem-Waltz* by John Childs, Debussy's in William Grant Still's impressionistic *Seven Traceries*, and Chopin's in R. Nathaniel Dett's *Barcarolle*. . . . The result, as the pianist no doubt intended, was to raise the listener's consciousness in respect to music by black composers. Along the way, one could also be entertained, no small thing."

WB136.5 ———. "A Pianist With a Touch of the Poet." *New York Times,* August 31, 1977.

Review of the August 29, 1977, piano recital by Leon Bates. "Mr. Bates handled each work on its own merits, skillfully taking care to differentiate between musical styles that lay only a few years apart but sometimes seemed to come from different worlds . . . in Mr. Still's *Traceries*, the pianist was not such a child of his time that he could not immerse himself in its Impressionistic day dreams."

W137 ***Sinner, Please Don't Let This Harvest Pass*** (California State Department of Education, *Let Music Ring,* edited by Peter W. Dykema, 1950; available from William Grant Still Music).
For solo voice (or voices) and piano, a cappella male quartet, or saxophone quartet.
Music education textbook edition (student's edition, p. 100).
Duration: 3 minutes.
Autograph location unknown.

W138 ***Sipping Cider Through a Straw*** (available from William Grant Still Music).
For SAT voices and piano for a music education textbook.
Autograph location unknown.

W139 ***Song for the Lonely*** (available from William Grant Still Music).
For voice and piano; also for voice and chamber orchestra; soprano, string quartet, and piano; soprano, string quartet, and harp; string quartet and piano; mezzo-soprano and harp.
Composed in Los Angeles, 1953.
Text by Verna Arvey.
Dedicated to Marie Powers.
Inscription by the composer on the autograph: "May this remind you that we were once lonely and you were one of those who offered us encourgement and understanding."
Instrumentation for chamber orchestra: solo voice with 2 flutes, 2 oboes, 2 clarinets, 2 bassoons; 3 horns, trumpet, 2 trombones, tuba; harp, celesta, strings.
Duration: 4 minutes.
Incomplete autograph of the conductor's score with orchestration notes and a facsimile of one page of a fair copy for piano and voice are in the William Grant Still and Verna Arvey Papers at the University of Arkansas Libraries, Fayetteville.
Autograph is in The William Grant Still Estate.

W139a **First Performance:** 1953 (December 9): Limoges, France; Salle Municipale-Limoges; Marie Powers, contralto; Alain Motard, piano.

Selected Performances

W139b 1954 (May 28): Perigueux, France; Casino de Paris; Marie Powers, contralto.
W139c 1961 (July 23): Los Angeles, CA; Los Angeles County Museum of Natural History; Sherrill-Whitelow Ensemble: Adrian Holland and William Henderson, violins; Russell Beckstead, viola; Constance Kelly, cello; Barbara Sherrill, piano; Pearl Whitelow, soprano.

W140 ***Song for the Valiant*** (R.D. Row Music Company, Boston, 1952, no. 794-6; available from William Grant Still Music).
For voice and piano; also for voice and orchestra, and voice and chamber group

Composed in Los Angeles, 1951.
Text by Verna Arvey.
Dedication: "For Jerome Hines."
Instrumentation for chamber group: high voice with 4 horns, 3 trombones, tuba; harp, strings.
Duration: 3 minutes.
Two autographs in open score of plans for orchestration for full orchestra in the keys of A-flat and E-flat major, an autograph of the piano vocal score in E-flat major, and a copy of the published song for high voice in A-flat major are in the William Grant Still and Verna Arvey Papers at the University of Arkansas Libraries, Fayetteville.

Selected Performances

W140a 1953 (May 22): San Jose, CA; Scottish Rite Temple; Robert Lancaster, bass; Richard Corbett, piano.

W140b 1953 (September 29): Palo Alto, CA; Palo Alto Community Center; Ruth Daniel, soprano; Margaret Thomas, piano.

W140c 1964 (May 24): Los Angeles, CA; First A.M.E. Church; Earl Green, tenor, Jonathan Collins, piano.

W140d 1973 (April 13): Malibu, CA; Pepperdine University, Wilshire Ebell Theatre; Shannon Goodwin, soloist.

W141 ***Song of a City,*** also known as *Rising Tide* and *Victory Tide* (J. Fischer & Brothers published the choral portion as *Rising Tide,* New York, 1939, no. 7525-4, for solo voice and piano; and no. 7809-7 for SSATBB, 1944; J.Fischer & Brothers published the choral version with the title, *Victory Tide,* New York, 1942, no. 7831 for SATB; no. 7837 for TTBB; J. Fischer & Brothers, New York; version for band, 1945, no. 8015; available from William Grant Still Music).
For chorus and orchestra; choral portion published for solo voice and piano; SSATBB, SATB, and TTBB choruses; band.
Composed in Los Angeles, 1939.
Commissioned for the Theme Exhibit by the New York World's Fair, 1939.
Text by Albert Stillman.
Played in the Perisphere for the duration of the Fair from 1939-1940.
Instrumentation for orchestra: chorus with 3 flutes (3rd doubles on piccolo), 2 oboes, English horn, 2 clarinets, 2 bassoons; 4 horns, 3 trumpets, 3 trombones, tuba; timpani, cymbals, xylophone, snare drum, triangles; piano or harp, strings.
Duration: 3 minutes.
Instrumentation for *Rising Tide:* SATBB or SSATBB chorus with clarinet, bassoon; alto and tenor saxophone; horns, 3 trumpets, trombone; strings.
Autograph with title *Victory Tide* in open score including orchestration notes, autograph of orchestration sketch with title *Song of a City,* and facsimiles with title *Song of a City* of instrumental parts in multiple copies for all instruments listed in "Instrumentation" section of this entry are in the William Grant Still and Verna Arvey Papers at the University of Arkansas Libraries, Fayetteville. The Still and Arvey Papers include a copy of the first sheet music publication of *Rising Tide* (J.F.&B. 7525-4) for solo voice and piano signed by the composer and a copy of the octavo edition for TTBB chorus and piano (J.F.&B. 7837-7).

Holograph of piano vocal score, *Rising Tide,* is in the Library of Congress, deposited for copyright March 25, 1939.
Autograph of the band arrangement location unknown.

W141a **First Performance:** 1939 (April 30): New York, NY; World's Fair, André Kostelanetz, conductor, with an orchestra of fifty-five musicians. A recording that was taped at the Fox Movietone News Building in New York in February 1939.

Selected Performances

W141b 1942 (May 8): Atlanta, GA; Spelman College Chorus, Kemper Harreld, director.

W141c 1945 (March 23): Detroit, MI; Robert Nolan Choir, Robert L. Nolan, director; Evelyn Davis, piano.

W141d 1945 (May 11): Atlanta, GA; Sisters Chapel; Atlanta-Morehouse-Spelman Chorus of Mixed Voices, Kemper Harreld, director.

W141e 1953 (May 22): San Jose, CA; Scottish Rite Temple; Choral Guild of San Jose, LeRoy V. Brant, conductor.

W141f 1961 (April 21): Orangeburg, SC; South Carolina State College, White Hall Auditorium; The Collegiate Chorale, James Marquis, director.

W141g 1968 (November 13): Grambling, LA; Grambling College, College Auditorium; Grambling College Choir, Robert W. Williams, director.

W141h 1969 (May 25): Tuskegee, AL; Tuskegee Institute, Logan Hall; Tuskegee Institute Concert Choir; C. Edouard Ward, conductor.

W141i 1971 (February 13): Orangeburg, South Carolina; South Carolina State University, Smith-Hammond-Middleton Memorial Center; Collegiate Chorale, H.H. Fleming, director; South Carolina All-State College Band, William Grant Still, guest conductor.

Bibliography

WB141.1 "Fair's Music Theme To Shun Stridency." *New York Times*, July 29, 1938.
Announcement that Still will be the composer of the theme music for Democracity, the topical center of the 1939 New York World's Fair.

WB141.2 Crawford, Lenore. "Draws Pictures of Joy, Sorrow." *Windsor Daily Star*, October 15, 1938.
Article on Still, providing background on him as the composer selected to write the theme music for the 1939 New York World's Fair. The author concludes by stating: "So in choosing William Grant Still the World's Fair has picked an able musician, one of the strongest forces in American music today and a sensitive interpreter of a nation's life."

WB141.3 "The Talk of the Town: Theme Center's Theme." *New Yorker* 15 (February 25, 1939): 10-11.
This article describes how the theme music for the 1939 New York World's Fair was recorded, under the direction of André Kostelanetz. "*Tomorrow's City* [*Song of a City*] is a stirring martial tune, so written that the beginning and the end blend, for continuous rendition. The film on which it is recorded will be spliced at the ends and will be played sixteen hours a day during the Fair for a total of 31,857 performances."

WB141.4 "Music for 50 Million People." *Crisis* (April 1939): 107-8.
Lengthy article on the music of the New York World's Fair and the

selection of Still as its composer. "Published and unpublished works of numerous composers were played in record form, without the jury knowing the names of the composers. It was finally agreed unanimously that the composer of *Lennox* [sic] *Avenue* and *From a Deserted Plantation*, seemed to be most capable of giving musical expression to the mood and color of the theme exhibit." Still had submitted two compositions to the contest. His works won first and second place in the competition.

W142 ***Song of the Hunter*** (Holt, Rinehart and Winston, *Exploring Music*, edited by Beth Landis; available from William Grant Still Music).
For voices with piano, drums, temple blocks, and gourd for a music education textbook.
Composed in Los Angeles, 1968.
Text by Verna Arvey.
Duration: 1 minute.
Facsimile of the published edition is in the William Grant Still and Verna Arvey Papers at the University of Arkansas Libraries, Fayetteville.

W143 ***Songs: A Medley*** (available from William Grant Still Music).
For instrumental chamber ensemble.
Contents: I. Song of the Rivermen (Father Mississippi), II. Slave Chant, III. Oh! Dem Golden Slippers, IV. I'm Goin' Where Nobody Knows My Name. V. Medley of Ain't Misbehavin' and Sweet Georgia Brown, VI. Some of These Days, VII. Love Will Find a Way, VIII. St. Louis Blues.
Instrumentation: clarinet; alto saxophone, tenor saxophone; trumpet; drums, conga drum, bongo drum; piano, guitar, banjo; strings.
Song of the Rivermen is also in **The American Scene,** Suite 5: A Mountain, A Memorial and A Song. **Songs: A Medley** and **Spirituals: A Medley** were once known as *A Look at Jazz*.
Manuscripts or fragments of manuscripts of all of the tunes in this group are in the William Grant Still and Verna Arvey Papers at the University of Arkansas Libraries, Fayetteville.

W144 ***Songs of Separation*** (Leeds, New York, 1949, no. 658-11; MCA Music Publishing, New York; available from William Grant Still Music).
A song cycle for voice and piano; also arranged for mezzo-soprano and harp; voice and orchestra; voice and string quartet.
Composed in Los Angeles; holograph of *Idolatry* dated 1945.
Dedicated to Freita Shaw (I), Hannah Bierhoff (II), Edyth and Eugene Pearson (III), Joyce Hansen (IV), and Luriel Rahn (V).
Contents: I. Idolatry, II. Poeme, III. Parted, IV. If You Should Go, V. A Black Pierrot.
Poems by Arna Bontemps (I), Philippe Thoby-Marcelin (II), Paul Laurence Dunbar (III), Countee Cullen (IV), Langston Hughes (V).
Duration for entire song cycle: 12 minutes.
If You Should Go (IV) arranged for voice with chamber orchestra; *A Black Pierrot* (V) arranged for chamber orchestra (without voice).
Instrumentation for *If You Should Go:* soprano soloist with 3 flutes (3rd doubles on piccolo), 2 oboes, English horn, 3 clarinets, 2 bassoons; 4 horns, (no trumpets), 3 trombones, tuba; timpani, cymbal; harp, celesta, strings.

Instrumentation for *A Black Pierrot:* 2 flutes, 2 oboes, 2 clarinets, 2 bassoons; 3 horns, 1 trumpet, 2 trombones, 1 tuba; harp, celesta, strings.

Holographs of each song and autographs of orchestration drafts are in the William Grant Still and Verna Arvey Papers at the University of Arkansas Libraries, Fayetteville. The holograph of *Idolatry* is dated August, 1945.

Facsimile of a manuscript of *A Black Pierrot* for voice and piano is in the James Weldon Johnson Memorial Collection of Negro Arts and Letters at Yale University.

W144a **First Performance:** 1946 (January 23): Delaware, OH; Herta Glaz, soloist.

Selected Performances

W144b 1946 (February 19): Herta Glaz, soloist. *Concert Time* program over the ABC Radio Network.

W144c 1953 (July 1): Stockton, CA; Civic Auditorium; Ruth Daniel, soprano; Margaret Thomas, piano.

W144d 1956 (March 11): Pasadena, CA; Pasadena Playhouse; Georgia Laster, soprano; Verna Arvey Still, piano.

W144e 1956 (March 22): Little Rock, AR; Dunbar Community Center; Georgia Laster, soprano; Myron Myers, piano.

W144f 1959 (June 7): Los Angeles, CA; Avalon Christian Church; Waldemar Hille, piano. (*See:* WB136.1)

W144g 1959 (July 5): Los Angeles, CA; Pepperdine College; Leonardo Watts, baritone; Waldemar Hille, piano. (*See:* WB136.2, WB136.3)

W144h 1964 (April 27): Los Angeles, CA; Lindy Opera House; Elissa Martini, soprano; Sara Robinson, piano.

W144i 1970 (April 22): Houston, TX; Texas Southern University, University Auditorium; Oakland Youth Chamber Orchestra; Robert Hughes, conductor; Cynthia Bedford, mezzo-soprano.

W144j 1970 (May 16, 17): Oakland, CA; Oakland Auditorium Theatre; Oakland Youth Chamber Orchestra, William Grant Still, guest conductor; Cynthia Bedford, mezzo-soprano.

W144k 1970 (November 9): Oberlin, OH; Oberlin College, Warner Concert Hall; Doris Mayes, mezzo-soprano; Natalie Hinderas, piano; Ronald Copes and John Schoening, violins; Noah Chaves, viola; Norman Fischer, cello. (*See:* WB155.2, WB155.3)

W144l 1972 (April 9): Grambling, LA; Grambling College, Dunbar Hall, Little Theatre; Beatrice Hilda Keys, soprano; T. Curtis Mayo, piano.

W144m 1975 (May 24): Los Angeles, CA; University of Southern California, Town and Gown Building; Michael Sell, tenor; Eudice Shapiro and George Kast, violins; Milton Thomas, viola; Gabor Rejto, cello; Andrian Ruiz, piano.

W144n 1975 (August 3): Hattiesburg, MS; University of Southern Mississippi, Marsh Auditorium; Martha Blanding Spence, soprano; Malcolm J. Breda, piano.

W144o 1976 (January 9): Buffalo, NY; Kleinhans Music Hall; Buffalo Philharmonic Orchestra, Frank Collura, conductor; Hilda Harris, mezzo-soprano.

W144p 1976 (June 6): New York, NY; Lincoln Center, Alice Tully Hall; Diane Randolph, soprano; John Morrison, tenor; Marjorie Lewis, piano.

W144q 1979 (October 18): Los Angeles, CA; Arnold Schoenberg Institute; Peggy Keller, soprano; Chris Arpin, piano. (*See:* WB112.4)

Bibliography

WB144.1 Hickman, C. Sharpless. "Composer Honored by Concert Here." *Pasadena Star-News*, March 12, 1956.
   Review of the March 11, 1956, performance. "His music is stamped with eloquence, good taste and an innate conservatism. . . . Miss Laster is a perfect interpreter of Still's vocal music, for she constantly mirrors his taste, expressiveness, and (in this day) unusual forbearance in setting song to a dramatic text. . . . Admitting that the very small 'baby grand' piano limited her tonal resourcefulness, Mrs. Still was sadly deficient in verve and proportion."

WB144.2 "Laster, Still Well Received In Concert Attended By 500." *Los Angeles Sentinel*, March 22, 1956, sec. B, p. 3.
   Review of the March 11, 1956, performance. "Both ladies [Georgia Laster and Verna Arvey Still] received a wild ovation at the conclusion of the concert and returned for encores."

WB144.3 Rosenburg, Josef. "Laster Recital Lends Interest To Waning Concert Season." *Arkansas Gazette*, March 23, 1956.
   Review of the March 22, 1956, performance. "Beautiful in lyricism and atmosphere in harmonic setting, the five songs [*Songs of Separation*] proved a fine contribution to the song literature. The soprano [Georgia Laster] sang them 'con amore.'"

WB144.4 Cunningham, Carl. "Youth orchestra stars singer." *Houston Post*, April 23, 1970.
   Review of the April 22, 1970, performance of the Oakland Youth Chamber Orchestra, Robert Hughes, conductor, and Cynthia Bedford, mezzo-soprano. "From the moment Miss Bedford began singing Still's *Songs of Separation* . . . hers was a wonderfully free, soaring and intelligently sensitive performance that held the listener's attention with magnetic appeal. . . . Still's song cycle was probably the most appealing work, by virtue of its masterful craftsmanship and sheer expressive naturalness."

WB144.5 Tucker, Marilyn. "Tribute to Black Composers." *San Francisco Chronicle*, May 18, 1970.
   Review of May 16, 1970, performance of the Oakland Youth Chamber Orchestra. The program included Still's *Songs of Separation*, which he conducted, and the *Scherzo* from the *Afro-American Symphony*. "His *Songs of Separation* . . . are art songs rich with the freedom of beautiful melody, dramatic force and lyric intensity."

WB144.6 DeCles, Diana. "Orchestra in All Black Program." *Berkeley Daily Gazette*, May 19, 1970.
   Review of the May 16, 1970, performance of the Oakland Youth Chamber Orchestra. "The exception to the extremely modern in sound was William Grant Still's *Songs of Separation*, conducted by the composer. This piece consisted of musical settings for the poems of five Negro poets, sung by Miss [Cynthia] Bedford, and was predominantly lush and warm in sound, with a sensitive attention to the line of the poetry. . . . Still's *Scherzo* [from the *Afro-American Symphony*] was lively, rhythmic, and ethnic in feeling rather than in any specific detail."

WB144.7 Putnam, Thomas. "Mezzo-Soprano Reaches With Pinchless Voice, Sharp Eye." *Buffalo Courier Express*, January 10, 1976.

Review of the January 9, 1976, performance of the Buffalo Philharmonic Orchestra. "Hilda Harris introduced the *Songs of Separation* by William Grant Still. . . . These orchestral songs have a bittersweet romanticism and French purity and warmth that Miss Harris communicated with lovely simplicity. The music of Still often is based on Negro spirituals, but these songs come from a different source, and are expressions of a noble spirit, with a pause for light amusement."

WB144.8 Davis, Peter G. "Triad Sings Black Composers' Works." *New York Times*, June 7, 1976.

Review of the June 6, 1976, Triad Choral performance at the Lincoln Center. "The cyclical *Songs of Separation* for two solo voices is a pleasantly bittersweet evocation of lost love, tinged slightly by salon sentimentality perhaps, but lovely statements in their own modest way. *From A Lost Continent* . . . is a four-movement choral suite conjuring up an aural image of Mu, a legendary continent engulfed by the Pacific Ocean eons ago. There is no text, simply vowel and consonant sounds designed to capture the archaic flavor of the subject. By using modal scales, open harmonies and primitive rhythmic motor patterns, Mr. Still has created an undeniably compelling piece of musical exotica."

W145 *Sorcerer: Fantastic Scene for pantomimists and dancers, The*
(piano score available from William Grant Still Music).
For orchestra, 3 actors, 2 solo dancers, and corps de ballet.
Composed in New York; holograph dated August 12, 1933.
Scenario by (Harold) Bruce Forsythe.
Inscription by the composer on the holograph says, "(With humble thanks to God for His aid.)—William Grant Still."
Argument on the holograph: "The Sorcerer, a gloomy, deformed, flamelike Being, by his mastery of the *six truths* has drawn into his cavern the Youth, who lies bound upon the floor, and the Maiden, through whom the Sorcerer plans to win Desire . . . [and finally] Throwing the Maiden roughly aside, the Sorcerer proceeds to the incantations he believes will cause him the release of Beauty within himself. . . . From behind the caldron arises a radiant and terrible Being, The Monster, Lord of the *seventh truth*. The Gnomes [dancers] drive the Sorcerer into his grasp, leaving the Maiden as best she may to free her Lover."
Instrumentation in holograph of orchestral version: piccolo, 3 flutes, oboes, English horn, 3 clarinets, bass clarinet, 2 bassoons, contrabassoon; 4 horns, 3 trumpets and 3 trombones (with Harmon mutes and flutter tonguing), tuba; percussion, timpani, cymbals, triangle; harp, piano, strings.
Holograph of the conductor's score with orchestration notes of "The Sorcerer: Fantastic Scene for 3 actors, 2 solo dancers, and corps de ballet" is in the William Grant Still and Verna Arvey Papers at the University of Arkansas Libraries, Fayetteville, and in The William Grant Still Estate. The Still and Arvey Papers also include a facsimile of an autograph piano score, complete with stage directions, the argument, a list of characters and dancers, stage directions, information on properties, and the complete scenario in typewritten manuscript.
Family papers indicate that this work was "discarded by the composer."

W146 ***Southern Interlude, A,*** see also ***Highway 1, U.S.A.,*** **W62.**
Opera in 2 acts; reduced orchestra, small chorus, 4 vocal soloists, 1 stage set.
Composed in Los Angeles; holograph dated June 1942.
Libretto by Verna Arvey.
Instrumentation in the holograph score: 2 flutes, 2 oboes, English horn, 3 clarinets, bass clarinet, 2 bassoons; 4 horns, 2 trumpets, 2 trombones; timpani, gong, snare drum; harp, strings.
Duration: 60 minutes.
Holograph, bound, of Acts I and II, titled ***A Southern Interlude,*** dated June 1942 is in the William Grant Still and Verna Arvey Papers at the University of Arkansas Libraries, Fayetteville. Verna Arvey's notes include a synopsis, stage set design, the libretto with notes from Arvey and Still (including thematic sketches), and a preliminary list of arias.
Family papers indicate that this work was "discarded by the composer" and the musical material incorporated into other works.

W147 ***Spirituals: A Medley*** (available from William Grant Still Music).
For flute, 2 clarinets, bassoon; harp, piano, strings.
Contents: I. Get on Board (*See:* W38, W54), II. Motherless Child (*See:* W39), III. Medley, IV. Nobody Knows the Trouble I've Seen, V. Jesus is a Rock (*See:* W101), VI. Were You There?, VII. He Rose, VIII. What a Morning, IX. Deep River (*See also:* W38), X. Finale.
Holograph, with the same instrumentation and corrections, of a group titled *Medley (III)* with text under the melody line is in the William Grant Still and Verna Arvey Papers at the University of Arkansas Libraries, Fayetteville. The spirituals in this medley are *We Are Climbing Jacob's Ladder; Little David, Play on Your Harp* (also in W83); and *Go Down Moses.* ***Spirituals: A Medley*** and ***Songs: A Medley*** were once known as *A Look at Jazz.*
Autograph of complete work is in The William Grant Still Estate.

W148 ***Steal Away to Jesus*** (available from William Grant Still Music).
Spiritual arrangement for vocal solo, SSATB chorus and piano.
Composed in New York, about 1923.
Performed by Helen Woodruff with violin, cello, and piano in a recording by The Black Swan Phonograph Company in the 1920s. (*See:* B113)
Holograph of solo with chorus and piano version is in The William Grant Still Estate.
Autograph location of The Black Swan version unknown.

W149 ***Suite for Violin and Piano*** (Delkas Music Publishing Company, Los Angeles, 1945; available from William Grant Still Music).
For violin and piano; also arranged by the composer for violin and orchestra (violin part edited by Louis Kaufman); *I* and *III* arranged by the composer for string orchestra, flute, and piano with the title *Preludes.*
Composed in Los Angeles; holograph dated 1943.
"Dedicated to my friends, Louis and Annette Kaufman."
Contents suggested by paintings of three contemporary Negro artists:
I. Majestically—Vigorously: Richmond Barthe's *African Dancer,* II. Slowly and expressive: Sargent Johnson's *Mother and Child,* and III. Rhythmically and humorously: Augusta Savage's *Gamin.*

Mother and Child movement arranged by the composer for string orchestra (no soloist), string quartet, string quintet, and cello and piano.

Instrumentation for the version for orchestra: solo violin and 2 flutes (2nd doubles on piccolo), 2 oboes, English horn, 3 clarinets, 2 bassoons (2nd doubles on contrabassoon); 4 horns, 3 trumpets, 3 trombones, tuba; timpani, bells, marimba, tom-toms, cymbals; harp, celesta, strings.

Duration: 15 minutes.

Holograph, dated May 1943, of the version for violin and piano with revisions and orchestration notes and a copy of the published version are in the William Grant Still and Verna Arvey Papers at the University of Arkansas Libraries, Fayetteville.

Holograph of *Preludes* (movements I and III) for string orchestra, flute, and piano is in The William Grant Still Estate.

W149a **First Performance:** 1944 (March 14): Boston, MA; Jordan Hall; Louis Kaufman, violin; Vladimir Padwa, piano.

Selected Performances

W149b 1944 (March 17): New York, NY; Town Hall; Louis Kaufman, violin; Vladimir Padwa, piano.

W149c 1946 (July 21): Washington, DC; National Gallery of Art; Stanley Weiner, violin; Charlotte Eisler, piano.

W149d 1947 (August 25): St. Louis, MO; City Art Museum of St. Louis; Samuel Marti, violin; Gunhild Nilsson, piano.

W149e 1948 (January 13): New York, NY; Times Hall; Stanley Weiner, violin; Elsa Fiedler, piano.

W149f 1948 (April 5): Kansas City, MO; U.S. Epperson Hall; Elma Eaton Karr, violin; Richard Canterbury, piano.

W149g 1949 (February 2): Los Angeles, CA; Wilshire Ebell Fine Arts Hall; Samuel Marti, violin; Gunhild Nilsson, piano.

W149h 1954 (January 14): Detroit, MI; Detroit Public Library; Noreen Smialek, violin; Mrs. Rose Polant, piano.

W149i 1955 (February 21): Baltimore, MD; Peabody Conservatory; Ronald Knudsen, violin; Gene Akers, piano.

W149j 1958 (June 15): Los Angeles, CA; Los Angeles County Museum of Natural History; Louis Kaufman, violin; Annette Kaufman, piano.

W149k 1972 (March 26): Santa Monica, CA; Santa Monica Bay Woman's Club; Louis Kaufman, violin; Annette Kaufman, piano.

W149l 1977 (April 4): New York, NY: Carnegie Recital Hall; Joyce Rasmussen Balint, violin; Louise Colusso Feinauer, piano.

W149m 1980 (January 14): Washington DC; Kennedy Center; Darwyn Apple, violin; Seth Carlin, piano.

W149n 1984 (February 15): Fayetteville, AR; University of Arkansas, Fine Arts Center Concert Hall; University Chamber Orchestra, Carlton R. Woods, conductor; Sandy Foster, flute; Norma Ortiz-Karp, piano.

Bibliography

WB149.1 R., J.W. "Music." *Boston Daily Globe*, March 15, 1944.
Review of the March 14, 1944, performance by Louis Kaufman. "Still's *Suite [for Violin and Piano]* never quite made its point."

WB149.2 S., D.W. "Music." *Boston Herald*, March 15, 1944.

Review of the March 14, 1944, recital by Louis Kaufman. "William Grant Still's *Suite [for Violin and Piano]* was pleasant enough to hear, while not showing any remarkable originality. The third movement . . . was most American in its idiom, being based on the type of jazz that was popular in the twenties."

WB149.3 Bennett, Grena. "Kaufman at Town Hall." *New York Journal-American*, March 18, 1944.

Review of the March 17, 1944, performance in New York by Louis Kaufman. "[*Suite for Violin and Piano*] was an adroit and interesting contribution to modern compositions. The piano accompaniments were effectively played by Vladimir Padwa."

WB149.4 Strauss, Noel. "Kaufman Presents Sonatina by Jones." *New York Times*, March 18, 1944.

Review of the March 17, 1944, performance by Louis Kaufman. "Mr. Still's [*Suite*] was not representative of the composer at his best."

WB149.5 de Sayn, Elena. "Stanley Weiner Offers Unusual Violin Suite." Washington *Evening Star*, July 22, 1946.

Review of a performance by Stanley Weiner in Washington D.C., on July 21, 1946. "[*Suite for Violin and Piano*] bears an unmistakable racial color, to the development of which the composer devoted himself in the last 20 years. . . . Mr. Still shows his expertness in the boldness of his harmonies and facile part-writing."

WB149.6 Green, Ellen Josephine. "Great American Composer To Be Given First Hearing In Kansas City." *Musical Bulletin* 36 (April 1948): 5.

Preview of the Kansas City Musical Club's April 5, 1948, program which includes Still's *Suite for Violin and Piano*. "In composing his *Suite*, Mr. Still took the joy of the Gamin, the grace and agility of the African Dancer, and the infinite tenderness of the Mother and Child and wove these qualities into a composition which—if your sense of hearing be fine enough and your imagination keen enough—will enchant you with its subtle and beautiful moods evoked by these qualities."

WB149.7 Slater, Richard. "Kaufman Duo Heard In Santa Monica Recital." *Los Angeles Times*, March 29, 1972.

Review of a March 26, 1972, recital by Louis and Annette Kaufman. "The final portion of the program paid homage to local composer William Grant Still with his picturesque and mildly modern *Suite for Violin and Piano* which is dedicated to the Kaufmans, and with two encores, *Blues*, from his *Lennox* [sic] *Avenue Suite*, and his arrangement of the spiritual *Here's One*. The composer acknowledged the applause of a moderately large, appreciative audience."

W150 ***Summerland*, from *Three Visions*** (available from William Grant Still Music in many arrangements; see also ***Three Visions***, W161).

For piano solo; arranged by the composer for chamber orchestra; 2 pianos; cello and piano; flute and piano; violin and piano; string quartet; string quintet; symphonic band with harp; flute, harp, and string quartet.

Composed in Los Angeles, 1935.

Instrumentation for chamber orchestra: flute, oboe, 2 clarinets, bassoon; 2 horns, 2 trumpets, trombone; drums, strings.

Duration: 6 minutes.
Autograph of *Summerland* arrangement for quintet (flute, violin, viola, cello, and harp) in open score with orchestration notes and the autograph of the piano solo version are in the William Grant Still and Verna Arvey Papers at the University of Arkansas Libraries, Fayetteville.
Autographs of other versions are in The William Grant Still Estate.

W151 *Swing Low, Sweet Chariot.*
Spiritual arrangement.
Composed in New York, about 1923.
Performed by C. Carroll Clark on a recording by The Black Swan Phonograph Company in the 1920s. (*See:* B113)
Autograph location unknown.

W152 *Symphony No. 2 in G Minor, "Song of a New Race"* (1937) (Carl Fischer, Inc., New York).
For orchestra.
Composed in Los Angeles; begun in 1936 and completed in 1937.
Dedicated to Isabel Morse Jones.
Inscription by the composer on the holograph: "Praying that this may receive the blessing of God."
Contents: I. Slowly, II. Slowly and Deeply expressive, III. Moderately fast, IV. Moderately Slow; the orchestral parts indicate there is to be no pause between the second and third movements.
Instrumentation: 3 flutes (3rd doubles on piccolo), 2 oboes, English horn, 3 clarinets, bass clarinet, 2 bassoons; 4 horns, 3 trumpets and 3 trombones (felt hats, cup mutes, and straight mutes), tuba; timpani, bells, vibraphone, wire brush, cymbals, snare drum; harp, celesta, strings.
Duration: 25 minutes.
Holograph of the complete work with orchestration notes and revisions by the composer, sketches, and an autograph labeled "revised version—Symphony in G minor," are in the William Grant Still and Verna Arvey Papers at the University of Arkansas Libraries, Fayetteville. The Still and Arvey Papers contain facsimiles of the conductor's score in manuscript and facsimiles of a complete set of fair copies of parts in manuscript for performance.

W152a **First Performance:** 1937 (December 10, 11): Philadelphia, PA; Academy of Music; Philadelphia Orchestra, Leopold Stokowski, conductor.

Selected Performances

W152b 1937 (December 14): New York, NY; Carnegie Hall; Philadelphia Orchestra, Leopold Stokowski, conductor.

W152c 1938 (October 19, 20): Rochester, NY; Kilbourn Hall; Rochester Civic Orchestra, Howard Hanson, conductor.

W152d 1939 (February 23): Rochester, NY; Kilbourn Hall; Rochester Civic Orchestra, Howard Hanson, conductor.

W152e 1939 (August 1): San Diego, CA; Ford Bowl, Balboa Park; San Diego Symphony Orchestra, William Grant Still, guest conductor.

W152f 1940 (January 4): Cleveland, OH; Severance Hall, Cleveland Orchestra, Rudolph Ringwall, conductor.

W152g 1940 (September 24): San Francisco, CA; Federal Plaza; San Francisco Symphony, William Grant Still, guest conductor. (*See:* WB76.8, WB76.9)

W152h 1941 (April 29): Rochester, NY; Eastman Theatre; Eastman School Senior Symphony Orchestra, Howard Hanson, conductor. (*See:* WB103.2)

W152i 1945 (November 19): Paris, France; Théâtre des Champs-Élysées; Orchestre National, Rudolph Dunbar, conductor.

W152j 1979 (January 20): Oakland, CA; Scottish Rite Auditorium; Ebony Symphony Orchestra, Wilton Jones, conductor.

Bibliography

WB152.1 Gilman, Lawrence. "Program Notes." *Journal of the Philadelphia Orchestra*, December 10-11, 1937.

Program notes for the first performance. "Mr. Still prefers to confine his commentary to the following observations: 'This *Symphony in G Minor*, begun in 1936 and completed in 1937, is related to my *Afro-American Symphony* (composed in 1930), being, in fact, a sort of extension or evolution of the latter. This relationship is implied musically through the affinity of the principal theme of the first movement of the *Symphony in G Minor* to the principal theme of the fourth, or last, movement of the *Afro-American*. It may be said that the purpose of the *Symphony in G Minor* is to point musically to changes wrought in a people through the progressive and transmuting spirit of America. I prefer to think of it as an abstract piece of music." A copy of the program in the Still and Arvey Papers bears the following note: "Dear Billie—Came to Phila to hear your Symphony. Enjoyed it [immensely] Congratulations! . . . [Your friend] Clarence Cameron White."

WB152.2 Martin, Linton. "Stokowski Mute in Exit from Phila. Orchestra." *Philadelphia Inquirer*, December 11, 1937.

Report on the December 10, 1937, concert including *Symphony No. 2 in G Minor*, which "was of absorbing interest, unmistakably racial in thematic material and rhythms, and triumphantly articulate in expression of moods, ranging from the exuberance of jazz to brooding wistfulness."

WB152.3 Pleasants, Henry. "Music in Review." Philadelphia *Evening Bulletin*, December 11, 1937.

Review of the December 10, 1937, concert. "[*Symphony No. 2 in G Minor*] is a weak work, composed of half an hour or more of sugared melancholy broken only by [a] lively third movement which is easily the most effective of the four. Despite the fact that Mr. Still is himself a Negro, the rich and inventive idiom of his race is hardly suggested."

WB152.4 Downes, Olin. "Stokowski Offers New Compositions." *New York Times*, December 15, 1937.

Review of the December 14, 1937, concert. "[The *Symphony No. 2 in G Minor*] . . . repeats itself, in style, in mood, in orchestral coloring and melodic utterance. Forty percent of it could have said all there is in it to say. . . . Here is an unquestionable gift, and warm feeling, now sad, now gay, characteristic and sincere in expression. . . . In many scores Mr. Still has shown a conspicuous talent. There is good reason to believe that as he gets more and more of his earlier inspiration out of his system he will find a style and form distinctively and completely his own."

WB152.5 Thompson, Oscar. "Stokowski Contrasts Eras." New York *Sun*, December 15, 1937.

Review of the December 14, 1937, concert. "[The *Symphony No. 2 in*

G Minor] . . . abounds in a species of likable exposition, but achieves little in the way of transformation of the basic material. Moreover, one movement is very much like another, irrespective of changes of tempo and dynamics. The symphony lacks essential contrast and inner organic growth."

WB152.6   Gilman, Lawrence. "Music." *New York Tribune*, December 16, 1937.
Review of the December 14, 1937, concert. "The ghost of Mélisande haunts the dusk of Mr. Still's imagination; and it is interesting to discover the nostalgic wraith of the Franco-English Delius returning once more to that Southern America where he dwelt long years ago. Mr. Still's music [*Symphony No. 2 in G Minor*], especially when he is under the influence of Delius, seems a trifle luscious for the America of today. Yet now and again it speaks with its native and unmistakable voice, and effects us by its sincerity and passion. Mr. Stokowski played it superbly, as though he believed in it; and the result was often moving."

WB152.7   "Music: Jazz Symphony." *Time* 30 (December 20, 1937): 44-45.
Review of the December 10, 1937, performance. The article includes a review of the premiere performance of the *Symphony No. 2 in G Minor* and background on Still. "Pleasantly sentimental in the moments when it was not jazzy, the score was more impressive in its clear professional instrumentation . . . than through its intrinsic musical qualities. Minus its jazz content it might possibly have been a better symphony; minus its symphonic pretensions, its jazz moments would certainly have been better jazz."

WB152.8   Simon, Robert A. "Musical Events." *New Yorker* 13 (December 25, 1937): 28.
Review of the December 14, 1937, performance. "[*Symphony No. 2 in G Minor*] . . . is a downright tuny affair, but not as enjoyable as it's long, because it's too long. A few cuts will help to make it eligible for general circulation."

WB152.9   Winton, Carl. "Famed Philadelphia Symphony Thrills New York Music Lovers." *Pittsburgh Courier*, January 1, 1938.
Review of the December 14, 1937, performance. "Mr. Still has undeniable experience in and talent for the orchestral idiom. But his art on the compositional side suffers tremendously from one-sidedness which took the direction last night of an abuse of lyricism almost to boredom. This was plainly visible throughout the audience which was kindly to say the least."

WB152.10   D., J. P. "American Works Played In Kilbourn Hall Recital." *Rochester Evening News*, February 24, 1939.
Review of the February 23, 1939, performance. "William Grant Still's *Symphony No. 2* [*in G Minor*] carried to ingenious length a resourcefulness and comfort in Negro and jazz tunes, to a degree of consonance and comfort in the present-day orchestral idiom which might make it a favorite with contemporary audiences. . . . It is a consequential, always clear development of themes in five and six tones, and the contrasts of moody woodwinds with lyric strings are masterful in the jazz-symphonic style."

WB152.11   Sabin, Stewart B. "American Works Rouse Interest at Civic Orchestra Concert." *Rochester Democrat and Chronicle*, February 24, 1939.
"Still's symphony [*No. 2 in G Minor*] was introduced in fashion to make it ingratiate itself on a first hearing. To the writer its two middle

movements are of the widely known Negro composer's best. The finale has dramatic consequence; the first movement with its inflexible rhythms and adherence to principal theme may be prolix. It appealed as a bit so last night."

WB152.12 Warner, A. J. "Composers' Concert Proves Interesting." *Rochester Times-Union*, February 24, 1939.

"The instrumentation [of *Symphony No. 2 in G Minor*] is often richly effective, and the thematic material has moments of beauty and color. Moreover, there was no excessive dissonance to afflict the ears of the listener in spite of the fact that the work is amply endowed with modernisms. The orchestra provided a spirited performance and the audience left no doubt of its approval."

WB152.13 Herreshoff, Constance. "Appealing Melody Charms Under Guest Conductor." *San Diego Sun*, August 2, 1939.

Review of the West Coast premiere of *Symphony No. 2 in G Minor* on August 1, 1939. "The Still Symphony abounds in appealing melody, interesting harmonic and rhythmic effects. No observer could fail to be interested in the novelty and bright colorings of its orchestration. . . . In spite of short rehearsal time, the symphony came over well last night."

WB152.14 Imgrund, Frances. "Acclaim Still Symphony." San Diego *Evening Tribune*, August 2, 1939.

Review of the West Coast premiere of *Symphony No. 2 in G Minor* on August 1, 1939. "Integrity of craftsmanship, as well as the thought and feeling of this very quiet, modest man, left its imprint upon his music. . . . The symphony was most difficult but the orchestra played with such sympathetic unanimity that its beautiful, tender spirit was never lost, and its strength and virility were obvious."

WB152.15 Moody, Sally Brown. "Sokoloff Wins Favor; Presents Negro Composer." *San Diego Union*, August 2, 1939.

"Review of the August 1, 1939, performance. Still conducted his *Symphony No. 2 in G Minor*. . . . To the writer the composer had little to say, and said it rather tamely. Greater familiarity with the score on the part of the players might have made for a more cohesive whole. . . . [W]e had the feeling that he had deliberately controlled himself in writing this work rather than allowing the music, which undeniably has a latent force and power, to express itself as it desired. Guest conductor Still was cordially received and recalled a number of times."

WB152.16 Wesley, E. B. "Wm. Grant Still Conducts Compositions in San Diego." *California Eagle*, August 10, 1939.

Review of the August 1, 1939, performance of the San Diego Symphony Orchestra. "The purpose of the Symphony was brought out beautifully and artistically by the brilliant composer and conductor [William Grant Still]. Nothing was lacking in praise of his performance."

WB152.17 Bacon, Elmore. "Levant's Jazz Makes Concert Hit." *Cleveland News*, January 5, 1940.

Report on January 4, 1940, concert. "In this [*Symphony No. 2 in G Minor*] Still gathers together many beloved Negro spirituals and has woven them into a musical tapestry whose sameness of pattern sometimes tends to monotony. . . . Its general atmosphere is tinged with repression and its melodies are mostly plaintive."

WB152.18 Elwell, Herbert. "Levant Frolics in Musical Pasture." *Cleveland Plain Dealer*, January 5, 1940.

Review of January 4, 1940, performance. "Heard here for the first time, it was disappointing. It is in G minor, unfortunately, almost all the way through. Had it modulated oftener it might have held attention better. As it was, its sweet, dreamy melodies soothed the nerves of those who never listen for structure anyway, and irritated those who do."

WB152.19 Loesser, Arthur. "Likes Home-Grown Music at Severance." *Cleveland Press*, January 5, 1940.

Review of January 4, 1940, concert. "[The *Symphony No. 2 in G Minor*] has a melodic vein of great warmth and sincerity, a rather luscious harmonic idiom which feels like an elaboration of that of our popular music. . . . Notwithstanding the composer's great skill in orchestration, his very positive gifts seem to be lyrical rather than symphonic."

WB152.20 Fairley, Lee. "Program Notes." Eastman School Senior Symphony Orchestra, April 29, 1941.

Program notes for *Symphony No. 2*. Still is quoted, in part, as follows: "This symphony is intended to suggest the American colored man of today. Yearning has progressed beyond the passive state; sorrow has given way to a more philosophic attitude; religious fervor and rough humor have been replaced by a more mundane form of emotional release; aspiration is now tempered with desire to give the best of African heritage."

W153 ***Symphony No. 3, "The Sunday Symphony"*** (1958) (Carl Fischer, Inc., New York).

For orchestra, in four movements.

Composed in Los Angeles, 1958; the composer's last symphony but numbered to fill the gap when the composer "discarded" his first *Symphony No. 3;* the other *Symphony No. 3* was composed in 1945 and later revised to become ***Symphony No. 5***. (*See:* W155)

Contents: I. Moderately: The awakening, II. Very Slow: Prayer, III. Gaily: Relaxation, IV. Resolutely: Day's end—and a new beginning.

Instrumentation: 3 flutes (3rd doubles on piccolo), 2 oboes, English horn, 2 clarinets, bass clarinet, 2 bassoons; 4 horns, 3 trumpets, 3 trombones, tuba; timpani,bells, triangle, tambourine, drums, 3 tom-toms, cymbals; celesta, harp, strings.

Duration: 25 minutes.

Two facsimiles of the conductor's score and facsimiles of a complete set of manuscript parts are in the William Grant Still and Verna Arvey Papers at the University of Arkansas Libraries, Fayetteville.

Autograph location unknown.

W153a **First Performance:** 1984 (February 12): Harrison, AR; North Arkansas Symphony Orchestra, Carlton R. Woods, conductor.

Selected Performances

W153b 1984 (February 18): Fayetteville, AR; First Baptist Church, North Arkansas Symphony Orchestra, Carlton R. Woods, conductor.

W153c 1995 (March 11): Fayetteville, AR; Walton Arts Center; North Arkansas Symphony Orchestra, Carlton R. Woods, conductor.

W154 ***Symphony No. 4, "Autochthonous (Indigenous)"*** (1947) (available from William Grant Still Music).
For orchestra, in four movements.
Composed in Los Angeles; holograph dated July 1947.
Dedicated to Maurice Kessler, Still's violin teacher at Oberlin College.
Contents: I. Moderately: The spirit of optimism and energy, II. Slowly: pensive, later animated in a folksy way, III. (Moderately fast) With a graceful lilt: humorous, IV. Slowly and reverently: love of mankind.
Instrumentation: 3 flutes (3rd doubles on piccolo), 2 oboes, English horn, 3 clarinets, 2 bassoons (2nd doubles on contrabassoon); 4 horns, 3 trumpets, 3 trombones, tuba; timpani, glockenspiel, resonator bell in G, triangle, wire brush, drums, military drum, cymbals, gong; harp, celesta, strings.
Duration: 27 minutes.
Holograph dated July 1947 with orchestration notes, revisions, and dedication is in the William Grant Still and Verna Arvey Papers at the University of Arkansas Libraries, Fayetteville. The Still and Arvey Papers also contain the initial melodic sketches with some harmonic progressions indicated for the first three movements.

W154a **First Performance:** 1951 (March 18): Oklahoma City, OK; Oklahoma City Orchestra, Victor Alessandro, conductor. Broadcast over the Mutual Radio Network.

Selected Performances

W154b 1951 (November 7): Brussels, Belgium; Institut National Belge de Radiodiffusion (INR) Symphony Orchestra, Franz Andre, conductor.

W154c 1959 (October 1): Denver, CO; Auditorium Theatre; Denver Symphony Orchestra, William Grant Still, guest conductor.

W154d 1968 (February 12): Seattle, WA; Seattle Center Opera House; Seattle Youth Symphony Orchestra, William Grant Still, guest conductor.

W154e 1971 (April 18): Los Angeles, CA; Widney High School; Southeast Symphony Orchestra, Louis Palange, conductor.

Bibliography

WB154.1 Baker, Ed. "Youth Symphony Plays Opera House Concert." *Seattle Times*, February 13, 1968.
Review of the February 12, 1968, performance of the Seattle Youth Symphony Orchestra. "His *Fourth Symphony* [which Still conducted] and a *Festive Overture*, which opened the concert, give hints of Negro spirituals and blues, but the hints are not developed. Romanticism, pleasantly written, is the dominant theme. *Out of the Silence*, a tone poem, came off best among the Still pieces. It featured solos by two Youth Symphony members: Pamela Snow, pianist, and Pamela Presley, flutist, whose sweet, clear playing was a brief delight. The fourth selection by Still was *Danzas de Panama*, a light holiday for strings."

W155 ***Symphony No. 5, "Western Hemisphere"*** (1945; revised 1958) (available from William Grant Still Music).
For orchestra.
Composed in Los Angeles, 1945, and revised after 1947 as "Third Symphony"; further revised as "Fifth Symphony" in 1958.

Dedicated to Christian Dupriez as "Third Symphony;" Dedicated to Victoria Juarez Burke as "Fifth Symphony."

Contents: I. The vigorous, life-sustaining forces of the Hemisphere (briskly), II. The natural beauties of the Hemisphere (slower, and with utmost grace), III. The nervous energy of the Hemisphere (energetically), IV. The overshadowing spirit of kindness and justice in the Hemisphere (moderately).

Instrumentation: 3 flutes (3rd doubles on piccolo), 2 oboes, English horn, 3 clarinets, 2 bassoons; 4 horns, 3 trumpets, 3 trombones, tuba; timpani, bells, chime, marimbaphone, snare drum, cymbals; harp, celesta, strings.

Duration: 25 minutes.

Autograph initial melodic sketches of a version called "Symphony—Western Continents" are in the William Grant Still and Verna Arvey Papers at the University of Arkansas Libraries, Fayetteville. Inscriptions by the composer on this sketch say, "A kindly land. Vigorous lands that invited men to thrive (grow strong) on their warm bosoms. 1. Physical development, 2. Spiritual growth, 3. Mental development—progress in science [and] mechanics—4—pointing to glorious future."

Autograph of final version is in The William Grant Still Estate.

W155a **First Performance:** 1970 (November 9): Oberlin, Ohio; Oberlin College; Warner Concert Hall; The Oberlin Orchestra, Robert Baustian, conductor.

Selected Performances

W155b 1971 (October 10): Santa Monica, CA; Santa Monica Civic Auditorium; The Santa Monica Symphony Orchestra; Victor Bay, conductor.

W155c 1973 (February 23, 25): Detroit, MI; Wayne County Community Arts Auditorium; Detroit Metropolitan Orchestra, Charles Sumner, conductor. (*See also:* WB172.9)

Bibliography

WB155.1 Finn, Robert. "Still Opus Premieres Tonight at Oberlin." *Cleveland Plain Dealer*, November 9, 1970.

An interview with Still on the eve of the premiere of *Symphony No. 5* by the Oberlin Orchestra. "Still has no quarrel with those who label him a 'conservative' composer. His work integrates Negro subjects and folk material with the symphonic process but he does not hold this up as a model of what other, younger black composers must do (Still always uses the term 'Afro-American' instead of 'black' or 'Negro'). 'All composers should write what they want,' he says. 'I do not see why anyone thinks they must all write alike, and I don't understand why a piece that was judged wonderful yesterday cannot still be wonderful today.'"

WB155.2 Price, Theodore. "Still Talent Revealed In Concert." *Akron Beacon Journal*, November 10, 1970.

Lengthy review of the seventy-fifth birthday concert in honor of Still at Oberlin. The all-Still program included the world premiere of *Symphony No. 5*. "Subtitled *Western Hemisphere*, the 20 minute, four-movement work was composed in 1958. A descriptive 'poeme' by Still envisions the end of a day in eternity, after a mighty civilization has begun, climaxed and declined and when the lands of the Western Hemisphere become endowed with new, positive qualities. . . . But his *Western Hemisphere Symphony* . . . somehow falls short of these earlier marks [*Danzas de*

WB155.3 Salisbury, Wilma. "Pop Element Diffused in Still Program at Oberlin." *Cleveland Plain Dealer*, November 11, 1970.

Review of the November 9, 1970, concert at Oberlin. The all-Still program included the world premiere of *Symphony No. 5, Western Hemisphere*. "Altogether, *Western Hemisphere* . . . gave the impression that it was intended as a background for something else. In greater or lesser degree, the same ingenuous tunes, sweet harmonies, thick textures, repetitious techniques and pictorial effects also characterized the other Still pieces performed: *To You, America!* . . . *Three Visions* . . . *Songs of Separation* . . . and *Danzas de Panama*."

WB155.4 Rockwell, John. "Americana in Santa Monica." *Los Angeles Times*, October 12, 1971, sec. 4, p. 12.

Review of the October 10, 1971, performance of the Santa Monica Symphony Orchestra, Victor Bay, conductor. "The concert ended with William Grant Still's *Symphony No. 5, Western Hemisphere*. . . . It sounded Sunday rather more like an unpretentiously engaging lyric suite than a symphony in the formal sense—tuneful, untroubled by harmonic adventuresomeness, fleshed out with deft but sometimes slightly simplistic scoring. The last movement, expanding songfully and rhetorically on a single, stirring theme made a particularly ingratiating effect.'"

WB155.5 Hale, Richard. "Americana Opens Symphony Season." *Evening Outlook*, October 15, 1971, p. 19.

Review of the October 10, 1971, performance of the Santa Monica Symphony Orchestra, Victor Bay, conductor. "For an important climax, Bay presented the West Coast premiere of *Symphony No. 5*. . . . Still was present and was called repeatedly to the stage to acknowledge the prolonged applause which greeted the excellent performance by the orchestra. If thematically the symphony was not particularly striking, the polished development however led to a strong climax."

WB155.6 Carr, Jay. "Metro Orchestra is remarkable." *Detroit News*, February 26, 1973, sec. D, p. 7.

Review of the February 25, 1973, performance of the Detroit Metropolitan Orchestra. It included *Festive Overture, Wood Notes*, and *Symphony No. 5*. "Sumner [the conductor] has played portions of the four-part *Wood Notes* here before, and the broadly expansive sections came across most affectingly. The *Symphony No. 5*, subtitled *Western Hemisphere*, was a Michigan premiere. Actually this was Still's Third Symphony of 1937 [actually 1945], extensively revised and reissued in 1970. . . . This so-called symphony actually is a suite, with scoring more sophisticated than that of the *Wood Notes* Suite, at its most affecting in the lovely section depicting natural beauties. Sumner elicited performances of a warmth that paralleled the warmth and good will in the music. These were vibrant, human performances of vibrant, human music."

W156 ***Those Who Wait*** (available from William Grant Still Music).
For SSATBB chorus and orchestra with bass solo and mezzo-soprano solo. Composed in Los Angeles; holograph dated February 4, 1943.
Poem by Verna Arvey.

Dedicated to Nimrod and Clara Allen.
"Inspired by a request from Leopold Stokowski."
Instrumentation (indicated by the composer on the holograph): 3 flutes (3rd doubles on piccolo), 2 oboes, English horn, 3 clarinets (3rd doubles on bass clarinet), 2 bassoons; 4 horns, 3 trumpets and 3 trombones (cup mutes), tuba; percussion: cymbals, drums, gong; harp, strings, piano.
Duration: 10 minutes.
Holograph of the piano vocal score with sketches for the orchestration and a typed poem are in the William Grant Still and Verna Arvey Papers at the University of Arkansas Libraries, Fayetteville.
Holograph score is in The William Grant Still Estate.

W156a **First Performance:** 1992 (November 29): Milwaukee, WI; St. Mark's AME Church; Nathaniel Dett Chorus, Wallace Cheatham, conductor; Evelyn and Byron Jones, soloists.

Bibliography

WB156.1 "Composer Honors Columbus Couple." *Columbus Dispatch*, June 1, 1947. Article announcing that *Those Who Wait* is dedicated to Mr. and Mrs. Nimrod B. Allen. Mr. Allen, executive secretary of the Columbus (OH) Urban League, and Still first met at Wilberforce University.

W157 ***Three Dances,*** also known as *Ballet Dances, Ballet Music,* or *Suite of Three Dances* (available from William Grant Still Music).
For orchestra.
Contents: I. Boy's Dance from *Miss Sally's Party,* II. Dance Before the Hut from *Sahdji,* III. Tribal Dance from an unfinished ballet.
Instrumentation: 2 flutes (2nd doubles on piccolo), 2 oboes, 2 clarinets; 3 horns, 2 trumpets, 2 trombones; timpani, bells, chimes, xylophone, tambourine, rattle, tom-toms, cymbals; piano, strings.
Duration: 8 minutes.
Autograph is in The William Grant Still Estate.

Selected Performance

W157a 1955 (March 4): Baton Rouge, LA; Southern University; University Auditorium; New Orleans Philharmonic-Symphony Orchestra, Alexander Hilsberg, conductor. (*See:* WB2.55-WB2-57)

W158 ***Three Negro Songs*** (conductor's score available from William Grant Still Music).
For orchestra, no texts.
Composed in New York, 1921.
Contents: I. Negro Love Song, II. Death Song, III. Song of the Backwoods.
Instrumentation: 3 flutes (3rd doubles on piccolo), 2 oboes (2nd doubles on English horn), 3 clarinets, 2 bassoons; 4 horns, 3 trumpets, 3 trombones, tuba; timpani, bells, triangle, drums, cymbals; harp, strings.
Duration: 10 minutes.
Autograph of conductor's score is in The William Grant Still Estate.

W159 ***Three Portraits.***
For orchestra.
Composed in Hollywood, California, 1929-1930.
Commissioned by Paul Whiteman for The Paul Whiteman Orchestra.

Contents: I. Lento, II. Andante, III. Moderato.

Instrumentation: flute (piccolo), 2 oboes, English horn, B-flat clarinet, alto and bass clarinets, tenor saxophone, baritone saxophone, bass saxophone, bassoon; 3 trumpets, 4 trombones, tuba; percussion, bells, triangle, cymbal, tom-tom; piano, celesta, banjo, strings.

Holograph parts are in The Paul Whiteman Collection, Williams College Archives and Special Collections, Williamstown, Massachusetts. The holograph parts identify the following specific players (last names only): Trumbauer, Hazlett, Daley, Strickfaden, Maier, Margulis, Goldfield, Lecrest, Cullen, Hall, Rank, and Fulton.

Autograph score location unknown.

W160 *Three Rhythmic Spirituals* (Bourne Company, Inc., New York, 1961, nos. 807, 808, and 809).

Spiritual arrangements for mixed chorus and piano; also for solo voice and piano (in manuscript) and solo voice with orchestra (performed by Mattiwilda Dobbs).

Holy Spirit Don't You Leave Me arranged in New York, 1930; this group dates from 1956.

Contents: I. Lord, I Looked Down the Road, II. Hard Trials, III. Holy Spirit, Don't You Leave Me.

Manuscript copy in The William Grant Still Estate has title page with the following inscription:

"During the years when I have been engaged principally in composing symphonic and operatic works, I have also made it a point to visit small Negro churches in different parts of America. For the purpose of observing at first-hand the growth of this kind of American music. In most instances, I have found that spirituals, when sung in such surroundings, are quite unlike those arranged for the public—though no less devout.

"In presenting these three spirituals, I have tried to arrange them as I heard them sung by folk singers, and to emphasize, as they did, the natural rhythmic content of the music. —William Grant Still—"

Manuscripts for *Hard Trial* (no "s") and *Holy Spirit, Don't You Leave Me* for solo voice and piano in Verna Arvey's hand are in the William Grant Still and Verna Arvey Papers at the University of Arkansas Libraries, Fayetteville.

Autograph location unknown.

Selected Performances

W160a 1973 (July 11): Chatauqua, NY; Amphitheater; Chatauqua Symphony Orchestra, Arthur Winograd, guest conductor; Mattiwilda Dobbs, coloratura soprano.

W160b 1975 (May 24): Los Angeles, CA; University of Southern California, Town and Gown Building; University of Southern California Chamber Singers, Charles C. Hirt, conductor; and Carl Haywood, piano.

W160c 1979 (October 18): Los Angeles, CA; Arnold Schoenberg Institute; University of Southern California Chamber Singers, Rodney Eichenberger, director. (*See:* WB112.4)

W160d 1984 (February 15): Fayetteville, AR; University of Arkansas, Fine Arts Center Concert Hall; University of Arkansas Schola Cantorum, Jack Groh, conductor, pianist not identified.

Bibliography

WB160.1 Morgan, Maritza. "Music In Review." *Chautauquan Daily* (Chautauqua, NY), July 14, 1973.

Review of the July 11, 1973, performance of the Chautauqua Symphony Orchestra. "The three rhythmic spirituals by William Grant Still, *Lord, I Looked Down The Road, Hard Trials*, and *Holy Spirit, Don't You Leave Me*, were as finely wrought as individual jewels in a rare setting. The orchestra accompaniment was extremely sophisticated in the diversified rhythm and complimented Miss [Mattiwilda] Dobbs' interpretation."

W161 *Three Visions* (J. Fischer & Brothers, New York, 1936, no. 7119; *Summerland* published separately for piano solo, 1936, no. 7119-12; published for small orchestra in 1938, no. 7326; some versions available from William Grant Still Music; see also *Summerland*, from *Three Visions*, W150).
For piano solo.
Composed in Los Angeles, 1935.
"Dedicated to my friends who have departed this life."
Contents: I. Dark Horseman, II. Summerland, III. Radiant Pinnacle.
First edition of 1936 J. Fischer publication of *Three Visions* for piano solo and a facsimile of a fair copy in manuscript with "COPYRIGHT 1936 BY J. FISCHER AND BRO." typed at the bottom are in the William Grant Still and Verna Arvey Papers at the University of Arkansas Libraries, Fayetteville.
Autograph is in the Los Angeles Public Library.

Selected Performances

W161a 1936 (October 12): Salt Lake City, UT; Trinity A. M. E. Church; Verna Arvey, piano.

W161b 1937 (January 10): Los Angeles, CA; Phillips Temple C.M.E. Church; Verna Arvey, piano.

W161c 1937 (May 25): Los Angeles, CA; Gibson Hall; Verna Arvey, piano.

W161d 1937 (November 21): Los Angeles, CA; Pacific Institute of Music and Fine Art; Verna Arvey, piano.

W161e 1937 (November 30): Memphis, TN; Centenary M.E. Church; William Duncan Allen, piano.

W161f 1937 (December 30): Portland, OR; Women's Club Building; William Duncan Allen, piano.

W161g 1939 (February 10): Nashville, TN; Fisk Memorial Chapel; William Duncan Allen, piano.

W161h 1939 (April 23): Salt Lake City, UT; Utah State Art Center; Verna Arvey, piano.

W161i 1939 (October 15): New York, NY; Town Hall; Roger Aubert, piano.

W161j 1945 (March 25): Pasadena, CA; Pasadena Civic Auditorium; John Pennington, piano.

W161k 1955 (February 6): Nashville, TN; Fisk University, Fisk Memorial Chapel; Matthew Kennedy, piano.

W161l 1956 (March 11): Pasadena, CA; Pasadena Playhouse; Verna Arvey, piano.

W161m 1969 (December 8): Grambling, LA; Grambling College, Woodson Auditorium; Geneva Handy Southall, piano.

194   William Grant Still: A Bio-Bibliography

W161n   1970 (January 7): Ruston, LA; Louisiana Tech University, Little Theatre; Geneva Handy Southall, piano.

W161o   1970 (November 9): Oberlin, OH; Oberlin College; Warner Concert Hall; Natalie Hinderas, piano. (*See:* WB155.2, WB155.3)

W161p   1972 (February 24): Petersburg, VA; Virginia State College, Owens Hall Auditorium; Althea Waites, piano.

W161q   1975 (March 16): Oakland, CA; Merritt College; Oakland Auditorium Theatre; William Duncan Allen, piano.

W161r   1980 (January 14): Washington, DC; Kennedy Center; Kay Pace, piano.

W161s   1982 (February 7): Talladega, AL; Talladega College, DeForest Chapel; William Duncan Allen, piano.

W161t   1984 (February 18): Fayetteville, AR; University of Arkansas, Fine Arts Center Concert Hall; Arthur Tollefson, piano.

Bibliography

WB161.1   McKinney, Howard D., ed. "Concerning William Grant Still." *Fischer Edition News* 11 (November-December 1935): 17-18.

Comments on the November 20, 1935, performance of the *Afro-American Symphony* by the New York Philharmonic-Symphony Orchestra. Also mentions that Still is writing a new piano suite for the Fischer Edition, namely, *Three Visions*, summing up the pieces thus: "There is certainly no lack of variety in these three numbers, and the work should prove a most interesting novelty for pianists."

WB161.2   Liebling, Leonard. "New Music of Interest Among Works." *Musical Courier* 114 (December 5, 1936): 16.

In a review of Still's *Three Visions*, which was published by J. Fischer & Brothers, Liebling says, "The music is sensitive and well made, harmonically resourceful, and with discernible melodic line, but does not give a complete impression of spontaniety. Rhythmic command and ability to 'color' on the keys, are required from the player who desires to show these *morceaux* at their best."

WB161.3   Saunders, Richard D. "Recital Fans Again Praise Native Music." *Hollywood Citizen-News*, May 26, 1937.

"Verna Arvey's skilled pianism feelingly interpreted three piano pieces [*Three Visions*] by William Grant Still. . . . They were capriciously rambling, with somewhat improvisatory qualities."

WB161.4   Grondahl, Hilmar. "Pianist Presents Unique Program." Portland *Oregonian,* December 31, 1937.

"It is because of Mr. Allen's distinction in the melodic emphasis of music that one will recall the chorale of the Franck opus, the *Summerland* section of Still's *Three Visions*, parts of the symphonic etudes and the choral lines of some of the Bach works above anything else of musical significance on the program."

WB161.5   Smith, Susie Aubrey. "Music Professor Delights Audience in Piano Recital." *Oregon Daily Journal*, December 31, 1937.

"The pianist [William Allen] was equally happy in his interpretations of more modern music. *Three Visions* . . . were unusually interesting, especially the first and third, *Dark Horsemen* and *Radiant Pinnacle*."

WB161.6   T.,O. "Roger Aubert, Pianist." *New York Sun*, October 16, 1939.

In this brief review, Still's *Three Visions*, performed on October 15, 1939, by Swiss pianist Roger Aubert, "were pleasant examples of this Negro composer's sophisticated idiom, in which suggestions of his racial origin appear, though not with any strong emphasis."

W162 ***Threnody: In Memory of Jan Sibelius*** (available from William Grant Still Music).
For orchestra, a tone poem.
Composed in Los Angeles; holograph dated January 1965.
Inscription by the composer says, "In memory of Jan Sibelius."
Commissioned by Dr. Fabien Sevitzky for the University of Miami Symphony Orchestra.
Contents of the holograph: "Slowly, Moderately slow: Resolutely, (in the style of a funeral [later changed to slow] march, a lyric style here, faster, in the style of a funeral march, singing: in a lyric style."
Instrumentation: 2 flutes, 2 oboes, 2 clarinets, 2 bassoons; 3 horns, 2 trumpets, 2 trombones, tuba; timpani, chime, cymbals, snare drum; harp, strings.
Duration: 4 minutes.
Holograph dated January 1965 in open score with orchestration notes and revisions, a three-staff reduction (as if for solo instrument and piano) which expands to six staves, and the initial melodic sketches indicating a formal plan are in the William Grant Still and Verna Arvey Papers at the University of Arkansas Libraries, Fayetteville.
Autograph of final version is in The William Grant Still Estate.

W162a **First Performance:** 1965 (March 14, 15): Miami, FL; University of Miami Symphony Orchestra, Fabien Sevitzky, conductor.

Bibliography

WB162.1 Bergh, Frances Hovey. "Program Notes." University of Miami Symphony Orchestra, March 14-15, 1965: 21+.
Review of the March 14, 1965, performance. "The composition, *In Memory of Jean Sibelius* was commissioned by Dr. [Fabien] Sevitzky only a few weeks ago, for the special purpose of introducing this concert. It is in the form of a dirge. It opens in moderate tempo in the key of e minor with a short introduction for brass. This is followed by a slow section in which the bassoon produces a bell-like sound. Here the melody is in the strings with harp accompaniment. The middle section is rhapsodic in form. The first theme is repeated and the composition comes to a slow finale."

WB162.2 Reno, Doris. "Sibelius Memorial Concert a Delight." *Miama Herald*, March 15, 1965.
Review of the March 14, 1965, performance of the University of Miami Symphony Orchestra. "Mr. Still can always be depended upon to write music that is listenable and meaningful, and his dirge in memory of Sibelius has mood, grace, and true feeling. It disclosed the American composer's admiration for, and comprehension of, the work of the late Finnish composer, which was beautifully expressed."

W163 ***To You, America!*** (Southern Music Publishing Company, Inc., New York, 1956; Peer Music Co., available from Theodore Presser).
For symphonic band in one movement (originally with organ).
Composed in Los Angeles; autograph dated October, 1951.

Dedicated to Lieutenant Colonial Francis E. Resta and the United States Military Academy Band.

Commissioned by the United States Military Academy, West Point, New York, in honor of the Sesquicentennial Celebration in 1952.

Winner of the George Washington Honor Medal, awarded by the 1952 National Awards Jury of the Freedoms Foundation Award (presented in 1953).

Contents: one movement, "Briskly" ending "Majestically."

Instrumentation for full band: D-flat piccolo, C piccolo, flutes, oboes, English horn, bassoons, E-flat clarinet, 4 B-flat clarinets, alto clarinet, bass clarinet; soprano, alto, tenor, and baritone saxophones; 4 B-flat cornets, 3 trumpets, 4 E-flat horns, 4 F horns, 3 trombones, baritone horns in treble and bass clefs, basses; string bass, harp, percussion, timpani.

Instrumentation for symphonic band (add additional parts for each of the following in addition to the full band instrumentation listed above): flutes, oboes, bassoons, 4 clarinets, alto clarinet, bass clarinet, 4 cornets, baritone horn in bass clef, basses, percussion.

Autograph in open score with orchestration notes and a second autograph labeled "revision" in the composer's hand, including the organ part, are in the William Grant Still and Verna Arvey Papers at the University of Arkansas Libraries, Fayetteville. The Still and Arvey Papers include initial melodic sketches with sketch of formal plan and a copy of the first published edition.

W163a **First Performance:** 1952 (February 17): West Point, NY; Army Theatre; United States Military Academy Band, William Grant Still, guest conductor.

Selected Performances

W163b 1952 (November 27): Pittsburgh, PA; Carnegie Music Hall; United States Military Academy Band, Captain Francis E. Resta, director; Marshall Bidwell, organ.

W163c 1954 (December 30): Pasadena, CA; Civic Auditorium; United States Military Academy Band, Lieutenant Colonel Francis E. Resta, director.

W163d 1966 (February 18): Houston, TX; Texas Southern University, University Auditorium; Texas Southern University Symphonic Band, William Grant Still, guest conductor.

W163e 1970 (November 9): Oberlin, OH; Oberlin College, Warner Concert Hall; The Oberlin Wind Ensemble; Kenneth Moore, conductor. (*See:* WB155.3)

Bibliography

WB163.1 Lewando, Ralph. "True Ability Shown By West Point Band." *Pittsburgh Press*, November 28, 1952.

   Review of the November 27, 1952, performance of the U.S. Military Academy Band. The program included *To You, America!* "Still's piece was more to the right but full of fervor and dignity and forthright appeal."

WB163.2 Lissfelt, J. Fred, "Varied Programs Mark Holiday Music Festival." *Pittsburgh Sun-Telegraph*, November 28, 1952.

   Review of the November 27, 1952, performance of the U.S. Military Academy Band. "William Grant Still's *To You, America!* wanders a long way until it finds the proper hymn (Marshall Bidwell contributing his bit at the organ)."

WB163.3 Hickman, C. Sharpless. "West Point Band Concert Thrills Pre-Fete

Crowd." *Pasadena Star-News*, December 31, 1954.
Review of the December 30, 1954, performance of the United States Military Academy Band. "The United States Military Academy Band from West Point, which played an exceptionally long but enthusiastically received free concert last night at Pasadena Civic Auditorium, is an admirably drilled unit of some 90 men which deserves its rating as one of the nation's best. . . . [*To You, America!*] is an overly-reiterative piece in the nature of an Indian war dance, and tends to become banal and monotonous—which is rather surprising for Still."

W164 *Troubled Island* (Peer Music Company, formerly Southern Music Publishing Company, Inc., New York; available from William Grant Still Music).
Opera in 3 acts with ballet, 4 stage sets; there is an arrangement for string quartet and contralto and one for full orchestra of the last scene.
Composed in Los Angeles; begun in 1937 and finished in 1941.
"Dedicated to Leopold Stokowski, in deep appreciation of his efforts to bring it to public attention."
Libretto by Langston Hughes.
For: Cast: Principle roles: baritone, bass, contralto, soprano, tenor; Secondary roles: 2 tenors, mezzo-soprano, baritone, soprano, 11 other minor roles; chorus and dancers.
Setting: Haiti, 1791.
Story: Based on the life of Haiti's first Emperor, Jean Jacques Dessalines.
Instrumentation: 2 flutes (2nd doubles on piccolo), 2 oboes (2nd doubles on English horn), 2 clarinets, 2 bassoons; 3 horns, 3 trumpets and 2 trombones (straight mutes, cup mutes, or soft hats), tuba; timpani, drums, special drums, tom-toms, cymbals, chime in F-sharp, bells, xylophone, gong, tambourine, gourd; harp, piano, strings.
Duration: 180 minutes.
Autograph sketches of themes identified with titles and additional sketches are in the William Grant Still and Verna Arvey Papers at the University of Arkansas Libraries, Fayetteville, along with a typed summary of the action and the text for *Fishermen's Song* with the names of William Grant Still and Langston Hughes typed at the bottom. The title page of the summary of the action says, "TROUBLED ISLAND, An Opera by William Grant Still and Langston Hughes."
Incomplete holograph score with indications for scoring is at the Library of Congress, deposited for copyright on December 13, 1941.
Autograph piano vocal score and autograph full orchestral score and parts are in The William Grant Still Estate.

W164a **First Performances:** 1949 (March 31, April 10, May 1): New York, NY; New York City Center; New York City Opera Company, Laszlo Halasz, conductor; Muriel O'Malley as Celeste; Nathaniel Sprinzena as Popo; Marie Powers as Azelia; Robert Weede as Dessalines; Oscar Natzka as Martel; Richard Charles as Vuval; Arthur Newman as Stenio; Robert McFerrin as Papaloi; Ruth Stewart as Mamaloi; Helena Bliss as Claire; Dorothy MacNeil as 1st Servant; Frances Bible as 2nd Servant and Mango Vendor; Rosalind Nadell as 3rd Servant; Richard Wentworth as Chamberlain; William Stanz as Messenger; Edwin Dunning as Steward and Fisherman; Mary Lesawyer as Melon Vendor; Eugene Bryden, stage; George Balanchine, choreographer for minuet; Jean-Leon Destiné, choreographer for voodoo dances; and H.A. Condell, scenic designer.

Selected Performances
(excerpts only)

W164b 1939 (April 23): Salt Lake City, UT; Utah State Art Center; A Reading of *Troubled Island: Prelude,* Verna Arvey; *Celeste's Lullaby,* Mrs. Gail Martin; *Love Scene* (with contralto solo), Mr. & Mrs. Gail Martin; *Minuet and Voodoo Dance,* Verna Arvey; *Drums in the Court,* Mr. Gail Martin; *Funeral March,* Verna Arvey.

W164c 1942 (February 1): Los Angeles, CA; YMCA, 28th and Paloma; Verna Arvey.

W164d 1945 (April 4): New York, NY; Town Hall; Muriel Rahn, soprano; William Lawrence, piano. Aria.

Bibliography

WB164.1 "New Opera on Haiti Is Topic." *Deseret News,* April 22, 1939.
Preview of a lecture-recital at Salt Lake City on April 23, 1939.

WB164.2 "Accomplished Pianist [Verna Arvey] Will Present Still Music." *Salt Lake Tribune,* April 23, 1939.
Preview of a lecture-recital that included excerpts from *Troubled Island,* and performances of *Kaintuck', Three Visions,* two dances from *Sahdji,* and *Quit Dat Fool'nish.* Still lectured at intermission.

WB164.3 M., G. "Recognition of American Music Urged." *Deseret News,* April 24, 1939.
Remarks on a lecture that Still gave on April 23, 1939, and a review of the excerpts from *Troubled Island,* both part of a lecture-recital at Salt Lake City. "[T]he music revealed originality and stark, dramatic power. Themes clearly created atmosphere and emphasized attributes of character. Arias are rich in melody. A phrase or an excerpt from a chorus had a way of investing a scene with life and color."

WB164.4 "New American Opera as Part of Concert." *Salt Lake Tribune,* April 24, 1939.
Review of a lecture-recital on April 23, 1939. "This dramatic opera [*Troubled Island*] was read and some of its most colorful themes given exposition by Verna Arvey, a young Los Angeles pianist, with several of the outstanding arias and scenes interpreted by Mr. and Mrs. Gail Martin in very interesting manner." The program included other works by Still, including *Kaintuck'* and *Three Visions,* and a lecture by Still. "[O]ften of haunting quality, *Kaintuck'* is in the nature of a tone poem, lovely and appealing."

WB164.5 "Stokowski Plans Variety of Music." *New York Times,* September 12, 1944.
In discussing the coming season of the New York City Opera Company, Stokowski says that the spring series will include *Troubled Island* "with an all Negro cast."

WB164.6 Le Berthon, Ted. "White Man's Views." *Pittsburgh Courier,* March 31, 1945.
Article on *Troubled Island* reporting, among other items, that Eleanor Roosevelt has become honorary chairperson of a committee to raise $30,000 to support the production.

WB164.7 Carter, Michael. "'Colored Play Better Music,' Stokowski Says, Yet None Measure up to Standards." Baltimore *Afro-American,* April 21, 1945.

In this lengthy article based on an interview with Leopold Stokowski, the reporter writes that Stokowski has not found any African American musicians to fill positions in the New York City Symphony. Stokowski elaborates on *Troubled Island:* "'It will be one of the most satisfying operas ever presented because it contains good music, dancing, plot, and poetry. I've been studying it and am eager to conduct it.' The opera will probably have an all-colored cast."

WB164.8 "La Guardia Backs Opera On Life of Jean Dessalines, Emperor of Haiti." *New York Amsterdam News*, June 9, 1945.

Long article on a meeting of editors, publishers, and music critics in the office of Mayor F.H. La Guardia on June 2, 1945, to launch a fund-raising drive and announce preparations to produce *Troubled Island* at the New York City Center.

WB164.9 "Newspapermen And Critics Hear Excerpts for 'Troubled Island.'" *New York Age*, June 9, 1945.

Announcement of a meeting held in Mayor F. H. La Guardia's office on June 2, 1945, to launch plans to produce *Troubled Island*. "Parts of the score were played . . . by Sylvan Levin, assistant conductor of the New York City Symphony, and arias were sung by Ella Belle Davis, soprano; Jean Handslik, contralto; George Randol, baritone and Paul Smith, tenor."

WB164.10 De Leighbor, Don. "Bill Still's 10-Year Hope Near Reality." *New York Amsterdam News*, July 7, 1945.

Long article on background of *Troubled Island*, written with the belief that it will be produced in 1946.

WB164.11 Greene, Marjorie E. "'Troubled Island' Production Postponed." *Miami Whip*, September 29, 1945.

Report on the postponement of *Troubled Island* "for another year."

WB164.12 "Ex-'Porgy' Baritone Now Ex-GI Will Appear in Coming Opera 'Troubled Island.'" Los Angeles *Criterion*, March 3, 1946.

Article on Lawrence Whisonant, a former alternate cast member of *Porgy and Bess*. Whisonant, the article claims, was discharged from the army, in part, to prepare for a lead role in the production of *Troubled Island*.

WB164.13 Straus, Noel. "Music: Two Operas." *New York Times*, September 15, 1946.

Background on the subject matter of two operas, Darius Milhaud's *Bolivar* and Still's *Troubled Island*. "There is full opportunity for pageantry in this work [*Troubled Island*], which boasts an elaborate orchestral score, especially rich in percussion and brass effects."

WB164.14 "Still Withdraws 'Troubled Island.'" *New York Sun*, June 5, 1947.

Short article announcing that Still has withdrawn *Troubled Island* from the New York City Center.

WB164.15 "Indifference of Producers Causes Withdrawal of Opera." *Baltimore Afro-American*, June 14, 1947.

Article on the withdrawal of *Troubled Island* from the New York City Center. "The reason, Mr. Still told the AFRO this week, is that City Center 'refuses to give definite commitment for it, meanwhile producing other new operas.'"

WB164.16 "William Grant Still Asks City To Refund Money For His Opera." *New York Age*, June 28, 1947, p. 1+.

The article contains the text of a letter from Still to the *New York Age*, elaborating on why he withdrew *Troubled Island* from the New York City Center, and asking that the money be returned. A lengthy response from Newbold Morris, chairman of the committee responsible for raising the money to produce Still's opera, is an attempt to explain the difficulties his committee has encountered.

WB164.17 "Wm. Grant Still's 'Troubled Island' Is Set for Mar. Opening." *Saint Louis Argus*, February 11, 1949.

In this short article, Camilla Williams and Laurence Winters—two African Americans—are rumored to be among those under consideration for the lead roles.

WB164.18 Campbell, Dick. "*Troubled Island* Set for New York; Salmaggi and San Carlo Aid Our Stars." *Pittsburgh Courier*, March 26, 1949.

Campbell writes about the progress African American opera performers, such as Catarina Jarboro, Edith Sewell, Jules Bledsoe, Minto Cato, Paul Smith, James Boxwell, Muriel Rahn, Muriel Smith, and others have made thanks to the Alfredo Salmaggi Opera Company, the San Carlo Opera Company, and Laszlo Halasz, director of the New York City Center Opera Company. Campbell asserts that Still's opera will "take its place besides *Aida, Carmen, Butterfly, Tosca, La Traviata, La Boheme* and the other masterpieces which have stood the test of time." Campbell concludes by asking, "How long will the hard-pressed Met continue to by-pass Negro artists, and yet have the crust to make a radio plea for funds from the 'general public' which includes nearly twenty million Americans of color? How long will this august institution subscribe to the policy of Constitution Hall? How long will it continue to bring hundreds of slightly talented mediocre aliens of Axis countries to its roster in preference to those whose heritage is deeply rooted in America? Time and perseverance and letters may hurry the ultimate goal which is inevitable."

WB164.19 Hughes, Langston. "*Troubled Island*: The Story of How An Opera Was Created." *Chicago Defender*, March 26, 1949.

Hughes describes how *Troubled Island* came to be. A Guggenheim Fellowship enabled Hughes to travel to California and collaborate on the opera with Still. After the libretto was finished Hughes traveled to Spain to cover the Civil War for the *Baltimore Afro-American*, and Still went to work on the music. The search for a presentation, although quite difficult, eventually proved successful when Laszlo Halasz agreed to direct it at the New York City Opera Company.

WB164.20 Affelder, Paul. "City Opera Company Gives World Premiere of *Troubled Island*." *Brooklyn Eagle*, April 1, 1949.

Review of the March 31, 1949, world premiere of *Troubled Island* by the New York City Opera Company. "The composer's treatment of the orchestra was one of the opera's strongest points. His scoring was always varied, highly colored, and original, with some particularly effective use of divided strings. Throughout the evening, however, there was always the conflict between grand opera and light opera, and when the performance ended, we couldn't make up our minds into which category to place *Troubled Island*."

WB164.21 Bagar, Robert. "*Troubled Island*, New Opera, Is Given Here." *New York World-Telegram*, April 1, 1949.

Review of the March 31, 1949, world premiere of *Troubled Island*.

"Often the music is melodious, though not expressive enough, and the dramatic interest is neither sustained effectively nor of better than average appeal. As a whole the score is faintly reminiscent of styles and musical manners well known in the Broadway musical theater of an earlier day—Gershwin, Romberg, and some others—and there are also occasional references to Delius, Puccini and Massenet."

WB164.22 Briggs, John. "*Troubled Island* Has City Center Premiere." *New York Post Home News*, April 1, 1949.

Review of the March 31, 1949, world premiere of *Troubled Island*. "William Grant Still's opera *Troubled Island*, to a libretto by Langston Hughes, was received with cheers, whistles and noisy applause at its premiere at the City Center last evening. . . . Yet for one listener the opera did not quite come off. . . . Last night one was never sure whether one was hearing a first-rate performance of an inferior work, or a second-rate reading of a good one."

WB164.23 Downes, Olin. "Halasz Presents New Still Opera." *New York Times*, April 1, 1949, p. 30.

Review of the March 31, 1949, world premiere of *Troubled Island*. "There are a good many clichés of Broadway and Hollywood in the score of William Grant Still's opera. . . . At the same time, as the piece goes on, there is evident in it an operatic talent, a structure of considerable breadth and melodic curve which commended the opera to the audience and which implied that a composer who is just entering the period of his maturity may attain a more integrated style and a less conventional facility in a later score."

WB164.24 Kastendieck, Miles. "An Interesting Operatic Work." *New York Journal-American*, April 1, 1949. (Essentially the same article was published in the *Christian Science Monitor* [April 9, 1949] under the title "Still's Opera Has Premiere.")

Review of the March 31, 1949, world premiere of *Troubled Island*. "It is a self-conscious work. He [Still] is still striving for something not yet within his grasp. There are flashes of imaginative writing, of skillful handling of choruses, of atmospheric effectiveness. There are also stretches of hybrid writing, of Hollywood orchestration, of Broadway musical comedy technique. The result is a mixture of styles signifying talent and a feel for opera but achieving little more than a suggestion of it."

WB164.25 Kolodin, Irving. "The Music Makers: *Troubled Island*, a Still-born Opera at the Center." *New York Sun*, April 1, 1949.

Review of the March 31, 1949, world premiere of *Troubled Island*. "Still's first and fatal limitation as a theater composer is a weakness in setting the narrative element of his task. When he arrived at a scene that could be treated melodically, he did that technically well, if with no compelling strength or originality. He was at his best in occasional bits of local color, such as a dance in the first act, a ceremonial in the second, a fisherwoman's chorus in the third—these had grace, a touch of charm, even gayety [sic] but always there was a dramatic story demanding his attention, to which he turned with a good deal less relish. . . . A partisan audience could find little to be partisan about."

WB164.26 Perkins, Francis D. "Tragedy in Haiti." *New York Herald Tribune*, April 1, 1949.

Review of the March 31, 1949, world premiere of *Troubled Island*. "Haiti and its tragic history have distinct possibilities as subjects for the lyric stage. In *Troubled Island* these possibilities have been realized to some if not to the fullest extent. . . . The music suggested that Mr. Still has a flair for opera, but one that is not fully developed; it also suggested intentions not yet fully realized in a musical idiom for this form."

WB164.27 Sabin, Robert. *"Troubled Island." Musical America* 69 (April 1, 1949): 5+.

Lengthy review of the March 31, 1949, world premiere of *Troubled Island*. "If ever a libretto called for music of tragic power and intensity, this one does. Yet Mr. Still's score is largely unsuited to the nature of the subject. It sounds more like operetta music than like opera, and it is dramatically inadequate for the grandeur of the subject."

WB164.28 Watt, Douglas. "Still's *Troubled Island* a Troubled Opera." *New York Daily News*, April 1, 1949.

Review of the March 31, 1949, world premiere of *Troubled Island*. "Although Langston Hughes' libretto is not a very good one, it has more power and meaning than William Grant Still has been able to summon in the way of musical expression. Too much of the time, even in the more dramatic scenes, the music seems to be leading up to a chorus from *Show Boat* or *The Desert Song*. Unfortunately, it does not even fulfill these promises."

WB164.29 Levine, Ben. "William Grant Still's Opera On Haiti Gets World Premiere." *Daily Worker* (New York, NY), April 6, 1949.

Review of the March 31, 1949, world premiere of *Troubled Island*. "[M]ost of the music was of a pallid, decorative quality, too heavily influenced by productions like *Porgy and Bess*. . . . The singers, naturally, were handicapped by the absence of definite melodies and musically dramatic climaxes. . . . But with all its handicaps, the opera is definitely worth hearing."

WB164.30 Hamburger, Philip. "Musical Events: Nobody Knows the Trouble I've Heard." *New Yorker* 25 (April 9, 1949): 110-11.

"There were moments when his music sounded operatic, all right, but for the most part it seemed to have been designed for a romantic operetta. Some of the score was unadulterated musical comedy, with snatches that were fetching but bore little or no relation to the whole. . . . Like Mr. Still, Mr. Hughes was working simultaneously on several planes. . . . I could not escape the conclusion that what should have been ringing truths became prosaic and perfunctory statements in the welter of plot and counterplot. . . . His [Weede's] was a miraculous performance, both vocally and dramatically."

WB164.31 Holt, Nora. "Freedom the Theme In *Troubled Island*." *New York Amsterdam News*, April 9, 1949.

Review of the March 31, 1949, world premiere of *Troubled Island*. "Mr. Still invests the score with music which he pours from his soul as he feels the frustration of Celeste the slave mother as she croons to her son 'Sleep . . . a flame will sweep our slavery away. . . sleep 'til the new day.' The opera is stirring drama, gripping music and moving text, which should be seen to enjoy the fullest."

WB164.32 Waldman, Mike. "*Troubled Island* Misses Its Mark, Reviewer Says." *Pittsburgh Courier*, April 9, 1949.

Review of the March 31, 1949, world premiere of *Troubled Island*.

The opera "fell short of the mark and thereby became an adjectiveless target for most of the aisle sitters. . . . From where I sat, *Troubled Island* seemed like the work of an artist who possessed all the tools, but in a Herculean effort to piece a masterpiece together, he puts nails where screws should have been and vice versa."

WB164.33 B., J. D. "Winters in 'Troubled Island.'" *New York Herald Tribune*, April 11, 1949.

Short review of the second performance of *Troubled Island* April 10. Laurence Winters played Dessalines. "Mr. Winters' delineation . . . was a highly impressive one viewed both vocally and dramatically. His characterization was a dignified and often genuinely affecting one."

WB164.34 P., R. "Winters Sings At Center." *New York Times*, April 11, 1949.

Short article on the second performance of *Troubled Island* on April 10. Laurence Winters played the role of Dessalines, with the rest of the cast unchanged.

WB164.35 "Troubled Opera." *Newsweek* 33 (April 11, 1949): 86.

Review of the March 31, 1949, world premiere of *Troubled Island*. "*Troubled Island* is troubled by far more than the Haitian fight for independence which motivates its story. Still's music for his first produced opera is derivative and leans too heavily on operetta-type clichés. Hughes's verse resorts too often to the old 'soonmoon' rhymes. Despite the obvious disadvantages of presenting grand opera in blackface, most of the cast performed rather well."

WB164.36 "Troubled Opera." *Time* 53 (April 11, 1949): 71.

Review of the March 31, 1949, world premiere of *Troubled Island*. "Poet Hughes's libretto turned out to have far more peroration . . . than punch. And Composer Still's music, sometimes lusciously scored, sometimes naively melodic, often had more prettiness than power. . . . Composer Still's first-night audience liked it fine, anyhow. Exultant, happy, and even more determined after taking six curtain calls with the cast, Still said he planned to keep on trying to write grand opera. Said he: 'You don't realize your mistakes until they stare you in the face. I discovered my weak points.'"

WB164.37 K., R. M. "Troubled Island, Opera by Still, Premiered at City Center." *Musical Courier* 139 (April 15, 1949): 5.

"In summation, the opera is highly melodious, possesses sensuous richness and charm, is well if not too originally scored. The writing for the voices is pleasing and not usually awkward. The chief flaw is that there are few flashes of invention that make episodes unforgettable."

WB164.38 Rogers, W. G. "Staging New Opera Gives Work The Works." *Oakland Tribune*, April 17, 1949, p. C11.

Description of what it takes to stage an opera using *Troubled Island* as an example. Laszlo Halasz remarks that, "Only an idiot would write an American opera, because . . . only an idiot would appreciate how small were chances of production."

WB164.39 Smith, Warren Storey. "Music." *Boston Post*, April 17, 1949.

Review of the second performance on April 10, 1949, of *Troubled Island*. "To say that it is better than the general run of American operas is to say very little. I shall therefore speak a real mouthful and pronounce it a better show than that current sensation of the Lyric Theatre, Benjamin

Britten's *Peter Grimes*. . . . Still's music is a bit facile and not a little derivative, though always apt and agreeable."

WB164.40 "City Opera Closes Its 'Best' Season." *New York Times*, May 2, 1949.
Includes brief report on the May 1 performance. "The attendance for the final opera—William Grant Still's 'The Troubled Island'—was relatively small. . . . The newcomers . . . were Julius Rudel, the conductor, who kept it moving along with a good surge of melody; Marguerite Piazza, who sang and acted well as the handsome mulatto empress, and Richard Wentworth, who got a special round of applause for the resonant tones, and the personal conviction of his aria, 'My World.'"

WB164.41 Smith, Cecil. "Music: Operas, Haitian and Egyptian." *New Republic* 120 (May 2, 1949): 28.
Review of the March 31, 1949, world premiere of *Troubled Island*. "It is not an impressive work, and public response to the music was friendly and sympathetic rather than genuinely enthusiastic. . . . The music creates little atmosphere; it is full of pale echoes of Gershwin, DeBussy [sic] and Delius, and it is frequently inanimate rhythmically."

WB164.42 Jefferson, Miles M. "The Negro On Broadway: 1948-1949." *Phylon* 10 (1949):103-11.
Under "Odds and Ends," the author has a few remarks on *Troubled Island*. "It must suffice here to report that the opera proved disappointing to music and drama lovers alike who had anticipated inspiration rather than labor in the first major opus of its kind completely composed by Negroes to be presented in New York."

W165 ***Twelve Negro Spirituals, Volumes 1 and 2*** (Handy Brothers Music Co., Inc., New York, 1937 and 1948; republished by Francis Day and Hunter in London, no. 21608; available from William Grant Still Music).
Spiritual arrangements for voice and piano, text in dialect.
First edition of *Volume 1* has a photograph of the composer with the following inscription: "To my friend W.C. Handy to remind him of my gratitude for what he has done for Negro music."
Contents: *Volume 1:* Gwinter Sing All Along de Way; All God's Chillun Got Shoes; Lis'en to de Lam's; Keep Me F'om Sinkin' Down; Lawd, I Wants to be a Christian; Great Camp Meeting. *Volume 2:* Great Day; Ah Got a Home in-a Dat Rock; Peter, Go Ring Dem Bells; Good News; Didn't Mah Lawd Deliver Daniel; Mah Lawd Gonna Rain Down Fiah.
The first edition, illustrated by Albert Barbelle with "Literary Treatments" by Ruby Berkley Goodwin, of Volume One (1937) by Handy Brothers Music Co., Inc., is in the William Grant Still and Verna Arvey Papers at the University of Arkansas Libraries, Fayetteville. The "Literary Treatments" are stories written in dialect. Biography of the composer in the first edition of *Volume 1* is by Verna Arvey.
First edition, with "Literary Treatments" by Ruby Berkley Goodwin, of *Volume 2* (1948) is in the Still and Arvey Papers. A facsimile of the published version for solo voice and piano of *Great Day* (F. & D. Ltd. 21608), and a facsimile of the SATB chorus with soprano solo and piano version of *Gwine to Sing All Along the Way,* are also in the Still and Arvey Papers.
Autograph locations unknown.

Bibliography

WB165.1   Robertson, Edythe. "Our Music Corner: William Grant Still's Arrangements of 12 Negro Spirituals Published in Book Form." *New York Age*, July 24, 1937.

"Volume 1 of the book *Twelve Negro Spirituals* . . . is quite unique. The stories and illustrations all depict the songs in a very realistic manner. The chordal treatment has modernistic flavor and seems to enhance the beauty of the spirituals rather than detract. The harmonization of the accompaniment has been carefully annotated for dynamics and expression by the composer."

W166   *Up There* (Silver Burdett Company, New York, 1951, in *World Music Horizons,* page 116).
For voice and piano in a music education textbook.
Composed in Los Angeles, 1950.
Text by Verna Arvey.
Partial autograph sketch of piano and voice part with text written in Verna Arvey's hand above and below the pitches of the melody is in the William Grant Still and Verna Arvey Papers at the University of Arkansas Libraries, Fayetteville.
Autograph location unknown.

W167   *Vignettes* (Southern Music Publishing Company, Inc., New York; available from William Grant Still Music).
Folk song arrangements for oboe, bassoon, and piano; *Carmela* has also been arranged for viola and piano by the composer.
Composed in Los Angeles, 1962.
For Lady Evelyn Barbirolli's Camden Trio.
Contents: I. Indian Moccasin Game (Wisconsin, U.S.A.), II. Carmela (California, U.S.A.), III. Inca Melody (also called Peruvian Melody), IV. Clinch Mountain (Southern Mountain region, U.S.A.), [V. Héla Grand-Père (Haiti),] VI. Gardé Piti Mulet Là, or M'sieu Banjo (Louisiana, U.S.A.).
Duration: 11 minutes, 30 seconds.
Autograph musical score for oboe, bassoon, and piano with notes on the origin of the folk music by Verna Arvey is in the William Grant Still and Verna Arvey Papers at the University of Arkansas Libraries, Fayetteville. (*Héla Grand-Père* is not in the published edition.)

Selected Performances

W167a   1975 (August 31): Los Angeles, CA; Los Angeles County Museum of Natural History; John Ellis, oboe; Don Christlieb, bassoon; Annette Kaufman, piano.

W167b   1979 (October 18): Los Angeles, CA; Arnold Schoenberg Institute; John Rojas, oboe; Sharon Brandolino, bassoon, Shari Rhoads Thompkins, piano. (*See:* WB112.4)

W168   *Voice of the Lord, The* (M. Witmark & Sons, New York, 1946, no. 20552-9, SATB arrangement; G. Schirmer, New York, 1951, no. 42272, in the collection, *Synagogue Music by Contemporary Composers;* available from William Grant Still Music).
For tenor, chorus, and organ (also piano).
Composed in Los Angeles, 1946.

Text of the 29th Psalm, "Mizmor Ledovid," (Hebrew) or "The Voice of the Lord."
Dedicated to Dr. Edwin R. Embree of the Rosenwald Foundation.
Composed for the Park Avenue Synagogue, New York.
Holograph of the full score for organ and voices with the composer's notes for revisions is in the William Grant Still and Verna Arvey Papers at the University of Arkansas Libraries, Fayetteville.
Facsimile of the score arranged for mixed chorus, tenor solo, and organ is in the James Weldon Johnson Memorial Collection of Negro Arts and Letters at Yale University.

W168a **First Performance:** 1946 (May 10): New York, NY; Park Avenue Synagogue; David J. Putterman, cantor.

Selected Performances

W168b 1949 (May 12): New York, NY: Columbia University, St. Paul's Chapel; David J. Putterman, cantor; and Park Avenue Synagogue Choir, Max Helfman, conductor.

W168c 1984 (February 15): Fayetteville, AR; University of Arkansas, Fine Arts Center Concert Hall; University of Arkansas Schola Cantorum, Roger Moore, tenor.

Bibliography

WB168.1 "N.Y. Synagogue to Give Still's Latest Work." *California Eagle*, April 18, 1946.
    Announcement that Still's *Voice of the Lord* will have its first performance at the Park Avenue Synagogue on May 10, 1946.

WB168.2 Kastendieck, Miles. "Columbia's Festival Presents Liturgical Music." New York *Journal-American*, May 13, 1949.
    Kastendieck reports that Putterman and the choir "imparted no special life to this music."

WB168.3 Perkins, Francis D. "Concert and Recital." *New York Herald Tribune*, May 13, 1949.
    "Mr. Still's settings of the Twenty-Ninth Psalm, which had a hint or two of the Negro spiritual in its melodic style, was expressively appropriate."

WB168.4 Straus, Noel. "Columbia Opens Music Festival." *New York Times*, May 13, 1949.
    "The compositions were delivered by the choir with a good understanding of their respective intentions and an enthusiastic approach."

W169 ***Wailing Woman*** (available from William Grant Still Music).
For orchestra, dramatic soprano solo, and SATB chorus; also in piano vocal score.
Composed in Los Angeles; holograph dated April 1946.
Poem by Verna Arvey (poem published in *Opportunity: A Journal of Negro Life* 17 [February 1939]: 54).
Dedicated to the memory of Jo-Jo Solomon (Izler Solomon's son).
Instrumentation: Soprano solo and SATB chorus with 3 flutes (3rd doubles on piccolo), 2 oboes, English horn, 3 clarinets (3rd doubles on bass clarinet), 2 bassoons; 4 horns, 3 trumpets, 3 trombones, tuba; celesta, piano, harp, strings .
Duration: 8 minutes, 36 seconds to 10 minutes.

Holograph sketches with orchestration notes and fair copy of piano vocal score are in the William Grant Still and Verna Arvey Papers at the University of Arkansas Libraries, Fayetteville.

W169a **First Performance:** 1991 (April 21): Ames, IA; Stephens Auditorium; Iowa State University Orchestra and Chorus, Kirk Smith, conductor, Robert Molison, choir director.

W170 *We Sang Our Songs: The Fisk Jubilee Singers: 1871-1971* (available from William Grant Still Music).
For SATB chorus and piano.
Text by Verna Arvey.
Commissioned for the Centennial of the Fisk Jubilee Singers in 1971.
Text begins: "We are the small voices out of the stillness of the past—Remembering, remembering! We sang our songs, So that you may now sing yours. We dreamed our dreams, So you may dream yours."
Holographs of sketches, autographs (one labeled master copy), and a fair copy in manuscript are in the William Grant Still and Verna Arvey Papers at the University of Arkansas Libraries, Fayetteville. The text with melodic sketches by the composer is typed on one page.

W170a **First Performance:** 1971 (October 6): Nashville, TN; Fisk University, War Memorial Auditorium; Fisk Jubilee Singers, Matthew Kennedy, director; Anne Gamble Kennedy, piano.

Selected Performances

W170b 1972 (April 23): Nashville, TN; Fisk University, Fisk Memorial Chapel; Fisk Jubilee Singers, Matthew Kennedy, director; Anne Gamble Kennedy, piano.

W170c 1973 (January 9): Los Angeles, CA; University of Southern California, Bovard Auditorium; Fisk Jubilee Singers, Matthew Kennedy, director; Anne Gamble Kennedy, piano.

W170d 1973 (February 20): Cincinnati, OH; University of Cincinnati, Patricia Corbett Theatre; Fisk Jubilee Singers, Matthew Kennedy, director; Anne Gamble Kennedy, piano.

W170e 1976 (June 6): New York, NY; Lincoln Center, Alice Tully Hall; Triad Chorale, Noel Da Costa, director, Marjorie De Lewis, piano.

Bibliography

WB170.1 Nicholas, Louis. "Emotion Fills Fisk Tribute to Singers." *Nashville Tennessee*, October 7, 1971.
Review of the centennial concert presented by the Fisk Jubilee Singers October 6, 1971. "The 18 singers, with the girls strikingly dressed in yellow, sang with great enthusiasm and intensity all evening. The group sound was vital and rich, and the more rhythmic songs inspired such exuberant reactions at times as to get almost out of control. . . . Anne Gamble Kennedy was the reliable and sensitive accompanist for several selections, including . . . William Grant Still's commissioned piece, *We Sang Our Songs*, a sweetly romantic setting of an inspirational text."

W171 *Winter's Approach* (G. Schirmer, 1928, publication no. 33805; available in *Romantic American Arts Songs*, New York, G. Schirmer).
For voice and piano.

Composed in New York, 1926.
Poem by Paul Laurence Dunbar.
Performed in 1927 in a set of three songs called "Dialect Songs" with *The Breath of a Rose* and *Mandy Lou*.
Holograph is in the Research Division, New York Public Library for the Performing Arts at Lincoln Center.

Selected Performances

W171a   1927 (April 16): New York, NY; New School of Social Research Auditorium; Jessie Zachary, soprano. (*See:* WB16.1)

W171b   1933 (August 31): Oakland, CA; College of the Holy Names; Radiana Pazmor, mezzo-contralto.

W171c   1933 (September 26): San Francisco, CA: Doris Barr Studio; "Program of Modern Songs" presented by the New Music Society of California; Radiana Pazmor, contralto; Katheryn Foster, piano.

W171d   1935 (May 5): Los Angeles, CA; Musart Theater; Leola Longress, soprano; John A. Gray, piano.

W171e   1935 (December 8): San Francisco, CA; Sorosis Club; Nathan Emanuel, tenor; Verna Arvey, piano.

W171f   1945 (September 12): Los Angeles, CA; Embassy Auditorium; Hortense Love, soprano; Paul Ulanowsky, piano.

W171g   1947 (April 25): Nashville, TN; Fisk Memorial Chapel; Lenora Lafayette, soprano; Harriet Cady, piano.

W171h   1956 (April 1): San Francisco, CA; First A.M.E. Zion Church; Ruth Daniel, soprano; Irving Pearson, piano.

Bibliography

WB171.1   Fisher, Marjory M. "Pazmor Gives Ultra-Modern Song Program." *San Francisco News*, September 28, 1933
    Review of the September 26, 1933, "Program of Modern Songs" presented by the New Music Society of California, Radiana Pazmor, contralto. "*Winter's Approach* by Still proved an altogether delightful and humorous song that could have been written by none but a Negro. Both text and music possess strong racial elements."

WB171.2   Garner, George. "Local Critic Praises Soprano's Artistry, Commends Sponsors." *Los Angeles Sentinel*, September 20, 1945.
    Review of the September 12, 1945, recital by Hortense Love. "The art songs by contemporary Negro composers were unusual. *Winter's Approach* . . . was a gem in the voice of Miss Love."

W172   **Wood Notes** (Southern Music Publishing Company, Inc., New York, 1959, no. 451-68; Peer Music Co., New York).
Suite for orchestra; also arranged for small orchestra by the composer.
Composed in Los Angeles; holograph dated 1947.
Inspired by the poems of J. Mitchell Pilcher (from Montgomery, Alabama).
Dedicated to F. J. Lehmann, Still's composition teacher at Oberlin.
Notes on the first performance program provide the following descriptions:
    I. "An American river flowing calmly and singing in the manner of the folk." II. "Rustling leaves and the song of the winds." III. "Lullaby of the wind." IV. "Droll fairies dance while a whippoorwill calls. These

fairies are natives of the western hemisphere." V. "The forest speaks of the creator."

Contents: I. Singing River, II. Autumn Night, III. Moon Dusk, IV. Whippoorwill's Shoes, V. Theophany. (V is not in the published version.)

Instrumentation: 2 flutes (2nd optional), 2 oboes (2nd optional), 2 clarinets, 2 bassoons (2nd optional); 2 horns, 3 trumpets, 2 trombones (no tuba); timpani, percussion, vibraphone, triangle, bells, drums, cymbals; harp or piano, celesta, strings (organ).

Duration: 20 minutes.

Holograph dated 1947 of score for full orchestra with revisions and notes on orchestration is in the William Grant Still and Verna Arvey Papers at the University of Arkansas Libraries, Fayetteville. This holograph includes the movement titled *Theophany*. The Still and Arvey Papers include an autograph of the arrangement for small orchestra and some orchestra parts.

W172a **First Performance:** 1948 (April 22, 23): Chicago, IL; Orchestra Hall; Chicago Symphony Orchestra; Artur Rodzinski, conductor. (Includes *Theophany* movement.)

Selected Performances

W172b 1949 (January 9): Oklahoma City, OK; Municipal Auditorium; Oklahoma Symphony Orchestra, Victor Alessandro, conductor.

W172c 1965 (April 18): Washington, DC; National Gallery of Art; National Gallery Orchestra, Richard Bales, conductor.

W172d 1973 (February 23, 25): Detroit, MI; Wayne County Community Arts Auditorium; Detroit Metropolitan Orchestra, Charles Sumner, conductor; University of Toledo Gospel Chorus, Joan Horton, director; Jimmy Byrd, organ. (*See also:* WB155.6)

W172e 1976 (June 20): Washington, DC; National Gallery of Art, East Garden Court; National Gallery Orchestra, Richard Bales, conductor.

Bibliography

WB172.1 Borowski, Felix. "Horowitz Night at Concert." *Chicago Daily Sun-Times*, April 23, 1948.

Review of a concert on April 22, 1948, by the Chicago Symphony Orchestra. "There can be no question that of all the Negro composers in our country Mr. Still is the most remarkable. He possesses a fund of melodic ideas, his harmony is sometimes in the modern manner, and his handling of the orchestra is expert and, occasionally, original and brilliant. It would be going too far, perhaps, to declare that *Wood Notes* is the most convincing of the scores which have been heard from him. The music, indeed, is somewhat naive, and lacking in force, and the Negro element—as it is represented characteristically in spirituals—makes a more or less deliberate, rather than a spontaneous entrance into it. Dr. Rodzinski and the orchestra gave an excellent performance of the new piece."

WB172.2 Cassidy, Claudia. "Horowitz, Rodzinski, and the Rachmaninoff 3d Share an Ovation in Orchestra Hall." *Chicago Tribune*, April 23, 1948.

Review of a concert on April 22, 1948, by the Chicago Symphony Orchestra. "What Mr. Rodzinski does with that orchestra continues to be a wonder of the music world. He tuned it up with William Grant Still's

Wood Notes, a lyrical exploration of the American landscape and some of its imaginative implications."

WB172.3 Buckley, Charles. "Rodzinski and Horowitz Co-Star in Spectacular Concert." *Chicago Herald American*, April 24, 1948.
Brief review of a concert on April 22, 1948, by the Chicago Symphony Orchestra. "An extremely good performance did little to alleviate the essential dullness of *Wood Notes* by William Grant Still."

WB172.4 Sablosky, Irving. "Horowitz Still The 1st Pianist." *Chicago Daily News*, April 24, 1948.
Review of a concert on April 22, 1948, by the Chicago Symphony Orchestra. "The program began with a cordial reading of William Grant Still's *Wood Notes*—pleasant music with an occasional flash of personality."

WB172.5 White, Garland. "Pilcher Pens Basic Lyrics For New Suite." *Montgomery Advertiser*, July 4, 1948, sec. B, p. 1+.
General article on J. Mitchell Pilcher, Montgomery, Alabama, poet, whose poems inspired Still to compose *Wood Notes*. "The opening movement, . . . *Singing River*, was inspired by Pilcher's lyric bearing the same epithet . . . [it] was written by Pilcher on the famous Bibb Graves Bridge, spanning the Coosa River at Wetumpka, Alabama. *Autumn Night*, the second movement, suggests rustling leaves and the song of the winds. The third movement bears the intriguing title, *Moon Dusk*, and expresses the composer's version of the poet's dreamy lullaby of the winds. The Scherzo, or fourth movement, of *Wood Notes*, is titled *Whippoorwill's Shoes*. It interprets Pilcher's poem for children, and depicts, in tonal effect and regional application, droll fairies dancing while a whippoorwill calls. The concluding movement, *Theophany*, relates in slow, retarding tempo, how the forest speaks of the Creator."

WB172.6 Beers, Marion. "Program Notes." (Oklahoma Symphony Orchestra), January 9, 1949.
Program notes for the Oklahoma City performance of *Wood Notes*. Still, in a letter to Victor Alessandro, conductor of the Oklahoma Symphony Orchestra, states that *Wood Notes* "is a suite of short pieces, melodic and simple in idiom because it deals with nature. It has a distinctly southern flavor also, because each of its sections was inspired by a separate poem by J. Mitchell Pilcher, a journalist who lives in Montgomery, Alabama."

WB172.7 Crowder, Charles. "Gallery Orchestra Displays Its Growing Versatility." *Washington Post* April 19, 1965, sec. B, p. 4.
Review of the April 18, 1965, performance of the National Gallery Orchestra. The program included *Wood Notes*. "They are pieces that have their roots in the dance tune and sentimental ballad style of Stephen Foster and that period. They might easily be the pieces written to be played on the south lawn of the old mansion—all of the romance is there—for the fair lady's 18th birthday. Ah me, had someone just hung a little Spanish moss on the fishtail palms in the East Garden Court!"

WB172.8 Lowens, Irving. "A Typical Different Evening at the Gallery." *Evening Star*, April 19, 1965.
Review of the April 18, 1965, performance of the National Gallery Orchestra. "The Pilcher poems which moved him [Still] are full of such dominant-seventh harmonies as 'pensive vale,' 'restless stream,' 'golden

yesterdays' 'shadowy night,' 'Languid strand' and 'lonely whippoorwill.' So is Still's score. It sounded old-fashioned, passe and pallid. It would have been kinder, to my mind, had Bales played something with a touch of youth and vigor, such as his *Afro-American Symphony*."

WB172.9 Cowden, Robert H. "Program Notes: A Tribute To William Grant Still." (Program notes for the Third Annual Afro-American Concert presented by the Detroit Metropolitan Orchestra, February 23 and 25, 1973.)

"These remarks by the composer might be helpful in understanding [*Wood Notes*]. 'Melody, in my opinion, is the most important musical element. . . . I prefer music that suggests a program to either pure or program music in the strict sense. . . . I am unable to understand how one can rely solely on feeling when composing . . . a fragment of a musical composition may be conceived through inspiration or feeling, but its development lies altogether within the realm of intellect.' The composer's own words offer us an insight into [*Symphony No. 5*]. 'There is one overall truth that I've learned. Probably it's best that I approach it by way of another truth. Although material means must be employed in the production of music, music is actually spiritual in nature, and its message is addressed to the truth that goes hand in hand with it. That is that the voice of inspiration is the voice of God, and the soul of man must first hear it before its message may be transferred to the intellect.'"

W173 ***Your World*** (Ginn and Company, 1971, *The Magic of Music, VI*, edited by Wersen Walters, et al.; available from William Grant Still Music.).
For SATB chorus with piano; SAA for a music education textbook.
Poem by Georgia Douglas Johnson, published in *American Negro Poetry*, edited by Arna Bontemps (New York: Hill and Wang: 1963): 23.
Holograph with revisions, an autograph of score for SATB chorus and piano, initial melodic sketches, and a facsimile of the fair copy with a biographical sketch of the composer are in the William Grant Still and Verna Arvey Papers at the University of Arkansas Libraries, Fayetteville.

WRITINGS BY WILLIAM GRANT STILL AND VERNA ARVEY

William Grant Still published in a variety of music journals, including *Australian Musical News and Musical Digest*, *Etude*, *Musical Journal*, and *Opera, Concert, and Symphony*. His views on race relations appeared in *Crisis*, *Opportunity*, and *Negro Digest*, as well as in numerous African American newspapers throughout the country (see entry **S22** for an example of how one of Still's letters, distributed by Calvin's News Service, was picked up by African American newspapers). He also collaborated on a number of articles with Verna Arvey, an accomplished journalist who unabashedly promoted the career of Still in her own writings about the life and work of the composer.

The writings in this section are in three groups: 1) those by Still; 2) those by Still and Arvey; and 3) those by Arvey. The articles are arranged in chronological order within each group. Some of the essays were reprinted in other publications, such as *William Grant Still and the Fusion of Cultures in American Music,* edited by Robert B. Haas (Los Angeles: Black Sparrow Press, 1972), the second edition of *William Grant Still and the Fusion of Cultures in American Music,* edited by Judith Anne Still, Celeste Anne Headlee, and Lisa M. Headlee-Huffman (Flagstaff: The Master-Player Library, 1995), and Jon Michael Spencer's "The William Grant Still Reader: Essays on American Music," a special issue of *Black Sacred Music: A Journal of Theomusicology* (Duke University Press, 1992). In such instances the Haas, Still, and/or Spencer source is identified within parentheses after the first citation.

Writings by William Grant Still

S1   Still, William Grant. "An Afro-American Composer's Point of View." In *American Composers on American Music*, Henry Cowell, ed., 182-83. Palo Alto, Calif.: Stanford University Press, 1933. (Also appears in Haas, *Fusion,* 112; Still, *Fusion,* 52; and Spencer, "Reader," 232, under the title "An Afro-American Composer's Viewpoint.")

This short article provides insight to his compositional process, as the following excerpt indicates: "Melody, in my opinion, is the most important musical element. After melody comes harmony; then form, rhythm, and dynamics. I prefer music that suggests a program to either pure or program music in the strict sense. I find mechanically produced music valuable as a means of study; but even at its best it fails to satisfy me completely."

S2 ———. "Three-Fold Purpose." *California Eagle*, June 12, 1936.
In this letter to the editor, Still writes to convey his respect to this African American newspaper for "its value as a bearer of real news, its dignity, its appearance, and its inspirational value," as well as to compliment one of its reporters and to become a subscriber.

S3 ———. "The Art of Musical Creation." *The Rosicrucian Fellowship Magazine* (July 1936): 297-99. (Also appears in Spencer, "Reader," 81-85.)
Musical composition is primarily a subjective process, Still maintains. This article describes the methods that Still employed when he composed.

S4 ———. "The American Composer" *The Baton* 2 (March 1937): 4. (Also appears in Spencer, "Reader," 86-87.)
Still suggests that the Works Progress Administration will advance the cause of American composers by devoting attention to programs devoted to their work and that Howard Hanson has done an exceptional job in presenting American compositions on a large scale at Rochester.

S5 ———. "Crescendo." Los Angeles *Daily News*, June 19, 1937.
Lengthy letter to the editor defending American music. In conclusion Still states: "Outside of the fact that critics and audiences have found much in it to praise, loyalty alone should make all those who live in this country desirous of appreciating its culture."

S6 ———. "Are Negro Composers Handicapped?" *The Baton* 1 (November 1937): 3. (Also appears in Spencer, "Reader," 88-90.)
The composer states that he does not believe that his race has deterred him in his profession. However, he also recognizes that prejudices do exist and that they can lead to harmful results.

S7 ———. "Afield In Music." *Deseret News*, April 29, 1939.
On April 23, 1939, Still gave a presentation in Salt Lake City at the Utah State Art Center as part of a lecture-recital program. This article is taken from his address and credited in the newspaper under the composer's name. The presentation focused on attitudes of Americans toward American music.

S8 ———. "For Finer Negro Music." *Opportunity: A Journal of Negro Life* 17 (May 1939): 137. (Also appears in Spencer, "Reader," 95-96.)
Still implores the people of his race to develop better opportunities for African American musicians and composers and outlines some of his suggestions.

S9 ———. "Modern World Challenges Contemporary Composers." *Los Angeles Times*, July 5, 1939, sec. 4, p. 4.
Still compares the challenges in composing music in his day against those of the old masters of yesteryear. While technology has created advancements in music, it has its limitations. "The form and method of creation differ greatly now, due to different mediums of transmission. The old masters were accustomed to developing each theme to its fullest extent. Nowadays, when a composer so often works with a stop watch in the knowledge that his music must fit a certain radio program or a certain film scene, and must be just so long and no longer, adequate development is impossible. He must work for beauty and interest despite this." Article identified "As Told to Verna Arvey."

S10 ———. "A Negro Symphony Orchestra." *Opportunity: A Journal of Negro Life* 17 (September 1939): 267, 286-87. (Also appears in Spencer, "Reader," 97-99.)
This article elaborates on one of Still's hopes, namely, to see "the realiza-

tion of a Negro Symphony Orchestra so fine that it would rank with—and perhaps surpass—the best in the world."

S11 ———. "Spirituals, Blues Important Section of American Music." *New York Amsterdam News*, June 29, 1940, p. 25. (Also appears in Spencer, "Reader," 100-101.)

Still writes that spirituals and blues occupy a significant place in the development of American music. He also states that, while much progress has been made by African American composers, much more could be done to support African American artists.

S12 ———. "Reader Opinions." *Pacific Coast Musician,* October 18, 1941.

Still writes, "[I] am writing to commend you for your courageous stand on behalf of American musicians. Best wishes to you for having the courage of your convictions and for having such fine convictions in the first place."

S13 ———. "Letters to the Editor." *Pacific Coast Musician*, October 3, 1942.

Letter to the editor. Still quotes from a letter that he received from Joseph Fischer and mentions "how nice it would be for American conductors to vie with each for first performances of native compositions."

S14 ———. "Composer Wants American Music to Build U.S. Morale." *Kansas City Call*, October 9, 1942.

The composer promotes the performance of American music as one avenue of building morale to support the war effort. This article was published in many other African American newspapers, including the *Chicago Defender*.

S15 ———. "Still Quits Film on 'Stormy Weather' Protests Race Slant." *Jersey Herald News*, February 20, 1943.

In this long letter released through Calvin's News Service, Still explains why he resigned from Twentieth Century-Fox. His letter caused quite an uproar in Hollywood and across the country, and it was reprinted in whole or part in numerous newspapers, but especially those representing African American views.

S16 ———. "Splendid Presentation." *Los Angeles Tribune*, February 22, 1943.

Still thanks the newspaper for its "accurate and excellently presented" facts relative to his resignation from Twentieth Century-Fox.

S17 ———. "Stresses Cooperation." *War Worker* 1 (October, 1943).

Still compliments the paper for its interracial approach and wishes it success.

S18 ———. "Still calls Nathaniel Dett one of our 'cultural pioneers.'" *Los Angeles Tribune*, November 8, 1943. (Also appears in Spencer, "Reader," 109-110.)

Still recounts some of the contributions to music made by R. Nathaniel Dett, who died in Battle Creek, Michigan, on October 2, 1943. Published in other African American newspapers through Calvin's News Service.

S19 ———. "Leopold Stokowski as I Know Him." *War Worker* 1 (November 1943, Last Half): 6, 8. (Also appears in Spencer, "Reader," 111-13.)

Still writes a glowing account of Stokowski, who championed performances of Still's music—especially the *Afro-American Symphony*—and that of William L. Dawson.

S20 ———. "Race Problem Study Needed." *New York Times*, January 19, 1944.

In this letter to the editor, Still states that racial unrest in the United States is a recognized fact. He believes that education has an important role to play and recommends that "every one of us devote thought to the matter immediately and do whatever we can do."

S21 ———. "The Men Behind American Music." *Crisis* 51 (January 1944): 12-15, 29. (Also appears in Spencer, "Reader," 114-23.)

The focus of this article is to explain that musical compositions have often been created by one individual yet claimed by another. As one example, Still states that many of the works of George Gershwin had their origin with African American composers and arrangers. Still provides additional examples of musicians and composers whose style was claimed by another.

S22 ———. "Propaganda's Place in the World Politics." *Louisville Defender*, July 8, 1944. (Also appears in the July 8, 1944, issue of Los Angeles *Spotlight* as "Time for Negro to Start Propaganda Campaign—Still," the July 17, 1944, issue of *Los Angeles Tribune* as "W. Grant Still Thinks Race Needs Artistic Propaganda;" in the first half of the August 1944, issue of *War Worker* as "Needed: More True Cultural Propaganda;" the July 8, 1944, issue of the *Shreveport Sun* as "Writer Urges Negroes to Start National Propaganda Campaign;" and the July 8, 1944, issue of the Jacksonville *Florida Tattler* as "Time for Negroes to Start Propaganda Campaign!")

Still indicates that the cultural contributions of African Americans must be emphasized better to improve interracial relations. He remarks, "Now is the time for us to show our best, most sincere, faces to the world. For if we concentrate on the cheap elements in our own lives, how can we expect the white man to do otherwise? We cannot afford to have one Negro who compromises." Articles written by Still that appear in African American newspapers received a wide distribution thanks to Calvin's News Service. This entry serves as an example in that regard.

S23 ———. "Another Musical Pioneer Passes." *Miami Whip*, August 19, 1944. (Also appears in the August 12, 1944, issue of the Norfolk *Journal and Guide* as "Still Sees Loss in Death of Cook.")

Still writes of the contributions to music that Will Marion Cook made during his lifetime. Cook died in New York on July 19, 1944. Published in other African American newspapers through Calvin's News Service.

S24 ———. "The Negro and His Music in Films." In *Writers' Congress; The Proceedings of the Conference held in October 1943 under the Sponsorship of the Hollywood Writers' Mobilization and the University of California*, 277-79. Berkeley and Los Angeles: University of California Press, 1944. (First appeared in print in the October 1943 issue of *War Worker* [p. 15] under the title "The Negro and his Music." Also appears in Spencer, "Reader," 105-8.)

As a participant for the session "Music and the War," Still concludes by stating, "The present war and its attendant crisis at home should wrest two major concessions from Hollywood: an open mind with regard to minority groups and their art forms, and the will to make a positive contribution to interracial understanding."

S25 ———. Review of *Unsung Americans Sung*, by W. C. Handy, ed. *Crisis* 52 (January 1945): 26.

Still has praise for this volume, which provides insight to the musical tributes and the literary work of thirty-seven writers and composers of African American heritage. Although Still is not a subject of *Unsung Americans Sung*, his personal copy, now in the William Grant Still and Verna Arvey Papers, University of Arkansas Libraries, Fayetteville, bears the inscription "To Mr. & Mrs. Wm. G. Still, with sincere appreciation of the wonderful work done by both to make this effort better understood. W. C. Handy, 8-8-1944."

S26 ——. "How Do We Stand in Hollywood?" *Opportunity: A Journal of Negro Life* 23 (Spring 1945): 74-77. (Also appears in Spencer, "Reader," 124-32.)

Still examines the Hollywood film industry and the racial stereotypes it promotes. "In short we would like to see the Negro presented to the world and to America as a normal American. If this were done, the films could make a real contribution to inter-racial understanding and a better world."

S27 ——. "The King Is Dead—Long Live The King!" *Stadium Concerts Reviews* 28 (June-July 1945): 7, 11, 41. (Also appears in Spencer, "Reader," 133-35.)

Still indicates that contemporary music has greater possibilities as a social expression due to its availability over the radio, at live concerts, and from recordings. Consequently, the public becomes the final judge of the value of a piece of music. "One of the manifestations of our changing society is the gradual but definite democratization of music. In the old days, folk music was the only truly communal music, for the sophisticated musical creations were enjoyed only by wealthy people. A King or a Queen might patronize a composer, and command gala performances of anything that suited the royal fancy. Through the years, more and more people have become associated with the production, management and enjoyment of music, until today it may rightly be said that the public is King."

S28 ——. "The Function of Piano Music in American Culture." *Fischer Edition News* 22 (June-July 1946): 8-10.

Still indicates that as America develops its native culture, its music, especially that written for piano, is a very important component. "There can be many interesting and unusual ideas built around American piano music for concerts, and for students' recitals. One of these might begin with American piano music of the eighteenth century, and progress through compositions written by Americans of the romantic and the modern schools of thought. . . . The styles in American music (which are reflected in the music written for piano) are many, and so varied that a tasteful arrangement of such concert material cannot fail to arouse audience interest."

S29 ——. "Composer Writes on Negro's Future in Serious Music." *Los Angeles Tribune*, October 5, 1946. (Also appears in the October 7, 1946, issue of the *Los Angeles Criterion* under the title "Serious Music a Challenge to Negro Youth.")

In citing examples of young African Americans pursuing careers in orchestras or as composers of orchestral works, Still believes that there are such opportunities for those who work hard and are dedicated.

S30 ——. "From the Podium." *Time* 48 (October 28, 1946): 8.

Letter to the editor. Still writes that he doesn't share Rudolph Dunbar's sentiments as contained in Dunbar's letter to the editor, published in the October 7, 1946, issue of *Time*. Dunbar's interview with the reporter from *Time*, Mr. Louis Banks, took place at the Still residence.

S31 ——. "Letter to the Editor." *Opera, Concert and Symphony* 11 (December 1946): 3.

The November 1946 issue of *Opera, Concert and Symphony* contained an article based upon an interview with Still. Upon receiving that issue, the composer wrote a letter of appreciation to the magazine as he "felt that you had correctly interpreted my thoughts."

S32 ——. "A Symphony of Dark Voices." *Opera, Concert and Symphony* 12 (May 1947): 18-19, 36, 38-39. (Also appears in Spencer, "Reader," 136-43.)

Still extols the influence that African American musicians and composers have on American music, including contributions of spirituals, symphonies, jazz, and folk music.

S33 ———. "Politics in Music." *Opera, Concert and Symphony* 12 (August 1947): 10-11, 30. (Also appears in Spencer, "Reader," 144-49.)

Still comments on political motives surrounding the work of some artists, especially as they may relate to communistic or capitalistic persuasions. He concludes that, "In my humble opinion, politics—as such—should not enter into the consciousness of a true artist when his work is concerned. He should, however, be interested in the human problems that are a part of our lives, and should balance this with his interest in the abstract elements of his art-form."

S34 ———. "American Music and the Well-Timed Sneer." *Opera and Concert* 13 (May 1948): 10-11, 26-27, 30. (Also appears in Spencer, "Reader," 150-56.)

Still presents critical viewpoints relative to the preponderance of European compositions being performed over American works. He also criticizes attempts by ultra-modernists to deprecate other composers' works.

S35 ———. "Music, A Vital Factor in America's Racial Problems." *Australian Musical News and Musical Digest* 29 (November 1948): 12-13. (Also appears in *Oberlin Alumni Magazine* [March 1950]: 9, 25, and Spencer, "Reader," 169-72, both under the title "A Vital Factor in America's Racial Problems.")

Still indicates that being African American has not hampered him in his musical aspirations, citing the assistance he received from people like George Chadwick and Edgard Varèse; however, life outside of music has proven difficult at times because of his race.

S36 ———. "'The Musical Workshop' Inspiration to Composer." *Los Angeles Mirror*, December 11, 1948.

Still writes a brief review of Frederick Dorian's *The Musical Workshop* and offers other titles for those interested in music or dance.

S37 ———. "Can Music Make a Career?" *Negro Digest* 7 (December 1948): 79-84. (Also appears in Spencer, "Reader," 157-63.)

Still draws upon his own background and experiences throughout this article, aimed primarily at African Americans. He concludes by saying, "In short, come on along! There is . . . always room at the top!"

S38 ———. "With and Without Honor." In *Music and Dance in California and the West*, edited by Richard Drake Saunders, 18-19. Hollywood, California: Bureau of Musical Research, Inc., 1948.

Still laments the circumstances surrounding the chances of composers of serious American music ("prophets with and without honor in their own country") in receiving performances of their works. In his mind "the unfortunate fact is that serious American music is still in the position of having to sell itself to the American public."

S39 ———. "The Composer Needs Determination and Faith." *Etude* 67 (January 1949): 7-8. (Also appears in Spencer, "Reader," 164-68.)

Biographical sketch and music philosophy of Still. "To me, the important elements in good music are (1) a *good* melody; (2) form; (3) variety (which may be attained by varying one's thematic material); and (4) harmonic treatment."

S40 ———. "Troubled History of 'The Troubled Island.'" *New York Times*, March 20, 1949.

Still recounts the difficulties encountered in producing an opera. After finally getting the opportunity to produce *Troubled Island*, Langston Hughes, who wrote the libretto, went to Spain and Verna Arvey was called upon to assist with the revisions.

S41 ———. "My Biggest Break." *Negro Digest* 7 (October 1949): 19.

Still looks back to 1911 when he first realized he wanted to write "serious music—more particularly operatic music—for a career for myself." The response elicited by the audience for *Troubled Island* "told me that my work had not been in vain."

S42 ———. "The Structure of Music." *Etude* 68 (March 1950): 17, 61. (Also appears in Southern, *Readings in Black American Music*, 276-79, and Spencer, "Reader," 173-76.)

Still writes that musical form is as important as it ever was, despite the atonalists. "There exists today a school of contemporary composers, some in Europe and some in America, which apparently—at least on first hearing—disregards the laws of form. No recurring themes are evident. Indeed, it is hard to detect the actual themes, since the members of this school actually scorn what we know as melody. They have directed their efforts mainly toward exploring new harmonic effects because that is so much easier than constructing a well-proportioned composition. . . . Because these composers scorn inspiration, I call them 'cerebral' composers. Other people refer to them as 'atonalists.' My feeling is that a composer should be tested, not by the bizarre sounds he can produce, but by his ability to construct a simple, satisfying piece of music, harmonically, melodically, and architecturally."

S43 ———. "Fifty Years of Progress in Music." *Pittsburgh Courier*, November 11, 1950, p. 15. (Also appears in *Dansk Musiktidsskrift* 26 [Argang 1951]: 91-95, as "Negrene: amerikansk musik," and in Spencer, "Reader," 177-88.)

In reviewing the progress of African American music, Still describes the contributions of Harry T. Burleigh, R. Nathaniel Dett, Roland Hayes, Marian Anderson, William L. Dawson, and others. He also credits people like Leopold Stokowski for advancing the works of African American composers. Still mentions his serious reservations relative to Leftist doctrines, especially as race relations are concerned, and encourages African Americans, as consumers, to become more aware of their importance in supporting African American artists in the world of music.

S44 ———. "Cliques and claques in music orbit." Los Angeles *Daily News*, December 2, 1950, p. 22+.

Review of *My Life in Music* by John Erskine. In his remarks Still discusses cliques in music, the need for a more democratic approach to music, and the exponents of ultra-modern or atonal music.

S45 ———. Review of *The Analytical Concert Guide*, by Louis Biancolli. Los Angeles *Daily News*, December 1, 1951.

S46 ———. Review of *The American Symphony Orchestra*, by John H. Mueller, and *Orchestral Music: An Armchair Guide*, by Lawrence Gilman. Los Angeles *Daily News*, December 22, 1951.

S47 ———. "Composer shows meaning of music." Los Angeles *Daily News*, April 5, 1952.

Review of Paul Hindemith's *A Composer's World* for which Still offers the following conclusion. "This writer wishes that Hindemith had not expressed his disapproval of the term 'American' as applied to our native composers. Granted that a few of his reasons are sound, the fact still remains that many of us are proud of being American composers, just as composers in other countries are proud of their heritage. We are interested in helping to build a great national culture, as has been built in other lands. Hindemith, a visitor who has been received here warmly, would do well to encourage us in our ambitions."

S48 ———. "Negro Composer Warns His Race About Reds' Lies." *Arkansas Gazette*, April 6, 1952. (Also appeared in the *Los Angeles Sentinel*, June 19, 1952, sec. B, p. 3, under the title "Composer Hits Red Baiters," and the *Columbus Evening Dispatch,* July 12, 1952, under the title "Negro Composer Warns Against Communist Lies.")

Letter to Dr. LeRoy Williams of Little Rock which was subsequently published in the editorial page. "The Communists pretend to be our friends when they come to us, yet I have learned that their friendship is only a mask. They cheerfully knife us in the back whenever and however it suits their purposes to do so. They are at present making a great show of being the only ones to fight our battles for us. In the first place, no one asked them to do so. In the second place, when it becomes known that they also suppress whenever possible the news of loyal Americans—white and colored—who also are fighting our battles, the complete falsity of their position will be seen clearly."

S49 ———. "Mmn. [sic] [Kirsten] Flagstad, woman of two personalities." *Los Angeles News*, November 30, 1952.

Review of Louis Biancolli's book *The Flagstad Manuscript*.

S50 ———. "Negro servicemen given compliment." Los Angeles *Daily News*, September 1, 1953. (Similar article appeared in the *Los Angeles Herald Express*, September 22, 1953, and the *Los Angeles Examiner*, September 3, 1953, both under the title "Good Americans.")

Letter to the editor. "We wish to express our pleasure at seeing among the American servicemen returning from Korea this morning the smiling faces of some of our colored Americans. We hope the American public will understand that it is these loyal young men—some of whom have returned and some of whom gave their lives overseas—who are representative of the millions of patriotic American Negroes. They are in decided contrast to those few misguided souls who refuse, under the protection of the U.S. Constitution's Fifth Amendment, and presumably under orders from Moscow, to assist our congressional investigators in their efforts to preserve our freedoms. Such reluctant witnesses deserve only scorn from their fellow-citizens, while the men who fought for their country are proudly acknowledged."

S51 ———. "Man has right to like the music he likes." Los Angeles *Daily News*, December 7, 1953.

Review of *Understanding Music* by William S. Newman. "The student and the lover of detail will find this book stimulating. The average music-lover, reading it in order to appreciate music better, is apt to feel that it is somewhat like making a chemical analysis of his food before sitting down to dinner!"

S52 ———. "Towards a Broader American Culture." American Symphony Orchestra League *Newsletter* 6 (July 1954): 1,7,13. (Also appears in *Southwestern Composers Journal* 1 [Season 1955-56]: 4, 16, and Spencer, "Reader," 189-91, and *Australian Musical News and Musical Digest* 45 [January 1955]: 2+.)

Excerpts of Still's keynote address at the national convention of the American Symphony Orchestra League, Springfield, Ohio, June 17, 1954. The thrust of Still's remarks is to encourage the performance of music written by American composers on concert programs, especially new works, which Still believes should be played repeatedly.

S53 ———. "Juke Box Royalty." *Times-Picayune*, October 22, 1954.

Letter to the editor. "Recently I became aware of a provision in our laws which makes it possible for juke boxes to earn large sums of money for their owners without anything being done to compensate the composers and lyricists without whose songs the juke boxes would be useless. Although my music is not played in juke boxes because I am a serious composer, I still feel that all of us, as colleagues, owe a duty to each other."

S54 ———. "The Greater Need for Choral Singing Today." *Fischer Edition News* 31 (February-April 1955): 1-2.

Still espouses the virtues of choral music in this short article. "America needs the solace, the spiritual strength and the unity of purpose that can come from choral singing. Whether people gather together to form a professional group, or whether they are amateurs singing for their own enjoyment, they are nevertheless creating a bond of sympathy and understanding between themselves and their fellow-countrymen."

S55 ———. "Regarding Some False 'Notes' in the Fine Arts." *Tones and Overtones* 3 (Fall 1955): 25-27.

This article was based on a presentation to the Allied Arts League of Los Angeles, California, on September 11, 1955. Still suggests that the membership—comprised of African American women—become active in cultural life in Los Angeles. He suggests working with the Los Angeles Philharmonic, for example. He also recommends "boycotting of everything which portrays the Negro in the stereotyped manner. . . . " He cites *Porgy and Bess* in that regard. As part of his conclusion, he states, "We welcome others who will join us in the fight against the stereotype, and against any sort of cultural segregation."

S56 ———. "The Juke Box Industry—And The Composer." *Arkansas Gazette*, January 16, 1958. (Similar letter appears in the *Los Angeles Times*, January 23, 1958, as "Juke Box Bill Plea Made.")

Still is asking for support of Senate Bill 1870 which, among other items, provides for the payment of royalties to composers whose music is played on juke boxes.

S57 ———. "The Composer's Creed." *Music of the West* 17 (October 1961): 13-15. (Also appears in Spencer, "Reader," 198-202.)

This is based upon a speech delivered at the annual meeting of the Music Teachers' Association of California, Pacific Grove, California, July 18, 1961. Still indicates that contemporary music is at a crossroads, and all those who play a role in the world of music are faced with a decision to make relative to the direction of music. He concludes by stating, "In summation, I would say these things: 1. Music's true function is greater than that of merely expressing harsh and uninteresting sounds; 2. The new is not necessarily better than the old; 3. Intellect isn't always more desirable than emotion; AND unintelligibility can never supplant simplicity and understandability."

S58 ———. "Turnabout" *Los Angeles Herald-Express*, November 17, 1961. (Also appeared under the title "Russian Music" in the *Los Angeles Times*, November 15, 1961, and under the title "Preference" in the *Los Angeles Examiner*, November 16, 1961.)

Letter to the editor. "I would like to comment on the fact that the music of the Soviet Russian composer, Shostakovich, was featured on the opening concert of our own Philharmonic Orchestra, while no American composition was presented. Since we are now having a cultural exchange with Russia, dare we hope that the music of American composers will be used to open the symphony season in Russia, and that no Russian works will be presented at that time?"

S59 ——. "Problems of the American Composer." *Lyric* 1 (December 1963): 7, 13.

In this short article, Still states that composers have difficulty finding audiences for their music and performers willing to present compositions. He goes on to champion the works of American composers.

S60 ——. "Negro Musicians." *Frontier* (March 1964): 27.

The January 1964 issue of *Frontier* contained an article (p. 21-22) by Henry Roth entitled "Hollywood and the Negro Musician" in which he suggests that the Hollywood entertainment industry—the motion picture studios, television, and the phonograph companies—should include more creative and performing musicians that are African American. Still, in a letter to the editor, states that, "To the best of our knowledge, Mr. Roth has done an excellent job of assembling and presenting the facts on an issue which, until now, has generally been ignored."

S61 ——. "Source of Pride." *Arizona Daily Star*, April 7, 1966, sec. D, p. 12.

Letter to the editor by Still commenting favorably on the Tucson Symphony Orchestra, which recently performed *Festive Overture*, and on the Tucson High School Symphonic Band, which recently performed *Little Red School House* and *American Scene*.

S62 ——. "Excellent Cartoon." *Los Angeles Herald Examiner*, October 30, 1966, sec. G, p. 4.

Letter to the editor. "We would like to thank you for publishing the excellent cartoon, 'But I Don't Want to Live Next Door to One,' on your October 19 editorial page. We are grateful for every recognition of the fact that the decent Negro citizens, while not giving up their drive for equal citizenship, are still not allied with the hate-mongers, the rioters and the self-appointed 'leaders' who lead no one but themselves. We prefer to reach our goals through friendship and accomplishment, and to respect our fellow-citizens, even as we ask them to respect us."

S63 ——. "Program Praised." *Los Angeles Times*, November 21, 1966.

Letter to the editor. "Recently, it was my privilege to participate in a program called, 'The Negro and the Arts,' a joint effort of the UCLA Extension and the University Fine Arts Production Department, on several Southern California campuses. Although the *Times* did report several aspects of this series, to our gratification, I would like to call attention to it again, simply because of the contrast between this constructive approach to a nationwide problem and the situations existing on other campuses. Most of us agree that the most effective solution to current racial matters is one of education—not only education of the masses so that they can take their places as responsible citizens, but also education of both races to the very real contribution made by Negroes who have already forged ahead."

S64 ——. "My Arkansas Boyhood." *Arkansas Historical Quarterly* 26 (Autumn 1967): 285-92. (Also appears in Haas, *Fusion*, 75-81; Still, *Fusion*, 9-14; and Spencer, "Reader," 245-51.)

Still recounts some of the people, scenes, activities, and interests associated with his boyhood and growing up in Little Rock.

S65 ———. "Praise for Seattle Youth Symphony." *Seattle Times*, February 21, 1968.

Letter to the editor subsequent to the February 12, 1968, performance of the Seattle Youth Symphony Orchestra. "Over a period of years I have heard wonderful reports about the Seattle Youth Symphony. . . . To my immense gratification, I discovered that all the glowing reports were fully justified and that Vilem Sokol and his fine young musicians had developed an organization deserving of national attention."

S66 ———. "The History And Future of Black American Music Studies: Practices And Potentials." *Music Bulletin* of Lincoln University, Pennsylvania, 2 (August 1969): 7-17. (Also appears in de Lerma, *Black Music in Our Culture*, 93-108; Haas, *Fusion*, 124-39; Still, *Fusion,* 64-79; and Spencer, "Reader," 215-31, as "A Composer's Viewpoint.")

Condensed version of the speech delivered by Still on June 21 at the "Seminar on Black Music in College and University Curricula," sponsored by Indiana University, June 18-21, 1969. Still provides a review of his background, including his education, experiences with W.C. Handy, his experiments with avant-garde music in the 1920s, and his thoughts on race relations.

S67 ———. "The Negro Musician in America." *Music Educators Journal* 56 (January 1970): 100-1, 157-61. (Also appears in Spencer, "Reader," 207-14.)

Still writes of the musical development of African Americans, tracing the history to the era of slaves and bringing it forward to accomplishments in the orchestral field in the mid-twentieth century. He concludes that the future of African Americans in the field of music is inextricably bound with their future in America, taking into account improvements in their economic situation.

S68 ———. "What I Owe to Oberlin." *Oberlin Alumni Magazine* 67 (January 1971): 14-15.

Still provides insight to his years at Wilberforce University, his decision to go to Oberlin, and his education and experiences at Oberlin.

S69 ———. "Black Composers." *Los Angeles Times*, April 15, 1973.

Letter to the editor. "When Martin Bernheimer wrote (April 9) 'I don't believe that there are no black composers who write serious, original significant music,' I couldn't agree with him more. I don't believe it either."

S70 ———. "On Composing for the Harp." *American Harp Journal* 4 (Winter 1974): 32-33.

Short article in which Still (as told to Verna Arvey) describes his experience on composing for the harp, especially with the composition *Ennanga*, and touches upon his associations with Ann Mason Stockton, Lois Adele Craft, and Mary Sevitzky Portanova.

S71 ———. "Horizons Unlimited." In Haas, *Fusion*, 113-23. (Also appears in Still, *Fusion,* 53-63, and Spencer, "Reader," 233-44.)

Still draws upon his own experiences in describing why variety is important to the world of music and musical compositions. He also suggests that the audience is a factor to consider.

S72 ———. "On Orchestration." In Haas, *Fusion*, 103-07. (Also appears in Still, *Fusion,* 35-39, and Spencer, "Reader," 252-56.)

Based upon a presentation in Rochester, New York, Still remarks, "The major problem confronting one who sets out to score for an orchestra is that of presenting the music most effectively." He then goes on to elaborate on what he believes is the solution: "clarity, balance and a tasteful variety of tone color."

S73 ———. "What a Composer Is." In Haas, *Fusion*, 108-11. (Also appears in Still, *Fusion,* 48-51, and Spencer, "Reader," 257-60.)

This article was developed from a presentation. The composer considers "first the qualities a composer must have, then . . . of my own approach to a new composition and of the steps taken in building the composition from its inception, illustrating this with excerpts from my *Afro-American Symphony*."

S74 ———. "Remembering Arkansas." In *William Grant Still Studies at the University of Arkansas: A 1984 Congress Report*, edited by Claire Detels, 44-46. Fayetteville, Ark.: University of Arkansas, 1985.

The article is based upon a presentation by Still at the University of Arkansas on March 22, 1972. Similar in content to "My Arkansas Boyhood," Still provides glimpses of his life while growing up in Little Rock.

Writings by Still and Verna Arvey

SA1 Still, William Grant and Verna Arvey. "Negro Music in the Americas." *Revue Internationale de Musique* 1 (May-June 1938): 280-88. (Also appears in Spencer, "Reader," 91-94.)

In this short article, the authors provide an overview of how African Americans have influenced music in the Americas. They incorporate jazz, blues, spirituals, and choral arrangements in the process.

SA2 ———. "La Música de Mi Raza." *Música* 1 (August 1941): 105, 107-08. (Also appears in Spencer, "Reader," 102-04, under the English language title "The Music of My Race.")

This article first appeared in *Música,* a publication of the Orquesta Sinfónica Nacional of Bogotá, Colombia. In this short article Still briefly mentions some of the merits and influences of African American music to American music as a whole. Still states that jazz, for example, conveys "a great variety and gracefulness in instrumental effects unknown to classic composers. It has developed a totally new orchestral style. It is a style having great dignity, if used with intelligence and discretion."

SA3 ———. "Does Interracial Marriage Succeed?" *Negro Digest* 3 (April 1945): 50-52.

The authors provide insight on interracial marriage through their own experience. "We married because, after five years of working together in an intellectual companionship that was and has continued to be far closer than any physical intimacy could ever be, we suddenly realized that we were only happy together, that together we wanted to build a home and to have children. In short, we married because we fell in love."

SA4 ———. "Added Orchids." *Los Angeles Tribune*, March 23, 1946.

Letter to the editor congratulating the *Tribune* on receiving the Willkie Award in journalism.

SA5 ———. "Serious Music: New Field for the Negro." *Variety* (January 5, 1955): 227. (Also appears in Spencer, "Reader," 192-93.)

Still comments on the challenges facing African American composers of serious music. "There was a time . . . when certain white people doggedly held to the stereotyped belief that every colored musician belonged to and should stay in popular music. . . . Today, it is no longer a novelty to hear the serious work of a Negro composer on concert programs. . . . In the beginning, Negro composers of serious music had to make a choice (a purely personal one) between several different styles of writing. Should they write abstract music, or should they make a conscious attempt to express a racial heritage in a higher form? Some of us have gone from one style to the other, according to the dictates of each new composition. . . . So, when we aspire to the heights on which Beethoven and Mozart dwelled, we have more than one reason for doing so. At present, we are simply writing music which we hope audiences will enjoy and America will be proud to own."

SA6 ———. "Modern Composers Have Lost Their Audience: Why?" *Australian Musical News and Musical Digest* 47 (July 1956): 15-16. (Also appears in Haas, *Fusion*, 99-101; Still, *Fusion,* 31-33; and Spencer, "Reader," 261-64.)

Still and Arvey suggest that dissonance in contemporary music may very well explain why fewer people frequent and support concert performances. The March 1957 issue of *Australian Musical News* (p. 36-37) contains the responses of twelve readers who express their agreement with the authors.

SA7 ———. "Our American Musical Resources." *Showcase: Music Clubs Magazine* 41 (Fall 1961): 7-9. (Also appears in Spencer, "Reader," 194-97.)

The authors indicate that a renewed interest in folk sources by American composers would enhance American music. "I think we should make a conscious effort to balance the intellectual approach to music with the emotional, or 'feeling' approach. One way to do this is to reconsider folk sources: not to use them consciously or exclusively, but to absorb them all and combine them in our inner being so that, unconsciously, a truly American idiom will emerge in our created serious music."

SA8 ———. "The Lost Audience For New Music." *Music Journal* (1966 Annual Anthology): 38-39.

The authors express their views on dissonant music and the negative effects they believe it holds. "When it first came to public notice, [dissonant] music was electrifying. What not everyone realized after that was that it succeeded because its dissonance had a reason for existing. For dissonance does have a value, and can be used with pleasing effects. Later, when some composers began to write dissonance just for the sake of dissonance, there arose a sameness in the greater part of the music that was composed."

Writings by Verna Arvey

A1 Arvey, Verna. "American Music." *Gateway* 1 (April 1935): 9, 31.

Arvey indicates that "America is just now coming into its own musically, through the efforts of strong individual composers," one of which she identifies as Still. "His birthright gives him the feeling of the negro [sic] and of the American Indian; his activities give him a firsthand knowledge of Jazz, and his studies give him a knowledge of orchestration and of fascinating instrumental effects possessed by few other living musicians."

A2 ———. *Choreographic Music: Music for the Dance*. New York: E.P. Dutton and Co., 1941.

Includes a chapter (p. 286-300) entitled "The Ballets of John Alden Carpenter and William Grant Still." Discusses *Lenox Avenue, La Guiablesse, Sahdji,* and excerpts from other works by Still.

A3 ———. "The Composer in Hollywood." *Musical America* 56 (November 10, 1936): 8.

The author describes what modern composers, such as Still, might face if they venture into the film business. In Still's case the author mentions that pieces composed by William Grant Still for the film *Lady of Secrets* were "dubbed down" and resulted in a situation that his music could scarcely be heard.

A4 ——. "The Significance of Composers in Hollywood." *Pacific Coast Musician* April 17, 1937, p. 3.

Review of composers who reside in Los Angeles. "The fact that audiences like Still's music so tremendously today shows that it says something to them that is real, something vital. 'Do you know what I think people are seeking in music?' declares this composer [Still], 'They want to be able to say, "This is a part of me!" European music is beautiful and well-scored, but I can *thrill* to something typically American—even a Blues song, if it is a good one.'"

A5 ——. "My Association With The Music of William Grant Still." *Hamitic Monthly* 3 (May 1937): 6.

Arvey recounts her initial interests in the life and compositions of Still, dating to the early 1930s when she performed some of his works in Los Angeles and Mexico City, where she played *The Dance of the Children* from *La Guiablesse*.

A6 ——. "William Grant Still: Afro-American Composer Sketched." *California Leader*, April 29, 1937.

Sketch of Still's life and a list of his compositions from 1924 to 1936. "Still's creative work in music is ranked among the finest of all American composers."

A7 ——. "The Ballets of William Grant Still." *New Challenge* 2 (Fall 1937): 75-80.

"Still's approach to the composition of dance music is unique. He had seen Pavlowa dance, and though her artistry impressed him deeply, he was even then searching for newer, broader forms of choreographic expression in music. Thus his music is rhythmic in such a distinctive way that it can only be adequately choreographed with modern, free movements: the realization of his mental vision. His music is also conducive to sustained movements, not erraticisms. Instead of mentally picturing actual dance steps, he visualized the general trend and feeling of each dance. Often he would conceive a dance in its elemental form and make the music, in pitch and in rhythmic values, correspond to that form: the pitch determining the dancer's movement in space; the rhythm determining the foot or floor patterns." Arvey goes on to describe Still's *Lenox Avenue, La Guiablesse, Sahdji,* and dance excerpts from other compositions.

A8 ——. "William Grant Still, Afro-American Composer." *Twelve Negro Spirituals.* Volume 1. Wellington Adams, editor. New York: Handy Brothers Music Co., Inc., 1937: [7].

In one page, Arvey provides a good chronological review of the compositions by Still up to 1937.

A9 ——. "William Grant Still: Creative Aspects of His Work." *Arts Quarterly* 1 (January-March 1938): 3-4, 22.

Arvey, based upon her working relationship with Still, describes some of the ways that the composer creates music. These include relatively simple steps, such as jotting down ideas or themes on notes and then developing a sketch from this material. Still worked slowly, perhaps developing only two or three good measures in a day. The final portion of the article includes random examples of Still's creative processes, such as the following excerpt. "'To me, it appears best to compose away from the piano, but to try out ideas or inspirations at the piano.'"

A10 ———. "Is There A Place For Negroes In Classical Music?" *UpBeat* 1 (January 1939): 7, 34.

Arvey briefly describes the career of William Grant Still, describing his years as a struggling musician, later making commercial arrangements, being a bandleader, and, finally, composing in the symphonic field.

A11 ———. "W.G.S. Creator of Indigenous American Music." *The Chesterian* 20 (May-June 1939): 134-38. (Also appears in *Fischer Edition News* 15 [January-September 1939]: 8-12.)

Arvey provides background on Still and his style of composition. "William Grant Still is an expression of the soul of Afro-America, from the vague wanderings about ancestral Africa to the human joys and spiritual sorrows of the present day. The sons of the soil speak in his music, as do the sophisticated intellectuals who congregate in metropolitan areas."

A12 ———. *Studies of Contemporary American Composers: William Grant Still.* New York: J.Fischer, 1939.

In reviewing the life and work of Still, the author provides a chronological narrative of the composer's significant works, accomplishments, and honors. She also includes a select list of publications and first performances of Still's more significant compositions.

A13 ———. "New Cantata By Still." *New York Times*, May 26, 1940.

Report on the development of *And They Lynched Him On A Tree*. "The composer has carefully avoided the obvious and has produced a musical document which should have increasing value as a historical portrait, quite apart from any political significance that may be attributed to it at this particular time."

A14 ———. "New Chapin-Still Collaboration." *New York Times*, September 14, 1941.

Report on the development of *Plain-Chant for America*. "From a stirring musical beginning emphasizing all that has been done to achieve and maintain our democracy, through a mechanical section picturing the ruthless regimentation of imagism which is foreign to our spirit and temperament, and a recitative indicating that America is not yet faultless, to an exultant promise that 'If freedom fails, we'll fight for more freedom!' The composition is a passionate affirmation of Americanism."

A15 ———. "William Grant Still: American Composer." *Co-Art Turntable* 2 (February 1942): 7-8.

Biographical sketch of Still. "A biographer would have to be a supreme creative artist to find glamour in the daily life of this American composer, for it contains few of those delightful little tid-bits that make interesting reading. The daily routine, with few exceptions, starts with breakfast. Then, until noon, creative work. After that, mechanical work (scoring, making orchestra parts or piano scores on the music typewriter) and so on until bedtime, with only a short break for dinner in the middle of the afternoon, and an hour to work out-of-doors. Once in bed, he reads—sometimes occult and sometimes travel books—before dropping off to sleep. Generally speaking, he has very little social life, in the accepted sense of the words—not because he doesn't enjoy it, but because he enjoys work more."

A16 ———. "Outstanding Achievements of Negro Composers." *Etude* 60 (March 1942): 171, 210.

Arvey examines some of the contributions to piano music of African American composers of serious music, including Harry T. Burleigh, Melville Charlton, Florence B. Price, R. Nathaniel Dett, Samuel Coleridge-Taylor, and William Grant Still, among others. She includes *The Black Man Dances* (1934) and *Kaintuck'* (1935) among Still's works for piano.

A17 ———. "Negro Culture in Retrospect." *Negro History Bulletin* 5 (June 1942): 207-9.

This article was based upon a presentation in Los Angeles at the Norma Gould Auditorium on March 15, 1942. Still is briefly mentioned, as is his *Muted Laughter* from *Seven Traceries* and *Blues* from *Lenox Avenue*.

A18 ———. "Britain Applauds Rudolph Dunbar." *Opportunity: A Journal of Negro Life* 20 (November 1942): 330-31.

In describing Dunbar's accomplishments, Arvey discusses his work conducting the *Afro-American Symphony*.

A19 ———. "Experiment In Americanism." *Dance* 17 (August 1943): 12-13, 24, 32.

Review of the development of the American Composers' Concerts at the Eastman School of Music in Rochester. Arvey highlights the work of Thelma Biracree, Eastman's choreographer of Still's *Sahdji*.

A20 ———. "Dunbar Thrills Liberated Paris." *Boston Chronicle*, January 6, 1945.

Report on the November 19, 1944, performance of the Pasdeloup Symphony Orchestra, in Paris, France. The conductor was Rudolph Dunbar. "The house was completely sold out, the French musicians agreed unanimously that the whole performance was unique in the musical history of Paris, and the *Afro-American Symphony* by William Grant Still, which was featured on the program, drew shouts of approbation and vigorous stamps from the enthusiastic French audience. Even the men in the orchestra, which played magnificently, cheered lustily after they had finished playing the work."

A21 ———. "La Guardia's Campaign For Opera Is Cultural Advance." Los Angeles *Criterion*, July 9, 1945, sec. A, p. 1.

Article on the announcement by Mayor La Guardia that funds will be raised to produce Still's *Troubled Island* at the New York City Center.

A22 ———. "A New Leaf for the Recording Co.'s." *Miami Whip*, February 9, 1946, p. 12.

Arvey notes that the general public has a good selection of records made by African American jazz artists. However, the same cannot be said for African American composers of "serious musical compositions." As one example, a Los Angeles radio station employee found only "two recordings of the *Scherzo* from William Grant Still's *Afro-American Symphony* . . . and one recording of the same composer's *Traceries*."

A23 ———. "Letter to the Editor." *Opera, Concert and Symphony* 12 (February 1947): 3.

Reference to the death of Charles Wakefield Cadman, who died at Los Angeles on December 30, 1946. Still was an honorary pallbearer.

A24 ———. "Mechanics or Composers?" *Musical Digest* 29 (November 1947): 7, 8, 14.

Arvey provides insight into what serious composers face when they try to work in the film industry. Her remarks include a lengthy paragraph on Still, who resigned from his position in the film industry due to serious disagreements with a music director.

A25 ———. "William Grant Still Teams Up With Southerner To Produce Musical Gem." *Chicago Defender*, May 29, 1948.

Article relative to the composition *Wood Notes*. "*Wood Notes*, which the composer dedicated to Professor F. J. Lehmann of Oberlin, who recognized and helped him with his talent in the very early years of his study, came to being in this [manner]. Several years ago, Mr. [J. Mitchell] Pilcher of Alabama wrote an article for the *Etude* Music Magazine in which he especially praised Mr. Still's music, although the composer was then a stranger to him. He called Mr. Still's attention to the article and then sent him his own book of poetry, called *War and Peace*. Mr. Still was so impressed with Mr. Pilcher's poems that he selected five of them as inspiration for the orchestral suite."

A26 ———. "Still Opera Points The Way." *Music Forum and Digest* 1 (August 1949): 16-18. (Also appears in Haas, *Fusion*, 94-98; Still, *Fusion*, 26-30; and the *Voice of Saint Louis* [British West Indies], April 17, 1951, p. 1+.)

Arvey provides observations on how *Troubled Island* developed. She mentions Still's love of opera dating to when he was a boy. She also describes Still's relationship with Langston Hughes who wrote much of the libretto. How Still created the music is discussed, and the production of the opera at the City Center is addressed.

A27 ———. "David Meets Goliath. . . . Or Songwriters Want Their Loot." *Pittsburgh Courier*, January 16, 1954, Pacific Coast edition.

Report on an anti-trust suit filed against the broadcasting industry and its affiliates by a group of thirty-three composers and song writers, of which Still is included. "The thirty-three plaintiffs ask $150,000,000 damages for past injuries to themselves and their colleagues. . . . They ask that BMI (Broadcast Music, Inc., which was formed by the broadcasters to monopolize the field of music in America) be separated from the broadcasting industry as a whole and be forced to operate independently as a simple performing rights society."

A28 ———. "Letter to the Editor." *Los Angeles Evening Herald Express*, December 28, 1961.

Arvey describes some of the friendly actions exhibited by people towards Still when he was on a recent trip to Miami, Florida, and suggests that if similar acts of kindness were displayed with more regularity, there would be far fewer problems between the races.

A29 ———. "With His Roots in the Soil." *International Musician* 62 (July 1963): 20-21, 41-42. (Also appears in Haas, *Fusion*, 82-87, and Still, *Fusion*, 15-20.)

This article serves as a very good general overview of Still and his music.

A30 ———. "Afro-American Music Memo." *Music Journal* 27 (November 1969): 36, 68.

Arvey reports on the influence that African American music, including that of Still, had on white composers, such as George Gershwin. "Gershwin felt that he was not 'borrowing' any musical material exactly. He was listening and absorbing, then transferring the Negro idiom to his own musical speech. Yet we might assume that sometimes there actually was unconscious borrowing, not only in the *I Got Rhythm* episode, but in others. How else can the similarity of the opening notes of his *Summertime* (in *Porgy and Bess*) to the opening notes of the *St. Louis Blues* be explained?"

A31 ———. "Symphonies In Black," *Music Journal* 32 (April 1974): 28-29, 32-36.

Arvey provides insight into the contributions and achievements associated with African American composers and serious music, including the Chevalier de St. Georges, George Augustus Polgreen Bridgetower, Samuel Coleridge-Taylor, William Grant Still, and others.

A32 ———. "Memo for Musicologists." In Haas, *Fusion*, 88-93, and Still, *Fusion*, 21-25.

Composers such as Gershwin and Dvořák benefitted by listening to and studying African American works and performances and, thereby, greatly enhanced their own compositions.

A33 ———. "Negro Dance and its Influence on Negro Music." In de Lerma's *Black Music in Our Culture*, 79-92.

Based upon a presentation at Indiana University's "Seminar on Black Music in College and University Curricula," June 18-21, 1969. Her treatment of the subject includes references to Still's four ballets: *Sahdji*, *La Guiablesse*, *Miss Sally's Party*, and *Lenox Avenue*.

A34 ———. *In One Lifetime*. Fayetteville, Arkansas: University of Arkansas Press, 1984. With "An Afterthought" by Judith Anne Still.

Verna Arvey's version of Still's life as only she could tell it. The appendices, including "A Glossary of Terms," "Who's Who in the Life of William Grant Still," "The Works of William Grant Still," and "Orchestras and Conductors Performing the Works of William Grant Still," are helpful. The second printing includes an index prepared by Judith Anne Still.

GENERAL BIBLIOGRAPHY

The General Bibliography is divided into two sections. Section One (entries **B1** through **B123**) contains information from bibliographies, catalogs, dictionaries, encyclopedias, guides, indexes, and other general reference works that direct researchers to other sources. Section Two (entries **B124** through **B450**) includes references to monographs, journals, newspaper and magazine articles, newsletters, and theses and dissertations that relate to Still.

A few articles appear in more than one publication, particularly in Jon Michael Spencer's "The William Grant Still Reader: Essays on American Music," a special issue of *Black Sacred Music: A Journal of Theomusicology* (Duke University Press, 1992), and in the second edition of *William Grant Still and the Fusion of Cultures in American Music,* edited by Judith Anne Still, Celeste Anne Headlee, and Lisa M. Headlee-Huffman (Flagstaff: The Master-Player Library, 1995). These will be cited as "Spencer, 'Reader'" and as "Still, *Fusion.*"

Section One

B1   *ASCAP Biographical Dictionary.* 4th ed. Compiled for ASCAP by Jaques Cattell Press. New York: R.R. Bowker Co., 1980: 487-88.

B2   *ASCAP Symphonic Catalogue.* 3d ed. New York: R.R. Bowker, 1977: 442-43.
Includes a listing, with instrumentation, of fifty-six compositions by Still representing most of his orchestral works.

B3   Abajian, James, comp. *Blacks and Their Contributions to the American West; A Bibliography and Union List of Library Holdings Through 1970.* Boston: G.K. Hall and Co., 1974.
Includes references to books, articles, letters, and compositions.

B4   Adkins, Cecil, and Alis Dickinson. *Doctoral Dissertations in Musicology.* 7th North American Edition/2d International Edition. Philadelphia: American Musicological Society and International Musicological Society, 1984.
Identifies dissertations on Still by Ralph Ricardo Simpson, Martha Ellen Blanding Spence, and Jon Michael Spencer.

B5   ———. *International Index of Doctoral Dissertations and Musicological Works in Progress.* Philadelphia: American Musicological Society and International Musicological Society, 1977.

Identifies dissertations on Still by Ralph Ricardo Simpson and Martha Ellen Blanding Spence.

B6 Anderson, E. Ruth, comp. *Contemporary American Composers: A Biographical Dictionary*. 2d ed. Boston: G.K. Hall and Co., 1982: 497.

B7 Arnold, Ben. *Music and War: A Research and Information Guide*. Garland Reference Library of the Humanities; Vol. 1581. Music Research and Information Guides; Vol. 17. New York: Garland Publishing, Inc. 1993.

The music included in this volume deals specifically with art compositions related to war, with an emphasis on Western art music. The title for each work, the date and place of its premiere performance, and a short description are provided for each entry. *In Memoriam: The Colored Soldiers Who Died for Democracy* is described as: "One of his [Still's] most popular works written to support the war effort, this B-flat minor lament is full of repeated notes, tempo fluctuations, and muted brass. It remains in 4/4 throughout and climaxes at the end with a *ffff* outburst on a B-flat minor chord (p. 204)."

B8 Arnold, Denis, ed. *The New Oxford Companion to Music*. Vol. 2. Oxford: Oxford University Press, 1983: 1749-50.

Contributor Mark Tucker states: "Still's music tends towards a conservative, tonal style; it is often attractive, well-constructed, lyrical, and readily accessible. . . . Still's work in art music helped break new ground for other Black composers, but his contribution to American musical life is better gauged by considering his sustained involvement in a wide range of musical styles and contexts."

B9 Arnowsky, S. *Performing Times of Orchestral Works*. London: Ernest Benn Ltd., 1959: 689.

Lists *Afro-American Symphony*, *Dismal Swamp*, and *La Guiablesse* and includes medium and duration for each work.

B10 Bagar, Robert, and Louis Biancolli. *The Concert Companion: A Comprehensive Guide to Symphonic Music*. New York: Whittlesey House, 1947.

This book is a compendium of program notes covering the period 1940-1946. The notes for Still's music (pp. 682-86) pertain to *And They Lynched Him on a Tree*, *Plain-Chant for America*, *Old California*, *Poem for Orchestra*, and *In Memoriam: The Colored Soldiers Who Died for Democracy*. The authors mistakenly state that *And They Lynched Him on a Tree* received its first performance on June 24, 1940. Because of rain, the premiere was actually on June 25.

B11 *Baker's Biographical Dictionary of Musicians*. 8th ed. Revised by Nicolas Slonimsky. New York: Schirmer Books, 1992: 1787-88.

B12 Barlow, Harold, and Sam Morgenstern. *A Dictionary of Musical Themes*. New York: Crown Publishers, 1948: 453-54.

Includes movements and themes for the *Afro-American Symphony*.

B13 Berry, Lemuel. *Biographical Dictionary of Black Musicians and Music Educators*. Vol. 1. Guthrie, Okla.: Midwest Publishing Co., in association with Educational Book Publishers, 1978: 180-81.

B14 *Bio-Bibliographical Index of Musicians In The United States of America Since Colonial Times*. Prepared by the District of Columbia Historical Records Survey, Work Projects Administration. Washington, D.C.: Pan American Union, 1941: 361.

B15 Block, Maxine, ed. *Current Biography: Who's News and Why*. New York: H.W. Wilson Co., 1941: 829-30.

B16 Bohle, Bruce, ed. *The International Cyclopedia of Music And Musicians.* New York: Dodd, Mead and Company, 1975: 2154.

B17 Borroff, Edith. *American Operas: A Checklist.* J. Bunker Clark, ed. Warren, Mich.: Harmonie Park Press, 1992: 288-89.

This bibliography includes the date of the work, its length, the identity of the librettist, and the type of work or type of subject matter when not suggested by the title. The date and place of premieres are also included. Still's operas are included.

B18 Brown, Rae Linda. *Music, Printed and Manuscript, in the James Weldon Johnson Memorial Collections of Arts and Letters: An Annotated Catalog.* Critical studies on Black life and culture, vol. 23; Garland reference library of the humanities, vol. 277. New York: Garland Publishing, Inc., 1982: 26.

Describes Still's scores for *Kaintuck'* and *Sahdji.*

B19 Bull, Storm. *Index to Biographies of Contemporary Composers.* Vol. 3. Metuchen, N.J.: Scarecrow Press, Inc., 1987: 735.

B20 Burkett, Randall K., Nancy Hall Burkett, and Henry Louis Gates, Jr., editors. *Black Biography 1790-1950.* 3 vols. Alexandria: Chadwyck-Healey, 1991.

Locating biographical information on African Americans can be exceedingly difficult. This reference tool, however, makes the task easier by serving as an index to biographical sources for nearly 31,000 individuals. The entry for Still lists his date of birth as May 11, 1894 or 1895 (it was 1895); his place of birth as Woodville, Mississippi; his occupation as a performing artist; and his religion as Presbyterian. The following biographical sources are listed for Still: Benjamin G. Brawley, *The Negro Genius* (New York: Dodd, Mead & Co., 1937): 303; Maud Cuney-Hare, *Negro Musicians and Their Music* (Washington: Associated Publishers, Inc., 1936): 333; Karl E. Downs, *Meet the Negro* (Pasadena: Login Press, 1943): 197; Edwin R. Embree, *13 Against the Odds* (New York: Viking Press, 1944): 197; Maude Wanzer Layne, *The Negro's Contribution to Music* (Mathews Printing & Lithographing Co., 1942): 75; Florence Murray, *The Negro Handbook* (New York: Wendell Malliet and Co., 1942): 218; Jessie Parkhurst Guzman, ed., *Negro Year Book; A Review of Events Affecting Negro Life, 1941-1946* (Tuskegee: Department of Records and Research, Tuskegee Institute, 1947): 430; Ben Richardson, *Great American Negroes* (New York: Thomas Y. Crowell Co., 1945): 50; J.A. Rogers, *World's Great Men of Color* (New York: J.A. Rogers, Futuro Press, 1947): 714; Harold W. Taylor, *One Tenth of a Nation* (Long Island, New York; Progressive Book Shop, 1946): 24; *Who's Who in Colored America, 1927* (New York: Who's Who in Colored America Corp., 1927): 350; *Who's Who in Colored America, 1930-1931-1932* (Brooklyn, New York; Thomas Yenser, 1933): 403; *Who's Who in Colored America, 1933-1934-1935-1936-1937* (Brooklyn, New York; Thomas Yenser, 1937): 492; *Who's Who in Colored America, 1938-1939-1940* (Brooklyn, New York; Thomas Yenser, 1940): 490; *Who's Who in Colored America, 1941 to 1944* (Brooklyn, New York: Thomas Yenser, 1944): 491; *Who's Who in Colored America, Supplement, 1950* (Yonkers-on-Hudson, New York: Christian E. Burckel & Assoc., 1950): 489.

B21 Butterworth, Neil. *A Dictionary of American Composers.* Garland Reference Library of the Humanities, vol. 296. New York: Garland Publishing, Inc., 1984: 446-47.

B22 *Catalog of the American Music Center Library.* Vol. 3. Music for Orchestra, Band and Large Ensemble. New York: American Music Center, 1982: 159-60.

Scores for Still's *Afro-American Symphony*, *Bells*, *Darker America*, and *Dismal Swamp* are listed.

B23 Claghorn, Charles Eugene. *Biographical Dictionary of American Music*. West Nyack, N.Y.: Parker Publishing Company, Inc., 1973: 421.

B24 Cummings, David. *The New Everyman Dictionary of Music*. Originally compiled by Eric Blom. New York: Weidenfeld and Nicolson, 1989: 729-30.

This provides a very brief biographical sketch and identifies some of Still's compositions, including *Blue Steel*, *La Guiablesse*, *Sahdji*, *Lenox Avenue*, *Afro-American Symphony*, and *Africa*, among others.

B25 Daniels, David. *Orchestral Music: A Handbook*. 2d ed. Metuchen, N.J.: Scarecrow Press, 1982: 281.

Lists the *Afro-American Symphony*, *Darker America*, and *Festive Overture* and provides instrumentation, duration, and source of performance materials.

B26 Davis, John P., ed. *The American Negro Reference Book*. Englewood Cliffs, N.J.: Prentice-Hall, Inc., 1966: 749+.

B27 de Lerma, Dominique-René. "A Concordance of Black-Music Entries in Five Encyclopedias." *Black Perspective in Music* 11 (Fall 1983): 190-209.

Includes entries in *Baker's Biographical Dictionary of Musicians*, 6th ed., revised by Nicolas Slonimsky, New York: Schirmer Books, 1978; *Musicians Since 1900: Performers in Concert and Opera*, compiled and edited by David Ewen, New York: H.W. Wilson, 1978; *The New Grove Dictionary of Music and Musicians*, edited by Stanley Sadie, London: Macmillan Publishers, 1980; *Die Musik in Geschichte und Gegenwart: Allgemeine Enzyklopädie der Musik*, edited by Friedrich and Ruth Blume, Kassel: Bärenreiter, 1949-1979; and *Who's Who in Opera*, compiled by Maria Rich, New York: Arno Press, 1976. Still's biography and a select list of his compositions are found in MGG, vol. 9, p. 1330-31 (written by Nicolas Slonimsky); in *Baker's*, p. 1666-67; and in Grove's, vol. 18, p. 145-46 (written by Eileen Southern).

B28 ———. *A Discography of Concert Music by Black Composers*. Afro-American Music Opportunities Association Resource Papers; Monographic Series, no. 1. Minneapolis: AAMOA Press, 1973.

B29 ———. *Bibliography of Black Music*. 4 vols. The Greenwood Encyclopedia of Black Music. Westport, Conn.: Greenwood Press, 1981-84.

These volumes provide a wealth of information. Numerous articles by or about Still are included. However, the omission of an effective index is a serious drawback.

B30 *Dictionary Catalog of the Schomburg Collection of Negro Literature and History*. New York Public Library. Volume 8, "S." Boston: G.K. Hall and Co., 1962.

Includes sixteen entries for articles, books, or published music by Still, none of which appears to be unique.

B31 Eagon, Angelo. *Catalog of Published Concert Music by American Composers*. 2nd supp. to 2nd ed. Metuchen, N.J.: Scarecrow Press, 1974.

Still's scores for *Christmas in the Western World* and the *Afro-American Symphony* are included.

B32 *Edwin A. Fleisher Collection of Orchestral Music in the Free Library of Philadelphia, The: A Descriptive Catalogue*. Vol. 2. Philadelphia: Free Library of Philadelphia, 1945.

Lists, with instrumentation, Still's *Afro-American Symphony*; *Dismal*

Swamp; *Ebon Chronicle*; *From the Journal of a Wanderer*; *Three Dances* (from *La Guiablesse*); *Kaintuck'*; and *From the Black Belt*.

B33 *Edwin A. Fleisher Music Collection in the Free Library of Philadelphia, The.* Philadelphia: Edward Stern & Co., Inc., 1933.
Lists, with instrumentation, Still's *Darker America*.

B34 Embree, Edwin R. *American Negroes: A Handbook*. New York: John Day Co., 1942.
The author states that "William Grant Still ranks with the best of modern composers (p. 63)."

B35 *Encyclopaedia Britannica*. Vol. 21. Chicago: Encyclopaedia Britannica, 1970: 246.
Brief sketch of Still's life by David Nicholas Fallows.

B36 *Encyclopedia Americana: International Edition*. Vol. 25. Danbury, Conn.: Grolier Inc., 1982: 714.

B37 Ewen, David. *American Composers: A Biographical Dictionary*. New York: G.P. Putman's Sons, 1982: 625-28.
Includes a general article on Still. Appended are a list of works and a very brief bibliography.

B38 ———, comp. and ed. *American Composers Today*. New York: H.W. Wilson Company, 1949: 232-34.

B39 ———, comp. and ed. *Composers of Today*. New York: H.W. Wilson Company, 1934: 258-59.

B40 ———, comp. and ed. *Composers Since 1900: A Biographical And Critical Guide*. New York: H.W. Wilson Company, 1969: 545-47.

B41 ———. *Composers Since 1900: A Biographical and Critical Guide. First Supplement*. New York: H.W. Wilson Company, 1981: 274-75.

B42 ———. *Encyclopedia of Concert Music*. New York: Hill and Wang, 1959: 450.

B43 ———. *New Complete Book of the American Musical Theater*. New York: Holt, Rinehart and Winston, 1970: 480.
The author mentions that Still, a member of the pit orchestra for *Shuffle Along*, later achieved fame as a serious composer.

B44 *Facts on File*. 38 (December 31, 1978): 1032. (obit.)

B45 Farish, Margaret K., ed. *Orchestral Music in Print*. Philadelphia: Musicdata, Inc., 1979: 778.
Lists, with instrumentation and duration, nineteen compositions by Still.

B46 Friedberg, Ruth C. *American Art Song and American Poetry. Volume 1. America Comes of Age*. Metuchen, N.J.: Scarecrow Press, 1981.
The author's chapter "Settings by Five 'Americanists'" includes information on Earnest Bacon, Aaron Copland, Roy Harris, Douglas Moore, and Still, whose *Winter's Approach, Breath of a Rose,* and *Songs of Separation* are treated (pp. 100-09).

B47 Gray, John, comp. *Blacks in Classical Music: A Bibliographical Guide to Composers, Performers, and Ensembles*. Music Reference Collection, no. 15. Westport, Conn.: Greenwood Press, 1988: 59-64.
This volume lists four monographs on Still, ten books with sections devoted to the composer, fifteen biographical directories that include Still, five dissertations and forty-nine magazine or newspaper articles on him, and twenty-one references to his obituary.

B48 Gray, Michael, comp. *Classical Music Discographies, 1976-1988: A Bibliography*. Discographies, No. 34. Westport, Conn.: 1989.
   This bibliography is the first cumulative supplement in a series that originated with *Bibliography of Discographies. Volume 1 Classical Music, 1925-1975*, published in 1977. This supplement identifies the discography in Verna Arvey's *In One Lifetime*, published by the University of Arkansas Press, 1984.

B49 Gray, Michael H., and Gerald D. Gibson. *Bibliography of Discographies. Volume 1: Classical Music, 1925-1975*. New York: R.R. Bowker Co., 1977.
   Identifies a discography in *William Grant Still and the Fusion of Cultures in American Music*, by Robert Bartlett Haas, ed., published in 1972.

B50 *Grove's Dictionary of Music*. 5th ed. Edited by Eric Blom. Vol. 8. New York: St. Martin's Press, 1955: 89.
   Contributor Nathan Broder provides a brief sketch of Still's life, no bibliography, but, at least, a listing of Still's "outstanding" works.

B51 Guzman, Jessie Parkhurst, ed. *The Negro Year Book: A Review of Events Affecting Negro Life, 1952*. New York: Wm. H. Wise & Co., Inc., 1952: 62.

B52 Hamilton, David, ed. *The Metropolitan Opera Encyclopedia*. New York: Metropolitan Opera Guild, 1987: 350.

B53 Haywood, Charles. *A Bibliography of North American Folklore and Folksong*. New York: Greenberg, 1951: 391, 461.
   Includes *Old California* and *Twelve Negro Spirituals*.

B54 Heintze, James R. *American Music Studies: A Classified Bibliography of Master's Theses*. Bibliographies in American Music, no. 8. Detroit: Information Coordinators, Inc., 1984: 52.
   Lists theses on Still by Mary Lou Simpson and Paul Harold Slattery.

B55 Hinson, Maurice. *Music for Piano and Orchestra: An Annotated Guide*. Bloomington and Indianapolis: Indiana University Press, 1993.
   Kaintuck' and *Dismal Swamp* are included. Of the former the author states: "An Impressionistic tone poem, contrasting sections, banjo figuration in piano part, cadenza, *pp* ending." And of the latter: "A colorful, somewhat Impressionistic tone poem. Piano partakes of the ensemble but also has some solo moments. Deserves hearing."

B56 ———. *The Piano in Chamber Ensemble: An Annotated Guide*. Bloomington: Indiana University Press, 1978: 229.
   Lists Still's *Incantation and Dance*.

B57 Holden, Amanda, ed., with Nicholas Kenyon and Stephen Walsh. *The Viking Opera Guide*. London: Penguin Group, 1993: 1011.
   The two-paragraph narrative on Still notes that "uncomplicated singable melodies" are characteristic of his operatic style. It also identifies his nine operas.

B58 Horne, Aaron, comp. *Keyboard Music of Black Composers: A Bibliography*. Music Reference Collection, No. 37. Westport, Conn.: Greenwood Press, 1992: 182-84.
   The author provides a biographical sketch of Still, a listing of twenty-four works, and seven sources for further reading.

B59 ———. *String Music of Black Composers: A Bibliography*. Music Reference Collection, No. 33. Westport, Conn.: Greenwood Press, 1991: 169-73.
   The entry for Still was based upon information provided by Verna Arvey. Fifty-three works are listed, excluding many identified in the biographical sketch.

B60 Howe, Mentor A., and Roscoe E. Lewis, comps. *A Classified Catalogue of the Negro Collection in the Collis P. Huntington Library, Hampton Institute.* St. Clair Shores, Mich.: Scholarly Press, Inc., 1971 (originally published by the Hampton Institute, 1940).
Identifies Still's *Twelve Negro Spirituals*.

B61 Hughes, Rupert, comp. *The Biographical Dictionary of Musicians*. Revised and edited by Deems Taylor and Russell Kerr. New York: Blue Ribbon Books, Inc., 1940: 419.

B62 *The Institute of American Music of the University of Rochester: American Composer's Concerts and Festivals of American Music, 1925-1971: Cumulative Report.* Rochester: University of Rochester, 1972.
As director of the Eastman School of Music from 1924 to 1964, Howard Hanson featured works by a great many young American composers, including Still, who had ten of his compositions premiered at the Eastman School.

B63 *Kaiser Index to Black Resources, 1948-1986.* 5 vols. Brooklyn, N.Y.: Carlson Publishing, Inc., 1992.
The *Kaiser Index* is a bibliographical guide to periodical literature, published articles, and ephemera located at the Schomburg Center for Research in Black Culture of the New York Public Library. Volume four (p. 417) includes forty citations under Still's name.

B64 Kennedy, Michael. *The Concise Oxford Dictionary of Music*. 3d ed. New York: Oxford University Press, 1985: 693.

B65 ———. *The Oxford Dictionary of Music*. 3d ed. London: Oxford University Press, 1980: 622.

B66 Kornick, Rebecca Hodell. *Recent American Opera: A Production Guide*. New York: Columbia University Press, 1991.
This guide provides information on 213 American opera/music theatre works. Each work is described in a format that includes the following: genre classification; number of acts; scenes; number of sets; length of work in minutes; style and structure of music; author and source of libretto; the commission, if any; the company, place, and date of the premiere; plot; production requirements; and short reviews. *A Bayou Legend, Highway 1, U.S.A.,* and *Minette Fontaine* are included.

B67 Koshgarian, Richard. *American Orchestral Music: A Performance Catalog*. Metuchen, N.J.: Scarecrow Press, 1992: 491-93.
This volume includes information on thirty-one Still compositions, including their title, date of composition, duration, instrumentation, and where performance materials are published.

B68 Krummel, D.W., Jean Geil, Doris J. Dyen, and Deane L. Root. *Resources of American Music History: A Directory of Source Materials from Colonial Times to World War II*. Music in American Life. Urbana: University of Illinois Press, 1981.
Institutions cited as having research materials associated with Still include the University of Arkansas; California State University, Long Beach; Stanford University; Yale University; Howard University; Library of Congress; University of Michigan; Jackson State University; University of Rochester, The Eastman School of Music; Syracuse University; Converse College; Moldenhauer Archives, Spokane, Washington; and the University of Wyoming.

B69 Low, W. Augustus, ed. *Encyclopedia of Black America*. New York: McGraw-Hill, Inc., 1981: 809.

This brief sketch of Still provides background on his education. Eleven of his compositions are listed.

B70 Lowery, Charles D., and John F. Marszalek, eds. *Encyclopedia of African-American Civil Rights: From Emancipation to the Present*. Westport, Conn.: Greenwood Press, 1992: 502.

Contributor Charles D. Lowery provides a basic biographical sketch of Still. Four references are provided for further reading.

B71 Machlis, Joseph. *Introduction To Contemporary Music*. New York: W.W. Norton, 1961: 491.

"William Grant Still . . . is a dedicated proponent of Negro nationalism. He bases his music on the folk songs of his people, expressing their sorrows and aspirations. His most fully realized works are the *Afro-American Symphony* (1931); the cantata *And They Lynched Him on a Tree* (1940); and *In Memoriam: The Colored Soldiers Who Died for Democracy* (1943)."

B72 Mattfeld, Julius. *A Handbook of American Operatic Premieres, 1731-1962*. Detroit Studies in Music Bibliography, No. 5. Detroit: Information Service, Inc., 1963: 105.

Identifies the premiere of *Troubled Island* at the New York City Center, March 31, 1949.

B73 Matthews, Geraldine O., comp. *Black American Writers, 1773-1949: A Bibliography and Union List*. Boston: G.K. Hall & Co., 1975: 122.

In the Fine Arts chapter, this volume identifies three Still compositions, from the many that were published, namely, *Plain-Chant for America*, *Seven Traceries*, and *Twelve Negro Spirituals*.

B74 McPherson, James M., Laurence B. Holland, James M. Banner, Jr., Nancy J. Weiss, Michael D. Bell. *Blacks in America: Bibliographical Essays*. Garden City, N.Y.: Doubleday and Co., Inc., 1971: 291-92.

B75 Moore, Elizabeth C. *An Almanac for Music-Lovers*. New York: Henry Holt and Co., 1940: 128.

The primary purpose of this volume is to supply what the author states as: "interesting anniversary dates in music." Thus, the birth of Still is included under those entries for May 11.

B76 Mueller, Kate Hevner. *Twenty-Seven Major American Symphony Orchestras: A History and Analysis of their Repertoires, Seasons 1942-43 through 1969-70*. Bloomington: Indiana University Studies, 1973: 326-27.

This volume includes information on thirteen Still compositions, including title, duration, year of performance, and orchestra which performed the piece. The author calculates that fifteen major orchestras performed Still compositions up to 1970.

B77 Murray, Florence, comp. and ed. *The Negro Handbook*. 1st ed. New York: Wendell Malliet and Co., 1942: 218, 251.

B78 *National Union Catalog of Manuscript Collections, 1959-1961*. Ann Arbor, Mich.: J.W. Edwards, Inc., 1962.

Based upon reports from libraries, archives, and other repositories that hold manuscripts, the National Union Catalog of Manuscript Collections (NUCMC) "represents another step toward achieving bibliographical control over the vast manuscript resources of American repositories. It contains reproductions of cards for nearly 7,300 manuscript collections, issued by the Library of Congress during 1959, 1960, and 1961, thus making the accumulated information readily available to scholars and repositories everywhere (p. iii)." Two collections that contain material on Still are identified in this volume, namely, the Julius Rosenwald Fund Archives (NUCMC entry number MS 61-1520) and the George Gershwin Memorial Collection of Music and Music Literature (MS 61-3149), both located in the library at Fisk University, Nashville, Tennessee.

B79 ———, *1970*. Washington: Library of Congress, [1972].

The papers of Nicolas Slonimsky (MS 70-2026), conductor, composer, and musicologist, located at the Library of Congress, include material by or about Still.

B80 ———, *1972*. Washington: Library of Congress, 1974.

The papers of the author and teacher Countee Cullen (MS 72-853), located at the Amistad Research Center, New Orleans, Louisiana, include correspondence of Grace and William Grant Still.

B81 ———, *1977*. Washington: Library of Congress, 1977.

The musical scores of William Grant Still (MS 77-1961) are located at the University of Arkansas Libraries, Fayetteville.

B82 ———, *1981*. Washington: Library of Congress, 1982.

The papers of music critic, pianist, and teacher Irving Schwerké (MS 81-99) and those of the musician William Treat Upton (MS 81-100), both located at the Library of Congress, contain correspondence associated with William Grant Still.

B83 *New Encyclopaedia Britannica: Micropaedia, The.* Vol. 11. Robert McHenry, Editor in Chief. Chicago: Encyclopaedia Britannica, Inc., 1993: 270.

B84 *New Grove Dictionary of American Music, The.* (H. Wiley Hitchcock and Stanley Sadie, eds.) Vol. 4, London: Macmillan Press Limited, 1986: 311-12.

The entry on Still, contributed by Eileen Southern, is essentially the same as that which appears in *The New Grove Dictionary of Music and Musicians*, except for minor revisions. The bibliography identifies nine sources.

B85 *New Grove Dictionary of Music and Musicians, The.* (Stanley Sadie, ed.) Vol. 18. London: Macmillan Publishers Limited, 1980: 145-46.

Contributor Eileen Southern provides an abbreviated sketch of Still's life and work. The list of works is arranged in three categories: orchestral, vocal, and instrumental. The bibliography identifies four sources.

B86 *New Grove Dictionary of Opera, The.* (Stanley Sadie, ed.) Vol. 4. London: Macmillan Press Limited, 1992: 544.

Contributor Thomas Warburton includes information on *Blue Steel*, *Troubled Island*, *A Bayou Legend*, *Highway 1, U.S.A.*, *Costaso*, *Mota*, *The Pillar*, and *Minette Fontaine*. The narrative concludes as follows: "All the operas reveal Still's gift of melody couched in a tonal, mildly dissonant harmonic idiom, but they avoid direct quotation of folk material."

B87 Newman, Debra L., comp. *Black History: A Guide to Civilian Records in the National Archives*. Washington: National Archives Trust Fund Board, 1984.

In the Records of the Work Projects Administration (Record Group 69), as part of the records of the WPA Division of Information, a folder of correspondence under Still's name exists among the general correspondence of the Radio Section for 1936 to 1942. (p. 148).

B88 Newman, Richard, comp. *Black Access: A Bibliography of Afro-American Bibliographies*. Westport, Conn.: Greenwood Press, 1984: 181.

It identifies Eileen Southern's article on Still's major works, found in the May 1975 issue of *The Black Perspective in Music*.

B89 Oja, Carol J., ed. *American Music Recordings: A Discography of 20th-Century U.S. Composers.* Booklyn, N.Y.: Institute for Studies in American Music, 1982.

This discography identifies thirty-five recordings that include Still compositions.

B90 Page, James A., comp. *Selected Black American Authors: An Illustrated Bio-Bibliography.* A Reference Publication in Black Studies. Dorothy Porter, ed. Boston: G.K. Hall and Co., 1977.

The entry (pp. 257-58) for Still includes very brief biographical information, a short list of writings, works, honors, and awards, and quoted information from the *Negro Almanac.*

B91 Parsons, Charles H. *Opera Composers and Their Works.* Vol. 4 of the Mellen Opera Reference Index. Lewiston, N.Y.: Edwin Mellen Press, 1986: 1736.

This source provides brief backgrounds on *Blue Steel, A Bayou Legend, A Southern Interlude, Troubled Island, Mota, The Pillar, Minette Fontaine, The Peaceful Land,* and *Highway 1, U.S.A.*

B92 Pebworth, James R., comp. *A Directory of 132 Arkansas Composers.* Fayetteville, Ark.: University of Arkansas Library, 1979: 67-69.

After his biographical sketch, the author provides a list of citations for further reading and a selected list of compositions by Still arranged by ballets, chamber music, choral music, operas, and orchestral music.

B93 Peterson, Bernard L., Jr. *A Century of Musicals in Black and White: An Encyclopedia of Musical Stage Works By, About, or Involving African Americans.* Westport, Conn.: Greenwood Press, 1993.

A Bayou Legend, Blue Steel, Sahdji, and *Troubled Island* are included. Also, Still is mentioned in *Shuffle Along* relative to its orchestration.

B94 Phemister, William. *American Piano Concertos: A Bibliography.* Bibliographies in American Music. No. 9. Detroit: Information Coordinators, Inc., 1985: 270-71.

Kaintuck' is included, with an early review of its performance by the Rochester Philharmonic Orchestra in 1936, with Harry Watts at the piano.

B95 Ploski, Harry A., and Roscoe C. Brown, comps. and eds. *The Negro Almanac.* 1st ed. New York: Bellwether Publishing Company, Inc., 1967: 727-28.

A biographical sketch of Still is included in the chapter "Famous Negro Personalities." *Darker America, Afro-American Symphony, Symphony No. 2 in G Minor,* and *Troubled Island* are identified.

B96 Porter, Dorothy B., comp. *The Negro in the United States: A Selected Bibliography.* Washington, D.C.: Library of Congress, 1970: 22.

Identifies Edwin R. Embree's *13 Against the Odds,* which includes a chapter on Still.

B97 Randel, Don Michael, comp. *Harvard Concise Dictionary of Music.* Cambridge: Belknap Press of Harvard University Press, 1978: 483.

B98 Rehrig, William H. *The Heritage Encyclopedia of Band Music.* Vol. 2. Edited by Paul E. Bierley. Westerville, OH: Integrity Press, 1991: 727.

After a short biographical sketch, this volume lists Still's *Folk Suite, From the Delta, Little Red Schoolhouse,* and *To You, America!*

B99 Robinson, Wilhelmena S. *Historical Negro Biographies.* International Library of Negro Life and History. New York: Publishers Co., Inc., [1968]: 250-51.

B100 Rosenthal, Harold, and John Warrack. *Concise Oxford Dictionary of Opera.* London: Oxford University Press, 1964: 383.

This volume identifies Still's date and place of birth, and includes one sentence as follows: "His four operas have met with success in U.S.A., his *Troubled Island* being given by the N.Y. City Opera in 1949."

B101 Ross, Anne, ed. *The Opera Directory*. New York: Sterling Publishing Co., Inc., 1961: 315.

B102 Scholes, Percy A. *The Oxford Companion To Music*. 10th ed. London: Oxford University Press, 1956: 983.

B103 Skowronski, JoAnn. *Black Music In America: A Bibliography*. Metuchen, N.J.: Scarecrow Press, 1981: 503-08.

Ninety-nine entries, arranged in chronological order by date of publication, are listed for Still. They include books, magazine articles, music journals, and dissertations.

B104 Slonimsky, Nicolas. *Music Since 1900*. 4th ed. New York: Charles Scribner's Sons, 1971.

Eleven of Still's works are identified in this volume, providing the reader with information relative to their premiere performances. The compositions are: *Afro-American Symphony*; *And They Lynched Him on a Tree*; *Darker America*; *From the Black Belt*; *La Guiablesse*; *Highway 1, U.S.A.*; *In Memoriam: The Colored Soldiers Who Died for Democracy*; *Lenox Avenue*; *Poem for Orchestra*; *Sahdji*; and *Troubled Island*.

B105 ———. *Supplement to Music Since 1900*. New York: Charles Scribner's Sons, 1986.

Five of Still's works are identified, and his death is noted. The compositions are: *A Bayou Legend; Minette Fontaine; Symphony No. 2 in G-Minor; Symphony No. 4, "Autochthonous;"* and *Symphony No. 5, "Western Hemisphere."*

B106 Smith, Dwight L., ed. *Afro-American History: A Bibliography*. Clio Bibliography Series. Santa Barbara, Calif.: ABC-CLIO, Inc., 1974: 63.

Identifies Still's article "My Arkansas Boyhood," published in the *Arkansas Historical Quarterly*.

B107 Smythe, Mabel M., ed. *The Black American Reference Book*. Englewood Cliffs, N.J.: Prentice-Hall, Inc., 1976: 696, 820.

B108 Southern, Eileen. *Biographical Dictionary of Afro-American And African Musicians*. The Greenwood Encyclopedia of Black Music. Westport, Conn.: Greenwood Press, 1982: 359-61.

Of all of the biographical sketches that appear on Still, this is certainly among the better ones, especially from the standpoint of his professional career as a composer and arranger.

B109 Spencer, Jon Michael. *As The Black School Sings: Black Music Collections at Black Universities and Colleges with a Union List of Book Holdings*. Music Reference Collection, No. 13. Westport, Conn.: Greenwood Press, 1987.

Spencer's volume enables researchers to locate articles, clippings, interviews, photographs, programs, recordings, and works by or about Still that are found at predominantly African American colleges and universities. Jackson State University and Tuskegee Institute each have a William Grant Still Collection, the Black Music Archive at North Carolina Central University includes facsimilies of thirteen compositions by Still, and Fisk University holds an oral history interview of Still. These are just a few examples from Spencer's valuable reference tool.

B110 Spradling, Mary Mace, ed. *In Black And White: A Guide to Magazine Articles,*

Newspaper Articles, and Books Concerning More than 15,000 Black Individuals and Groups. 3d ed. Vol. 2. Detroit: Gale Research Co., 1980: 921-22.

B111 Stevenson, Rosemary M., comp. *Index to Afro-American Reference Resources.* Bibliographies and Indexes in Afro-American and African Studies, No. 20. Westport, Conn.: Greenwood Press, 1988: 236.

Cites Skowronski's *Black Music in America: A Bibliography.*

B112 Toppin, Edgar A. *A Biographical History of Blacks In America Since 1528.* New York: David McKay Co., Inc., 1971: 415-18.

B113 Turner, Patricia. *Dictionary of Afro-American Performers.* New York: Garland Press, 1990: 355-65.

This volume includes a biographical sketch of Still, a bibliography of selected publications and works, selected references to obituaries, and a brief discography that identifies some of the early recordings of Still's works and arrangements.

B114 Warrack, John, and Ewan West. *The Oxford Dictionary of Opera.* Oxford: Oxford University Press, 1992: 679.

This source provides a very brief entry for Still and only lists *A Bayou Legend*, *Troubled Island*, and *Highway 1, U.S.A.*

B115 Wenk, Arthur, comp. *Analyses of Nineteenth- and Twentieth-Century Music: 1940-1985.* MLA Index and Bibliography Series, No. 25. Boston: Music Library Association, 1987: 274.

Dissertations by Ralph Ricardo Simpson and Martha Ellen Blanding Spence are the only citations pertaining to Still.

B116 ———. *Analyses of Twentieth-Century Music, 1940-1970.* MLA Index and Bibliography Series, No. 13. Ann Arbor: Music Library Association, 1975:69.

Lists Ralph Ricardo Simpson's dissertation on Still.

B117 Westrup, J.A., and F. Ll. Harrison. *The New College Encyclopedia of Music.* Revised by Conrad Wilson. New York: W.W. Norton and Co., Inc., 1976: 520.

Identifies Still as "the world's first Negro symphonist. . . . His music, much of which has a distinctive Negro stamp, includes . . . operas, of which *Troubled Island* . . . is perhaps the most important."

B118 White, Evelyn Davidson, comp. *Choral Music by Afro-American Composers: A Selected Bibliography.* Metuchen, N.J.: Scarecrow Press, 1981.

Includes *And They Lynched Him on a Tree*; *The Blind Man*; *Christmas in the Western World*; *Ev'ry Time I Feel the Spirit*; *Hard Trials* and *Lord, I Looked Down the Road* (from *Three Rhythmic Spirituals*); *Here's One*; *I Feel Like My Time Ain't Long*; *Is There Anybody Here*; *Lawd, Ah Wants to be a Christian*; *Toward Distant Shores*; *Victory Tide*; and *The Voice of the Lord.*

B119 *Who's Who Among Black Americans.* 1st ed. Vol. 1. William C. Matney, editor. Northbrook, IL: Who's Who Among Black Americans, Inc., 1976: 597.

B120 *Who's Who in America.* Vol. 22. Chicago: The A.N. Marquis Company, 1942: 2096.

This is the first edition of *Who's Who* that contains an entry for Still. From 1942 to 1977, each edition of Who's Who contains an entry for Still, although the earlier editions tend to provide more information on his works.

B121 *Who's Who In Colored America: A Biographical Dictionary of Notable Living Persons of African Descent in America.* 2d ed. 1928-1929. New York: Who's Who In Colored America Corp., 1929: 350.

Identifies Still's date and place of birth, his father and mother, his wife and children, and aspects of his professional career stating that, "In addition to his work as a composer of serious music Mr. Still is also an arranger, having orchestrated a number of successful musical shows. *Running Wild, Dixie to Broadway*, and the 5th Edition of Earl Carroll's *Vanities,* are among these." The entry (pp. 490-91) for Still in the fifth edition of *Who's Who in Colored America* (1940) is essentially the same.

B122 *Who's Who in Music and Musicians.* International Directory. London: Burke's Peerage, 1962: 203.

Includes a brief sketch with information on Still's honors, compositions, colleges attended, and organizations.

B123 Wilson, Charles Reagan, and William Ferris, eds. *Encyclopedia of Southern Culture.* Sponsored by the Center for the Study of Southern Culture at the University of Mississippi. Chapel Hill: University of North Carolina Press, 1989.

Contributor Berkley Hudson's biographical sketch (pp. 1084-85) of Still provides information on his early life and education, notes his many "firsts" and mentions some of his compositions and awards. Contributor Ronald L. Davis, who wrote the section "Classical Music and Opera," states: "*A Southern Interlude* and especially *A Bayou Legend*, both dating from the 1940s, have solidified Still's reputation among opera enthusiasts (p. 1001)." *A Southern Interlude* was actually "discarded" by Still, who used portions as source material for *Highway 1, U.S.A. Troubled Island* is not mentioned.

Section Two

B124 Adams, Stanley. "Birthday Greetings to William Grant Still." *Black Perspective in Music* 3 (May 1975): 133-34.

As president of ASCAP, Adams mentions some of Still's accomplishments in conveying his best wishes on Still's seventy-fifth birthday.

B125 *Africa And The United States: Images and Realities.* Final Report of the 8th National Conference of the U.S. National Commission for UNESCO, Boston, October 22-26, 1961, p. 65.

Still appeared as a panelist for the session "African Music and Dance," and a portion of his remarks appeared in the published final report. "William Grant Still, a composer, was concerned with the influence of African music on Western music. He states that the music of the American Negro, which is a fusion of African and other elements, is now recognized in Europe as one of the great contributions of the United States to the arts of the world. Cultural fushion [*sic*] such as this brings with it a harmony of living. African music has actually succeeded in realizing some of the ideals of the United Nations and of UNESCO and of those who believe in the brotherhood of man, and African composers can look forward to a 'new era' in African music."

B126 "Afro-American composer will be honored at OC." *Elyria Chronicle-Telegram,* November 7, 1970.

Preview of activities and events associated with the seventy-fifth birthday concert in honor of Still at Oberlin College Conservatory of Music.

B127 Alexander, Ruth. "Left-Wing Musicians Use All Marxist Tricks." *Los Angeles Examiner*, November 1, 1953. (A similar article entitled "Our America" appeared in the *New York Sunday Mirror*, November 1, 1953.)

Article describing communism in music and Still's attempts to fight it. "The present leader of the fight against Communism in music is Dr. Still . . . Dr. Still has had the courage to put country before art. On platform and in press he has called attention to Communist efforts to use Negroes as the *shock troops* of the revolution they hope to bring about here. He has found that his race as a whole has resisted Communist pressure, but his art, music, has not resisted it."

B128 Allen, Walter C. *Hendersonia: The Music of Fletcher Henderson and His Musicians*. Jazz Monographs, No. 4. Highland Park, N.J.: 1973.

The early period of Still's professional career is largely undocumented. This volume has useful information on that part of Still's life. The first page, for example, provides the following: "There were also symphonic organizations Uptown, such as the New Amsterdam Orchestra, conducted by Alfred W. 'Allie' Ross, which gave a concert on February 6, 1921, at the New Star Casino. Its personnel of at least 52 Negro musicians included William Grant Still (oboe)."

B129 Allen, William Duncan. "Performing Arts." *Berkeley Post*, September 29, 1972, p. 12.

Lengthy article on Still written on the occasion of Robert Haas' book *William Grant Still and the Fusion of Cultures in American Music*. The author reviews aspects of the book, and mentions some of the recent performances of Still's compositions.

B130 Ardoyno, Dolores. "William Grant Still." *Musical America* (October 1984): 18-20.

The author, general manager of the Baton Rouge Opera, provides a biographical sketch of Still and background information on *A Bayou Legend* and *Minette Fontaine*.

B131 *Arkansas: A Guide To The State*. Compiled by Workers of the Writers' Program of the Work Projects Administration in the State of Arkansas. New York: Hastings House, 1941.

In the chapter "Music," Still is identified among the "well-known Arkansas musicians . . . Negro composer of the *Afro-American Symphony* and other orchestral and ballet music (p. 123)."

B132 Baker, David N., Lida M. Belt, and Herman C. Hudson, eds. *The Black Composer Speaks*. Metuchen, N.J.: Scarecrow Press, 1978.

This volume "consists of interviews with fifteen contemporary black composers and gives us an insight into their personal backgrounds, their philosophies, their motivations, and their attitudes toward their work (p. v)." Although Still is not one of the interviewees, his name comes up in some of the responses. For example, Ulysses Simpson Kay remarked that Still was one of the three people that influenced him in his life (p. 141).

B133 Baldwin, Lillian. *A Listener's Anthology of Music*. Volume 2. New York: Siver Burdett Co., 1948.

Brief biographical information on the composer, with special emphasis on the *Afro-American Symphony*.

B134 Bardolph, Richard. *The Negro Vanguard*. Westport, Conn.: Negro Universities Press, 1959.

The author provides insights on perceptions of Still's career. "William L. Dawson . . . and William Grant Still, easily the best-known Negro composers of symphonic music, are important figures in the vanguard. . . . Sympathetic whites helped [Still] with scholarships, fellowships and free tuition at crucial points in his career, and courageously put his music before the public; he became, indeed, more intimately associated, socially and professionally, with whites than with

Negroes. . . . Both [Still and Dawson] . . . continued to be productive in the 1940's and 1950's. Still . . . has repeatedly refused to produce music in the 'Uncle Tom' tradition when his radio and motion-picture employers called for music that conformed to the stereotype of 'Negro Music.' Dawson and Still, though performed by venturesome conductors like Stokowski and Barbirolli, and despite their demonstrated capacity for abstract and universal materials, are still largely identified in the public mind with African and Negro American themes."

B135 "Be Optimists, McNutt Tells Howard Grads." *Washington Post*, June 14, 1941.

Review of commencement exercises at Howard University. Still received an honorary degree of doctor of music, *in absentia*.

B136 Bethune, Mary McLeod. "Says Spiritual Has Paved Way For Greater Accomplishments In Music." *Chicago Defender*, September 5, 1953.

Article describing the importance of the spiritual in American music. "I recall William Grant Still who today is writing much of the classical music of our times. We do not hear much of his work but it is exerting a tremendous influence on the field of music. His work bespeaks the theme of our age. It is not necessarily Negro music. It is recognized because of its quality and its excellence."

B137 "Black Composer, Conductor Dies At Los Angeles At 83." *Arkansas Gazette*, December 13, 1978, sec. A, p. 13.

In a lengthy obituary, the *Gazette* discusses the career and compositions of Still. "Former University of Arkansas President David W. Mullins described Mr. Still as a man of talent and sensitivity 'who is held in high esteem by professional people throughout the world, regardless of their race, creed or color. His outlook is not racial in nature, but rather one of love for all humanity, and the depth of this feeling is expressed in his music, which is reflective of the best in American history and tradition,' Mullins said."

B138 "Blues in California." *Time* 51 (June 7, 1948): 55.

"[Still] is the U.S.'s leading Negro composer. His melodic, sometimes fiercely rhythmic symphonies and tone poems have been performed by Stokowski, Rodzinski and Monteux. . . . But somehow, the big breaks that have brought fame and fortune to less deserving composers have never seemed to come Still's way. . . . He has hopes that New York's energetic City Opera . . . will perform one of his operas: 'Now that I have one foot in the grave [he is in good health at 53], I guess I've got a better chance.'"

B139 Braithwaite, Coleridge Alexander. "A Survey of the Lives and Creative Activities of Some Negro Composers." Ed. D. diss. Columbia University, 1952.

Still is one of eighteen composers who are the subjects in this survey. Each chapter—one per composer—is arranged in a single pattern: a biographical sketch, a photograph, a list of creative activities in music and literature, and a bibliography relative to each composer. The chapter on Still (pp. 137-49) includes seventy compositions arranged in the following groups: orchestral; chamber; keyboard; operatic; choral; and vocal. The bibliography includes thirty-eight books and eight articles.

B140 Brooks, Tilford. *America's Black Musical Heritage*. Englewood Cliffs, N.J.: Prentice-Hall, Inc., 1984.

In the chapter "American Black Composers in the European Tradition," a section (pp. 214-20) is devoted to Still and his *Afro-American Symphony*. The volume also includes a list of Still's compositions (pp. 294-296) and a short list (p. 308) of recordings of his music.

B141 "Brush Stokes." *Los Angeles Times*, September 3, 1939, Part 3, p. 8.

Mentions that "Portraits have recently been made here of Composer William Grant Still by Painter Adrian Tucker and Sculptor Joseph D. Portanova."

B142 Butcher, Margaret Just. *The Negro in American Culture*. New York: Alfred A. Knopf, 1956: 86-87.

Still is mentioned quite a few times in this volume, especially for his contributions to music. "Much of Still's work, especially his *Sahdji* . . . and *Ebon Chronicle*, is ultra-modern, too sophisticated for the uninitiated. The [*Afro-American Symphony*], however, has moving simplicity and directness of musical speech. Its folk theme is treated in contrasted moods, with corresponding rhythms, making for a combined symphony and tone-poem of Negro experience. It is less programistic than Dawson's [*Negro Folk Symphony*], and gains by its nearer approach to pure music."

B143 Butler, Henry. "Still Is Grateful For Tin Pan Alley Days." *Indianapolis News*, March 6, 1970.

Still comments on his relationship with Fabien Sevitsky, one-time conductor of the Indianapolis Symphony, W. C. Handy, and Still's regard for American popular music. "'I'm glad for the experience I had in Tin Pan Alley. The music that came from there has genuine American qualities. Popular composers write for money, of course, but they also try to please the public, to find out what the public really wants and likes.' And he added, 'One thing America has given the world is rhythm.'"

B144 Calloway, Earl. "Black Music and Dance." In *The 1973 Compton Yearbook*. Chicago: F.E. Compton Co., 1973: 80-87.

In describing Still's position in the sphere of African American contributions to music, the author states, "Still is the most famous of the black nationalist composers, those who drew upon traditional Negro music as a source of thematic inspiration."

B145 ———. "A great musician sleeps and this generation never knew him." *Chicago Defender*, December 16, 1978.

Lengthy article on Still after his death on December 3, 1978.

B146 Calvin, Dolores. "New York Theatrical Comments." *Oklahoma City Black Dispatch,* April 3, 1943.

"It was funny to find how William Grant Still came to write *Quit Dat Foolish'ness* [sic]. It happened that his dog, Shep, kept chasing his tail one day, so the composer was driven to write it in music."

B147 ———. "There'll Be Far Greater Music After This War, Handy." *New York Black Dispatch,* January 30, 1943.

Lengthy interview with W.C. Handy, who has praise for Still's music. "Mr. Handy says there is a 'freshness'—something different and vital in the music of Mr. Still. He definitely feels something that the other fellow can't feel, but can only imitate."

B148 ———. "William Grant Still, Noted Musician, Writes Short Opera." *New York Black Dispatch,* February 6, 1943.

In a very long article reviewing Still's accomplishments, the composer notes that he has just finished the short opera, *A Southern Interlude*, which was later revised as *Highway 1, U.S.A.*

B149 Cariaga, Daniel. "Composer William Grant Still Dies." *Los Angeles Times*, Dec. 6, 1978, sec. 4, p. 29.

Obituary on Still, who died December 3, 1978. ". . . Called by one critic 'an American Grieg,' Still merited the comparison through the direct melodious appeal and superb craftmanship of his compositions . . . "

B150 ———. "William Grant Still Tributes." *Los Angeles Times*, May 18, 1975, p. 65.
Preview of musical events in Los Angeles associated with celebrations of Still's 80th birthday.

B151 "Carter, Persichetti, Still to be Honored at Commencement." *Peabody Notes* 28 (June 1974): 1.
Article on the recipients of honorary degrees from the Peabody Conservatory of Music, where Still received an honorary Doctor of Music. Because of ill health, Still could not travel, and his degree was conferred *in absentia* for the first time in the school's history.

B152 "Charles S. Johnson, William Grant Still, Arthur B. Spingarn Honored by Howard." *New York Amsterdam News*, June 7, 1941.
Announcement of recipients of honorary degrees from Howard University for 1941. Brief biographical sketches are included. Still received a Doctor of Music degree, *in absentia*.

B153 Chase, Gilbert. *America's Music: From The Pilgrims To The Present*. Rev. 2d ed. New York: McGraw-Hill Book Co., 1966. 511-12.
Includes two long paragraphs on Still that review his more significant compositions.

B154 "Citations by President Johnson." *Howard University Bulletin* 21 (July 1, 1941): 8.
Comments presented by Mordecai W. Johnson, president of Howard University, during commencement exercises as an honorary Doctor of Music was conferred upon Still, *in absentia*. "You have become the creative pioneer in the establishment of an intensely American music and the star of your glowing genius is ascending toward world magnitude."

B155 Clad, Michele. "Life of Composer is not Unrecorded." *Arkansas Gazette*, May 26, 1985, p. 8C.
Review of Verna Arvey's *In One Lifetime*, published by the University of Arkansas Press in 1984. This general review offers little substance.

B156 Cobbs, Paul-Elliott. "William Grant Still's 'The Afro-American Symphony,' A Culturally Inclusive Perspective." D.M.A. diss., University of Washington, 1990.
In the author's words, the purpose of this study is to "examine the possibility of culturally inclusive musical analysis as part of score preparation of syncretic music, using Still's *Afro-American Symphony* as the example." The study includes: (1) background information regarding the composer which might have relevance for a culturally authentic performance of his work; (2) a traditional musical analysis of the score; (3) culturally specific African American components of the work; (4) performance practices involving some specific idiomatic African American components in the Symphony; and (5) the identification of areas of concern that need to be addressed in order for the work to be successfully programmed.

B157 Cody, Carlos Bernard. "A Study of Selected Band Compositions of Three Twentieth Century Composers: William Grant Still, Ulysses Kay, and Hale Smith." Ph.D. diss. University of Southern Mississippi, 1990.
"The primary purpose of this study was to demonstrate that selected band compositions of William Grant Still, Hale Smith, and Ulysses Kay can provide awareness, knowledge, and understanding about compositional styles of Afro-

American composers to wind literature." Still's *Folk Suite for Band* is part of the study.

B158 Collaer, Paul. *A History of Modern Music*. Translated from the French by Sally Abeles. Cleveland: World Publishing Company, 1961.

In his chapter "Nationalism and Eclecticism," the author includes Still among the composers who wanted "to throw off the traditions imported from Europe." He goes on to remark of the *Afro-American Symphony*, "In this work Negro Spiritual melodies are included in a style halfway between that of Dvořák's *New World Symphony* and that of César Franck's *Symphony*."

B159 "College Graduates Largest Class." *Oberlin Review*, June 24, 1947, p. 1.

Report on commencement exercises at Oberlin College, during which Still received the honorary degree of Doctor of Music.

B160 "Composer Analyzes Spirituals: Blues from Cotton Fields Our Music, Says William Still." *Los Angeles Herald*, April 5, 1940.

Speaking at the annual convention of the Music Educators of America, Still suggests that spirituals will have a greater influence on American music in the future.

B161 "Composer Dies." *Music Notes* 35 (Winter 1978-1979): 15.

Obituary in the official publication of the Arkansas Federation of Music Clubs.

B162 "Composer Gives Scholarship." *California Eagle*, September 4, 1936.

Short piece noting that Still will provide for two scholarships, one in voice and another in piano, at the Gray Conservatory of Music.

B163 "Composer's Corner." *Lyric* 4 (February 1967): 16-17.

Brief article from a very general standpoint, tracing Still's life and touching upon his major accomplishments.

B164 *Composers of the Americas*. Volume 5. Washington, D.C.: Union Panamericana, 1959.

Contains biographical data and a catalog of the composer's works (pp. 85-97).

B165 Cook, J. Douglas. "Visits to the Homes of Famous Composers, No. 3, William Grant Still." *Opera, Concert and Symphony* 11 (November 1946): 8-9+.

Lengthy interview with Still touching upon composing, orchestration, race, and highlights of his career.

B166 Copland, Aaron. *Copland On Music*. Garden City, N.Y.: Doubleday & Co., Inc., 1960 [first published in 1944]: 158-59.

"William Grant Still began about twelve years ago as the composer of a somewhat esoteric music for voice and a few instruments. Since that time he has completely changed his musical speech, which has become almost popular in tone. He has a certain natural musicality and charm, but there is a marked leaning toward the sweetly saccharine that one should like to see eliminated."

B167 Cowell, Henry, ed. *American Composers on American Music*. Palo Alto: Stanford University Press, 1933.

This volume is the product of a symposium, one which Still attended. Cowell, in the first chapter, entitled "Trends in American Music," has this to say about Still: "William Grant Still, Negro, uses his people's themes and feelings as a base for his music, which is otherwise in modern style with some rather vague European influence. Perhaps he possesses the beginnings of a genuine new style. At present, however, his works are unformed and contain many crudities. Only later developments will show whether or not his present promise will be fulfilled." Still's own remarks are presented in chapter 27 (pp. 182-83) under the title "An Afro-American Composer's Point of View."

B168 Craven, Robert R., ed. *Symphony Orchestras of the United States*. Westport, Conn.: Greenwood Press, 1986: 361.

In describing the Rhode Island Philharmonic Orchestra, the author discusses the influence of conductor, Francis Madeira, who encourages the performance of works of native American composers such as Still.

B169 [Dabrishus, Michael J.]. "William Grant Still Is Honored for Classical Music Contribution." *Arkansas News*, Fall 1989, p. 5.

A general overview of the life of Still, in a newspaper published by the Old State House at Little Rock, primarily for use in schools and other educational activities.

B170 Dabrishus, Michael J. "William Grant Still's Papers Opened at the University." *Grapevine*, October 30, 1992, p. 7.

Announcement that the papers of William Grant Still and Verna Arvey will be formally opened at a dedication in the reading room of the Special Collections Division of the University of Arkansas Libraries on November 5, at which time the composer's daughter, Judith, will be a special guest.

B171 Dalrymple, Jean. *From The Last Row*. Clifton, N.J.: James T. White & Company, 1975: 101.

The author describes her twenty-five year career with City Center. "[*Troubled Island*] was splendidly produced and extraordinarily well-cast, taking into consideration that white singers were playing black parts, which probably would be unheard of in the New York City Opera today. Robert Weede was Dessalines, the leader of the revolt, and Marie Powers was Azelia, his wife. They were unforgettable. Azelia's lament when Dessalines was slain still haunts me. The critics were a bit pro and con in their opinions, but our audiences loved it all, including the 'authentic voodoo dances' by Jean Leon Destine and his group and the ominous thudding of the distant drums."

B172 Davidson, Celia Elizabeth. "Operas by Afro-American Composers: A Critical Survey and Analysis of Selected Works." Ph.D. diss., Catholic University, 1980.

Eight operas by six composers are examined for detailed historical and analytical discussion. They are: *The Martyr*, *Vendetta*, and *Voodoo* by Harry Laurence Freeman; *Treemonisha* by Scott Joplin; *Ouanga* by Clarence Cameron White; *A Christmas Miracle* by Mark Fax; *Jubilee* by Ulysses Kay; and *Highway 1, U.S.A.* by Still. Short biographies of each composer precede the discussion of their opera(s). Scores, newspaper articles, reviews, and interviews were used as a basis of the author's research.

B173 Davie, Maurice R. *Negroes In American Society*. McGraw-Hill Series in Sociology and Anthropology. New York: McGraw-Hill Book Co., Inc., 1949: 378.

The author identifies Still among the African American composers and arrangers who have attained artistic achievement.

B174 de Lerma, Dominique-René. *Black Music in Our Culture*. Kent, OH: Kent State University Press, 1970.

This publication is based, in large part, on a conference entitled "Seminar on Black Music in College and University Curricula," held at Indiana University, June 18-21, 1969. Still and Arvey attended, and their presentations were among those published in this volume. Still's is entitled "A Composer's Viewpoint" (pp. 93-108) and Arvey's "Negro Dance and Its Influence on Negro Music," (pp. 79-92).

B175 ———. "A Concordance of Scores and Recordings of Music by Black Composers." *Black Music Research Journal* (December 1984): 60-140.

Identified by the author as a "preliminary biblio-discography," fifteen compositions by Still are included. (pp. 102-05).

B176 ———. *Reflections on Afro-American Music*. Kent, OH: Kent State University Press, 1973.

Based largely on a seminar held at Indiana University in 1971, this volume contains the edited papers and remarks that were presented. Still is mentioned on numerous occasions, as is evident in the index.

B177 ———. Review of "The William Grant Still Reader: Essays on American Music," A Special Issue of *Black Sacred Music: A Journal of Theomusicology*, Vol. 6 (Fall 1992). Edited by Jon Michael Spencer. (Durham, NC: Duke University Press, 1992). In the *Arkansas Historical Quarterly* 52 (Summer 1993): 191-92.

The reviewer provides context for readers unfamiliar with Still's life, as well as comments on Spencer's "Reader." Of the latter he states: "The sixty-page introduction by the editor, more than a sketch of Still's life, is an exceptionally important evaluation of the composer as a musician and of his musical credo. It is more the latter subject which is addressed in the thirty-five reprinted articles by Still, the focus of this anthology."

B178 ———. "A Selective List of Choral Music by Black Composers." *Choral Journal* 12 (April 1972): 5-6.

The list includes Still's *Christmas in the Western World (Las Pascuas), A Psalm for the Living*, and *The Voice of the Lord*, with descriptive information by arrangement and publication.

B179 de Toledano, Ralph. "The Music Giant: William Grant Still." *Lincoln Review* 5 (Winter 1985): 47-49.

The author writes that Still was not given the recognition he deserved because of Still's views on race and on politics. "As a working composer, he found himself involved in the flesh-tearing politics of the music world. Because he would have no part of the back-stabbing and in-fighting of that world, the self-aggrandizement and the compromise of principle, he did not achieve the status that should have been his."

B180 "'Dean of Negro Composers' to Visit the UA, Give Papers to University Library." *Arkansas Gazette*, March 12, 1972, sec. A, p. 7.

Preview of activities associated with Still's visit to the University of Arkansas, Fayetteville, at which time the composer "will formally announce the donation of his personal and professional papers and manuscripts to the U of A Library."

B181 Detels, Claire. "Still, the Traditionalist." In *William Grant Still Studies at the University of Arkansas: A 1984 Congress Report*. Claire Detels, ed. Fayetteville: University of Arkansas.

Based upon remarks from a pre-concert lecture on February 18, 1984, at Fayetteville, Arkansas. Detels provides insight into Still's belief in traditional personal values—such as patriotism, freedom, democracy, and religious faith—as well as his traditional values as a composer, including form, tonal structure, and emphasis on melody.

B182 ———, ed. *William Grant Still Studies at the University of Arkansas: A 1984 Congress Report*. Fayetteville: University of Arkansas.

On February 15-19, 1984, the University of Arkansas held a William Grant

Still Festival at which time scholars, musicians, and community members met to discuss the life and works of Still and to hear performances of his music. This report serves as a record of the scholarly papers, as well as of some of the excerpts from pre-concert lectures. "The contributors include the most distinguished scholar in the field of Black American music—Eileen Southern of Harvard University—as well as specialists in certain areas of William Grant Still's life and compositional output—Ruth Friedberg on the literature of the art song, Barbara Garvey Jackson on Arkansas composers contemporary with Still, Thomas Warburton on Still's operas, and Southern historian Willard Gatewood on 'William Grant Still's Little Rock,' among others (p. iv)." Still's "Remembering Arkansas," an essay delivered at the University of Arkansas on March 22, 1972, is included.

B183 Dierks, Donald. "William Grant Still . . . Craftsman, Artist." *San Diego Union*, January 24, 1971, sec. E, p. 1+. (Reprinted as "William Grant Still: Dean of Black Composers." *Cincinnati Enquirer*, March 19, 1971, p. 12.)

Article based upon an interview of William Grant Still and Verna Arvey. In 1934 Still traveled to Southern California to begin work on an opera, *Blue Steel*. He extended his stay to the point that he became a permanent resident. "He now says *Blue Steel* was not to his liking, 'so I finally discarded it.' 'But only as a whole opera, Billy.' Mrs. Still said, 'You have used material from it in other things, you know.' 'Yes, I do quite a lot of revising and discarding, but I never really destroy anything.' Still said. 'I guess I could use that expression that is so popular nowadays—I "recycle" some of my music when I have gotten the good out of it.'"

B184 Dietz, Betty. "American Culture Is In Danger, Says Still." *Dayton News*, June 20, 1954.

Report on an address entitled, "Toward A Broader American Culture," by William Grant Still, presented at the national convention of the American Symphony Orchestra League, Springfield, Ohio, June 17, 1954. Still deplores the practice by U.S. orchestras of performing foreign music over American works. "[Still] waged U.S. orchestras to include in each concert one American work and one contemporary work by a foreign composer (not necessarily Russian, he added). He further charged them with the responsibility of seeking out local composers and performers. 'Every famous composer was local once, somewhere,' he pointed out."

B185 Dixon, W. Randy. "Rudolph Dunbar Can't Write About Himself." *Pittsburgh Courier*, March 6, 1943, p. 21.

During the course of a lengthy interview, Rudolph Dunbar "considers Still as America's greatest living composer, bar none."

B186 Dobbins, Sharon E.A. "Oberlin College: an early contributor to black music and black musicians." *Oberlin Alumni Magazine* 70 (May/June 1974): 5-7.

Article on the influence of Oberlin College to the development of black music and musicians. William Grant Still is included in this general survey.

B187 Dorr, Donald. "Chosen Image: The Afro-American Vision in the Operas of William Grant Still." *Opera Quarterly* 4 (Summer 1986): 1-23. (Also appears in Still, *Fusion,* 144-61.)

The author writes from the perspective of a producer, director, and librettist. His working introduction to Still's operas came as stage director for the Opera/South production of *Highway 1, U.S.A*. Dorr uses diary excerpts, performance reviews, and interviews with effective results.

B188 Dougan, Michael B. *Arkansas Odyssey: The Saga of Arkansas from Prehistoric Times to Present*. Little Rock: Rose Publishing Co., 1994.
In the section "Music in Arkansas Culture," the author provides brief information on Scott Joplin, Florence Price, and Still. Of Still he states, in part, that "his *Afro-American Symphony* [is] the single most frequently performed major composition by an American black (p. 554)."

B189 Douglass, Fannie Howard. "A Tribute to William Grant Still." *Black Perspective in Music* 2 (Spring 1974): 51-3.
General overview of the life and accomplishments of Still.

B190 Doving, Richard. "Two Gifts to Modern Music American, Thinks Still." *San Francisco People's World*, February 28, 1938.
In an interview, Still states that American composers have made important contributions to the development of music, "the first, a greater flexibility of instrumental technique. By that I mean an ability to perform passages that were unheard of a few years ago. For example, in Ferde Grofé's orchestration of *Rhapsody in Blue*, he uses a clarinet glissando that was previously considered impossible. The second is more vague—an idea of greater rhythmic freedam [sic]."

B191 Drummond, Andrew H. *American Opera Librettos*. Metuchen, N.J.: Scarecrow Press, Inc., 1973.
The author includes *Troubled Island* in his work and provides background on its development, a synopsis, and excerpts from the reviews of the premiere by critics Olin Downes, Philip Hamburger, and Francis D. Perkins.

B192 Dunbar, Rudolph. "Negroes." *World Review* (March 1942): 61-64.
In this British publication, Dunbar discusses some of the challenges and accomplishments of African Americans. Still is referred to as: "One of the greatest composers in America."

B193 Duncan, John. "Negro Composers of Opera." *Negro History Bulletin* 29 (January 1966): 79-80+.
General article on black composers of opera, including, H. Laurence Freeman, William Grant Still, Antonio de Assis Republicano, Clarence Cameron White, Shirley Graham, Samuel Coleridge-Taylor, Ulysses Kay, Julia Perry, and Esteban Pena Morell.

B194 Dunn-Powell, Rosephanye. "The Solo Vocal Writing Style of William Grant Still." D.M. thesis, Florida State University, 1993.

B195 *Eastman School Festival of American Music. Bulletin*. Rochester, N.Y.: Eastman School of Music, 1939.
In addition to the programs of the Ninth Annual Festival of American Music, it contains a complete list of compositions performed in the nine Festivals and the fifty-four American Composers' Concerts (1925-1939). Sixteen of Still's compositions are listed.

B196 "Editorials." Hollywood *Citizen News*, September 25, 1951.
Report that Still "asked Rep. Donald L. Jackson to let him testify before the Congressional Committee on Un-American Activities. . . . Communists, said the Negro composer, do not speak for the Negro race."

B197 Edwards, Benjamin Griffith. "The Life of William Grant Still." Ph.D. diss., Harvard University, 1987.
This is the first dissertation completed on Still from the field of American history. The author relies heavily on the letters, scrapbooks, diaries, inter-

views, speeches, and publications of the composer as sources of information. He also consulted pertinent collections at the University of Arkansas, the Library of Congress, the New York Public Library, Yale University, and other institutions, as well as numerous secondary research materials, to produce his study on the life of Still.

B198 Embree, Edwin R. *13 Against The Odds.* New York: Viking Press, 1945: 196-210.

The success stories of this book, of which Still is one, are short biographies of African-Americans.

B199 Emery, Lynne Fauley. *Black Dance in the United States from 1619 to 1970.* Palo Alto, Calif.: National Press Books, 1972:

Mentions Still as a musician in the orchestra for *Shuffle Along.*

B200 Everett, Thomas. "Concert Band Music by Black-American Composers: A Selected List." *Black Perspective In Music* 6 (Fall 1978): 143-50.

The author includes *From the Delta* and *Folk Suite for Band* among his selected list.

B201 Everett, Tom. "Five Questions: 30 Answers." *The Composer* 8 (1977): 21-24.

T.J. Anderson, Jack Beeson, Paul Earls, Ulysses Kay, William Grant Still, and Julian Work respond to questions by Everett. When asked how his music may have been influenced by elements of black tradition Still had this to say: "'When I studied in Conservatories as a young man, I absorbed the traditions of music. Then, when I became a pupil of Edgard Varèse, my horizons broadened, and I wrote in a very dissonant style. Then I began to feel that this idiom was not fully expressing *me*, so I composed quite a few works expressive of Afro-Americans, consciously using Negro musical idioms. There then came a period when I considered this to be a limited objective, so I began to write in a more universal idiom, suiting the style of each composition to its subject matter. If I wished to write in a Negroid idiom I did so, and if I wanted to express a different subject, I felt free to do that too.'"

B202 "Exhibit Will Show Original Music Manuscripts." *Pasadena Star-News,* June 7, 1941.

Announcement that an exhibit of original manuscripts by American composers will be held at the Los Angeles Museum in conjunction with the annual convention of the National Federation of Music Clubs, June 18-26, 1941. Still's *Kaintuck'* was part of the display.

B203 Ferguson, Blanche E. *Countee Cullen and the Negro Renaissance.* New York: Dodd, Mead and Co., 1966: 180.

"*If You Should Go* attracted the attention of another composer, William Grant Still, who created a musical setting for them [*Songs of Separation*]. Still's career was an inspiration to the Renaissance and the post-Renaissance Negro. Even in the early thirties he was composing and arranging music for motion pictures, radio, and the theater."

B204 Fields, Bernice. "Kaufman to Play New Works By Still, Gifted Negro Composer." *New York Daily Worker,* February 20, 1943.

Lengthy interview with violinist Louis Kaufman, who remarks that "Still can afford to be unpretentious because of his sure mastery of the forms of composition and his extraordinary sensitivity to melodic and harmonic elements."

B205 "58 Fellowships of Guggenheim Fund Granted." *New York Herald Tribune,* April 4, 1939.

Announcement of the recipients of Guggenheim awards for 1938, including a brief background on each person. Still is among them.

B206 "Five Honorary Degrees Given at Commencement." *Oberlin Alumni Bulletin* (Third Quarter 1947): 4.
Full page article on the recipients of honorary degrees, of which Still is one.

B207 Fleming, John. "Composer Proves There's No Color Line in Music World." *Arkansas Gazette*, August 9, 1953.
Lengthy article touching upon Still's life as a boy growing up in Little Rock through a description of his major compositions and accomplishments.

B208 Floyd, Samuel A,. Jr., ed. *Black Music in the Harlem Renaissance*. Knoxville: University of Tennessee Press, 1993.
Includes a chapter (pp. 71-86) by Rae Linda Brown entitled "William Grant Still, Florence Price, and William Dawson: Echoes of the Harlem Renaissance," and a list of compositions by Still (pp. 208-12).

B209 Foreman, Clark. "The Negro In American Life." *Times* (London), June 8, 1939, p. 10.
In this extensive article on the position of the African-American in American life, Still is identified as a composer "whose symphony has been played by great orchestras."

B210 Fortenberry, L.C. "Renowned Composer Dies." *Los Angeles Sentinel*, December 7, 1978, sec. A, p. 1+.
Obituary on Still, who died December 3, 1978.

B211 "Four Composers Get Guggenheim Fellowships. " *Musical America* 58 (April 10, 1938): 4.
General article on the recipients, one of which was Still.

B212 Friedberg, Ruth. "William Grant Still—His Songs and His Poets." In *William Grant Still Studies at the University of Arkansas: A 1984 Congress Report*. Fayetteville: University of Arkansas, 1985: 34-39.
This article is based upon a lecture-recital given by Ruth Friedberg and Verleen Reese on February 17, 1984, at Fayetteville, Arkansas. The author provides background and context to Still's *Winter's Approach, The Breath of a Rose, Songs of Separation*, and *Grief*.

B213 Gatewood, Willard. "William Grant Still's Little Rock." In *William Grant Still Studies at the University of Arkansas: A 1984 Congress Report*. Claire Detels, ed. Fayetteville: University of Arkansas, 1985: 10-12.
Based upon a presentation on February 15, 1984, at Fayetteville, Arkansas. Gatewood provides a good account of the African American influences in Little Rock between 1895 and 1911, the period of Still's formative years in the "City of Roses," as it was known.

B214 Gehrkens, Karl W. "Questions and Answers." *Etude* 66 (August 1948): 478.
"William Grant Still is probably the foremost of our Negro composers, and has made significant contributions to contemporary musical literature. Rather early in his career he wrote in what was then an ultra-modern style, but he has since discarded that idiom and his later works are written in a more orthodox, almost romantic vein, and are not highly dissonant. He is not interested in musical experimentation, but rather in the expressing of emotions. His music has a strong racial flavor, and he has, in fact, devoted himself to the development of Negro idioms and the treatment of Negro subjects in his program works."

B215 Goss, Madeleine. *Modern Music-Makers: Contemporary American Composers.* New York: E.P. Dutton & Co., Inc., 1952.

Includes a chapter (pp. 207-21) on Still that provides basic biographical information. Many of the composer's works are included in a list by genre.

B216 Greene, Patterson. "Bridging a Musical Gap." *Los Angeles Herald-Examiner*, September 8, 1963, p. D-6.

Brief article on Still and his interest in folk music of South America, Africa, and the United States. "The composer feels a rich source of material in the Creole folk songs of Louisiana has been overlooked by composers, and has made use of several products of the mingling of French and Spanish settlers in the South. Louis Moreau Gottschalk based piano compositions on them a century ago, but he has had few followers."

B217 ———. "William Grant Still . . . An American Composer Who Happens To Be Black." *High Fidelity/Musical America* (March 1975): MA27.

"'In order to be Negro music,' Still says, 'music has to have some of the *characteristics* of Negro music. You can't just have a black putting something on paper and have it become "black music."' The composer and his librettist wife, writer Verna Arvey, both feel strongly on the matter. 'At Oberlin,' Mrs. Still says, 'when they had his seventy-seventh birthday celebration, they called up and asked, "how do you feel about the black music thing?" Well, we don't like it. In the first place, we have always been for brotherhood, for integration. We intermarried, and our children intermarried, and if you say "black" don't you automatically think "white?" It's a separatist thing. Back when Billy's music was being heard, all the big conductors—Stokowski, Rodjinski [sic], Hanson, Szell— presented him as an American composer who happened to be black.'"

B218 Griggs-Janower, David. "The Choral Works of William Grant Still." *Choral Journal* 35 (May 1995): 41-44. (A short version of this article appears in the October 1994 issue of *Troubadour*, the Eastern Division newsletter of the American Choral Director's Association.)

Of Still's larger choral works, the author discusses the following: *And They Lynched Him on a Tree*; *Christmas in the Western World*; *Caribbean Melodies*; *A Psalm for the Living*; *Plain-Chant for America*; and *From A Lost Continent*. Of Still's smaller choral works, the following are discussed: *Three Rhythmic Spirituals*; *Little David, Play on Your Harp*; *Steal Away to Jesus*; and *We Sang Our Songs*, among others. The author concludes his article thus, "Still combined a great richness of compositional inspiration with a wealth of musical traditions to create new flavors. Too long overlooked, Still's music deserves to become better known among choral conductors."

B219 "Guggenheim Fellowships Given To Five Southlanders." *Los Angeles Times*, April 4, 1939.

Announcement that five people from Southern California, one of which was Still, were awarded Guggenheim Fellowships.

B220 Haas, Robert Bartlett, ed. *William Grant Still and the Fusion of Cultures in American Music*. Los Angeles: Black Sparrow Press, 1972.

An important resource for scholars, this volume includes: a biographical sketch of Still; a comprehensive study of the *Afro-American Symphony*; a review of *Symphony No. 4, "Autochthonous;"* ten articles by or about Still (included in the bibliography of articles by or about Still); a catalogue of works (1921-1972); a discography; and a short bibliography, among other components. (*See also:* B411)

B221 Hall, Frederick. Introduction to *William Grant Still and the Fusion of Cultures* *in American Music*. Los Angeles: Black Sparrow Press, 1972. (Also appears in Still, *Fusion,* ii.)

Hall remarks on the significance of Still to American music, especially from an African American perspective (p. xi).

B222 "Handy, Still Appear at Jefferson Hi[gh]." *California Eagle*, October 3, 1940.

Still and W. C. Handy appeared as speakers at a Los Angeles high school on September 27, 1940. Still, during his introduction of Handy, said, "young people of today have no right to cry over the lack of opportunity when Handy had succeeded in spite of extremely limited opportunities."

B223 Handy, W. C. *Father of the Blues*. New York: Macmillan Co., 1941.

In writing of his life, Handy mentions Still from time to time.

B224 ———. *Negro Authors and Composers of the United States*. New York: Handy Brothers Music Co., Inc., [1947]: 23.

Still is identified, along with his works, *Africa*, *Afro-American Symphony*, *Blue Steel*, and *Twelve Negro Spirituals*.

B225 Hanson, Howard. Introduction to *William Grant Still and the Fusion of Cultures in American Music*. Los Angeles: Black Sparrow Press, 1972. (Also appears in Still, *Fusion,* i.)

Hanson remarks on the significance of Still to American music (p.ix).

B226 Harris, Carl G., Jr. "A Study of Characteristic Stylistic Trends Found in the Choral Works of a Selected Group of Afro-American Composers." D.M.A., University of Missouri-Kansas City, 1972.

The purpose of this study is to: "1) trace the development of choral music by certain Afro-American composers and arrangers from the late nineteenth century to contemporary times; and 2) to delineate certain characteristic trends found in the choral works of a selected group of Black composers and arrangers, who because of their different styles of writing have been labeled by this writer as Black Trailblazers, Black Nationalists and Black Innovators." Still is included among those in the category of Black Nationalists. The Still works that are part of this study are *And They Lynched Him on a Tree*, *A Psalm for the Living*, *Three Rhythmic Spirituals*, *Victory Tide*, and *Christmas in the Western World*.

B227 ———. "Three Schools of Black Choral Composers and Arranger, 1900-1970." *Choral Journal* 14 (August 1974): 11-18.

This article discusses the notable African American composers and arrangers. It includes Still among the "Black Nationalists," and provides a short sketch of his life and career.

B228 Harton-Brown, Connie Y. "African-American Influences in Selected Compositions by American Composers." M.A. thesis, Eastern Michigan University, 1993.

"The purpose of this project is to reveal the African-American influences on selected compositions by five American composers: four African-American—Harry Thacker Burleigh; Scott Joplin; William Grant Still; William Levi Dawson; and one Russian born White American—Louis Gruenberg."

B229 Havel, O'Dette. "Librarian Brings Order to Composer's Papers." *The University* 3 (April 10, 1992): 4.

Article on the cataloging of the papers of William Grant Still and Verna Arvey at the University of Arkansas, a project funded by the National Endowment for the Humanities. Norma Ortiz-Karp served as project archivist.

B230 Headlee, Judith Anne Still. "William Grant Still: A Voice High-Sounding." *Music Educators Journal* 70 (February 1984): 24-30.

This article, written by the composer's daughter, is based upon interviews of Still by R. Donald Brown and includes significant excerpts from those interviews. (*See also* Still, Judith Anne)

B231 Hinson, Maurice. *Guide to the Pianist's Repertoire.* Bloomington: Indiana University Press, 1973: 623-24.

Identifies four of Still's works: *Three Visions*, as "Short character pieces in varied moods;" *Seven Traceries*, as "Somewhat impressionistic;" *Fairy Knoll*, as "A filigree tinkling scherzo;" and *Phantom Chapel*, as "Deep, sonorous, bell-tone qualities."

B232 Holt, Nora. "Dunbar Fresh from Berlin Triumph Off to Hollywood." *New York Amsterdam News*, August 24, 1946.

Lengthy article based upon an interview of Rudolph Dunbar, who provides background on his life, education, and admiration for the work of Still. "When asked if Mr. Still's works merited a whole program, he replied, 'Most assuredly. Not because he is a Negro and a friend, but because he is a great composer.'"

B233 ———. "Music" *New York Amsterdam News*, February 16, 1946, p. 23.

The writer laments what she believes to be a paucity of African-American composers. "Covering the last ten years, we can point with pride to but one musician who has resolved to work for a high goal in composition regardless of economic slavery, prejudice and contiguous deterrents. . . . William Grant Still continues to hold a niche unmatched in the field of major composition. . . . We wonder where the composers are who can or are striving to reach Mr. Still's pinnacle?"

B234 Howard, John Tasker. *Our Contemporary Composers: American Music in the Twentieth Century.* New York: Thomas Y. Crowell Co., 1942: 280-82.

The author devotes considerable space to Still in describing the composer's work and accomplishments, opening his description with the remark, "By far the most widely recognized Negro composer today."

B235 Hudgins, Mary D. "An Outstanding Arkansas Composer." *Hot Springs News*, August 31, 1972, p. 2.

Article reviewing the many accomplishments of Still.

B236 ———. "An Outstanding Arkansas Composer, William Grant Still." *Arkansas Historical Quarterly* 24 (Winter 1965): 308-14.

This general article was written to honor Still on the occasion of his seventieth birthday.

B237 ———. Book Review of *William Grant Still and the Fusion of Cultures in American Music*, by Robert Bartlett Haas, ed. *Arkansas Historical Quarterly* 32 (Spring 1973):102-04.

In addition to providing a review of the volume in question, Hudgins includes a concise biographical sketch of the composer.

B238 ———. "William Grant Still—The Dean of Negro Composers." *Arkansas Gazette*, January 30, 1966, sec. E, p. 4.

Lengthy sketch of Still's life noting his major compositions and accomplishments.

B239 Huggins, Nathan Irvin. *Harlem Renaissance.* New York: Oxford University Press, 1971.

Mentions that Still wrote the music to *If You Should Go*, by Countee Cullen, and includes the verse (pp. 212-13).

B240 Hughes, Langston. *Famous Negro Music Makers*. New York: Dodd, Mead and Co., 1955: 85-89.

Hughes' chapter on Still is a good five-page biographical sketch, and concludes as follows. "A quiet, golden-skinned, rather distraught looking man, Still lives with his wife, two children, and a dog, in a house behind a high wire fence with a locked gate, in Los Angeles. He avoids visitors who have no appointments. He composes for several hours in the morning, and arranges or copies in the afternoon, working on a musical typewriter. For recreation, he tends his vegetable garden, makes much of his own furniture, and carves out little wooden toys—animals, trains, and whole villages—for his youngsters. Occasionally he writes an article for some musical magazine. Still is a religious man and at the end of every new composition, when the last note is down on the manuscript, he writes, 'With humble thanks to God, the source of inspiration (p. 89).'" *Troubled Island* is only noted.

B241 Hughes, Langston, and Milton Meltzer, eds. *Black Magic: A Pictorial History of the Negro in American Entertainment*. Englewood Cliffs, N.J.: Prentice-Hall, 1967.

In the discussion of *Troubled Island*, the authors state: "The characters were all Negro. Robert McFerrin was among the singers, but the leading roles were performed by white artists, Robert Weede, Helena Bliss, and Marie Powers in blackface. They looked odd, but sang beautifully (p. 147)."

B242 "I Pity Negro Communists." *Los Angeles Tidings*, June 13, 1952.

Lengthy article on Still's views pertaining to communists and their attempts to use members of his own race for the communist cause.

B243 Illidge, Cora Gary. "Music News." *New York Amsterdam News*, September 17, 1930, p. 10.

The columnist notes the publication of *American Composers of Today and Their Works* by Claire Reis, and then touches upon Still. "Among the fifty-five composers represented, William Grant Still, composer, conductor and wind instrumentalist, and who lives in Jamaica, L.I., is the only Negro. Besides his many other notable works, Mr. Still is widely known for the music written for the Broadway production, *Rain or Shine*."

B244 ———. "Music News." *New York Amsterdam News*, December 31, 1930, p. 9.

In a lengthy column, the writer touches upon some of the achievements of Still. She also mentions that Still "has written and arranged sacred music, some of which is frequently used in the services of Grace Congregational Church, of which he is an active member." She then quotes Still: "'I am not seeking to give the impression that I lead an exemplary life, for this is not true. But I do depend solely on God for inspiration and for avenues through which my efforts may be presented.'" The article also notes that Still's orchestrations may be heard over WJZ during the *Maxwell House Hour*.

B245 "In Memoriam: William Grant Still (1895-1978)." *Black Perspective in Music* 7 (Fall 1979): 235-43.

Photographs, messages of condolences, and copies of programs brought together as a memorial article after the composer's death.

B246 "In Retrospect . . . A Pictorial Survey." *Black Perspective in Music* 3 (May 1975): 207-34.

Sixteen photographs of Still and memorabilia are brought together in this article.

B247 "In Retrospect: Letters from W.C. Handy to William Grant Still." *Black Perspective in Music* 7 (Fall 1979): 199-234.

With notes and an introduction by Eileen Southern, this article brings together seventeen letters from Handy to Still from April 2, 1941 to October 28, 1944, illustrated with seven photographs. The Spring 1980 issue of *Black Perspective* contains Part 2 of this article (pp. 65-119). It includes twenty-five letters from Handy from January 9, 1945 to March 7, 1958, illustrated with ten photographs.

B248 Jackson, Barbara Garvey. "William Grant Still and Some Contemporary Arkansas Composers." In *William Grant Still Studies at the University of Arkansas: A 1984 Congress Report*. Claire Detels, ed. Fayetteville: University of Arkansas, 1985: 13-14.

Based upon a presentation on February 15, 1984, at Fayetteville, Arkansas, Jackson provides background to the lives of Scott Joplin, Harriet Gibbs Marshall, and Florence Price.

B249 Jackson, Clyde Owen. *The Songs of Our Years: A Study of Negro Folk Music*. New York: Exposition Press, 1968.

This modest publication (54 pp.) includes an appendix created by a letter from Still, which the author received and published in its entirety. The letter addresses a number of subjects, including Antonin Dvořák's possible influence in the use of African-American folk themes in promoting larger works; the effects of Fisk, Tuskegee, Hampton and other choral groups towards a better understanding and appreciation of African-American folk music; and Still's views on the future of African-American folk music.

B250 James, Shaylor Lorenza. "Contributions of Four Selected Twentieth-Century Afro-American Classical Composers: William Grant Still, Howard Swanson, Ulysses Kay, and Olly Wilson." Ph.D. diss., Florida State University, 1988.

The purposes of this study were: "(1) to develop a sourcebook which explores the contributions of four selected twentieth-century Afro-American composers . . . and (2) to provide a perspective through which scholars and educators may become more aware of orchestral compositions by these composers and explore musical and philosophical influences on the composers, particularly those arising from ethnic heritage."

B251 John Simon Guggenheim Memorial Foundation. *Directory of Fellows, 1925-1974*. New York: JSGMF, 1975.

Still is included (p. 381) as a Fellow for 1934, 1935, and 1938. His first award covered a twelve-month period, beginning on May 14, 1934, and the second was technically considered a renewal, beginning on June 3, 1938 and lasting six months.

B252 John Simon Guggenheim Memorial Foundation. *Reports of the Secretary and of the Treasurer*. 1933 and 1934. New York: JSGMF, [1935].

In 1934 Still received a Guggenheim award for creative work in musical composition. It was renewed in 1938 for a period of six months. The *Reports* are valuable as they contain a record of each Fellow's accomplishments, publications, honors, and awards during the biennium covered. *Reports* (and pages therein) that provide substantive information on Still cover the following bienniums: 1933-1934: 121-22; 1935-1936: 34, 117-18, 121, 151; 1937-1938: 49, 136-38, 141-42; 1939-1940: 170-72, 176, 178; 1941-1942: 207-10, 217-19, 281; 1943-1944: 222-27; and 1945-1946: 298-302. When combined with Marguerite Kelly Kyle's compilations for "AmerAllegro" in *Pan Pipes of*

Sigma Alpha Iota, these two sources provide the best chronological review of Still's works and accomplishments from 1925 to 1977.

B253 Johnson, Carl, comp. *Paul Whiteman: A Chronology (1890-1967)*. Williamstown, MA: Williams College, rev. ed. (1979).

For the year 1927, the author states: "Bill Challis had left Goldkette to team up with Ferde Grofé and William Grant Still as Whiteman's chief arrangers (p. 19)."

B254 Johnson, Herbert. "The Piano Music of William Grant Still." D.M.A. thesis, Manhattan School of Music, 1992.

B255 Jones, Isabel Morse. "American Composition Now Being Granted Place in Sun." *Los Angeles Times*, October 27, 1935.

Lengthy article on the recognition that American music is beginning to receive, including information on Still, who relocated to Los Angeles. "He is radical and racial in his composing but emotional and melodic too. His Afro-American music made a distinct impression in the cities of Germany. He says Wagner has influenced him more than any other composer. He still is excessively modest and never seeks the lime light. He has lived here two years and is one of America's outstanding composers but few knew he was here."

B256 ———. "Composers' Society To Organize Here." *Los Angeles Times*, July 12, 1936.

The article provides background on why composers, performers, and others in music believe that an organization in Southern California is necessary "to promote performances and to make contributions to the music life of the community through concerted effort." The name of William Grant Still is included as one of those who may become part of the group.

B257 ———. "Controversy Rages Over *Porgy and Bess*." *Los Angeles Times*, February 20, 1937.

Article outlines viewpoints over the debate as to whether George Gershwin is an artist or an arranger. Still is mentioned in this regard: "Duke Ellington is at one end of the Negro musical rainbow, probably the beginning end of good rich, earth, and William Grant Still is at the other, where modern color blends with Anglo-Saxon hymn-tunes. Ellington actually does write new arrangements of new shapes. Still is as skillful with orchestral color as Ravel. Neither of these men could have written anything like *Porgy and Bess*, however, because they are too close to the life pictured in that opera."

B258 ———. "Meet the Composer: (12) William Grant Still." *Musical America* 64 (December 25, 1944): 7, 25. (Later published in *Negro Digest* [May 1945]: 55-58 under the title "From Tin Pan Alley To Opera.")

In this biographical sketch, Jones touches upon Still's youth, his present family life in California, his symphonies and operas, and his interest in racial struggles.

B259 Jones, Jack. "'Daddy of the Blues' visits his lovin' chillun in L.A." Los Angeles *Daily News*, June 25, 1954.

Report on a trip to Los Angeles by W.C. Handy, who reminisced with William Grant Still, Frank Drye, L. Wolfe Gilbert, and Andy Razaf. "Still said of Handy: 'He's a wonderful musician. We meet on common ground. Jazz or classical . . . there isn't much distinction.'"

B260 Jones, Julia B. "Talk O'Town." *Pittsburgh Courier*, February 27, 1943.

The author, a classmate of Still while at Wilberforce, writes in her column that his resignation from Twentieth Century-Fox "was a very fine and courageous act."

B261 Kamarck, Edward L., ed. "Artist in an Age of Revolution: A Symposium." *Arts and Society* 5 (Summer-Fall 1968): 219-22. (Also appears in Spencer, "Reader," as "Answer to a Questionnaire," 203-06.)

William Grant Still was one of a number of African Americans who responded to a questionnaire. Take, for example, the first question: "Do you think of yourself as a Negro artist or an artist who happens to be a Negro?" Still responded: "I think of myself first as an American, then as an artist who happens to be a Negro. After all, I have Indian, Irish, Spanish and Scotch blood in veins in addition to the African—I don't consider any of them more important than the other."

B262 Kass, Carole. "Still and Freeman Blend Talents for Concert Today." *Richmond Times-Dispatch*, March 21, 1971, sec. J, p. 1+.

Interview with William Grant Still, Verna Arvey Still, and Paul Freeman prior to a program performed by the Richmond Symphony which included Still's *Cumbia y Congo* from *Danzas de Panama* and *Scherzo* from *Afro-American Symphony*. In response to a criticism that Still's attitude was not ethnic enough, he replied, "'I have been a Negro every day for 75 years, and you are not going to tell me how to be one. I do not believe in a white culture and a black culture. That is separatism. I believe we should all be citizens of the United States. . . . I was in Memphis, working for W.C. Handy, and I used to go to this disreputable street [Beale Street] and hear the sounds the people sang in their back yards. Some listeners thought they were only singing about sex, but I heard them singing about hard times, and hard work, and pains of the heart and hope.'" Of a South American influence in some of his music he indicates, "'I communicate with my unconscious. I know what I need. I sit back, don't think and it comes through to me. Of course, much South American music has African origins.'"

B263 Kaufman, Annette and Louis. "Notes on the Violin, its Composers and Players." *Violins and Violinists* 6 (August 1944): 48-52.

Still is identified among those composers in the United States who are "beginning to have a clear voice" relative to compositions for the violin.

B264 Kaufman, Schima. *Everybody's Music*. New York: Thomas Y. Crowell Co., 1938.

This volume includes synopsis of the eleven episodes of *Lenox Avenue* (pp. 242-44).

B265 Kaufmann, Helen L. *The Story of One Hundred Great Composers*. New York: Grosset and Dunlap, 1943: 213-14.

Still is described as: "One whose voice is being effectively lifted in serious music today. . . . The first Negro to write a significant symphony and conduct a major orchestra, he is extremely modest; in him racial pride goes hand in hand with intense personal humility." The appendix includes eleven compositions by Still (p. 288).

B266 Kellner, Bruce. *The Harlem Renaissance: A Historical Dictionary for the Era*. Westport, Conn.: Greenwood Press, 1984.

Includes a lengthy sketch of Still (pp. 342-45) by Desmond Arthur. Mentions Still as music director of the Black Swan Phonograph Corporation, as well as Still performing on the oboe for the musical comedy *Shuffle Along*.

B267 ———, ed. *Keep A-Inchin' Along: Selected Writings of Carl Van Vechten about Black Art and Letters*. Contributions in Afro-American and African Studies, No. 45. Westport, Conn.: Greenwood Press, 1979.

Notes one of Still's scores (p. 126) in the James Weldon Johnson Memorial Collection of Negro Arts and Letters at Yale University. "Another of the more interesting items in this department of the collection is the manuscript orchestral score of William Grant Still's ballet, *Sahdji*, in which is laid autobiographical comment in longhand by Alain Locke and Bruce Nugent, who collaborated on the scenario for this dance-drama." Also included is a letter (pp. 264-65) from Carl Van Vechten to Langston Hughes, dated March 1, 1939, stating "please tell William Grant Still to call me when he comes East as I MUST photograph him."

B268 Kennan, Clara B. "Native of Little Rock Is Widely Celebrated Negro Composer." *Arkansas Gazette Magazine*, August 5, 1951, p. 1.

Lengthy article on Still tracing his youth in Little Rock to prominence in the world of music.

B269 Kernodle, Tammy Lynn. "Still's *Troubled Island*, A Troubled Opera: Its Creation, Performance, and Reception." Master's thesis, Ohio State University, 1993.

Troubled Island premiered in 1949 at the New York City Center. Although it met with a favorable response by the audience, critics were very harsh on it. This thesis is an attempt to answer some of the questions surrounding this controversial production, including one that certain critics plotted together to "pan" it.

B270 Kinscella, Hazel Gertrude. *Music On The Air*. Garden City, N.Y.: Garden City Publishing Co., Inc., 1934: 210.

In her work associated with radio broadcasts of music the author has the following to provide on Still: "we are slowly developing a group of gifted Negro composers. Such men as William Grant Still, a composer of the highest sincerity, would naturally be moved by the songs of his people. This influence gives to his music not only an individuality which could be found only in America, but also a moving force resulting from the man's highly sensitive and powerfully emotional nature. This music can justly be called one branch of American music."

B271 Koppes, Clayton R., and Gregory D. Black. "Blacks, Loyalty, and Motion-Picture Propaganda in World War II." *Journal of American History* 73 (September 1986): 383-406.

In their treatment of the film *Stormy Weather*, a picture that had a turbulent development, the authors mention Still and quote a portion of his January 25, 1945, letter to Walter White, executive secretary of the NAACP. "Musical supervisor William Grant Still . . . charged that producer Alfred Newman threw out his arrangements because they were 'not authentic' and refused to hire the black musicians Still wanted. The composer noted sardonically: 'The usual excuse in Hollywood [is] if it's Negro music it has to be crude to be authentic.' The alternate musicians, he said, could barely sight-read, 'clowned for the audition,' and made a 'pitiful' impression."

B272 Krueger, Karl. "Homage to William Grant Still." *Black Perspective in Music* 3 (May 1975): 134.

When Krueger, a conductor, wrote "Homage" he was the founder and director of the Society for the Preservation of the American Musical Heritage. His short paragraph concludes with: "The nobility of his character, his steadfastness and generosity, and the wise philosophy that has guided him through the tangled ways and byways of this world—these have contributed to making him one of the most memorable and cherished human beings I have known."

B273 Kyle, Marguerite Kelly. "AmerAllegro." *Pan Pipes of Sigma Alpha Iota* 42 (December 1949): 112.

Kyle's "AmerAllegro" compendiums are significant because they serve as a compilation of premieres and recent performances, publications, recordings, honors and awards, and other news in the form of a summary for the year. The information is provided by the composers themselves and edited by Kyle. Summaries of Still's activities can be found in the following volumes of *Pan Pipes*: 42 (December 1949): 112; 43 (December 1950): 131; 44 (January 1952): 45; 45 (January 1953): 67-68; 46 (January 1954): 62; 47 (January 1955): 68-69; 48 (January 1956): 74; 49 (January 1957): 70; 50 (January 1958): 73-74; 51 (January 1959): 86; 52 (January 1960): 73; 53 (January 1961): 77; 54 (January 1962): 72-73; 55 (January 1963): 71; 56 (January 1964): 81; 57 (January 1965): 80-81; 58 (January 1966): 86; 59 (January 1967): 97; 60 (January 1968): 94; 61 (January 1969): 77-78; 62 (January 1970): 84; 63 (January 1971): 79-80; 64 (January 1972): 80; 65 (January 1973): 74; 66 (January 1974): 74; 67 (January 1975): 74; 68 (January 1976): 74-75; 69 (January 1977): 73-74; and 70 (January 1978): 64-65. When combined with information from the John Simon Guggenheim Memorial Foundation *Reports of the Secretary and of the Treasurer*, these two sources provide the best chronological review of Still's works and accomplishments from 1925 to 1977.

B274 LaMar, Lawrence F. "Film Studios Break Precedent—Randol, Still Sign Contracts." *California Eagle*, June 5, 1936, p.1, 10.

Article announcing, in part, that Still signed a contract with Columbia Studios to write and score music, working directly under Morris Stoloff, head of the music department. "Part of this interest is undoubtedly heightened by the fact that the learned composer is a Negro. . . . The general assignment handed Mr. Still gives him full opportunity to familiarize himself with studio routine work of scoring and composing for current film productions."

B275 Le Berthon, Ted. "White Man's Views." *Pittsburgh Courier*, May 18, 1946.

The writer, in his weekly column, believes that Still's music transcends race. "What impinges on his consciousness daily is the modern American scene, which is polyglot, in flux, uncrystallized, multiracial. . . . He is stalking dreams and visions and seeking to clothe them in beautiful sound."

B276 Leab, Daniel J. *From Sambo to Superspade*. Boston: Houghton Mifflin Company, 1975.

This monograph on the African American experience in the motion picture industry mentions Still (p. 122). "There were aspects of [*Stormy Weather*] that verged on the ridiculous and the patronizing. William Grant Still . . . resigned as the film's music supervisor in protest against studio attitudes that, he said, 'degraded colored people.' Still charged that some of his orchestrations for post-World War I music were thrown out because, according to the studio's white music director, 'Negro bands didn't play that well then.' Still also assailed the studio for emphasizing 'crude' black music and 'erotic' black dancing, and for frustrating attempts to counter the 'Hollywood stereotype as regards colored people.'"

B277 Lebrecht, Norman. *The Companion to 20th-Century Music*. New York: Simon and Schuster, 1992: 335.

This volume provides a short biographical sketch of Still, stating that he was the "first black American to win symphonic recognition." It identifies his *Afro-American Symphony, Symphony No. 2 in G Minor, Troubled Island, And They Lynched Him on a Tree*, and *Symphony No. 5, "Western Hemisphere,"* but mistakenly identifies his place of birth as Missouri.

B278 Levette, Harry. "New angle in Wm. Still case." *Los Angeles Sentinel*, March 4, 1943.

Still provides additional information on his resignation from Twentieth Century-Fox in this interview for the Associated Negro Press.

B279 ———. "Stokowski Gets First Race Press Confab." *California Eagle*, June 3, 1943.

Lengthy article based upon an interview with reporters representing the African American press, on May 27, 1943, at the home of Still. Mention is made of *Those Who Wait*, which Still wrote for Stokowski.

B280 Levine, Morton. "Music Composer's Life in a Minor Key." *Estwood Hills Press*, January 22, 1948, p. 7+.

General article on Still. "The other night, with personal program notes and an occasional interjection of 'I don't want to bore you' or 'Are you getting tired?' Still played excerpts from his *Afro-American Symphony*, *Lenox Avenue*, *Poem for Orchestra*, *Sahdji* ballet and *In Memoriam: The Colored Soldiers Who Died for Democracy*. In these works you get a Cross-section of Still's musical personality. He writes for orchestra with a flair. His music is lively with rhythm and pungent with instrumental color. He likes brilliant violins and shining brass and very individualistic woodwinds."

B281 Lewis, Ellistine Perkins. "The E. Azalia Hackley Memorial Collection of Negro Music, Dance, and Drama: A Catalog of Selected Afro-American Materials." Ph.D. diss. University of Michigan, 1978.

The purpose of this study was "to scrutinize the holdings of the E. Azalia Hackley Collection of Negro Music, Dance, and Drama as a source of Afro-American music materials for use in the development and implementation of multicultural music curricula (p. 154)." The Hackley Collection is a special collection of African American materials located in the Music and Performing Arts Department of the Detroit Public Library. The "Catalog of Selected Afro-American Materials" that Lewis created contains 1,120 titles of published music, books, and sound recordings, including many relating to Still.

B282 Lewis, Emery Jerome. "A Comprehensive Analysis of the Melodic Structure of the Afro-American Symphony." M.A. thesis, Ohio State University, 1977.

B283 Lewis, Iris. "Famed Composer Is Guest at Final Symphony Salon of Year; Mr. Hartshorn Is Speaker." *Long Beach Press-Telegram,* April 2, 1943.

Still was the guest of honor at the April 1, 1943, symphony salon of the Long Beach Women's Committee for the Philharmonic Orchestra of Southern California. He commented on and played recorded excerpts of some of his compositions.

B284 "Liberian Research Society Awards Blue Ribbons at Annual Dinner." *California Leader*, April 22, 1937.

On April 16, 1937, Still was awarded a Blue Ribbon by the Liberian Research Society for his success in music. "In accepting the award the famous composer said: 'It is dangerous to think too much of race; rather, think of America. If the colored man is to survive he must compete with the best in America.'"

B285 Lindstrom, Carl E. "Music Needs to Get Away from New York." *Hartford (Connecticut) Times,* July 21, 1947, p. 22.

Lindstrom believes that critics and others in the world of music from New York command an undue influence over what is performed. He includes a lengthy portion of a letter from Still on the subject, who raises the same objections.

B286 ———. "Musicians Point Out Two Kinds of Critics." *Hartford (Connecticut) Times*, October 6, 1947, p. 14.

Second in a series of three articles on music critics, Still is quoted twice, one of which is as follows: "'A critic should have a thorough musical foundation combined with journalistic training—neither is complete without the other. If there is a tendency to over-emphasize either of these, it's best to lean toward the musical side. Some of our accredited schools should offer special courses of study for those who would like to become music critics.'"

B287 ———. "Reportorial Function of Critic Recognized." *Hartford (Connecticut) Times*, October 13, 1947, p. 16.

Last in a series of three articles on music critics, Still is quoted as follows: "'Newspaper criticism should have a dual function, that of reporting what takes place and that of offering a critical evaluation with no personal bias. Yes, all fair, intelligent criticism should and does help performer and composer.'"

B288 ———. "Victims Turn Tables on the Music Critic." *Hartford (Connecticut) Times*, September 29, 1947.

First in a series of three lengthy articles on music critics. Still is quoted twice. "'A critic should be able to forget his personal taste and to write objectively. Music should be evaluated for what it is rather than for what someone thinks it should be. . . . Unfortunately, a composer does have need of a literary interpreter. When something is new, it needs all the elucidation possible so that it may have the best chance to attain audience and critical understanding.'"

B289 Lippey, Joyce, and Walden E. Muns. "William Grant Still." *Music Journal* 21 (November 1963): 34+.

General interview with Still. Includes list of compositions.

B290 Locke, Alain. *The Negro and His Music*. Kennikat Press Series in Negro Culture and History. Port Washington, N.Y.: Kennikat Press, 1968: 132-33.

La Guiablesse and *Sahdji* are included among a group of compositions by Locke that suggest: "A healthier primitivism and a more dignified tradition . . . when we are trying to develop the deeper possibilities of our music."

B291 ———. *The Negro in America*. Reading With A Purpose Series, No. 68. Chicago: American Library Association, 1933:47.

In his chapter "The Negro As Man And Artist," Locke includes Still among those who have developed strong and positive reputations for their work.

B292 ———. "Negro Music Goes To Par." *Opportunity: Journal of Negro Life* 17 (July 1939): 196+.

The author provides insight to new perceptions on African-American music, especially as they relate to technical analysis, criticism, and scholarship. Of Still, Locke writes that he "is more and more taking his place as one of the most original and outstanding of the younger American composers. As his style matures the folk idiom crops out more and more, tempering his earlier, too intellectualized, ultra-modernistic style."

B293 "Los Angeles Musicians Mark 25th Anniversary." *Pittsburgh Courier*, September 22, 1945.

Article describing activities at the twenty-fifth meeting of Musician's Local 767, American Federation of Musicians. The highlight of the meeting was the presentation of a trophy to William Grant Still for "Outstanding Achievement in Music Composition."

B294 Lott, R. Allen. "'New Music for New Ears': The International Composers'

Guild." *Journal of the American Musicological Society* 36 (Summer 1983): 266-86.

Identifies Still among the American composers presented by the Guild; the others included Henry Cowell, Henry Eichheim, Carl Ruggles, and Emerson Whithorne. As an appendix, the article includes programs of the Guild from 1922 to 1927, of which Still's music is found on three: *From the Land of Dreams* (1925), *Levee Land* (1926), and *Darker America* (1926).

B295 Lovoos, Janice. "The Portrait Sculpture of Joseph Portanova." *American Artist* 29 (January 1965): 38-43+.

Article on the sculptor, including illustrations of some of his pieces—one of which shows Still, one of his first sitters.

B296 MacLeod, Lynne L. "A Life Full of Music." *Mississippi* 13 (May-June 1995): 93-96.

The article is written for a popular magazine whose audience constitutes the general public. The piece weaves together facts, questionable statements, and inaccuracies. For example, the *Afro-American Symphony* premiered in 1931, not 1933 (p. 95). Still's list of honorary degrees, as provided by the author, is both deficient and in error. He received nine honorary degrees, not five. One of them was an honorary Master of Music from Wilberforce University in 1936, not an earned degree as stated by the author (p. 95).

B297 "Mail Bag." *Woodville Republican*, July 4, 1980.

In their attempts to learn more about the family history of Still, Donald and Dolores Dorr visited Woodville, Mississippi, the birth place of Still, and spoke with a number of people in the area. They wrote a long letter to the editor of the local paper, thanking those who assisted them, and described some of the things that they learned during their trip.

B298 "Marksville Poet Featured On Radio Network." *Marksville (Louisiana) Weekly News,* July 17, 1948.

General article, including biographical sketch, on J. Mitchell Pilcher, Montgomery, Alabama, poet and Marksville, Louisiana, native, whose poems inspired Still to compose *Wood Notes*.

B299 Martin, Donald. "Current Films with Worth While Music." *Etude* (January 1940): 14+.

Still is mentioned as one of a handful of composers who were hired by Hollywood film companies to work on films.

B300 "Mastery . . . William Grant Still." *Tones and Overtones* 1 (Spring 1954): 49-58.

This lengthy article provides background on Still's career, a brief listing of articles by Still, a list of his compositions, and a list of books and periodicals containing information on the composer.

B301 Matthews, Miriam. "Phylon Profile, XXIII: William Grant Still—Composer." *Phylon* 22 (Second Quarter 1951): 106-12. (Also appears in Still, *Fusion,* 189-96.)

Good profile of the composer, including background on his education, highlights of his career, and short list of awards and prizes.

B302 McBride, Jessica Lundy. "The Blues Theme in William Grant Still's *Afro-American Symphony*." "Mini" thesis, Texas A and I University, 1975.

The author of this brief (15 p.) study, identified as a "Mini Thesis," concludes by stating that Still "uses the blues theme as a basis of unification with the work [*Afro-American Symphony*]. He does this chiefly through the two elements of music—*Time* and *Tone* [p. 14]."

B303 McCorvey, Everett David. "The Art Songs of Black American Composers." D.M.A. University of Alabama, 1989.

Still is one of eleven composers who are included in this study. The others are Camille Lucille Nickerson, Edgar Rogie Clark, Henry T. Burleigh, Coleridge-Taylor Perkinson, Florence B. Price, George T. Walker, Leslie Adams, John E. Price, Margaret A. Bonds, and Cedric Carl Dent. The author provides a biographical sketch of each and "a complete catalogue of art songs composed by these composers." There are twenty-one art songs attributed to Still.

B304 McGehee, Charles White. "Mississippi's Foremost Composer." *Summit (Mississippi) Sun,* August 17, 1939.

Lengthy article on Still, noting his accomplishments and experience.

B305 "Men Who Do Things: William Grant Still." *Opportunity: Journal of Negro Life* 16 (September 1938): 273, 284-85.

The article begins with a description of what a visitor to the perisphere at the 1939 New York World's Fair will see and hear, including Still's music. It then moves to a review of Still's life and accomplishments, including his orchestrations for *Vanities*, *Rain or Shine*, and the second *Americana*, as well as his work for the *Deep River Hour*.

B306 "Message From William Grant Still." *Peabody Notes* 29 (October 1974): 4.

Since Still could not attend commencement exercises, because of ill health, when an honorary Doctor of Music was conferred upon him, he sent a letter of acceptance that was printed in this issue of the Peabody Conservatory of Music newsletter.

B307 Meyers, Robert. "Still Elevating the Blues." *Washington Post,* May 18, 1975, p. G-6.

Article based upon an interview of the composer at his home on the occasion of his eightieth birthday. Of the *Afro-American Symphony*, the composer remarks, "I wanted to demonstrate how the blues, so often considered a lowly expression, could be elevated to the highest musical level."

B308 Michaelis, Adrian. "Still Music on the Western Air." *Black Perspective in Music* 3 (May 1975): 177-89.

Michaelis served for forty years as program manager for the Standard Oil Company's public service radio broadcasts. From that perspective, he discusses the performance of Still's music over the *Standard Symphony Hour* and the *Standard School Broadcast*. Eight photographs accompany the article.

B309 Miles, Melvin N. "A Transcription for Concert Band of the First Movement from William Grant Still's *Afro-American Symphony*." Master's thesis. Morgan State University, 1978.

B310 Moe, Orin. "William Grant Still: *Songs of Separation*." *Black Music Research Journal* (December 1980): 18-36.

An excellent analysis of the original voice and piano version of Still's *Songs of Separation*. A brief version of this subject first appeared in the Spring 1980 *Black Music Research Newsletter*, a piece that was re-printed in the Spring 1990 issue of *Black Music Research Journal* under the title "Black Music and Musical Analysis: William Grant Still's *Song of Separation* As A Point of Departure." Moe places this song cycle within the context of Black Music Scholarship through a textual and musical exegesis that is both scholarly and convincing.

B311 Monson, Karen. "Still Has Lived Through Musical Changes." *Los Angeles Herald-Examiner,* January 24, 1970, sec. B, p. 5.

General interview with Still touching upon his work with W.C. Handy, Edgard Varèse, and the blues idiom. Still provides the following background for his association with Varèse. "'I was working for the Negro record company in New York, Black Swan. One morning I read a letter that one of the secretaries was typing. Mr. Varèse had wanted someone to teach his ultramodern music. The secretary was replying that we had nobody who could do it, but I ripped the letter from her typewriter and told her that Varèse had found his man.'" Still summarizes: "'There are elements of that music that can be adopted, such as the expanded view of harmonies. But sound isn't enough for music. You need the spiritual side too'"

B312 Morch, Al. "ASCAP 'Greats' Decry American Music Trends." *Newslife* (Beverly Hills, Calif.), June 29, 1954: 2.

Interview with William Grant Still, W.C. Handy, and L. Wolfe Gilbert. Still, commenting on serious American music, states, "The modern writers are imitating the decadent European masters instead of creating a living American musical culture. If the composers were giving audiences what they want—the common touch, so to speak—attendance figures at contemporary concerts would be much higher."

B313 Morgan, Lena Moon. "An Interview with William Grant Still." *Pan Pipes of Sigma Alpha Iota* 53 (January 1962): 35, 38.

A general overview on the education, accomplishments, honors and awards of Still.

B314 Morton, Tim. "Still Remembered." *Norfolk Virginian-Pilot,* March 16, 1975.

Review of Still's major accomplishments the week before his *Highway 1, U.S.A.* is to be produced at Norfolk State College.

B315 "The Motion Picture As A Weapon of War." *People's World*, March 27, 1943, p. 5.

In response to a question on the contributions of the motion picture industry to the war effort, posed to a number of people in that industry, Still responds, "Properly carried out, it would amount to an education of the American people for the full responsibilities and privileges of our democracy and a greater respect for our nation abroad."

B316 Muns, Monty. "Metronome." *Los Angeles City News*, March 31, 1960.

Review of a lecture presented by Still entitled "Audience Reaction to Contemporary Music." "Dr. Still took umbrage at labellers—the people who would stamp a period with the term 'contemporary,' thus making this a style or school of music rather than a period of time [in] which music is being composed. Said Still: 'Is it wrong to consider the term contemporary anything other than what it is, which is right now, when music is being written.'"

B317 Murchison, Gayle. "'Dean of Afro-American Composers' or 'Harlem Renaissance Man': *The New Negro* and the Musical Poetics of William Grant Still." *Arkansas Historical Quarterly* 53 (Spring 1994): 42-74.

The author is a musicologist specializing in American and African American music. She effectively uses information drawn from the William Grant Still and Verna Arvey Papers at the University of Arkansas with that of primary and secondary sources on the Harlem Renaissance to provide a new assessment of Still, his artistic and aesthetic ideals, and his music.

B318 "Music in Films." *Films* 1 (Winter 1940): 7.

Still responded to a questionnaire sent out in an attempt to establish information for students and critics of film music as follows: "The films for which I composed part of the music were: *Theodora Goes Wild*, *Pennies from Heaven*, *Lady of Secrets*. I also composed about 29 sketches for the stock catalogue at Columbia Studios, and of course I don't know how these have been used since I left the studio."

B319 "Music Journal Adds Eight New Members To Its Advisory Council." *Music Journal* 32 (July 1974): 10-11.

Sketches of the accomplishments of new advisory board members, of which Still is one.

B320 Myers, Marcus. "UA celebrates composer's centennial." *Arkansas Traveler*, March 13, 1995, p. 13+.

Article on the activities that took place at the University of Arkansas, Fayetteville, as part of the "William Grant Still Centennial Week," March 8-11, 1995. Lectures, recitals and performances, and an exhibit of materials from the William Grant Still and Verna Arvey Papers were part of the program.

B321 "Negro Historical and Cultural Society Negro History Week Observance." *San Francisco Sun Reporter*, January 31, 1970, p. 28.

Article describing the events which will take place during Negro History Week, including a list of Still's contributions to music. "[Still] is extremely critical of his own works, but he admittedly prefers his compositions based on Negro spirituals. 'Spirituals are just as universal as any other form of music,' he says. 'I believe in that type of melody and harmony.'"

B322 "Negro Performers Brightened the Decades!" *Pittsburgh Courier*, September 17, 1960, sect. 3, p. 7.

Lengthy article on the contributions of black musicians, singers, and composers to American Culture. "William Grant Still and William Dawson, the best-known Negro composers, won recognition with the aid of a few courageous American conductors like Leopold Stokowski, John Barbirolli, Arthur Judson and Eugene Goossens. . . . The obstacles facing Negro composers are so great that only 10 years ago, William Grant Still called the creative barrier 'the most difficult of all.' Of prejudiced critics he said, 'These opponents are not only biased people, they are scared people. When they hear music by a Negro composer that is successful from an audience standpoint, they become desperately afraid. They have seen Negroes rise to prominence in so many fields; they hope it won't happen in the creative world.'"

B323 Nelson, Boris. "William Grant Still: 50 Years Of Music." *Toledo Blade*, May 2, 1965, sec. E, p. 4.

General biographical sketch and a review of Still's major accomplishments. "Technically, he uses atonality if it can be effective, yet he sees the need for tonality—and he is particularly appreciative of the characteristics of individual national schools. Thus his music covers all imaginable styles—in works for large and small orchestra, for band, instrumental combinations, organ, piano, voice, chorus, ballet, and his first and best love, opera."

B324 Neurath, Herbert. "Orchestra Problems Discussed." *Musical America* 74 (July 1954): 5.

Report on the national convention of the American Symphony Orchestra League, held in Springfield, Ohio, June 17-19, 1954. Still presented the opening address, entitled "Toward A Broader American Culture." "[Still] stressed the importance of a conscious effort to emphasize national culture in this country. He noted the role American orchestras are playing in disseminating knowledge of American music, particularly of works of composers living in their own region. He maintained that works of all categories and styles should be heard—not in one, but two or three performances, as one presentation does not give an adequate impression of a new composition."

B325 Nichols, Charles H. *Arna Bontemps-Langston Hughes Letters, 1925-1967*. New York: Dodd, Mead and Co., 1980.

Between 1925 and 1967 Bontemps and Hughes exchanged about 2,300 letters, from which the author has selected about 500 for this publication. Still worked closely with both, so it is not surprising that his name surfaces in some of the letters. For example, in a letter to Bontemps dated February 14, 1941, Hughes says, "Still tells me rehearsals for *Troubled Island* have begun in Los Angeles, mixed cast, chorus of one hundred, orchestra of seventy which he will conduct (p. 75)." In a letter to Hughes dated November 19, 1945, Bontemps writes, "My first song just came through, a poem called *Idolatry*, set by Still. A very impressive job for the more profound music lovers. I hear there are some more to come, by him as well as a few others (p. 200)." Although Still is mentioned less than ten times in these selected letters, it leads one to believe that research in their collections would reveal additional letters associated with Still.

B326 "Notes for *Notes*." *Notes: The Quarterly Journal of the Music Library Association* 36 (June 1980): 873-74.

The papers of critic, pianist, and teacher Irving Schwerké are noted as a donation to the Music Division of the Library of Congress. Significant correspondence from numerous individuals in the field of music is part of the collection, including forty-three letters from William Grant Still.

B327 "Oberlin College honors composer William Grant Still." *Pittsburgh Courier*, November 7, 1970 (Detroit Edition). (Also published in the *Chicago Defender*, October 31, 1970 and the *Akron Reporter*, November 7, 1970.)

Extensive article on activities scheduled for the seventy-fifth birthday concert in honor of Still at Oberlin College Conservatory of Music, including a list of his accomplishments and "firsts."

B328 "Oberlin Honors Wooster Head, Four Others." *Cleveland News*, June 24, 1947.

Announcement on honorary degrees conferred by Oberlin College. Still received a Doctor of Music.

B329 "Oberlin Marks William Grant Still's 75 1/2th Birthday." *Oberlin Alumni Magazine* 67 (January 1971): 12-13.

A brief review of the activities held at Oberlin College November 8 and 9, 1970, associated with the belated celebration of Still's 75th birthday. A biographical sketch is included.

B330 "Oberlin to Honor Black Composer-Music." *Lorain Journal*, November 7, 1970.

Preview of activities and events associated with the seventy-fifth birthday concert in honor of Still at Oberlin College Conservatory of Music.

B331 O'Connor, Tom. "Los Angeles Life: Portrait No.17—William Grant Still." Los Angeles *Evening News*, September 26, 1936, p.3.

Biographical sketch of Still, number seventeen in a series of thirty sketches of distinguished Los Angeles citizens. The article is accompanied with a portrait sketched by Georges Schreiber, the noted Belgian American artist.

B332 Oderigo, Néster R. Ortiz. *Panorama De La Música Afroamericana*. Buenos Aires: Editorial Claridad, 1944.
Includes a section (pp. 242-44) on Still.

B333 Oja, Carol J. "'New Music' and the 'New Negro': The Background of William Grant Still's *Afro-American Symphony*." *Black Music Research Journal* 12 (Fall 1992): 145-69.
The author examines the *Afro-American Symphony* within the context of the broad artistic movements of its era. *Darker America, Dismal Swamp, From the Land of Dreams, Kaintuck'*, and *Levee Land* are brought within the author's discussion.

B334 Oliver, Elizabeth M. "Afro Visits With The Allens And The Stills." *Baltimore Afro-American*, June 14, 1960, p. 9.
Article on the lives of Nimrod Allen, founder of the Frontiers of America, and William Grant Still, who first met as students at Wilberforce University in 1911.

B335 Oney, Tom. "Black Composer, 75, Begins Working on Seventh Opera." *Lorain Journal*, November 11, 1970.
Interview with Still while he was in Oberlin for an all-Still concert at the Oberlin College Conservatory of Music. "'I really don't know what my favorite (music) would be, but my preference is opera. I wrote one on New Orleans [*Minette Fontaine*] and, after a year and one half of research, I fell in love with the city. . . . But a change has taken place. . . . I wouldn't want to write that way anymore,' he said and smiled. . . . 'I think already there's a germ of a different style having its effect on me—a new type of music.' Still said he would like to pursue a new field called musical dissonance. 'As I see it, that would be ideal and offer new scope of harmony for me. . . . It [a new opera] will be a departure from any I have written before,' he said. 'It will be our [includes Verna Arvey Still] own story and will not come from the conscious, but from the subconscious.'"

B336 "Opera for Broadway: An Outlet for the Contemporary Composer?" *Musical Digest* (November 1947): 5, 18.
Is Broadway the best outlet for the production of contemporary operas? Still was among those who responded "no." Still remarks: "'If an American opera can find a place for itself on Broadway, then by all means let it be produced there. But do not saddle us with the thought that Broadway is the *only* place for our operas.'"

B337 Ortiz-Karp, Norma. "NEH Supports Still-Arvey Project." *Books and Letters* 6 (Spring 1992): 2.
The author, project archivist for the arrangement, description, and preservation of the papers of Still and Arvey, describes the significance of the collection, housed in the Special Collections Division of the University of Arkansas Libraries, Fayetteville.

B338 Ottley, Nevilla E. *Still's Life in Pictures*. Takoma Park, MD: Classics of Ebony Publishing, 1995.
Published for the centennial celebration of the birth of Still, this publication includes fifty-five photographs with accompanying text surrounding the life, works and accomplishments of the composer.

B339 Ottley, Roi, and William J. Weatherby, eds. *The Negro in New York: An Informal Social History*. New York: New York Public Library, 1967.
In their chapter "The Black Bourgeoisie," the editors devote attention to Harry

Pace and the Black Swan Phonograph Company. Pace is quoted extensively, in part as follows: "'William Grant Still . . . was Musical Director . . . who arranged the material necessary to be recorded and took charge of the recordings at the laboratory. . . . The pressure of arranging and recording became so great that I hired Fletcher Henderson who became Recording Manager and worked under Mr. Still, so that Still would only arrange while Henderson played in the orchestra and handled recordings at the factory (p. 234).'"

B340 Palevoda, Walter. "Keynotes." *Miami Beach Reporter,* May 2, 1963.
Based upon a series of questions posed to Still in an interview, the reporter presents his column in a question and answer format.

B341 Palmer, Zuma. "Radio Programs Personalities." *Hollywood Citizen-News,* August 17, 1942.
Still remarks that radio can do much more to develop interests in American music. He touches upon his work with the *Deep River Hour.*

B342 ———. "Radio Programs Personalities." *Hollywood Citizen-News,* August 18, 1942, p. 14.
Article reflecting the personal side of Still, including his work habits and gardening.

B343 Parker, John B. "Composer praises individuality he developed at OC." *Elyria Chronicle-Telegram,* November 10, 1970.
Interview with Still. "'As important as the technical foundation one can develop at the Oberlin Conservatory is the individuality one can develop there,' Still said. 'The tendency to go along with the herd doesn't bring anything new. The composer would be failing his purpose in life without this individuality. . . . In spite of the importance of individuality, however, the composer must remember that he is writing for the people. . . . Most younger contemporary composers are still writing in the avant garde style that saw its infancy in the early 1920s. . . . Many new composers fail to see avant garde's true value, which can only be realized when it is contrasted with other idioms. . . . Inventive ability is the composer's most important gift,' Still said."

B344 Parmenter, Ross. "The World Of Music: Still Works At New Opera." *New York Times,* October 2, 1949.
Brief article indicating Still at work on an opera (*Costaso*) set in the American Southwest. The libretto was written by Verna Arvey.

B345 Patterson, Lindsay, comp. and ed. *The Negro In Music And Art.* International Library Of Negro Life And History. New York: Publishers Company, Inc., 1970.
"Other Negro composers, such as William Grant Still, confined their efforts to the classical arena. Dr. Still, winner of several fellowships and holder of many honorary degrees, dipped into the realm of popular music to arrange and conduct for radio and television, but remained steadfast to his loftier ambitions (pp. 123-24)."

B346 "Peabody to honor three composers." *Baltimore Sun,* May 24, 1974, p. B4.
Article on the 1974 recipients of honorary degrees from the Peabody Conservatory of Music, to be awarded during the 106th commencement on May 29. Still received an honorary Doctor of Music, *in absentia.* It was the first *in absentia* honorary degree in the 106-year history of the school.

B347 Peattie, Donald Culross. "Grubstaking the Best Folks." *Readers Digest* (August 1939): 71-74. (Condensed from an article that appears in the August, 1939, issue of *Survey Graphic.*)

Overview on the history and benefits of the Guggenheim Foundation. Still is identified as a Guggenheim Fellow.

B348 Perlee, Charles D. "Book, LPs Honor Black Composer." *San Bernardino (California) Sun-Telegram,* March 25, 1973, sec. D, p. 5.

Article devoted to Still, mentioning recent recordings and the publication of *William Grant Still and the Fusion of Cultures in American Music.*

B349 "Persons and Achievements to be Remembered in February." *Negro History Bulletin* 2 (February 1939): 36+.

Still is included among a select group of African Americans whose accomplishments are worthy of note.

B350 Pipkin, Viki. "Remembering William Grant Still." *Los Angeles Mesa Wave,* May 10, 1979.

Review of the life and accomplishments of Still with remarks by his widow, Verna Arvey, who stated, "Although his musical accomplishments made him a pioneer, I feel that in a much greater sense of the word he was a pioneer because he created music of interest to many great conductors of the day. His music was serious and had a definite American flavor."

B351 Portanova, Mary Spaulding Sevitsky. "Music Is Beauty." *Black Perspective in Music* 3 (May 1975): 196-98.

The author describes her association with Still, which began when they met in Indianapolis where Portanova was principal harpist with the Indianapolis Symphony Orchestra.

B352 Prattis, P.L. "Horizon." *Pittsburgh Courier,* June 18, 1955.

Article pertaining to a recent New York banquet staged by the National Negro Opera Foundation to promote the New York production of *Ouanga,* the opera written by Clarence Cameron White. The author laments the absence of Still, whose "presence . . . could not have but been an inspiration to everyone present." The article then goes on to describe Still's latest accomplishments.

B353 Price, Theodore. "Night of Nostalgia for Dr. Hanson." *Rochester Democrat and Chronicle,* May 8, 1971.

In this lengthy article relative to the Festival of American Music, Howard Hanson reminisces on the history of the Festivals. Mention is made of his early support of Still.

B354 Rampersad, Arnold. *The Life of Langston Hughes.* 2 vols. New York: Oxford University Press, 1986 and 1988.

In this enormous study of Hughes, the author effectively uses letters between Hughes and Still to document the history of their relationship, one which ended in controversy after the production of *Troubled Island* in 1949.

B355 Ratliff, William. "A Resurgence of Interest in Composer Still." *Los Angeles Times* (Calendar Section), November 24, 1985, p. 58.

Full page article on the composer, based upon an interview with his wife Verna and daughter Judith.

B356 Ray, Russell. "University Recalls Works of Composer W.G. Still." *Springdale Morning News,* March 6, 1995.

Preview of activities scheduled during the "William Grant Still Centennial Week" at the University of Arkansas, March 8-11, 1995. Lectures, recitals and performances, and an exhibit are included in the festivities.

B357 Razaf, Andy. "The Negro's Past, Present And Future in Songwriting." *Pittsburgh Courier,* June 18, 1960, p. 18.

General article on the accomplishments of black songwriters. "Negro writers have written art, classical and serious music. The symphonies of our own Dr. William Grant Still have been acclaimed as some of the finest music ever written by an American. How often do you hear them played? An all-out drive to awaken us to the greatness and cultural value of our musical achievements has been long overdue."

B358 ———. "Time Out For Thinking." *Los Angeles Herald-Dispatch*, September 1, 1955.

Article on the contributions of black musicians and composers. "Negro writers have created many art and classical songs, even symphonic music. The great symphonies of our own composer and arranger, Dr. William Grant Still, have been acclaimed as some of the finest music ever composed by an American. Yet, when have you ever heard one of Dr. Still's symphonies?"

B359 Reasons, George, and Sam Patrick. "Classical Compositions Won Acclaim." *Kansas City Star*, September 7, 1974.

Article highlighting Still's life touching upon his milestones and significant accomplishments.

B360 Reis, Claire R. *Composers, Conductors and Critics*. New York: Oxford University Press, 1955.

The author, who served as executive chairman of the League of Composers for twenty-five years, provides a personal account of her association with the world of music. She recounts one memory associated with an excerpt of Still's *Troubled Island* sung by a small group of performers in the office of Mayor La Guardia for the benefit of a group of African-American newspaper and magazine editors from all over the country.

B361 Reno, Doris. "I Compose With Pain I Enjoy." *Miami Herald*, October 29, 1961, sec. E, p. 19.

An interview with William Grant Still, who was in Miami to attend the premiere performance of the University of Miami Symphony Orchestra's production of *The Peaceful Land*. "'I don't think anything I've written is really 'racial.' All my compositions are for all people. I intend them to say something to everyone. Certainly *The Peaceful Land* is full of the hope of peace for us all, Americans and Africans and every person alive. . . . Now I can spend all my time composing serious music, and I try to make the most of it. But when I was doing popular arranging and orchestrating, I always determined not to let it master me. I always got everything out of it I could. And I got a lot—I learned to really orchestrate through my *Deep River Hour* on CBS in New York, for instance. . . . I only compose with great pain, but I enjoy the pain. . . . When I'm composing the music moves along so fast I used to have trouble remembering my themes until I got to the development. I learned to control its movement. But there are still quite a few of my works I've never heard and never want to hear; they'll be better forgotten. . . . I think the processes of fusion, growth and learning go on eternally, even in our after-life.'"

B362 ———. "Sounds of Music—in Three Parts." *Miami Herald*, May 10, 1963.

An interview with composers Edward M. Goldman, William Grant Still, and Frances Thorne, who were in Miami for the Fourth American Contemporary Music Festival at the University of Miami.

B363 Review of *William Grant Still and the Fusion of Cultures in American Music*, edited by Robert Bartlett Haas, ed. *Choice* 9 (February 1973): 1600.

"Still is recognized as the Nestor of American black composers. This 'source-book miscellany,' with a laudatory spirit suggestive of an 'authorized biography,' contains a useful assemblage of information on Still's career, reprints of his articles . . . bibliography, discogarphy, and suggested programs for an all-Still festival. . . . The structure of the text is too loosely conceived, the scholarship often amateurish. . . . Still deserves a more serious book than this one, which bears too many of the hallmarks of the vanity press."

B364 Rhodes, Don. "Black Composer's Best Work Is Still To Be Performed." *Augusta Herald*, March 20, 1972.

Interview with Still in which he discusses his early life and how he became interested in classical music. "Asked about his best work . . . Still responded, 'I guess I could cite my *Afro-American Symphony*, but my best work really has not been performed yet. It's called *Minette Fontaine* and is an opera based on a woman of the same name. The original story is set in New Orleans. I completed it several years ago before I had even visited New Orleans.' Asked why the opera hasn't been produced, Still sadly commented, 'It costs so much to produce an opera these days.'"

B365 Richardson, Ben Albert. *Great American Negroes*. New York: Thomas Y. Crowell Co., 1945: 50-61.

In part, the author states that Still "has proved that the Negro's particular contribution to the musical culture of our country can be more than spirituals and much of our dance music. There are wellsprings of music deep within Negroes which when tapped by knowledge, inspiration, and perseverance, are capable of producing major compositions that can rank with the finest orchestral music the world has ever known (p. 61)."

B366 Roach, Hildred. *Black American Music: Past and Present*. Malabar, Florida: Krieger Publishing Co., 1992. 2d edition.

Includes a section (pp. 122-24) on Still within the chapter "Art Music: Its Definition, Trends and Traditional Composers."

B367 Roberts, Enid Yvette. "Classical Music Not Limited To Whites." *Washington Informer*, November 29, 1979, p. 8+.

Very sketchy outline of the exposure of music to African Americans drawing upon Eileen Southern's research, and touching upon some of Still's accomplishments, including the recent performance of *Highway 1, U.S.A.* at the Gateway Theater, Washington, D.C.

B368 Robertson, Bill. "William Grant Still, Distinguished Composer, Lives Quietly In Area." *Los Angeles City News*, January 28, 1960.

Lengthy biographical sketch describing Still's boyhood interests in music, his educational background, and listing Still's major compositions, achievements, and awards.

B369 Robinson, Louie. "38 Years of Serious Music." *Ebony* 19 (February 1964): 102-06.

Lengthy report on the work and accomplishments of Still, based upon an interview. Notes how life was culturally but not financially rewarding. Still's philosophy of life and music included.

B370 Rockwell, John. "Still's 75th Birthday Today." *Los Angeles Times*, May 11, 1970, sec. 4, p. 16.

Interview with Still on the occasion of his seventy-fifth birthday. "'I used to have my music played a lot more in Los Angeles back in the 30s' and 40s,' he recalls, without bitterness. 'But now most people seem to want only this ultra-modern stuff. . . . I don't worry much about being out of fashion,' he smiles. 'Everybody has to be true to himself, to express himself in the way he believes is best. I'm content.'"

B371 Rodriquez, José, ed. *Music and Dance in California*. Compiled by William J. Perlman. Hollywood, Calif.: Bureau of Musical Research, 1940: 178-79.

B372 Rogers, J.A. "Your History." *Pittsburgh Courier*, May 17, 1941.

With an illustration of Still by Samuel Milai, Rogers provides a brief sketch of the composer describing him as "One of the greatest of living American composers."

B373 "Rosenwald Fellowship Goes to Still." *California Eagle*, May 9, 1940.

Announcement that Still received a Rosenwald Fellowship, one of sixty-eight but the only one from California, out of more than six hundred applicants.

B374 Rossi, Nick, and Robert A. Choate. *Music Of Our Time: An Anthology of Works of Selected Contemporary Composers of the 20th Century*. Boston: Crescendo Publishing Co., 1969.

Includes a chapter (pp. 236-44) on Still and a focus on the *Afro-American Symphony*.

B375 Rothe, Friede F. "Twenty Years of American Composers." *Musical Courier* 128 (August 1943): 16.

This is the sixth part of the author's series. In it, Still is identified as a "Spokesman for His People." The author asserts that "once he is oriented towards the expression of the feeling and background of his people, only works of inner sincerity and deep musical purpose can have value and significance."

B376 Ryder, Georgia A. "Another Look at Some American Cantatas." *Black Perspective in Music* 3 (May 1975): 135-40.

Included in this article are the following: *Highway 1, U.S.A.*; *And They Lynched Him on A Tree*; and *Plain-Chant for America*.

B377 ———. "Melodic and Rhythmic Elements of American Negro Folk Songs as Employed in Cantatas by Selected American Composers Between 1932 and 1937." Ph.D. diss., New York University; 1970.

The purpose of this study was to identify American Negro folk music idioms and to determine the nature of their use in cantatas by William Grant Still, Robert Nathaniel Dett, Earl Robinson, Roy Ringwald, Charles Haubiel, Wynn York, and Elie Siegmeister. *And They Lynched Him on a Tree* and *Plain-Chant for America* are included in this study.

B378 Saal, Hubert. "Black Composers." *Newsweek* (April 15, 1974): 82.

Article relative to the Black Composers Series of Columbia Records, of which Still is included in volume two. "Another important contributor is 78-year-old William Grant Still, dean of black American composers, originally a jazz man, whose gay *Afro-American Symphony* reflects not only Still's blackness but his ambivalent years as a commercial arranger (he put together *Frenesi* for Artie Shaw) and as a student of Edgard Varèse."

B379 Sabin, Robert. "A Survey of Our Orchestral Repertoire." *Musical America* 65 (July 1945): 8.

Based upon a survey of twenty-three orchestras representing a cross-section across the United States, the author found Still to be among the top ten American composers whose works were performed. The time period for the survey is not identified.

B380 Saltzberg, Geraldine. "Composer Needs 'God In Works.'" *Arizona Daily Star*, March 29, 1966.

An interview with Still prior to a performance by the Tucson Symphony which included Still's *Festive Overture*. "[Still's] philosophy of composing became apparent after a few minutes of conversation. 'A composer needs inspiration,' he explained. 'Not the mood of the moment, but the permanent breath of life, emanating from the life source itself. No amount of technique can make up for this God-given sense of life. Somewhere in his nature, the real composer must have a spiritual quality which enables him to come close to God. At the end of my works I always write 'With humble thanks to God, the source of inspiration.'"

B381 Sanjek, Russell. *American Popular Music and Its Business: The First Four Hundred Years*. Vol. 3, 1900-1984. New York: Oxford University Press, 1988: 402.

Still is listed among thirty-three plaintiffs in the lawsuit Schwartz v. BMI, of which the chief concern was to prosecute "an action against BMI, the interlocking radio and television broadcasters, and networks, which control it, those recording companies which are part of it, and all those others who have directly, and indirectly injured writers by placing American music in a strait jacket manipulated through BMI."

B382 Scarborough, Charles. "Honors For Negro Music." *Richmond News Leader*, March 20, 1971, sec. A, p. 30.

Lengthy article on William Grant Still, Paul Freeman, and the contributions of African American composers to the field of classical music.

B383 Schuyler, George. "Views and Reviews." *Pittsburgh Courier*, March 27, 1943.

Lengthy article on Still's resignation from Twentieth Century-Fox. "We should also praise, honor and support those Negro artists like William Grant Still who refuse to lend their talents to such productions [as *Stormy Weather*]."

B384 Scott, Phyllis. "NANM Convention Ends On Note Of Triumph." *California Eagle*, September 1, 1949.

Review of highlights associated with the National Association of Negro Musicians which held its annual meeting, August 21-26, in Los Angeles. "William Grant Still's *Archaic Ritual* was a pleasant blending of harmonious movements. It was listenable and enjoyably pleasant on a hot summer evening."

B385 Seidenbaum, Art. "Harmony Aim of Negro Composer." *Los Angeles Times*, September 7, 1963, sec. 3, p. 7.

Lengthy article on Still. "Musically, he is a gradualist. Socially, without dissonance, Still has been a constant force for progress. His tempo, without toadying, has been upbeat. He claims that any changes have grown out of love, received and reciprocally given. 'If I'm ever given credit for having taught,' says composer Still, 'it will have been by example.'"

B386 *Selected Items from the George Gershwin Memorial Collection of Music and Musical Literature*. Nashville: Fisk University Library, [1947].

Among the manuscripts listed is the "complete manuscript of full score" for *La Guiablesse*.

B387 Sewell, George Alexander. *Mississippi Black History Makers*. Jackson: University Press of Mississippi, 1977: 186-94.

Includes a chapter on Still.

B388 Shank, William. Review of *William Grant Still and the Fusion of Cultures in*

American Music, by Robert Bartlett Haas, ed. *Library Journal* 97 (November 15, 1972): 3715.

"There is much of value here, but it is organized in a manner that has neither focus nor direction. The absence of an index makes the book particularly cumbersome to use. However, in spite of its weaknesses, it will almost certainly be essential for any collection on American music, in view of the paucity of material on the subject."

B389 Shaw, Arnold. *Black Popular Music in America: From the Spirituals, Minstrels, and Ragtime to Soul, Disco, and Hip-Hop.* New York: Schirmer Books, 1986.

In the chapter on *Shuffle Along*, the author states that Will Henry Bennett Vodery, the African American theater composer/conductor, "was revered as a man who was generous in opening doors for others. Among these was a young William Grant Still . . . whose first rewarding assignments as an arranger came through Vodery's intervention (p. 81)."

B390 Shirley, Wayne D. "William Grant Still's Choral Ballad *And They Lynched Him on a Tree.*" *American Music* 12 (Winter 1994): 425-61.

The author draws upon the Francis and Katherine Biddle Papers at Georgetown University, the Katherine Garrison Chapin Papers at the Library of Congress, the Alain L. Locke Papers at Howard University, the William Grant Still and Verna Arvey Papers at the University of Arkansas, and papers in the possession of Judith Anne Still to present a masterful history of the development and premiere of *And They Lynched Him on a Tree.*

B391 Simpson, Mary Lou. "William Grant Still: A Review of Literature, A Proposed Unit of Study." Master's thesis, Texas Woman's University, 1972.

The purpose of this study was "to review the biographical literature on William Grant Still and to develop a proposed teaching unit appropriate for fourth grade students (p. 1)." Simpson's bibliography lists only thirty-two sources. The author's list of works, arranged by genre, includes fifty-seven compositions.

B392 Simpson, Ralph Ricardo. "William Grant Still—The Man and His Music." Ph.D. diss., Michigan State University, 1964.

This study, the first dissertation completed on Still, is valuable from a number of standpoints. It provides a very good background of the composer from his formative years through the early 1960s. It also includes a harmonic analysis of some works and provides insight to the influence of jazz. It is an important source on the works of Still, since much of the information came from family files.

B393 Slattery, Paul Harold. "A Comparative Study of the First and Fourth Symphonies of William Grant Still." Master's thesis, San Jose College, 1969.

As described by the author: "The purpose of this study is to present a comprehensive portrayal of William Grant Still, the man, his style of musical composition, his compositional philosophy, and his place in the historical style continuum of American music. . . . The *Afro-American Symphony* (1930) and Autochthonous [*Symphony No. 4, "Autochthonous"*] (1947) will be submitted to analysis and comparison . . . in the following areas: (1) Formal structure; (2) Harmonic structure and vocabulary; (3) Origin of themes and thematic development; (4) Factors that unify the symphonies; (5) Methods used to obtain variety of expression; (6) Orchestration technique; (7) Rhythmic devices employed; (8) Accomplishment of the tension-release cycle; (9) The basic compositional style of the symphonies."

B394 Slepian, Dorothy. "The Use of Polyphonic Forms and Devices by Contemporary American Composers." Ph.D. dissertation. Boston University, 1946.

"The purpose of this study is to present a comprehensive review and analysis of one of the most important technical factors in the music of modern composers [the use of polyphonic forms and devices]." As part of her research, Slepian sent questionnaires to leading American composers to solicit their opinions. She also reviewed selected compositions. In the case of Still, she examined *Darker America, Three Visions, Dismal Swamp,* and the *Afro-American Symphony.* Citing a letter from Still (the date is not provided) and her own research, Slepian has this to say: "William Grant Still's works, based on the *Darker America,* contain no evidence of polyphonic forms at all. He writes that the type of polyphony existing in the fugue, canon, etc., has not been used by him since it does not appeal to him. He states, however, that he has employed the polyphony of two or more independent voices appearing simultaneously in a rather free manner but not for a great length of time (p. 258)."

B395 Smallwood, Bill. "The Delightful Side." *Los Angeles Tribune,* November 29, 1943.

In his regular column the author provides snippets of information on a wide variety of people and subjects, including Still, who is ". . . so absorbed in his hobby of toymaking that he finds the days too short in which to work."

B396 Smith, Randolph. Review of *Studies of Contemporary American Composers: William Grant Still* by Verna Arvey. *Philadelphia Tribune,* February 16, 1939.

Very favorable review. "In short, Miss Arvey makes this Negro composer a distinctive personality thru his music, which has been lauded by America's severest critics."

B397 Soucek, Carol. "Composer Stills [*sic*] Honored by USC." *Los Angeles Herald-Examiner,* May 29, 1975, sec. B, p. 1.

Review of festivities associated with the University of Southern California's "Tribute to William Grant Still" May 24, 1975.

B398 Southern, Eileen. "America's Black Composers of Classical Music." *Music Educators Journal* 62 (November 1975): 46-59.

Southern's lengthy article includes a short paragraph on Still. "The influence of [Edgard] Varèse is negligible in Still's music, but Still credited the avant-garde composer with having 'opened new horizons' for him and having loosened up his music. After working with [George] Chadwick, Still was inspired to move in the direction of nationalistic music, finding it more 'suitable' to his nature."

B399 ———. Book review of *In One Lifetime,* by Verna Arvey. *Black Perspective in Music* 13 (Spring 1985): 122-24.

While Southern qualifies her enthusiasm for the publication, she leaves no doubt of her admiration for Still. "*In One Lifetime* is a warm and personal portrait of the composer William Grant Still . . . it offers intimate details that only she could provide, drawing upon her own relationship and as well upon conversations and interviews with others who were close to Still. The book reads like fiction. . . . At times this can be quite disturbing, for instance, when the author puts into the mouths of persons statements that she could not possibly have actually heard, since the events being described occurred before she met Still. But leaving such quibbles aside, the book is a spell-binder. Once begun, it is difficult to put down."

B400 ———. "Conversation with . . . William Grant Still." *Black Perspective in Music* 3 (May 1975): 165-76.

This article is based upon conversations with the composer that took place, largely, on June 20-22, 1969, at Bloomington, Indiana, where Still and Southern were attending the "Seminar on Black Music in College and University Curricula" at Indiana University.

B401 ———. *The Music of Black Americans: A History.* New York: W.W. Norton and Co., 1971.

In her chapter "Composers: From Nationalists to Experimentalist," Southern includes background on Still and the *Afro-American Symphony* (pp. 454-62). In the second edition, published in 1983, Southern includes Still in the chapter "The Black Renaissance" under the sub-heading "The Dean of Afro-American Composers" (pp. 423-27). In addition, Still is mentioned on numerous occasions in both editions.

B402 ———, comp. and ed. *Readings in Black American Music.* New York: W. W. Norton and Co., 1971.

Includes a reprint (pp. 276-79) of Still's article "The Structure of Music," which first appeared in the March 1950 issue of *Etude*.

B403 ———, comp. "William Grant Still: List of Major Works." *Black Perspective in Music* 3 (May 1975): 235-38.

Included is a select list of compositions and articles by Still.

B404 ———. "William Grant Still—Trailblazer." In *William Grant Still Studies at the University of Arkansas: A 1984 Congress Report.* Claire Detels, ed. Fayetteville, University of Arkansas, 1985: 1-9.

Based upon a paper delivered in February 16, 1984, at Fayetteville, Arkansas. Southern traces Still's life from his birth on May 11, 1895, at Woodville, Mississippi, through his travels with W.C. Handy, and on to his career as a professional composer. This is one of the best accounts surrounding Still's early activities, information that is based, in part, on conversations with Still.

B405 Spence, Martha Ellen Blanding. "Selected Song Cycles of Three Contemporary Black American Composers: William Grant Still, John Duncan, and Hale Smith." Ph.D. diss., University of Southern Mississippi, 1977.

The author presents biographical information and career data on Still. *Songs of Separation* is the song cycle studied. Spence believes that the work is a fine example of the Black Art Song and that the composition is worthy of inclusion in Black Studies Programs.

B406 Spencer, Jon Michael, ed. "The William Grant Still Reader: Essays on American Music." A Special Issue of *Black Sacred Music: A Journal of Theomusicology* 6 (Fall 1992).

This issue brings together thirty-six articles by Still that "capture the full breadth of Still's compositional thought and social critiques of America over the course of his thirty-six years of publishing (p. xiii)." The author places Still in context with a sixty-page introduction that is a significant addition to the body of literature on the composer.

B407 ———. "The Writings of Robert Nathaniel Dett and William Grant Still on Black Music. Part 2." Ph.D. diss. Washington University, 1982.

The main purpose of this project is to interpret the writings of the composers. The author presents factors which might have influenced their writings. The author then examines the writings to see if they could shed information on the following questions: What is Black Music?; What is the role of the Black musician and the Black educational institution in the preservation of Black musical culture?; and What effect does the avant-garde idiom have on Black music. This study has a very good bibliography of Still's writings.

B408 Still, Judith Anne. "Carrie Still Shepperson: The Hollows Of Her Footsteps." *Forum Magazine* 15 (Spring 1977): 60-65. (Later published in *Phi Delta Gamma Journal* 43 [May 1981]: 40-45, under the name Judy Anne Headlee.)

While the article is chiefly concerned with Still's mother, it is valuable for an appreciation of the influence she had upon the composer during his youth.

B409 ———. "From Composer to Composition: The Visionary Path." *Piano Guild Notes* 34 (September-October 1984): 8, 40-41.

The composer's daughter suggests that many errors and misconceptions exist pertaining to the life and career of her father, providing some examples in her article.

B410 ———. "In My Father's House . . . " *Black Perspective in Music* 3 (May 1975): 199-206.

As the daughter of William Grant Still, the author provides many warm and personal observations about her father.

B411 Still, Judith Anne, Celeste Anne Headlee, and Lisa M. Headlee-Huffman, eds. *William Grant Still and the Fusion of Cultures in American Music.* 2d ed. Flagstaff, AZ: The Master-Player Library, 1995.

This edition, a revised and updated version of Robert B. Haas's 1972 edition of the same title, was prepared to help celebrate the one hundred anniversay of the birth of Still. In addition to the contents of the first edition, this enlarged edition includes the following: "William Grant Still's Musical Style: A Monumental Contribution to American Music," by Anne Simpson; "Essays of Bias: Blesh, Mellers and 'Black Music'" and "Chosen Image: The Afro-American Vision in the Operas of William Grant Still," by Donald Dorr; "William Grant Still: The Folk Suites and Other Compositions in the Educational Setting," by Jean F. Matthew; "Fusion of Styles in the Piano Works of William Grant Still," by Carolyn L. Quin; "Phylon Profile XXIII: William Grant Still—Composer," by Miriam Matthews; "William Grant Still," by Howard Hanson; "Of One Blood, Thou and I," by Charles W. McGehee; "Recalling Still," by Grant D. Venerable II; and "Out of the Wilderness, or 'The Last Best Hope of the Earth,'" by Judith Anne Still. (*See also:* B220)

B412 Still, William Grant. Interview by R. Donald Brown, November 13, 1967, and December 4, 1967. Tape recording and edited transcript, California State University, Fullerton, as part of the California Black Oral History Project. The transcript, comprised of fifty-two pages, includes a four-page biographical sketch by Miriam Matthews and an index. Transcript edited by Judith Anne Still.

B413 "Still To Speak On Black Music." *Indiana Daily Student*, June 21, 1969.

General article on the "Seminar on Black Music in College and University Curricula," sponsored by Indiana University, June 18-21, 1969. Still was the featured speaker at the closing session.

B414 "Stormy weather lies ahead." *Los Angeles Sentinel*, February 18, 1943.

Lengthy editorial applauding Still for his resignation as musical director of *Stormy Weather*.

B415 "*Strange Fruit* Highly Praised." *Los Angeles Sentinel*, March 9, 1944.

The novel *Strange Fruit* was written by Lillian Smith, editor of the quarterly, *South Today*. The book received praise from people throughout the country who were interested in seeing race relations improved, including Still who said, "It is important for all of us to know this strong, sympathetic voice that has come out of the white south. *Strange Fruit* is 'must' reading for every American in these crucial times."

B416 Swift, Kay. "None But the Brave." *Black Perspective in Music* 3 (May 1975): 190-92.

The author describes her first encounters with Still, focusing primarily on their work with *Rising Tide (Song of a City)* and the 1939 New York World's Fair.

B417 "Talent of Race Recognized in Inscriptions on Wall of Honor at N.Y. World Fair." *Pittsburgh Courier*, July 20, 1940.

Announcement that the names of forty-one African Americans, including William Grant Still, have been inscribed on the "Wall of Honor" of the American Common at the New York World's Fair.

B418 Thompson, Leon E. "A Historical and Stylistic Analysis of the Music of William Grant Still and a Thematic Catalog of His Works." Ph.D. diss., University of Southern California, 1966.

The author provides a good biographical sketch of the composer, placing Still in historical perspective. The stylistic analysis covers a selection of compositions rather than being comprehensive. The larger portion of the study is devoted to the thematic catalog, which provides information on principal theme or themes, date and place of composition, location of original composition at the time of this study, date and place of first performance, and date and place of publication, among other data.

B419 Tremblay, George. "Co-Art Forum." *Co-Art Turntable* 2 (August 1942): 11-14.

Based upon a recorded interview, Still and Arthur Lange provide commentary on a variety of subjects associated with American music.

B420 Trimborn, Harry. "Talented Negroes Find Few Barriers in Musical World." *Los Angeles Times*, June 24, 1968.

Lengthy article on the prospects for the black musician seeking a career in serious music. William Grant Still is quoted as saying, "'In all my long career, the fact that I'm Negro has not made any significant difference. I honestly believe this.' Still could recall only one occasion in which race prevented a performance of one of his works. 'That was about 20 years ago when a Southern orchestra refused to perform a suite "inspired" by a work of a Louisiana-born white poet.' Still said the conductor in a peculiar twist of logic, wrote that performance of the piece might result in integration of schools.'But this is hardly worth mentioning,' Still said. 'There were so many good things that happened to us in the South.'"

B421 Tucker, Mark. "The Genesis of *Black, Brown and Beige*." *Black Music Research Journal* 13 (Fall 1993): 67-86.

The author suggests that works by African American composers may have been sources of inspiration for Duke Ellington when he composed *Black, Brown and Beige*. Tucker notes that Still's *Darker America*, *Levee Land*, and *Africa* might be included.

B422 *Twentieth Century Composers on Fugue*. Chicago: DePaul University, 1966.

Still is one of forty-three composers who responded to a survey on the validity of the fugue in twentieth-century music (p. 47). Still's response is as follows: "In my opinion, it is true that the Fugue is a relic of a bygone era. yet in it there could be a challenge to a comtemporary composer, if he felt that he would like to attempt a wedding of an old form and a new idiom, which would also be *interesting*. This would be a possibility, though modern composers' minds do not often run in such channels. Certainly the result of this fusion would be far from what we have come to expect from the traditional writing of Fugue, for all the imaginative and creative devices which have developed in the past few centuries would have to play a part in its concept."

B423 "UA To Present Honorary Degrees To Three June 5." *Northwest Arkansas Times* (Fayetteville), May 29, 1971, p. 1+.
Preview of activities associated with commencement ceremonies at the University of Arkansas. Still received an honorary Doctor of Law.

B424 "U.S. Reds Use Music To Push Dogma, Says William Grant Still." *San Jose Mercury*, May 23, 1953.
Article detailing Still's views on communism, especially as it relates to American musicians and their work. Still's remarks were made at a San Jose Chamber of Commerce luncheon, where he was the guest speaker.

B425 Ussher, Bruno David. "Music." *Los Angeles Daily News,* February 17, 1939.
Music column which touches upon Still. "Still has made history for the Afro-American, but it is as an artist, irrespective of antecedents, that he takes his place. He has spoken musically for his own people, yet, ultimately, his is a key giving voice in that great chorus which is the voice of America."

B426 Van Vechten, Carl. "The J. W. Johnson Collection at Yale." *Crisis* (July 1942): 222+.
Article describing the James Weldon Johnson Memorial Collection of Negro Arts and Letters, founded by Carl Van Vechten, at Yale University. One Still score is described. "Another of the more interesting items . . . is the manuscript orchestral score of . . . *Sahdji,* in which is laid autobiographical comment in longhand by Alain Locke and Bruce Nugent, who collaborated on the scenario for this dance-drama."

B427 Varèse, Louise. *Varèse: A Looking-Glass Diary.* Vol. 1: 1883-1928. New York: W.W. Norton and Co., Inc., 1972: 226-27.
"His [Still's] score, *Land of Dreams*, won him several adverse criticisms for his having fallen prey to the unorthodox precepts of Edgard Varèse. . . . However, after the concert he wrote Varèse: 'That was one of the greatest moments of my life. . . . Through it all I never lost sight of the one who befriended me.'"

B428 Warburton, Thomas. "The Operas of William Grant Still." In *William Grant Still Studies of the University of Arkansas: A 1984 Congress Report*. Fayetteville: University of Arkansas, 1985: 16-33.
This article is based upon a presentation delivered on February 17, 1985, at Fayetteville, Arkansas. The author provides thoughtful insight and observations pertaining to Still's operas. The accompanying tables and samples from the music, for example, Table 2 is an outline of *Costaso* with motivic analysis, provide a welcome dimension to the discussion.

B429 Weisenberg, Charles. "Negro Impact Minimal." *Los Angeles Times*, October 28, 1966, sec. 4, p. 11.
Article reviewing a panel discussion entitled "The Negro Idiom in American Music" which was held on October 25, 1966, at UCLA as part of a series entitled "The Negro and the Arts." William Grant Still was a member of the panel. "Still . . . said that serious composers of his race are rarely recognized by the public at large or even other Negroes. 'I have always wanted the

freedom to compose within the Negro idiom when I wanted to or compose abstract music,' said Still. He told the UCLA audience that the Negro composer must be able to handle the music of other races and nationalities if he is to become a truly American composer. The Negro idiom must be only a part of his American background. . . . 'The difference between Negro composers in America and Europe is that in America they are Negroes first and in Europe they are known by their nationality first,' said Still."

B430 Westerman, George W. *High Lights on the Life of William Grant Still*. Panama: Private Printing, 1944.

This mimeograph copy highlighting the accomplishments of Still includes "Notes of Interest" about the composer, background on the development of *In Memoriam: The Colored Soldiers Who Died for Democracy*, references to Rudolph Dunbar conducting Still's compositions, and notes on some of the first performances of Still's works.

B431 ———. "The Passing Review." *Isthmian Negro Youth Congress Bulletin* 1 (December 19, 1943): 5-6.

This Panamanian publication provides an overview of Still's work and accomplishments.

B432 "William Grant Still." *Oberlin Alumni Magazine* (Winter 1979): 46.

Lengthy obituary highlighting most of Still's major accomplishments.

B433 "William Grant Still." *Southern California Music Record* 1 (June 20, 1940): 13-15.

The inaugural number of this modest publication, it contains a fairly good biographical sketch of the composer.

B434 "William Grant Still Choice for Carver Award." *Los Angeles Sentinel*, January 15, 1953.

Article announcing Still as the recipient of the George Washington Carver Achievement Award presented by Phi Beta Sigma fraternity.

B435 "William Grant Still—The Successor To George Gershwin?" *Flash* 2 (November 15, 1938): 8-9.

Two pages of photographs showing Still involved in a variety of activities, from playing with his dog Shep, to rehearsing with the orchestra at the Hollywood Bowl.

B436 "William Grant Still to visit OC campus Nov. 8-9 for belated birthday fete." *Oberlin News-Tribune*, November 5, 1970.

Preview of activities and events associated with the seventy-fifth birthday concert in honor of Still at Oberlin College Conservatory of Music.

B437 *William Grant Still: Trailblazer from the South*. Arkansas Educational Television Network, 1984. Alex Haley, host and narrator. 30 min.

This documentary on Still draws heavily from the William Grant Still and Verna Arvey Papers at the University of Arkansas Libraries, as well as from the composer's own music. Judith Anne Still, Eileen Southern, and Laszlo Halasz appear as interviewees.

B438 "William Grant Still's Music at the Center." *Art Cetera* 4 (November 1992): 1.

In conjunction with the official opening of the William Grant Still and Verna Arvey Papers at the University of Arkansas Libraries, a special concert of Still's music was presented at the Walton Arts Center at Fayetteville on November 5. *Seven Traceries*, *Miniatures*, *From the Delta*, and selections from *Preludes* were part of the program.

B439 "William Grant Still's Orchestral Work Is Winning Composition." *Music Notes* 18 (October-November 1961): 11.

Article announcing Still's composition *The Peaceful Land* as the winner of the National Federation of Music Clubs contest for an orchestral work dedicated to the United Nations, providing Still with a $1500 cash award. "Mr. Ray Green, Chairman of the Committee, said that 86 scores were entered in the competition; they were of unusually high calibre and many were by well-known composers. He also said the winning composition was a beautiful and significant addition to symphonic literature; and practical for all symphony orchestras—major, metropolitan, college, and community."

B440 "William Still, 83, Black Composer." *New York Times*, December 6, 1978.

Obituary on Still, who died December 3, 1978. "Mr. Still was a pioneer in his field. . . . His main aim was always to develop a symphonic type of black music, which he did in his *Afro-American Symphony*, a work played throughout the United States. This ideal persisted in all his music, which was melodious and conservatively styled, and was based on black spirituals, although these were seldom quoted directly."

B441 Williams, Leroy E. "A Tribute to W. Grant Still." *Arkansas State Press*, January 21, 1944.

Short article in tribute to Still by one of his friends in Little Rock, Arkansas.

B442 Williford, Stanley. "William Grant Still: Time To Discover A Musical Giant." *Los Angeles Sentinel*, February 8, 1973, sec. A, p. 10.

Lengthy feature article on Still based upon an interview and excerpts from *William Grant Still and the Fusion of Cultures in American Music*. "Many more of his works remain unpublished or unperformed. It is still a sore spot with him.'Everything has not been recorded,' said Still. 'That's been a big problem. I've had to face active enemies who have been about to keep me pushed out. I have some operas that I would like to see performed very much' . . . Still continues to believe that the masses of blacks are moving toward more serious music. 'They lean toward good music,' he said. 'They sing the *Messiah* in church, the *Stabat Mater* and the *Seven Last Words of Christ*. There is a natural feeling for good music. A lot of people contend it isn't so, but I believe it is'"

B443 Willoughby, Diana. "Broken Chains: A Brief Analysis of Famous Negro Personalities—Part II." *Horoscope* (March 1947): 17-18.

The following serves as a sample of the author's interpretations. "Mr. Still's chart is the chart of a careful, patient, hard-working and sensitive composer, who, while he soars to great heights of musical expression, of symphonic feeling and inspiration, is still able to keep himself chained to the exigencies demanded of the composer."

B444 "Wm. Grant Still, James Luvalle Get '39 Rosenwald Fellowships." *California Eagle*, May 4, 1939.

Announcement on the recipients of Rosenwald Fellowships with a short background of each.

B445 Woll, Allen. *Black Musical Theatre: From 'Coontown' to 'Dreamgirls.'* Baton Rouge: Louisiana State University Press, 1989: 233.

In his chapter "Langston Hughes and the New Black Musical," the author provides a paragraph on *Troubled Island* describing its early history and eventual performance by the New York City Opera Company.

B446 Woodson, Carter G., and Charles H. Wesley. *The Negro In Our History*. 11th ed. Rev. and enlarged. Washington, D.C.: Associated Publishers, Inc., 1966: 700-03.

In their chapter on education and cultural attainment, the authors state: "The list of modern Negro composers manifests its best with William Grant Still whose name ranks high in original American music. *Africa*, the *Afro-American Symphony*, the *Symphony No. 2 in G Minor*, *Blue Steel*, *Troubled Island*, *A Bayou Legend*, and *Lenox Avenue* are noted.

B447 "WPA Project Will Present Premiere of Opera by Famous Negro Musician." *Chattanooga Times*, November 15, 1936.

During the course of a lengthy interview, Clarence Cameron White remarks that William Grant Still is "the most talented symphonic writer, white or colored, in America today."

B448 Yellen, Jack. "Songwriters In Top Ranks As Creators Of Our Music." *New York Amsterdam News*, June 4, 1966.

Extensive article on African American musicians and composers, including William Grant Still.

B449 Young, A. S. Doc. "Reports on the Image Awards." *Los Angeles Sentinel*, January 24, 1974.

Report on the Seventh Annual NAACP Image Awards presentations, held on January 19 at the Hollywood Palladium. Still received the first NAACP President's Award.

B450 Young, Amanda. "Black Musicians Leading the Way." *Music Educators Journal* 68 (February 1982): 46-48.

In recognition of Black History Month, this article highlights the careers of twenty-three outstanding African American composers, one of which is Still. The *Afro-American Symphony* and *Levee Land* are the only works identified, although a lengthy quote from a letter written by Howard Hanson to Still is included.

DISCOGRAPHY

This *selected* list includes commercially-produced discs, whether or not currently available. Because of their significance, a few privately-produced discs are included and some recordings of spiritual arrangements; but, to a large extent, recordings of arrangements and radio air checks have been omitted due to space limitations.

Entries are arranged by genre: Opera, Music for Ballet and Stage, Orchestral Music, Choral Music, Chamber Music, Music for Soloist with Accompaniment, Music for Solo Piano, Music for Wind Ensemble (Band), and Music for Music Education Textbooks.

Opera

D1   *A Bayou Legend.* Opera/South. Cassette. (1974). From the world premiere by Opera/South. Available from William Grant Still Music. (*See:* W9a)

D2   *Columbia Black Composers Series. William Grant Still/Samuel Coleridge-Taylor.* Columbia Records (Masterworks) CBS-M 32782. (1974). Reissued by The College Music Society (CBS Special Products) P19426. (1986).
London Symphony Orchestra, Paul Freeman, conductor; William A. Brown, tenor; performing *What Does He Know of Dreams?* and *You're Wonderful, Mary,* arias from *Highway 1, U.S.A.*

D3   *Highway 1, U.S.A.* Cassette. (1963). From the world premiere by the University of Miami Opera. Available from William Grant Still Music. (*See:* W62a)

D4   *Minette Fontaine: An Opera in Two Acts.* 2 cassettes. (1984). From the world premiere by the Baton Rouge Opera Company. Available from William Grant Still Music. (*See:* W99a)

D5   *Troubled Island: An Opera in Three Acts.* Southern Music and The Voice of America. 2 cassettes. (1990). From the 1949 dress rehearsal. Available from William Grant Still Music. For information on cast and performers, see W164a.

Music for Ballet and Stage

D6   *Artie Shaw.* RCA Victor 27411 A & B. (1940-41).
Artie Shaw, clarinet, and his orchestra, performing *Blues* from *Lenox Avenue.*

D7 *The Complete Artie Shaw, 1940-41, Volume IV.* RCA Bluebird AXM2-5572-1-B (1980).
   Artie Shaw and his orchestra, performing *Blues* from *Lenox Avenue*.

D8 *Columbia Black Composer Series. Volume 7, William Grant Still/Fela Sowande and George Walker.* Columbia Records (Masterworks) M33433, (1975). Reissued by The College Music Society (CBS Special Products) P19431. (1986).
   London Symphony Orchestra, Paul Freeman, conductor; the Morgan State College Choir; performing *Sahdji*.

D9 *Hancock Ensemble.* University of Southern California, Hancock Foundation No. 395. (1942).
   The Hancock Ensemble, Loren Powell, director, performing *The Flirtation* from *Lenox Avenue*.

D10 *Howard Hanson/Eastman-Rochester Orchestra.* Mercury Records MG 50257-B. (1960).
   Eastman-Rochester Orchestra, Howard Hanson, conductor; The Eastman School Chorus; performing *Sahdji*.

D11 *Lenox Avenue: The Music of William Grant Still.* Bay Cities Disc 1033. CD. (1991).
   CBS Symphony Orchestra, Howard Barlow, conductor (1938), performing *Lenox Avenue*.

D12 *My Concerto/Artie Shaw.* RCA Victor (Collector's Issue) LPT 1020 (EAVP-8414). (1955).
   Artie Shaw, clarinet, and the Artie Shaw Orchestra; Billy Butterfield, trumpet; Jack Jenny, trombone; Jerry Jerome, saxophone; Johnny Guarnieri, piano; performing *Blues* from *Lenox Avenue*.

D13 *William Grant Still.* Koch International Classics. CD 7154. (1993). Recorded April 1992 at Siemens-Villa, Berlin.
   Berliner Symphoniker, Isaiah Jackson, conductor, performing *La Guiablesse* and *Danzas de Panama*.

D14 *William Grant Still Conducts William Grant Still.* Glendale Records (Legend) GL-8011. Cassette GLC-8011. (1984). Recorded September 25, 1940.
   Members of the San Francisco Symphony Orchestra, William Grant Still, conductor, performing *Entrance of Les Porteuses* from *La Guiablesse*. • The Los Angeles WPA Symphony Orchestra and Chorus, Verna Arvey, piano, performing *Lenox Avenue*.

D15 *William Grant Still: Strings, Keyboard and Harp.* William Grant Still Music WGSM 1001. Cassette. (1987). Reissue of Orion ORS 7278 and OC 633.
   Louis Kaufman, violin; Annette Kaufman, piano, performing *Blues* from *Lenox Avenue*.

Orchestral Music

D16 *Afro-American Symphony.* Chandos Records Ltd. CD 9154.(1992). Recorded September 29, 1992.
   Detroit Symphony Orchestra, Neeme Järvi, conductor; performing *Afro-American Symphony*.

D17 *Angel City Symphony.* Ball Records CAM-1502.
   Angel City Symphony, Leroy E. Hurte, conductor, performing *Summerland* from *Three Visions*.

D18 *Arthur Bennett Lipkin Conducts.* Composers Recordings, Inc., CRI SD 259-B, Cassette CAS 259. (1970).
The Royal Philharmonic Orchestra, Arthur Bennett Lipkin, conductor, performing *Festive Overture.*

D19 *Autochthonous Symphony.* National Association of Educational Broadcasters tape. (1959). A reel-to-reel tape distributed to educators only of a live performance at a UNESCO concert in Denver, Colorado.
The Denver Symphony Orchestra, William Grant Still, conductor, performing *Symphony No. 4, "Autochthonous" (Indigenous)* (1947).

D20 *Columbia Black Composers Series. Volume 2, William Grant Still/Samuel Coleridge-Taylor.* Columbia Records (Masterworks) CBS-M 32782. (1974). Reissued by The College Music Society (CBS Special Products) P19426. (1986).
London Symphony Orchestra, Paul Freeman, conductor, performing *Afro-American Symphony.*

D21 *The Contemporary Composer in the U.S.A.* Vox (Turnabout) TV-S 34546. (1974).
Westchester Symphony Orchestra, Siegfried Landau, conductor, performing *From the Black Belt* and *Darker America.*

D22 *Instrumental Music in the 20th Century.* The Society for the Preservation of the American Musical Heritage MIA-118. (1965).
The Royal Philharmonic Orchestra of London, Karl Krueger, conductor, performing *Afro-American Symphony.*

D23 *National Music Camp* (Interlochen, Michigan). Silver Crest Records NMC-1971-3A. (1971).
The University of Michigan All-State Intermediate Orchestra, G. Anderson White, conductor, performing excerpts from *The American Scene:* Suite 3, *The Old West: Song of the Plainsmen, Sioux Love Song,* and *Tribal Dance.*

D24 *Our Musical Past. Volume 5.* Library of Congress OMP 106CD.
The Royal Philharmonic Orchestra, Karl Krueger, conductor, performing *Afro-American Symphony.*

D25 *Scherzo/Fugue in G-Minor.* Columbia Records (Masterworks) 11992-D (1944).
The All-American Orchestra, Leopold Stokowski, conductor, performing *Scherzo* from *Afro-American Symphony.*

D26 *Scherzo/Joe Clark Steps Out.* Victor Records (Red Seal) 2059B. (1940-41).
Eastman-Rochester Symphony Orchestra, Howard Hanson, conductor, performing *Scherzo* from *Afro-American Symphony.*

D27 *Symphony No. 2 in G Minor (Song of a New Race).* Chandos Records Ltd. CD 9226. Cassette 1604. (1993).
Detroit Symphony Orchestra, Neeme Järvi, conductor, performing *Symphony No. 2 in G Minor, "Song of a New Race"* (1937).

D28 *William Grant Still, 1895-1978.* Fayetteville, Arkansas: Opus I Productions (1984).
North Arkansas Symphony Orchestra, Carlton R. Woods, conductor, performing *Symphony No. 3, "The Sunday Symphony"* (1958).

D29 *William Grant Still Conducts William Grant Still.* Glendale Records (Legend) GL-8011. Cassette GLC-8011. (1984). Recorded September 25, 1940.
Members of the San Francisco Symphony Orchestra, William Grant Still,

conductor, performing movements II and III of *Symphony No. 2 in G Minor, "Song of a New Race"* (1937).

Choral Music

D30 *Eye of the Storm.* Fisk University NR 2597A. (1972).
Fisk Jubilee Singers, Matthew Kennedy, director, performing *We Sang Our Songs.*

D31 *The Paine College Concert and Gospel Choirs.* Century Records 40598. (1972).
The Paine College Choir, Victor Bilanchone, director, performing *Plain-Chant For America.*

D32 *Walk as Children.* CD (1991). Recorded live at Trinity Cathedral, Phoenix, Arizona, March 12, 1991.
Northern Arizona University Chorale, Dr. Jo-Michael Scheibe, conductor, Kelly Sanford, piano, performing *All That I Am.*

D33 *William Grant Still, 1895-1978.* Fayetteville, Arkansas: Opus I Productions (1984).
University of Arkansas Schola Cantorum, Jack Groh, conductor, pianist unknown, performing *Three Rhythmic Spirituals* and *I Feel Like My Time Ain't Long.*

D34 *William Grant Still: Voices and Piano.* The William Grant Still Performing Arts Society. (1989). Cassette. Available from William Grant Still Music.
William Grant Still Chorus, Paul Smith, director, Byron Smith, piano, performing *The Blind Man; Where Shall I Be?; Is There Anybody Here?; Sinner, Please Don't Let This Harvest Pass; Lis'en to de Lam's; Here's One; Glory to the Newborn King; A Maiden Was Adoring God, The Lord; Jesous Ahatonhia; Tell Me, Shepherdess; Sing! Shout! Tell the Story!; Citadel; Pastorale* from *Rhapsody; Radiant Night* from *Minette Fontaine; Oh, Sorrow* from *And They Lynched Him on a Tree; A Psalm for the Living; Dance from Costaso;* and *Dance of the Porteuses* from *La Guiablesse.*

Chamber Music

D35 *Get on Board! American Music for Winds.* Cambria Master Recordings. CD-1083. (1995).
Sierra Winds: Richard Soule, flute, piccolo; Stephen Caplan, oboe; Felix Viscuglia, clarinet; Bernard Kolle, bassoon; Carol Urbah-Stivers, piano; Kim DeLibero, harp; Teresa Ling, violin; Rebecca Ramsey, violin; John Peskey, viola; Kelley Mikkelsen, cello; performing *Folk Suite No. 2; Folk Suite No. 3; Folk Suite No. 4; Get on Board; Miniatures for Flute, Oboe, and Piano;* and *Vignettes.*

D36 *Lenox Avenue: The Music of William Grant Still.* Bay Cities Disc 1033. CD. (1991).
Louis Kaufman and George Berres, violins; Alexander Neiman, viola; and Terry King, cello; performing *Mejorana y Socavon* and *Cumbia y Congo* from *Danzas de Panama.*

D37 *Louis Kaufman—Violin.* Orion ORS 793S9. (1972).
Lois Adele Craft, harp; Annette Kaufman, piano, and the Kaufman String

Quartet: Louis Kaufman and George Berres, violins; Alexander Neiman, viola; Terry King, cello; performing *Ennanga* for harp, piano, and string quartet.

D38 *The Music of William Grant Still.* Orion ORS 7278, Cassette OC 633. (1972).
Lois Adele Craft, harp; Annette Kaufman, piano; and the Kaufman String Quartet: Louis Kaufman and George Berres, violins; Alexander Neiman, viola; and Terry King, cello; performing *Danzas de Panama* for string quartet and *Ennanga* for harp, piano, and string quartet.

D39 *Oboist Peter Christ.* Crystal Records. CD 321. (1986). Recorded in Los Angeles in 1978.
Gretel Shanley, flute; Peter Christ, oboe; Sharon Davis, piano; performing *Miniatures for Flute, Oboe, and Piano.*

D40 *Summerland. William Grant Still.* Koch International Classics. CD 7192. (1994). Recorded May 1993 at Symphony House, Wellington, New Zealand.
Alexa Still, flute; Susan DeWitt, piano; New Zealand String Quartet; Michael Steer, double bass; performing *Folk Suite No. 1; Preludes for String Orchestra, Flute and Piano* (movements II and III from *Suite for Violin and Piano*).

D41 *20th Century American Violin Works in Historic Recordings.* Music & Arts. CD 638. (1990).
Lois Adele Craft, harp; Annette Kaufman, piano; and the Kaufman String Quartet: Louis Kaufman and George Berres, violins; Alexander Neiman, viola; Terry King, cello; performing *Danzas de Panama,* Nos. 1 and 3, for string quartet and *Ennanga* for harp, piano, and string quartet.

D42 *William Grant Still, 1895-1978.* Fayetteville, Arkansas: Opus I Productions (1984).
Leonard Garrison, flute; Robert Umiker, clarinet; Samuel Magill, cello; Arthur Tollefson, piano; performing *Folk Suite No. 4.*

D43 *William Grant Still: Strings, Keyboard and Harp.* William Grant Still Music WGSM 1001. Cassette. (1987). Reissue of Orion ORS 7278 and OC 633.
Lois Adele Craft, harp; Annette Kaufman, piano; and the Kaufman String Quartet: Louis Kaufman and George Berres, violins; Alexander Neiman, viola; Terry King, cello; performing *Danzas de Panama* for string quartet and *Ennanga* for harp, piano, and string quartet.

D44 *Works by William Grant Still.* New World Records. CD 80399-2. (1990).
Videmus: Jean DeMart, flute; Ann Hobson Pilot, harp; Lynn Chang and Lydia Forbes, violins; George Taylor, viola; and Mark Churchill, cello; performing *Summerland.* • Jean DeMart, flute; Vivian Taylor, piano; Lynn Chang and Lydia Forbes, violins; George Taylor, viola; and Mark Churchill, cello; performing *Out of the Silence.*

Music for Soloist with Accompaniment

D45 *An American Tribute to Sigurd Rascher.* Crystal Records, Inc. CD 652. (1994).
Lawrence Gwozdz, alto saxophone, and Lois Leventhal, piano, performing *Romance for Saxophone.*

D46 *Art Songs by Black American Composers.* University of Michigan Records SM 0015. (1980).
Willis Patterson, artistic director; Susan Matthews, mezzo-soprano; unidentified pianist; performing *Grief.*

D47 ***The Black Composer in America.*** Desto Records DC 7107-A. Cassette X47107. (1970).
   Cynthia Bedford, mezzo-soprano; the Oakland Youth Orchestra, Robert Hughes, conductor; performing *Songs of Separation.*

D48 ***Black Spirituals and Art Songs.*** Narthex Recording N64085, 827N4581.
   John Patton, tenor; C. Edward Thomas, piano; performing *Lawd, I Wants to Be a Christian.*

D49 ***Contemporary American Violin Music.*** Concert Hall Records H-1640, CHS 1140. (1950). Reissue of Vox 667-A.
   Louis Kaufman, violin; Annette Kaufman, piano; performing *Blues* from *Lenox Avenue* and *Here's One.*

D50 ***Get on Board! American Music for Winds.*** Cambria Master Recordings. CD-1083. (1995).
   Sierra Winds: Richard Soule, flute; Stephen Caplan, oboe; Felix Viscuglia, alto saxophone; Carol Urbah-Stivers, piano; performing *Incantation and Dance* (oboe and piano), *Quit Dat Fool'nish* (alto saxophone and piano), and *Summerland* from *Three Visions* (flute and piano).

D51 ***Volume 2, The Kaufman Legacy.*** World Records (Discopaedia) WRC1-13SS, MB 1032. (1983).
   Louis Kaufman, violin; Annette Kaufman, piano; performing *Blues* from *Lenox Avenue* and *Here's One.*

D52 ***Lenox Avenue: The Music of William Grant Still.*** Bay Cities Disc 1033. CD. (1991).
   Louis Kaufman, violin; Annette Kaufman, piano; performing *Carmela, Here's One, Pastorela,* and *Summerland.* • Claudine Carlson, mezzo-soprano, and George Akst, piano, performing *Songs of Separation* and *Song for the Lonely.*

D53 ***Louis Kaufman.*** Vox 667B (Set 627-5, VX81044). (1948).
   Louis Kaufman, violin; Annette Kaufman, piano; performing *Here's One.*

D54 ***Music of Afro-American Composers.*** CD. (1995).
   Northern Arizona University Wind Symphony, Patricia J. Hoy, conductor; Celeste Anne Headlee (granddaughter of William Grant Still), soprano; performing *Levee Land.*

D55 ***The Music of William Grant Still.*** Orion ORS 7152. Cassette OC 633. (1971).
   Louis Kaufman, violin; Annette Kaufman, piano; performing *Blues* from *Lenox Avenue, Carmela, Here's One, Pastorela, Suite for Violin and Piano,* and *Summerland* from *Three Visions.*

D56 ***Summerland. William Grant Still.*** Koch International Classics. CD 7192. (1994). Recorded May 1993 at Symphony House, Wellington, New Zealand.
   Alexa Still, flute; Susan DeWitt, piano; performing *Suite for Violin and Piano* (movements II and III), edited for flute solo by Alexa Still; the following also edited by Alexa Still: *Bayou Home, Here's One, If You Should Go,* and *Song for the Lonely.*

D57 ***William Grant Still, 1895-1978.*** Fayetteville, Arkansas: Opus I Productions (1984).
   Robert Umiker, alto saxophone; Arthur Tollefson, piano; performing *Romance for Saxophone.*

D58 ***Works by William Grant Still.*** New World Records. CD. 80399-2. (1990).
   Videmus: Lynn Chang, violin; Vivian Taylor, piano; performing *Suite for*

Violin and Piano. • Robert Honeysucker, baritone; Vivian Taylor, piano; performing *Citadel, Here's One, Song for the Lonely,* and *Songs of Separation.* • Robert Honeysucker, baritone; Jean DeMart, flute; Vivian Taylor, piano, Lynn Chang and Lydia Forbes, violins; George Taylor, viola; and Mark Churchill, cello; performing *Lift Ev'ry Voice and Sing.* • Jean DeMart, flute; Vivian Taylor, piano; performing *Incantation and Dance.*

Music for Solo Piano

D59 *An Anthology of Piano Music by Black Composers.* Opus One 39. (1977).
Ruth Norman, piano, performing, from *Seven Traceries: Muted Laughter* and *Wailing Dawn;* and *Summerland* from *Three Visions.*

D60 *Black American Piano Music.* Da Camera Magna SM 94144.
Felipe Hall, piano, performing *Three Visions.*

D61 *Black Piano: A Treasury of Works for Solo Piano by Black Composers.* Music & Arts Programs of America. CD 737. (1992).
Monica Gaylord, piano, performing *Seven Traceries* and *Three Visions.*

D62 *Natalie Hinderas Plays Music of Black Composers, 2 Volumes.* Desto CMS Records DC-7102B-2. Cassette X47103-2. (1970). Recorded at Rutgers Church, New York, 1970. Reissued by Composers Recordings, Inc. CD 629 (1992).
Natalie Hinderas, piano, performing *Three Visions.*

D63 *Pathways to Music: From Jazz to Rock.* Keyboard Publications, and CBS Records (REP 1) PV 12063. (1973).
Verna Arvey, piano, performing *Blues* from *Lenox Avenue.*

D64 *Piano Music of William Grant Still.* Koch International Classics. CD 7192.
Denver Oldham, piano, performing *Africa, Bells, Blues* from *Lenox Avenue, Preludes, Seven Traceries, Summerland* from *Three Visions,* and *Swanee River.*

D65 *Richard Fields Plays Piano Music of William Grant Still.* Orion ORS 82442. (1982).
Richard Fields, piano, performing *Bells, Quit Dat Fool'nish,* and *Three Visions.* • Richard Fields, piano; Gary Steigerwalt, piano; performing *Kaintuck'.*

D66 *Samuel Coleridge-Taylor/William Grant Still.* Orion ORS 78305/306. (1978).
Frances Walker, piano, performing *Seven Traceries.*

D67 *Seven Traceries for Piano by William Grant Still.* Co-Art Records 5037 A & B (ACA181-2, 182-2). (1940-41).
Verna Arvey, piano, performing, from *Seven Traceries: Cloud Cradles, Muted Laughter, Out of the Silence,* and *Woven Silver.*

D68 *Summerland. William Grant Still.* Koch International Classics. CD 7192. (1994). Recorded May 1993 at Symphony House, Wellington, New Zealand.
Susan DeWitt, piano, performing *Pastorela, Quit Dat Fool'nish,* and *Summerland* from *Three Visions.*

D69 *William Grant Still/Afro-American Symphony.* New Records (AAO) NRLP 105. (1952).
Gordon Manley, piano, performing *Blues* from *Lenox Avenue;* from *Seven Traceries: Cloud Cradles, Muted Laughter, Mystic Pool, Out of the Silence,* and *Woven Silver;* and *Three Visions.*

D70 ***William Grant Still Piano Music.*** William Grant Still Music WGSM 1002, Cassette. (1987).
Albert Domingues, piano, performing *Bells, Blues* from *Lenox Avenue, Quit Dat Fool'nish, Seven Traceries,* and *Three Visions.*

Music for Wind Ensemble (Band)

D71 ***Barber/Still/Ravel/Stravinsky/Milhaud.*** American Society of Composers, Authors and Publishers CB 177. (1952). Pittsburgh International Contemporary Music Festival.
U.S. Military Academy Band, Captain Francis E. Resta, conductor, performing *To You, America!*

D72 ***From the Delta.*** Columbia Records 4519-M CO 39622. (1948).
Morton Gould and his Symphonic Band, performing *Work Song from the Delta.*

D73 ***Music of Afro-American Composers.*** CD. (1995).
Northern Arizona University Wind Symphony, performing excerpts from *The American Scene: Berkshire Night, A New Orleans Street, Tribal Dance, Grand Teton, Tomb of the Unknown Soldier;* and *Summerland* from *Three Visions.*

Music for Music Education Textbooks

D74 ***God's Goin' to Set This World on Fire.*** *Exploring Music/ The Junior Book Song Recordings.* Holt, Rinehart and Winston THS2, SYB 107. (1968).

D75 ***Sound, Beat and Feeling.*** *New Dimensions in Music.* American Book Company (Litton Educational Publishing) SAAB-1003. (1972). Album to be used with an educational textbook of the same name. • Includes *My Brother American.*

D76 ***Two Songs by Contemporary Composers.*** *Songs from American Music Horizons* (part of the *New Music Horizons* textbook series). Columbia Records MJV-119, CO 45872. (1951). • Includes *Lament.*

D77 ***William Grant Still.*** *American Composers* (an educational kit of records, tapes, booklets and filmstrips for sale to schools). Keyboard Publications and CBS Records (REP 1) PV 12063. (1973). • Includes an excerpt from *Danzas de Panama* and *Scherzo* from *Afro-American Symphony.*

APPENDIX A: ALPHABETICAL LIST OF WORKS

The list below includes all titles of works and movements within works by William Grant Still. Boldface type identifies titles with entries in this volume. Those with a **W** number direct the reader to the specific entry in the "Works and Performances" section.

	Adolorida, see ***Miniatures for Flute, Oboe, and Piano***
	Africa, see ***Pages from Negro History***
W1	***Africa,*** variants of title: ***Darker Africa*** and ***Darkest Africa***
	African Dancer, see ***Suite for Violin and Piano***
W2	***Afro-American Symphony*** (1930), also known as ***Symphony No. 1***
	Aguinaldo, see ***Christmas in the Western World***
	Ah Got a Home in-a Dat Rock, see ***Twelve Negro Spirituals, Volume 2***
	Ah, La Sa Wu!, see ***Caribbean Melodies***
	Ain't Misbehavin', see ***Songs: A Medley***
	All God's Chillun Got Shoes, see ***Twelve Negro Spirituals, Volume 1***
W3	***All That I Am***
W4	***Alnados de España, Los***
W5	***American Scene, The,*** includes five suites: *The East; The South; The Old West; The Far West;* and *A Mountain, A Memorial, and A Song*
W6	***And They Lynched Him on a Tree***
	Anda Buscando de Rosa en Rosa, see ***Folk Suite No. 4***
W7	***Archaic Ritual***
W8	***Aria*** (for accordion)
	Arkansas, see ***Mississippi***
	Aurore Pradere, see ***Little Folk Suite from the Western Hemisphere No. 3***
	Autochthonous Symphony, The, see ***Symphony No. 4, "Autochthonous"*** (1947)
	Autumn Night, see ***Wood Notes***
	Ave Maria, see ***Costaso***
	Awful Truth, The (lost)
	Backslider, The, see ***Levee Land***
	Baintown, see ***Caribbean Melodies***
	Ballad, see ***Costaso***
	Ballet Dances, see ***Three Dances***
	Ballet Music, see ***Three Dances***
	Bambalelé e Espingarda Pá Pá Pá, see ***Folk Suite No. 1***
	Bayou Home, see ***I'm Pickin' My Last Row of Cotton***
W9	***Bayou Legend, A***
	Bellamina, see ***Caribbean Melodies***
W10	***Bells***
	Beneaf de Villers, see ***Log Cabin Ballads***
	Berkshire Night, see ***The American Scene***
W11	***Beyond Tomorrow,*** also known as *A Song at Dusk*
	Bit of Wit, A, see ***Seven Traceries***
	Black Belt Suite, see ***From The Black Belt***
W12	***Black Bottom***
	Black Land, The, see ***From the Furnace of the Sun***

- W13 **Black Man Dances, The,** also known as *Four Negro Dances*
- *Black Pierrot, A,* see **Songs of Separation**
- *Blind Man, The,* see **Four Octavo Songs**
- *Blind Man Stood on the Road and Cried, The,* see **Four Octavo Songs**
- *Blue,* see **From the Black Belt**
- W14 **Blue Steel**
- W15 **Blues, The,** from **Lenox Avenue**
- *Bow and Arrow Dance,* see **Folk Suite No. 3**
- *Boy's Dance,* see **Miss Sally's Party** and **Three Dances**
- W16 **Breath of a Rose, The**
- *Brother Lowdown* (lost)
- W17 **Brown Baby**
- *Brown Girl,* see **From the Black Belt**
- *Cake Walk,* see **Miss Sally's Party**
- W18 **Can'tcha Line 'Em,** variant of title: *Can't You Line 'Em*
- *Capotin, El,* see **Little Folk Suite from the Western Hemisphere No. 1**
- *Captain Kidd,* see **Little Red Schoolhouse**
- W19 **Caribbean Melodies**
- *Carmela,* see **Vignettes**
- W20 **Carry Him Along,** see also **Caribbean Melodies**
- *Celeste's Lullaby,* see **Troubled Island**
- *Central Avenue,* see **Lenox Avenue**
- *Chamber Music for Brass and Percussion,* see **Fanfare for the 99th Fighter Squadron**
- *Chink, Pink, Honey,* see **Folk Suite No. 2**
- W21 **Choreographic Prelude**
- W22 **Christmas in the Western World (Las Pascuas)**
- W23 **Citadel**
- *Clap Yo' Han's,* see **From the Black Belt**
- *Clinch Mountain,* see **Vignettes**
- *Cloud Cradles,* see **Seven Traceries**
- *Colleen Bawn,* see **Little Red Schoolhouse**
- *Corrido,* see **Costaso**
- W24 **Costaso**
- *Crap Game, The,* see **Lenox Avenue**
- *Crawdad Song, The,* see **Little Folk Suite from the Western Hemisphere No. 4**
- *Croon,* see **Levee Land**
- *Cross Eyed Monkey* (lost)
- *Cumbia y Congo,* see **Danzas de Panama**
- *Dance,* see **A Deserted Plantation, From the Black Belt,** and **From the Delta**
- *Dance Before the Chieftain,* see **Sahdji**
- *Dance Before the Hut,* see **Sahdji** and **Three Dances**
- *Dance from Costaso,* see **Costaso**
- *Dance of Love* (lost)
- *Dance of the Carnal Flowers* (lost)
- *Dance of the Children,* see **La Guiablesse**
- *Dance of the Porteuses,* see **La Guiablesse**
- *Dance of the Priestesses,* see **Blue Steel**
- *Dance of the Warriors,* see **Sahdji**
- *Dance of Yzore and Adou,* see **La Guiablesse**
- W25 **Danzas de Panama**
- *Dark Horseman,* see **Three Visions**
- *Darker Africa,* see **Africa**
- W26 **Darker America**
- *De Virgin Mary Had a Baby Boy,* see **Christmas in the Western World**
- *Death* (lost)
- *Death Chant,* see **Sahdji**
- *Death Dance of Sahdji,* see **Sahdji**
- *Death Song,* see **Three Negro Songs**
- *Deep River,* see **Spirituals: A Medley** and **Folk Suite for Band**
- *Dénouement,* see **Troubled Island**
- *Des Keep on Shovin',* see **From the Black Belt**
- W27 **Deserted Plantation, A,** see also **Down Yonder**
- *Devil's Hollow,* see **From a Journal of a Wanderer**
- *Devotion of a People, The* (lost)
- *Dialect Songs,* see **The Breath of a Rose, Mandy Lou,** and **Winter's Approach**
- *Didn't Mah Lawd Deliver Daniel,* see **Twelve Negro Spirituals, Volume 2**
- W28 **Dismal Swamp**
- *Do an' Nannie,* see **Caribbean Melodies**
- *Doo Ma,* see **Caribbean Melodies**
- W29 **Down Yonder,** see also **A Deserted Plantation**
- *Dream Wasted, A,* see **Highway 1,**

Alphabetical List of Works   297

U.S.A.
Drums in the Court, see **Troubled Island**
East, The, see **The American Scene**
W30 **Ebon Chronicle**, also known as *A Negro Epic*
Egyptian Princess, see **Little Red Schoolhouse**
Eh, Bi Nango, see **Caribbean Melodies**
El Capotin, see **Little Folk Suite from the Western Hemisphere No. 1**
El Monigote, see **Folk Suite No. 4**
El Nido, see **Little Folk Suite from the Western Hemisphere No. 2**
El Zapatero, see **Folk Suite No. 2**
W31 **Elegy**
Emancipation, see **Pages from Negro History**
En Roulant Ma Boule, see **Little Folk Suite from the Western Hemisphere for Brass Quintet**
W32 **Ennanga**
Entrance of Les Porteuses, see **La Guiablesse**
Entrance of Priests, see **Blue Steel**
Evalina, see **Caribbean Melodies**
W33 **Ev'ry Time I Feel the Spirit**, see also **Four Octavo Songs**
W34 **Fanfare for American War Heroes**
W35 **Fanfare for the 99th Fighter Squadron**
Far West, The, see **The American Scene**
Father Mississippi, see **The American Scene** and **Songs: A Medley**
Festive Dance, see **Sahdji**
W36 **Festive Overture**
Finale, see **Spirituals: A Medley**
First Dance of the Children, see **La Guiablesse**
W37 **Five Animal Sketches**
Florida Night, see **The American Scene**
W38 **Folk Suite for Band**
W39 **Folk Suite No. 1**
W40 **Folk Suite No. 2**
W41 **Folk Suite No. 3**
W42 **Folk Suite No. 4**
Four Dances from Sahdji, see **Sahdji**
W43 **Four Indigenous Portraits**
Four Negro Dances, see **The Black Man Dances**
W44 **Four Octavo Songs**

Frog Went A-Courtin', A, see **Miniatures for Flute, Oboe, and Piano**
W45 **From a Lost Continent**
W46 **From the Black Belt**
W47 **From the Delta**
W48 **From the Furnace of the Sun**
From the Gaiety of a People (lost)
W49 **From the Heart of a Believer**
W50 **From the Hearts of Women**
W51 **From the Journal of a Wanderer**
W52 **From the Land of Dreams**
From the South, see **The American Scene**
Funeral March, see **Troubled Island**
Gamin, see **Suite for Violin and Piano**
Gardé Piti Mulet Là, see **Vignettes**
W53 **Gateway to the Temple**
W54 **Get on Board**, see also **Spirituals: A Medley** and **Folk Suite for Band**
Glad Christmas Bells, see **Christmas in the Western World**
W55 **Glory to the Newborn King**
Go Down Moses, see **Spirituals: A Medley**
W56 **Go Get it**
W57 **God's Goin' to Set This World on Fire**
Going to My Old Home, see **Caribbean Melodies**
Golden Days, see **Costaso**
Good News, see **Twelve Negro Spirituals, Volume 2**
W58 **Good Night**
Grand Teton, see **The American Scene**
Great Camp Meeting, see **Twelve Negro Spirituals, Volume 1**
Great Day, see **Twelve Negro Spirituals, Volume 2**
W59 **Grief**
Guiablesse, La, see **La Guiablesse**
Gwinter Sing All Along de Way, variant of title: *Gwine to Sing All Along the Way*, see **Twelve Negro Spirituals, Volume 1**
W60 **Hallelujah 'Tis Done**
Hand A' Bowl, see **Caribbean Melodies**
Hard Trials, see **Three Rhythmic Spirituals**
He Rose, see **Spirituals: A Medley**
Héla Grand-Père, see **Caribbean Melodies** and **Vignettes**

W61 *Here's One*
Hey-Hey, see **Levee Land**
W62 *Highway 1, U.S.A.*, see also *A Southern Interlude*
W63 *Hiking Song*
Holy Spirit Don't You Leave Me, see **Three Rhythmic Spirituals**
Honeysuckle, see **From the Black Belt**
W64 *How I've Got Dem Twilight Blues*
W65 *I Feel Like My Time Ain't Long*
I Ride an Old Paint, see **Miniatures for Flute, Oboe, and Piano**
I Want Jesus to Walk with Me, see *A Deserted Plantation*
W66 *I Want To*
Idolatry, see **Songs of Separation**
If You Should Go, see **Songs of Separation**
W67 *Igama Lo Kusina*
I'm Goin' Where Nobody Knows My Name, see **Songs: A Medley**
I'm Gonna Tell What Ma Lawd Has Done fo' Me, see **Lenox Avenue**
W68 *I'm Pickin' My Last Row of Cotton*, also known as **Bayou Home**
In a Pioneer Settlement, see **Lyric Quartette; Musical Portraits of Three Friends: Impressions**
W69 *In Memoriam: The Colored Soldiers Who Died for Democracy*
In Memory of Jan Sibelius, see **Threnody: In Memory of Jan Sibelius**
In the Mountains of Peru, see **Lyric Quartette; Musical Portraits of Three Friends: Impressions**
Inca Dance, see **Folk Suite No. 3**
Inca Melody, see **Vignettes**
Inca Song, see **Folk Suite No. 3**
W70 *Incantation and Dance*
Indian Moccasin Game, see **Vignettes**
Indios and Yaravi, Los, see **Little Folk Suite from the Western Hemisphere No. 4**
Introduction to Desert Scene, see **Costaso**
Invitation Dance, see **Sahdji**
W71 *Is There Anybody Here (Who Loves My Jesus)?*
Jes Keep on Shovin', see *From the Black Belt*
Jesous Ahatonhia, see **Christmas in the Western World**
Jesus is a Rock in a Weary Land, see **Miniatures for Flute, Oboe, and Piano** and **Spirituals: A Medley**
Juba (lost)
W72 *Jungle Drums*
W73 *Jungle Episode: The Origin of Jazz*
W74 *Kaintuck'*
W75 *Keep Me F'om* [or *From*] *Sinkin' Down*, see also **Twelve Negro Spirituals, Volume 1**
W76 *La Guiablesse*
La Piñata, see **Christmas in the Western World**
La Varsoviana, see **Little Folk Suite from the Western Hemisphere No. 5**
W77 *Lament*
Land of Peace, see **Africa**
Land of Romance, see **Africa**
Land of Superstition, see **Africa**
W78 *Lawd, I Want(s) to be a Christian*, see also **Twelve Negro Spirituals, Volume 1**
W79 *Legend*
W80 *Lenox Avenue*
W81 *Levee Land*
Levee Land, see **The American Scene**
Levee Song, see **Levee Land**
Li'l Scamp, see **From the Black Belt**
W82 *Lilt* (for accordion)
Lis'en to de Lam's, see **Twelve Negro Spirituals, Volume 1**
Little Conqueror, see **Little Red Schoolhouse**
W83 *Little David, Play on Your Harp*, see also **Spirituals: A Medley**
W84 *Little Folk Suite from the Western Hemisphere for Brass Quintet*
W85 *Little Folk Suite from the Western Hemisphere No. 1*
W86 *Little Folk Suite from the Western Hemisphere No. 2*
W87 *Little Folk Suite from the Western Hemisphere No. 3*
W88 *Little Folk Suite from the Western Hemisphere No. 4*
W89 *Little Folk Suite from the Western Hemisphere No. 5*
Little Mother, see **From the Hearts of Women**
W90 *Little Red Schoolhouse*
W91 *Little Song That Wanted to Be a Symphony, The*
W92 *Log Cabin Ballads*
Long To'ds Night, see **Log Cabin**

Alphabetical List of Works

Ballads
Look at Jazz, A, see *Songs: A Medley* and *Spirituals: A Medley*
Lord, I Looked Down The Road, see *Three Rhythmic Spirituals*
Los Indios and Yaravi, see *Little Folk Suite from the Western Hemisphere No. 4*
Los Reyes Magos, see *Christmas in the Western World*
W93 *Lost Out Blues*
Love Bids Me Stay at Home, see *Costaso*
W94 *Love Me in Your Old Time Way*
Love Scene, see *Troubled Island*
Love Will Find a Way, see *Songs: A Medley*
Lullaby, see *Rhapsody*
W95 *Lyric Quartette; Musical Portraits of Three Friends: Impressions*
Lyric String Quartette, see *Lyric Quartette*
Magic Bells, see *From the Journal of a Wanderer*
Magic Crystal, see *Patterns*
Mah Bones is Creakin', see *From the Black Belt*
Mah Lawd Gonna Rain Down Fiah, see *Twelve Negro Spirituals, Volume 2*
Maiden Was Adoring God, The Lord, A, see *Christmas in the Western World*
Mama, I Saw a Sailboat, see *Caribbean Melodies*
W96 *Mandy Lou*
Manhattan Skyline, see *The American Scene*
March Finale, see *Mississippi*
W97 *Marionette*
Medley, see *Songs: A Medley* and *Spirituals: A Medley*
Mejorana y Socavon, see *Danzas de Panama*
W98 *Memphis Man*
Men of the Army, see *Mississippi*
W99 *Minette Fontaine*
W100 *Miniature Overture*
W101 *Miniatures for Flute, Oboe, and Piano*
W102 *Minorities: Minorities and Majorities*
Minuet and Voodoo Dance, see *Troubled Island*
Miss Malindy, see *Log Cabin Ballads*
Miss M'Lindy (lost)
W103 *Miss Sally's Party*
W104 *Mississippi*
Mister Brown, see *Caribbean Melodies*
Mizmor Ledovid, see *The Voice of the Lord*
Mol'e, see *Folk Suite No. 2*
Mom'selle Zizi, see *Folk Suite No. 2*
Monigote, El, see *Folk Suite No. 4*
Moon Dusk, see *Wood Notes*
W105 *Mota*
Mother and Child, see *Suite for Violin and Piano*
Motherless Child, see *Spirituals: A Medley* and *Folk Suite No. 1*
Mountain, A Memorial, and A Song, A, see *The American Scene*
Musical Portraits of Three Friends: Impressions, see *Lyric Quartette*
Musieu Banjo, see *Vignettes*
Muted Laughter, see *Seven Traceries*
W106 *My Brother American*
Mystic Moon, see *From the Journal of a Wanderer*
Mystic Pool, see *Seven Traceries*
Navaho Country, see *The American Scene*
Negro Epic, A, see *Ebon Chronicle*
Negro in America, The: A Revue of the Race, see *From the Furnace of the Sun*
Negro Love Song, see *Three Negro Songs*
New Orleans Street, A, see *The American Scene*
Nido, El, see *Little Folk Suite from the Western Hemisphere No. 2*
W107 *Nigeria, We Hail Thee*
W108 *No Matter What You Do*
Nobody Knows the Trouble I've Seen, see *Spirituals: A Medley*
Oh! Dem Golden Slippers, see *Songs: A Medley*
Oh, Sorrow, see *And They Lynched Him on a Tree*
W109 *[Ohio, Ohio: Your Beacon Burns Brightly]*
Old Ark's a Moverin, The, see *Folk Suite for Band*
W110 *Old California*
Old West, The, see *The American Scene*
On a Plantation, see *Lyric Quartette;*

Musical Portraits of Three Friends: Impressions
On the Village Green, see **The American Scene**
Only Angels Have Wings (lost)
Out of the Silence, see **Seven Traceries**
Paean, see **Rhapsody**
Pages from a Mother's Diary, see **Little Red Schoolhouse**
W111 **Pages from Negro History**
Parted, see **Songs of Separation**
Pastorale, see **Rhapsody**
W112 **Pastorela**, variant of title: **Pastorella**
W113 **Path of Glory, The**
W114 **Patterns**
W115 **Peaceful Land, The**
Peas and Rice, see **Caribbean Melodies**
Peruvian Melody, see **Folk Suite No. 2** and **Vignettes**
Peter, Go Ring Dem Bells, see **Twelve Negro Spirituals, Volume 2**
Petey, see **Little Red Schoolhouse**
Petite Suite, see **Little Red Schoolhouse**
Phantom Chapel, see **Bells**
Phantom's Trail, see **From A Journal of a Wanderer**
W116 **Pillar, The**
Piñata, La, see **Christmas in the Western World**
W117 **Plain-Chant for America**
Plaza, The, see **The American Scene**
W118 **Poem for Orchestra** (1944)
Poeme, see **Songs of Separation**
W119 **Pompous March**
Prelude, see **Troubled Island**
Prelude (for piano), see **Preludes I-V** (for piano)
W120 **Preludes I-V** (for piano)
W121 **Preludes for String Orchestra and Piano**
Preludes for String Orchestra, Flute and Piano, see **Suite for Violin & Piano**
W122 **Pretty Ways**
W123 **Prince and the Mermaid, The**
Promenade, see **Costaso**
W124 **Promised Land**
Psalm 29, see **The Voice of the Lord**
W125 **Psalm for the Living, A**
Punto, see **Danzas de Panama**
Puritan Epic (lost)
W126 **Quit Dat Fool'nish**

Radiant Night, see **Minette Fontaine**
Radiant Pinnacle, see **Three Visions**
W127 **Reverie**
Reyes Magos, Los, see **Christmas in the Western World**
W128 **Rhapsody**
W129 **Ring Play**
Rising Tide, see **Song of a City**
W130 **Ritual**
Romance, see **Romance for Saxophone** and **Rhapsody**
W131 **Romance for Saxophone**
W132 **Sahdji**
St. Louis Blues, see **Songs: A Medley**
Salangadou, see **Little Folk Suite from the Western Hemisphere No. 1**
W133 **Scherzo**, from **Afro-American Symphony** (1930)
Second Dance of the Children, see **La Guiablesse**
W134 **Sentimental Song**
W135 **Serenade**
Serenade, see **From the Black Belt**
W136 **Seven Traceries**
Sing! Shout! Tell the Story! see **Christmas in the Western World**
Singing River, see **Wood Notes**
W137 **Sinner, Please Don't Let This Harvest Pass**, see also **Folk Suite for Band**
Sioux Love Song, see **The American Scene**
W138 **Sipping Cider Through a Straw**
Sister Heavy Hips (lost)
Slave Chant, see **Songs: A Medley**
Slavery, see **Pages from Negro History**
Soft Shoe Dance, see **Lenox Avenue**
Some of These Days, see **Songs: A Medley**
Sometimes I Feel Like a Motherless Child, see **Folk Suite No. 1**
Song at Dusk, A, see **Beyond Tomorrow**
W139 **Song for the Lonely**
W140 **Song for the Valiant**
W141 **Song of a City**, also known as Rising Tide and Victory Tide
Song of a New Race, see **Symphony No. 2 in G Minor** (1937)
Song of the Backwoods, see **Three Negro Songs**
W142 **Song of the Hunter**
Song of the Plainsmen, see **The American Scene**

Song of the Rivermen, see *The American Scene* and *Songs: A Medley*
Song of Worship, see *From a Lost Continent*
Songs, composed for Madame Marya Freund (lost)
W143 *Songs: A Medley*
W144 *Songs of Separation*
W145 *Sorcerer, The*
Sorrow Song, see *From the Black Belt*
South, The, see *The American Scene*
W146 *Southern Interlude, A*, see also *Highway 1, U.S.A.*
Spiritual, see *A Deserted Plantation*
Spiritual, see *From the Delta*
W147 *Spirituals: A Medley*
W148 *Steal Away to Jesus*
Still, My Heart, see *Blue Steel*
W149 *Suite for Violin and Piano*
Suite of Three Dances, see *Three Dances*
W150 *Summerland*, from *Three Visions*
Sunday Symphony, The, see *Symphony No. 3* (1958)
Sundown Land, see *The American Scene*
Sweet Betsy from Pike, see *Little Folk Suite from the Western Hemisphere No. 2*
Sweet Georgia Brown, see *Songs: A Medley*
W151 *Swing Low, Sweet Chariot*
Symphony in G Minor, see *Symphony No. 2 in G Minor* (1937)
Symphony No. 1, see *Afro-American Symphony* (1930)
W152 *Symphony No. 2 in G Minor, "Song of a New Race"* (1937)
W153 *Symphony No. 3, "The Sunday Symphony"* (1958)
W154 *Symphony No. 4, "Autochthonous (Indigenous)"* (1947)
W155 *Symphony No. 5, "Western Hemisphere"* (1945; revised 1958)
Tamborito, see *Danzas de Panama*
Tant Sirop est Doux, see *Little Folk Suite from the Western Hemisphere No. 3*
Tayêras, see *Folk Suite No. 4*
Tell Me, Shepherdess, see *Christmas in the Western World*
Ten Poun' Ten, see *Caribbean Melodies*
Theophany, see *Wood Notes*
This Day Must Come, see *Poem for Orchestra* (1944)
W156 *Those Who Wait*
W157 *Three Dances*, also known as *Ballet Dances*, *Ballet Music*, or *Suite of Three Dances*
Three Dances from *La Guiablesse*, see *La Guiablesse*
Three Fantastic Dances for Chamber Orchestra (lost)
W158 *Three Negro Songs*
W159 *Three Portraits*
W160 *Three Rhythmic Spirituals*
W161 *Three Visions*
W162 *Threnody: In Memory of Jan Sibelius*
W163 *To You, America!*
Tomb of the Unknown Soldier, see *The American Scene*
Toward Distant Shores, see *Four Octavo Songs*
Tribal Dance, see *The American Scene* and *Three Dances*
W164 *Troubled Island*
Tumblebug's Lament (lost)
Tutu Maramba, see *Little Folk Suite from the Western Hemisphere No. 5*
W165 *Twelve Negro Spirituals, Volumes 1 and 2*
Two Banana, see *Caribbean Melodies*
Two Hebraic Songs, see *Folk Suite No. 1*
W166 *Up There*
Valley of Echoes, see *From the Journal of a Wanderer*
Varsoviana, La, see *Little Folk Suite from the Western Hemisphere No. 5*
Ven, Niño Divino, see *Christmas in the Western World*
Victory Tide, see *Song of a City*
W167 *Vignettes*
Virgin Mary Had a Baby Boy, De, see *Christmas in the Western World*
W168 *Voice of the Lord, The*
Wade in the Water, see *Little Folk Suite from the Western Hemisphere No. 3*
W169 *Wailing Woman*
Waltz, see *Costaso*

We Are Climbing Jacob's Ladder,
see **Spirituals: A Medley**
W170 **We Sang Our Songs, The Fisk Jubilee Singers: 1871-1971**
Were You There? see **Spirituals: A Medley**
Western Hemisphere, The, see **Symphony No. 5** (1945)
What a Morning, see **Spirituals: A Medley**
What Does He Know of Dreams? see **Highway 1, U.S.A.**
Where Shall I Be (When the Great Trumpet Sounds)? see **Little Folk Suite from the Western Hemisphere for Brass Quintet** and **Four Octavo Songs**
Whippoorwill's Shoes, see **Wood Notes**
Whoopee Ti Yo Yo, see **Little Folk Suite from the Western Hemisphere No. 2**
W171 **Winter's Approach**
Woman Sweeter Than Man, see **Caribbean Melodies**
W172 **Wood Notes**
Work Song from the Delta, see **From the Delta**
Woven Silver, see **Seven Traceries**
Yaravi, see **Folk Suite No. 3**; **Little Folk Suite from the Western Hemisphere No. 4**; and **Miniatures for Flute, Oboe and Piano**
Young Missy, see **A Deserted Plantation**
W173 **Your World**
You're Wonderful, Mary, see **Highway 1, U.S.A.**
Zapatero, El, see **Folk Suite No. 2**

APPENDIX B: PRELIMINARY LIST OF ARRANGEMENTS AND ORCHESTRATIONS

BS   Pace Phonograph Company, Black Swan label, recordings
CW   Correspondence with the Clarence Williams Music Publishing Company (See WGS/VAS Papers, Box 9) University of Arkansas Libraries, Fayetteville
Diary   William Grant Still, Diary 1930 (See WGS/VAS Papers, Box 54), University of Arkansas Libraries, Fayetteville
HJA   Paul Hogan Jazz Archive, Tulane University, New Orleans, Louisiana
Handy   Pace and Handy Music Company or Handy Brothers Music Company
PWC   The Paul Whiteman Collection, Williams College Archives and Special Collections, Williamstown, Massachusetts
UN   location or publisher unknown, title referred to in a written or printed source
VG   personal collection of Vince Giordano, Brooklyn, New York
WGS   William Grant Still Music, Flagstaff, Arizona
WR   Willard Robison Letters (See WGS/VAS Papers, Box 39), University of Arkansas Libraries, Fayetteville

"Musical theatre" includes musical revues, follies, vaudeville, Broadway, and off-Broadway shows. Along with the song and musical theatre titles from the sources listed above are the names of radio and television programs (but not specific arrangements made for those shows) and movies on which Still worked. He also composed and orchestrated many background sequences for Columbia, Universal, Warner, and Fox Studios, which are not listed here.

Each entry lists title, composer (in parentheses, if known), source, and date (n.d. indicates no date).

50 Million Frenchmen Medley (Porter), PWC, 1930
After You've Gone (Creamer), missing from PWC, n.d.
All That I'm Asking Is Sympathy (Davis & Burke), PWC, n.d.
Alone In My Dreams (Archer), PWC, n.d.
Americana (McEvoy), musical theatre, n.d.
Ancient History Medley (various), PWC, 1929
Aunt Hagar's Blues, Diary, 1930
Battleship Kate (Sweatman & Rives), VG, 1924
Beautiful (Leonard, Stern & Stern), PWC, 1929
Blue (Riesman), Diary, 1930
Blue Eyes Get Red Red Ready for Love (Hoffman), PWC, n.d.
Blue Turning Grey Over You (Waller), PWC, n.d.
Broken Idol (Squires), PWC, 1929
Cameo Kirby Medley (Donaldson), PWC, 1930
Camp Meeting Blues (Canoll), HJA, Handy, n.d.
Can It Be True (Maxwell), PWC, n.d.
Can't Forget Medley, PWC, 1929
Can't Get Away From Medleys, PWC, 1929

Caribbean Love Song (Berton), PWC, n.d.
Carmela (Valente), PWC, n.d.
Carolina in the Morning (Donaldson), PWC, n.d.
Carolina Medley, PWC, 1929
Chantez les bas (Handy), PWC, n.d.
Chicago Blues (Biese, Altiere & Williams), Handy, VG, 1924
Chinatown Medley, PWC, 1929
Chinese Lullaby, Diary, 1930
College Medley (various), PWC, n.d.
Cooking Breakfast for the One I Love (Tobias), PWC, 1930
Cottage for Sale (Robison), PWC, 1930
Creole Follies (Creamer & Johnson), musical theatre, n.d.
Cut Out, CW, n.d. [about 1920]
Dance Away the Night (Stamper), PWC, n.d.
Dance of the Babes in the Woods, PWC, n.d.
Dance of the Paper Dolls (Tucker, Schuster & Siras), PWC, n.d.
Danse Barbare from *Congo Sketches* (Donaldson), WGS, 1928
Danse Barbaric (Donaldson), UN, [1928]
Dark Madonna (Donaldson), UN, [1928]
Deep River, Diary, 1930
Deep River Hour with Willard Robison, WOR Radio, New York, 1931-1934
Diane (Rapee & Pollack), PWC, n.d.
Dixie to Broadway, musical theatre, 1924
Dream Lover (Schertzinger), PWC, n.d.
Erotic Medley, PWC, 1929
Evangeline Waltz Medley, PWC, 1929
Fantasy on St. Louis Blues (Handy), UN, 1927
Feelin' the Way I Do (Gillespie, Cook & Moret), PWC, 1929
Fiddlin' Joe (Bagar, Cavanaugh & Mills), PWC, 1929
50 Million Frenchmen Medley (Porter), PWC, 1930
Florida Blues, The (Phillips), VG and HJA, Handy, 1916
Flying High Selection (DeSylva, Brown & Henderson), PWC, 1930
French Medley, PWC, 1929
Frenisi, UN, 1940
Frisco Jazz Band Blues (Rich), HJA, Handy, VG, 1919
From Beale Street to Broadway (Handy), Handy, VG, 1920
From the Land of the Sky Blue Water (Cadman), PWC, n.d.

Glow-Worm, Diary, 1930
Gospel Train, De, PWC, 1929
Gypsy Love Song (Herbert), PWC, n.d.
Heigh Ho Everybody (Woods), PWC, 1929
Here We Are (Warren), PWC, n.d.
Here's Another Medley, PWC, n.d.
He's a Good Man to Have Around (Ager), PWC, 1929
Hesitating Blues, The (Handy), Handy, 1916
Hindustan (Wallace & Weeks), PWC, 1929
Hit the Deck Medley (Youmans), PWC, 1930
I Belong to That Band, UN, 1941
I Can Do Wonders with You, PWC, 1929
I Heard from Heaven Today, UN, 1941
I Need Atmosphere, PWC, 1930
I Never Had the Blues (Williams), Handy, VG, 1919
I Think You'll Like It (Whiting), PWC, 1929
I Want to Meander in the Meadow (Woods), PWC, 1929
If I Had You (Shapiro, Campbell & Connelly), PWC, n.d.
If You Believed in Me (Baer), PWC, 1929
I'm Following You (Dreyer & MacDonald), PWC, 1929
I'm Looking All Around for a Vampire (Creamer & Layton), Handy, VG, 1920
I'm Sailing on a Sunbeam (Dreyer & MacDonald), PWC, 1929
In My Chateau of Love (Burton), VG, 1924
Irving Berlin Inc. (Berlin), PWC, 1929
Jazz Me Blues, The (Delaney), HJA, Handy, VG, 1921
Just an Hour of Love (Ward), PWC, 1930
Just One More Day (Thompson & Williams), VG, 1923
Kentucky Home, Diary, 1930
Khartum (Marcus), VG, 1922
Kissing Daddy (Marcus), VG, 1923
Lady of Secrets, movie soundtrack, n.d.
Let's Do Something Different Tonight (Frisch & Motzan), PWC, 1930
Lift Ev'ry Voice and Sing (Johnson), WGSM, n.d.
Lonely Troubadour (Klenner), PWC, 1929
Lonesome Sal (Bellin, Cox, Gillespie), HJA, Handy, n.d.
Long Gone (Smith & Handy), VG, 1920
Long Gone from Bowling Green (Smith & Handy), HJA, Handy, VG, 1920
Lost Horizons, "Death of the Lama" section, movie, 1937
Love Your Spell Is Everywhere (Goulding), PWC, 1929

Marines Hymn (Offenbach), PWC, n.d.
Maxwell House Hour, WJZ Radio, New York, 1930
Mean to Me (Turk & Ahlert), PWC, n.d.
Medley, PWC, 1929
Miss You (Tobias), PWC, 1929
Modernistic (Johnson), PWC, 1929
Moonlight & Roses Medley, PWC, 1929
Moonlight Reminds Me of You (Crawford), PWC, 1929
Music in May Medley, PWC, n.d.
My Dear (Garber and Large), PWC, 1929
My Girl, PWC, 1929
My Hero Waltz Medley, PWC, 1929
My Kinda Love (Alter), PWC, 1929
My Madonna, PWC, 1929
My Mother's Eyes (Baer), PWC, 1929
My Mother's Eyes Waltz (Baer), PWC, 1929
New York Glide (DeLaney), HJA, n.d.
Nina Rosa Selection (Romberg), PWC, 1930
Nobody's Using It Now (Schertzinger), PWC, 1930
Nocturnal Medley, PWC, 1929
Off Time-Dixie Cinderella Medley, PWC, 1929
Ol' Man River, Diary, 1930
Old Gold Hour, KFI Radio, California, 1929-1930
Old Miss (Handy), Handy, VG, 1916
One Moment More Medley, PWC, n.d.
One More Medley, PWC, n.d.
Over There Medley, PWC, n.d.
Passionate (Willie Smith), CW, n.d. [about 1920]
Passionate (Willie Smith), CW, 1937
Passionate Medley (Willie Smith), PWC, 1929
Peg O' My Heart, Diary, 1930
Pennies From Heaven, movie soundtrack, 1936
Perry Mason Show (the original), television, n.d.
Prehistoric Medley, PWC, n.d.
Puttin' on the Ritz Selection (Berlin), PWC, n.d.
Rain or Shine, musical theatre, n.d.
Reminiscent Medley, PWC, 1929
Rhythm King (Hoover & Trent), PWC, 1929
Romance (Donaldson), PWC, 1930
Romantic Medley, PWC, 1929
Rumba Rhythm (Remick), Diary, 1930
Runnin' Wild (Johnson), musical theatre, 1923
Safety in Numbers Medley, PWC, n.d.
Sally Medley (Kern), PWC, n.d.
Sally Medley #2 (Kern), PWC, 1929
Saxophone Blues (Bernard & Weidoeft), Handy, VG, 1919
Shadrack (MacGimsey), UN, n.d.
Show Boat Medley (Kern), PWC, 1929
Siboney (Lecuona), PWC, 1929
Singin' River (Moret), PWC, 1929
Sleepy Valley Medley, PWC, 1929
Sleepy Water, PWC, n.d.
Slow Drag Blues (Snowden), Handy, VG, 1919
Sociable, PWC, 1929
Song of Songs Medley, PWC, 1929
Sons of Guns Selection, PWC, 1930
Sorella, La (Clerc), PWC, 1929
South Sea Medley, PWC, n.d.
Sphinx, The (Barbour), Handy, VG, 1919
Spirituale (Trent), PWC, 1929
St. Louis Blues (Handy), UN, 1916
St. Louis Blues (Handy), PWC, 1929
Steal Away (spiritual), BS, [1923]
Steppin' Along Medley, PWC, 1929
Stormy Weather, movie soundtrack (not used), 1943
Struttin' Time (Hunter, Rogers & Roberts), musical theatre, n.d.
Sud Bustin' Blues (Lewis, Bocage & Piron), CW, VG, 1924
Suez (Stout), Handy, VG, 1919
Summer Medley, PWC, n.d.
Sunshine of Your Smile, Diary, 1930
Suwanee River, Diary, 1930
Swamp, The, CW, n.d. [about 1920]
Swanee Shuffle (Berlin), PWC, 1929
Sweet Mama Papa's Getting Mad (Little, Frost & Rose), VG, 1920
Sweetheart of Sigma Chi (Vernor), PWC, 1929
Swing Low, Sweet Chariot (spiritual), BS, [1923]
Tango Medley, PWC, n.d.
Telephone Blues or *Those Doggone Telephone Blues* (Marcus), VG, 1926
That Thing Called Love (Bradford), Handy, VG, 1920
Theodora Goes Wild, movie soundtrack, n.d.
They're Hunting A Husband for Helen (St. Leon & Spicer), Handy, VG, 1919
Trixie (John), HJA, Handy, n.d.
Vagabond King Selection (Friml), PWC, 1930
Vanities (Earl Carroll), musical theatre, n.d.
Waters of Perkiomen, Diary, 1930
Weary River (Silvers), PWC, 1929

We're on God's Side, CW, 1942
Western Sea Medley, PWC, 1929
What Wouldn't I Do for That Man (Gorney), PWC, 1929
What'll I Do Waltz Medley, PWC, 1929
When Summer is Gone (Wilhite), PWC, 1929
Where the For-Get-Me-Nots Remember, PWC, 1929
Where Were You Medley, PWC, 1929
Whistling (or *Whistlin'*) *Blues* (Diamond, Barnett & Holtsworth), HJA, Handy, VG, 1921
White Dove (Lehar), PWC, 1930
Who Discovered Medleys Medley, PWC, n.d.
Worrying Over You (DeRose), PWC, 1930
Would I Love to Love You (Dreyer & Clare), PWC, 1929
Wouldn't It Be Wonderful (Akst), PWC, 1929
Yamekraw (Johnson), VG, 1928
Year From Today (Jolson, MacDonald & Dreyer), PWC, 1929
You Want Lovin', PWC, 1929

INDEX

Page numbers are listed first, followed by bibliographic entry numbers, coded by letter: A for writings by Verna Arvey, B for entries from the general bibliography, D for entries from the discography, S for writings by William Grant Still, SA for writings by Still and Arvey, and W or WB (the two are interfiled) for entries from "Works and Performances." However, the main entry to each work found in the "Works and Performances" section is not indexed. *Festive Overture,* for example, has no index entry for W36 (*Festive Overture*) because that is where one would expect to find it. It has, however, an entry for WB91.9 because one would not look for it in the review of a performance of W91, *The Little Song That Wanted to Be a Symphony.*

369th Infantry Regiment Band, 19
A.B.C. Symphony (Australia), 11
Abajian, James, B3
Abdul, Raoul, WB62.17
Adair, James, W114c
Adams, Leslie, B303
Adams, Stanley, B124
Adams, Wellington, A8
Addison, Adele, W16g
Adkins, Cecil, B4, B5
Aeolian Music Foundation, 39, W115
 eolian String Quartet, W32e
ffelder, Paul, WB164.20
 ica, 1, 21, 25, 28, 30, 32, B24, B224,
  B421, B446, D64. *See also* Land of
  uperstition
 can Methodist Episcopal Church, 16
 -American Chorale (Washington, DC),
  V45g
 -American Symphony, 8, 25-29, 31-32,
  7-38, 40, A18, A20, A22, B7, B12,
  i22, B24, B25, B31, B32, B71, B95,
  i104, B131, B133, B140, B142, B156,
  i158, B188, B220, B224, B262, B277,
  B280, B282, B296, B302, B307, B309,
  B333, B364, B378, B393, B394, B401,
  B440, B446, B450, D16, D20, D22,
  D24-D26, D77, S19, S73
 ter You've Gone (arr.), 18

Ager, Milton, 21
Aida (Giuseppe Verdi), WB164.18
Akers, Gene, W149i
Akst, George, D52
Alabama Agricultural and Industrial College, 15, 17
Alcorn Agricultural and Mechanical College (Lorman, MS), 15
Alessandro, Victor, W154a, W172b
Alexander, Otis, W62f
Alexander, Ruth, B127
Alfredo Salmaggi Opera Company, WB164.18
Ali, Susan, W9e
All-American Orchestra, 37, D25
All That I Am, D32
Allen, Chris, W9e
Allen, Clara: dedication to, W156, WB156.1
Allen, David, W6d
Allen, Donald Vail, WB6.20
Allen, Nimrod, B334; dedication to, W156, WB156.1
Allen, Thomasena Davis, W62h
Allen, Walter C., B128
Allen, William Duncan, 34, B129, W61e, W126e, W161e-W161g, W161q, W161s; dedication to, 34, W136
Allied Arts League of Los Angeles, S55
Almond, Dale, W25p
American Accordionists' Association, 39, W8,

WB8.3, WB8.6, W82, WB82.1; National
Convention, 39
American Composers' Concerts, 25, 27
American Composers of Today and Their Works
(Claire Reis, comp.), 25
American Composers' Orchestra, 8
American Federation of Musicians: Local 767,
B293; Local 802, W30
American Guild of Organists, 39, W31
American Harp Society of Los Angeles, W32e
American in Paris, An (George Gershwin), 29
American Scene, The, D23, D73, S61
American School of the Air (radio program),
W18a
American Society of Composers, Authors, and
Publishers (ASCAP), 31, 37
American Symphony Orchestra (John H. Mueller),
S46
American Symphony Orchestra League, 38,
B184, B324, S52
Americana (musical show), 21, B305
Amistad Research Center (New Orleans, LA),
B80
Amos, Gloria, W62f
Analytical Concert Guide (Louis Biancolli), S45
Ancient History Medley (arr.), 24
And They Lynched Him on a Tree, 35, A13,
B10, B71, B104, B118, B218, B226,
B277, B376, B390, D34
Anderson, E. Gilbert, 21
Anderson, E. Ruth, B6
Anderson, Harry, 15
Anderson, Marian, S43
Anderson, T. J., B201
Andre, Franz, W2bb, W154b
Andrews, George Whitfield, 18
Andrews, Richard, W132b
Angel City Symphony Orchestra (Los Angeles,
CA), D17, W117i, W135b
Annual Music Week Effort (Harlem), 28
Apple, Darwyn, W149m
Archaic Ritual, B384
Ardoin, John, WB25.4
Ardoyno, Dolores, B130, W9d, W99a
Aria, 39
Arkansas Federation of Music Clubs, B161
Arlen, Walter, W25c.1, WB136.2
Armstrong, George, WB62.4
Arndal, Ernst, W111d
Arnold, Ben, B7
Arnold, Denis, B8
Arnowsky, S., B9
Arpin, Chris, W144q
Arthur, Desmond, B266
Arvey, Dr. Bessie: dedication to, W125
Arvey, Dale, W74a, W74c
Arvey, Verna, 2, 3, 9-12, 31, 35-36, B48,
B59, B155, B175, B183, B217, B262,
B335, B344, B350, B396, B399, W13,
W40, W60, W80f, W109; dedications to,

29, W30, W74; librettos by, 39, W9,
W24, W62, W99, W105, W116, W146;
as performer, 30, 33, 35, 39, D14, D63,
D67, W1h, W1j, W1l, W14b, W15b,
W15c, W16c, W32a-W32e, W50a,
W74a-W74c, W74f-W74k, W76c, W76d,
W76f-W76h, W80a, W80c-W80f, W80g,
W80h, W126c, W126d, W144d, W161a-
W161d, W161h, W161l, W164b,
W164c, W171e; poems by, W50, W69,
W118, W156, W169; text and other writing
by, 25, 30-31, 33, 35, S40, W3, W19,
W22, W30, W53, W68, W77, W80,
W91, W102-W104, W106, W111,
W113, W128, W139, W140, W142,
W164, W165, W166, W170 (*see also In
One Lifetime*). William Grant Still and Verna
Arvey Papers: *see* Still, William Grant
Assaf, Nancy Ross, W99a
Ashworth, Jody L., W9e
Atherton, Roy, W123a
Atkinson, Swales, W117f-W117h
Atlanta-Morehouse-Spelman Chorus of Mixed
Voices, W141d
Atlanta University, 15
Aubert, Roger, W161i
Avery, Bennet, W62g
Azhderian, Edward, W90a

B.B.C. Orchestra, 11
BMI. *See* Broadcast Music, Inc.
Babb, Edith, W91c
Babich, Arthur, W110i
Bach, Johann Sebastian, WB161.4
Bacon, Earnest, B46
Bacon, Elmore, WB118.2, WB152.17
Bagar, Robert, B10, WB69.2, WB117.2,
WB118.3, WB164.21
Bakaleinikoff, Constantin, W46f
Bakaleinikoff, Vladimir, W46h
Baker, David N., B132
Baker, Ed, WB154.1
Baker, Josephine, 19
Balanchine, George, W164a
Balazs, Frederic, W5a, WB36.13, W103b
Baldwin, Lillian, B133
Bales, Richard, W25c, W25l, W111c, W133i,
W172c, W172e
Bales, William, W9b
Balint, Joyce Rasmussen, W149l
Ballard, Clavis, W25p
Ballinger, Cathryn Flewellyn, W16h
Balthrop, Carmen, W9d
Baltimore Symphony Orchestra, W132f
Bamboula (Samuel Coleridge-Taylor), 30
Banks, Louis, S30
Banner, James M., Jr., B74
Barbelle, Albert, 33, W165
Barbirolli, Lady Evelyn, W101a, W101b;
Camden Trio, W167; dedication to, W101

Index   309

Barbirolli, Sir John, 35, B134, B322, W117a, W117d, W117h; dedication to, W101
Barclay, Bob, W32g
Bardolph, Richard, B134
Barlow, Harold, B12
Barlow, Howard, 32-33, D11, W80a, W80b
Barnett, Jack, 19
Barnett, John, W133j
Barra, Donald, W9e
Barrère, Georges, 23, 25, W1a, W46a, W46b, W92a; dedication to, W1
Barrère Little Symphony Orchestra, 23, 25, W1a, W46a, W46b, W92a
Barthe, Richmond, W149
Barzin, Leon, W15a, W36q
Bass, John Quincy, W74e
Bates, Leon, W136e
Bates College (Lewiston, ME): honorary doctorate, 38
Baton Rouge Opera Company, B130, D4, W99a
Baustian, Robert, W155a
Bay, Victor, W155b
Bay Region Federal Symphony (San Francisco, CA), W74g, W74h, W80d, W80e
Bayou Home, D56
Bayou Legend, A, 3, 35, 40, B66, B86, B91, B93, B105, B114, B123, B130, B446, D1
Beale Street, B262
Beatty, Harry, W76b
Beaufort, Robert, WB2.54
Beckstead, Ross, W32c, W32e
Beckstead, Russell, W139c
Bedford, Cynthia, D47, W144i, W144j
Beers, Marion, WB172.6
Beeson, Jack, B201
Beethoven, Ludwig van, SA5
Beiderbecke, Bix, 25
Bell, Eleanor, WB36.3
Bell, Frederick, W61f, W125e
Bell, Michael D., B74
Bell, William Service, W58a; dedication to, W58
Bells, 37, B22, D64, D65, D70
Belt, Lida M., B132
Bennett, Denise, W62e
Bennett, Elsie M., WB8.2, WB8.6
Bennett, Gordon, W62a
Bennett, Grena, WB69.3, WB149.3
Bennett, Robert Russell, 29, WB8.1, WB80.5
Berens, Fritz, W90c, W90d
Bergh, Frances Hovey, WB8.4, WB115.1, WB162.1
Berkshire Night, D73
Berlin, Irving. See *Irving Berlin, Inc.*
Berlin Philharmonic Orchestra, 28, W2c, W2x, W133a
Berliner Symphoniker, D13
Bernheimer, Martin, S69, WB36.20

Bernstein, Leonard, 39, WB62.3
Berres, George, D36-D38, D41, D43, W121a, W135d
Berry, Lemuel, B13
Bethune, Mary McLeod, B136
Beverly Hills Symphony Orchestra, W5c
Beyond Tomorrow, 25. See also *Song at Dusk*
Biancolli, Louis, B10, S45, S49, WB69.2, WB110.6, WB110.8
Bible, Frances, W164a
Biddle, Francis, W6, W117; Francis and Katherine Biddle Papers (Georgetown University), B390. *See also* Chapin, Katherine Garrison
Bidwell, Marshall, W163.2
Bierhoff, Hannah: dedication to, W144
Bierley, Paul E., B98
Bigelow, Stanley, WB2.15
Bilanchone, Victor, D31
Billups, Reginald, W62b
Biracree, Thelma, 26, 29, A19, W76a, W76i, W103a, W132a-W132c; dedication to, W103; The Thelma Biracree Schnepel Collection, W76, W103, W132
Birchard, C. C. See C. C. Birchard, Publisher
Bishop, Dorothy, W70c
Black, Gregory D., B271
Black, Brown and Beige (Duke Ellington), B421
Black Man Dances, The, 4, 31-32, A16
Black Swan Dance Masters, 20
Black Swan Dance Orchestra, W122
Black Swan label. *See* Pace Phonograph Company
Blackman, Bessie Lawson: dedication to, 39, W43
Blake, Eubie, 4, 7, 8, 19
Bledsoe, Jules, WB164.18
Blind Man, The, B118, D34
Bliss, Helena, B241, W164a
Blitzstein, Marc, 29
Block, Maxine, B15
Blom, Eric, B50
Blue Steel, 9, 30-31, B24, B86, B91, B93, B183, B224, B446
Blues (From the Black Belt), 23
Blues, The, from *Lenox Avenue*, 25, A17, D6, D7, D12, D15, D49, D51, D55, D63, D64, D69, D70
Blume, Friedrich, B27
Blume, Ruth, B27
Bohle, Bruce, B16
Bohm, Jerome D., WB6.4, WB6.7, WB36.9, WB69.4
Bohnert, Carol, W62b
Boise Philharmonic Orchestra, W115b
Bolivar (Darius Milhaud), WB164.13
Bolm, Adolph, 23, W76
Bonds, Margaret A., B303
Bonds, Samuel, W62h
Bonomo, Octave, W111e, W111f
Bontemps, Arna, 35, 37, B325, W144, W173
Booth, Alan, W70d

Bornn, Hugo, W126f
Borowski, Felix, WB2.21, WB172.1
Borroff, Edith, B17
Boston Pops Orchestra, W133h
Boston Symphony Orchestra, 11, W69d
Boutelse, Phil, W72
Bowers, Violet George, WB36.23
Boxwell, James, WB164.18
Bradford, Harold, W62b
Braithwaite, Coleridge Alexander, B139
Brandolino, Sharon, W167b
Brant, LeRoy V., W45a, W45b, W59, W141e; dedication to, W135
Brant, Ruth: dedication to, W135
Brasier, Virginia, W23
Brawley, Benjamin G., B20
Brawner-Floyd, Alpha, W16l
Brazzel, Mary Ann, W62c
Breath of a Rose, The, 23, 31, B46, B212
Breda, Malcolm J., W144n
Brice, Carol, W6d
Brice, Jonathan, W6d
Bridgetower, George Augustus Polgreen, A31
Briggs, John, 8, 37, WB6.18, WB69.5, WB117.3, WB164.22
Britten, Benjamin, WB164.39
Broadcast Music, Inc., A27, B381
Broder, Nathan, B50
Broekman, David, W2m
Bronson, Carl, WB2.47, WB80.7, WB117.6
Brooks, Tilford, B140
Brother Lowdown, 4
Brourman, Jacques, W115b
Brown, R. Donald, B230, B412
Brown, Rae Linda, B18, B208
Brown, Ray C. B., WB117.12
Brown, Roscoe C., B95
Brown, William A., D2, W9c, W62d, W62g
Brown Baby, 20
Browning, David A., W131a
Bruce, Richard (pseud.). *See* Nugent, Bruce
Bryant, James, W62e
Bryden, Eugene, W164a
Buckley, Charles, WB172.3
Buffalo Philharmonic Orchestra, W133k, W144o
Bull, Storm, B19
Bullock, August, W62e
Bundy, Grace. *See* Still, Grace Bundy
Bunge, Jean, WB9.4
Burge, Louise, 35, W6a-W6c
Burgess, Gary, W9d
Burke, Harry R., WB10.1
Burke, Victoria Juarez: dedication to, W155
Burkett, Nancy Hall, B20
Burkett, Randall K., B20
Burleigh, Henry Thacker, 17, A16, B228, B303, S43
Bush, Elmer, W6f
Bush, Ronald, W132e

Butcher, Margaret Just, B142
Butler, Henry, B143, WB36.11
Butterfield, Billy, D12
Butterworth, Neil, B21
Byrd, Jimmy, W172d

CBS Radio Network, 28, 33-34, 36, W18a. *See also* Columbia Broadcasting System
C. C. Birchard, Publisher, 25
Cadman, Charles Wakefield, 33, A23
Cady, Harriet, W171g
Cage, Earl, W132c
California Black Oral History Project, B412
California Society of Composers, 32-33
California State University, Fullerton, B412
California State University, Long Beach, B68
Callin, Owen, WB69.17
Calloway, Earl, B144, B145
Calvin, Dolores, B146-B148; dedication to, W10
Calvin's News Service, 35, S22, S23
Camden Trio, W167
Campbell, Cynthia V., WB99.2
Campbell, Dick, WB164.18
Canterbury, Richard, W149f
Cantrell, Roger, W9b
Capitol Hill School, 16
Caplan, Stephen, D35, D50
Cariaga, Daniel, B149, B150, WB9.15, WB9.25, WB118.15
Caribbean Melodies, 35, B218
Carlin, Seth, W149m
Carlson, Claudine, D52
Carmela, D52, D55
Carmen (Georges Bizet), WB164.18
Carozza, Carmen, W8b
Carpenter, John Alden, 23, 38, A2
Carr, Jay, WB155.6
Carroll, Earl, 21. *See also* Earl Carroll's *Vanities*
Carter, Charles, W132e
Carter, John, W16g
Carter, Michael, WB164.7
Casagrande, Efram, W15g
Casella, Alfredo, 22
Cassidy, Claudia, WB172.2
Caston, Saul, W36c
Castro, Washington, W7c
Cato, Minto, WB164.18
Central Avenue, 31, 33
Centro de Cultura (Benevento, Italy), W25d
Chadwick, George Whitefield, 7, 20, 40, B398, S35
Challis, Bill, B253
Chamberlain, Carl, WB9.23
Chambers, Martin, W9e
Chang, Lynn, D44, D58
Chapin, Katherine Garrison, 35, A14, W6, WB6.3, W117; Francis and Katherine Biddle Papers (Georgetown University), B390; Katherine Garrison Chapin Papers (Library of

Congress), B390. *See also* Biddle, Francis
Charles, Clayton, W62a
Charles, Richard, W164a
Charleston Symphony Orchestra (Charleston, WV), 11, 36, W36r, W46i, W46j, W62b
Charlton, Melville, A16
Chase, Frank, 8
Chase, Gilbert, B153
Chassman, Joachim, W135d; dedication to, W95
Chatauqua Symphony Orchestra, W160a
Chatman, Floyd, W132d
Chaves, Noah, W25j, W144k
Chavez, Carlos, 24
Cheatham, Wallace, W156a
Chicago (IL): Allied Arts, Inc., 22-23, W76; Civic Opera, 27, 30; Grand Opera Company, 30, W76e; International Film Festival, WB9.27; North Shore Festival Association, Orchestral Composition Contest, 22, W51; Opera Ballet, 30; Symphony Orchestra, 11, 22, 37, W2h, W51a, W76b, W118f, W172a
Chism, Olin, WB133.3
Choate, Robert A., B374
Chocolate Soldier (Oscar Strauss), 17
Choral Guild of San Jose (San Jose, CA), W45a, W45b, W141e
Chow, Alan, W136g
Christ, Peter, D39
Christlieb, Don, W167a
Christmas Carol (Charles Dickens), 23
Christmas in the Western World (Las Pascuas), B31, B118, B178, B179, B218, B226
Chuck Davis Dance Company, W45f
Churchill, Mark, D44, D58
Cincinnati Musicians' Association Symphony, W27b
Cincinnati Symphony Orchestra, 11, 36, W36, W36a, W74e; Golden Jubilee Season Composition Competition, 36, WB36.1
Citadel, D34, D58
Citrus College Community Opera Association (Azusa, CA), W62c
Civic Arts Orchestra (Los Angeles, CA), W132d
Clad, Michele, B155
Claghorn, Charles Eugene, B23
Claiborne, Cheryl, W62a
Clarence Williams Music Publishing Company, 33
Clark, C. Carroll, 20, W151
Clark, Edgar Rogie, B303
Clark, J. Bunker, B17
Clarke, Catherine, W62f
Clef Club, 19
Clemmons, Francois, W9a, W9d
Cleveland, Linda, W62d
Cleveland Symphony Orchestra, 11, 36, W69h, W69i, W69l, W69m, W69o, W69p, W118, W118a, W133e, W152f

Cloud Cradles, D67, D69
Cobbs, Paul-Elliott, B156, W2
Cody, Carlos Bernard, B157
Coleridge-Taylor, Samuel, 17, 30, 40, A16, A31, B193, D2, D20, WB1.7, WB25.7, WB76.6, WB117.15
Collaer, Paul, B158
Collegiate Choir, W6c
Collins, Jonathan, W59c, W140c
Collura, Frank, W144o
Colored Chorus of Oakland (CA), W80c, W80d, W80e
Columbia Broadcasting System, 33; commissioned by, W18, W80; CBS Symphony Orchestra, D11, W80a, W80b, W112b. *See also* CBS
Columbia recording, 23, 37; Columbia Records/AAMOA (Afro-American Music·Opportunities Association) Black Composers Series, 40
Columbia Studios, 32, B274, B318. *See also* Motion picture industry
Columbus International Film Festival, WB9.27
Columbus Urban League, W156.1
Combs, Mary, W131b
Communism, B127, B196, B242, B424, S33, S43, S48, S50
Compinsky, Manuel, W2i
Composers' Protective Society, 29
Composer's World (Paul Hindemith), S47
Concerts Pasdeloup, 28
Condell, H.A., W164a
Conrad, Barbara, W9a, W9c
Converse College, B68
Convington, Ferman, W62f
Cook, J. Douglas, B165
Cook, Will Marion, S23, W96
Cooper, Bobby G., W9d
Copes, Ronald, W25j, W144k
Copland, Aaron, B46, B166, WB80.5
Coppin, John, W32c
Coppin, Margaret, W32c, W32e
Coppin String Quartet, W32c
Corbett, Richard, W33a, W61d, W140a
Cornell, Dorothy, W80f
Cort, John, 19
Costaso, Ramon, W24
Costaso, 38, B86, B344, B428, D34
Couch, Alice, W76a, W76i, W132b, W132c
Councill, William Harper, 15, 17
Couser, William, W132e
Covarrubias, Miguel, 28
Covell, George, W126h
Cowden, Robert H., WB172.9
Cowell, Henry, 24, 29, 34-35, 38, B167, B294, S1
Craft, Lois Adele, D37, D38, D41, D43, S70, W32a-W32g; dedication to, 39, W32
Craven, Robert R., B168
Crawford, Lenore, WB6.11, WB141.2

Crawford, Ruth, 24
Creamer, Henry, 21
Crenshaw-Leimert Chorus, W132d
Creole Follies (musical revue), 21
Creston, Paul, WB8.3
Crosby, Bing, 28, 31
Cross-Eyed Monkey, The, 4
Croughton, Amy H., WB2.1, WB2.4
Crowder, Charles, WB172.7
Csaky, Nelly, W15g; Accademia Csaky, W15g; Csaky Ensemble, W114, W136; Nelly Csaky String Quartet, W25d
Cullen, Countee, 28, B80, B203, B239, W144
Cumbia y Congo, B262, D36
Cumbo, Clarissa, 4
Cumbo, Marion, 21
Cummings, David, B24
Cuney-Hare, Maud, B20
Cunningham, Carl, WB144.4

Da Costa, Noel, W16l, W45f, W170e
Dabrishus, Michael J., B169, B170
Dallas Symphony Orchestra, 37, W25i, W118c, W118d, W133m
Dalrymple, Jean, B171
Dance from Costaso, D34
Dance of Love, 24
Dance of the Carnal Flowers, 24
Dance of the Children, A5
Dance of the Porteuses, D34
Dance Theater on LaBrea (Los Angeles, CA), W80f
Dance Theatre Group of Los Angeles, 33
Daniel, Ruth, W16e, W16f, W140b, W144c, W171h
Daniels, David, B25
Danse Nègre (Samuel Coleridge-Taylor), WB25.7
Danzas de Panama, 37, B262, D13, D36, D38, D41, D43, D77
Dark Horseman, 33
Darker America, 23, 25-26, B22, B25, B33, B95, B104, B294, B333, B394, B421, D21
Davidson, Celia Elizabeth, B172
Davidson, Marie Hicks, WB2.19
Davie, Maurice R., B173
Davis, Curtis W., W9d
Davis, Ella Belle, WB164.9
Davis, Evelyn, W141c
Davis, John P., B26
Davis, Peter G., WB25.7, WB62.16, WB144.8
Davis, Ronald L., B123
Davis, Sharon, D39
Dawson, William Levi, B134, B142, B208, B228, B322, S19, S43, W36h
De Leighbor, Don, WB164.10
de Lerma, Dominique-René, B27-29, B174-178
De Lewis, Marjorie, W16k
de Paur, Leonard, W9a, W9c, W9d, WB9.2, WB9.4, WB9.5, WB9.9, WB9.10, WB9.13, WB9.16, WB9.17
De Pinto, Geraldine, WB90.3
de Sayn, Elena, WB149.5
de Toledano, Ralph, B179
Deal, John, W113a
DeArmand, Peggy, W131c
Death Song, 21
DeBose, Tourgee, W58a
Debussy, Claude, 28, WB136.4, WB164.41
DeCles, Diana, WB144.6
Deep River (song), 1, WB2.55
Deep River Hour (radio program), 4, 8, 28, 33, B305, B341, B361
Deep River Orchestra (Willard Robison), 27-28
Deermont, Helen, WB99.1
Del Solar, Tomas, W132c
Delaplain, Theresa, W101f
DeLibero, Kim, D35
Delius, Frederick, WB9.11, WB152.6, WB164.21, WB164.41
Delkas, 37
DeMart, Jean, D44, D58
DeMers, John, WB9.10, WB9.19
Denney, Jane, WB123.1
Dent, Cedric Carl, B303
Denver Symphony Orchestra, 36, D19, W36c, W154c
Deserted Plantation, A, 25, 29, 34
Dessalines, Jean Jacques, W164
Destine, Jean Leon, B171, W164a
Detels, Claire, B181, B182, S74
Detroit: Metropolitan Orchestra, 36, W36o, W155c, W172d; Musicians Association, W101d; Public Library, B281; Symphony Orchestra, 11, D16, D27, W2dd, W91c, W133l
Dett, Robert Nathaniel, A16, B377, B407, S18, S43, WB80.5
DeWitt, Susan, D40, D56, D68
Diamond, Jack Legs, 22
Diamond, Joe, 19
Dickens, Charles, 23
Dickinson, Alis, B4, B5
Dierks, Donald, B183
Dietz, Betty, B184
Dillard University Choir, W117j
Diron's Swan Song, 3
Dismal Swamp, 31-32, B7, B22, B32, B55, B333, B394
Dixie to Broadway (musical show), 21, B121
Dixon, Dean, W110h
Dixon, W. Randy, B185, WB2.37
Dobbins, Sharon E. A., B186
Dobbs, Mattiwilda, W111d, W128, W160, W160a
Dobish, Gail, W99a

Doernberg, Jerry, WB132.5
Domingues, Albert, D70
Dorati, Antal, 37, W118c, W118d
Dorian, Frederick, S36
Doris Barr Studio, W171c
Dorr, Dolores, B297
Dorr, Donald, B187, B297, B411, W9a, W9c, W9d, W62d, W99a
Dorsey, Abner, 35, W6b
Dougan, Marjorie, W80f
Dougan, Michael B., B188
Douglass, Fannie Howard, B189
Douglass, Frederick, 17
Doving, Richard, B190
Down Yonder, 25
Downes, Olin, 23, 26, B191, WB2.8, WB26.1, WB36.8, WB52.1, WB69.1, WB69.6, WB81.1, WB117.4, WB118.4, WB132.1, WB152.4, WB164.23
Downs, Karl E., B20
Dragon, Carmen, W5b
Drummond, Andrew H., B191
Drums of Haiti (Langston Hughes), 34
Drye, Frank, B259
DuBois, W. E. B., 17, WB6.12
Dufour, Charles L., WB36.17
Dunbar, Paul Lawrence, 17-18, 21, 26, W2, W27, W58, W144, W171
Dunbar, Rudolph, 21, 36, A18, A20, B185, B192, B232, B430, S30, W2n-W2z, WB2.40, W36b, W69e, WB69.11, W76k, W110g, W117f, W117g, W152i; dedication to, 36, W36
Duncan, Geraldyne, W16i
Duncan, John, B193
Dunham, Katherine, 29-30, 36, W76e
Dunn-Powell, Rosephanye, B194
Dunning, Edwin, W164a
Dupriez, Christian: dedication to, W155
Durrett, C. William, WB62.12
Dvořák, Antonin, 17, A32, B158, B249
Dyen, Doris J., B68
Dykema, Peter W., W137

Eagon, Angelo, B31
Earl Carroll's Vanities (musical show), 8, 21, B121, B305
Earls, Paul, B201
East Los Angeles Junior College, W9b; Chorus, W9b; Concert Choir, W6f; Dancers, W9b; Orchestra, W9b
Eastman School of Music (University of Rochester), 23, 27, 29, B62, B68, B195, W26, W76, W91, W103; American Composers' Concerts, A19; Chorus, D10; Little Symphony, W14a, W46c; Senior Symphony Orchestra, W152h; Summer Orchestra, W111b; Symphony and Chorus, W1g
Eastman-Rochester Symphony Orchestra, D10, D26, W91e, W132c

Ebon Chronicle, 25, 29, 32, B32, B142
Ebony Symphony Orchestra, W152j
Edwards, Benjamin Griffith, B197
Edwards, Miss Robert V., W74b
Eggler, Bruce, WB9.9
Eichenberger, Rodney, W160c
Eichheim, Henry, B294
Einstein, Alfred, 8
Eisler, Charlotte, W149c
El Paso Symphony Orchestra, W91f
Elie, Jr., Rudolph, WB69.9
Elixir of Love (Gaetano Donizetti), 16
Ellegaard, Mogens, W8c
Ellington, Duke, B257, B421
Ellis, John, W101e, W167a
Elwell, Herbert, WB69.14, WB69.24, WB152.18
Emanuel, Nathan, W16c, W76a, W171e
Embree, Edwin R., B20, B34, B96, B198; dedication to, W168
Emery, Lynne Fauley, B199
Ennanga, 39, D37, D38, D41, D43, S70
Ennis, Bayard F., WB62.5
Entrance of Les Porteuses, D14
Erskine, John, S44
Esposito, Vincent, W112j
Ethel Waters and Her Jazz Masters, 20, W17, W93, W98
Ettore, Eugene, WB8.1
Europe, James Reese, 19
Eva Jessye Choir, W6b, W6c
Evans, Mary Jane, W123a
Evans, Wanda, W132e
Evans, Wilbur, W117a, W117c
Everett, Chestyn, WB136.1, WB136.3
Everett, Thomas, B200
Everett, Thomas G., W47h
Everett, Tom, B201
Eversman, Alice, WB111.1, WB117.13
Ev'ry Time I Feel the Spirit, 25, B118
Ewen, David, B27, B37-43
Eymann, Dale, W38a
Ezmirlian, Diana, W32e

Faber, Charles, WB25.3
Fairley, Lee, WB152.20
Fairy Knoll, 37, B231
Fallows, David Nicholas, B35
Fambro, Anne (William Grant Still's grandmother), 5, 16
Fantasy on St. Louis Blues (arr.), 23
Farberman, Harold, W26g
Farish, Margaret K., B45
Farrar, Reginald, W16j
Faulkner, Dee Tankersley, W91a
Fax, Mark, B172
Feinauer, Louise Colusso, W149l
Feldman, Goldie, WB91.1
Fentress, J. Cullen, WB2.50, WB2.52
Ferguson, Blanche E., B203

Fernandez, O. Lorenz, W28d
Ferris, William, B123
Festival Ensemble Chorus, W125e
Festive Overture, 36, B25, B380, D18, S61, WB91.9
Fiedler, Arthur, W133h
Fiedler, Elsa, W149e
Fields, Bernice, B204
Fields, Richard, D65
Fine, Vivian, 29
Finn, Robert, WB155.1
Fischer, Carl, 36
Fischer, George: dedication to, W110
Fischer, J., 33, W80
Fischer, Joseph, S13
Fischer, Norman, W25j, W144k
Fisher, Charles, W70f
Fisher, Gary, W9b
Fisher, Marjory M., WB1.11, WB74.11, WB76.8, WB171.1
Fisk Jubilee Singers, 17, D30, W170, W170a-W170d
Fisk University, B78, B109, B249, B386
Flagstad Manuscript (Louis Biancolli), S49
Fleary, Dingwall, W62h
Fleming, H. H., W141i
Fleming, John, B207
Flippin, Jay, W131b
Flirtation, The, D9
Floren, Myron, W8a
Florida Blues (arr.), 18
Floyd, Samuel A., Jr., B208
Folk Suite for Band, 39, B98, B157, B200
Folk Suite, No. 1, 39, D40
Folk Suite, No. 2, 39, D35
Folk Suite, No. 3, 39, D35
Folk Suite, No. 4, 39, D35, D42
Forbes, Lydia, D44, D58
Foreman, Clark, B209
Foreman, T.E., WB32.2
Forsythe, Harold Bruce, 25, 29-32, WB1.7, W13, W14, WB76.6, W126a, W145; dedication to, 31, W126
Fort Worth Symphony Orchestra, 32, W30a
Fortenberry, L. C., B210
Foster, Katheryn, W171c
Foster, Sandy, W149n
Four Indigenous Portraits, 39
Four Nocturnes (Robert Russell Bennett), WB8.1
Fourth Symphony. See *Symphony No. 4, "Autochthonous (Indigenous)"*
Fox, Russell, W9b
Fox Studio, 36. *See also* Motion picture industry
Franck, César, B158, WB132.7, WB161.4
Frankenstein, Alfred, WB1.12
Frankfurter Rundfunk Symphonie Orchestra, 26
Frankie and Johnnie (arr.), 28
Franusich, Melita, W45b
Freedoms Foundation Award, 38, W163
Freeman, Harry Lawrence, 28, B172, B193

Freeman, Paul, 40, B262, B382, D2, D8, D20, W25i, W25k, W132f, W133m, W133o
Frenesi (arr.), B378
Fried, Alexander, WB74.12
Friedberg, Ruth C., B46, B182, B212
Frisco Jazz Band Blues (arr.), 19
From a Lost Continent, 37, B218
From the Black Belt, 21, 23, 38, B32, B104, D21
From the Delta, 37, B98, B200, B438
From the Journal of a Wanderer, 21-22, B32
From the Land of Dreams, 21, B294, B333
Frontiers of America, B334
Fulton, Corliss, W62f
Funkhouser, Barbara, WB91.9
Fynette H. Kulas American Composers' Fund, 36, W118

G. Schirmer, Inc., 23, W96
Gagnard, Frank, WB9.1, WB9.6, WB117.18
Galkin, Elliott, WB132.7
Ganz, Rudolph, W133g
Garner, George, WB171.2
Garrison, Leonard, D42, W40a, W42a
Gates, Henry Louis, Jr., B20
Gatewood, Willard, B182, B213
Gaulmon, Cornell, W62e
Gault, Arthur, W50a
Gayle, Westley, W132e
Gaylord, Monica, D61
Gebert, Ernst, W114a, W114b; dedication to, W114
Gedney, Irene, W28b
Gehrkens, Karl W., B214
Geil, Jean, B68
Gentilesca, Franco, W62g
George, Collins, WB2.58
George, Donald, W99a
George Washington Carver Achievement Award, B434
Georges Barrère's Little Symphony. *See* Barrère Little Symphony Orchestra
Georgetown University, B390
Gerrard, Bernard, W25e
Gershwin, George, 8, 29, 32, 34, A30, A32, B257, B435, S21, WB2.58, WB25.5, WB74.17, WB164.21, WB164.41; George Gershwin Memorial Collection of Music and Music Literature (Fisk University, Nashville, TN), B78, W76
Get on Board, D35
Giannini, Vittorio, WB80.5
Gibson, Gerald D., B49
Gilbert, L. Wolfe, B259, B312
Gill, Frank P., WB91.4
Gillam, Professor, 6
Gilman, Lawrence, S46, WB2.9, WB152.1, WB152.6
Gilmore, Teresa, W62h

Giordano, Vince, 41n
Glackin, William C., WB90.2
Glaz, Herta, W144a, W144b
Gleason, Eleanor, W80f
Gleason, James, 21
Glenn, Larry, W123a
Glory to the Newborn King, D34
Go Get It, 20
Goins, Eddie, W9a, W9c
Goldberg, Albert, WB69.18, WB112.4
Goldkette, Jean, B253
Goldman, Anita, W91c
Goldman, Edward M., B362
Goldman, Edwin Franko, W110c
Goldman, Harris, W25e
Goldman, Richard Franko, W38b, W47a, W47d-W47f, W110j
Goldman Band, W38b, W47a, W47d-W47f, W110c, W110j
Golschmann, Vladimir, W10a
Good Night (Langston Hughes), 18-19
Goodwin, Ruby Berkley, 33, W165
Goodwin, Shannon, W140d
Goossens, Eugene, 22-23, 36, B322, W26a, W36a, W74e, W81a; dedication to, 36, W36
Gordon, Joseph, W62d
"Gordons of Berkeley:" dedication to, W45
Goss, Madeleine, 12, B215
Gottschalk, Louis Moreau, B216
Gould, Charles, W70h
Gould, Morton, 29; and his Symphonic Band, D72
Gould, Norma, 33, W80f
Gowdy, Alma, WB1.13
Grace Congregational Church (Harlem), 24, B244
Graham, Shirley, B193
Grainger, Percy, 29
Grambling College (LA): Band and Orchestra, W117k; Choir, W141g
Grand Forks [ND] Symphony, W113a
Grand Teton, D73
Grant, Willy M. (pseudonym for William Grant Still), 20, W17, W56, W64, W66, W93, W94, W98
Gray, John, B47
Gray, John A., 31, W16b, W171d
Gray, Michael H., B48, B49
Gray Conservatory of Music (Los Angeles, CA), B162; Library of Music, 31
Great Falls (MT) High School Symphony Orchestra, W135, W135a
Greater Miami Philharmonic Orchestra, W100a
Green, Earl, W59c, W140c
Green, Ellen Josephine, WB149.6
Greenbrook, Reginald G., W127b
Greene, Elvira, W62g
Greene, Marjorie E., WB164.11
Greene, Patterson, B216, B217, WB125.2

Greenwich Sinfonietta, W46d
Grief, B212, D46
Grieg, Edvard, B149, WB9.11, WB9.13
Griffes, Charles, 26, 28
Griffin, Alison, WB62.14
Griggs, Anthony, W50
Griggs-Janower, David, B218
Grimes, Evelyn, W91c
Grofé, Ferde, 25, 29, 32, B190, B253
Groh, Jack, D33, W125d, W125f, W160d
Gromko, William, W32f
Grondahl, Hilmar, WB161.4
Gross, Ben, WB80.3
Gruenberg, Louis, B228, WB80.5
Guarnieri, Johnny, D12
Guggenheim Fellowship, 9, 29, 31, 34, B205, B211, B219, B252, WB2.16, WB74.2; dedication to the founders of, W14
Guggenheim Foundation. *See* John Simon Guggenheim Memorial Foundation
Guiablesse, La. *See La Guiablesse*
Gunn, Glenn Dillard, WB117.14
Gunsmoke (television program), 13
Guse, Harriet, W62c
Gusman, Suzanna, W99a
Guthrie, James K., W36i
Guzman, Jessie Parkhurst, B20, B51
Gwozdz, Lawrence, D45

Haas, Robert Bartlett, B49, B129, B220, B237, B363, B388
Hackley, E. Azalia: E. Azalia Hackley Memorial Collection of Negro Music, Dance, and Drama (Detroit Public Library), B281
Hague, Robert A., WB47.3, WB118.6
Hainke, Rudolph E., W74k
Hains, Frank, 39, WB9.2, WB9.3, WB9.5, WB9.7, WB9.13, WB62.8, WB62.13
Haiti, 34
Halasz, Laszlo, B437, W164a, WB164.18, WB164.19, WB164.38
Hale, Richard, WB155.5
Haley, Alex, B437
Hall, Clarence J., W76a, W76i, W132b, W132c
Hall, Felipe, D60
Hall, Frederick, B221
Hall, James H., WB69.16
Hall Johnson Choir, 33, W80f
Hamburger, Philip, B191, WB164.30
Hamilton, Betty, W62b
Hamilton, David, B52
Hampton Institute, B249
Hancock Ensemble, D9
Handslik, Jean, WB164.9
Handy, W. C. (William Christopher, "Father of the Blues"), 7, 17-19, 22, 26-28, 38, B143, B222-224, B247, B259, B262, B311, B312, B404, S25, S66, W103, W165

Handy Brothers Music, Inc., 33, W75
Hansen, Joyce: dedication to, W144
Hanson, Howard, 8, 14, 23-26, 28-29, 38, 40, B62, B217, B225, B353, B411, B450, D10, D26, S4, W1b, W1g, W2a-W2d, W26b, W26c, W28a, W28b, W74d, W76a, W76i, WB80.5, W91e, W103a, WB103.3, W132a-W132c, W133a, W133c, W152c, W152d, W152h; dedication to, W132
Happy Feet (Paul Whiteman; recording), 8
Hard Trials, B118
Hardwick, Linda, W45f
Hardy, Lloyd, W132e
Harford, Margaret, WB61.1
Harlem Orchestra, 21, 36
Harlem Renaissance, 26
Harmon Award. *See* William E. Harmon Awards for Distinguished Achievement Among Negroes in Music
Harmonians String Quartet, W25p
Harper, Leonard L., 21
Harreld, Josephine: dedication to, W136
Harreld, Kemper, W141b, W141d
Harris, Carl G., Jr., B226, B227
Harris, Hilda, W144o
Harris, Margaret, 39, W62d, W62g
Harris, Roy, 24, B46, WB80.5
Harris, Terry Patrick, W99a
Harrison, F. Ll., B117
Harrison, Guy Fraser, W69b
Harrison, Richard B., 6
Harth, Sidney, W2ii
Harton-Brown, Connie Y., B228
Harvard University Concert Band, W47h
Hatchett, Starling, W62h
Haubiel, Charles, B377
Hauri, Erin, WB36.18
Have Gun Will Travel (television program), 13
Havel, O'Dette, B229
Hay, Gabriel, W101c
Hayes, Roland, S43
Haywood, Carl, W160b
Haywood, Charles, B53
Headlee, Celeste Anne, B411, D54
Headlee, Daniel: dedication to, W62
Headlee, Judith Anne (Still), B230, W44; dedication to, W62. *See also* Still, Judith Anne
Headlee, Larry Allyn, 13; dedication to, W62, W128
Headlee-Huffman, Lisa M., B411; dedication to, W62
Headley, George, W6b
Hearn, Lafcadio, W76
Heintze, James R., B54
Heldenleben, WB118.15
Helfman, Max, W168b
Hellfighters. *See* 369th Infantry Regiment Band
Helsinki Municipal Orchestra, 11, W2aa
Hemeter, Mark, WB62.9

Henahan, Donal, WB136.4, WB136.5
Henderson, Fletcher, 20-21, B128, B339, W66, W122
Henderson, W. J., WB2.10
Henderson, William, W139c
Henry, Laurence, W132d
Henry, Paul, W17, W98
Here's One, B118, D34, D49, D51-D53, D55, D56, D58
Herreshoff, Constance, WB80.14, WB80.15, WB152.13
Herrington, Tommy, WB91.2
Herrman, Bernard, W112b
Hess, Howard W., WB36.4
Hess, Mary Jean, W91c
Hiawatha's Wedding Feast (Samuel Coleridge-Taylor), 17, WB117.15
Hickman, C. Sharpless, WB144.1, WB163.3
Hight, Walter, W45f
Highway 1, U.S.A., 2, 39-40, B66, B86, B91, B104, B114, B123, B148, B172, B187, B314, B367, B376, D2, D3
Hill, Gloria, W16i
Hille, Waldemar, W136a, W136b, W144f, W144g
Hilsberg, Alexander, W157a
Hindemith, Paul, S47
Hinderas, Natalie, D62, W144k, W161o
Hines, Jerome, 37, W117d; dedication to, W140
Hinson, Maurice, B55, B56, B231
Hirt, Charles C., W160b
Hogan, Kerry, W9e
Holden, Amanda, B57
Holger, Oscar, 26
Holland, Adrian, W139c
Holland, Laurence B., B74
Hollywood Bowl [CA] Symphony Orchestra, 36, W2z, W7a, W36d, W110f
Hollywood [CA] Symphony Orchestra, W114b
Holt, Ben, W9d
Holt, Nora, B232, B233, WB164.31
Holtsworth, Saxi, 19
Holy Spirit, Don't You Leave Me, 25
Honeysucker, Robert, D58
Horne, Aaron, B58, B59
Horne, Lena, 36
Horton, Joan, W172d
Houston, Elsie, W43
Houston International Film Festival, WB9.27
How I Got Dem Twilight Blues, 20
Howard, John Tasker, B234
Howard, Wardell, W9b
Howard University, B68, B390; honorary doctorate, 35, B135, B152, B154
Howe, Mentor A., B60
Hoy, Patricia J., D54
Hruby, Frank, WB69.22
Hubbard, Charles, W50a
Hudgins, Mary D., B235-B238

Hudson, Berkley, B123
Hudson, Herman C., B132
Huggins, Nathan Irvin, B239
Hughes, Albert D., WB80.6
Hughes, Jonathan, W62h
Hughes, Langston, 33-35, 37, A26, B240, B241, B267, B325, B354, B445, S40, W16, W144, W164, WB164.19, WB164.36
Hughes, Revella E., 19, W58b
Hughes, Robert, D47, W144i
Hughes, Rupert, B61
Hull, Glenn, W62f
Hunter, Eddie, 21
Hurston, Zora Neale, 35, W19, W20, W67, W130
Hurte, Leroy E., D17, W117i, W135b

INR. *See* Institut National Belge de Radiodiffusion
I Feel Like My Time Ain't Long, B118, D33
I Got Rhythm (George Gershwin), 8, A30, WB2.29, WB25.5
I Never Had the Blues (arr.), 19
I Want Jesus to Walk with Me, 29
I Want To, 20
Idolatry (Arna Bontemps), 37, B325. *See also Songs of Separation*
If You Should Go (Countee Cullen), B203, B239, D56. *See also Songs of Separation*
Il Trovatore (Giuseppe Verdi), 16
Illidge, Cora Gary, B243, B244
Imgrund, Frances, WB152.14
In Memoriam: The Colored Soldiers Who Died for Democracy, 36, B7, B10, B71, B104, B280, B430
In One Lifetime (Verna Arvey), A34, B48, B155, B399
Incantation and Dance, B56, D50, D58
Indiana University, A33, B175, B176, B400, B413; Seminar on Black Music in College and University Curricula: 1969, A33, B175, B400, B413, S66; Seminar, 1971, B176
Indianapolis Symphony Orchestra, B143, B351, W36f, W74l
Ingle, John, W132d
Inglewood Philharmonic, W5d
Inglewood Symphony Orchestra, W114a; dedication to, W114
Institut National Belge de Radiodiffusion (INR), 38, W45c; Symphony Orchestra, 11, W2bb, W154b
Instituto Brasil-Estados Unidos, W28d
International Composers' Guild, 21-23, 27, B294, W26a, W52; Orchestra, 8, W52a, W81a
International Film and Television Festival of New York, WB9.27
International Society for Contemporary Music, 23, 25
Irish, Mrs. Leiland Atherton, 9; dedication to, W116
Irvin, Richard, W80f
Irving Berlin, Inc. (arr.), 24
Is There Anybody Here?, B118, D34
Isaekes, Richard, W62g
Ives, Charles, 24

Jackson, Barbara Garvey, B182, B248
Jackson, Clyde Owen, B249
Jackson, Donald L., B196
Jackson, Hanley, W123a
Jackson, Howard, 32
Jackson, Isaiah, D13
Jackson State University, B68, B109, W9c, W9d; Chorale, W62d
Jackson Symphony Orchestra (Jackson, MS; now Mississippi Symphony), 38, W91a
Jackson Symphony Orchestra (Jackson, TN), W2, W2kk, W125g
James, Shaylor Lorenza, B250
Janssen, Werner, W110, W110a, W110b, W110d
Janzen, Eldon, W90f
Jarboro, Catarina, 19, WB164.18
Jarcac, Dorothee, W80f
Järvi, Neeme, D16, D27
Jefferson, Miles M., WB164.42
Jenkins, Walter D., WB32.3
Jenny, Jack, D12
Jerome, Jerry, D12
Jesous Ahatonhia, D34
Jessye, Eva, 28, W6c. *See also* Eva Jessye Choir
John Simon Guggenheim Memorial Foundation, 29, 31, 34, B251, B252, B273, B347. *See also* Guggenheim Fellowship.
Johnson, Campbell, W31c, W127d
Johnson, Carl, B253
Johnson, Charles S., B152
Johnson, Georgia Douglas, W173
Johnson, Hall, 19, 27-28. *See also* Hall Johnson Choir
Johnson, Herbert, B254
Johnson, James P., 21
Johnson, James Weldon, 19; James Weldon Johnson Memorial Collection of Negro Arts and Letters (Yale University), B267, B426, W74, W132, W144, W168
Johnson, Leavata, W62g
Johnson, Louis J., W117i
Johnson, Mordecai W., B154
Johnson, Raymond I., W9a, W9c, W9d
Johnson, Sargent, W149
Jones, Alicia, W9b
Jones, Byron, W156a
Jones, Evelyn, W156a
Jones, Herbert V. R. P., W113a
Jones, Isabel Morse, B255-258, WB1.7, WB1.14, WB2.16, WB2.22, WB2.26, WB2.48, WB36.6, WB46.4, WB74.2,

WB74.10, WB74.14, WB76.5, WB76.6,
WB80.5, WB80.8, WB80.12, WB110.2,
WB110.7, WB117.8; dedication to, W152
Jones, Jack, B259
Jones, Julia B., B260
Jones, Marilyn, W101d
Jones, Samuel, W2hh
Jones, Wilton, W152j
Joplin, Scott, B172, B188, B228, B248
Joyner, Maurice, W62f
Juba, 24
Jubal (Bruce Forsythe), 30
Judson, Arthur, B322; dedication to, W118
Juilliard Foundation, 25
Juilliard School of Music Orchestra, W117b
Julius Rosenwald Foundation, W103, W168;
    Fellowship, 35. See also Rosenwald
    Fellowship
Julius Rosenwald Fund Archives (Fisk University,
    Nashville, TN), B78. See also Rosenwald
    Fellowship
Jungle Episode: The Origin of Jazz, 25

Kahgan, Philip, W5d
Kahn, Erich Itor, W112a
Kaintuck', 12, 30, 35, A16, B18, B32, B55,
    B94, B202, B333, D65
Kamarck, Edward L., B261
Kamei, Yukiko, W112i
Kansas City Philharmonic Orchestra, W2k
Kappa Alpha Psi, 16
Karr, Elma Eaton, W149f
Kass, Carole, B262
Kast, George, W144m
Kastendieck, Miles, WB47.1, WB164.24,
    WB168.2
Katz, David, W6d
Kaufman, Annette, 36, B263, D15, D37, D38,
    D41, D43, D49, D51-D53, D55, W15f,
    W61b, W101e, W112c-W112g, W149j,
    W149k, W167a; dedication to, W149
Kaufman, Carol, W132d
Kaufman, Louis, 36, B204, B263, D15, D36-
    D38, D41, D43, D49, D51-D53, D55,
    W15, W15a, W15d, W15f, W61b,
    W61c, W112, W112a, W112c-W112g,
    W126g, W149, W149a, W149b, W149j,
    W149k; dedication to, W149
Kaufman, Schima, B264
Kaufman String Quartet, D37, D38, D41, D43
Kaufmann, Helen L., B265
Kay, Ulysses Simpson, 34, B132, B157,
    B172, B193, B201, B250, W27c, W126b
Keene, John, W74m, W112k
Keith, Ed, W62c
Keller, Peggy, W144q
Kellner, Bruce, B266, B267
Kelly, Constance, W139c
Kendall, Raymond, WB7.1
Kennan, Clara B., B268

Kennedy, Anne Gamble, W170a-W170d
Kennedy, John F., WB2.58
Kennedy, Matthew, D30, W161k, W170a-
    W170d
Kennedy, Michael, B64, B65
Kenworthy, Ruth, W6b
Kenyon, Nicholas, B57
Kernodle, Tammy Lynn, B269
Kessler, David, WB2.2, WB2.5, WB28.1,
    WB74.3
Kessler, Maurice, 18, W26e; dedication to, 18,
    W154
Keys, Beatrice Hilda, W144l
Kimball, George H., WB91.7
Kimball, Robert, WB36.22
King, Terry, D36-D38, D41, D43
King, William G., WB6.6
King of Jazz, The (motion picture), 24-25
Kinscella, Hazel Gertrude, B270
Kirschke, William, W91f
Klemperer, Otto, 2, 12, 35, W74j
Kniest, John, W62c
Knorr, James, W62b
Knudsen, Ronald, W149i
Kolb, Harold, W76i
Kolle, Bernard, D35
Kolodin, Irving, 29, WB164.25
Koppes, Clayton R., B271
Korn, Richard, W69k
Kornick, Rebecca Hodell, B66
Koshgarian, Richard, B67
Kostelanetz, André, 34, WB2.55, W141a,
    WB141.3
Kramer, William W., 2, W62e
Krueger, Karl, B272, D22, D24, W2k
Krummel, D. W., B68
Kubelik, Rafael, 37, W118f
Kyle, Marguerite Kelly, B252, B273

La Boheme (Giacomo Puccini), WB164.18
La Guardia, Fiorello, 12, A21, B360,
    WB164.8, WB164.9
La Guiablesse, 22-24, 29-30, A2, A5, A7,
    A33, B9, B24, B104, B290, B386, D13,
    D14, D34
La Traviata (Giuseppe Verdi), WB164.18
LaBrew, Arthur, W101d
Laciar, Samuel L., WB1.9
Ladd, Tom, W80f
Lady of Secrets (motion picture), A3, B318
Lafayette, Lenora, W171g
LaMar, Lawrence F., B274, WB1.19
Lament, D76
Lamentations (Virgil Thomson), WB8.3
Lancaster, Kevin, W25o
Lancaster, Robert, W33a, W61d, W140a
Land of Dreams, B427
Land of Romance, 32
Land of Superstition, 25, 28, 32
Landau, Siegfried, D21, W26f

Lane College Concert Choir (Jackson, TN), W125g
Laney, Ben, W62a
Lange, Arthur, W7b
Lange, Hans, W2e, W2h
Lange, Marjorie, W5
Laris, Ralph, W59b
LaRose, Joseph, WB9.8, WB62.10
Las Pascuas. See Christmas in the Western World (Las Pascuas)
Las Vegas Studio Orchestra, W32g
Lasher, John C., W62c
Laster, Georgia, W144d, W144e; Branch Chorus, W117i
Laurence, Wilton, W132c
Laury, Otis, W62b
Lawd, Ah Want(s) to be a Christian, B118, D48
Lawrence, Catherine Mary: dedication to, W90
Lawrence, Florence, WB1.20
Lawrence, Robert, WB6.19
Lawrence, William, W164d
Layne, Maude Wanzer, B20
Le Berthon, Ted, B275, WB164.6
Leab, Daniel J., B276
Leacacos, John P., WB69.23
League of Composers, B360, W69, W74
Lebow, Roger, WB118.14
Lebrecht, Norman, B277
Lee, Everett, W2jj
LeGon, Jeni, W132d
Lehmann, Friedrich J., 18, A25; dedication to, W172
Lehrman, Phillip, W118h
Leib, Julius, W1m
Leighton, Mary, WB36.5
Lemay, Paul, W18b
Lenox Avenue, 2, 12, 31-34, 38, A2, A7, A17, A33, B24, B104, B264, B280, B446, D9, D11, D14. *See also: Blues, The, from Lenox Avenue*
Lert, Richard, W1d, W118e
LeSane, John, W62h
Lesawyer, Mary, W164a
Levee Land, 21-22, B294, B333, B421, B450, D54
Leventhal, Lois, D45
Levette, Harry, B278, B279
Levin, Sylvan, WB164.9
Levine, Ben, WB164.29
Levine, Morton, B280
Levister, Norma J., W61e
Lewando, Ralph, WB117.5, WB163.1
Lewis, Daniel, W118i
Lewis, Edward, W80f
Lewis, Ellistine Perkins, B281
Lewis, Emery Jerome, B282
Lewis, Iris, B283
Lewis, Marjorie, W144p
Lewis, Roscoe E., B60
Leydon, Joe, WB9.16, WB9.17

L'Histoire du Soldat (Igor Stravinsky), 23
Liberian Research Society, B284
Library of Congress, B68, B79, B82, B197, B326, B390, W1, W2, W14, W34, W46, W104, W110, W117, W127
Liebling, Leonard, WB161.2
Lift Ev'ry Voice and Sing, D58
Lightfoot, Peter, W9d
Lilt, 39
Lindstrom, Carl E., B285-B288
Ling, Teresa, D35
Linstead, Dr. George F., WB2.34
Lipkin, Arthur Bennett, D18
Lippey, Joyce, B289
Lis'en to de Lam's, D34
Lissfelt, J. Fred, WB163.2
Little David, Play on Your Harp, B218
Little Red Schoolhouse, B98, S61
Little Rock, Arkansas, 5, 16, 31, 34, B182, B213, S64, S74
Little Song that Wanted to be a Symphony, The, 12, 38
Little Symphony (Los Angeles, CA), W114c
Liverpool Philharmonic Orchestra, 11, W2p, W2u, W117g
Livingston, Fud, W1
Locke, Alain, 26, 36, B267, B290-292, B426, WB6.5, WB6.15, W132; Alain L. Locke Papers (Howard University), B390
Loesser, Arthur, WB69.15, WB152.19
Log Cabin Ballads, 23
Lomax, Alan, 34, W18
Lomax, John A., W18
London Philharmonic Orchestra, W2n
London Symphony Orchestra, 11, D2, D8, D20, W2o, W117h
Long, Yvonne, W45a
Long Beach Women's Committee for the Philharmonic Orchestra of Southern California, B283
Longress, Leola, 30, W16b, W171i
Lord, I Looked Down the Road, B118
Los Angeles (CA): Bureau of Music Symphonic Band, W38a; Federal Colored Chorus, W80g; Federal Music Project Orchestra, W2i; Federal Symphony Orchestra, W1l, W2j, W80c; Jubilee Singers, W6e, W6f, W125c; Philharmonic Orchestra, 11, 32, 35-36, S55, W1k, W2m, W2ii, W35a, W36i, W36m, W46h, W69c, W69j, W74j, W117d, W133b, W133c, W133j; Philharmonic Society, 9; WPA Symphony Orchestra and Chorus, D14
Los Angeles County (CA): Symphonic Band, W110i; Museum, B202
Lost Horizon (motion picture), 4, 32
Lost Out Blues, 20
Lott, R. Allen, B294
Love, Hortense, W171f
Love Me in Your Own Time, 20
Lovoos, Janice, B295

Low, Elspeth, W101c
Low, W. Augustus, B69
Lowe, Elgin, W62e
Lowens, Irving, WB172.8
Lowery, Charles D., B70
Lucas, Helen, W80f
Lupkiewicz, Joseph, W111b
Lyles, Aubrey, 19

M. Elise, Sister, S.B.S., W62d
M. W. Gibbs High School, 6, 16
MacDowell, Edward, 26
Machlis, Joseph, B71
MacIntyre, Arpha, W59b
Mack, Cecil, 21
MacLeod, Lynne L., B296
MacNeil, Dorothy, W164a
Madama Butterfly (Giacomo Puccini), WB164.18
Maddaford, Lina, W62a
Madeira, Francis, B168
Maganini, Quinto, W1e; dedication to, W28
Magill, Margaret, W112k
Magill, Samuel, D42, W40a, W42a
Mahler, Gustav, WB118.14
Maiden, Cullen, W9d
Maiden Was Adoring God, The Lord, A, D34
Mandy Lou, 23
Mangum, David, WB62.7
Manley, Gordon, D69
Margetson, Edward, 28
Margetts, David, W32c, W32e
Mariani, Hugo, W2ee
Marks, Maurice, 21
Markuson, Stephen, W99a
Marquis, James, W141f
Marsh, William J., WB118.11
Marshall, Harriet Gibbs, B248
Marshall, William, W111f
Marszalek, John F., B70
Martens, Frederick, W124
Marti, Samuel, W28c, W149d, W149g; dedication to, W112
Martin, Bob, 12
Martin, Donald, B299
Martin, Gail, W164b
Martin, Mrs. Gail, W164b
Martin, Linton, WB152.2
Martini, Elissa, W144h
Mason, Bobbie, W9a, W9c, W9d
Mason, Jack, WB80.10
Massenet, Jules, WB164.21
Massey, Andrew, W36s
Mathews, Patrick, W62a
Matney, William C., B119
Mattfeld, Julius, B72
Matthew, Jean F., B411
Matthews, Geraldine O., B73
Matthews, Justus, W123a
Matthews, Michael, W25o

Matthews, Miriam, B301, B411, B412, W5
Matthews, Susan, D46
Maxwell House Hour (radio program), B244
Mayer, Martin, WB9.21
Mayes, Doris, W144k
Mayo, T. Curtis, W144l
McBride, Jessica Lundy, B302
McBride, Robert, W70a, W70b
McCorvey, Everett David, B303
McCullough, James, W70g
McEvoy, J. P., 21
McFerrin, Robert, B241, W164a
McGarrahan, Gerald, W46d
McGehee, Charles White, B304, B411
McKernan, Felix, W110n
McKinley, Carl, 26
McKinney, Howard D., W161.1
McMahon, Robert Young, W8e, W82a, W82b
McNeil, Albert J., W6e, W6f, W125b, W125c; Albert McNeil Singers, W117i, W125b
McPhee, Colin, 24
McPherson, James M., B74
McPhierson, Dr.: dedication to, W61
Mehta, Zubin, W36m
Mejorana y Socavon, D36
Mélisande, WB152.6
Meltzer, Milton, B241
Memphis Man (arr.), 20
Merchant of Venice (William Shakespeare), 16
Meredith, Ted, W80f
Metropolitan Opera, 2, 29
Meyer, Paul, W61c
Meyers, Robert, B307
Michaelis, Adrian, B308; dedication to, W76
Michell, Phyllis, W62c
Middleton, Emanuel, WB117.10
Midsummer Night's Dream (William Shapespeare), 16
Miers, Virgil, WB118.9
Mikkelsen, Kelley, D35
Milai, Samuel, B372
Miles, John, W9a
Miles, Josie, 20, W64, W94
Miles, Melvin N., B309
Milhaud, Darius, 23, WB164.13
Milici, Luis, W25h
Miller, Flournoy, 19
Mills, Florence, 19, 21-22, W81, W81a
Mines, Harry, WB2.17
Minette Fontaine, 3, B66, B86, B91, B105, B130, B335, B364, D4, D34
Miniatures for Flute, Oboe, and Piano, 37, B438, D35, D39
Minorities: Minorities and Majorities, 13
Mirza Ali Muhammad, the Bab, W53
Miss Sally's Party, A33
Mississippi Center for Educational Television, W9d
Mitchell, Bob, W132e

Mittauer, Frank, WB76.15
Modarelli, Antonio, W46i
Moe, Henry Allen: dedication to, W6
Moe, Orin, B310
Mohler, Steven, W25o
Moldenhauer Archives (Spokane, WA), B68
Monson, Karen, B311, WB36.21
Monteux, Pierre, B138, W110e
Moody, Sally Brown, WB152.15
Moore, Douglas, B46
Moore, Elizabeth C., B75
Moore, Kenneth, W163e
Moore, Kermit, W36p
Moore, Mary Carr, 33
Moore, Robin, W25p
Moore, Roger, W168c
Morch, Al, B312
Morgan, Lena Moon, B313
Morgan, Maritza, WB160.1
Morgan, Marta, WB36.19, WB90.1
Morgan State College Choir, D8, W132f
Morgenstern, Sam, B12
Moross, Jerome, WB80.5
Morris, Barbara, W91e
Morrison, John, W144p
Morton, Tim, B314, WB62.15
Mosley, Robert, W9a, W9c
Moss, Carlton, 9, 30, W14
Moss, Eileen, W9b
Mota, 38, B86, B91
Motard, Alain, W139a
Motion picture industry, 4, 24, 29, 31-32, 36, A3, A4, A24, B203, B271, B274, B276, B299, B315, B318, B383, B414, S15, S16, S24, S26, S60
Moussorgsky, Modest Petrovich, 23
Mozart, Wolfgang Amadeus, 13, SA5
Mueller, Florian, W70f
Mueller, John H., S46
Mueller, Kate Hevner, B76
Mueller, Robert, W101f
Mullins, David W., B137
Muns, Monty, B316
Muns, Walden E., B289
Murchison, Gayle, B317
Murphy, Owen, 21
Murray, Florence, B20, B77
Muse, Clarence, W80c
Music Educators of America, B160
Music Goes 'Round and 'Round, The, 4
Music Teachers' Association of California, S57
Musical Workshop (Frederick Dorian), S36
Mute, Mabel (later Mabel Mute White), 16-17
Muted Laughter, A17, D59, D67, D69
Mutual Radio Network, 34, 38, W154a
My Brother American, D75
My Girl (arr.), 24
My Kinda Love (arr.), 28
My Life in Music (John Erskine), S44
Myers, Marcus, B320

Myers, Myron, W144e
Mystic Pool, D69

NAACP Image Awards, B449; President's Award, B449
NBC (radio), 28, W15e; Symphony Orchestra, W6c
NYA Orchestra, W26d
Nadell, Rosalind, W164a
Nashville Symphony Orchestra, 36, W36h
Nathaniel Dett Chorus, W156a
National Association for American Composers and Conductors, citation from, 37
National Association for the Advancement of Colored People. *See* NAACP
National Association of Negro Musicians, Inc., 28-29, B384, WB7.3
National Endowment for the Humanities, B229
National Federation of Music Clubs, 39, B202, B439, W115
National Gallery [Washington, DC] Orchestra, W25c, W172c, W172e; Sinfonietta, W111c; Strings, W25l
National Negro Opera Foundation, B352
National Opera/Ebony, W62g
National Orchestra (Paris), W2y
National Orchestral Association, W15a
National Philharmonic Orchestra, W2q-W2t
National Symphony (Panama), 11
National Symphony Orchestra (London), W117f
National Symphony Orchestra (Washington, DC), W133i
Natzka, Oscar, W164a
Negro Epic, A, 29
Negro Folk Symphony (Dawson), B142
Negro in Art (Alain Locke), 36
Negro Symphony Orchestra, W2l
Neiman, Alexander, D36-D38, D41, D43
Nelson, Boris, B323
Nelson, Burt, WB125.1
Neurath, Herbert, B324
New Amsterdam Orchestra, B128
New England Conservatory of Music, 7, 19, 20; honorary doctorate, 40
New Music Society of California, WB1.11, WB1.12, W28, W171c
New Negro: An Interpretation, The (Alain Locke), 26
New Orleans (LA): Opera Company, W99; Philharmonic-Symphony Orchestra, 36, W2cc, W2ff, W5e, W36k, W36s, W110l, W117j, W157a; Theatre of the Performing Arts, W36s
New Orleans Street, A, D73
New Star Casino, B128
New World Symphony (Antonin Dvořák), B158
New York (NY): Chamber Orchestra, W110h; City Center, 37, A26, B269; City Opera Company, B138, B171, B445, W164a, WB164.18, WB164.19; Philharmonic

Chamber Orchestra, W25n; Philharmonic-Symphony Orchestra, 11, 32, 35-37, W2e, W6a, W6b, W36e, W36q, W69a, W69f, W69g, W110e, W117, W117a, W118b; Public Library, B197, W16, W171
New York World's Fair, 1939, 34-35, B305, B416, B417, W141
New Zealand String Quartet, D40
Newman, Arthur, W164a
Newman, Debra L., B87
Newman, John, WB2.30
Newman, Richard, B88
Newman, William S., S51
Nicholas, Louis, WB36.15, WB170.1
Nichols, Charles H., B325
Nickerson, Camille Lucille, B303
Nigeria: national anthem, W107
Nilsson, Gunhild, W149d, W149g
No Matter What You Do, 24
Nolan, Robert L., W141c
Norfolk State College, B314; Orchestra, W62f
Norman, Ruth, D59
Norris, J. Weldon, W45g
North Arkansas Symphony Orchestra, D28, W153a-W153c
North Carolina A. & T. State University Choir, W45e
North Carolina Central University, B109
North Shore Festival Association. *See* Chicago
Northern Arizona University: Chorale, D32; Wind Symphony, D54, D73
Northwestern University Library, W2
Norton, Mildred, WB1.15, WB2.49, WB7.2, WB36.7, WB69.8, WB69.19
Nugent, Bruce (pseud.: Richard Bruce), 26, B267, B426, W132

Oakland (CA): Symphony Orchestra, W26g; Youth Chamber Orchestra, W133n, W144i, W144j; Youth Orchestra, D47
Oberlin College, 18, B159, B186, B206, B328, B329, S68, W58, W154, W172; Conservatory of Music, 7, B126, B327, B330, B335, B343, B436; Conservatory Orchestra, W26e; Conservatory Symphony Band, W47b, W47c; honorary doctorate, 37; Oberlin Orchestra, W155a; Wind Ensemble, W163e
Occidental College Band, W110n
O'Connor, Tom, B331
Oderigo, Néster R. Ortiz, B332
Oh, Miss Hannah, 4
Oh, Sorrow, D34
Oja, Carol J., B89, B333
Oklahoma City Orchestra, W154a
Oklahoma Symphony Orchestra, 11, 38, W172b
Old Black Joe, WB2.29
Old California, 38, B10, B53
Old Gold Hour (radio program), 24, W73

Old Miss (arr.), 18
Old State House (Little Rock, AR), B169
Old West, The, D23
Oldham, Denver, D64
Oliver, Elizabeth M., B334
O'Malley, Muriel, W164a
Oney, Tom, B335
Opera Workshop (Virginia Union University), W62e
Opera/South, 39-40, B187, D1, W9a, W9c, W9d; Opera/South Ballet, W9a; Opera/South Chorus, W9a; Opera/South Orchestra, W9d
Orange and Lemon (Carrie Still Shepperson), 16
Orchestra of America, W69k
Orchestral Music: An Armchair Guide (Lawrence Gilman), S46
Orchestre de la Société des Concerts Du Conservatoire (Paris), W2w, W69e
Orchestre National (Paris), 36, W36b, W76k, W110g, W152i
Ormandy, Eugene, W117e
Orquesta Sinfónica Nacional (Bogotá, Colombia), SA2, W46g
Orquesta Sinfónica Nacional de Costa Rica, W2ee
Orquesta Sinfónica Provincial de Rosario (Argentina), W25h, W25m
Orquesta Sinfónica Provincial de Santa Fe (Argentina), W7c
Ortiz-Karp, Norma, B229, B337, W149n
Osgood, Henry O., WB81.3
Ottley, Nevilla E., B338
Ottley, Roi, B339
Ouanga (Clarence Cameron White), B352
Out of the Silence, D44, D67, D69
Ozzie and Harriet (television program), 11

Pace, Harry, 20, B339
Pace, Kay, W161r
Pace and Handy Music Publishing Company, 18-19
Pace Phonograph Company, 7, 20-21, B266, B311, B339, W17, W56, W64, W66, W93, W94, W98, W122, W148, W151
Pacific Institute Symphony Orchestra, W46f, W74f
Padmore, George, WB117.16
Padwa, Vladimir, W15d, W126g, W149a, W149b
Paeff, Spinoza, W25e
Page, James A., B90
Page, Ruth, 22, 29, 30, W76, W76b
Paine College Choir, D31
Palange, Louis, W36n, W46k, W110k, W132e, W135e, W154e
Palevoda, Walter, B340
Palevsky, Joan: dedication to, W99
Palmer, Zuma, B341, B342
Pan American Association of Composers, 24
Pan Pipes of Sigma Alpha Iota, 31, 38, B252,

B273
Pappy, Consuelo, 28; dedication to, W120
Paramount Records, 20
Park Avenue Synagogue (New York, NY), W168; Synagogue Choir, W168b
Parker, Cynthia, W99a
Parker, Gail, W62e
Parker, John B., B343
Parmenter, Ross, B344
Parron, Manuel, W24
Parsons, Charles H., B91
Pasadena Civic Orchestra, W118e
Pasadena Inter-racial Women's Club, W5
Pasdeloup Symphony Orchestra (Paris), 11, A20, W1d, W2v
Pasmore, Jean, W45b
Passionette (arr.), 33
Pastorale, D34
Pastorela, 37, D52, D55, D68
Pastorini, Stefani Wells, W9e
Patrick, Corbin, WB2.59, WB36.12
Patrick, Lee, W131a-W131c
Patrick, Sam, B359
Patterson, Lindsay, B345
Patterson, Willis, D46
Patton, John, D48
Patton, Willy, W62d
Paul Whiteman Orchestra, The, 24, 28, W1, W1c, W1f, W1i, W27, W27a, W27b, W30a, W30b, W159. *See also* Whiteman, Paul
Pavillard, Dan, WB36.13
Pazmor, Radiana, W171b, W171c
Peabody Conservatory of Music: honorary doctorate, 40, B151, B306, B346
Peaceful Land, The, 39, B91, B361, B439
Pearce, Judy, W91b
Pearsall, Howard T., W45e
Pearson, Edyth: dedication to, W144
Pearson, Eugene: dedication to, W144
Pearson, Irving, W16f, W171h
Pearson, William P., W6f
Pease, James, W117e
Peattie, Donald Culross, B347
Pebworth, James R., B92
Pedigo, Alan, W112h
Pedigo, Billigene, W112h
Pedigo, William, W45b
Pelkey, James, W45a, W45b
Pena Morell, Esteban, B193
Pendleton, Edmund J., WB2.39
Pennies from Heaven (motion picture), 31, B318
Pennington, John, W161j
Pepperdine University: honorary doctorate, 40
Perkins, Francis D., B191, WB6.17, WB8.1, WB8.3., WB46.1, WB47.2, WB61.3, WB112.1, WB118.5, WB164.26, WB168.3
Perkinson, Coleridge-Taylor, B303
Perlee, Charles D., B348, WB91.3, WB110.9, WB118.12
Perlmutter, Donna, WB9.24
Perry, John, W101d
Perry, Julia, B193
Perry Mason (television program), 11, 13
Peske, Wilbert, WB2.24
Peskey, John, D35
Peter Grimes (Benjamin Britten), WB164.39
Peterson, Bernard L., B93
Peyser, Herbert F., WB133.2
Phantom Chapel, 37, B231
Phemister, William, B94
Phi Beta Sigma Fraternity: George Washington Carver Award, 38, B434
Philadelphia Symphony Orchestra, 11, 32, W1f, W1i, W2f, W2g, W30b, W91d, W117e, W152a, W152b
Philharmonic Orchestra of Indianapolis, W2gg
Philharmonic Orchestra of Southern California, Long Beach Women's Committee for, B283
Phillips, Helen, W61f
Phillips, Walton, W70e
Phillips, William King, 18
Piazza, Marguerite, WB164.40
Pickens, James Vincent, W9b
Pierre, Dorathi Bock, WB80.13
Pierson, Larry, W70e
Pilapil, Beatriz, W70g
Pilcher, J. Mitchell, A25, B298, W172, WB172.5
Pillar, The, B86, B91
Pilot, Ann Hobson, D44
Pipkin, Viki, B350
Pippin, Hollis, W62d
Pirtle, Caleb, III, WB9.14
Piston, Walter, WB80.5
Pittsburgh Symphony Orchestra, 11, 35, W117c
Pizzetti, Ildebrando, WB9.21
Plain-Chant for America, 35, A14, B10, B73, B218, B376, D31
Pleasants, Henry, WB152.3
Ploski, Harry A., B95
Plow That Broke the Plain (Virgil Thomson), WB110.7
Poe, Harry, W62h
Poem for Orchestra, 36, 38, B10, B104, B280
Polant, Mrs. Rose, W149h
Polo, Mark O., 39, WB62.3
Poole, Valter, W91c, W133l
Porgy and Bess (George Gershwin), 40, A30, B257, S55, WB2.55, WB62.8, WB62.13, WB80.5, WB164.12, WB164.29
Portanova, Joseph D., B141, W5
Portanova, Mary Spaulding Sevitzky, B351, S70
Porter, Dorothy B., B90, B96
Porter, Quincy, WB80.5
Potter, Raeschelle, W9d
Poulard, Annette Pierson, W62h
Powell, Loren, D9

Powers, Marie, B171, B241, W139a, W139b, W164a; dedication to, W139
Prattis, P. L., B352
Prelude and Dance (Paul Creston), WB8.3
Preludes, B438, D64
Preludes for String Orchestra, Flute and Piano, D40
Presley, Pamela, WB154.1
Pretty Ways (Still/Henderson), 20
Price, Florence B., A16, B188, B208, B248, B303
Price, John E., B303
Price, Theodore, B353, WB155.2
Price, William, 16
Prichard, Robert, W127a
Pritchett, Wendell, W16j
Pro Musica, W46e; All American Program, W74b
Psalm for the Living, A, B178, B218, B226, D34
Puccini, Giacomo, WB9.11, WB164.21
Purser, Geraldine, W101c
Putnam, Thomas, WB144.7
Putterman, David J., W168a, W168b

Quarm, Joan, WB91.10
Quin, Carolyn L., 43n, B411
Quinn, Alfred Price, WB25.2
Quit Dat Fool'nish, 4, 31, B146, D50, D65, D68, D70

Radiant Night, D34
Radiant Pinnacle, 33
Ragsdale, Chalon, W47i
Rahn, Muriel, W16d, W164d, WB164.18; dedication to, W144
Rain or Shine (musical show), 21, B243, B305
Rampersad, Arnold, B354
Ramsey, Rebecca, D35
Randel, Don Michael, B97
Randol, George, WB164.9
Randolph, Diane, W144p
Rascher, Sigurd: dedication to, W131
Rathbun, Loyd, W70c; dedication to Mr. and Mrs. Loyd Rathbun, W70
Ratliff, William, B355
Ravel, Maurice, B257
Ray, Russell, B356
Rayam, Curtis, W9c
Razaf, Andy, B259, B357, B358
Reasons, George, B359
Red Seal records, 16
Reese, Irwin, W9d
Reese, Verleen, B212
Rehrig, William H., B98
Reichard, Carolyn, WB1.5, WB2.6, WB14.1
Reiner, Fritz, 35, W117c
Reis, Claire R., 23, 25, B243, B360
Rejto, Gabor, W144m
Remisoff, Nicholas, W76b

Reno, Doris, B361, B362, WB8.5, WB62.1, WB115.2, WB162.2
Republicano, Antonio de Assis, B193
Respighi, Elsa, 22
Respighi, Giuseppe, 22
Respighi, Ottorino, 23
Resta, Francis E., D71, W163b, W163c; dedication to, W163
Rhapsody, D34
Rhapsody in Blue (George Gershwin), 29, B190, WB2.29, WB2.30, WB2.56
Rhode Island Philharmonic Orchestra, B168
Rhodes, Don, B364
Rhodes, John P., WB74.7
Rhythm Boys, 28, 31
Rich, Freddie, 19, 29
Rich, Maria, B27
Richardson, Ben Albert, B20, B365
Richmond (VA) Symphony, 36, B262, W25k, W36l, W133o
Riegger, Wallingford, 24, 29
Rigoletto (Giuseppe Verdi), 16
Ringwald, Roy, B377
Ringwall, Rudolph, 36, W118a, W133e, W152f
Rising Tide, 2, 34, B416. See also *Song of a City*
Roach, Hildred, B366
Robbins, Jack, 24
Robert Nolan Choir, W141c
Roberts, C. Lucketh, 21
Roberts, Enid Yvette, B367
Roberts, Pamela, W123a
Robertson, Bill, B368
Robertson, Edythe, WB165.1
Robertson, Irene, W31b, W127c
Robeson, Paul, 19, WB6.17
Robinson, Bill "Bojangles," 36
Robinson, Earl, B377
Robinson, Louie, B369
Robinson, Richard, W132d
Robinson, Sara, W144h
Robinson, Vernon, W2j
Robinson, Wilhelmena S., B99
Robison, Willard, 4, 27-28. See also Willard Robison's Deep River Orchestra
Rochester (NY): Civic Orchestra, 32, W28a, W69b, W76a, W76i, W103a, W132a, W133f, W152c, W152d; Philharmonic Orchestra, 23, 25, B94, W1b, W2a, W2b, W2d, W2hh, W26b, W26c, W28b, W74d, W132b
Rockwell, John, B370, WB155.4
Rodriguez, Rod, W9b
Rodriquez, José, B371
Rodzinski, Artur, 35, 37, B138, B217, W6a, W69a, W118b, W172a
Rogers, Alex, 21
Rogers, Bernard, 29
Rogers, J. A., B20, B372

Rogers, W. G., WB164.38
Rojas, John, W167b
Romance for Saxophone, D45, D57
Romberg, Sigmund, WB9.11, WB164.21
Roosevelt, Eleanor, 12, WB6.10, WB6.16, WB164.6; dedication to, W117
Roosevelt, Franklin Delano: dedication to, W117
Roossin, Isaiah, W91d
Root, Deane L., B68
Rosekrans, Charles, W99a
Rosenburg, Josef, WB144.3
Rosenfeld, Paul, W16a
Rosenfield, John, WB118.10
Rosenthal, Harold, B100
Rosenwald Fellowship, B373, B444, WB6.5. *See also* Julius Rosenwald Foundation; Julius Rosenwald Fund Archives
Roses of Picardy, 18
Ross, Alfred W. "Allie," B128
Ross, Anne, B101
Ross, Hugh, W6b
Rossi, Nick, B374
Roth, Henry, S60
Rothe, Friede F., B375
Rotter, Jorge, W25m
Rowe, Billy, WB80.2, WB80.4
Rowell, Anastine, W80f
Rower, Walter, W50a
Roy, Klaus G., WB69.21
Roy, Tom, W9e
Royal Philharmonic Orchestra, D18, D22, D24
Royall, Archie, W80f
Royer, Philip, W111a
Rudel, Julius, WB164.40
Ruggles, Carl, 22, 24, B294
Ruiz, Andrian, W144m
Runnin' Wild (musical show), 21, B121
Russell, Theodore, W91a
Ruth Page Ballet Company, W76b
Ryder, Georgia A., B376, B377

Saal, Hubert, B378
Sabin, Evelyn, W76a, W76i
Sabin, Robert, 37, B379, WB164.27
Sabin, Stewart B., 23, WB1.1, WB2.3, WB2.7, WB14.2, WB26.2, WB28.2, WB46.2, WB74.4, WB76.2, WB132.2, WB152.11
Sablosky, Irving, WB118.13, WB172.4
Sacramento Philharmonic Orchestra, W90c, W90d
Sadie, Stanley, B27
Saggus, James, WB9.12
Sahdji, 1, 22, 25-26, 31, 38, A2, A7, A19, A33, B18, B24, B93, B104, B142, B267, B280, B290, B426, D8, D10
Saint-Georges, [Joseph Boulogne], Chevalier de, A31
St. Louis Blues (arr.), 19, 25, A30
St. Louis [MO] Symphony Orchestra, W10a, W133p
Salisbury, Wilma, WB155.3
Saltzberg, Geraldine, B380, WB36.14, WB103.4
Salzedo, Carlos, 22, 29
Samuels, Marvin, W9b, W132d
Sanborn, Pitts, WB2.11, WB6.5
San Carlo Opera Company, WB164.18
San Diego State University (CA): Ensemble, W9e; Orchestra, W9e
San Diego Symphony Orchestra, 12, W1m, W74i, W80g, W152e
San Francisco Symphony Orchestra, D14, D29, W76j, W133g, W152g
Sanford, Kelly, D32
Sanjek, Russell, B381
San Jose (CA): Chamber of Commerce, B424
Sano Accordion Symphony, WB8.1
Santa Clara County [CA] Symphonette, W90a
Santa Monica [CA] Symphony Orchestra, W7b, W155b
Sargeant, Winthrop, WB69.20
Saunders, Richard D., WB1.16, WB2.18, WB5.1, WB46.3, WB74.1, WB74.16, WB76.4, WB76.7, WB76.16, WB110.3, WB110.4, WB114.2, WB117.9, WB161.3
Savage, Augusta, W149
Scarborough, Charles, B382, WB25.5
Scheibe, Jo-Michael, D32
Scherzo, from *Afro-American Symphony*, 28, 32, 37-38, A22, B262, D25, D26, D77
Schirmer, Inc. *See* G. Schirmer, Inc.
Schnepel, Thelma Biracree. *See* Biracree, Thelma
Schoening, John, W25j, W144k
Schola Cantorum, 35
Scholes, Percy A., B102
Schomburg Center for Research in Black Culture (New York Public Library), B63
Schubert, Franz, WB118.14
Schuller, Gunther, 8
Schultz, Thomas, W62c
Schuyler, George, B383
Schuyler, Philippa, 37; dedication to, 37, W10
Schwartz v. BMI, B381
Schwerké, Irving, 26, 28, 29, 32-33, B82, B326, W1, WB1.3; dedication to, 28-29, W2
Scott, Barbara, W111e
Scott, Carlyle, W80g
Scott, Gladys, W62d
Scott, Phyllis, B384, WB7.3
Seattle Youth Symphony Orchestra, 13, 36, S65, W25g, W36j, W154d
Second Baptist Church Choir (Los Angeles, CA), W45d
Segal, Lewis, WB132.6
Seidenbaum, Art, B385
Sell, Michael, W144m
Seven Traceries, 35, A17, A22, B73, B231,

B438, D59, D61, D64, D66, D67, D69, D70
Sevitsky, Fabien, 39, B143, W62a, W100a, W115a, W162, W162a, W74l; dedication to, W40
Sevitzky, Mrs. Fabien: dedication to, W40
Sewell, Edith, WB164.18
Sewell, George Alexander, B387
Shakesnider, Wilma, W62d
Shank, William, B388
Shanley, Gretel, D39, W126h
Shapiro, Eudice, W144m
Shavitch, Vladimir, W52a
Shaw, Arnold, B389
Shaw, Artie, 8, B378, D6, D7, D12
Shaw, Freita: dedication to, W144
Shaw, John, W45d
Shaw, Robert, W6c
Shep, 2, 4, 9, B146, B435; dedication to, 31, W126
Shepard, Richard F., WB9.26
Shepperson, Carrie Lena Fambro Still (William Grant Still's mother), 5, 15-16, 21, 23-24, B408; dedication to, W11
Shepperson, Charles Benjamin (William Grant Still's stepfather), 6, 16-17, 23
Sherman, Robert, WB2.60
Sherman, Thomas B., WB10.2
Sherrill, Barbara Geyen, W16h, W50b, W139c
Sherrill-Whitelow Ensemble, W139c
Shipskie, Nicholas, W62a
Shirley, Wayne D., B390, W117
Shoemake, Shouna, W9e
Shostakovich, Dimitri Dimitrievich, S58
Shuffle Along (musical show), 4, 8, 19-22, 30, B43, B93, B199, B266, B389
Shull, Paul, W135a
Shulsky, Samuel, WB1.2, WB1.6, WB14.3
Sibelius, Jan: in memory of, W162
Siegmeister, Elie, 29, B377
Sierra Winds, D35, D50
Simcock, Margaret, W80f
Similä, Martti, W2aa
Simmons, Barbara, W45a, W45b, W59a
Simmons, Calvin, W9b
Simmons, Leon G., W61g
Simmons, Susan, W91c
Simmons, Theodore, W45a, W45b, W59a
Simon, Janice, W8d
Simon, Robert A., WB2.13, WB6.13, WB15.1, WB36.10, WB47.4, WB69.7, WB118.7, WB152.8
Simpson, Anne, B411
Simpson, Mary Lou, B54, B391
Simpson, Ralph Ricardo, B4, B5, B115, B116, B392, W31a
Sims, Charmaine, W62e
Sinfónica de Yucatán (Mexico), W28c
Sinfonietta of New York, W1e
Sing! Shout! Tell the Story!, D34

Singer, Samuel L., WB91.5
Sinner, Please Don't Let This Harvest Pass, D34
Sioux Love Song, D23
Sissle, Noble, 19
Sister Heavy Hips, 4
Skowronski, JoAnn, B103, B111
Slater, Richard, WB149.7
Slatkin, Leonard, W133p
Slattery, Paul Harold, B54, B393
Slepian, Dorothy, B394
Slonimsky, Nicolas, B11, B27, B79, B104, B105, W46e, W46g
Smallwood, Bill, B395
Smialek, Noreen, W149h
Smith, Byron, D34
Smith, Cecil, WB164.41
Smith, Donald, W62a
Smith, Dwight L., B106
Smith, Edward, W62e
Smith, Esther, W111a
Smith, Hale, B157
Smith, Jack, W76b
Smith, Jewell, W80g
Smith, Jonnie, W97a
Smith, Leroy, 22
Smith, Lillian, B415
Smith, Marc Jack, W91b
Smith, Muriel, WB164.18
Smith, Nina Pugh, WB74.8
Smith, Paul, D34, WB164.9, WB164.18
Smith, Randolph, B396
Smith, Susie Aubrey, WB161.5
Smith, Warren Storey, WB164.39
Smith, William, W91d
Smithwick, Catheryn Lynne: dedication to, W90
Smyles, Harry, W70d
Smythe, Mabel M., B107
Snebly, Sandra, W91b
Snow, Pamela, WB154.1
Society for the Preservation of the American Musical Heritage, B272
Sokol, Vilem, S65, W25g
Solomon, Izler, W7a, W36d, W36f, W169
Solomon, Jo-Jo: dedication to, W169
Solstad, Harold M., W30
Song at Dusk, A, 25
Song for the Lonely, D52, D56, D58
Song of a City, 34, B416. See also *Rising Tide*; *Victory Tide*
Song of the Bayou, WB2.29
Song of the Plainsmen, D23
Songs of Separation, 37, B46, B203, B212, B310, B405, D47, D52, D58
Sonneck, G. C., 23, W96
Sorcerer: Fantastic Scene, The, 24, 29
Soucek, Carol, B397
Soule, Richard, D35, D50
Sound Off (radio program), W104a
South Bay-Torrance [CA] Symphony Orchestra, W110m

Index   327

South Carolina All-State College Band, W47g, W141i
South Carolina State College: Collegiate Chorale, W141f, W141i
Southall, Geneva Handy, W161m, W161n
Southeast Symphony Orchestra (Los Angeles, CA), W36n, W46k, W69n, W110k, W118g, W132e, W135e, W154e
Southern, Eileen, 16, 19, 20, B27, B84, B85, B88, B108, B182, B247, B398-404, B437, WB25.6
Southern Interlude, A, 2, 39, B91, B123, B148
Southern Music, D5
Southgate, Harvey, WB91.8
Southwest Philharmonic, W62h
Southwide Conference Educational Fund, W128
Sowande, Fela, D8
Sowerby, Leo, 28, WB80.5
Spears, Wood, W80f
Speer, David, WB9.22
Spelman College Chorus, W141b
Spence, Martha Ellen Blanding, B4, B5, B115, B405, W144n
Spencer, Jon Michael, B4, B109, B177, B406, B407
Spingarn, Arthur B., B152
Spinoza Paeff Quartet, W25e
Spivak, Rose, WB1.17
Spofford, Charles W., 42n
Spradling, Mary Mace, B110
Sprinzena, Nathaniel, W164a
Stadifer, Glenn, W132d
Standard School Broadcast (radio program), B308; Standard School Broadcast Symphony Orchestra, W5b
Standard Symphony Hour (radio program), B308; Standard Symphony Orchestra, W15e, W18b, W110a
Stanford University, B68
Stanz, William, W164a
Steal Away to Jesus, 20, B218
Stearns, Phillip, W80d, W80e
Steele, Emmett, W132c
Steer, Michael, D40
Steigerwalt, Gary, D65
Steinberg, Ben, W26d
Sterrett-Bryant, James, W9b
Stevenson, Delcina, W9b
Stevenson, Doris, W112i
Stevenson, Joseph, W80f
Stevenson, Rosemary M., B111
Stewart, Ruth, W164a
Still, Alexa, D40, D56
Still, Caroline Elaine (daughter of Still and Bundy), 21; dedication to, 25
Still, Carrie Lena Fambro. *See* Shepperson, Carrie Lena Fambro Still
Still, Duncan Allan (son of Still and Arvey), 3, 36; dedication to, W111

Still, Elaine (daughter of Still and Bundy), 27; dedication to, W11
Still, Gail Lynton (daughter of Still and Bundy), 18, 27, 31; dedication to, 25, W11
Still, Grace Bundy (first wife), 1, 6, 7, 9, 17, 20-21, 24, 26-27, 34-35, B80, W11, W108
Still, Judith Anne (daughter of Still and Arvey), 3, 13, 36, A34, B390, B408-412, B437, WB32.4. *See also* Headlee, Judith Anne (Still)
Still, June Allen (daughter of Still and Bundy), 20; dedication to, 25, W11
Still, Verna Arvey (second wife). *See* Arvey, Verna
Still, William Bundy ("Billy," son of Still and Bundy), 17; dedication to, 25, W11
Still, William Grant: as guest conductor, D14, D19, D29, W1k, W1l, W2l, W2cc, W2dd, W2ff, W5e, W21, W21a, W25f, W32e, W36g, W36j, W47g, W50a, W74f-W74i, W76j, W80c-W80e, W80g, W90e, W110m, W117k, W125a, W133b, W133n, W141i, W144i, W152e, W152g, W154c, W154d, W163a, W163d; honorary degrees, 35, 37, 40, B135, B151, B152, B154, B159, B186, B206, B296, B306, B328, B346, B397, B423; obituaries, B44, B137, B145, B149, B161, B210, B432, B440; William Grant Still and Verna Arvey Papers (Special Collections Division, University of Arkansas Libraries, Fayetteville), B170, B180, B197, B229, B317, B320, B337, B390, B437, B438, S25
Still, William Grant, Sr., 5, 15, 17
Stillman, Albert, W141
Stinson, Eugene, WB2.20, WB76.3
Stock, Frederick, 22, W51a
Stockton, Ann Mason, S70
Stoessel, Albert, W117b
Stoetzer, Robert, W62a
Stokes, Sheridan, W101e
Stokowski, Leopold, 32, 37-38, B134, B138, B217, B279, B322, D25, S19, S43, W2f, W2g, W6c, W35a, W36e, W110f, W152a, W152b, W156, WB164.5, WB164.7; dedication to, 37, W164
Stoloff, Morris, B274
Stomberg, Rolf, 14n
Stone, Carol, W123, W123a
Stormy Weather (motion picture), 36, B271, B276, B383, B414, S15
Strange Fruit (Lillian Smith), B415
Straus, Noel, WB110.5, WB149.4, WB164.13, WB168.4
Strauss, Oscar, 17
Strauss, Richard, WB9.13
Stravinsky, Igor, 23
Strickfaden, Charles, 25, W1, W29, W30, W159

Struttin' Time (musical show), 21
Stutsman, Grace May, WB69.10
Sueing, Oliver, W9c
Suite for Violin and Piano, 36, D40, D55, D56, D58
Summerland, 33, D17, D44, D50, D52, D55, D59, D64, D68, D78
Summertime (George Gershwin), A30
Summerville, Cynthia, W136f
Summo, Beverly, WB114.1
Sumner, Charles, W36o, W155c, W172d
Swanee River, D64
Swanson, Howard, B250, WB36.22
Swift, Kay, 34, B416; dedication to, W136
Swing, Sally, WB2.45
Swing Low, Sweet Chariot, 20
Swisher, Viola Hegyi, WB80.11
Sykes, Clarence, W62f
Symphony (César Franck), B158
Symphony for Small Orchestra (Darius Milhaud), 23
Symphony No. 2 in G Minor, "Song of a New Race," 32, B95, B105, B277, B446, D27, D29
Symphony No. 3, "The Sunday Symphony." D28. See also Third Symphony
Symphony No. 4, "Autochthonous (Indigenous)," 18, 38, B105, B220, B393, D19
Symphony No. 5, "Western Hemisphere," 2, B105, B277
Symphony of the New World, W2jj, W36p
Syracuse University, B68
Szell, George, B217, W69c, W69d, W69f-W69i, W69l, W69m, W69o, W69p

Tailleferre, Germaine, 22
Tang, Jordan, W2kk, W125g
Taubman, Howard, WB2.25, WB6.8
Taylor, Davidson, 33
Taylor, Deems, 33, WB1.8, WB80.4
Taylor, Earl, W9a
Taylor, George, D44, D58
Taylor, Harold W., B20
Taylor, Vivian, D44, D58
Tchaikovsky, Pëtr Ilich, 8, WB69.5
Teagarden, Charles, 25
Tell Me, Shepherdess, D34
Terry, Lesa, W25p
Teske, Charles, W80f
Tetley-Kardos, Richard, W46h
Texas Southern University: String Quartet, W25f; Symphonic Band, W163d
Theodora Goes Wild (motion picture), B318
Third Symphony, 3. See also Symphony No. 3, "The Sunday Symphony"
Thoby-Marcelin, Philippe, W144
Thomas, Anthony David, W61g
Thomas, C. Edward, D48
Thomas, Margaret, W16e, W140b, W144c
Thomas, Milton, W144m

Thomas, Naymond, W9a, W9c
Thomas, Rube, W30
Thomason, Ann, W91b
Thompkins, Shari Rhoads, W167b
Thompson, Arthur, W62g
Thompson, Helen, W5
Thompson, Janet, W91c
Thompson, Leon E., B418, W25n, W36l, W36r, W46j, WB46.5, W62b, W69n, W118g
Thompson, Oscar, WB6.9, WB152.5
Thomson, John, W9d
Thomson, Virgil, WB8.3, WB110.7
Thorne, Frances, B362
Those Who Wait, B279
Three Dances from *La Guiablesse*, B32
369th Infantry Regiment Band, 19
Three Portraits, 25
Three Rhythmic Spirituals, B118, B218, B226, D33
Three Stooges (television program), 13
Three Visions, 33-34, B231, B394, D17, D50, D55, D59, D60-D62, D64, D65, D68-D70, D73
Tietze, Philip, W25o
Tihmar, David, W80f
Tin Pan Alley, B143
Tiompkin, Dimitri, 4, 36
Tipton, Nancy, WB9.18
To You, America! 38, B98, D71
Tollefson, Arthur, D42, D57, W40a, W42a, W74m, W131d, W161t
Tomb of the Unknown Soldier, D73
Toppin, Edgar A., B112
Torkanowsky, Werner, W110l, W117j, W36k
Tosca (Giacomo Puccini), WB164.18
Toward Distant Shores, B118
Trask, Sherwood, W48
Treasure Island (Robert Louis Stevenson), 11
Trebacz, Iris, W50a
Trebacz, Leon, W50a
Tremblay, George, B419
Triad Chorale, W16l, W45f, W170e
Tribal Dance, D23, D73
Trimborn, Harry, B420
Tritt, Edward C., W90b, W91b
Troubled Island, 2, 3, 12, 33-35, 37-38, A21, A26, B72, B86, B91, B93, B95, B100, B104, B114, B117, B123, B171, B191, B240, B241, B269, B277, B325, B354, B360, B445, B446, D5, S40, S41
Trumbauer, Frankie, 25, W1, W30, W159
Tucker, Adrian, B141
Tucker, David, III, W9e
Tucker, Gregory, W70a, W70b
Tucker, Marilyn, WB144.5
Tucker, Mark, 41n, B421
Tucker, Sophie, 8
Tucson (AZ): High School Symphonic Band, S61, W90e; Symphony Orchestra, S61,

W5a, W36g, W103b
Tumblebug's Lament, 4
Turner, Patricia, B113
Tuskegee Institute, B109, B249; Tuskegee Institute Concert Choir, W141h
Twelve Negro Spirituals, 33, A8, B53, B60, B73, B224
Twentieth Century-Fox, B260, B278, B383, S15, S16. *See also* Motion picture industry

UCLA. *See* University of California at Los Angeles
Ulanowsky, Paul, W171f
Umiker, Robert, D42, D57, W40a, W42a, W131d
Understanding Music (William S. Newman), S51
United Nations, B439; dedication to, 39, W115
United States. Work Projects Administration, 35, B447, S4
United States Military Academy Band, D71, W163a-W163c; dedication to, W163
Universal Studios, 25. *See also* Motion picture industry
University of Arkansas, Fayetteville, B68, B170, B181, B182, B197, B212, B213, B229, B248, B317, B320, B356, B390, B404, B428; Chamber Ensemble, W125d; Chamber Orchestra, W25q, W149n; Concert Choir, W125f; honorary doctorate, 40, B423; Libraries, B81, B337, B437, B438; Schola Cantorum, D33, W65a, W71a, W125f, W160d, W168c; Symphonic Winds, W90f; University Band, W47i; William Grant Still Centennial Week, 1995, B320, B356; William Grant Still Festival, 1984, B182
University of California at Los Angeles, B429; McNeil Singers, W125b
University of Miami: American Contemporary Music Festival (1963), B362; Festival of American Music (1962), WB8.5; Opera, 39, D3, W62a; Symphony Orchestra, 39, B361, W 62a, W115a, W162, W162a
University of Michigan, B68; All-State Intermediate Orchestra, D23
University of Nevada, Las Vegas: University String Symphony, W32f
University of Redlands (CA): University-Community Symphony Orchestra, W90b, W91b
University of Rochester. *See* Eastman School of Music
University of Southern California, B397; Chamber Singers, W160b, W160c; String Quartet, W25o; Symphony Orchestra, W118h, W118i; Tribute to William Grant Still (and honorary doctorate), 1975, 40, B397
University of Toledo Gospel Chorus, W172d
University of Wyoming, B68
Upton, William Treat, B82
Urbah-Stivers, Carol, D35, D50

Urseth, Alfred LeRoy, W117d
Ussher, Bruno David, B425, WB6.1, WB76.17, WB117.1
Utah State Art Center, S7
Utica Junior College, W9c, W9d

Vacano, Wolfgang, W2gg
Van Cleef, Ed, W9d
Van Den Burg, William, W25e
Van Grove, Isaac, W76b
Van Hoesen, Karl D., W14a, W46c, W111b
Van Vechten, Carl, B267, B426
VanGundy, Palmer, WB80.9
Vanities (musical show). *See Earl Carroll's Vanities*
Varèse, Edgard, 7, 21, 23-25, 35, 39-40, B201, B311, B378, B398, B427, S35; dedication to, 25 (of Harold Bruce Forsythe's 1930 biography of Still), W52, WB52.1
Varèse, Louise, 21-22, 35, B427
Variety, 19
Varney, J. Arnold, W135d
Vaughn Williams, Ralph, 23
Venerable, Grant D., B411
Verdi, Giuseppe, 16, WB9.11, WB9.13, WB164.18
Verongos, Helen, WB9.20, WB9.27
Victor Symphonic Contest, 24
Victory Tide, 34, B118, B226. *See also Rising Tide; Song of a City*
Videmus, D44, D58
Vignettes, D35
Villa-Lobos, Heitor, 24, WB1.7, WB76.6
Virginia Union University, University Players, W62e
Viscuglia, Felix, D35, D50
Vodery, Will Henry Bennett, B389
Vogt, Martin, W132b
Voice of America (radio), 37, D5
Voice of the Lord, The, B118, B178
Voorhees, Don, 8, 22-24, 27; dedication to, W24

WABC (radio station), 29, 32
WEEI Boston (radio station), 24
WNAC Boston (radio station), 24
WNYC New York (radio station), W26d
WOR New York (radio station), 24, 27-28; Symphony Orchestra, W133d
WPA. *See* United States. Work Projects Administration
Wailing Dawn, D59
Waites, Althea, W161p
Waldman, Mike, WB164.32
Waldo, Elisabeth, 37, W25, WB25.1
Waldo Latin American String Quartet, W25a, W25b
Walker, Clyde, W62d
Walker, Frances, D66, W136c, W136d
Walker, George, D8

Walker, George G., WB36.2
Walker, George T., B303
Walker, James, W58b
Wallace, Inez, 20, W56
Wallenstein, Alfred, W69j, W133d
Waller, Thomas Wright ("Fats"), 33
Waller, Juanita, W9a, W9c
Walsh, Stephen, B57
War and Peace (J. Mitchell Pilcher; poetry), A25
Warburton, Thomas, B86, B182, B428
Ward, C. Edouard, W141h
Warner, A.J., WB103.1, WB152.12
Warrack, John, B100, B114
Washington, Booker T., 17
Washington, Isabelle, 20, W66
Watanabe, Ruth, WB91.6
Waters, Ethel, 20, 36, W17, W93, W98. See also Ethel Waters and Her Jazz Masters
Watt, Douglas, WB164.28
Watts, Harry, B94
Watts, Henry, W74d
Watts, Leonardo, W33b, W144g
Watts [CA] Symphony Orchestra, W111e, W111f
Way Down Yonder in de Co'nfiel', 4
We Sang Our Songs, B218, D30
Weatherby, William J., B339
Webster, Paul, W68
Weede, Robert, B171, B241, W164a, WB164.30
Weill, Kurt, WB9.13
Weiner, Stanley, W149c, W149e
Weisenberg, Charles, B429
Weiskopf, Herbert, W5c
Weiss, Adolph, 24
Weiss, Nancy J., B74
Wen Talbot Negro Choir, 35, W6a
Wenk, Arthur, B115, B116
Wentworth, Richard, W164a, WB164.40
Wentzel, Andrew, W99a
Werner Janssen Symphony Orchestra, W110b, W110d
Wesley, Charles H., B446
Wesley, E. B., WB152.16
West, Ewan, B114
West Los Angeles Chorus, W132d
West Valley [CA] Chorus, W132d
Westchester (NY): Interracial Fellowship Chorus, W6d; Symphony Orchestra, D21, W26f
Westchester [CA] String Symphony Orchestra, W121a, W135d
Westerman, George W., B430, B431
Western Hemisphere. See *Symphony No. 5, "Western Hemisphere"*
Western Maryland College Little Symphony Orchestra, W111a
Westrup, J. A., B117
Weyland, John, WB69.25
What Does He Know of Dreams?, D2
Where Shall I Be?, D34

Whisonant, Lawrence, W6c, WB164.12
Whistling Blues (arr.), 19
White, Clarence Cameron, 6, B172, B193, B352, B447, WB152.1
White, Evelyn Davidson, B118
White, G. Anderson, D23
White, Garland, W172.5
White, Paul, W133f
White, Virginia, W6f
White, Walter, B271
Whitelow, Pearl, W50a, W50b, W139c
Whiteman, Paul, 8, 9, 24-29, 32, 38, B253, W1c, W1f, W1i, WB2.58, W27a, W27b, W30a, W30b; commissioned by, W11, W13, W27, W29, W73, W159; dedication to, W29; Paul Whiteman Collection, The (Williams College, Williamstown, MA), 25, W1, W11, W13, W27, W29, W30, W73, W159. See also Paul Whiteman Orchestra
Whithorne, Emerson, B294
Whitlock, E. Clyde, WB16.2
Whitney, Frances Maddaford, W62a
Widder, Roger, W70g
Wilberforce University, 6, 16, 32, B334, S68; honorary degree, B296
Will, Mary Ertz, WB103.2
Willard Robison's Deep River program, 28; Orchestra, 27
William, Ralph Vaughn, 23
William E. Harmon Awards for Distinguished Achievement Among Negroes in Music, 24
William Grant Still: Chorus, D34; Ensemble, W50a
Williams, Arthur L., W47b, W47c
Williams, Camilla, WB164.17
Williams, Clarence, 33. See also Clarence Williams Music Publishing Company
Williams, LeRoy, S48
Williams, Leroy E., B441
Williams, Renee, W62f
Williams, Robert W., W141g
Williams, Rudy, W132e
Williams, Sophie, W125e
Williams, Straight P., 19
Williford, Stanley, B442
Willkie Award, SA4
Willoughby, Diana, B443
Willson, Meredith, W15e
Wilson, Candace, W91e
Wilson, Charles Reagan, B123
Wilson, Diane, W16k
Wilson, Olly, B250
Wilson, Russell, W62e
Wincenc, Joseph, W133k
Winograd, Arthur, W160a
Winstead, Adelaide and Kenneth: dedication to, W97
Winters, Laurence, WB164.17, WB164.33, WB164.34
Winter's Approach, 23, 31, B46, B212

Winthrop, Fredrick, W9b
Winton, Carl, WB152.9
Woll, Allen, B445
Wolter, Beverly, WB2.56
Wood, Judith, W132d
Wood Notes, A25, B298
Woodbeck, Wilson, W61a
Woodruff, Helen, 20, W148
Woods, Bernard, W45a
Woods, Carlton R., D28, W25q, W149n, W153a-W153c
Woodson, Carter G., B446
Woodville, Mississippi, 5, 15-16, 18, B297
Work, Julian, B201
Work Song from the Delta, D72
Woven Silver, D67, D69
Wright, Mrs. John, 13

Yale University, B68, B197, B267, B426
Yeiser, Frederick, WB74.6, WB74.9
Yellen, Jack, B448
Yervanian, Ann, W91e
York, Wynn, B377
You Made Me Love You, 18
Young, A. S. Doc, B449
Young, Amanda, B450
You're Wonderful, Mary, D2

Zachary, Jessie, 23, W16a, W96a, W171a
Zepernick, Werner, WB36.16
Zephyr Trio, W101a, W101b
Ziegfield Follies, 28; dressing room door, 28
Zinger, Pablo, W112j
Zoloth, Alan, W101f

About the Authors

JUDITH ANNE STILL is the daughter of William Grant Still and the owner/manager of William Grant Still Music. Ms. Still has written many articles (some award-winning) about her father, music, and inspirational topics. She is the widow of mini-submarine pioneer Larry Allyn Headlee.

MICHAEL J. DABRISHUS is Head of the Special Collections Division and Professor at the University of Arkansas Libraries, Fayetteville, where the papers of William Grant Still and Verna Arvey are located. He is past president of the Society of Southwest Archivists.

CAROLYN L. QUIN is a member of the Music faculty at Riverside Community College in Riverside, California. She was formerly Chair of the Department of Music at Winthrop University and has been on the faculty at Lane College. Her other research interests as a musicologist include Fanny Mendelssohn Hensel, multicultural education, and women and music.

Recent Titles in
Bio-Bibliographies in Music

Germaine Tailleferre: A Bio-Bibliography
Robert Shapiro

Charles Wuorinen: A Bio-Bibliography
Richard D. Burbank

Elliott Carter: A Bio-Bibliography
William T. Doering

Leslie Bassett: A Bio-Bibliography
Ellen S. Johnson

Ulysses Kay: A Bio-Bibliography
Constance Tibbs Hobson and Deborra A. Richardson, compilers

John Alden Carpenter: A Bio-Bibliography
Joan O'Connor, compiler

Paul Creston: A Bio-Bibliography
Monica J. Slomski, compiler

William Thomas McKinley: A Bio-Bibliography
Jeffrey S. Sposato

William Mathias: A Bio-Bibliography
Stewart R. Craggs

Carl Ruggles: A Bio-Bibliography
Jonathan D. Green

Gardner Read: A Bio-Bibliography
Mary Ann Dodd and Jayson Rod Engquist

Allen Sapp: A Bio-Bibliography
Alan Green